D1229344

Business and Human Rights

In a global economy, multinational companies often operate in jurisdictions where governments are either unable or unwilling to uphold even the basic human rights of their citizens. The expectation that companies respect human rights in their own operations and in their business relationships is now a business reality that corporations need to respond to.

Business and Human Rights: From Principles to Practice is the first comprehensive and interdisciplinary textbook that addresses these issues. It examines the regulatory framework that grounds the business and human rights debate and highlights the business and legal challenges faced by companies and stakeholders in improving respect for human rights, exploring such topics as:

- the regulatory framework that grounds the business and human rights debate
- challenges faced by companies and stakeholders in improving human rights
- industry-specific human rights standards
- current mechanisms to hold corporations to account
- future challenges for business and human rights

With supporting case studies throughout, this text provides an overview of current themes in the field and guidance on practical implementation, demonstrating that a thorough understanding of the human rights challenges faced by business is now vital in any business context.

Dorothée Baumann-Pauly is Research Director at the NYU Stern Center for Business and Human Rights, New York and a member of the Editorial Board of the *Business and Human Rights Journal*.

Justine Nolan is an Associate Professor in the Faculty of Law at the University of New South Wales and Deputy Director of the Australian Human Rights Centre. She is a Visiting Scholar at NYU Stern Center for Business and Human Rights and a member of the Editorial Board of the *Business and Human Rights Journal.*

An important contribution to a vital subject, this excellent primer on business and human rights offers valuable insight for both current and future practitioners. Recognizing the challenges and preparing effectively are vital to drive responsible and sustainable business.

Paul Polman, *CEO, Unilever*

Baumann-Pauly and Nolan have written an important and ambitious book, tackling a topic that remains increasingly urgent and still understudied: how to integrate human rights concerns into global business. The editors skillfully examine the complex history of this topic and sketch out a number of realistic strategies that stakeholders can use to bring human rights issues more forcefully into the corporate environment. The book will be a useful tool for educating both future and current business leaders.

Debora Spar, *President, Barnard College*

Business and Human Rights

From Principles to Practice

Edited by Dorothée Baumann-Pauly and Justine Nolan

WITHDRAWN

SEP 15 2016

PROPERTY OF
SENECA COLLEGE
LIBRARIES
NEWNHAM CAMPUS

Routledge
Taylor & Francis Group

LONDON AND NEW YORK

First published 2016
by Routledge
2 Park Square, Milton Park, Abingdon, Oxon OX14 4RN

and by Routledge
711 Third Avenue, New York, NY 10017

Routledge is an imprint of the Taylor & Francis Group, an informa business

© 2016 selection and editorial matter, Dorothée Baumann-Pauly and Justine Nolan; individual chapters, the contributors

The right of Dorothée Baumann-Pauly and Justine Nolan to be identified as editors of this work has been asserted by them in accordance with sections 77 and 78 of the Copyright, Designs and Patents Act 1988.

All rights reserved. No part of this book may be reprinted or reproduced or utilized in any form or by any electronic, mechanical, or other means, now known or hereafter invented, including photocopying and recording, or in any information storage or retrieval system, without permission in writing from the publishers.

Crown copyright material is licensed under the Open Government license v2.0.

Trademark notice: Product or corporate names may be trademarks or registered trademarks, and are used only for identification and explanation without intent to infringe.

British Library Cataloguing-in-Publication Data
A catalogue record for this book is available from the British Library

Library of Congress Cataloging-in-Publication Data
Names: Baumann-Pauly, Dorothée, editor. | Nolan, Justine, editor.
Title: Business and human rights : from principles to practice / edited by Dorothée Baumann-Pauly and Justine Nolan.
Description: Abingdon, Oxon ; New York, NY : Routledge, 2016. | Includes bibliographical references and index.
Identifiers: LCCN 2015041655| ISBN 9781138833586 (hbk) | ISBN 9781138833562 (pbk) | ISBN 9781315735429 (ebk)
Subjects: LCSH: International business enterprises–Law and legislation. | Corporate governance–Law and legislation–Social aspects. | Social responsibility of business. | Human rights.
Classification: LCC K1322 .B874 2016 | DDC 343.07–dc23
LC record available at http://lccn.loc.gov/2015041655

ISBN: 978-1-138-83358-6 (hbk)
ISBN: 978-1-138-83356-2 (pbk)
ISBN: 978-1-315-73542-9 (ebk)

Typeset in Times New Roman
by Wearset Ltd, Boldon, Tyne and Wear

Printed and bound in the United States of America by Publishers Graphics, LLC on sustainably sourced paper.

Outline contents

Detailed contents

Notes on contributors

Christine Bader is a speaker, adviser and writer on corporate responsibility and sustainability. She is the author of *The Evolution of a Corporate Idealist: When Girl Meets Oil* (Bibliomotion, 2014). She was most recently an adviser to BSR and a Visiting Scholar at Columbia University, where she co-taught human rights and business. Christine's writing has appeared in the *New York Times, The Atlantic, Fast Company, Harvard Business Review* and numerous other publications. Christine was an adviser to the UN Secretary-General's Special Representative for Business and Human Rights from 2006 to 2011. She holds an MBA from Yale University.

Joanne Bauer is Senior Researcher, Institute for the Study of Human Rights and Adjunct Professor, School of International and Public Affairs, Columbia University. She is the editor of *Forging Environmentalism: Justice, Livelihood, and Contested Environments* (Routledge, 2006) and co-editor (with Daniel A. Bell) of *The East Asian Challenge for Human Rights* (Cambridge University Press, 1999). From 2006 to 2012 she was Senior Researcher, Business and Human Rights Resource Centre, and from 1993 to 2005, Director of Studies at the Carnegie Council for Ethics and International Affairs. She is a Senior Fellow at Melbourne University Law School, an adviser and consultant to a number of NGOs, including Inclusive Development International and Accountability Counsel, and co-leads the Teaching Business and Human Rights Forum.

Dorothée Baumann-Pauly is a business ethics scholar and has worked extensively on the implementation of human rights in multi-stakeholder settings. She is currently the Director of Research at the NYU Stern Center for Business and Human Rights and on the Editorial Board of the *Business and Human Rights Journal*. She has published widely on topics at the intersection of business ethics, corporate responsibility and human rights and is the author of *Managing Corporate Legitimacy* (Greenleaf, 2013). Dorothée received a PhD in economics from the University of Zurich, Switzerland.

Mattie J. Bekink is an Amsterdam-based consultant working on human rights, institutional strategy and communications. Mattie is currently affiliated with NYU Stern's Center for Business and Human Rights, where she focuses on ethical investing. Prior to establishing her consultancy, Mattie was the Deputy Country Director of the American Bar Association's Rule of Law Initiative China Program. She has also worked as an associate in the international arbitration and litigation group at Skadden, Arps, Slate, Meagher & Flom LLP, as a fellow at the Center for Human Rights and Global Justice and as policy associate at the Center for American Progress. Mattie has a BA in International Relations from Stanford University and a JD from Georgetown University Law Center.

Louis Bickford is the Global Human Rights Program Officer at the Ford Foundation, with a focus on strengthening the international human rights movement. Prior to joining the Ford Foundation in 2012, he was on the executive leadership team at Robert F. Kennedy Human Rights and, before that, was a founding staff member and director of the Policymakers and Civil Society unit at the International Center for Transitional Justice (ICTJ). Bickford is also an Adjunct Professor at Columbia University and New York University. He received a PhD from McGill University in Political Science.

Sara Blackwell is the Legal and Policy Coordinator of the Frameworks Programs at the International Corporate Accountability Roundtable (ICAR), where she leads ICAR's initiatives to build and implement legal frameworks to prevent business-related human rights harms. Sara has previously worked with the Fair Labor Association, EarthRights International, the Center for International Environmental Law, Green Advocates in Liberia and the Peace Corps in Zambia. She holds a JD from Georgetown University Law Center and a BA in Political Science and Human Rights from Barnard College of Columbia University, where she graduated summa cum laude and Phi Beta Kappa.

Anne-Marie Buzatu is Deputy Head of the Public–Private Partnerships division at the Geneva Centre for the Democratic Control of Armed Forces. Working under a mandate of the Swiss government, she led the elaboration of the International Code of Conduct for Private Security Service Providers (ICoC; January 2009–November 2010). She subsequently led the development of the ICoC Association, a multi-stakeholder governance and oversight mechanism for the ICoC, which began operations in September 2013. Current projects include working with the ICRC to develop security sector reform–security sector governance (SSR-SSG) guidance for multinational companies, as well as supporting better governance approaches for the Internet/cyber security.

Rachel Davis has been the Managing Director of Shift since it was founded in 2011. Previously, she served as Senior Legal Adviser to Professor John Ruggie, the former Special Representative of the UN Secretary-General, and helped develop the UN Guiding Principles on Business and Human Rights. Rachel is also a Research Fellow with the CSR Initiative at Harvard Kennedy School. She clerked at the UN International Criminal Tribunal for the former Yugoslavia and at the High Court of Australia, and served in the Australian Attorney-General's Department. She is a graduate of Harvard Law School and the University of New South Wales.

Surya Deva is an Associate Professor at the School of Law of City University of Hong Kong. His primary research interests lie in business and human rights, corporate social responsibility and India–China constitutional law. He has published extensively in these areas. Surya's books include *Socio-Economic Rights in Emerging Free Markets: Comparative Insights from India and China* (editor) (Routledge, 2015); *Human Rights Obligations of Business: Beyond the Corporate Responsibility to Respect?* (co-edited with David Bilchitz) (Cambridge University Press, 2013); and *Regulating Corporate Human Rights Violations: Humanizing Business* (Routledge, 2012). He is one of the founding Editors-in-Chief of the *Business and Human Rights Journal*.

William S. Dodge is Professor of Law at the University of California, Davis, School of Law and an expert on international business and international disputes. He is co-author of *Transnational Business Problems* (5th ed., 2014) and co-editor of *International Law in the U.S. Supreme Court: Continuity and Change* (2011). Professor Dodge has written extensively about the Alien Tort Statute and authored the amicus brief followed by the Supreme Court in *Sosa*. He served as Counselor on International Law to the Legal Adviser at the US Department of State while *Kiobel* was before the Supreme Court.

Mary Dowell-Jones is an Honorary Fellow of the Human Rights Law Centre at the University of Nottingham. Her work focuses on ethics and conduct in the financial markets, and the impact of the financial system on economic and social rights around the world. She has written on financial regulation, the austerity crisis, financial stability and financial crises, resilience and sustainable finance and the challenges of implementing the corporate responsibility to respect in the financial sector. She has advised and consulted on these issues with various international, national and non-governmental organizations.

Anthony P. Ewing is a Lecturer at Columbia Law School, where he teaches Transnational Business and Human Rights, and a Senior Advisor at Logos Consulting Group in New York. Anthony has served as an independent expert for the International Labour Organization and is a member of the United Nations Global Compact Human Rights and Labour Working Group. He co-directs the Teaching Business and Human Rights Forum, a platform for collaboration among teachers worldwide. Anthony holds a BA from Yale University and a JD from Columbia University. Monika Bukelskyte (Columbia LLM, 2014) provided research assistance for his chapter.

Bennett Freeman was Senior Vice President – Sustainability Research and Policy at Calvert Investments, the largest family of sustainable and responsible (SRI) mutual funds in the US from 2006 to 2015. He led the firm's environmental, social and governance analysis and its shareholder advocacy and public policy initiatives on issues such as Sudan divestment and responsible investment in Burma; extractive revenue transparency and conflict minerals; Internet freedom of expression and privacy. As US Deputy Assistant Secretary of State for Democracy, Human Rights and Labor from 1999 to 2001, he led the development of the Voluntary Principles on Security and Human Rights.

Arvind Ganesan is the Director of Human Rights Watch's Business and Human Rights Division. He leads the organization's work to expose human rights abuses linked to business and other economic activity, hold institutions accountable and develop standards to prevent future abuses. This work has included research and advocacy on a wide range of issues including the extractive industries; public and private security providers; international financial institutions; freedom of expression and information through the Internet; labour rights; supply chain monitoring and due diligence regimes. He is a founding member of the Voluntary Principles on Security and Human Rights and the Global Network Initiative where he also serves on the board. He serves on the board of EG Justice, an NGO that promotes good governance in Equatorial Guinea, and is a member of the International Corporate Accountability Roundtable (ICAR)'s steering committee.

Kristen Genovese is a senior researcher at the Centre for Research on Multinational Corporations (SOMO) in the Netherlands, where she coordinates the Human Rights & Grievance Mechanisms Programme. Prior to joining SOMO in 2014, Kris was the Director of the People, Land, and Resources Program at the Center for International Environmental Law. She has also worked for Defenders of Wildlife and the Environmental Law Institute. Kris received her law degree from New York University School of Law in 2004 and her BS in Environmental Policy and Behavior from the University of Michigan School of Natural Resources and the Environment.

Ben W. Heineman, Jr. was GE's Senior Vice President – General Counsel from 1987 to 2005. He is currently a Senior Fellow at Harvard Law School and Harvard Kennedy School, and a lecturer at Yale Law School. His book, *High Performance with High Integrity*, was published by the Harvard Business Press (2008). He is also the author of books on British race relations and the American presidency and the forthcoming, *The Inside Counsel Revolution*. He writes and speaks frequently on corporate ethics, anti-corruption, corporate governance and the global economy.

Scott Jerbi is a Senior Advisor and Geneva Representative at the Institute for Human Rights and Business. From 1997 to 2002 he worked for the United Nations Office of the High Commissioner for Human Rights, where his duties included leading the development of the Office's policies and interactions with the private sector. From 2002 to 2010 he served as Senior Advisor to former UN High Commissioner Mary Robinson at Realizing Rights: the Ethical Globalization Initiative.

Chris Jochnick is the CEO of Landesa, the rural development institute that works to secure land rights for the world's poorest. Prior to joining Landesa in August 2015, Jochnick was the Director of the Private Sector Department at Oxfam America, where he managed partnerships and adversarial campaigns targeting Fortune 500 companies. He has worked for two decades on issues of human rights, development and corporate accountability, including seven years in Latin America. He is the co-founder of the Center for Economic and Social Rights and is the Chair of the Board of the Business and Human Rights Resource Centre. Jochnick is a graduate of Harvard Law School, where he teaches a course on business and human rights.

Christine Kaufman is Professor of International and Constitutional Law at the University of Zurich Law School, Switzerland. Before joining the law faculty in Zurich, Kaufmann served at the Swiss Central Bank and later at the World Trade Institute (WTI) in Berne. In 2013 she was appointed Co-president of the newly set up Federal Advisory Committee of the National Contact Point for the OECD Guidelines for Multinational Enterprises. Kaufmann's main research interests include the interactions between human rights and business, the relationship between the international trade and the international financial system as well as the related implications on global governance.

Sarah Labowitz is the Co-director of the NYU Center for Business and Human Rights and a Research Scholar in Business and Society at NYU Stern. She has worked on business and human rights from within leading NGOs, the US government, a company and now in academia. She leads the centre's project-based work and has developed its methodology for linking research and practical advocacy with companies. Prior to joining Stern in 2013, she worked at the US State Department on cyber policy, Internet freedom and human rights. Sarah is a fellow of the Truman National Security Project and a member of the Council on Foreign Relations. She holds an MA in International Relations from the Fletcher School of Law and Diplomacy at Tufts University and a BA in History from Grinnell College.

Richard M. Locke is the 13th Provost of Brown University. He is an internationally respected scholar and authority on international labour markets, worker rights, comparative political economy, labour relations and corporate responsibility. He has published five books as well as numerous articles on economic development, labour relations and corporate responsibility. For his ongoing research on fair and safe working conditions in global supply chains, Locke was named the 2005 Faculty Pioneer in Academic Leadership by the Aspen Institute. He currently chairs the Apple Academic Advisory Board, a group of independent academics who are working with Apple to improve labour conditions among the company's suppliers.

Amol Mehra, Esq. is an international human rights lawyer and current Director of the International Corporate Accountability Roundtable. Amol has worked to build accountability frameworks in both domestic and international arenas, including over private military and security companies, around supply chains and extractives industries, and has worked to strengthen measures related to non-financial disclosure, anti-corruption, procurement and due diligence regimes. Amol holds a Bachelor of Commerce degree from McGill University and a JD with Honors in International Law from the University of San Francisco School of Law.

Felicitas Morhart is Professor of Marketing at the University of Lausanne, Switzerland. She graduated in Communication Science at the University of Munich and earned her PhD in Business Administration (2008) from the University of St Gallen, Switzerland. Her work lies at the intersection of marketing, positive leadership and business ethics, such as her work on brand-specific transformational leadership, brand authenticity and eudaimonic consumption. Her work has been published in the *Journal of Marketing*, *Journal of Consumer Psychology*, *Journal of Management Inquiry*, *Journal of Advertising Research* and *Harvard Business Manager*, among others.

John Morrison is the Executive Director of the Institute for Human Rights and Business. John has extensive experience working with leading companies on issues of corporate responsibility and human rights. He worked previously with The Body Shop International plc and led the Business Leaders Initiative on Human Rights from 2003 to 2009. He has also worked for a number of civil society and governmental organizations on issues of migration, human trafficking and forced labour. John has acted as an adviser to a number of governments during their presidencies of intergovernmental organizations and has chaired a wide range of conferences and initiatives in many parts of the world. He is the author of *The Social License: How to Keep Your Organization Legitimate* (Palgrave Macmillan, 2014).

Justine Nolan is an Associate Professor in the Faculty of Law at UNSW Australia and Deputy Director of the Australian Human Rights Centre. She is a Visiting Scholar at the NYU Stern Center for Business and Human Rights. She is a co-author of *The International Law of Human Rights* (2011) and has published widely in the area of business and human rights. Prior to her appointment at UNSW in 2004 she was the Director of the Business and Human Rights Program at the Lawyers Committee for Human Rights (now Human Rights First) in the US. She is on the Editorial Board of the *Australian Journal of Human Rights* and the *Business and Human Rights Journal.*

Guido Palazzo is Professor of Business Ethics at the University of Lausanne, Switzerland. He graduated in Business Administration at the University of Bamberg, Germany and earned his PhD in Political Philosophy (1999) from the University of Marburg, Germany. His research interests are in corporate social responsibility, (un)ethical decision-making and organized crime. His work has appeared in journals such as *Academy of Management Review, Academy of Management Journal, Business Ethics Quarterly* and *Journal of Management Studies.*

Chip Pitts teaches CSR/BHR and Leadership at Stanford, Oxford and in Asia. Former top executive of a major multinational and leading startups, he serves as independent expert for the UN Human Rights Council, UN Global Compact Adviser, current EPIC Board Chair and former board leader of Fairtrade International and Amnesty International USA, among others. Current Advisory board service includes the ABA Center for Human Rights BHR Project and the Business and Human Rights Resource Centre. Co-author of a pioneering textbook in the field, Pitts has helped shape the field as teacher, author and norm entrepreneur for the last three decades.

Michael Posner is the Co-director of the NYU Center for Business and Human Rights and the Jerome Kohlberg Professor of Ethics and Finance at NYU Stern. From September 2009 until March 2013, he served in the Obama Administration as Assistant Secretary of State for Democracy, Human Rights and Labor at the US State Department. From 1978 to 2009, he was the Executive Director and the President of Human Rights First, a US-based human rights advocacy organization. As Assistant Secretary of State, Michael travelled to more than 40 countries where he represented the US government on a wide range of human rights issues. Michael holds a JD from the University of California, Berkeley Law School, and a BA with distinction and honours from the University of Michigan. He taught human rights at Yale and Columbia law schools.

Caroline Rees has been President of Shift since 2011. She was a lead adviser to Professor John Ruggie during his UN mandate, and from 2009 to 2011 was Director of the Governance and Accountability Program at the Harvard Kennedy School's Corporate Social Responsibility Initiative. Caroline previously spent 14 years as a British diplomat. From 2003 to 2006 she led the UK's human rights negotiating team at the UN. Her prior foreign service career covers Iran, Slovakia, the UN Security Council and the European Union. She is a graduate of Oxford University and the Fletcher School of Law and Diplomacy.

John Gerard Ruggie is the Berthold Beitz Professor in Human Rights and International Affairs at Harvard's Kennedy School of Government and Affiliated Professor in International Legal Studies at Harvard Law School. From 1997 to 2001, he served as UN Assistant Secretary-General for Strategic Planning, and from 2005 to 2011 as UN Special Representative for Business and Human Rights. A Fellow of the American Academy of Arts & Sciences, his most recent book is *Just Business: Multinational Corporations and Human Rights*. In 2014 he received the Harry LeRoy Jones Award of the Washington Foreign Law Society, honouring 'an individual who has made an outstanding contribution to the development and application of international law'.

Michael Samway is an adjunct faculty member at Georgetown University and a former Visiting Scholar at the Center for Business and Human Rights at NYU. He spent 10 years at Yahoo! where he was a Vice President and Deputy General Counsel, founded Yahoo!'s Business & Human Rights Program and was a founding board member of GNI. Previously, he practised law at White & Case. Michael received his BSFS/MSFS from Georgetown, was a Fulbright Scholar in Chile and received his JD/LLM from Duke. He has published commentary on law, business, human rights and technology and has testified before Congress on Internet freedom.

Judith Schrempf-Stirling is Assistant Professor of Management at the University of Richmond, USA. She graduated in International Business at the University of Maastricht, the Netherlands, and earned her PhD (2010) from the University of Lausanne, Switzerland. Her research interests focus on corporate social responsibility, business and human rights and responsible consumption. Her work has appeared in journals such as *Academy of Management Review*, *Business & Society*, *Business Horizons* and *Journal of Business Ethics*.

Barbara Shailor is internationally recognized for her work to secure economic, social and political rights for workers throughout the world. Shailor served as the Special Representative for International Labor Affairs at the Department of State. She was responsible for labour issues and the impact of American foreign policy and programmes on labour rights and living standards. Shailor, a union member for over 40 years, also served as the Director of the International Department of the AFL-CIO and senior adviser on international policy and programmes. She is a member of the Council on Foreign Relations and served on the Board of Directors of the American Center for International Solidarity, the German Marshall Fund, the International Rescue Committee, the Franklin and Eleanor Roosevelt Institute, the Global Reporting Initiative and numerous labor advisory committees. She continues to speak, write, advise and consult on international labour issues.

Auret van Heerden has 40 years' experience in labour and human rights issues worldwide. He began as a student leader and anti-apartheid activist in South Africa before being recruited by the International Labour Organization to work on the Programme of Action against Apartheid. In 1994 he was appointed

Labour Attaché at the South African Mission to the UN in Geneva. He returned to the ILO to head the Action Programme on Social and Labour Issues in EPZs. In 2001 he joined the Fair Labor Association and served as its President and CEO for 13 years. He now consults and teaches.

Florian Wettstein is Professor and Chair of Business Ethics and Director of the Institute for Business Ethics at University of St Gallen, Switzerland. He has published widely on topics at the intersection of business ethics, corporate responsibility and human rights and is the author of *Multinational Corporations and Global Justice: Human Rights Obligations of a Quasi-Governmental Institution* (Stanford University Press, 2009). Florian is Editor-in-Chief of Cambridge University Press's new *Business and Human Rights Journal*.

Simon Zadek is Co-director of the UNEP Inquiry into the Design of a Sustainable Financial System, a Visiting Professor and DSM Senior Fellow in Partnerships and Sustainability at Singapore Management University, a Senior Fellow at the International Institute for Sustainable Development, and Distinguished Senior Fellow of the Academy of Business in Society. He founded and was Chief Executive of the international think tank, AccountAbility. His publication, 'The Civil Corporation', received the Academy of Management Social Issues in Management Award, and his *Harvard Business Review* 'Paths to Corporate Responsibility' is widely cited and used by business.

Preface

The business and human rights field has developed rapidly in the last two decades. In the mid-1990s most corporations were questioning the relevance of human rights to their businesses. But a combination of factors has brought more companies in different industries to this discussion. For many of them the question now is *how* they can address the human rights challenges they face in a competitive business environment. This volume seeks to help them and others explore this question.

The United Nations Human Rights Council's endorsement of the UN Guiding Principles on Business and Human Rights in June 2011 accelerated the development of corporate and civil society activities and academic scholarship on the subject. Business and human rights is now taught at a number of law and public policy schools around the world. And more recently some business schools have also started to add business and human rights courses to their curricula. In 2013 the New York University Stern School of Business became the first business school to create a centre on business and human rights, a centre with which we are both affiliated. Networks of business and human rights teachers and researchers have formed in the United States and Europe to discuss teaching approaches, exchange teaching materials and discuss research.[1] In 2014, Cambridge University Press announced the launch of the *Business and Human Rights Journal* – the first of its kind – which will publish academic research on business and human rights but also integrate perspectives from the field.[2] These are all indicators that the academic field is maturing.

This book includes the work of more than 30 authors from diverse academic and practice perspectives. Included in this volume are works by academic experts from the fields of business, law and political science. We also have included contributions from business leaders, non-governmental organizations and other practitioners whose perspectives reinforce the comprehensive, interdisciplinary approach adopted in this book. This collaboration also allowed us to bridge several divides that currently characterize the field. Business and human rights is by definition a multidisciplinary field that cuts across several social science disciplines. Legal approaches to business and human rights are of longer standing but the perspectives of business scholars, political scientists and others are becoming increasingly central to the debate. We invited these diverse contributions based on our view that an understanding of this field requires a truly interdisciplinary examination. The book also reflects differences in the approach to these issues in different regions: for example, in Western Europe and the United States. There are widely divergent views as well on the appropriate role for companies to be addressing these issues in juxtaposition with governments. We explore a number of other still unresolved issues in this embryonic field, ranging from whether a state-centric or a shareholder value maximizing focus is most appropriate for corporations today. This book deliberately does not always offer answers to these questions, but rather presents a range of perspectives and questions to consider in the teaching of these important topics.

The contrast between academic perspectives and those of business and human rights practitioners also helps to highlight some of the challenges in making practical progress in the implementation of human rights standards for global businesses. Corporations need to justify their engagement in human rights by creating a business case for human rights mindful of their business models. They also need to develop internal systems that infuse respect for human rights in all the places they operate and throughout their internal hierarchies.

In compiling this volume we greatly enjoyed the interactions with the authors and owe a great debt of gratitude to each of these contributors who took time from their busy lives to enable us to create this volume. We created this book in less than a year, an achievement that was only possible thanks to the exemplary commitment of all of our contributors. We thank you all for your commitment, patience and shared sense of purpose.

We are indebted to our colleagues at the NYU Stern Center for Business and Human Rights, and especially the Co-Directors of the Center Sarah Labowitz and Michael Posner. Their continuous support and perspective was an invaluable resource. We also owe a special note of thanks to Luke Taylor who worked tirelessly as our outstanding copy-editor over the course of the past months.

Finally, we would like to thank our future readers, whether teachers, students or practitioners, who we hope will both learn from it and be inspired to take this emerging field to the next level. The time is ripe for a textbook on business and human rights and we are grateful to Routledge for giving us the chance to publish this volume. What we have produced aims to capture the history of this field and the main themes in this rapidly evolving area. This may be the first such volume but it surely will not be the final word as these issues will continue to play a larger role in the corporate landscape in the years to come.

Dorothée Baumann-Pauly
Justine Nolan

Notes

1   For instance, the Teaching Business and Human Rights Forum, a platform for collaboration among individuals teaching business and human rights worldwide, formed in May 2011, http://TeachBHR.org. A similar network of BHR teachers and scholars has existed in Europe since 2014 (The BHRights Initiative, www.cbs.dk/en/research/departments-and-centres/department-of-intercultural-communication-and-management/ research/research-projects).
2   Cambridge University Press, *Business and Human Rights Journal*, http://journals.cambridge.org/action/displayJournal?jid=BHJ.

Chapter 1

The relationship of human rights to business

The role that corporations play in domestic and international economies is fundamental and over the last few decades the impact of business on human rights has become increasingly visible. The growth and interest in business and human rights issues has in part stemmed from recurring examples of corporate irresponsibility but business can also be a transformative force for good. The opening chapter by Justine Nolan provides an overview of the relevance of human rights to business and their intrinsic interconnectedness. This contribution highlights how far some companies have come in their acknowledgement and acceptance of the relevance of human rights to their business operations and how far some companies still have to go.

A threshold question for companies' engagement is how to justify potential investments in human rights. There is a long-standing debate on whether there exists a 'business case' whereby companies can quantify the benefits or costs of investments in human rights. Some scholars point out this normative question cannot be answered empirically and therefore the basis for demanding corporate action is ethics or morality. Yet, in corporate practice engagement with human rights needs to be linked to the long-term vision of a sustainable business model. Baumann-Pauly and Posner suggest broadening the debate that is currently narrowly focused on financial returns and risk mitigation. They present an argument that industry-specific standards for human rights both reduce reputational risk and provide affirmative benefits to companies.

Finally, this chapter features two prominent case studies that are commonly featured in any classroom discussion of business and human rights. Workplace incidents that violate individuals' human rights have become commonplace features in the media over the last few decades. Every day, there are occurrences on a farm, in a factory, around a mine that are contrary to accepted workplace standards. Once every generation, there is a disaster that captures the world's attention. The two case studies in this chapter – focusing on the toxic chemical spill at a factory in Bhopal, India in 1984 and the collapse of the Rana Plaza building in Dhaka, Bangladesh in 2013 nearly 30 years later – illustrate the devastating impact of a failure to protect human rights. These two examples showcase multiple failures of regulation involving both government and corporate actors. While these dramatic cases are indicative of what might be perhaps the worst that can happen when human rights are not protected, they are also representative of the many workplace problems that occur on a much smaller scale every day, which can cumulatively have a negative impact on an individual's ability to work and live with dignity.

Section 1.1

Business and human rights in context

Justine Nolan

1 Introduction

Recent decades have witnessed the exponential growth of global corporations; at the same time, the power and resources of many governments has eroded. Many of the top Fortune 500 companies have revenues equivalent to and often significantly larger than the gross domestic product (GDP) of many nation states.[1] With the increasing centrality of the role played by corporations in driving global commerce and trade comes increasing levels of corporate power – political and social, as well as economic – which suggests the need for a reappraisal of the appropriate role for business in an increasingly globalized world.

Writing over four decades ago, economist Milton Friedman argued that a company's only social responsibility is 'to use its resources and engage in activities designed to increase its profits so long as it stays within the rules of the game, which is to say, engages in open and free competition without deception or fraud'.[2] He also wrote:

> In a free enterprise, private property system, a corporate executive is an employee of the owners of the business. He has direct responsibility to his employers. That responsibility is to conduct the business in accordance with their desires, which generally will be to make as much money as possible while conforming to the basic rules of the society, both those embodied in law and those embodied in ethical custom.[3]

While Friedman referenced a narrow legal definition of a corporation's potential social responsibility, he did recognize each company's responsibility to conform to the basic rules of society including those based in ethical customs. Using this as a starting point, recent decades have seen the emergence of a broader understanding of a corporation's social responsibility that seeks to embed respect for human rights in business operations. Significant developments have been taking place in factories, fields and workplaces all over the world where a variety of stakeholders have been pushing and prodding corporations to adopt operational changes that will lead to sustained compliance with international human rights standards. Sometimes business has been proactive in seeking such changes; at other times it has been reluctant or simply absent. The acceptance by the United Nations Human Rights Council in 2011 of the Guiding Principles on Business and Human Rights[4] (Guiding Principles), which affirms that companies have a responsibility to respect human rights, solidifies the centrality of rights to business. For many (but not all) companies, the question is no longer: 'Do we have an obligation to address human rights?' Rather, it is: 'How do we do it, at what cost, and with whom do we collaborate in addressing the problems that exist?'

The role that corporations play in domestic and international economies is fundamental. Their impact on human rights is equally important as they have the potential to make a direct and enduring impact on people's lives. Business can be a transformative force for good. Through commercial activity driven by corporations, jobs and wages are made available, goods and services are provided and taxes are paid enabling governments to provide further goods and services. A globalized economy has generated millions of jobs over the last quarter-century. It has lifted hundreds of millions of people out of extreme poverty.[5] Thereby, directly or indirectly, a vast array of human rights may be supported – from rights to work, welfare, food and shelter, health and education, to freedoms involving speech, association and movement. In short, corporations are central to the provision of many of the things that make human life more tolerable, enjoyable and fulfilling; indeed, the work and wages that corporate enterprise brings to many communities are key elements to the establishment and maintenance of individual human dignity – to which end human rights strive to meet.[6]

But some business practices have also eroded respect for or simply disregarded human rights. Corporations, both local and transnational, have been and continue to be minor and major abusers of human rights. Some corporations are guilty of treating workers badly – in terms of pay, conditions and working environments; some pollute the environment in ways that have dramatic and serious effects far beyond their immediate surroundings; some discriminate against indigenous peoples, or certain ethnic or religious groups, or against women, or people with disabilities, or on grounds of sexuality; and some work alongside (or inside) governments that perpetrate gross human rights abuses, such as in Nazi Germany, Apartheid South Africa and in the many authoritarian and repressive states in the world today.[7]

Today, many governments lack the will or capacity to protect the basic rights of their own people. Often they lack both. Companies are being forced to adjust to a much larger role – financially, socially and politically – than they have ever played or are comfortable playing. Various legal and non-legal initiatives have sprouted in the last few decades in an attempt to attach some sense of corporate responsibility to the protection of human rights. Understanding the roles and responsibilities of these companies in this new landscape and determining the practical 'rules of the road' for implementing such roles and responsibilities is a significant challenge. What the appropriate role is for business in an increasingly globalized world is a question that will draw diverse responses. A brief survey of some corporate approaches towards accepting (or not) the relevance of human rights to their business operations reveals both how far (some) companies have come, and how far some have to go.

2 Changing role of companies in society

2.1 Corporate catastrophe in Bhopal[8]

An early catalyst for recalibrating the role of companies in society was the 1984 disaster in Bhopal, India, in which more than 3,000 people were killed and tens of thousands injured in an industrial gas leak accident at a Union Carbide pesticide plant. In the aftermath of this catastrophe some blame was rightly attributed to the central and state Indian governments and their lax enforcement of safety laws and haphazard planning permissions.[9] However, attention also focused on the plant operator, Union Carbide India Limited (UCIL), and its United States (US) based parent company, Union Carbide Corporation (UCC). Although UCC exercised extensive control over its Indian subsidiary (evidenced not simply by share ownership or representation on the board of directors but also by involvement in 'key decisions regarding issues such as, technology, plant design, safety … training of employees'[10]), it attempted to shift the blame for the accident to its subsidiary UCIL. The reaction of these companies was generally one of obfuscation and a denial of responsibility for the calamity that ensued; liability was strictly defined by UCC and UCIL in terms of their legal accountability for the disaster. Litigation was pursued in both the American and Indian courts with mixed results.[11] An action brought in the US against UCC was ultimately dismissed by the Second Circuit Court of Appeals;[12] the case brought in India against UCC settled for US$470 million. Bhopal remains one of the modern world's worst industrial accidents and, as a legal precedent, it is most noteworthy for highlighting the limitations of the law and the lack of justice ultimately delivered to those worst affected.[13] In the more than 30 years since Bhopal, as corporate violations of human rights have continued to occur, what, if anything, has changed in terms of corporate and public perceptions of a company's responsibility to act and provide redress in the face of corporate human rights abuses?

2.2 Managing global supply chains

In most industries, large companies now rely on a series of contractors and suppliers in a range of countries to produce and transport their products. Today's global supply chains link individual workers with large and small companies across national, political and cultural boundaries. Companies do not generally own or operate the factories in which their goods are produced and they may contract with hundreds, sometimes thousands, of different suppliers annually. Nike,[14] for example, sources its products from over 700 factories, engaging nearly one million workers across more than 40 countries.[15] The problems associated with regulating multi-jurisdictional supply chains, along with civil society and public pressure to improve working conditions, has caused (some) companies to take a more proactive role in regulating the workplaces producing their goods.

In the mid-1990s, Nike faced allegations of using 'sweatshop labour' to produce its goods in factories throughout Asia. Under a barrage of media criticism, Nike first denied that it had any responsibility for the factory working conditions that allegedly included 'physical and verbal abuse of workers, hazardous working conditions, pennies per hour wages, and anti-union efforts throughout Indonesia, China, and Vietnam, where Nike employ[ed] over 350,000 workers'.[16]

In response, Nike established a department tasked with working to improve factory conditions. Continuing criticism of the company led to protests on US college campuses, and in 1998, then CEO of Nike, Phillip Knight, acknowledged that '[t]he Nike product has become synonymous with slave wages, forced overtime, and arbitrary abuse … I truly believe the American consumer doesn't want to buy products made under abusive conditions'.[17]

The 1990s was a tumultuous time for many companies flirting with the notion of corporate social responsibility (CSR). The decade was notable for the expansive adoption of corporate codes of conduct, the appearance of glossy CSR reports and experimentation in self-regulation – led by high-profile brands producing consumer goods such as Nike, Disney, Gap, Reebok, Levi Strauss and Mattel. Corporate self-regulation was the key buzzword but internal codes of conduct were generally developed with limited stakeholder input and few, if any, independent or transparent monitoring and reporting mechanisms to assess compliance with international human rights and labour and environmental standards. Unsurprisingly, these modes of self-governance were soon criticized for their lack of robustness, legitimacy and effectiveness.[18]

A change in strategy saw a limited number of companies engage external stake-holders and join multi-stakeholder initiatives[19] to develop and implement compliance with human rights and environmental standards in the workplace. Nike today participates in the Fair Labor Association (FLA), a non-profit which is a collaborative effort of companies, universities and colleges and civil society organizations, aimed at improving working conditions in global supply chains.[20] Such external collaboration can also lead to ongoing advances in corporate policies that do more to embrace human rights as part of corporate culture. In 2005, Nike was the first company in the apparel and footwear sector to disclose the names and locations of its contract factories, and that information is still publicly available on its website.[21] In 2009, Nike joined three other apparel companies (Adidas, Gap and Knights Apparel) all with business interests in Honduras, in adopting an advocates approach to human rights by sending a letter to then US Secretary of State, Hillary Clinton, urging support for the restoration of democracy in Honduras (which would have the flow-on effect of stabilizing the local economy).[22]

The public criticism and media attention that forced apparel and footwear companies to act in the 1990s has more recently been centred on one of the world's giants in the electronics sector – Apple – and the working conditions in its supplier factories in Asia. In the last decade, Apple has become one of the richest and most successful companies in the world, in part by mastering global manufacturing. However, a series of media and non-governmental organization (NGO) reports[23] highlighted allegations that factory workers employed by Foxconn (a principal but not exclusive supplier for Apple) assembled iPhones, iPads and other devices while labouring in onerous and sometimes unsafe work environments. One report argued that

> [e]mployees work excessive overtime, in some cases seven days a week, and live in crowded dorms. Some say they stand so long that their legs swell until they can hardly walk. Under-age workers have helped build Apple's products, and the company's suppliers have improperly disposed of hazardous waste and falsified records.[24]

In 2010, employee suicides at Foxconn plants in China garnered significant attention for both Apple and Foxconn and, to a lesser extent, other global electronic brands also producing in those factories.[25] Like Nike before it, Apple took a closer look at its supplier code of conduct (first made publicly available in 2005) and the mechanisms designed to monitor workplace conditions. In 2012, Apple also joined the FLA in an effort to improve its factory auditing process.

The death of more than 1,100 workers in the collapse of the Rana Plaza building (which housed several garment factories) in Dhaka, Bangladesh in April 2013 is another example of the many problems still lurking in global supply chains.[26] The Rana Plaza tragedy spurred factory owners, associations, international buyers, international organizations and the governments of Bangladesh, the US and the European Union to involve themselves (to different degrees) in various public–private partnerships to address the safety and regulation of Bangladesh's garment factories. Bangladesh is now the world's number two garment exporter, second only to China: it has somewhere between 5,000 and 6,000 factories[27] manufacturing for export operating in a somewhat ad hoc regulatory landscape.

These examples reaffirm the fact that substandard working conditions are a global problem. Regulating and improving working conditions in global supply chains is a work in progress. Multiple motives (including reputation protection) and pressure points (media, trade unions, NGOs, consumers, workers, investors) and internal leadership within some companies have influenced, and continue to influence, corporate approaches to improving compliance with human rights standards. There has been a significant shift in corporate attitudes from 30 years ago in the wake of Bhopal. Initial public denial of responsibility is still a default response for some companies but others acknowledge that they bear some responsibility for ensuring fair and humane working conditions throughout their globalized supply chain. What remains is disagreement about the most effective means of achieving respect for and compliance with international human rights standards.

2.3 Working in and/or with repressive states

Companies operating in industries as diverse as the extractive sector and the information and communication technology (ICT) sector have been accused of complicity with repressive regimes. The difficult political and social environments in places such as Nigeria and China have created, and continue to pose, challenges for companies in these (and other) sectors, where the relationship between government and private enterprise is more closely linked and mutually reliant and reinforcing than is the case in, for example, the garment industry. In the extractive sector, companies often operate through joint ventures with host governments. In the ICT sector, companies may be forced to choose between operating in a manner that does not fully respect human rights and exiting the market (for example, Google's decision to cease operations in China in 2010).

Shell's operations in Nigeria are an example of the challenges often faced by companies in the extractive sector. Through its Nigerian subsidiary, Shell Petroleum Development Company, Shell has operated in Nigeria for over 50 years. Shell has consistently faced significant community opposition to some of its operations in Nigeria[28] and security risks (including sabotage of its pipelines) are a fundamental challenge to its business. Shell, like many companies operating in this sector, routinely hires security forces to protect its assets, including employing local government police and military forces. In a series of high-profile lawsuits, Shell, along with other extractive sector companies including Unocal, Total, Talisman, Chevron and Exxon, has been accused of complicity in a host of human rights violations including coercive appropriation of land, torture, extrajudicial killing, arbitrary detention, forced labour and infringements of the rights to peaceful assembly and association.[29] The claims against Shell also alleged complicity in the detention and execution of the Ogoni 9 (including Ken Saro-Wiwa, one of the leaders of the Movement for the

Survival of the Ogoni People).[30] That case was settled in 2009 for US$15.5 million, on the eve of a trial in a US court.[31] A subsequent case against Shell, decided by the US Supreme Court in 2013, significantly limited the future of litigation in this field.[32]

In 1999, in response to consistent public criticism about its corporate approach to environmental and human rights issues, Shell adopted a corporate policy designed to guide the company's operation in a more 'stakeholder-sensitive' manner[33] and participated in multi-stakeholder dialogues that led to the establishment of the Voluntary Principles on Security and Human Rights.[34] However, despite increasing sensitivity on the part of some companies to human rights issues and a willingness to participate in multi-stakeholder dialogues, achieving more systemic change in the way business operates and interacts with stakeholders in a manner that theoretically and practically respects human rights in the extractive sector still seems some way off.

Companies in the ICT sector may also face the challenges of operating in difficult political and social environments and of balancing the tension between adhering to international human rights standards and conforming to the wishes of host governments. Governments around the world have long censored access to information and the Internet offers ongoing challenges both to governments that are determined to limit access to information, and companies whose existence relies on the transmission of information. Just as the Internet has the potential to empower and educate and provide individuals with a gateway to limitless information, it also has the ability to 'become a tool of repression ... enhanc[ing] the ability of repressive governments to restrict the freedoms and basic human rights of their citizens'.[35]

In February 2006 a very contemporary human rights dilemma arose when companies such as Yahoo!, Google, Microsoft and Cisco were called to a US congressional hearing and subjected to a public interrogation about their cooperation with the Chinese government in censoring Internet content.[36] As it does with offline media, the Chinese government seeks to limit online content including restricting access to information concerning human rights. Because not all of the Internet traffic in China goes through government-monitored Internet exchange points ('the great firewall of China'), the Chinese government also relies on third parties to execute surveillance and filtering on its behalf (or what might be referred to as 'state-induced self-censorship').[37] China has sought and received the cooperation of local and global Internet companies in limiting access to information. In 2002, Yahoo! signed China's 'Public Pledge on Self-discipline for the Chinese Internet Industry' (sponsored by the government-affiliated Internet Society of China) that required Yahoo! to 'refrain from producing, posting or disseminating harmful information that may jeopardize state security and disrupt social stability, contravene laws and regulations and spread superstition and obscenity' and to 'monitor the information publicized by users on websites according to law and remove the harmful information promptly'.[38] In 2007, Yahoo! faced intense public scrutiny when it was accused of providing information about the online activities of particular users to Chinese law enforcement, which led to their detention.[39]

In recent times, following the revelations of US whistle-blower Edward Snowden, major US technology companies like Google, Microsoft and Yahoo! have had their reputations hurt by allegations of involvement (even if unwilling or perhaps unknowing) in the mass collection of data by the US National Security Agency.[40] Partly in an attempt to win back consumer trust, a growing number of companies have increased the transparency of their operations by issuing reports on the number of government requests they receive to share data or user information.[41]

The challenge for companies operating in the ICT sector 'arises where the law, or the day-to-day practice by government entities and officials ... in which the company is doing business comes into conflict with internationally recognized human rights'.[42] Failure to follow local laws can mean fines or imprisonment for locally based employees of the global company. In 2008, Yahoo! was the first ICT company to launch its business and human rights programme and was one of the leading corporate protagonists behind the launch of the Global Network Initiative. During this period of corporate introspection, Yahoo! publicly posed questions on its corporate blog which gave a sense of the issues it was/is grappling with in merging human rights standards with its business operations. For example, Yahoo! asked:

> [Are] partially censored results, with notice to users better than no results at all in a challenging market? Should companies draw the line on doing business somewhere based on the type of speech a government limits?... How do companies design product approaches that balance legitimate government rights and requirements for data access with adequate protections for user privacy?... Should we design an approach that works in Beijing, Paris, Sao Paulo, Sydney, Toronto and Washington DC all at once? Is that possible? How far can a company go in challenging local laws and orders?[43]

These thoughtful and difficult questions demonstrate the challenges ICT companies continue to face when operating in environments where local laws conflict with international human rights standards. Companies can no longer sit back and wait for the next problem to emerge but must proactively develop operational standards that guide the company with respect to human rights. For instance, during the Arab Spring uprising in January 2011, when hundreds of thousands of protesters in Egypt were demanding an end to the 30-year rule of President Mubarak, and to the state of emergency that prevailed, the government ordered the three main voice and data communication providers in Egypt – Vodafone, Mobini and Etisalat – to suspend services in selected areas. Vodafone acceded to the government's orders and also followed 'requests' to send out a series of pro-government SMS messages. It was only after Vodafone's network was disrupted and corrupted in this manner that the company began to develop procedures to ensure operational compliance with international human rights standards.[44] Demonstrating and implementing corporate respect for human rights requires companies to be proactive not simply responsive.

3 Multi-layered, multi-pronged, multi-stakeholder approach

Recent decades have witnessed an evolution in societal and (to a lesser extent) legal notions of corporate responsibility. The notion that business has a responsibility to respect human rights is generally accepted. From the time when Friedman was writing about CSR in 1970 to today, there has been a notable shift in the approach of many companies from avoidance and denial of the relevance of human rights to their business, to acknowledgement and engagement with the issues and with external stakeholders. However, the mechanisms for implementing that responsibility are less clear-cut.

What is becoming increasingly apparent is that for sustained improvements to occur, a multiplicity of stakeholders must be involved. Recourse to local laws and a system of enforcement and judicial relief in the host countries where global corporations operate should always be an option for ensuring greater respect for human rights. However, the reality is that in many countries this simply is not happening. In developing countries (but not exclusively so), laws are sometimes weak, and enforcement weaker still, whether due to corruption or institutional fragility. Thus, reliance on host governments to ensure that human rights are protected remains a long-term proposition. Instead, a multi-pronged, multi-layered and multi-stakeholder approach that institutionalizes a networked form of governance is required. Cooperation between business, NGOs, governments, unions and international institutions (like the International Labour Organization) is key to implementing improved protections for workers. The focus should be both on implementing practical industry-specific standards as well as refining an improved regulatory framework that may operate across sectors. This book highlights a variety of initiatives that have begun to address these challenges in practical ways that allow businesses to thrive while at the same time addressing the most pressing human rights problems in their core business operations.

Notes

1   For example, in 2014, the revenue of Walmart (US$485 billion). Walmart employs over 2.2 million people worldwide; as the world's third-largest employer it 'has a workforce that trails only the militaries of the United States and China in size'. See Human Rights Watch, *World Report 2013* (2013), p. 29. Comparisons between the revenues of top Fortune 500 companies and the GDPs of states show: Exxon Mobil (US$382 billion) and Colombia (US$377 billion); Chevron (US$203 billion) and Qatar (US$210 billion); Berkshire Hathaway (US$194 billion) and New Zealand (US$197 billion); and Apple (US$182 billion) and Vietnam (US$185 billion). For revenue figures, see Fortune, 'Fortune 500 2015', http://fortune.com/fortune500/wal-mart-stores-inc-1. For GDP figures, see United States, Central Intelligence Agency, 'The World Factbook', www.cia.gov/library/publications/the-world-factbook/fields/2195.html.

2   M. Friedman, 'The Social Responsibility of Business Is to Increase Its Profits', *New York Times Magazine*, 13 September 1970.

3   Ibid.

4   Human Rights Council, 'Guiding Principles on Business and Human Rights: Implementing the United Nations "Protect, Respect and Remedy" Framework', Report of the Special Representative of the Secretary-General on the Issue of Human Rights and Transnational Corporations and Other Business Enterprises, UN Doc. A/HRC/17/31 (21 March 2011).

5   World Bank Group, *A Measured Approach to Ending Poverty and Boosting Shared Prosperity: Concepts, Data, and the Twin Goals* (Policy Research Report, 2015); *The Economist*, 'Towards the End of Poverty', 1 June 2013.

6   In an influential study conducted for the World Bank in 2000 involving data collected from more than 60,000 poor people from countries all over the world, the number one mentioned answer to the question of what they needed to improve their lives was 'employment': D. Narayan *et al.*, *Voices of the Poor: Crying Out for Change* (New York: Oxford University Press for the World Bank, 2000).

7   See B. Stephens, 'The Amorality of Profit: Transnational Corporations and Human Rights' (2002) 20 *Berkeley Journal of International Law* 45. For a wealth of information on all aspects of corporate interaction on human rights issues, see Business & Human Rights Resource Centre, www.business-humanrights.org.

8   See S. Deva in this volume, 'Bhopal: the saga continues 31 years on', p. 22.

9   S. Deva, *Regulating Corporate Human Rights Violations* (New York: Routledge, 2012) p. 30.

10 Ibid., p. 28.

11 In the United States, see *In Re Union Carbide Corporation Gas Plant Disaster at Bhopal, India in December 1984*, 634 F. Supp. 842 (1986); affirmed, *In Re Union Carbide Corporation Gas Plant Disaster at Bhopal,*

India in December 1984, 809 F. 2d 195 (2d Cir. 1987). In India, see *Union Carbide Corporation v Union of India*, AIR 1990 SC 273; *Union Carbide Corporation v Union of India*, AIR 1992 SC 248.

12 *In Re Union Carbide Corporation Gas Plant Disaster at Bhopal, India in December 1984*, 809 F. 2d 195 (2d Cir. 1987).

13 Litigation is still ongoing in this matter and victims are still waiting for justice. See Amnesty International, '28 Years Later, Women in Bhopal Still Waiting for Justice', 3 December 2012, www.amnestyusa.org/news/news-item/28-years-later-women-in-bhopal-still-waiting-for-justice; Amnesty International, 'India: Court Decision Requires Dow Chemical to Respond to Bhopal Gas Tragedy', 23 July 2013, www.amnesty.org/en/articles/news/2013/07/india-court-decision-requires-dowchemical-respond-bhopal-gas-tragedy.

14 Nike is one of the world's largest suppliers of athletic shoes and apparel and a major manufacturer of sports equipment, with revenues in excess of US$25 billion in 2014: Nike, 'Nike, Inc. Reports Fiscal 2014 Fourth Quarter and Full Year Results', 26 June 2014, http://news.nike.com/news/nike-inc-reports-fiscal-2014-fourth-quarter-and-full-year-results-fiscal-2014-fourth-quarter-and-full-year-results.

15 As of December 2014: Nike, 'Frequently Asked Questions', http://nikeinc.com/pages/frequently-asked-questions.

16 Dara O'Rourke, *Smoke from a Hired Gun: A Critique of Nike's Labor and Environmental Auditing in Vietnam as Performed by Ernst & Young* (San Francisco: Transnational Resource and Action Center, 1997) p. 6, http://nature.berkeley.edu/orourke/PDF/smoke.pdf. Note that although this quotation references Nike as 'employing' some 350,000 workers, the workers were not employed directly by Nike but rather were employed by the company operating the factory in which the garments were produced. See also the reproduction of the leaked Ernst & Young 'Environmental and Labor Practice Audit' report of 13 January 1997: Corpwatch, 'Ernst & Young Environmental and Labor Practice Audit of the Tae Kwang Vina Industrial Ltd Co, Vietnam', www.corpwatch.org/article.php?id=2488.

17 M. Nisen, 'Why the Bangladesh Factory Collapse Would Never Have Happened to Nike', *Business Insider Australia*, 9 May 2013, www.businessinsider.com/how-nike-solved-its-sweatshop-problem-2013-5.

18 P. Utting, *Rethinking Business Regulation: From Self-Control to Social Control* (United Nations Research Institute for Social Development, Technology, Business and Society, Programme Paper No. 15, 2005) p. 1, www.unrisd.org/unrisd/website/document.nsf/462fc27bd1fce00880256b4a0060d2af/f02ac3db0ed406e0c1257 0a10029bec8/$FILE/utting.pdf.

19 According to Utting,

   the term 'multistakeholder initiatives' is often used to refer to voluntary CSR initiatives where two or more stakeholders, actors of interest groups cooperate in the design and application of standards. Such stakeholders often include companies, industry associations, NGOs, trade unions, government agencies and international organizations. Multistakeholder institutions are sometimes legally constituted as not-for-profit organizations, with different interests and actors in their governance structures.

   (Rethinking Business Regulation)

   See also D. Baumann-Pauly *et al.* in this volume, 'Setting and enforcing industry-specific standards for human rights: the role of multi-stakeholder initiatives in regulating corporate conduct', p. 107.

20 See Fair Labor Association, www.fairlabor.org. See also A. van Heerden in this volume, 'The Fair Labor Association: improving workers' rights in global supply chains', p. 128.

21 Nike, 'Global Manufacturing', http://manufacturingmap.nikeinc.com.

22 Letter from Nike Inc, the Adidas Group, Gap Inc and Knights Apparel to The Hon. Hillary R. Clinton, 27 July 2009, www.adidas-group.com/media/filer_public/2013/08/13/2009_07_27_adidasgroup_letter_clinton.pdf.

23 'Apple under Fire Again for Working Conditions at Chinese Factories', *Guardian*, 19 December 2014; C. Duhigg and D. Barboza, 'In China, Human Costs Are Built into an iPad', *New York Times*, 25 January 2012; China Labor Watch, *Beyond Foxconn: Deplorable Working Conditions Characterize Apple's Entire Supply Chain* (27 June 2012), www.chinalaborwatch.org/upfile/2012_8_13/2012627-5.pdf; R. Litzinger, 'Labor in China: A New Politics of Struggle' (2013) 112 (1) *South Atlantic Quarterly* 172.

24 Duhigg and Barboza, 'In China, Human Costs Are Built into an iPad'.

25 A. Chakrabortty, 'The Woman Who Nearly Died Making Your iPad', *Guardian*, 6 August 2013. In 2010, 18 Foxconn employees attempted suicide, with 14 deaths. The suicides drew media scrutiny, and employment practices at Foxconn, a large contract manufacturer, were investigated by several of its customers including Apple and HP: ibid. Foxconn is a major manufacturer that has catered to such companies as Apple, Dell, HP, Motorola, Nintendo, Nokia and Sony.

26 See J. Nolan in this volume, 'Rana Plaza: the collapse of a factory in Bangladesh and its ramifications for the global garment industry', p. 27.

27 S. Labowitz and D. Baumann-Pauly, *Business as Usual Is Not an Option: Supply Chains and Sourcing after Rana Plaza* (New York University: Stern Center for Business and Human Rights, 2014) p. 23.

28 R. Boele, H. Fabig and D. Wheeler, 'Shell, Nigeria and the Ogoni: A Study in Unsustainable Development. I. The Story of Shell, Nigeria and the Ogoni People: Environment, Economy, Relationships – Conflict and Prospects for Resolution' (2001) 9 *Sustainable Development* 74.

29 C. Kaeb, 'Emerging Issues of Human Rights Responsibility in the Extractive and Manufacturing Industries: Patterns and Liability Risks' (2008) 6(2) *Northwestern Journal of International Human Rights* 327. For a discussion of the diamond industry and its challenges, see I. Smillie, 'Blood Diamonds and Non-State Actors' (2013) 46(4) *Vanderbilt Journal of Transnational Law* 1003.

30 Kaeb, 'Emerging Issues of Human Rights Responsibility', p. 332.

31 Shell did not admit liability and stated the payment was a 'humanitarian gesture': J. Mouawad, 'Shell to Pay $15.5 Million to Settle Nigerian Case', *New York Times*, 8 June 2009.

32   *Kiobel v Royal Dutch Petroleum Co*, 133 S. Ct. 1659 (2013).
33   Shell International, *The Shell Report 1999: People, Planet and Profit – An Act of Commitment* (1999), http://reports.shell.com/sustainability-report/2011/servicepages/previous/files/shell_report_1999.pdf.
34   See S. Jerbi in this volume, 'Extractives and multi-stakeholder initiatives: the Voluntary Principles on Security and Human Rights; the Extractive Industries Transparency Initiative; the Kimberley Process Certification Scheme', p. 147.
35   Amnesty International, *Undermining Freedom of Expression in China: The Role of Yahoo!, Microsoft and Google* (2006) p. 4, www.amnesty.org/en/documents/pol30/026/2006/en. See also Human Rights Watch, *'Race to the Bottom': Corporate Complicity in Chinese Internet Censorship* (Vol. 18, No. 8(C), August 2006), www.hrw.org/reports/2006/china0806/china0806web.pdf.
36   T. Zeller Jr., 'Web Firms Are Grilled on Dealings in China', *New York Times*, 16 February 2006. Tom Lantos, California Democrat and House Foreign Affairs Committee Chairman, has been quoted as saying to representatives of Yahoo!, 'While technologically and financially you are giants, morally you are pygmies'. Z. Coile, 'Lawmakers Blast Yahoo Executives for Helping China Jail Dissident', *San Francisco Chronicle*, 7 November 2007.
37   J. Nolan, 'The China Dilemma: Internet Censorship and Corporate Responsibility' (2009) 4(1) *Asian Journal of Comparative Law*, article 3.
38   Amnesty International, *Undermining Freedom of Expression in China*, p. 18. The pledge was signed by Yahoo!'s wholly owned subsidiary based in Hong Kong.
39   *Wang Xiaoning v Yahoo! Inc*, No. 07-cv-2151 (ND Cal. filed 18 April 2007). In 2007, the parties agreed to a private settlement and issued a joint stipulation of dismissal in which Yahoo! agreed to bear the plaintiffs' legal costs and establish a fund 'to provide humanitarian and legal aid to dissidents who have been imprisoned for expressing their views online': see, e.g. Business & Human Rights Resource Centre, 'Yahoo! Lawsuit (re China)', http://business-humanrights.org/en/yahoo-lawsuit-re-china-0?page=3. The case concerned the detention and imprisonment of Chinese activist Wang Xiaoning and Chinese journalist Shi Tao, who were each subsequently sentenced to 10 years' imprisonment in China on respective charges of incitement to subvert state power and of illegally providing state secrets to foreign entities. Wang was found guilty on the basis of essays advocating democratic reform and multi-party democracy in China that he distributed via email and through Yahoo! Shi was convicted on the basis of an email he sent from his Yahoo! account to an Internet forum. The email contained his comments on a Chinese government circular prepared in advance of the 15th anniversary of the Tiananmen Square uprising outlining restrictions on the media.
40   J. Vijayan, 'Snowden Leaks Erode Trust in Internet Companies, Government', *ComputerWorld*, 4 April 2014, www.computerworld.com/article/2489544/data-privacy/snowden-leaks-erode-trust-in-internet-companies--government.html.
41   S. Rosenblatt, 'Tech Firms Reveal Even More about FISA Requests', Cnet, 4 February 2014, www.cnet.com/au/news/tech-firms-reveal-even-more-about-fisa-requests.
42   M. Samway, 'Business, Human Rights and the Internet', in A.C. Arend and M.P. Lagon (eds), *Human Dignity and the Future of Global Institutions* (Washington, DC: Georgetown University Press, 2014) pp. 295, 300.
43   Ibid.
44   I. Brown and D. Korff, 'Digital Freedoms in International Law', Global Network Initiative, 14 June 2012, p. 4J, https://globalnetworkinitiative.org/sites/default/files/Digital%20Freedoms%20in%20International%20Law.pdf; J. Garside, 'Vodafone under Fire for Bowing to Egyptian Pressure', *Guardian*, 27 July 2011.

Section 1.2

Making the business case for human rights: an assessment

Dorothée Baumann-Pauly and Michael Posner

1 Doing business in the 21st century: the relevance of human rights for companies

Companies, particularly globally operating companies, are confronted with human rights issues in their day-to-day business practices. For example, in the manufacturing sector, corporations have been struggling to ensure compliance with labour rights in their global supply chains for decades. Similarly, companies in the information and communication technology (ICT) sector are today increasingly expected to respond to privacy concerns and complicity allegations when operating in repressive regimes that restrict freedom of expression. These human rights issues affect the companies' core business processes and not addressing them is for many companies, particularly those in the media spotlight, no longer an option. Yet effectively installing human rights policies and procedures may be costly. It may even affect the very business model on which these companies have thrived. In these circumstances, the question becomes: How can corporations make the business case for human rights and explain to their shareholders and stakeholders why changes are potentially beneficial to their businesses? This chapter reviews the business case debate in academia and practice and assesses how some corporations have begun to explain their investment in human rights. The chapter concludes with an agenda that can assist in creating an 'enabling environment' for corporations to adopt human rights policies and practices.

For many large multinational companies in the 21st century, global expansion is central to their business model. Many of these companies are powerful global actors, some with annual revenues that match or exceed the gross domestic product of nation states where they do business.[1] The process of globalization, in which transnational corporations (TNCs) have played and continue to play a major role, has been a driver of development in less developed countries, lifting hundreds of millions of people out of extreme poverty over the last 30 years.[2]

The primary motivation for the global expansion of TNCs is profit. Some TNCs depend heavily on natural resources obtained in far-flung places: for example, companies in the energy sector. Others go abroad in an effort to lower manufacturing or other production costs, particularly companies operating in industries with thin profit margins. Increasingly, many global brands are also seeking to expand their customer bases by appealing to rapidly growing emerging markets, like China and India.

As they extend their geographic reach, these companies have come to recognize that doing business in a globalized world presents a series of social and environmental challenges that they cannot ignore. Operating across many national borders, they struggle to adapt in countries that do not offer predictable, safe operating conditions. All too often they find themselves doing business in countries where local governments are either unwilling or unable to provide a stable, business-friendly environment, where corruption is endemic and where commercial systems are not subject to the rule of law.[3]

In many less developed countries, environmental safeguards and standards are lax. Yet in the last 20 years a significant number of companies have responded to growing international demands for them to minimize their environmental footprints by investing in various environmental safeguards. At the same time, these companies have moved far more cautiously in addressing the human rights challenges they face, even when there is clear evidence that their actions are contributing to these often very serious problems. This reticence is beginning to change. In particular, the responsibility of global businesses to ensure respect for human rights in their places of operation has solidified since the adoption of the UN Guiding Principles on Business and Human Rights[4] in 2011. These responsibilities are especially acute when governments cannot or will not regulate corporate conduct in ways that protect the rights of people. But the exact nature and scope of those obligations is still far from well-defined. Human rights advocates within companies need greater clarity and better data as they strive to make the business case within their companies for adopting more ambitious human rights programmes.

In addressing human rights challenges, the first step companies must take is to assess the full range of human rights challenges they face in their core business operations. Once they have assessed these risks they need to develop plans of action for addressing these challenges. If there are added costs, as there often will be, the company must decide whether and at what level it is willing to invest the necessary resources. In some instances, this may require a company to decline certain business deals where the risks of doing business are too great. In other instances, companies may face the prospect of continuing existing work-streams but applying different business models to them. Often a single company will not have the authority or capacity to act alone, so it will need to develop cooperative approaches with its business competitors and coordinate with leaders in the communities in which it operates.

Addressing the human rights risks of corporate activity is often hard, particularly where human rights challenges derive from state practice. Internet companies operating in places like China or Russia face these challenges on a daily basis. In other industries, doing the right thing for human rights is likely to require financial and strategic investments on the part of companies. Why then should companies proactively respect human rights? And how do they make the business case for doing so?

2 The academic debate on the business case for human rights

In academia, the focus of myriad studies has been on measuring the link between a company's broad commitment to corporate responsibility (of which addressing human rights challenges may be a part) and financial performance.[5] Evidence from one of the most comprehensive meta-studies to date, which analysed the results of close to 200 studies on the topic, showed a small but positive correlation between corporate responsibility and financial performance.[6] A new meta-study that was published in 2015 further supports earlier findings and shows that there is a positive relationship between companies' commitments to corporate social responsibility (CSR) and their financial performance, at least for Western companies.[7] However, considering the methodological challenges and the reporting biases that underlie many of these studies, the overall question of whether corporate engagement with CSR truly pays off remains at best inconclusive.[8]

To date, these systematic studies have focused on CSR broadly and not specifically on human rights. Some studies have focused on corporate engagement with environmental issues; these studies show quite consistently that there is at least some positive effect from environmentally sound policies on a firm's performance.[9] From a methodological standpoint, the business case for environmental sustainability is easier to analyse than the case for commitment to human rights.[10] Energy savings, for example, are measurable and the cost reductions often create a win–win situation for society and the company.[11] Systematically overcoming human rights challenges, by contrast, often requires a company to make additional investments in training, social compliance audits or enhanced infrastructure.[12] The benefits for these investments may come over the longer term, but will not be evident in the short term. Longitudinal studies that would measure such long-term benefits for corporations do not yet exist and assessing the qualitative impact of human rights initiatives will be a challenge.[13]

Accordingly, it remains an open question as to whether the relative costs and economic benefits of adopting strong human rights policies can be quantified empirically. Normative business ethics scholars would argue that the question of whether there is a business case for human rights is the wrong starting point to motivate and justify the engagement of corporations in human rights. While these scholars are not against making the business case, they start from the premise that human rights are a normative imperative and that no economic rationale is needed for companies to devote resources to addressing these challenges.[14]

To illustrate their thinking, take the issue of child labour, which is often a profitable alternative in specific environments such as family farming. Business case sceptics would say that even if there is a strong economic rationale for using child labour, it is not an acceptable practice.[15]

While these normative arguments are convincing in theory, they are unlikely to win the day inside most corporations where chief executive officers (CEOs) must justify added costs to their shareholders. The current framing of the debate, with its narrow focus on negative risks weighed against short-term corporate financial performance, is the wrong frame to discuss and decide these issues. What is needed instead is a broadening of the debate by taking a longer-term horizon and also exploring the affirmative aspects of the business case for undertaking a serious engagement with human rights.

3 Making the business case for addressing human rights

The question of whether there is a business case for adopting human rights programmes is also debated internally within large corporations.[16] It revolves around a consideration of the costs of making commitments relating to human rights and weighing those costs against the benefits that will accrue to the company and its relevant stakeholders.

Inside each company the business case for human rights has both negative and positive dimensions. The negative business case focuses on avoiding human rights risks and violations through corporate operations and public relations exercises; the positive business case points to the potential benefits of proactively addressing human rights issues that are linked to core business operations.

3.1 The negative business case for human rights

The key negative dimension of the business case for human rights engagement is the risk to a company's reputation if action is not taken. This risk is especially real for consumer-facing companies; it is also growing as the expansion of the Internet, mobile phones and social media links more people globally and allows negative words and images exposing company practices to become exponentially more accessible. Companies that have become the target of media attention, non-governmental organization and consumer campaigns and occasional litigation resulting from their association with human rights problems know the potential costs associated with this negative public attention. By developing credible human rights programmes companies will be in a stronger position to manage these reputational, operational and legal risks. At a time when public polls show great fluctuations in public trust in companies (and since 2014 a sharp decline), the need to address human rights problems in a credible manner is an increasingly important element of a company's larger effort to maintain and restore public trust. The Edelman Trust Barometer captures the nuances of these developments on an annual basis and has in this context become an important reference for companies.[17]

The following case from the mining sector illustrates the costs that can accrue when human rights concerns are not taken into account.

Snapshot

Negative business case: cost of conflict

A 2014 report entitled *Costs of Company–Community Conflict in the Extractive Sector* explores the full range of costs to extractive companies from failing to prevent or mitigate conflict with local communities around their operations.[18] The research shows that:

- the most frequent costs were those arising from lost productivity due to temporary shutdowns or delays;
- the single most often overlooked cost was staff time spent managing conflicts with local communities, including the CEO's time; and
- the greatest cost of conflict according to the report was the opportunity costs in terms of the lost value linked to future projects, expansion plans or sales that did not go ahead.

The report also points out that managing conflict with local communities is delicate as such conflicts can easily spin out of control and turn into international campaigns against the company and in some cases result in costly litigation. Community conflicts can also have a knock-on effect on the company's ability to recruit and/or retain top talent. The report concludes that extractive companies generally do not identify, understand and aggregate these costs. As a result, this information does not receive attention from senior management or boards of directors and is therefore not taken into account in business decision-making.

While human rights risks are substantial and often costly for many corporations, such companies typically opt to address these risks as legal or public relations problems rather than tackling the underlying problems. This is a short-sighted but all too familiar approach to these challenges, particularly for companies that are not in the public spotlight. When companies apply a purely economic rationale to their operations, and focus only on the pressure to achieve maximum short-term financial returns, they often decide that the potential negative impact of human rights problems simply does not outweigh the time, money and attention it would take to deal effectively with the complex issues that underlie many business and human rights challenges. In effect, they decide to accept such costs as unavoidable but manageable costs of doing business.[19]

The development of marketing-oriented CSR departments in many large companies is one manifestation of this approach. Companies that park the human rights portfolio in their CSR offices, rather than in their central operations departments, are marginalizing these issues and opting to view them through this public relations prism. The alternative these companies seek to avoid is to address human rights challenges effectively and as a central business objective. They recognize that doing so may require investments and even changes in the company's business model.[20] A risk mitigation-oriented approach alone, however, will not justify such a substantial review of corporate operations. How can engaging in human rights make good business sense?

3.2 The affirmative business case for human rights: responding to 21st-century challenges

Leading companies that are beginning to address human rights challenges consider their firms as part of an increasingly integrated global community. They incorporate human rights into their core business strategies and see their engagement as part of their future business models. They acknowledge both the challenges and opportunities that come with doing business globally in the 21st century. They also recognize that their companies will be most likely to thrive in increasingly healthy, rights-respecting societies. Consider Hewlett Packard's sustainability strategy called 'Living Progress', which is built upon this model. Their CEO, Meg Whitman, says:

> HP Living Progress is our framework for thinking about how we do business. It's the way we integrate sustainability into our business strategy, building on a commitment we articulated in our company objectives in 1957 and have reaffirmed every year since. We consider human, economic, and environmental impacts across our entire value chain as we develop our products, services, and solutions, manage our operations, and drive interactions with our customers, partners, and communities.[21]

In a very different industry, athletic shoes and apparel, Nike, an industry leader, describes its business model based on principles of sustainability:

> We understand that innovation through the lens of sustainability is fundamental to achieving our vision of growth that is not dependent upon constrained resources. Indeed, creating and building business models that not only recognize and accommodate but thrive on the constraints of the natural world is the only way we can achieve growth in the present that won't compromise our ability to grow and succeed for decades to come.[22]

With the objective of ensuring its long-term success, Unilever has developed a sustainability strategy in the food and beverage sector. In support of that approach, Unilever's CEO Paul Polman argues that the fiduciary duty of corporations is not simply to prioritize short-term shareholders returns but to invest in business models that serve both business and society:

I don't think our fiduciary duty is to put shareholders first. I say the opposite. What we firmly believe is that if we focus our company on improving the lives of the world's citizens and come up with genuine sustainable solutions, we are more in synch with consumers and society and ultimately this will result in good shareholder returns. Why would you invest in a company which is out of synch with the needs of society, that does not take its social compliance in its supply chain seriously, that does not think about the costs of externalities, or of its negative impacts on society?[23]

Unilever's 'Sustainable Living Plan' was launched in November 2010. It decouples growth from environmental impact while endeavouring to increase the company's positive social impact.[24] One element in this 10-year strategy is to advance human rights across the company's operations and extended supply chain by 2020. To implement this long-term strategy, Polman has, for example, abandoned quarterly profit reporting as part of a long-term strategy:

We have aligned management incentives for the long term and invested heavily in R&D to build our pipeline of innovations. In addition, we have moved away from quarterly profit reporting; since we don't operate on a 90-day cycle for advertising, marketing, or investment, why do so for reporting?[25]

Polman also highlights the business case for this rationale. He points out that the so-called 'licence to operate' means that corporations need to operate in a way that is socially acceptable:

Increasingly with governments being gridlocked, the need for change increasingly has to come from responsible business. If businesses understand that, they'll have a bright future. If businesses don't understand that, I think the consumer will increasingly vote them out of business.[26]

CEOs and senior managers of other companies echo Polman's long-term vision and his optimism in terms of a long-term positive return on investment (ROI). For example, Brian Krzanich, CEO of Intel Corporation, said in the context of a discussion on conflict minerals: 'I believe that, in the long-run, if you build a company to do the right thing, you'll get a return on investment.'[27]

Tim Cook, CEO of Apple, goes even further than Krzanich, arguing that an economic rational alone cannot be the only driver for business's engagement in societal matters. In a response to a question by a representative of the conservative National Center for Public Policy Research at a shareholder meeting, he said:

When we work on making our devices accessible by the blind, I don't consider the bloody ROI. The same thing applies to environmental issues, worker safety, and other areas where Apple is a leader. If you want me to do things only for ROI reasons, you should get out of this stock.[28]

For these and other leading companies, respecting human rights is becoming an integral part of an innovative business strategy that is also good for the overall health of the company. Ed Potter, Coca-Cola's Director for Global Workplace Rights, argues that respect for human rights within the global business community is maturing[29] and Coke's human rights engagement is visible to external and internal audiences and has positive effects:

> Coca-Cola has been a path maker. We are now sought after as a company to learn from, based on our tools and framework for respecting human rights. Everyone at Coca-Cola can feel very good every day because we're solving problems and improving workplace conditions across the business system and our supply chain.[30]

These policy statements alone do not prove that these, or any other companies, are perfect role models for implementing human rights programmes. In fact, these and virtually all other global companies confront persistent human rights challenges and do not always act in a rights-respecting manner. What these statements do show is that some companies apply a broader understanding to the business case question. The statements also reflect a longer-term, holistic perspective on the elements that will define future business success. Leading companies acknowledge the changing business landscape and highlight a mix of reasons that drive their search for alternative business models and their human rights engagement. While they are well aware of the risks associated with failing to address human rights challenges, they also see major potential benefits by adopting strong human rights practices. While each industry is very different, companies across the spectrum talk about their greater ability to hire and retain outstanding employees drawn to them by the inclusion of CSR (including human rights) in their business models.[31] They see good human rights policies as enhancing the quality control of their products and increasing worker retention throughout their supply chains.

Many of these companies have developed inclusive approaches to sustainability, which in turn shape their efforts to promote a clean environment, respect human rights, challenge corruption and improve community relations in an integrated approach. The positive business case for human rights also focuses on creating an environment where employees feel greater freedom to innovate and improve product quality, and ultimately to attract investors focused on social issues. Good human rights practices also ensure what is typically called the company's 'licence to operate'. In the academic discourse, scholars refer to the social acceptance of a corporation as 'corporate legitimacy'. The corporate legitimacy concept is based on how critical stakeholders perceive corporate operations. Managing corporate legitimacy is a business challenge for global corporations that operate in increasingly diverse environments and empirical studies show that respecting human rights has become a core requirement for corporate legitimacy.[32]

While references to each of these benefits are still largely anecdotal, it is clear that they are becoming important elements of the business culture for visionary companies. In some specific contexts, there are early efforts to measure benefits attributable to a positive business case for human rights. One example is a 2012 Berenschot report written for the Dutch Ministry of Foreign Affairs. It shows a positive connection between fair wages and increased productivity and decreases in labour turnover.[33] These findings were confirmed by a 2014 white paper published by the Fair Labor Association (FLA), a multi-stakeholder initiative (MSI) whose mission is to improve workers' rights. The FLA white paper concludes, '[s]uppliers that pay living wages are generally professionally managed companies who in turn should have a better chance to become a preferred supplier. Fair wages are a strong underpinning to more sustainable supply chains'.[34]

4 Shared responsibility to foster the business case for human rights

While some leading companies have started to address human rights challenges in their business operations, it is clear that they cannot address governance gaps on their own. To drive change in the field of corporate human rights conduct and to foster the positive business case for human rights, several things need to change.

First, companies will be much more likely to invest in human rights initiatives in a financial environment where large investors are willing to make longer-term investments that give CEOs greater latitude to develop and apply resources to build programmes to protect the environment, human rights and other social aspects into their business operations. Typically, there are no quick fixes for overcoming human rights challenges. Successful programmes also will require some initial investments, which will incur costs. And global businesses, acting alone, cannot be expected to absorb all of these costs. New models of shared responsibility and accountability are therefore required. Shared responsibility means that global brands will help identify the human rights risks and costs associated with their core businesses and then participate in collective efforts to share these costs with local business partners, local and foreign governments, international financial institutions and others. Developing new business models that embrace notions of shared responsibility will be a foundation for the sustainability of business and the willingness of global companies to engage seriously with human rights. Creating platforms that allow key industry stakeholders to come together to jointly develop a formula by which they can determine the fair share of responsibility for each individual actor is therefore of paramount importance for (cost-)effectively addressing human rights challenges as well as for business sustainability.

Companies also need to recognize that each business sector has specific human rights challenges, which need to be addressed across the industry. To date about 400 companies have adopted and published their own human rights policies.[35] But many of these 'policies' are very general and modest in scope, and much work still needs to be done on an industry-by-industry basis to develop concrete human rights standards and metrics that companies will use in their business operations. Clarifying which core business practices have an impact on human rights and defining industry-specific standards and metrics for addressing them will ensure that there is a level playing field for what is expected from each company. This is important as it allows individual companies to make concrete cost calculations of how to reach the industry benchmark that applies to all industry players equally.

In some industries, MSIs have been created to help set standards and to provide both a framework for evaluating company performance and a pooled resource for companies in implementing human rights programmes. These MSIs, typically involving civil society, academic and other private actors, and in some cases also involving governments, help to reduce the costs and risks of human rights compliance by allowing companies to pool resources as they address complex human rights challenges in their industry. These MSIs also provide a safe forum where each company can benefit from lessons learned across their industry and they help companies to credibly show their systematic progress with respect to human rights challenges.[36] This is particularly valuable in a context in which an increasing number of companies report on their human rights activities but where it also remains difficult for critical external observers to set apart and reward the companies that make serious and systematic efforts to address human rights.

On a parallel track, each individual company needs to ensure that their internal organizational structures and procedures are aligned with their broader commitment to human rights. For human rights issues to be addressed on a routine basis at all levels of a company, internal human rights policies and procedures need to be defined and enforced. This requires the full support of senior management, global dissemination by training employees and a clear articulation of the real consequences if these policies and procedures are not followed. Such measures help to ensure that respecting human rights becomes part of a company's internal culture and those human rights risks are indeed effectively mitigated.

Companies that are building credible human rights programmes also need to build trusted relationships with critical stakeholders. Regular engagement with key stakeholders facilitates the identification of emerging human rights issues and allows a company to address them proactively. It opens the door to include local community leaders and other outside experts who can help define and assist in the implementation of human rights policies and to increase their effectiveness. A 2013 study published in the *Strategic Management Journal* provided preliminary evidence of the direct positive link between stakeholder engagement and the financial markets' evaluation of firms.[37] It showed that 'the social licence to operate' can be empirically tested and that maintaining such a licence is in the enlightened self-interest of corporations.[38]

Finally, companies have an important role to play in educating consumers and investors. Clear industry standards, metrics and benchmarks will create meaningful reference points for reporting and evaluating company performance, both in terms of internal processes and actual outcomes. It will increase transparency over corporate conduct and promote a race to the top, which will benefit industry leaders and enable consumers and investors to make informed purchasing and investing decisions.[39]

In a world in which business is increasingly called upon to address broader social and environmental issues, corporate engagement with human rights goes beyond acting upon a moral obligation. Embedding human rights in core business processes becomes a business imperative to ensure the company's licence to operate. An increasing number of business leaders recognize the potential business benefits that accrue to their companies when they develop strong human rights standards and compliance programmes. Models of shared responsibility as outlined above can help to foster an 'enabling environment' for the affirmative business case for human rights.[40]

Notes

1   For a comparison of national GDP and TNC revenue, see V. Trivett, '25 US Mega Corporations: Where They Rank If They Were Countries', *Business Insider*, 27 June 2011, www.businessinsider.com/25-corporations-bigger-tan-countries-2011-6?op=1&IR=T.

2   *The Economist*, 'Towards the End of Poverty', 1 June 2013, www.economist.com/news/leaders/21578665-nearly-1-billion-people-have-been-taken-out-extreme-poverty-20-years-world-should-aim.

3   The academic literature is divided on whether a stable environment is necessary for business to be successful. Some businesses may actually thrive in or take advantage of unstable political or security environments and

be profitable in doing so. See, e.g. M. Guidolin and E. La Ferrara, 'Diamonds Are Forever, Wars Are Not: Is Conflict Bad for Private Firms?' (2007) 97(5) *The American Economic Review* 1978; V.H. Hoffmann, T. Trautmann and J. Hamprechts, 'Regulatory Uncertainty: A Reason to Postpone Investments? Not Necessarily' (2009) 46(7) *Journal of Management Studies* 1227. However, in most industries, if corporations are focused on mitigating risks, stable environments are preferable to unstable environments.

4   Human Rights Council, 'Guiding Principles on Business and Human Rights: Implementing the United Nations "Protect, Respect and Remedy" Framework', Report of the Special Representative of the Secretary-General on the Issue of Human Rights and Transnational Corporations and Other Business Enterprises, UN Doc. A/HRC/17/31 (21 March 2011).

5   For reviews of the academic literature, see J.J. Griffin and J.F. Mahon, 'The Corporate Social Performance and Corporate Financial Performance Debate: Twenty-Five Years of Incomparable Research' (1997) 36(1) *Business and Society* 5; M. Orlitzky, F.L. Schmidt and S.L. Rynes, 'Corporate Social and Financial Performance: A Meta-analysis' (2003) 24(3) *Organization Studies* 403; J.D. Margolis and J.P. Walsh, *People and Profits: The Search for a Link between a Company's Social and Financial Performance* (Mahwah, NJ: Lawrence Erlbaum, 2001); J.D. Margolis and J.P. Walsh, 'Misery Loves Companies: Rethinking Social Initiatives by Business' (2003) 48(2) *Administrative Science Quarterly* 268; J.D. Margolis, H.A. Elfenbein and J.P. Walsh, 'Do Well by Doing Good? Don't Count on It' (2008) 86(1) *Harvard Business Review* 19.

6   J.D. Margolis, H.A. Elfenbein and J.P. Walsh, 'Does It Pay to Be Good? A Meta-Analysis and Redirection of Research on the Relationship between Corporate Social and Financial Performance', 1 November 2007, www.hks.harvard.edu/m-rcbg/papers/seminars/margolis_november_07.pdf.

7   Q. Wang, J. Duo and S. Jia, 'A Meta Analytical Review of Corporate Social Responsibility and Corporate Financial Performance: The Moderating Effect of Contextual Factors', *Business & Society* (published online 4 May 2015).

8   K. Rost and T. Ehrmann, 'Reporting Biases in Empirical Management Research: The Example of Win–Win Corporate Social Responsibility', *Business & Society* (published online 15 February 2015).

9   S. Ambec and P. Lanoie, 'Does It Pay to Be Green? A Systematic Overview' (2008) 22(4) *Academy of Management Perspectives* 45.

10 D. De Felice, 'Business and Human Rights Indicators to Measure the Corporate Responsibility to Respect: Challenges and Opportunities' (2015) 37 *Human Rights Quarterly* 511.

11 Ambec and Lanoie, 'Does It Pay to Be Green?'

12 See, e.g. the estimated costs for making the garment sector in Bangladesh safe and sustainable: S. Labowitz, 'Garment Factory Repairs' (Letter to the Editor), *New York Times*, 22 October 2014, www.nytimes.com/2014/10/23/opinion/garment-factory-repairs.html?module=Search&mabReward=relbias%3Aw%2C{%221%22%3A%22RI%3A8%22}&_r=1.

13 De Felice, 'Business and Human Rights Indicators to Measure the Corporate Responsibility to Respect'.

14 For an overview of the normative business ethics debate, see F. Wettstein, 'Human Rights as a Critique of Instrumental CSR: Corporate Responsibility beyond the Business Case' (2012) 18 *Notizie di Politeia* 18.

15 See A. Crane *et al.*, 'Contesting the Value of "Creating Shared Value"' (2014) 56(2) *California Management Review* 130.

16 For example, the Action 2020 plan of the World Business Council for Sustainable Development, a CEO-led organization of large well-known companies, summarizes why human rights are good for business here: http://action2020.org/business-solutions/operationalize-the-un-guiding-principles-on-business-and-human.

17 See Edelman, '2015 Edelman Trust Barometer', www.edelman.com/2015-edelman-trust-barometer.

18 R. Davis and D.M. Franks, *Costs of Company–Community Conflict in the Extractive Sector*, CSR Initiative Report No. 66 (Cambridge, MA: Harvard Kennedy School, 2014).

19 See, for example, the example of BP described in M.J. Bekink in this volume, 'Thinking long term: investment strategies and responsibility', p. 231.

20 In the context of sourcing practices in the garment sector, see, e.g. S. Labowitz and D. Baumann-Pauly, *Business as Usual* Is *Not an Option: Supply Chains and Sourcing after Rana Plaza* (2014), www.stern.nyu.edu/cons/groups/content/documents/webasset/con_047408.pdf.

21 HP's CEO Meg Whitman: www8.hp.com/us/en/hp-information/global-citizenship/ceoletter.html.

22 Nike, Inc, 'Our Sustainability Strategy', www.nikeresponsibility.com/report/content/chapter/our-sustainability-strategy#sthash.ErIBlWCW.dpuf.

23 See J. Confino, 'Unilever's Paul Polman: Challenging the Corporate Status Quo', *The Guardian*, 24 April 2012, www.theguardian.com/sustainable-business/paul-polman-unilever-sustainable-living-plan.

24 Unilever, 'Sustainable Living', www.unilever.com/sustainable-living-2014/our-approach-to-sustainability/unilever-sustainable-living-plan-summary.

25 McKinsey & Company, 'Paul Polman: The Remedies for Capitalism', www.mckinsey.com/features/capitalism/paul_polman.

26 K. Ryssdal, 'Unilever CEO: For Sustainable Business, Go against "Mindless Consumption"', Marketplace, 11 June 2013, www.marketplace.org/topics/sustainability/consumed/unilever-ceo-paul-polman-sustainable-business.

27 NYU Stern Center for Business and Human Rights, 'In Pursuit of Conflict Free: A Conversation on Corporate Responsibility', 19 September 2014, www.stern.nyu.edu/experience-stern/news-events/in-pursuit-of-conflict-free.

28 K. Russell, 'Tim Cook Erupts after Shareholder Asks Him to Focus Only on Profit', *Business Insider*, 28 February 2014, www.businessinsider.com/tim-cook-versus-a-conservative-think-tank-2014-2#ixzz3amX018fg.

29 J. Moye, 'Coke's Ed Potter Reflects on 33 Years at the ILO Conference', Coca-Cola, 17 November 2014, www.coca-colacompany.com/stories/cokes-ed-potter-reflects-on-33-years-at-the-ilo-conference.

30 Ibid.
31 See S. Gargiulo, 'Why Everyone Wants to Work for the "Good Guys"', CNN, 7 November 2012, www.cnn.com/2012/11/07/business/global-office-csr-volunteer.
32 See D. Baumann-Pauly, *Managing Corporate Legitimacy: A Toolbox* (Sheffield: Greenleaf Publishing, 2013); D. Baumann-Pauly, A.G. Scherer and G. Palazzo, 'Managing Institutional Complexity: A Longitudinal Study of Legitimacy Strategies at a Sportswear Brand' (2015) *Journal of Business Ethics* (forthcoming).
33 Berenschot, *Living Wage in International Supply Chains: An Inventory Report* (2012), www.berenschot.com/publish/pages/2787/living_wage_12-07.pdf.
34 Fair Labor Association, 'Organizational Strategy on Wages, Draft for Discussion', 8 October 2014, http://origin.library.constantcontact.com/download/get/file/1103529695246-223/FLA+Wage+Strategy+Draft.pdf.
35 For a list of corporations that have issued a corporate human rights policy, see Business & Human Rights Resource Centre, 'Company Policy Statements on Human Rights', http://business-humanrights.org/en/company-policy-statements-on-human-rights.
36 See D. Baumann-Pauly *et al.* in this volume, 'Setting and enforcing industry-specific standards for human rights: the role of multi-stakeholder initiatives in regulating corporate conduct', p. 107.
37 W.J. Henisz, S. Dorobantu and L.J. Nartey, 'Spinning Gold: The Financial Returns to Stakeholder Engagement' (2013) 35(12) *Strategic Management Journal* 1727.
38 See J. Morrison in this volume, 'The social licence: one way of thinking about business and human rights', p. 101.
39 See G. Palazzo, F. Morhart and J. Schrempf-Stirling in this volume, 'Shopping for a better world: how consumer decisions can help to promote sustainability and human rights', p. 200.
40 M. Lazala and J. Bardwell, '"What Human Rights?" Why Some Companies Speak out While Others Don't', Open Democracy, 17 June 2015, www.opendemocracy.net/openglobalrights/mauricio-lazala-joe-bardwell/%E2%80%9Cwhat-human-rights%E2%80%9D-why-some-companies-speak-out-while.

Section 1.3

Bhopal: the saga continues 31 years on

Surya Deva

1 Factual matrix

Union Carbide India Ltd (UCIL), a subsidiary of Union Carbide Corporation (UCC) – a multinational corporation (MNC) based in the US – had a chemical plant in Bhopal, a city in central India. On the night of 2 December 1984, there was a massive leakage of toxic gases from methyl isocyanate (MIC) storage tank number 610 of the Bhopal chemical plant.[1] The immediate cause for reaction and consequent leakage of gases was the introduction of water into the MIC storage tank.[2] However, there is no consensus on how water entered the tank.[3] Whereas UCC tried to explain this through a sabotage theory,[4] the Indian government suggested that water might have entered the tank during routine washing of pipes on that night.[5]

For a number of reasons, the precise number of people who died and who were injured from exposure to the leaked gases is unknown.[6] According to Amnesty International's estimate, 'between 7,000 and 10,000 people died within three days of the gas leak' and over 20,000 have died to date.[7] Out of the then estimated total population of Bhopal (894,539), more than 62 per cent (559,835) were affected by the gas leakage.[8] Many survivors still suffer from a range of medical conditions including respiratory illness, eye disease, immunity impairment, neurological damage, neuromuscular damage, cancers, gynaecological disorders, miscarriages and compromised mental health.[9] The leak at Bhopal also led to environmental pollution in the vicinity of the plant, including contamination of the ground water.[10]

Many different terms have been used to describe what happened in the city of Bhopal on the night of 2 December 1984 – from incident to accident, disaster, catastrophe, crisis, tragedy, sabotage, massacre and industrial genocide.[11] But I prefer to simply call it 'Bhopal' because this term has now acquired a secondary meaning: Bhopal symbolizes corporate impunity for human rights violations and the timid response of a government to such impunity.[12]

2 The ongoing battle for accountability

Bhopal resulted in complex litigation both in India and the US to impose civil as well criminal liability on UCC and UCIL.[13] In fact, the litigation saga continues in both jurisdictions, though victims should not have much hope for justice from this battle.

As UCC controlled UCIL, had supplied technology for the Bhopal plant as well as trained personnel working there, and UCIL had minimal assets with which to compensate a large number of victims, it made sense to sue UCC. Considering the undeveloped nature of Indian tort law and endemic delays in courts in India, it was also logical to sue UCC before the US courts. However, it was almost impossible for poor and non-English-speaking victims to go after the parent company in the US. This led to the Indian government acting as *parens patriae* and enacting a law in 1985 to claim an 'exclusive' right to represent all victims both within and outside India.[14]

In the first round of litigation in the US, the Indian government relied on two notable principles: absolute/strict liability for ultra-hazardous and inherently dangerous activity, and enterprise liability for MNCs. Neither of these arguments prevailed, as Judge Keenan on 12 May 1986 dismissed the suit on the ground of *forum non conveniens*.[15] The legal proceedings then began before Indian courts. In February 1989, the Indian Supreme Court approved a settlement under which UCC agreed to pay US$470 million to the Indian government in exchange for quashing all civil and criminal liabilities of UCC/UCIL.[16] The settlement order was heavily criticized as being unfair and unreasoned.[17]

The Indian Supreme Court later reinstated criminal cases against UCC/UCIL.[18] But no conviction took place until June 2010, when a court in the state of Madhya Pradesh found UCIL and seven of its executives guilty of criminal negligence.[19] The factory site as well as the waste disposal site is still highly contaminated with 'pesticides, chlorinated benzenes and heavy metals'.[20] While the United Nations Environment Programme has offered to undertake a full evaluation of the spread of toxic waste in and around the Bhopal plant,[21] the agency cannot operate without the consent and cooperation of the Indian government. Based on the government's previous failure to discharge its duty to respect, protect and fulfil human rights in relation to Bhopal, the future prospects of tough state actions in cleaning the site or providing continuous medical help to the affected victims do not appear to be very promising.

One can then conclude that Bhopal, 31 years on, continues to be a live example of corporate impunity for human rights violations.[22] UCC/UCIL never admitted any legal liability for Bhopal; UCC has in fact tried to avoid facing legal proceedings before Indian courts. Despite continuous civil society pressure, Dow Chemical, which took over UCC in 2001, continues to deny any responsibility for the loss of lives and subsequent environmental contamination.[23] Dow Chemical has also not responded to multiple summons issued by an Indian court pleading that it has no responsibility for Bhopal.[24]

3 Why is Bhopal still relevant?

Why does Bhopal continue to occupy a central space in the discourse on business ethics, corporate social responsibility and more recently business and human rights? There are several reasons.[25] First, Bhopal depicts the political economy within which companies typically violate human rights: an MNC based in a developed country passes on the risks of its profit-maximizing activities to the poor people of a developing country. It should be noted, though, that this dynamic is changing in the 21st century with the emergence of MNCs from developing countries as global players. These MNCs, say from BRIC (Brazil, Russia, India and China) countries, could externalize risks at the horizontal level (when operating in another developing country) or at an inverse vertical level (when operating in a developed country).

Second, victims' quest to hold UCC accountable for Bhopal brought to the fore almost all the substantive, procedural, conceptual and practical hurdles that arise in dealing with human rights violations by non-state actors operating at a transnational level. The illustrative examples of these hurdles include inadequate articulation of precise corporate human rights obligations, the difficulty in piercing the corporate veil, misuse of the doctrine of *forum non conveniens*, lack of legal aid to victims, the presence of a large number of victims, insufficiency of civil and criminal sanctions against corporations, and the involvement of corrupt state agencies.

Third, Bhopal illustrated that companies generally tend to deny any responsibility for human rights abuses linked to their actions unless they are subjected to significant pressure, whether inside the court through litigation or outside the court through civil society campaigns. Most of the more recent settlements that MNCs have reached with victims are offshoots of this 'pressure' narrative.[26]

Fourth, Bhopal remains relevant because the world community has not yet been able to put in place a regulatory framework that could both prevent and provide effective redress for corporate human rights abuses. In this way, Bhopal continues to serve as a touchstone to test the efficacy of regulatory initiatives aimed at ensuring that companies comply with their human rights obligations.

In short, Bhopal was, and remains, a stark reminder of the difficulties that victims of corporate human rights abuses experience in seeking justice, especially when an MNC is involved and both the home and the host governments lack the political will or capacity to pursue all means to hold the MNC accountable.

4 Lessons learned: what if Bhopal were to occur today?

What has changed since Bhopal? Have India and the global community learned any lessons from Bhopal? Would the outcomes for victims and the involved MNCs be any different if Bhopal were to occur today?

When Bhopal occurred in 1984, Edward Freeman has just published his famous book on the stakeholder theory, outlining why and how corporations should give due regard to the interests of their stakeholders.[27] But still there was no clear articulation of the human rights responsibilities of business. Nor were there many regulatory initiatives occupying this field in the early 1980s. The situation is much different now, most notably with the United Nations Human Rights Council endorsing the Guiding Principles on Business and Human Rights in June 2011.[28]

We have also seen that, since the 1990s, many MNCs have been sued in several jurisdictions for their involvement in human and labour rights violations or polluting the environment, something that was not common before Bhopal. Post-Bhopal, the reliance on courts to hold MNCs accountable has become a regular feature with elements of innovation, for instance, employing the 18th-century Alien Tort Claims Act[29] against corporations, and relying on a parent company's direct duty of care to bypass the need to pierce the corporate veil.[30]

Reliance on courts to hold companies accountable for human rights abuses has also been complemented by civil society-led complaints (for example, the use of National Contact Points under the OECD Guidelines for Multinational Enterprises[31]), advocacy and campaigns in multiple fora. As compared to the 1980s, civil society is now much more connected at the transnational level, greatly facilitated by the evolution of the Internet and other technologies. Consequently, a global network of civil society is much better placed to counter the influence of MNCs and to exert pressure on them.

The rise in the power of civil society in the last two decades or so has also made another difference. Unlike Bhopal, victims now no longer need to rely on state institutions to negotiate compensation with MNCs. Direct corporate settlements with victims – when the latter are empowered by the civil society and/or public interest-oriented law firms – have proved to be effective because they greatly reduce corruption possibilities in the distribution of compensation by state agencies.[32]

These differences should have *some* positive bearing on the access to justice outcomes if Bhopal were to occur today. Nevertheless, the location of a putative Bhopal would still have significant bearing on victims' access to effective remedies. If Bhopal occurred now not in the city of Bhopal but in a developed country, the response of the company as well as the relevant government is likely to be much different, as illustrated by the 2010 BP oil spill in the Gulf of Mexico. However, the very fact that the location of corporate human rights abuses and the identity of victims still has a bearing on access to justice indicates that we have not yet met all the challenges illustrated by Bhopal.

Notes

1   J. Cassels, *The Uncertain Promise of Law: Lessons from Bhopal* (Toronto: University of Toronto Press, 1993) p. 3; Amnesty International, *Clouds of Injustice: Bhopal Disaster 20 Years On* (London: Amnesty International, 2004) p. 10.
2   Cassels, *The Uncertain Promise of Law*, p. 4.
3   T. Kletz, *Learning from Accidents* (Oxford: Butterworth-Heinemann, 2nd ed., 1994) pp. 98–9; D. Kurzman, *A Killing Wind: Inside Union Carbide and the Bhopal Catastrophe* (New York: McGraw-Hill, 1987) pp. 185–9.
4   K. Fortun, *Advocacy after Bhopal: Environmentalism, Disaster, New Global Orders* (Chicago: University of Chicago Press, 2001) pp. 101–3.
5   Cassels, *The Uncertain Promise of Law*, pp. 8–11.
6   Amnesty International, *Clouds of Injustice*, pp. 10–12; M. Galanter, 'Legal Torpor: Why So Little Has Happened in India after the Bhopal Tragedy' (1985) 20 *Texas International Law Journal* 273, 282–3.
7   Amnesty International, *Clouds of Injustice*, p. 12.
8   Government of Madhya Pradesh, Bhopal Gas Tragedy Relief and Rehabilitation Department, Bhopal, 'Facts & Figures', http://bgtrrdmp.mp.gov.in/facts.htm.
9   Amnesty International, *Clouds of Injustice*, pp. 12–18; B. Dinham and S. Sarangi, 'The Bhopal Gas Tragedy of 1984 to? The Evasion of Corporate Responsibility' (2002) 14(1) *Environment and Urbanization* 89, 92–6.
10 Amnesty International, *Clouds of Injustice*, pp. 22–6.
11 S. Deva, *Regulating Corporate Human Rights Violations: Humanizing Business* (Oxford and New York: Routledge, 2012) pp. 25–6.
12 S. Deva, 'From 3/12 to 9/11: Future of Human Rights?' (2004) 39 *Economic & Political Weekly* 5198, 5200.
13 For an account of the five phases of the Bhopal litigation, see Deva, *Regulating Corporate Human Rights Violations*, pp. 36–44.
14 Bhopal Gas Leak Disaster (Processing of Claims) Act (No. 21 of 1985), s. 3.
15 *In Re Union Carbide Corporation Gas Plant Disaster at Bhopal, India in December 1984, 634 F. Supp. 842 (1986). Affirmed by the US Court of Appeal in In Re Union Carbide Corporation Gas Plant Disaster at Bhopal, India in December 1984*, 809 F. 2d 195 (2d Cir. 1987). *Forum non conveniens* is a legal doctrine whereby courts may decline to hear a case if a more appropriate/convenient forum is available to the parties.
16 *Union Carbide Corporation v Union of India*, AIR 1990 SC 273. It is worth noting that UCC to date has not admitted any liability/responsibility for Bhopal. The settlement order, inter alia, read: 'The aforesaid payments [US$470 million] shall be made to the Union of India as claimant and *for the benefit of all victims* of the Bhopal gas disaster ... and *not as fines, penalties, or punitive damage*.' Ibid., p. 275 (emphasis added).
17 See Amnesty International, *Clouds of Injustice*, pp. 60–1.
18 *Union Carbide Corporation v Union of India*, AIR 1992 SC 248.
19 *State of Madhya Pradesh v Anderson & Ors*, Cr. Case No. 8460/1996; 'Bhopal Trial: Eight Convicted over India Gas Disaster', BBC News, 7 June 2010, http://news.bbc.co.uk/2/hi/south_asia/8725140.stm.
20 Centre for Science and Environment, *Contamination of Soil and Water inside and outside the Union Carbide India Limited, Bhopal* (2009), www.cseindia.org/userfiles/Bhopal%20Report%20Final-3.pdf.
21 The Bhopal Medical Appeal, 'UNEP Offers Contamination Assessment of Bhopal Disaster Site to Government of India', 25 February 2015, http://bhopal.org/unep-offers-contamination-assessment-of-bhopal-disaster-site-to-government-of-india.
22 See Dinham and Sarangi, 'The Bhopal Gas Tragedy', p. 89.
23 Dow, 'Bhopal', www.dow.com/sustainability/issues/bhopal/general.htm.
24 Amnesty International, 'Dow Chemical Must Comply with new Indian Court Summons on Bhopal Disaster', 4 August 2014, www.amnesty.org/en/articles/news/2014/08/dow-chemical-must-comply-new-indian-court-summons-bhopal-disaster.
25 Deva, *Regulating Corporate Human Rights Violations*, pp. 24–5.
26 See, e.g. the settlement reached by Shell for Nigeria oil spills. 'Shell Announces £55m Payout for Nigeria Oil Spills', *Guardian*, 7 January 2015, www.theguardian.com/environment/2015/jan/07/shell-announces-55m-payout-for-nigeria-oil-spills.
27 E. Freeman, *Strategic Management: A Stakeholder Approach* (Boston: Pitman, 1984).
28 Human Rights Council, 'Guiding Principles on Business and Human Rights: Implementing the United Nations "Protect, Respect, Remedy" Framework', Report of the Special Representative of the Secretary-General on the Issue of Human Rights and Transnational Corporations and Other Business Enterprises, UN Doc A/HRC/17/31 (21 March 2011). For a critique, see Deva, *Regulating Corporate Human Rights Violations*, pp. 109–15. See generally S. Deva and D. Bilchitz (eds), *Human Rights Obligations of Business: Beyond the Corporate Responsibility to Respect?* (Cambridge: Cambridge University Press, 2013).
29 28 USC §1350. See W.S. Dodge in this volume, 'Business and human rights litigation in US courts before and after *Kiobel*', p. 244
30 See, e.g. *Chandler v Cape plc* [2012] EWCA Civ 525.
31 Organisation for Economic Co-operation and Development, 'Guidelines for Multinational Enterprises' (2011 ed.), www.oecd.org/daf/inv/mne/48004323.pdf.
32 For example, part of the compensation offered by Shell to Nigerian oil spills' victims will be transferred directly to their bank accounts.

Section 1.4

Rana Plaza: the collapse of a factory in Bangladesh and its ramifications for the global garment industry

Justine Nolan

1 Background

On 24 April 2013, an eight-storey factory building – Rana Plaza – collapsed in the industrial outskirts of Dhaka, the capital of Bangladesh, killing more than 1,100 workers and crippling hundreds more. The disaster dominated global headlines for a few weeks but the public's attention eventually waned. The collapse of the Rana Plaza building was the worst industrial accident anywhere in the world for the last 30 years (since a toxic gas leak in Bhopal, India, in 1984 that killed thousands of people) and highlighted the poor conditions in Bangladesh's garment factories where many workers continue to labour in unsafe conditions and work long hours for low pay.

Thirty years ago in Bangladesh there were fewer than 400 garment factories employing about 120,000 workers.[1] Today, there are estimated to be somewhere between 5,000 and 6,000 factories[2] with more than four million workers, and these jobs have lifted many people out of the destitution that village life might otherwise offer them.[3] There is no doubt that the garment business has been a driving force for social development in Bangladesh but industrialization has also come with significant costs, especially for the health, safety and well-being of workers. Just six months prior to the collapse of the Rana Plaza building, in November 2012, the Tazreen garment factory in Bangladesh caught fire and killed 112 of its workers and wounded another 200.[4] In October 2013, six months after governments, companies and civil society were mobilized into action following the Rana Plaza tragedy, seven workers died in a fire at a knitting factory in Dhaka.[5]

2 Garment industry: low wages and lax regulation

The global garment manufacturing industry is a business built on low wages and lax regulation. While minimum wages for workers in Bangladesh have risen post-Rana Plaza – from US$34 to US$68 per month at the end of 2013 – they are still among the lowest-paid garment workers in the world.[6] Today's global supply chains – many of which sometimes seem not only ungoverned but ungovernable – link (often opaquely) individual workers with large and small companies across national, political and cultural boundaries.

The practice of indirect sourcing[7] – non-transparent subcontracting conducted with little oversight and extremely tight margins – is an essential feature of the export garment sector in Bangladesh. While brands maintain relationships with one group of 'known' factories, those factories subcontract orders to a much wider group of 'unknown' factories to complete production. This practice is what has made Bangladesh so competitive on volume and price.[8]

Western buyers and ultimately consumers profit from this indirect system of sourcing and many global brands devote little time and attention to understanding the nature and scope of this practice. '[Some] brands want to ignore subcontractors. They have their targets, too – 98 per cent on-time shipment – and they don't care how they get the products.'[9] Attempts to regulate this 'independent republic of the supply chain'[10] are challenging and necessitate the involvement of a variety of government and non-state actors. The reaction to the Rana Plaza disaster epitomizes this.

3 Reforming Bangladesh's garment industry

In the aftermath of the catastrophe a number of new initiatives were launched with the aim of improving worker safety in Bangladesh. More than 170 mainly European businesses joined the Accord on Fire and Building Safety in Bangladesh,[11] which involves Bangladeshi authorities, trade unions, non-governmental organizations (NGOs) and the International Labour Organization (ILO). American businesses (including Gap, Target and Walmart) subsequently launched the Alliance for Bangladesh Worker Safety.[12] Factory inspections are claimed to have increased by 70 per cent, a number of garment facilities and factories were closed for inadequate safety standards,[13] and the government of Bangladesh increased the legal minimum wage and made other labour law reform commitments to improve workplace safety (including strengthening the labour inspectorate,[14] simplifying registration of trade unions, establishing safety committees and improving the compensation regime).[15] However, Bangladeshi labour law provisions still fall short of international labour standards on freedom of association and collective bargaining,[16] particularly in Export Processing Zones. The tragedy also led to a decision by President Obama of the United States to suspend trade preferences to Bangladesh under the Generalized System of Preferences.[17] These initiatives saw a confluence of stakeholders coming together to attempt to address and strengthen the regulatory landscape of Bangladesh's garment sector.

While the government of Bangladesh should be the principal regulator of the garment sector, like many other governments hosting the operational end of various supply chains, it 'lacks the political will, technical capacity and resources necessary to protect the basic rights of its own workers'.[18] Close ties between the government and the garment sector and pervasive corruption[19] also weaken the regulatory landscape.[20] Many practical regulatory responsibilities have been outsourced to trade associations, especially the Bangladesh Garment Manufacturers and Exporters Association.

4 Global supply chains need global rules

Substandard working conditions are not just a Bangladeshi problem but also a global problem.[21] Global supply chains in industries as diverse as garments, toys, coffee, tomatoes, shoes, chocolate and palm oil have developed at a frenetic pace. Business demands, inadequate regulation, corruption and weak institutions result in weak protection of workers' rights. Current business practices often undermine efforts to improve compliance with human rights. Business sourcing models that establish tight manufacturing schedules for producing 'fast fashion' set compelling incentives for subcontracting, which comes with increased risks for workers. Reform efforts being trialled in Bangladesh that employ a combination of private voluntary and state regulation are attempting to tackle these labour problems. How this unfolds in a world of volatile consumer markets that require increased flexibility in production, rigid labour markets that do not allow flexibility, and rising costs that incentivize cost-cutting, remains to be seen.

Improvements to working conditions in Bangladesh's garment facilities are a work in progress. The solution is not to abandon Bangladesh or other countries like it but rather for business to practically reassess how manufacturing is done, the time-line for doing it and for each of us to increase our awareness as consumers of the way our goods are made. Governments must also be prepared not only to enact improvements in legal safety standards but to commit to enforcing them. Most importantly, workers must have a voice. This means not simply creating more unions but creating effective unions and forums for workers to be heard. None of these components can succeed in isolation. For too long, much of the focus has been on developing codes of conduct and social audits without factoring in the business practices that can undermine these well-intentioned efforts. A blend of private and public actors working within a multi-dimensional, multi-stakeholder framework that assesses differing responsibilities along global supply chains is required to tackle these inherent problems. Business as usual must no longer be an option.

Notes

1 S. Labowitz and D. Baumann-Pauly, *Business as Usual Is Not an Option: Supply Chains and Sourcing after Rana Plaza* (2014) p. 14, www.stern.nyu.edu/cons/groups/content/documents/webasset/con_047408.pdf.
2 Media reports estimate there are between 5,000 and 6,000 factories in Bangladesh but the exact number remains unclear. See, e.g. J. Burke, 'Bangladesh Factory Fires: Fashion Industry's Latest Crisis', *Guardian*, 8 December 2013.
3 Labowitz and Baumann-Pauly, *Business as Usual* Is *Not an Option*, p. 16.
4 J.A. Manik and J. Yardley, 'Bangladesh Finds Gross Negligence in Factory Fire', *New York Times*, 17 December 2012.
5 'Timeline: Deadly Factory Accidents in Bangladesh', CBC News, 9 October 2013, www.cbc.ca/news2/interactives/timeline-bangladesh.
6 See, e.g. J. Yardley, 'Bangladesh Takes Step to Increase Lowest Pay', *New York Times*, 4 November 2013.
7 Labowitz and Baumann-Pauly define indirect sourcing as

> the routine practice of subcontracting, often through purchasing agents and in a manner that is not transparent to buyers.... As orders are subcontracted and in some cases re-subcontracted, production moves into facilities that are outside the scope of current regulation and often are 'noncompliant' with minimum standards for safety and workers' rights.

(*Business as Usual Is Not an Option*, p. 9)

8 D. Baumann-Pauly, S. Labowitz and N. Banerjee, 'Closing Governance Gaps in Bangladesh's Garment Industry: The Power and Limitations of Private Governance Schemes', SSRN Working Paper, March 2015, p. 13.

9 Labowitz and Baumann-Pauly, *Business as Usual* Is *Not an Option*, p. 20.
10 See A. van Heerden, 'Making Global Labor Fair', TEDGlobal, July 2010, www.ted.com/talks/auret_van_heerden_making_global_labor_fair/transcript?language=en.
11 Accord on Fire and Building Safety in Bangladesh, http://bangladeshaccord.org.
12 Alliance for Bangladesh Worker Safety, www.bangladeshworkersafety.org/about/about-the-alliance. For a comparison of the Alliance and Accord initiatives, see Labowitz and Baumann-Pauly, *Business as Usual* Is *Not an Option*, pp. 53–6; B. Ter Haar and M. Keune, 'One Step Forward or More Window-Dressing? A Legal Analysis of Recent CSR Initiatives in the Garment Industry in Bangladesh' (2014) 30(1) *International Journal of Comparative Labour Law and Industrial Relations* 5.
13 Trade for Development Centre, *Made in Misery: Ethics in the Garment Industry after Rana Plaza* (2014) p. 1, www.befair.be/sites/default/files/all-files/brochure/Ethics%20in%20the%20garment%20industry_0.pdf.
14 However, implementation of the reforms has been slow. In 2013, the Bangladesh government identified

> the need to hire 800 additional labor inspectors to conduct factory inspections. Almost two years later, the government had created 392 new positions (almost half of the target number of inspectors). However, as of October 2014, the government had only been able to fill 50 of these positions.
>
> (D. Baumann-Pauly, S. Labowitz and N. Banarjee 'Closing Governance Gaps in Bangladesh's Garment Industry – The Power and Limitations of Private Governance Schemes', 12 March 2015, available at http://papers.ssrn.com/sol3/papers.cfm?abstract_id=2577535)

15 See International Labour Organization, 'ILO Statement on Reform of Bangladesh Labour Law', 22 July 2013, www.ilo.org/global/about-the-ilo/media-centre/statements-and-speeches/WCMS_218067/lang--en/index.htm. It is to be noted, though, that important sections of the Bangladesh Labour Act 2006 still fall short of international labour standards found in International Labour Organization, Convention Concerning Freedom of Association and Protection of the Right to Organise, San Francisco, 9 July 1948, in force 4 July 1950, C087 (ILO Convention No. 87); and International Labour Organization, Convention Concerning the Application of the Principles of the Right to Organise and to Bargain Collectively, Geneva, 1 July 1949, in force 18 July 1951, C098 (ILO Convention No. 98).
16 See especially ILO Convention No. 87; ILO Convention No. 98.
17 Office of the United States Trade Representative, 'US Trade Representative Michael Froman Comments on President's Decision to Suspend GSP Benefits for Bangladesh', press release, June 2013, https://ustr.gov/about-us/policy-offices/press-office/press-releases/2013/june/michael-froman-gsp-bangladesh. According to the Office of the United States Trade Representative:

> US trade preference programs such as the Generalized System of Preferences (GSP) provide opportunities for many of the world's poorest countries to use trade to grow their economies … GSP is the largest and oldest US trade preference program. Established by the Trade Act of 1974, GSP promotes economic development by eliminating duties on up to 5,000 types of products when imported from one of 122 designated beneficiary countries and territories.

See Office of the United States Trade Representative, 'Generalized System of Preferences (GSP)', https://ustr.gov/issue-areas/trade-development/preference-programs/generalized-system-preference-gsp.
18 Labowitz and Baumann-Pauly, *Business as Usual* Is *Not an Option*, p. 30.
19 Corruption is not confined to Bangladesh. Nine of the world's 10 biggest clothing producers score less than 50 out of 100 in Transparency International, *Corruption Perceptions Index 2012*, www.transparency.org/cpi2012/results.
20 S.N. Mawla, S.A. Chawdhury and N.H. Mina, *The Readymade Garment Sector: Governance Problems and Way Forward* (Transparency International Bangladesh, 2013), www.ti-bangladesh.org/beta3/images/max_file/es_rmg_en_07112013.pdf.
21 Centre for Sustainable Work and Employment Futures, University of Leicester, *New Industry on a Skewed Playing Field: Supply Chain Relations and Working Conditions in UK Garment Manufacturing* (2015), www2.le.ac.uk/offices/press/for-journalists/media-resources/Leicester%20Report%20-%20Final%20-to%20publish.pdf.

Chapter 2

Regulatory framework and Guiding Principles

In recent years, much has been written about the positive and negative impact of business on human rights, and how, why and if the corporate sector should be more engaged in respecting and protecting rights. Beginning in earnest in the 1990s, the debate has now largely moved from 'if' business should be engaged with human rights to 'how'. But, as the role and influence of corporations has increased globally, so too has the confusion around what specifically is required of them, and what the best mechanisms are to encourage companies to engage more substantially with human rights.

This chapter provides an overview of the principal regulatory developments in this field; those developments encompass a broad array of tools including international and national laws, soft norms and stakeholder-led initiatives. A reference to 'regulating' corporate conduct will mean different things to different people. Regulation is used here in a broad sense to incorporate formal and informal and legal and non-legal mechanisms, designed to influence or at times press corporations to better respect and/or protect human rights. Indeed, the business and human rights field is remarkable for the diversity of techniques that have been employed to regulate corporate conduct along with the breadth of stakeholders involved in using varied strategies.

The contribution by Justine Nolan spans the breadth of this movement and reinforces the apt statement of the former Special Representative of Business and Human Rights, that 'there is no single silver bullet solution to the institutional misalignments in the business and human rights domain. Instead, all social actors – States, businesses, and civil society – must learn to do many things differently'.[1] The adoption by the UN Human Rights Council in 2011 of the Guiding Principles on Business and Human Rights (Guiding Principles) was a major development in the business and human rights field. Chip Pitts describes the Guiding Principles and their impact. John Ruggie discusses his foundational premises in the development of the Guiding Principles and what, in his view, are the crucial next steps to be addressed in the business and human rights field.

What is becoming increasingly apparent is that in striving for greater protection for human rights, a multiplicity of stakeholders (both state and non-state actors) must be involved. Some of the most powerful global actors today are companies, not governments. Logically, recourse to international or local laws and a system of enforcement and judicial relief in the host countries where global corporations operate should be the primary option for ensuring greater protection for human rights. However, the reality is that in many countries this simply is not occurring. Laws are sometimes weak but enforcement is weaker still. Soft-law and stakeholder-led initiatives have an important role to play in engendering greater corporate respect for human rights and many of these mechanisms highlighted in this chapter must necessarily work in collaboration with each other.

Note

1   Human Rights Council, 'Protect, Respect and Remedy: a Framework for Business and Human Rights', Report of the Special Representative of the Secretary-General on the Issue of Human Rights and Transnational Corporations and Other Business Enterprises, John Ruggie, UN Doc. A/HRC/8/5 (7 April 2008), para. 7.

Section 2.1

Mapping the movement: the business and human rights regulatory framework

Justine Nolan

1 Introduction

Traditionally, responsibility for protecting and advancing respect for human rights has been assumed to be the duty of the state (national governments), with rules drawn predominantly from international treaties that might then be translated into national laws, such as health and safety or anti-discrimination legislation. It is only quite recently that discussion has expanded to focus on the human rights responsibilities of companies. In response to the evolution of the global business and human rights agenda in the last three to four decades, private (or public–private) regulation[1] has become a central means of driving consensus on how corporations can and should advance respect for (and sometimes protect) human rights. International law and its state-centric framework for protecting rights is proving inadequate to stem and redress corporate rights violations and has led to protection or governance gaps.

Writing in 2008, then United Nations (UN) Special Representative for Business and Human Rights (SRSG), John Ruggie noted that 'the root cause of the business and human rights predicament today lies in the governance gaps created by globalization – between the scope and impact of economic forces and actors, and the capacity of societies to manage their adverse consequences'.[2] That is, corporations often operate in countries that do not have the capacity or will to protect the rights of those within their jurisdiction; as a result, their activities are difficult to monitor and regulate, and wrongs often remain without redress. All around the global marketplace, non-state actors such as non-government organizations (NGOs), international institutions, unions, companies, multi-stakeholder groups and industry bodies, have stepped in to develop governance mechanisms that attempt to fill such gaps.[3]

The adoption by the UN Human Rights Council in 2011 of the Guiding Principles on Business and Human Rights[4] (Guiding Principles) signalled acceptance of the notion that corporate responsibility to respect human rights exists independently of, and as a complement to, states' duties to protect human rights. While the Guiding Principles provide a useful foundation for future action, many stakeholders were already involved in developing non-state-based regulatory initiatives – such as the Fair Labor Association or the Global Network Initiative – to develop industry standards, metrics and implementing procedures that give substantive content to corporate human rights responsibilities. This transfer or sharing of regulatory authority between states and non-state actors utilizes a combination of hard and soft laws[5] to establish relevant standards for corporate activity, including compliance mechanisms to monitor implementation of these standards.

This chapter provides an overview of the history of international, state and non-state efforts to regulate corporate compliance with human rights standards. It begins by highlighting the central obligations of states to protect human rights on the basis of international human rights and labour laws and national laws. The chapter then takes note of the corollary development of soft law (both from a top-down international institutional perspective and from a bottom-up stakeholder driven process) that has arisen in response to gaps in state protection mechanisms. What is becoming increasingly apparent is that for sustained improvements to occur, a multiplicity of stakeholders and mechanisms must be used to both prevent and redress the impact of business on human rights.

2 The human rights framework and its traditionally state-centric focus

The international human rights framework has been a touchstone for many seeking to attach human rights responsibilities to corporations. The relevance of human rights to business is now more generally accepted,[6] but the extent of corporate responsibilities (or perhaps even obligations) flowing from that symbiotic relationship is more contested. Understanding the human rights framework helps attach content to the rights themselves and gives a broader basis for understanding the independent but also interdependent responsibilities of both states and business in protecting and respecting these rights.

2.1 Universal Declaration of Human Rights

The Universal Declaration of Human Rights (UDHR) lists 30 substantive human rights that are promulgated as a common standard of achievement for all peoples and all nations: every 'individual and organ of society' shall strive by teaching and education to promote respect for these rights and by progressive measures secure their universal and effective recognition and observance.[7] Motivated by the experiences of the preceding world wars, the UDHR was the first time that countries agreed on a comprehensive statement of inalienable human rights. The UDHR is expressed entirely in terms of entitlements for individuals and peoples rather than obligations on states or other entities. As a declaration of the UN General Assembly, it does not create legal obligations of itself. Nevertheless, the UDHR is frequently cited as the source of human rights obligations that corporations are urged to follow.

The expression 'every individual' in the UDHR can be taken to include juridical persons. Thus 'every individual and organ of society' excludes no one, including corporations.[8] Furthermore, the phrase 'every organ of society' indicates that the human rights in the UDHR are to be respected, protected and promoted not only by states but also by all social entities capable of affecting the enjoyment of human rights, including corporations.[9]

Extending the moral, if not legal, authority of the UDHR to corporations relies on art. 29, which acknowledges that 'everyone' has 'duties' to the community, and art. 30, which prohibits any 'group' from engaging in any activity or performing any act aimed at destroying any of the rights and freedoms in the UDHR. Ultimately, however, the UDHR's provisions arguably express no more than a desire that corporations might 'strive' to promote respect for human rights rather than directly imposing any binding legal obligations on these non-state entities.[10]

2.2 International human rights treaties

While the UDHR identifies human rights entitlements rather than explicit legal obligations, international human rights treaties transform those rights into binding legal obligations upon states. The International Covenant on Civil and Political Rights (ICCPR)[11] and the International Covenant on Economic, Social and Cultural Rights (ICESCR)[12] make all the rights in the UDHR, other than the right to property, obligations of states party to them. Human rights obligations are also contained in subject-specific treaties including conventions of the International Labour Organization (ILO),[13] agreements concerning slavery[14] and racial discrimination[15] and the rights of particular groups including women,[16] children[17] and migrant workers.[18]

The state-centric framework of international human rights law emphasizes the primary responsibility of governments to protect human rights while remaining partially blind to the opportunity to speak more directly to influential non-state actors including corporations. The size, revenues and global reach of some corporations now means that their potential power to impact communities is commensurate with those of states; yet they are not directly bound by international human rights laws.[19] More recent treaties, and occasionally treaty bodies, have begun to refer more directly to the role of states in specifically preventing human rights abuses by corporations.[20] It is commonly assumed that these treaties do not themselves create direct obligations for corporations[21] but instead require states to regulate and adjudicate the acts of corporations in order to fulfil their duty to protect human rights as outlined in the treaties. Thus, a state failure to ensure compliance by private employers with basic international (or comparable national) labour standards could amount to a violation of the right to work or to just and favourable working conditions. However, the fact that a treaty imposes an obligation on a state to protect private persons from the actions of another does not automatically enable an individual to seek legal recourse from another private actor (such as a company) for violating his or her rights. Without direct obligations for companies, any allegation of a violation of human rights needs to be framed in terms of the responsibility of the state to protect human rights from violations by private actors.

2.2.1 A business and human rights treaty?

The resolution adopted by the UN Human Rights Council in 2014[22] to explore the development of a business and human rights treaty raises anew the issue of whether the international human rights law framework can accommodate corporate liability. Questions arise as to the necessity for a treaty, the potential effectiveness of a treaty and the theoretical and practical feasibility of establishing a framework to hold hundreds of thousands of corporations to account.[23] The current debate harks back to that which began in the 1970s (with respect to the development of a UN Draft Code to regulate transnational corporations) and perhaps illustrates how little has changed in certain respects. This issue is discussed in more detail in Sections 2.3, 2.4 and 2.5.

2.3 ILO conventions and guidelines

Core labour standards are a subset of fundamental human rights, some of which are expressly recognized in human rights treaties. However, it is a 'regrettable paradox that the human rights movement and the labor movement run on tracks that are sometimes parallel and rarely meet',[24] despite the substantial overlap between the two. The right to work has direct intersections with many other rights, including civil and political rights, such as the right to life and freedom of expression, and also economic, social and cultural rights, such as the rights to health and an adequate standard of living.

The ILO (the establishment of which pre-dates the UN by more than 25 years) liaises closely with UN charter-based and treaty-based bodies, and reports on issues such as child labour, discrimination, forced labour, migrant workers and freedom of association. Although the essence of both the UN and ILO compliance mechanisms is based on dialogue and persuasion, the systems of supervision (ILO) and monitoring (UN) differ. The ILO's unique tripartite structure aims to ensure the full participation of not only governments but also employer and employee representatives in the drafting and implementation of labour standards. Tripartite governance is not a panacea, however, and its effectiveness relies on the ability of each of the parties to negotiate as independent entities. In some regions of the world,

> industrial relations law and practice are closely bound up with industrialisation and development strategies that are generally accompanied by state control over labour unions in order to maintain the stability that national governments may feel is needed for rapid economic development.[25]

China is but one example of a country where the independence of the three delegate factions to the ILO is compromised.

International labour standards take the form of conventions (legally binding treaties) that may be ratified by member states, which are then monitored for compliance. Recommendations (non-binding guidelines) may supplement a particular convention or provide more general guidance on labour standards and their implementation. In the nearly 100 years since its creation, the ILO has drafted numerous conventions and recommendations covering a diverse range of topics but it has been less effective in enforcing standards than creating them. The ILO has enunciated four 'core labour standards' – freedom of association and collective bargaining, elimination of discrimination, elimination of forced labour and elimination of child labour – which are linked to eight conventions, commonly referred to as the ILO's fundamental or core conventions.[26] Like international human rights treaties, ILO conventions legally and directly bind states, rather than business. However, in 1977 the ILO attempted to speak more directly to business and launched its Tripartite Declaration of Principles Concerning Multinational Enterprises and Social Policy.[27] The Declaration aims to provide guidance concerning how corporations can positively contribute to economic and social progress. It encourages companies to implement labour rights but does not contain any enforcement mechanisms to ensure they do so.

Snapshot

The ILO and the Cambodian garment sector

Cambodia's Better Factories programme is illustrative of a departure from the ILO's traditional approach and highlights the potential value of involving a multiplicity of stakeholders and approaches (i.e. both 'carrot and stick') in improving working conditions.[28] The programme developed out of the 1999 US–Cambodia Bilateral Textile Trade Agreement, which provided Cambodia with increased access to the US market (via increased quotas) based upon tangible improvements in working conditions in Cambodia's garment factories.[29] The project, launched in 2001, monitors factory performance against international and national labour standards and was established by the ILO in cooperation with the US and Cambodian governments. It is not strictly a multi-stakeholder initiative in terms of its governance and structure but the participation of non-state actors (including business, NGOs and unions) in the programme is crucial.

Monitoring reports concerning the labour standards have been used by the US government to assess quota increases, as well as by global corporate buyers to determine where they should place their orders. Quotas were eliminated in 2005, but the ILO programme continues with the ongoing support of the Garment Manufacturers' Association in Cambodia, international buyers and unions; however, concerns have been raised about progress since 2005.[30] Key to the continuation of the programme are global buyers who are conscious of their own reputations and who, 'in the continuing absence of a [local] well-funded labor inspectorate ... appear to be driving improved compliance with ILO labor standards'.[31]

While international standards, such as those found in ILO and human rights treaties, are the appropriate baselines against which to monitor corporate compliance, they have meaning only if effective remedies and enforcement mechanisms are put in place or if they are taken up by local governments. The Better Factories project has the potential to showcase a concrete example of how international standards, together with strong monitoring and trade incentives and encouragement (in the form of orders) by global buyers and the involvement of civil society and unions, could be combined to form a sustainable basis for improving working conditions. However, some dispute the continued improvements in Cambodian factories, in part due to the fact that with the elimination of the quotas in 2005, the programme became 'non-binding and unenforceable'.[32] Some argue that 'by implementing non-binding programmes that offer carrots without wielding a stick, poverty wages and precarious work continue to be the norm in Cambodia's garment factories'.[33]

2.4 National laws

In most jurisdictions, national laws regulate specific corporate activities that affect human rights through provisions dealing with labour rights, anti-discrimination, environmental protection and crime. National laws can and do directly target corporations as subjects of law, although domestic legislation typically does not apply extraterritorially. Responsibilities of states as bounded by territorial limits do not match the transnational operations of the companies based or operating within their territory. The Guiding Principles adopted a rather modest approach to the prospect of states regulating corporate activities extraterritorially by noting only that '[s]tates must protect against human rights abuse within their territory and/or jurisdiction by third parties, including business enterprises'.[34] The Commentary to Guiding Principle No. 2 elaborates on these territorial and jurisdictional limits by noting the possibilities open to states to broaden and deepen the scope of the duty to protect under international human rights treaties, but it does not go so far as to suggest that states are obliged to act in this regard.[35] However, in contrast, several UN bodies have taken a more expansive approach regarding who and what a state might regulate in the pursuit of protecting human rights.[36] The barriers to regulating corporate activity extraterritorially are more likely to be political than legal.[37]

Snapshot

US Foreign Corrupt Practices Act

When looking for examples of how a state might reasonably regulate corporate activities beyond its borders, one model of extraterritorial legislation that has had a widespread impact on the private sector is the US Foreign Corrupt Practices Act (FCPA).[38] Adopted in 1977,[39] the FCPA has influenced the way in which US businesses operate abroad, and has changed the global business environment more generally with respect to corruption. Setting a precedent for how a legislative model can reverberate globally, the FCPA was followed into operation by the OECD Convention on Combating Bribery of Foreign Public Officials in International Business Transactions, and the UN Convention Against Corruption,[40] which established international standards for combating corruption. Companies have responded to these global anti-corruption laws by developing due diligence programmes to proactively identify potential risks. The global implementation of laws to combat corruption is a useful model for assessing how greater rigour could be brought to bear in applying international human rights standards to business, and the mandated due diligence requirements showcase how the Guiding Principles could be hardened into a national legislative model with extraterritorial reach.

Another way states can 'regulate' corporate activities that take place outside their territory is to mandate increased transparency in global business operations. For example, s. 1502 of the US Dodd–Frank Act requires all listed companies to report on the sources of minerals used in their products that originate from the Democratic Republic of Congo (DRC) or adjoining countries.[41] The purpose of this provision is to provide greater transparency about how the trade in minerals is potentially fuelling and funding the armed struggle in the DRC; functionally, it relies on the adverse reputational impact of such disclosure rather than mandating penalties for actually sourcing minerals from conflict-afflicted regions.

Reporting requirements are a first step in linking transparency with accountability, but much depends on the quality of the reports and to what use the information is then put. A study of the first set of Conflict Minerals Reports submitted to the Securities Exchange Commission up to June 2014 argues that these reports exhibited a low level of compliance with due diligence requirements and identified several obstacles to achieving broader compliance, including that:

> (i) international norms on supply chain due diligence are in their infancy; (ii) the proliferation of certification standards and in-region sourcing initiatives are still evolving and often competing; and (iii) inadequate local security and weak governance inhibit the mapping of mineral trade and the tracing of minerals in the region.[42]

Ultimately, however, laws – whether national or international – are only as strong as their enforcement capacity. In many countries, labour laws, in particular, are hampered by the inability or unwillingness of the state to enforce them. For example, in 2013 the US 'federal Occupational Health and Safety Administration ha[d] just two thousand inspectors to monitor over eight million workplaces in the United States, meaning that it [could] inspect each workplace only once every 131 years'.[43] In 2013, the Bangladeshi government identified

> the need to hire 800 additional labor inspectors to conduct factory inspections. Almost two years later, the government had created 392 new positions (almost half of the target number of inspectors). However, as of October 2014, the government had only been able to fill 50 of these positions.[44]

Likewise, reporting regulations with no sanctions attached for non-compliance are likely to result in partial compliance.[45] Such regulatory enforcement gaps have led to increased reliance on tools developed by non-state actors to monitor and report on workplace conditions.

3 International institutional initiatives

There have been a variety of attempts, particularly since the mid-1970s, to use 'soft law' to regulate the impact of business practices on human rights, for instance, through multi-stakeholder guidelines, declarations or codes of conduct. The institutional initiatives highlighted below are examples of attempts by various international organizations to harness the power of business to positively impact human rights by providing broad frameworks that assist companies in understanding what constitutes responsible business conduct. The utility of these initiatives is not their ability to act as a tool of legal accountability or as a means of providing sector-specific advice on how to respect and protect human rights; rather, the initiatives engage with companies to assist them to better understand the general contemporary responsibilities of business with respect to human rights and in promoting ethical leadership on human rights.

3.1 The UN Draft Code of Conduct on Transnational Corporations

In 1973 the UN Economic and Social Council charged a 'Group of Eminent Persons' with the task of advising on matters related to transnational corporations (TNCs) and their impact on the international development process. In 1974 the UN established the Centre on Transnational Corporations, which, by 1977, was coordinating the negotiation of the Draft Code of Conduct on Transnational Corporations (Draft Code). The text of the Draft Code contained duties for TNCs to respect host countries' development goals, observe their domestic laws, respect fundamental human rights and observe consumer and environmental protection objectives. The Draft Code was never officially adopted and its legal nature was never established. There were proponents of both a universally applicable, legally binding code and a voluntary code. If binding, the Draft Code would have served as a convention with both national and international mechanisms for implementation. If voluntary, it would have merely served as a set of broad guidelines to be observed by participating parties. That decades-old debate is now being reinvigorated with the 2014 resolution by the UN Human Rights Council to explore a treaty to regulate corporate activity.

3.2 The Organisation for Economic Co-operation and Development Guidelines for Multinational Enterprises[46]

The OECD Guidelines for Multinational Enterprises (OECD Guidelines) are 'recommendations addressed by governments to multinational enterprises operating in or from adhering countries'.[47] First launched in 1976 with only a passing reference to human rights, they were updated in 2011 to incorporate the tenets of the Guiding Principles. OECD members and adhering states are obliged to set up a National Contact Point (NCP) to promote the OECD Guidelines. The OECD Guidelines are voluntary in their application and multinational enterprises are invited to adopt the guidelines in their management systems and incorporate the OECD Guidelines into their corporate operations. In the 2000 update of the OECD Guidelines a new complaint procedure was introduced that allows NGOs and others to submit complaints concerning alleged breaches of the OECD Guidelines to a government's NCP.[48] To date, approximately 300 complaints have been addressed by NCPs but the extent of the remediation that has resulted from these complaints is unclear.[49] The OECD Guidelines have been widely criticized in part because of the inconsistent manner in which they have been applied by NCPs; nevertheless, the fact remains that the OECD Guidelines are one of the few institutional initiatives that includes a dispute resolution mechanism.[50]

Snapshot

United Kingdom (UK) National Contact Point and Gamma

Gamma International UK is part of the Gamma Group of companies that supplies and trains government agencies in the areas of communications monitoring, data recovery and forensics, and technical surveillance. In 2013 a complaint was lodged with the UK NCP by a number of NGOs (including Privacy International). It was alleged that Gamma supplied a spyware product (Finfisher) to agencies of the Bahrain government, which had used it to target pro-democracy activists in Bahrain. It was alleged that these activists were subsequently detained and in some cases tortured by the Bahrain security forces.[51] The complainants did not suggest that Gamma had a role in deciding who was targeted; rather, it was argued that the company should have made a judgement about the general risk that supplying Finfisher to Bahrain would lead to the product being used for internal repression.[52]

The UK NCP made a first assessment of the complaint in 2013 and offered the parties mediation but they were unable to reach agreement. In 2015 the UK NCP issued its findings[53] that Gamma's actions were not consistent with the general obligations in the Guidelines to respect human rights, that it had failed to develop a company policy on human rights and that it did not conduct appropriate due diligence.

The decision acts as a recommendation to the company and while it attracted media attention and was useful in 'naming and shaming' Gamma, the NCP does not have the power to ensure that Gamma's practices change in accordance with its recommendations. The NCP will issue a follow-up report one year after the release of its findings, which may again be useful in focusing public attention on the practices of one particular company.

3.3 UN Global Compact

In 2000 the UN established the Global Compact, which calls on companies to voluntarily 'embrace and enact' a set of 10 principles relating to human rights, labour rights, the environment and anti-corruption. By participating, companies agree to incorporate the principles in their day-to-day operations and issue an annual public Communication on Progress, which reports on the company's progress in implementing the principles. A failure to report could eventually lead to the expulsion of the company from the Global Compact.[54]

While the Global Compact has been successful in attracting a large number of participants, now estimated at more than 12,000 participants, including over 8,000 businesses,[55] its attempt to build a broad and inclusive tent has attracted some criticism, including with respect to the generality of its provisions, its participants' lack of commitment and the limited accountability that participation entails.[56] The Global Compact is not a vehicle to push companies beyond their comfort zone in confronting their human rights responsibilities; nor is it a tool for holding corporations to account for human rights violations. It is an educational initiative that raises awareness around business and human rights issues and, as such, can be a useful basis for peer learning. The Global Compact was significant for squarely placing human rights on the corporate agenda and welcoming business into the fold of the UN, but arguably the Global Compact has never reached its full potential as a learning platform and legitimately attracts criticism that it has instead been captured by 'big business'.[57]

Snapshot

The Global Compact's principles

Human rights
- Principle 1: Businesses should support and respect the protection of internationally proclaimed human rights; and
- Principle 2: make sure that they are not complicit in human rights abuses.

Labour standards
- Principle 3: Businesses should uphold the freedom of association and the effective recognition of the right to collective bargaining;
- Principle 4: the elimination of all forms of forced and compulsory labour;
- Principle 5: the effective abolition of child labour; and
- Principle 6: the elimination of discrimination in respect of employment and occupation.

Environment
- Principle 7: Businesses should support a precautionary approach to environmental challenges;
- Principle 8: undertake initiatives to promote greater environmental responsibility; and
- Principle 9: encourage the development and diffusion of environmentally friendly technologies.

Anti-Corruption
- Principle 10: Businesses should work against corruption in all its forms, including extortion and bribery.

3.4 The UN Norms on the Responsibilities of Transnational Corporations and Other Business Enterprises with Regard to Human Rights

In 1998 the UN Sub-Commission on the Promotion and Protection of Human Rights established a five-member Working Group to 'draft Norms ... on the responsibilities of transnational corporations and other business enterprises with regard to human rights'.[58] The Group embarked on a series of consultations during which various versions of the Norms were circulated and commented on by a diverse group including representatives from governments, intergovernmental organizations, NGOs, business, the UN and other interested parties. In 2003 the Working Group presented to the Sub-Commission a set of draft Norms on the Responsibilities of Transnational Corporations and Other Business Enterprises with Regard to Human Rights.[59] Although the Sub-Commission unanimously adopted the Norms,[60] the UN Commission on Human Rights in its 2004 session took note of the Norms, but resolved, much to the relief of many in the business community and many governments, that the Norms had 'no legal standing'.[61] The Commission then, in its 2005 session, effectively curtailed any further debate about the Norms by requesting the UN Secretary-General to appoint a Special Representative of the Secretary-General on human rights and transnational corporations and other business enterprises (SRSG) to, among other things, clarify the standards of corporate responsibility.[62] The SRSG later described the Norms endeavour as a 'train wreck' and declared the Norms dead.[63]

The Norms identified specific human rights relevant to the activities of business, such as the right to equal opportunity and non-discrimination, the right to security of person, the rights of workers and the rights of particular groups such as indigenous peoples. The Norms were based on the concept that:

> [E]ven though States have the primary responsibility to promote, secure the fulfilment of, respect, ensure respect of, and protect human rights, transnational corporations and other business enterprises, as organs of society, are also responsible for promoting and securing the human rights set forth in the Universal Declaration of Human Rights.[64]

The Norms provoked heated debate between business, government, human rights organizations and international and corporate lawyers. A number of key business organizations objected to the Norms on a variety of fronts and lobbied strongly against any moves by the Commission to adopt the Norms.[65] In contrast, many NGOs stridently welcomed the Norms.[66]

The main objections to the Norms were documented in a 2005 report prepared by the UN Office of the High Commissioner on Human Rights.[67]

Critics of the Norms argued that: the legal responsibilities placed on business were more extensive than those placed on states; the Norms privatized the protection of human rights by shifting the responsibility from states to business; the implementation provisions were unworkable; some of the standards vague and duplicative of other initiatives; and the binding nature of the Norms could be counterproductive, potentially jeopardizing other voluntary efforts such as the UN Global Compact, which was established during the Norms' drafting process.

Proponents of the Norms argued that the Norms could: fill a regulatory gap where states were failing to legislate effectively or were unable to protect human rights; address the shortcomings of the various voluntary initiatives that were inconsistent in their treatment of human rights and insufficient to mitigate corporate violations of rights; and offer the possibility of a remedy to victims of human rights violations.

The introduction of the Norms altered the framework of the business and human rights/corporate social responsibility debate. Some of the more amorphous corporate social responsibility dialogues now had to accommodate a debate on the role and relevance of international human rights to business. The divisive fracas spurred by the Norms gave way in 2005 to the consensus-seeking approach of the SRSG as he sought to build bridges between the various stakeholders and forge a different framework for addressing business and human rights challenges.

3.5 UN 'Protect, Respect, Remedy' Framework and the Guiding Principles

In July 2005 the UN Secretary-General appointed Professor John Ruggie as the SRSG. In the following years, Ruggie undertook an extensive consultation process and in 2008 presented the UN Human Rights Council with a Framework to anchor the business and human rights debate. The Framework comprises three core pillars (or principles):

1 the state's duty to protect against human rights abuses by third parties, including business;
2 the corporate responsibility to respect human rights; and
3 the need for more effective access to remedies.

The 2011 Guiding Principles aim to provide guidance in operationalizing this Framework (and are discussed further in Section 2.2). In July 2011 the UN Human Rights Council endorsed the Guiding Principles and announced the formation of a Working Group 'to promote the effective and comprehensive dissemination and implementation of the Guiding Principles'.[68]

The Guiding Principles have quickly become a 'common reference point in the area of business and human rights'.[69] States, international institutions (such as the OECD), multi-stakeholder initiatives, companies and NGOs have used the Guiding Principles in different ways.[70] A 2014 survey by *The Economist* of 853 senior corporate executives found that 83 per cent of respondents agreed that human rights are a matter for business as well as governments;[71] it seems reasonable to infer that the work of the SRSG influenced this majority opinion. However, the same survey revealed that '[w]hile corporate attitudes are evolving fairly quickly, concrete steps to reform company policies and to communicate such changes externally are slower to follow'.[72] Of course, the survey was not concerned with the particular impact of the Guiding Principles. Nevertheless, it does capture the essence of some of the critiques of the Guiding Principles, which argue that the broadly framed principles encourage, but do not oblige, companies to respect human rights.[73] Other criticisms[74] of the Guiding Principles centre on the following issues:

- *Extraterritorial protection of human rights.* One of the key issues regarding state enforcement of human rights (pillar 1) is the potential to protect human rights extraterritorially (that is, outside a state's territory). The fact that states have a duty to protect from third-party violations is non-controversial. How far that obligation extends and whether it should be applied extraterritorially is far less settled. The Guiding Principles note that 'States must protect against human rights abuse within their territory and/or jurisdiction by third parties, including business enterprises'.[75] The Commentary to Guiding Principle No. 2 notes the possibilities open to states to broaden and deepen the scope of the duty to protect but does not go so far as to suggest states are obliged to act in this regard. This approach does not reflect increasing international recognition, including by UN treaty bodies,[76] of the legal obligation on states to take action to prevent abuses by their companies overseas.

- *Flexibility and ambiguity around the commitment for companies to respect human rights*. The Guiding Principles have been criticized for providing 'far too much wiggle room [and including] too many "should" in place of "shalls"'.[77] The language used in the Guiding Principles when framing the corporate responsibility to respect human rights (pillar 2) stems from a social expectation (not legal obligation) to respect human rights and this is reflected in the recommendatory nature of the language employed.[78] The flexibility of the language may be welcomed by some stakeholders to allow for specific idiosyncratic tailoring of responses at a corporate level; however, the looseness of the language may also invite inaction and a business-as-usual approach from companies that remain hesitant about their responsibility to act.

- *Access to remedy must be mandated*. The Guiding Principles provide valuable guidance for developing state and non-state based systems to provide access to remedy (pillar 3) for victims of corporate abuses. As the Guiding Principles note, the concept of access to remedy is multi-pronged and includes judicial and non-judicial mechanisms. However, as one commentator observed back in 1999, 'only a selected few among private corporations are likely to willingly submit to new responsibilities without being legally compelled to do so'.[79] More than a decade later, this comment still rings true, particularly with respect to the provision of reparations for victims of corporate abuse. While the number of corporations prepared to adopt human rights policies may have risen, the limited mechanisms for enforcing such policies remain largely embedded in soft law that, unless hardened, will have a very limited effect in preventing future violations of human rights by corporations.

The SRSG has often stated that 'there is no single silver bullet solution to the institutional misalignments in the business and human rights domain. Instead, all social actors – States, businesses, and civil society – must learn to do many things differently'.[80] The development of the Framework and the Guiding Principles was a deliberate attempt to break from the divisive discussion of the previous years and build a more consensual approach to involving all stakeholders, but particularly business, in building greater respect for human rights. The Guiding Principles reaffirm the relevance of all human rights to business but do not end the debate on how best to address and redress corporate violations of human rights. The Guiding Principles instead set the stage for further elaboration of industry-specific standards and mechanisms (both state and non-state based) to protect and respect human rights.

4 Stakeholder initiatives on human rights

Prior to the development of the Guiding Principles, many NGOs and companies were already involved in establishing or working within practically focused private or public–private regulatory initiatives to improve respect for human rights. This section provides an overview of some of these initiatives (which are discussed more extensively in Chapter 4) that were generally developed at the behest of NGOs, unions, companies and/or governments with the aim (in part) of filling the regulatory lacuna that emerged from the inability or unwillingness of many states to protect human rights in the workplace.

One of the earliest initiatives was the Sullivan Principles, developed by Reverend Sullivan in 1977, which was a South African code of conduct aimed at ending discrimination against blacks in the workplace. The 1970s also saw a high-profile boycott campaign against the Swiss-based Nestlé corporation over concerns about its marketing campaign of breast milk substitutes in developing countries.[81]

Beginning in the 1990s, many companies began to adopt codes of conduct to guide responsible business practices and, perhaps, to pre-empt tactics such as those used against Nestlé. Initially, many of these codes were company-specific (and were often developed in-house without input from external stakeholders) or drafted exclusively by industry.[82] Over time, however, concerns around the content, legitimacy and accountability of such codes has seen a trend towards the development of 'multi-stakeholder' codes of conduct. Multi-stakeholder initiatives (MSIs) bring together a multiplicity of stakeholders to work together to achieve their goals collectively. MSIs may include representatives from groups as diverse as worker representatives, consumer groups, customers, investors, NGOs, business and governments.

Early MSIs in the corporate responsibility space were initially focused on environmental issues and include some that are still operating today, such as the Forest Stewardship Council (1993) and the Marine Stewardship Council (1997). Other MSIs soon emerged that targeted human rights more specifically and often focused on particular sectors (such as apparel or mining). Some of the earlier MSIs focused largely on apparel and footwear, including Social Accountability International (1997), the Fair Labor Association (1998) and the Ethical Trading Initiative (1998). Each of these was, in its own way, attempting to regulate what was seen as a (partially) unregulated market. Since 2000, a number of industry-specific MSIs have emerged, including the Voluntary Principles on Security and Human Rights (2000), the Kimberley Process Certification Scheme (2002), the Extractive Industries Transparency Initiative (2003), the Global Network Initiative (2008) and the nascent International Code of Conduct for Private Security Providers (2010). What these MSIs have in common is an attempt to forge consensus on a sector-specific set of standards. However, they differ vastly in terms of their structure, membership, governance, transparency, monitoring and reporting requirements.[83] While the proliferation of codes of conduct – whether company-specific or as part of an MSI – in the last two decades has meant that hundreds of companies have now publicly committed to upholding basic human rights, the challenge is to ensure that the standards espoused in codes or guidelines adopted by business are consistent, comprehensive and, most importantly, implemented.

Another response to the absence of effective regulation of international labour standards (particularly in supply chains) has been the development of international framework agreements (IFAs), which are agreements signed by global union federations (GUFs) and TNCs. The first IFA was signed by the French food multinational Danone in 1988 and by 2013 there were 88 IFAs operating globally.[84]

Like codes of conduct, IFAs can differ from company to company but they consistently reference the ILO core conventions. While some IFAs include monitoring mechanisms and some do not, their purpose is to provide a framework for labour negotiations to take place with a minimum floor. IFAs are generally distinguishable from other codes in the corporate responsibility field because they result from negotiation with international workers' representatives. The focus of IFAs on labour rights mean that they represent a strong possibility for protecting the rights of workers in far-flung areas around the globe. However, they too can suffer from some of the same problems that beset codes of conduct, such as failures in implementation and a top-down approach that would be strengthened by greater connection to local organizing.[85]

It is arguable that the increasing reliance on codes of conduct and/or stakeholder initiatives to regulate human rights is linked to the lack of better mechanisms, such as an enforceable international agreement or stronger state protection of human rights, though their popularity may also be construed as a tactic for avoiding government regulation. More positively, the use of these initiatives can also be seen as a deliberate strategic choice to involve key participants (particularly business) in developing solutions to business and human rights challenges. The attraction of adopting a code of conduct can be easily understood if the standards are viewed as containing only aspirational goals that aim for the best possible scenario with limited accountability if such goals are not met. But the simple adoption of a code by a company is very different from a commitment to be involved in an MSI with rigorous monitoring and reporting requirements or signing an IFA with a global union. The reality is that, not unlike the global state-centric framework for enforcing international human rights law, such initiatives are only as strong as their participants choose to make them, and they do not apply to those that do not want to join them. However, stakeholder initiatives have emerged as an effective regulatory technique for addressing corporate impacts on human rights and are not only an important supplement to international and national laws but perhaps a more immediate and practicable mechanism for protecting human rights.

5 Conclusion

Multiple mechanisms and stakeholders have been involved in the decades-long struggle to improve corporate respect for human rights. The acceptance by many companies in recent years of the relevance of human rights to business has been driven in part by campaigns involving unions, NGOs, consumers, investors and workers themselves. This push from the 'ground up' has caught the attention of companies, many of which have been forced into the spotlight to defend or redress their practices. Such stakeholder initiatives often make reference to the international framework of human rights and labour laws that provide a 'top-down' set of standards that enunciate the rights that are to be respected and protected. National laws that reiterate such standards are also crucial to developing an environment and business culture that values human rights. Accepting that rights must be respected by corporations, wherever in the world they operate, is one thing, making it happen is quite another. Utilizing the involvement of multiple stakeholders and mechanisms in a co-regulatory manner does not absolve a state from protecting rights but rather recognizes that, at times, a joint regulatory effort may be more effective than simply relying solely on the traditional state-centric tactics of yesteryear.

Activities in the last 30 to 40 years have seen significant advances in both the legal and quasi-legal basis for holding corporations to account for human rights violations. The steady evolution of a global social expectation that companies should respect international human rights standards, combined with the occasional foray by states in adopting an expansive extraterritorial approach to protecting rights, is changing the nature and possibility of developing a firmer basis for corporate legal accountability for human rights. The growth and depth of soft-law stakeholder-led initiatives that have developed around the theme of corporate responsibility have come about partly in recognition of the failure of legal regulation (both internationally and domestically) to hold corporations to account, but these soft-law initiatives have become and will continue to be an important tool in attempting to prevent and remedy corporate rights violations.

Notes

1   Regulation as referred to in this chapter incorporates formal and informal, legal and non-legal mechanisms designed to influence or at times coerce corporations to better respect and/or protect human rights.
2   Human Rights Council, 'Protect, Respect and Remedy: A Framework for Business and Human Rights', Report of the Special Representative of the Secretary-General on the Issue of Human Rights and Transnational Corporations and Other Business Enterprises, John Ruggie, UN Doc. A/HRC/8/5 (7 April 2008) para. 3.
3   L. Baccaro and V. Mele, 'For Lack of Anything Better? International Organizations and Global Corporate Codes' (2011) 89 *Public Administration* 451; R.M. Locke, *The Promise and Limits of Private Power* (New York: Cambridge, 2013); D. O'Rourke, 'Outsourcing Regulation: Analysing Nongovernmental Systems of Labour Standards and Monitoring' (2003) 31(1) *Policy Studies Journal* 1.
4   Human Rights Council, 'Guiding Principles on Business and Human Rights: Implementing the United Nations "Protect, Respect and Remedy" Framework', Report of the Special Representative of the Secretary-General on the Issue of Human Rights and Transnational Corporations and Other Business Enterprises, UN Doc. A/HRC/17/31 (21 March 2011).
5   Hard law refers to actual binding legal instruments and laws. By contrast,

> there is no entrenched definition of what constitutes soft law, in this context it might commonly include instruments as diverse as those internationally formulated (other than a treaty) that contain 'principles, norms, standards or other statements of expected behaviour' but also widely accepted codes of conduct that have been developed by a group of stakeholders as a mechanism to prevent corporate rights abuses.
> (J. Nolan, 'Refining the Rules of the Game: The Corporate Responsibility to Respect Human Rights' (2014) 30(78) *Utrecht Journal of International and European Law* 7, 9)

See also D. Shelton, 'Normative Hierarchy in International Law' (2006) 100(2) *American Journal of International Law* 291, 319; J. Ellis, 'Shades of Grey: Soft Law and the Validity of Public International Law' (2012) 25(2) *Leiden Journal of International Law* 313, 334; D. Vogel, 'Private Global Business Regulation' (2008) 11 *Annual Review of Political Science* 261, 262, who refers to civil regulation as soft law and defines it as 'socially focused voluntary global business regulations'.
6   The Economist Intelligence Unit, 'The Road from Principles to Practices: Today's Challenges for Business in Respecting Human Rights', *The Economist*, 16 March 2015.
7   Paris, 10 December 1948, GA Res. 217A (III), Preamble, Recital 8.
8   L. Henkin, 'The Universal Declaration at 50 and the Challenge of Global Markets' (1999) 25 *Brooklyn Journal of International Law* 17.
9   P. Muchlinski, 'The Development of Human Rights Responsibilities for Multinational Enterprises' in R. Sullivan (ed.), *Business and Human Rights: Dilemmas and Solutions* (Sheffield: Greenleaf Publishers, 2003) p. 39. See also UN General Assembly, Declaration on the Right and Responsibility of Individuals, Groups and Organs of Society to Promote and Protect Universally Recognized Human Rights and Fundamental Freedoms, UN Doc. A/Res/53/144 (8 March 1999); Commission on Human Rights, 'Implementation of the Declaration on the Right and Responsibility of Individuals, Groups and Organs of Society to Promote and Protect Universally Recognized Human Rights and Fundamental Freedoms', Report of the Secretary-General, UN Doc. E/CN.4/2000/95 (13 January 2000).
10 D. Kinley and J. Tadaki, 'From Talk to Walk: The Emergence of Human Rights Responsibilities for Corporations at International Law' (2004) 44(4) *Virginia Journal of International Law* 931, 948.
11 New York, 16 December 1966, in force 23 March 1976, 999 UNTS 171.
12 New York, 16 December 1966, in force 3 January 1976, 999 UNTS 3.
13 The core ILO Conventions are as follows: Convention Concerning Forced or Compulsory Labour (C29), Geneva, 28 June 1930, in force 1 May 1932; Convention Concerning Freedom of Association and Protection of the Right to Organise (C87), San Francisco, 9 July 1948, in force 4 July 1950; Convention Concerning the

Application of the Principles of the Right to Organise and to Bargain Collectively (C98), Geneva, 1 July 1949, in force 18 July 1951; Convention Concerning Equal Remuneration for Men and Women Workers for Work of Equal Value (C100), Geneva, 29 June 1951, in force 23 May 1953; Convention Concerning the Abolition of Forced Labour (C105), Geneva, 25 June 1957, in force 17 January 1959; Convention Concerning Discrimination in Respect of Employment and Occupation (C111), Geneva, 25 June 1958, in force 15 June 1960; Convention Concerning Minimum Age for Admission to Employment (C138), Geneva, 26 June 1973, in force 19 June 1976; Convention Concerning the Prohibition and Immediate Action for the Elimination of the Worst Forms of Child Labour (C182), Geneva, 16 June 1999, in force 19 November 2000.

14 Slavery Convention, Geneva, 25 September 1926, in force 9 March 1927, 60 LNTS 253.

15 International Convention on the Elimination of All Forms of Racial Discrimination, New York, 21 December 1965, in force 4 January 1969, 660 UNTS 195.

16 Convention on the Elimination of All Forms of Discrimination against Women, New York, 18 December 1979, in force 3 September 1981, 1249 UNTS 13.

17 Convention on the Rights of the Child, New York, 20 November 1989, in force 2 September 1990, 1577 UNTS 3. See further Committee on the Rights of the Child, 'Report on the Thirty-First Session', UN Doc. CRC/C/121 (11 December 2002), paras 630–53 (discussing Day of General Discussion, 'The Private Sector as a Service Provider and Its Role in Implementing Child Rights', 20 September 2002).

18 International Convention on the Protection of the Rights of All Migrant Workers and Members of Their Families, New York, 18 December 1990, in force 1 July 2003, 2220 UNTS 3.

19 V. Trivett, '25 US Mega Corporations: Where They Rank If They Were Countries', *Business Insider*, 27 June 2011, www.businessinsider.com/25-corporations-bigger-tan-countries-2011-6?op=1&IR=T.

20 For example, the Convention on the Rights of Persons with Disabilities provides that states parties have an obligation to take all appropriate measures to eliminate discrimination on the basis of disability by any person, organization or private enterprise: Convention on the Rights of Persons with Disabilities, New York, 13 December 2006, in force 3 May 2008, 2515 UNTS 3, art. 4(e). In 2004 the UN Human Rights Committee, commenting on the nature of a state's obligations under the ICCPR, affirmed that the obligation is only discharged if individuals are protected by the state, not just against human rights violations by its agents, but also against acts committed by private persons or entities: Human Rights Committee, 'General Comment 31, The Nature of the General Legal Obligation on States Parties to the Covenant', UN Doc. CCPR/C/21/Rev.1.Add.13 (29 March 2004), para. 8. Similarly, General Comments from the UN Committee on Economic, Social and Cultural Rights addressing the rights to work, health and water confirm the state's duty to protect against abuse by corporations in the context of economic, social and cultural rights: Committee on Economic, Social and Cultural Rights, 'General Comment 18, Article 6: The Equal Right of Men and Women to the Enjoyment of All Economic, Social and Cultural Rights', UN Doc. E/C.12/GC/18 (24 November 2005), para. 35; Committee on Economic, Social and Cultural Rights, 'General Comment 15, The Right to Water (Arts. 11 and 12 of the International Covenant on Economic, Social and Cultural Rights)', UN Doc. E/C.12/2002/11 (20 January 2003), para. 23; Committee on Economic, Social and Cultural Rights, 'General Comment 14, The Right to the Highest Attainable Standard of Health (Art. 12 of the International Covenant on Economic, Social and Cultural Rights)', UN Doc. E/C.12/2000/4 (11 August 2000), para. 35.

21 For an alternative view arguing that treaty obligations do apply directly to corporations, see D. Bilchitz, 'A Chasm between "Is" and "Ought"? A Critique of the Normative Foundations of the SRSG's Framework and the Guiding Principles' in S. Deva and D. Bilchitz (eds), *Human Rights Obligations of Business: Beyond the Corporate Responsibility to Respect?* (Cambridge: Cambridge University Press, 2013) p. 107.

22 Human Rights Council, 'Elaboration of an Internationally Legally Binding Instrument on Transnational Corporations and Other Business Enterprises with Respect to Human Rights', UN Doc. A/HRC/26/L.22/Rev.1 (25 June 2014).

23 J. Ruggie, 'Quo Vadis? Unsolicited Advice to Business and Human Rights Treaty Sponsors' (Institute for Human Rights and Business, 9 September 2014), www.ihrb.org/commentary/quo-vadis-unsolicited-advice-business.html. For broad commentary on the potential treaty, see http://business-humanrights.org/en/binding-treaty.

24 V.A. Leary, 'The Paradox of Workers' Rights as Human Rights' in L.A. Compa and S.F. Diamond (eds), *Human Rights, Labor Rights, and International Trade* (Philadelphia: University of Pennsylvania Press, 1996) p. 22 at 22.

25 W.R. Simpson, 'The ILO and Tripartism: Some Reflections' (September 1994) *Monthly Labor Review* 40.

26 See above n. 13.

27 International Labour Organization, 'Tripartite Declaration of Principles Concerning Multinational Enterprises and Social Policy', Geneva, November 1977 (as amended at its 279th (November 2000) and 295th Session (March 2006)).

28 Better Factories Cambodia, http://betterfactories.org.

29 The US–Cambodia Bilateral Textile Trade Agreement was the first agreement of its kind to link increased access to US markets to improved working conditions in an exporting country: Agreement Relating to Trade in Cotton, Wool, Man-made Fiber, Non-Cotton Vegetable Fiber and Silk Blend Textiles and Textile Products between the Government of the United States of America and the Royal Government of Cambodia, Phnom Penh, 20 January 1999. Textile and garment quotas were eliminated in January 2005 with the end of the GATT Multi-Fiber Agreement (in force 1 January 1974).

30 P. Harpur, 'Better Work: Problems with Exporting the Better Factories Cambodia Project to Jordan, Lesotho, and Vietnam' (2011) 36(4) *Employee Relations Law Journal* 98; D. Arnold, 'Workers' Agency and Re-working Power Relations in Cambodia's Garment Industry' (Capturing the Gains Working Paper 24), www.capturingthegains.org/pdf/ctg-wp-2013-24.pdf.

31 Locke, *The Promise and Limits of Private Power*, p. 171.

32 D. Arnold, 'Better Work or "Ethical Fix"? Lessons from Cambodia's Apparel Industry', *Global Labour Column*, http://column.global-labour-university.org/2013/11/better-work-or-ethical-fix-lessons-from.html.
33 Ibid.
34 Guiding Principle No. 1.
35 The Commentary to Guiding Principle No. 2 states:

> At present States are not generally required under international human rights law to regulate the extraterritorial activities of businesses domiciled in their territory and/or jurisdiction. Nor are they generally prohibited from doing so, provided there is a recognized jurisdictional basis. Within these parameters some human rights treaty bodies recommend that home States take steps to prevent abuse abroad by business enterprises within their jurisdiction. There are strong policy reasons for home States to set out clearly the expectation that businesses respect human rights abroad, especially where the State itself is involved in or supports those businesses. The reasons include ensuring predictability for business enterprises by providing coherent and consistent messages, and preserving the State's own reputation.

36 See above n. 20.
37 D. Augenstein and D. Kinley, 'When Human Rights "Responsibilities" Become "Duties": The Extra-territorial Obligations of States That Bind Corporations' in Deva and Bilchitz, *Human Rights Obligations of Business*, p. 271.
38 (1977) 15 USC §§78dd-1 et seq.
39 A number of subsequent amendments have been made to the FCPA including those in the Omnibus Trade and Competitiveness Act 1988, which arguably weakened the FCPA by enacting

> a 'knowing' standard in order to find violations of the Act. This standard was intended to encompass 'conscious disregard' and 'willful blindness.' The amendments provided certain defenses against finding violations of the act, such as that the gift is lawful under the laws of the foreign country and that the gift is a bona fide and reasonable expenditure or for the performance or execution of a contract with the foreign government.
> (M.V. Seitzinger, *Foreign Corrupt Practices Act (FCPA): Congressional Interest and Executive Enforcement* (Congressional Research Service, 7 February 2012), www.fas.org/sgp/crs/misc/R41466.pdf)

40 OECD Convention on Combating Bribery of Foreign Public Officials in International Business Transactions (21 November 1997); UN Convention against Corruption, 31 October 2003, in force 14 December 2005, 2349 UNTS 41.
41 Dodd–Frank Wall Street Reform and Consumer Protection Act, Pub. L. No. 111-203, 124 Stat. 1376 (2010). In addition, s. 1504 of the Act addresses financial transparency by requiring all listed oil and mining companies to disclose the revenues they pay to governments worldwide. See further A.P. Ewing in this volume, 'Mandatory human rights reporting', p. 284.
42 G.A. Sarfaty, 'Shining Light on Global Supply Chains' (2015) 56 *Harvard International Law Journal* (forthcoming), citing US Government Accountability Office, *SEC Conflict Minerals Rule: Information on Responsible Sourcing and Companies Affected* (Report to Congressional Committees, July 2013) 21. In addition, there are those who argue that the costs of such transparency initiatives (including funding the reporting and due diligence requirements and potentially directing trade away from developing countries in need of foreign investment) outweigh any potential benefits. For a summary of the pros and cons of such arguments, see 'Transparency, Conflict Minerals and Natural Resources: What You Don't Know about Dodd–Frank', transcript of a discussion hosted by the Brookings Institution and Global Witness, 13 December 2011, www.brookings.edu/research/opinions/2011/12/20-debating-Dodd-Frank-kaufmann.
43 P.J. Spiro, 'Constraining Global Corporate Power: A Short Introduction' (2013) 46 *Vanderbilt Journal of Transnational Law* 1101, 1116, citing R. Rabinowitz, 'OSHA Has a Big Job, on a Tiny Budget', *New York Times*, 29 April 2013, www.nytimes.com/roomfordebate/2013/04/28/where-osha-falls-short-andwhy/osha-has-a-big-job-on-a-tiny-budget.
44 D. Baumann-Pauly, S. Labowitz and N. Banerjee, 'Closing Governance Gaps in Bangladesh's Garment Industry: The Power and Limitations of Private Governance Schemes' (SSRN Working Paper, 12 March 2015) p. 4, http://papers.ssrn.com/sol3/papers.cfm?abstract_id=2577535.
45 Amnesty International and Global Witness, *Digging for Transparency: How US Companies Are Only Scratching the Surface of Conflict Minerals Reporting* (April 2015), www.globalwitness.org/campaigns/democratic-republic-congo/digging-transparency.
46 OECD Guidelines for Multinational Enterprises (2011).
47 Ibid., para. 1.
48 See L.C. Backer, 'Rights and Accountability in Development ("RAID") v DAS Air and Global Witness v Afrimex: Small Steps towards an Autonomous Transnational Legal System for the Regulation of Multinational Corporations' (2009) 10(1) *Melbourne Journal of International Law* 258. See further K. Genovese in this volume, 'Access to remedy: non-judicial grievance mechanisms', p. 266.
49 For a database of the complaints, see OECD Guidelines for Multinational Enterprises, Database of Specific Instances, http://mneguidelines.oecd.org/database.
50 See OECD Watch, www.oecdwatch.org.
51 United Kingdom Department for Business Innovations & Skills, 'Initial Assessment by the UK National Contact Point for the OECD Guidelines for Multinational Enterprises: Complaint by Privacy International and Others against Gamma International UK Ltd', June 2013, www.gov.uk/government/uploads/system/uploads/attachment_data/file/208112/bis-13-947-complaint-from-privacy-international-and-others-against-gamma-international-uk-ltd.pdf.

52 Ibid., para. 41.
53 UK National Contact Point for the OECD Guidelines for Multinational Enterprises, 'Privacy International & Gamma International UK Ltd: Final Statement after Examination of Complaint', December 2014, www.gov. uk/government/uploads/system/uploads/attachment_data/file/402462/BIS-15-93-Final_statement_after_ examination_of_complaint_Privacy_International_and_Gamma_International_UK_Ltd.pdf.
54 J. Lee, 'UN Global Compact Expels Hundreds for Non-Compliance', Triple Pundit, 22 January 2015, www. triplepundit.com/2015/01/un-global-compact-expels-members-non-compliance (reporting that in 2014 the UN Global Compact expelled 657 companies for not submitting their Communication on Progress).
55 From UN Global Compact, Participants & Stakeholders, www.unglobalcompact.org/ParticipantsAndStake-holders/index.html © United Nations. Reprinted with the permission of the United Nations.
56 S. Deva, 'Global Compact: A Critique of UN's "Public–Private" Partnership for Promoting Corporate Citizenship' (2006) 34 *Syracuse Journal of International Law & Commerce* 107; J. Nolan, 'United Nations' Compact with Business: Hindering or Helping the Protection of Human Rights' (2005) 24(2) *University of Queensland Law Journal* 445.
57 A. Rasche, '"A Necessary Supplement": What the United Nations Global Compact Is and Is Not' (2009) 48(4) *Business & Society* 511.
58 Sub-Commission on the Prevention of Discrimination and Protection of Minorities, 'The Relationship between the Enjoyment of Economic, Social and Cultural Rights and the Right to Development, and the Working Methods and Activities of Transnational Corporations', UN Doc. E/CN.4/Sub.2/Res/1998/8 (20 August 1998), para. 4.
59 United Nations Sub-Commission on the Promotion and Protection of Human Rights, 'Norms on the Responsibilities of Transnational Corporations and Other Business Enterprises with Regard to Human Rights', UN Doc. E/CN.4/Sub.2/2003/12/Rev.2 (2003).
60 Sub-Commission on the Promotion and Protection of Human Rights, 'Responsibilities of Transnational Corporations and Other Business Enterprises with Regard to Human Rights', Res. 2003/16 (13 August 2003), in Sub-Commission on the Promotion and Protection of Human Rights, 'Report of the Sub-Commission on the Promotion and Protection of Human Rights on Its Fifty-Fifth Session', UN Doc. E/CN 4/Sub 2/2003/43 (20 October 2003) pp. 51–3.
61 Commission on Human Rights, 'Report on the Sixtieth Session (15 March–23 April 2003)', UN Doc. E/CN.4/2004/127, Part I, ch. 42, p. 28, para. (c).
62 Commission on Human Rights, 'Human Rights and Transnational Corporations and Other Business Enterprises', Human Rights Resolution 2005/69, UN Doc. E/CN.4/RES/2005/69 (20 April 2005).
63 J.G. Ruggie, 'Remarks Delivered at a Forum on Corporate Social Responsibility Co-Sponsored by the Fair Labor Association and the German Network of Business Ethics', Bamberg, Germany, 14 June 2006, www. reports-and-materials.org/Ruggie-remarks-to-Fair-Labor-Association-and-German-Network-of-Business-Ethics-14-June-2006.pdf.
64 Norms on the Responsibilities of Transnational Corporations and Other Business Enterprises with Regard to Human Rights, Preamble, 3rd Recital.
65 Commission on Human Rights, 'Joint Views of the IOE and ICC on the Draft Norms on the Responsibilities of Transnational Corporations and Other Business Enterprises with Regard to Human Rights', joint written statement submitted by the International Chamber of Commerce and the International Organization of Employers, non-governmental organizations in general consultative status, UN Doc. E/CN.4.Sub.2.2003/ NGO/44 (29 July 2003), www.unhchr.ch/Huridocda/Huridoca.nsf/0/918bbd410b5a8d2cc1256d78002a535a? Opendocument. See also D. Kinley, J. Nolan and N. Zerial, 'Reflections on the United Nations Human Rights Norms for Corporations' (2007) 25(1) *Companies and Securities Law Journal* 30.
66 Amnesty International, *The United Nations Human Rights Norms for Business: Towards Legal Accountability* (2004). See also Human Rights Watch, *Nongovernmental Organizations Welcome the New UN Norms on Transnational Business* (2003).
67 Commission on Human Rights, 'Report of the United Nations High Commissioner on Human Rights on the Responsibilities of Transnational Corporations and Related Business Enterprises with Regard to Human Rights', UN Doc. E/CN.4/2005/91 (15 February 2005), paras 21–2.
68 Human Rights Council, 'Human Rights and Transnational Corporations and Other Business Enterprises', UN Doc. A/HRC/RES/17/4 (6 July 2011), para. 6(a).
69 D. Bilchitz and S. Deva, 'The Human Rights Obligations of Business: A Critical Framework for the Future' in Deva and Bilchitz, *Human Rights Obligations of Business*, p. 2.
70 R.C. Blitt, 'Beyond Ruggie's Guiding Principles on Business and Human Rights: Charting an Embracive Approach to Corporate Human Rights Compliance' (2012) 48(1) *Texas International Law Journal* 33.
71 The Economist Intelligence Unit, 'The Road from Principles to Practices', p. 4.
72 Ibid., p. 5.
73 Human Rights Watch, 'UN Human Rights Council: Weak Stance on Business Standards', 16 June 2011, www.hrw.org/news/2011/06/16/un-human-rights-council-weak-stance-business-standards.
74 See generally Deva and Bilchitz, *Human Rights Obligations of Business*.
75 Guiding Principle No. 1.
76 See above n. 20.
77 C. Jochnick, 'Making Headway on Business and Human Rights', Oxfam America, *The Politics of Poverty*, 11 February 2011, http://politicsofpoverty.oxfamamerica.org/2011/02/making-headway-on-business-and-human-rights.
78 For example, Guiding Principle No. 11 ('Business enterprises ... *should address* adverse human rights impacts'); Guiding Principle No. 13 ('The responsibility to respect human rights requires that business

enterprises: ... (b) *Seek to* prevent or mitigate adverse human rights impacts'); Guiding Principle No. 23 ('In all contexts, business enterprises *should*: ... (b) *Seek* ways to honour the principles of internationally recognized human rights when faced with conflicting requirements'); or Guiding Principle No. 24 ('business enterprises *should first seek* to prevent') (emphasis added).

79   M.K. Addo, 'Human Rights and Transnational Corporations: An Introduction' in M.K. Addo (ed.), *Human Rights and Transnational Corporations* (The Hague: Kluwer Law International, 2001) p. 11.

80   Human Rights Council, 'Protect, Respect and Remedy: A Framework for Business and Human Rights', para. 7.

81   Some boycotts against Nestlé are still ongoing despite the fact that in 1981 the World Health Organization adopted a set of recommendations (partly due to the campaigning around the boycott) for member states to regulate the marketing of breast milk substitutes: World Health Organization, International Code of Marketing of Breast-milk Substitutes, Resolution WHA34.22, Annex., www.who.int/nutrition/publications/code_english.pdf.

82   See, e.g. Worldwide Responsible Accredited Production, www.wrapcompliance.org.

83   See S. Jerbi in this volume, 'Extractives and multi-stakeholder initiatives: the Voluntary Principles on Security and Human Rights; the Extractive Industries Transparency Initiative; the Kimberley Process Certification Scheme', p. 147.

84   M. Fichter and D. Stevis, *Global Framework Agreements in a Union-Hostile Environment: The Case of the USA* (Friedrich Ebert Stiftung, November 2013) p. 3, http://library.fes.de/pdf-files/id/10377.pdf.

85   M.P. Thomas, 'Global Industrial Relations? Framework Agreements and the Regulation of International Labor Standards' (2011) 36(2) *Labor Studies Journal* 269.

Section 2.2

The United Nations 'Protect, Respect, Remedy' Framework and Guiding Principles

Chip Pitts[1]

1 Introduction

The United Nations (UN) 'Protect, Respect, and Remedy' Framework (Framework)[2] and associated Guiding Principles on Business and Human Rights[3] (Guiding Principles) were developed by former Special Representative of the Secretary-General on the Issue of Human Rights and Transnational Corporations (SRSG), Harvard Professor John G. Ruggie. The Guiding Principles were developed with input from independent experts and multi-stakeholder consultation from 2005 to 2011. Constructed on the heels of an ultimately contentious effort by the UN to create new standards,[4] Professor Ruggie adopted a more focused approach that emphasized the responsibility of business to respect human rights. The endorsement by the UN Human Rights Council (HRC) of the Framework (in 2008) and the Guiding Principles (in 2011) achieved what prior efforts had failed to achieve: broad multi-stakeholder consensus[5] and an authoritative UN imprimatur on implementing minimum standards regarding state duties to protect and business responsibilities to respect human rights. After the endorsement of the Guiding Principles in 2011, the HRC established a five-member, regionally diverse Working Group to help oversee and guide the implementation of the Guiding Principles.

2 The UN Framework and the Guiding Principles

2.1 Overview

In 2008 the HRC unanimously welcomed the 'Protect, Respect, Remedy' Framework. These three pillars constitute its 'differentiated but complementary responsibilities':

1   the state duty to protect against human rights abuses by third parties, including business;
2   the corporate responsibility to respect human rights; and
3   the need for more effective access to remedies.[6]

This simplified description may mislead slightly,[7] perhaps suggesting that states merely have duties to protect[8] and that businesses merely have responsibilities to respect. In actuality, in situations involving state-owned, controlled or substantially supported enterprises,[9] privatizations, contracts when businesses stand in the shoes of states[10] or that involve contracted state functions,[11] businesses may also have other duties including to protect, fulfil or promote human rights.[12]

After the Framework was accepted by the HRC in 2008, the SRSG focused on 'operationalizing' the three-pronged Framework. This work culminated in the Guiding Principles, which were unanimously endorsed by the HRC in June 2011. The Guiding Principles have since become a common reference point in business and human rights.

The Guiding Principles apply to all states and to all (not only transnational) business enterprises, regardless of business size, sector, location, ownership or structure. Guiding Principle 1 provides that '[s]tates must protect against human rights abuse within their territory and/or jurisdiction by third parties, including business enterprises. This requires taking appropriate steps to prevent, investigate, punish and redress such abuse through effective policies, legislation, regulations and adjudication'. The question of the jurisdictional and territorial reach of a state's duty to protect under the Guiding Principles is not definitively determined. The Commentary to Guiding Principle No. 2 notes:

> At present States are not generally required under international human rights law to regulate the extraterritorial activities of businesses domiciled in their territory and/or jurisdiction.[13] Nor are they generally prohibited from doing so, provided there is a recognized jurisdictional basis. Within these parameters some human rights treaty bodies recommend that home States take steps to prevent abuse abroad by business enterprises within their jurisdiction.
>
> There are strong policy reasons for home States to set out clearly the expectation that businesses respect human rights abroad, especially where the State itself is involved in or supports those businesses. The reasons include ensuring predictability for business enterprises by providing coherent and consistent messages, and preserving the State's own reputation.[14]

Guiding Principle No. 7 explicitly supports states taking greater extraterritorial steps in conflict-affected areas, where the risk of gross abuses is seen as especially high.

Guiding Principle No. 12 states that the responsibility to respect human rights 'refers to internationally recognized human rights', including, 'at a minimum', those expressed in the *International Bill of Human Rights*[15] and the International Labour Organization (ILO) *Declaration on Fundamental Principles and Rights at Work*,[16] but also other standards and instruments as circumstances require (as when rights of certain groups may be adversely affected).[17]

2.2 Meaning of 'respect'

The Framework's second pillar focuses on the business responsibility to *respect* human rights, which exists independently, over and above mere compliance with national laws and regardless of states ability or willingness to fulfil their own human rights obligations.[18] While primarily a negative responsibility – to refrain from harm – it also includes proactive, positive responsibilities: 'business enterprises should act with due diligence to avoid infringing on the rights of others and to address adverse impacts with which they are involved.'[19]

The Guiding Principles note that this responsibility applies not only to adverse impacts that are directly linked to business operations, products or services but also to linkages via '*their business relationships, even if they have not contributed to those impacts*'.[20] The UN Global Compact has developed a flowchart[21] summarizing actions to be taken given the Guiding Principles' distinctions between causing,

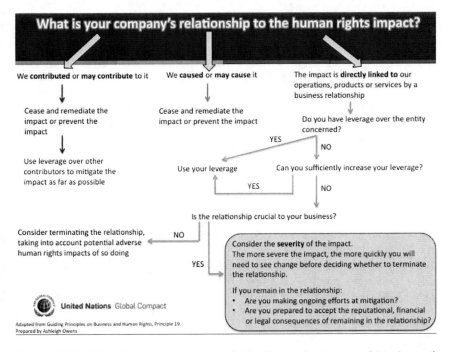

Figure 2.2.1 What is your company's relationship to the human rights impact? (source: UN Global Compact, www.unglobalcompact.org/docs/issues_doc/human_rights/Resources/Guiding_Principle_19_Flow_Chart.pdf (prepared by Ashleigh Owens))

contributing and being directly linked through relationships – all elaborations of the Guiding Principles' initial references to being 'involved' in adverse impacts:[22]

'Leverage' (the 'ability to effect change in the wrongful practices of an entity that causes harm'[23]) is a key factor in determining the appropriate action for the enterprise to take in preventing or mitigating harms beyond those it causes or may cause. Even when the business does not cause or contribute but is merely directly *linked to* adverse impacts through its operations, products or services by a business relationship, it should use its leverage to prevent or mitigate the harm.[24] Guiding Principle No. 19 notes that

> there are situations in which the enterprise lacks the leverage to prevent or mitigate adverse impacts and is unable to increase its leverage. Here, the enterprise should consider ending the relationship, taking into account credible assessments of potential adverse human rights impacts of doing so.[25]

The Framework and the Guiding Principles clarify and elevate to a state-endorsed agreement[26] the social expectations around businesses respecting human rights and provide guidance for them to do so. They thus complement, strengthen and provide further elaboration to the more general approach of the UN Global Compact, as well as the approaches of the ILO conventions, and a multitude of non-governmental organization (NGO), multi-stakeholder, academic and other initiatives[27] in harnessing increasingly powerful businesses to build rights-respecting business, governmental, political, legal[28] and social cultures.[29] The Guiding Principles are intended to develop greater normative clarity,[30] convergence and operationalization concerning the obligation to respect; in this way, the Guiding Principles create the potential for positive change. They reinforce minimum standards and serve as a valuable starting point for change-agents from business,[31] civil society[32] and various stakeholders. The Guiding Principles are being referenced in and influencing legislation,[33] agency regulations,[34] judicial[35] and quasi-judicial decisions,[36] and in some situations may help empower victims to achieve redress.

The Guiding Principles have also been used by treaty bodies,[37] special rapporteurs,[38] and mechanisms such as the Organisation for Economic Co-operation and Development's (OECD) National Contact Points and the International Finance Corporation's (IFC) Compliance Advisor Ombudsman. They have influenced other global norms forming part of the 'regulatory ecosystem',[39] including ISO's 26000 CSR standard, the OECD Guidelines for Multinationals and the IFC Performance Standards. Guiding Principle No. 23 expressly expects that businesses will treat the risk of gross human rights abuses 'as a legal compliance issue wherever they operate'. Some companies use the Guiding Principles as the basis for their 'compliance' programmes, although the ways they interpret and implement the Guiding Principles vary widely, and are usually not subject to independent external oversight.[40] Professor Ruggie has stated that the adoption of the Guiding Principles is the 'end of the beginning'[41] in the ongoing process of clarifying business and human rights norms.

3 Operationalization of the Guiding Principles by business

3.1 Organizational integration and due diligence

Guiding Principles No. 16–24 focus on internal company processes and the need to embed human rights and these principles into business practices throughout the extended enterprise (including business relationships). This begins with a publicly available policy 'approved at the most senior level of the enterprise'. The Guiding Principles also stress that these internal processes should be informed by stakeholder and internal as well as external expertise,[42] widely communicated internally and externally to 'all personnel, business partners and other relevant parties', clarifying 'lines and systems of accountability', and embedded enterprise-wide in operational policies and procedures.[43] Such integration is crucial, since otherwise the prevailing conflicts of interest between different business departments (e.g. between the corporate social responsibility (CSR) department and procurement) will continue to subvert the company's CSR objectives.

Guiding Principle No. 17 states that businesses should carry out human rights due diligence in order to identify, prevent, mitigate and account for how they address their adverse human rights impacts. The Guiding Principles expect ongoing human rights due diligence to identify and assess risks to rights-holders (and not merely the company)[44] to be completed 'as early as possible in the development of a new activity or relationship',[45] so that potential adverse impacts can be prevented or mitigated at early stages like contractual structuring or in due diligence for mergers or acquisitions.[46] There is now extensive guidance on this human rights impact assessment (HRIA) process.[47] While the Guiding Principles urge companies to assess and address all adverse impacts simultaneously, they acknowledge that prioritization based on severity may be necessary where simultaneous action is impossible as a practical matter.[48] For business enterprises with large, complex value chains where it is unreasonably difficult to conduct due diligence simultaneously across all adverse impacts, the Guiding Principles leave some room for flexibility:

> Where business enterprises have large numbers of entities in their value chains it may be unreasonably difficult to conduct due diligence for adverse human rights impacts across them all. If so, business enterprises should identify general areas where the risk of adverse human rights impacts is most significant.[49]

3.2 Tracking, reporting and publicly communicating on responses

The Guiding Principles call on companies to 'know and show'[50] whether the business has effectively addressed actual and potential adverse impacts, especially with respect to vulnerable individuals and groups. They ask businesses to track their responses using appropriate qualitative and quantitative indicators, integrated into reporting/disclosure processes.[51] A number of companies have begun Guiding Principles-compatible reporting.[52] An example of transparency is Nestlé's recent report on its due diligence and HRIA processes, describing seven HRIAs done with Nestlé subsidiaries in perceived high-risk countries (Angola, Colombia, Kazakhstan, Nigeria, Russia, Sri Lanka and Uzbekistan).

Snapshot

Nestlé's approach

Nestlé, a company with historical CSR troubles, especially regarding breast milk substitutes, adopted the Framework[53] in 2010 and, in the same year, conducted its first HRIA (with the assistance of the Danish Institute for Human Rights), focusing mainly on labour rights issues. The Guiding Principles have now been embedded into an integrated human rights due diligence (HRDD) system, beginning with Nestlé's Management and Leadership Principles (which, along with the Corporate Business Principles, have been described by Nestlé's CEO as the 'non-negotiable' principles 'we expect each and every one' of Nestlé's more than 340,000 employees 'to live by, every day, wherever they are in the world'[54]) and extending to 15 other key Nestlé policies/procedures.[55]

Nestlé's Human Rights Working Group meets every two months[56] to give sustained top-level management support to its one full-time human rights person. Major department heads participate (Compliance; Human Resources; Safety, Health and Environment; Legal; Public Affairs; Responsible Sourcing; Risk Management; Security).[57] Nestlé's HRDD[58] consists of eight interrelated, interdependent pillars: (i) mainstreaming operational policies; (ii) engaging with stakeholders; (iii) training; (iv) evaluating material risks; (v) assessing impacts; (vi) coordinating across other functions; (vii) working with external experts and partners; and (viii) monitoring and reporting.[59] Pillar (iv) identifies risks at five different levels: corporate; country operations; tier-one suppliers; upstream suppliers; and local communities.[60] Pillar (v), on HRIAs, focuses on eight different functional areas (Human Resources; Health and Safety; Security Arrangements; Business Integrity; Community Impacts; Procurement; Sourcing of Raw Materials; Product Quality/Marketing Practices).[61] Among lessons Nestlé learned are the advantages of open versus closed questions[62] and the importance of distinguishing more complex, comprehensive and functionally cross-cutting HRIAs from 'audits'.[63]

One may question Nestlé's HRDD approach – whether it is the correct prioritization strategy (beginning with labour rights and high-risk countries, as opposed to a more nuanced view of risks from the rights-holder's perspective), whether risks to rights-holders truly take precedence over risks to the business and whether this is fully understood to be a compliance issue beyond the headquarters' human rights function and other Nestlé Human Rights Working Group members. But such questions arise because the company has attempted to implement the Guiding Principles and has publicly shared the results.

3.3 Access to remedy

The third prong of the Framework and Guiding Principles is the need for access to effective remedies. This continues to remain elusive for most victims of business-related human rights violations. The state duty to provide effective remedies in the case of adverse impacts by business is paralleled by the responsibility of businesses to remedy impacts with which they are involved.[64] Yet states in reality often fail to implement their duty to provide effective remedy, because of lack of either resources or will. The business remedy responsibility strictly applies only to impacts that the business 'caused' or to which it 'contributed', as opposed to those with which the business is merely linked or involved (although such fine distinctions are unlikely to be appreciated by victims, increasing risks for businesses that do not broadly attend to remedies). In addition to cooperating with judicial mechanisms,[65] businesses are expected to establish or participate in 'legitimate' (for example, accessible, fair, transparent)[66] operational-level non-judicial grievance mechanisms.[67] But to date, the adequacy of company grievance mechanisms remains hotly contested, with many NGOs and victims sceptical that these will ever be adequate.[68]

4 Current implementation of the UN Guiding Principles

4.1 Implementation by businesses

Implementation of the Guiding Principles by businesses remains at an early stage, although some initiatives have started in certain sectors (like the Thun Group of financial institutions)[69] and among major companies.[70] The Business & Human Rights Resource Center (BHRRC) listed fewer than 400 companies with a specific and elaborated human rights policy as of May 2015,[71] but relatively little is known about the quality of the implementation of such policies. This seems a small number, vis-à-vis the estimated 80,000 multinational corporations globally, including most of the world's 50 largest and most powerful corporations.[72] Thousands more companies have committed to human rights via the UN Global Compact, which asks companies to embrace and report on 10 principles relating to human rights, labour, the environment and anti-corruption but has limited evaluation of substantive implementation attached to the process.

Snapshot

Hitachi[73]

Hitachi, a Japanese company, found that it first had to 'translate' the Guiding Principles and 'human rights' themselves into Japanese and into its business awareness and culture as it conducted workshops to educate its senior executives at corporate headquarters and from its major subsidiaries. The company found that risk management offered the most motivational lens through which to emphasize the importance of respect for human rights, and that the classic management 'Plan, Do, Check, Act' process, which Hitachi uses, offered a familiar entry point to help executives and relevant employees to understand the Guiding Principles. Embedding its policy commitment into corporate governance, Hitachi clarified that human rights compliance was obligatory for each of its global businesses, which have been undergoing training in effective due diligence to address adverse impacts.

4.2 Implementation by states

While the Guiding Principles repeatedly exhort states to enhance 'policy coherence'[74] both 'vertically' (to have the laws, policies and processes to implement their international human rights obligations) and 'horizontally' (among their different agencies and governmental levels and between their human rights obligations and their business-oriented trade and commerce policies), the impact of the Guiding Principles in this area appears to be limited to date. For example, state behaviour has changed very little when participating in international financial institutions (such as the World Trade Organization, World Bank or International Monetary Fund),[75] despite state obligations to protect human rights.[76]

Several states have developed or are developing National Action Plans (NAPs), as urged by the Working Group as a means of operationalizing the Guiding Principles.[77] NAPs are relevant not only for state implementation, but also to encourage business implementation.[78] Nevertheless, drafting progress has been slow, with quality varying widely. The current NAPs lack 'law and policy coherence' within states as there are tensions between the ministries handling commerce, trade, investment, sovereign wealth funds and government procurement, and those focused on human rights.

The BHRRC[79] currently identifies eight countries that have written and published NAPs: Colombia, Denmark, the United Kingdom, Finland, Lithuania, Norway, Sweden and the Netherlands. A number of other countries are currently developing NAPs, including Argentina, Azerbaijan, Belgium, Brazil, France, Germany, Greece, Indonesia, Ireland, Italy, Jordan, Latvia, Lithuania, Malaysia, Mauritius, Mexico, Morocco, Mozambique, Myanmar, Portugal, Slovenia, South Korea, Spain, Switzerland and the United States.[80]

To date, the NAPs have devoted relatively little attention to improving access to remedy as compared to preventive measures. The commitments and deadlines included in these reports are often vague or ambiguous, with little content that is concrete or measureable. Finally, the needs of vulnerable groups, such as indigenous people, are often overlooked.[81] While NAPs have the potential to foster progress, especially if used by mechanisms such as the HRC's universal periodic review, the UN treaty bodies, Special Rapporteurs and reviews by civil society, the media and others, developments to date have been limited.[82]

4.3 Working Group on business and human rights' role in implementation

To address the implementation challenges associated with the Framework and the Guiding Principles, the Working Group was established in 2011 to cooperate with treaty bodies and other HRC special procedures, and to recommend enhancements to domestic legislation, policies and access to remedy. Empowered to conduct country visits, the Working Group conducts regional forums as a source of information as well as education, and with the Office of the High Commissioner for Human Rights (OHCHR) guides the annual Forum on Business and Human Rights.

The Working Group has been criticized for focusing mostly on state action under Framework pillar 1 (the state duty), with too little attention given to pillars 2 and 3. The Working Group could do more to identify effective metrics for progress beyond anecdotal and small survey evidence, in addition to more effectively and publicly connecting the Framework/Guiding Principles to macro issues such as inequality, persistent poverty, tax avoidance, counterproductive business lobbying and corruption.

5 Assessment of the Guiding Principles

The Guiding Principles have generally been embraced by governments and global companies but have been criticized by a number of NGOs and academics, especially for their lack of specificity and inadequate ability to provide access to remedy.[83] The frequent critique[84] of the soft-law[85] Guiding Principles as merely 'non-legal' and/or 'voluntary' arguably neglects the legal nature of soft law, overlooks the complex hard- and soft-law interplay in this area[86] and misses the extent to which the Guiding Principles evolved under pressure to embrace existing and emerging hard as well as soft-law obligations.[87]

Some of the criticisms levied against the Guiding Principles are hard to reconcile with the plain language of the Guiding Principles' text, such as the claims that they apply only to (i) the narrowly bounded firm and not the extended enterprise including the firm's subsidiaries, affiliates or supply/value chain,[88] or (ii) some subset of firms or of internationally recognized universal human rights.[89] To the heftier criticism that victims were inadequately consulted,[90] the former SRSG argues that the consultations were extremely wide and legitimate.[91]

Other critiques expressed while the Guiding Principles were in draft form, including those from 125 civil society organizations and several experts,[92] argued that they did not adequately close the governance gaps identified and were in some ways regressive from the SRSG's own prior reports and existing international human rights law.[93] These criticisms were significantly addressed during the Guiding Principles' finalization (if not perfectly or to everyone's satisfaction).

Residual aspects of these long-standing concerns,[94] however, endure. What the SRSG said of prior standards is also true of the Framework and Guiding Principles: they still 'lack sufficient scale to truly move markets'.[95] Business implementation remains limited and often selective, although defenders of the Guiding Principles point out that progress takes time and that perfect compliance even with hard law is a fantasy. Victims still suffer tremendously from insufficient and ineffective remedies, so critics complain that the Guiding Principles have spurred insufficient progress. Better laws – and stronger monitoring, enforcement and implementation – are needed to ensure better compliance.[96]

In 2013, Human Rights Watch (HRW) noted that while the Guiding Principles 'provide some useful guidance to businesses interested in behaving responsibly they also represent a woefully inadequate approach to business and human rights issues'. In HRW's view:

> That is because without any mechanism to ensure compliance or to measure implementation, they cannot actually *require* companies to do anything at all. Companies can reject the principles altogether without consequence – or publicly embrace them while doing absolutely nothing to put them into practice.[97]

Similar concerns were reiterated very powerfully by Audrey Gaughran of Amnesty International in the closing session of the December 2014 UN Forum on Business and Human Rights, when she highlighted that the Guiding Principles will not change the reality that most victims of corporate abuses remain without effective remedy most of the time.[98]

As the SRSG has repeatedly noted, no 'single silver bullet'[99] will solve the problem of continued corporate abuse of human rights. While the Guiding Principles are a useful foundation for companies developing a framework to address human rights issues, their development does not bring business and human rights challenges to an end. What is required is a multi-pronged, multi-stakeholder approach – one that deploys all the major levers affecting corporate behaviour (including hard and soft law, incentives *and* values and corporate culture) – to effectively prevent and redress human rights violations.

Notes

1   Sung Gyu Yun of Yonsei University, South Korea, provided helpful research assistance.
2   Human Rights Council, 'Protect, Respect and Remedy: A Framework for Business and Human Rights', Report of the Special Representative of the Secretary-General on the Issue of Human Rights and Transnational Corporations and Other Business Enterprises, John Ruggie, UN Doc. A/HRC/8/5 (7 April 2008).
3   'Guiding Principles on Business and Human Rights: Implementing the United Nations "Protect, Respect, Remedy" Framework', by United Nations Human Rights, Office of the High Commissioner, © 2011 United Nations. Reprinted with the permission of the United Nations.
4   See United Nations Sub-Commission on the Promotion and Protection of Human Rights, 'Norms on the Responsibilities of Transnational Corporations and Other Business Enterprises with Regard to Human Rights', UN Doc. E/CN.4/Sub.2/2003/12/Rev.2 (26 August 2003). See also D. Kinley, J. Nolan and N. Zerial, 'The Politics of Corporate Social Responsibility: Reflections on the United Nations Human Rights Norms for Corporations' (2007) 25(1) *Company and Securities Law Journal* 30.
5   However, some commentators criticize the extent, quality and implications of what Deva has called a 'façade of consensus'; see S. Deva, 'Treating Human Rights Lightly: A Critique of the Consensus Rhetoric and the Language Employed by the Guiding Principles' in S. Deva and D. Bilchitz (eds), *Human Rights Obligations of Business: Beyond the Corporate Responsibility to Respect* (Cambridge: Cambridge University Press, 2013) pp. 79, 81.
6   Framework, para. 9.
7   See, e.g. Deva, 'Treating Human Rights Lightly'.
8   The Guiding Principles note at the outset that they are grounded in recognition of states' 'existing obligations to respect, protect and fulfil human rights and fundamental freedoms', p. 1.
9   Guiding Principle No. 4.
10   For example, the corporations established by the US Central Intelligence Agency to carry out extraordinary renditions. See, e.g. J. Mayer, 'Outsourcing Torture', *New Yorker*, 14 February 2005, www.newyorker.com/magazine/2005/02/14/outsourcing-torture.
11   For instance, involving private military contractors. For a discussion of this issue see A.-M. Buzatu in this volume, 'The emergence of the International Code of Conduct for Private Security Service Providers', p. 160.
12   See, e.g. F. Wettstein, 'CSR and the Debate on Business and Human Rights: Bridging the Great Divide' (2012) 22(4) *Business Ethics Quarterly* 739; O.F. Williams, *Corporate Social Responsibility: The Role of Business in Sustainable Development* (London and New York: Routledge, 2013) pp. 51–71 (arguing for additional moral duties of business).
13   This understates the status of current international law with respect to state-owned enterprises. See, e.g. D. Augenstein, *State Responsibilities to Regulate and Adjudicate Corporate Activities under the European Convention on Human Rights*, Submission to the Special Representative of the United Nations Secretary-General (SRSG) on the issue of Human Rights and Transnational Corporations and Other Business Enterprises (2011); C. Wee, *Regulating the Human Rights Impact of State-Owned Enterprises: Tendencies of Corporate Accountability and State Responsibility* (International Commission of Jurists, 2008).
14   In addition to the Guiding Principles' 'policy' reasons, there are perhaps legal reasons as well. See, e.g. D. Augenstein and D. Kinley, 'When Human Rights "Responsibilities" Become "Duties": The Extra-Territorial Obligations of States that Bind Corporations' in Deva and Bilchitz, *Human Rights Obligations of Business*, pp. 271, 283, 288. For further discussion on this point, see O. de Schutter, *Extraterritorial Jurisdiction as a Tool for Improving the Human Rights Accountability of Transnational Corporations* (Business & Human Rights Resource Centre, 2006). See also *Maastricht Principles on Extraterritorial Obligations of States in the Area of Economic, Social and Cultural Rights* (28 September 2011); O. de Schutter, A. Eide, A. Khalfan, M. Orellana, M. Salomon and I. Seiderman, 'Commentary to the Maastricht Principles on Extraterritorial Obligations of States in the Area of Economic, Social and Cultural Rights' (2012) 34 *Human Rights Quarterly* 1084.
15   The *International Bill of Rights* comprises the *Universal Declaration of Human Rights*, Paris, 10 December 1948, GA Res. 217A(III); the *International Covenant on Civil and Political Rights*, New York, 16 December 1966, in force 23 March 1976, 999 UNTS 171; and the *International Covenant on Economic, Social and Cultural Rights*, New York, 16 December 1966, in force 3 January 1976, 999 UNTS 3.
16   International Labour Conference, 86th sess., Geneva, 18 June 1998. The Declaration covers the core labour rights including free association and collective bargaining, forced and child labour, and non-discrimination.

17   Guiding Principle No. 12, Commentary.
18   Guiding Principle No. 11 and Commentary.
19   Guiding Principles, para. 6.
20   Guiding Principle No. 13 and Commentary (emphasis added). The Commentary clarifies that business relationships include 'business partners, entities in its value chain, and any other non-state or state entity directly linked to its businesses operations, products or services'.
21   UN Global Compact, 'What Is Your Company's Relationship to the Human Rights Impact?' (prepared by Ashleigh Owens), www.unglobalcompact.org/docs/issues_doc/human_rights/Resources/Guiding_Principle_19_Flow_Chart.pdf.
22   See Guiding Principle No. 11.
23   Ibid.
24   Ibid.
25   Guiding Principle No. 19.
26   J.G. Ruggie, *Just Business: Multinational Corporations and Human Rights* (New York: W.W. Norton & Co., 2013) p. 125.
27   Such as, among others, the Business & Human Rights Resource Centre (BHRCC), http://business-humanrights.org; the Institute for Human Rights and Business, www.ihrb.org; the Global Business Initiative, www.global-business-initiative.org; and the UN Principles for Responsible Management Education, www.unprme.org.
28   See, e.g. International Bar Association, 'IBA Publishes Business and Human Rights Guidance for Bar Associations and Lawyers', 23 October 2014, www.ibanet.org/Article/Detail.aspx?ArticleUid=c9bd50c6-c2b3-455b-b086-a7efbfe1f6a5.
29   Oliver Williams has lamented that the Framework and Guiding Principles, and Professor Ruggie, 'missed a teachable moment' by not more explicitly making the moral as well as the business case for such compliance: Williams, *Corporate Social Responsibility*, pp. 51–71.
30   Not all agree that this goal of greater normative clarity was achieved. See, e.g. D. Bilchitz, 'A Chasm between "Is" and "Ought"? A Critique of the Normative Foundations of the SRSG's Framework and the Guiding Principles' in Deva and Bilchitz, *Human Rights Obligations of Business*, p. 121.
31   See, e.g. China Chamber of Commerce of Metals, Minerals & Chemicals Importers & Exporters, 'Guidelines for Social Responsibility in Outbound Mining Investments', October 2014, www.srz.com/files/upload/Conflict_Minerals_Resource_Center/CCCMC_Guidelines_for_Social_Responsibility_in_Outbound_Mining_Operations_English_Version.pdf.
32   NGOs can use the Guiding Principles to evaluate gaps in state duties to protect, and in the broad spectrum of advocacy from confrontation to engagement with businesses. See, e.g. Oxfam, *Business and Human Rights: An Oxfam Perspective on the UN Guiding Principles* (June 2013), www.oxfam.org/sites/www.oxfam.org/files/tb-business-human-rights-oxfam-perspective-un-guiding-principles-130613-en.pdf; see also International Commission of Jurists – Danish Section and Reprieve, *Constructive Campaigning: Applying the UN Guiding Principles on Business and Human Rights to Civil Society Campaigning*, www.global-csr.com/fileadmin/Our_Approach/13_Constructive_Campaigning_NGOs_UNGPs.pdf.
33   For example, EU Directive 2014/95/EU of the European Parliament and of the Council of 22 October 2014 amending Directive 2013/34/EU as regards disclosure of non-financial and diversity information by certain large undertakings and groups, OJ 2014 No. L 330, in force 6 December 2014.
34   J.G. Ruggie, 'Closing Plenary Remarks', Third United Nations Forum on Business and Human Rights, Geneva, 3 December 2014, p. 3, www.ohchr.org/Documents/Issues/Business/ForumSession3/Submissions/JohnRuggie_SR_SG_BHR.pdf (referring to the establishment of the Peruvian Superintendency of Banks, Insurers and Private Pension Funds).
35   See, e.g. *Choc v Hudbay Minerals Inc*, 2013 ONSC 1414; *Adolfo Agustin Garcia et al. v Tahoe Resources Inc*, Notice of Civil Claim (filed 18 June 2014), http://business-humanrights.org/sites/default/files/documents/Notice_Civil_Claim.pdf.
36   See, e.g. UK National Contact Point, 'Final Statement by the UK National Contact Point for the OECD Guidelines for Multinational Enterprises: Afrimex (UK) Ltd', 28 August 2008, www.oecd.org/investment/mne/43750590.pdf.
37   See, e.g. Committee on the Rights of the Child, General Comment No. 16 (2013) on state obligations regarding the impact of the business sector on children's rights, UN Doc. CRC/C/GC/16 (17 April 2013), paras 7, 71.
38   See, e.g. J. Ezeilo, 'Report of the Special Rapporteur on Trafficking in Persons, Especially Women and Children', UN Doc A/67/261 (7 August 2012), paras 25–7, 50.
39   Ruggie, 'Closing Plenary Remarks', p. 2.
40   See, e.g. World Business Council for Sustainable Development (WBCSD), *Scaling up Action on Human Rights: Operationalizing the UN Guiding Principles on Business and Human Rights* (2014) pp. 16–18, www.wbcsd.org/Pages/EDocument/EDocumentDetails.aspx?ID=16382&NoSearchContextKey=true (referring to corporations such as Nestlé, Unilever, Heineken, DSM and ArcelorMittal treating the Guiding Principles as a compliance matter). See also D. Scheffer and C. Kaeb, 'The Five Levels of CSR Compliance: The Resiliency of Corporate Liability under the Alien Tort Statute and the Case for a Counterattack Strategy in Compliance Theory' (2011) 29(1) *Berkeley Journal of International Law* 334.
41   Ruggie, 'Closing Plenary Remarks', p. 1.
42   Guiding Principle No. 19, Commentary.
43   Guiding Principle No. 16 and Commentary.
44   Guiding Principle No. 17, Commentary.
45   Ibid.

46 Guiding Principle No. 17 and Commentary; Guiding Principle No. 18 – HRIAs should be undertaken prior to a new activity or relationship; prior to major decisions or changes in the operation (e.g. market entry, product launch, policy change, or wider changes to the business); in response to or anticipation of changes in the operating environment (e.g. rising social tensions); and periodically throughout the life of an activity or relationship.

47 See, e.g. Office of the High Commissioner for Human Rights, 'List of Tools', www.ohchr.org/EN/Issues/ Business/Pages/Tools.aspx; UN Global Compact, 'Tools and Resources', www.unglobalcompact.org/issues/ human_rights/tools_and_guidance_materials.html; International Petroleum Industry Environmental Conservation Association (IPIECA), 'Resources', www.ipieca.org/topic/human-rights/resources; International Centre for Human Rights and Democratic Development, 'Getting It Right: Human Rights Impact Assessment Guide', http://hria.equalit.ie/en.

48 Guiding Principles Nos 17 and 24 and Commentaries.

49 Guiding Principle No. 17, Commentary.

50 Guiding Principle No. 15, Commentary.

51 Guiding Principles Nos 17 and 20 and Commentaries. See further A. Mehra and S. Blackwell in this volume, 'The rise of non-financial disclosure: reporting on respect for human rights', p. 276.

52 See Shift and Mazars, 'First Comprehensive Guidance for Companies on Human Rights Reporting Launches in London', press release, 24 February 2015, www.ungpreporting.org/early-adopters/press-release.

53 Danish Institute for Human Rights and Nestlé, *Talking the Human Rights Walk: Nestlé's Experience Assessing Human Rights Impacts in Its Business Activities* (2013) p. 11, www.nestle.com/asset-library/documents/ library/documents/corporate_social_responsibility/nestle-hria-white-paper.pdf.

54 P. Bulcke, 'Keynote Statement', Third United Nations Forum on Business and Human Rights, Geneva, 2 December 2014, p. 3, www.ohchr.org/Documents/Issues/Business/ForumSession3/Submissions/20141202-PaulBulcke_opening.pdf.

55 Private Communications with Y. Wyss (February 2015); see also R. Song, *International Human Rights Impact Assessment Practices: Looking into the Case of Nestlé* (Seoul: National Human Rights Commission of Korea, 2014) p. 17. For an overview on the governance structure and the position of Nestlé's Human Rights Working Group, see Nestlé, *Nestlé in Society: Creating Shared Value and Meeting Our Commitments 2013* (2013) p. 21, http://storage.nestle.com/Interactive_CSV_Full_2013/index.html#22.

56 Bulcke, 'Keynote Statement', p. 3.

57 WBCSD, *Scaling up Action on Human Rights*, p. 13.

58 For a detailed description of Nestlé's HRDD, see Nestlé, 'Human Rights', www.nestle.com/csv/human-rights-compliance/human-rights.

59 CSR Europe and Econsense, *Business and Human Rights Workshop: Putting the Ruggie-Framework and the Guiding Principles into Practice* (2013) pp. 13–14, www.csreurope.org/sites/default/files/BHR Workshop Report - Ruggie Framework and UNGP - CSR Europe (2013).pdf.

60 WBCSD, *Scaling up Action on Human Rights*, p. 15. The business obligation to respect is not restricted to first-tier suppliers, but extends to business relationships in the value chain: Guiding Principle No. 13 and Commentary.

61 Danish Institute for Human Rights and Nestlé, *Talking the Human Rights Walk*, pp. 7–8, 18–19.

62 Ibid., pp. 9, 20.

63 Ibid., pp. 14, 29. HRIAs should not be adversarial, and Nestlé's Yann Wyss confirms that Nestlé treats human rights as a compliance matter globally while also recognizing that unlike the simple binary process of audit compliance for other areas, more time and in-depth analysis may be required for complex human rights situations; private communication with Y. Wyss (February 2015).

64 Guiding Principle No. 11 and Commentary ('Addressing adverse human rights impacts requires taking adequate measures for their prevention, mitigation and, where appropriate, remediation'); Guiding Principle No. 15(c) (the responsibility to respect includes having in place 'processes to enable the remediation of any adverse human rights impacts they cause or to which they contribute'); Guiding Principle No. 22 (obligation to provide or cooperate in remedies for adverse impacts the business caused or to which it contributed).

65 Guiding Principle No. 22, Commentary.

66 See the legitimacy criteria in Guiding Principle No. 31.

67 Guiding Principle No. 29.

68 See K. Genovese in this volume, 'Access to remedy: non-judicial grievance mechanisms', p. 266. Compare Barrick, *The Porgera Joint Venture Remedy Framework* (1 December 2014), www.barrick.com/files/porgera/ Porgera-Joint-Venture-Remedy-Framework-Dec1-2014.pdf, with MiningWatch Canada and Rights and Accountability in Development (RAID), *Privatized Remedy and Human Rights: Re-thinking Project-Level Grievance Mechanisms* (1 December 2014), www.miningwatch.ca/sites/www.miningwatch.ca/files/privatized_remedy_and_human_rights-un_forum-2014-12-01.pdf.

69 See the Thun Group of Banks, *UN Guiding Principles on Business and Human Rights: Discussion Paper for Banks on Implications of Principles 16–21* (October 2013), www.credit-suisse.com/media/cc/docs/responsibility/thun-group-discussion-paper.pdf; see also D. de Felice, 'Banks and Human Rights Due Diligence: A Critical Analysis of the Thun Group's Discussion Paper on the UN Guiding Principles on Business and Human Rights' (2015) *International Journal of Human Rights* 1.

70 Aim-Progress is one initiative, involving 40 member companies at the time of writing, to promote responsible sourcing and building capacity among its member companies to implement the Guiding Principles. See Aim-Progress, 'Business and Human Rights', www.aim-progress.com/page.php?pmenu=2&id=85. See also IPIECA, Resources.

71 S.A. Aaronson and I. Higham, 'Putting the Blame on Governments: Why Firms and Governments Have Failed to Advance the Guiding Principles on Business and Human Rights' (Institute for International Economic Policy Working Paper Series 2014-6), www.gwu.edu/~iiep/assets/docs/papers/2014WP/Aaronson Hingham201406.pdf.

72 A. Short, 'Shedding Light on Human Rights: Do Businesses Stand up to Scrutiny?' *Guardian*, 25 February 2015, www.theguardian.com/global-development-professionals-network/2015/feb/25/shedding-light-on-human-rights-do-businesses-stand-up-to-scrutiny.

73 Drafted by author and confirmed via email and interviews with company officials in February 2015 (on file with author).

74 Guiding Principle No. 8.

75 As urged by Guiding Principle No. 10.

76 Although the Guiding Principles apparently influenced UNCITRAL's new investor–state arbitration rules to enhance accountability through greater transparency. See J. Salasky, 'The New UNCITRAL Rules and Convention on Transparency', LSE Human Rights Blog, 6 August 2014, http://blogs.lse.ac.uk/investment-and-human-rights/portfolio-items/transparency-in-investment-treaty-arbitration-and-the-un-guiding-principles-on-business-and-human-rights-the-new-uncitral-rules-and-convention-on-transparency.

77 UN Working Group on Business and Human Rights, 'State National Action Plans', www.ohchr.org/EN/Issues/Business/Pages/NationalActionPlans.aspx.

78 S.A. Aaronson and I. Higham, 'Re-righting Business: John Ruggie and the Struggle to Develop International Human Rights Standards for Transnational Firms' (2013) 35(2) *Human Rights Quarterly* 264.

79 BHRRC, 'National Action Plans', http://business-humanrights.org/en/un-guiding-principles/implementation-tools-examples/implementation-by-governments/by-type-of-initiative/national-action-plans.

80 Ibid.

81 L.C. Backer, 'The Guiding Principles of Business and Human Rights at a Crossroads: The State, the Enterprise, and the Spectre of a Treaty to Bind Them All' (Coalition for Peace & Ethics, Working Papers (2014) No. 7(1)) pp. 1, 4, 10–11, 14–16.

82 See D. de Felice and A. Graf, 'The Potential of National Action Plans to Implement Human Rights Norms: An Early Assessment with Respect to the UN Guiding Principles on Business and Human Rights' (2015) 7(1) *Journal of Human Rights Practice* 40. See also International Corporate Accountability Roundtable (ICAR) and European Coalition for Corporate Justice (ECCJ), *Assessments of Existing National Action Plans (NAPs) on Business and Human Rights* (2014), http://accountabilityroundtable.org/wp-content/uploads/2014/10/ICAR-ECCJ-Assessments-of-Existing-NAPs.pdf.

83 See, e.g. Deva and Bilchitz, *Human Rights Obligations of Business*; R.C. Blitt, 'Beyond Ruggie's Guiding Principles on Business and Human Rights'; G. Skinner, R. McCorquodale and O. de Schutter, *The Third Pillar: Access to Judicial Remedies for Human Rights Violations by Transnational Business* (ICAR, CORE and ECCJ, 2013), http://accountabilityroundtable.org/wp-content/uploads/2013/02/The-Third-Pillar-Access-to-Judicial-Remedies-for-Human-Rights-Violation-by-Transnational-Business.pdf.

84 See, e.g. J. Nolan, 'All Care, No Responsibility?' in L. Blecher, N. Kaymar Stafford and G. Bellamy (eds), *Corporate Responsibility for Human Rights Impacts: New Expectations and Paradigms* (Chicago: ABA Publishing, 2014) pp. 5, 13–14.

85 Authoritative and influential (including on courts) but technically non-binding.

86 See, e.g. C. Pitts (ed.), M. Kerr and R. Janda, *Corporate Social Responsibility: A Legal Analysis* (Ontario: Butterworths-Lexis Nexis, 2009).

87 Ruggie, *Just Business*, p. 124.

88 See, e.g. Deva and Bilchitz, *Human Rights Obligations of Business*, p. 15.

89 See, e.g. ibid., p. 9.

90 Deva, 'Treating Human Rights Lightly', pp. 83–4.

91 See, e.g. Ruggie, *Just Business*, pp. 142–8.

92 Including the author.

93 ESCR-Net, 'Joint Civil Society Statement on the Draft Guiding Principles on Business and Human Rights – 2011', January 2011, www.escr-net.org/docs/i/1473602.

94 See, e.g. Human Rights Watch, 'UN Human Rights Council: Weak Stance on Business Standards', 16 June 2011, www.hrw.org/news/2011/06/16/un-human-rights-council-weak-stance-business-standards (no clear enforcement mechanism); Amnesty International, 'Comments on the United Nations Special Representative of the Secretary General on Transnational Corporations and Other Business Enterprises' Draft Guiding Principles and on Post-mandate Arrangements', 17 December 2010, www.amnesty.org/en/documents/IOR50/002/2010/en (Guiding Principles are 'voluntary', only for companies 'willing to ensure their activities respect human rights').

95 Guiding Principles, para. 5.

96 See, e.g. R.C. Blitt, 'Beyond Ruggie's Guiding Principles on Business and Human Rights'.

97 Human Rights Watch, *World Report 2013* (2013), www.hrw.org/world-report/2013/essays/without-rules?page=2.

98 This concern with persistent barriers to remedy has been validated by independent academic studies including those conducted by the OHCHR; see Skinner *et al.*, *The Third Pillar*; J. Zerk, *Corporate Liability for Gross Human Rights Abuses: Towards a Fairer and More Effective System of Domestic Law Remedies* (Report prepared for the Office of the UN High Commissioner for Human Rights, February 2014), www.ohchr.org/Documents/Issues/Business/DomesticLawRemedies/StudyDomesticeLawRemedies.pdf.

99 Framework, p. 4.

Section 2.3

Incorporating human rights: lessons learned, and next steps

John Gerard Ruggie

1 Introduction

In March 2015, the Economist Intelligence Unit published a report entitled 'The Road from Principles to Practice: Today's Challenges for Business in Respecting Human Rights'. It drew on a global survey of 853 senior executives. Among the headline findings was this:

> 83% of respondents agree (74% of whom do so strongly) that human rights are a matter for business as well as governments. Similarly, 71% say that their company's responsibility to respect these rights goes beyond simple obedience to local law.[1]

The report quotes Arvind Ganesan, who directs business and human rights at Human Rights Watch, as saying that as recently as the late 1990s 'there was no recognition that companies had human rights responsibilities'.[2] While many factors contributed to this shift, the 'watershed event', as the report puts it, was 'the UN Human Rights Council's endorsement in 2011 of the Guiding Principles on Business and Human Rights'[3] (Guiding Principles).

The Guiding Principles are the first official guidance the Council and its predecessor, the Commission on Human Rights, have issued for states and business enterprises on their respective obligations in relation to business and human rights. This marked the first time that either body 'endorsed' a normative text on *any* subject that governments did not negotiate themselves, and endorsement was unanimous. I developed the Guiding Principles over the course of a six-year mandate as Special Representative of the Secretary-General for Business and Human Rights, through nearly 50 international consultations, voluminous research reports and pilot projects.[4] UN High Commissioner for Human Rights, Zeid Ra'ad Al Hussein, describes the Guiding Principles as 'the global authoritative standard, providing a blueprint for the steps all states and businesses should take to uphold human rights'.[5] Compared with normative and policy developments in other highly complex and contested domains, like climate change, uptake of key elements of the Guiding Principles has been relatively swift: by other international standard-setting bodies, states, businesses, civil society and workers' organizations and bar associations.

Needless to say, much more needs to be done. When I presented the Guiding Principles to the Human Rights Council in 2011, I stated that 'I am under no illusion that the conclusion of my mandate will bring all business and human rights challenges to an end. But Council endorsement of the Guiding Principles will mark the end of the beginning'.[6] By this I meant that the Guiding Principles would provide an authoritative foundation on which to build. They were intended to trigger an evolution, not as the final word on the subject.

Our task now is to identify plausible paths ahead. But it is equally important to understand how we got here, why the Guiding Principles succeeded where previous such efforts failed. Critics believe it is because the Guiding Principles do not, in themselves, impose new legal obligations on states or businesses.[7] This is a partial and therefore misleading answer. More to the point is the recognition by John Tasioulas, Professor of Moral and Legal Philosophy at King's College London, that the Guiding Principles' success lies in breaking through certain conventional conceptual and doctrinal 'shackles'.[8] These contributed to past failures, and they would do so again if turned loose on future developments. Hence this chapter is divided into two parts: the premises underlying the Guiding Principles, and how to build on them.

2 Foundational logics

I drew the first premise from Harvard colleague and Nobel Laureate Amartya Sen: the need to rigorously distinguish human rights from human rights law. Sen maintains that treating human rights merely as the parents or progeny of law unduly constricts – he actually uses the term 'incarcerate' – the social logics and processes other than law that drive enduring public recognition of rights.[9] What were some practical implications of this premise?

The debate around the initiative preceding my mandate, the 'Norms on the Responsibilities of Transnational Corporations and Other Business Enterprises with Regard to Human Rights',[10] was bogged down by doctrinal differences concerning whether international human rights law applies directly to business enterprises. Advocates and the Norms said yes; businesses and most states said no. The Commission (now Council) rejected the Norms and created my mandate instead. I saw no reason to replicate the debate. Instead, I adopted the position that companies should look to internationally recognized rights for an authoritative enumeration not of human rights *laws* that might apply to them, but of human *rights* they should respect.

This had three decisive consequences. It permitted a clear differentiation between state duties and corporate responsibilities, satisfying a demand by states and businesses alike. It shifted the debate from doctrine to the practical question of how businesses can know and show they respect rights, to which the Guiding Principles provided the answer: through the human rights due diligence process the Guiding Principles stipulate for business enterprises to avoid infringing on the rights of others and address adverse impacts with which they are involved. And it made it possible for states to endorse the Guiding Principles even if they had not ratified all of the core human rights conventions – importantly including China in relation to the civil and political covenant,[11] and the United States vis-à-vis the economic, social and cultural covenant.[12]

The second premise underlying the Guiding Principles reflects the growing fragmentation of international law into separate and autonomous spheres of law. Human rights discourse is infused with the assumption of a rights-based hierarchy – the idea that human rights trump not only in a moral sense but that they also do, or at least should, in terms of the law. Yet in an influential report to the UN General Assembly, the authoritative International Law Commission concluded that 'no homogenous hierarchical meta-system is realistically available' within the international legal order to resolve the problem of incompatible provisions among different bodies of law, including when different tribunals that have overlapping jurisdictions address exactly the same set of facts and yet reach different conclusions.[13] In other words, resolution cannot be deduced from first principle. It has to be worked out in concrete realms of practice, where objectives are defined and can be aligned to achieve greater normative compatibility.[14] Thus, the Guiding Principles stress the importance of national policy coherence, of addressing cognate areas of policy and law that should be amended to provide greater space for human rights protection, and of states carrying that policy coherence with them when they participate in intergovernmental organizations.

Third, I observed that since the late 1990s the number of new multilateral treaties has dropped precipitously; not one has been deposited with the United Nations since 2010 and the most recent were targeted.[15] Earlier comprehensive treaties in complex and contested areas, such as the Kyoto Protocol,[16] have not fared well. Current indications are that Kyoto's top-down specification of emission cuts will be replaced by national pledges coupled with peer pressure – essentially an intergovernmental naming-and-shaming regime. Yet soft-law instruments and informal lawmaking are flourishing, as are many multi-stakeholder initiatives.[17] The causes are numerous, but among the main factors are the sheer complexity of transnational challenges, and global geopolitical/geo-economic shifts, generating a larger number and greater diversity of interests.

The inference I drew from this observation is that a trade-off exists between the 'comprehensiveness' of international instruments in complex and contested domains, and their 'binding-ness'. If you want comprehensiveness, go the soft-law route. If you aspire to binding-ness, take a targeted approach. I chose comprehensiveness in establishing a foundation, with follow-up binding instruments conceived as 'precision tools'.[18] In contrast, a non-governmental organization business and human rights 'treaty alliance' is demanding comprehensiveness (all rights and all businesses), binding-ness (a hard-law instrument) and universal jurisdiction.[19] This is so far beyond being feasible or reasonable as to constitute a purely symbolic gesture.

Fourth, the Guiding Principles rest on the recognition that global corporate conduct is shaped by three distinct governance systems. The first is the traditional system of public law and governance, domestic and international. Important as it is, by itself it has been unable to do all the heavy lifting on this and many other global challenges. The second is a system of civil governance involving stakeholders affected by business enterprises and their representatives, employing such social compliance mechanisms as advocacy campaigns, law suits and other forms of pressure, and also partnering with companies to induce positive change. The third is corporate governance, which internalizes elements of the other two as constraints, risks and opportunities. While the doctrine of separate legal personality between parent company and subsidiaries may govern the partitioning of assets and legal liability by multinational enterprises, risk management and identifying strategic opportunities typically are enterprise-wide functions.

Developing the Guiding Principles involved participants from each of these governance systems; it was an instance of polycentric governance. The intellectual and policy challenge was to construct a conceptual and normative platform whereby the three governance systems become better aligned in relation to business and human rights, compensate for one another's shortcomings and play mutually reinforcing roles from which cumulative change can evolve over time.

To foster that alignment the Guiding Principles invoke the different discourses and rationales that reflect the different social roles these governance systems play in regulating corporate conduct. Thus, for states the emphasis is on their legal obligations under the international human rights regime to protect against human rights abuses by third parties, including business, as well as policy rationales that are consistent with, and supportive of, meeting those obligations. For businesses, beyond compliance with legal obligations, the Guiding Principles focus on the need to manage the risk of involvement in human rights abuses, which means that enterprises must act with due diligence to avoid infringing on the rights of others and address adverse impacts that occur. For affected individuals and communities, the Guiding Principles reinforce ways for their further empowerment to realize their right to remedy.

Finally, I sought to ensure that promoting implementation and building on the Guiding Principles would not be limited to the UN. Other actors have their own and often more powerful sources of leverage over business-related matters. Thus, I worked with individual governments and businesses, as well as civil society and workers' organizations. I also promoted uptake of the Guiding Principles with other international standard-setting bodies: the International Organization for Standardization (ISO); the Organisation for Economic Co-operation and Development (OECD); the International Finance Corporation; the European Union; the Association of South East Asian Nations; the African Union; and the Organization of American States. The result is implementation (highly variable, to be sure) through, and cascading effects beyond, these distributed networks, national and international, public and private – even as the expert working group that succeeded my mandate promotes the Guiding Principles from within the UN human rights machinery.

In sum, the answer to the question of why the Guiding Principles succeeded where other such initiatives have failed is far more complex than the dichotomy of voluntary vs mandatory measures that critics invoke. And if, going forward, these premises are ignored and the process reverts to prior conventional modalities, it could well revert to prior failures as well.

3 Next steps

Implementation of what is already on the table of course comes first. Let me illustrate how the dynamics of implementation unfold and should be reinforced in two areas in which the Guiding Principles have enjoyed rapid and widespread uptake: human rights due diligence and non-judicial grievance mechanisms. I then address three areas of law that should be prioritized.

Human rights due diligence is central to the corporate responsibility to respect human rights. Mark Taylor traced its path from my mandate into conflict minerals legislation even before the Guiding Principles were finalized.[20] Recently, the European Union adopted mandatory non-financial reporting requirements referencing the Guiding Principles,[21] and several governments and stock exchanges have moved in a similar direction. But there was no reporting framework based specifically on the Guiding Principles. As noted elsewhere in this book,[22] Shift, the non-profit founded by former members of my UN team, has produced such a framework.[23] It helps companies take a deep dive into whether and how well they are aligning their due diligence practices with the Guiding Principles. The results, in turn, will provide information for sophisticated benchmarking.[24] Beyond that, governments requiring and companies conducting due diligence on their own accord are likely to find the need for more specific sectoral standards than exist in most industries. This is the focus of the NYU Stern Center for Business and Human Rights. The demand for assurance frameworks may come next. In short, due diligence has a built-in dynamic that should be reinforced because it helps reduce the incidence of corporate-related human rights harm.

The Guiding Principles also promote effective non-judicial grievance mechanisms, state-based and firm-level. Among the former, the National Contact Points (NCPs) under the OECD Guidelines for Multinational Enterprises have the greatest global reach. The Guidelines were updated in 2011 and now include the Guiding Principles' corporate responsibility to respect provisions. The number of human rights complaints has since spiked, and the fraction of such cases accepted for NCP consideration is higher than for other types of complaint.[25] But NCP findings against companies generally have had no material consequences. Canada recently adopted new corporate responsibility requirements to change that, referencing the Guiding Principles. Extractive companies listed in Canada that do not comply with the requirements now can lose government support through export credits and consular services.[26] Other governments should adopt comparable policies.

I turn next to three priority areas for further legal development. One is international investment law, contained in nearly 3,000 bilateral investment treaties and investment chapters of free trade agreements. These allow multinational corporations to sue states for damages, not only in cases of expropriation without prompt and adequate compensation, but also if the economic equilibrium that existed when the investment was made is upset through policy measures that an arbitration panel might construe as regulatory takings, which can include labour regulations, human rights standards and environmental requirements. Moreover, there is a far higher degree of speculative litigation under the investment regime – trying to push the boundaries in favour of investors – than in the World Trade Organization.[27] A priority for business and human rights should be to ensure that bona fide public interest considerations gain greater protection as investment agreements come up for renewal.

A second area is corporate law, particularly the interpretation it has been given in recent decades in the Anglo-American system: as requiring maximizing short-term shareholder value. This has raised the incentive for CEOs to manage to the share price, discounting other factors, including harm to people and planet. A broader social conception of the corporation is necessary if we are to meet these challenges. Towards that end, University of London Professor Peter Muchlinski has outlined how the Guiding Principles' due diligence requirements could lead towards a more robust corporate duty of care.[28]

My final point concerns judicial remedy for harm done. The current treaty proposal seeks a comprehensive and binding instrument coupled with extraterritorial jurisdiction.[29] This raises serious practical problems. First, given the complex and contested nature of business and human rights, a comprehensive and legally binding instrument would have to be pitched at so high a level of generality that it would be of little use to real people in real places. Second, the proposal excludes national companies from its scope. This virtually guarantees opposition from multinational firms and their home states, thus polarizing the process and undermining the hard-won consensus that has been achieved. Consequently, 'success' at best would mean ending up with the functional equivalent of the UN migrant workers convention.[30] Adopted in 1990, it has yet to provide needed protection for migrant workers because, as expected, it has not been ratified by any country receiving significant numbers of migrant workers. Third, even that scenario may be overly optimistic because there is little indication that most *host* states of multinationals are prepared to accept home state judicial intrusion into their jurisdiction covering the entire range of internationally recognized rights, from extrajudicial killings to providing an adequate work/life balance.

Recognizing these constraints, I have advocated a 'precision tools' approach to further international legalization in this space. One obvious candidate is corporate involvement in 'gross abuses'.[31] This is because of the severity of the harms; because the underlying prohibitions in relation to natural persons already enjoy widespread consensus among states yet there remains considerable confusion about how they should be implemented in practice when it comes to legal persons; and because the knock-on effects for other aspects of the business and human rights agenda would be considerable, as was true of the US Alien Tort Statute before the Supreme Court gutted it.[32] To those who say this does not go far enough, Stanford Law Professor Jenny Martinez, who supports my proposal, provides a compelling response: 'a first step is better than no step at all'.[33] In effect, 'no step' would result from insisting on an 'all-in' treaty.

Notes

1   The Economist Intelligence Unit, 'The Road from Principles to Practices: Today's Challenges for Business in Respecting Human Rights', *The Economist*, 16 March 2015.
2   Ibid.
3   Ibid.
4   Human Rights Council, 'Guiding Principles on Business and Human Rights: Implementing the United Nations "Protect, Respect and Remedy" Framework', Report of the Special Representative of the Secretary-General on the Issue of Human Rights and Transnational Corporations and Other Business Enterprises, UN Doc. A/HRC/17/31 (21 March 2011).
5   Z. Ra'ad Al Hussein, 'Ethical Pursuit of Prosperity', *Law Society Gazette*, 23 March 2015, www.lawgazette.co.uk/analysis/comment-and-opinion/ethical-pursuit-of-prosperity/5047796.fullarticle.
6   See 'Presentation of Report to United Nations Human Rights Council, Professor John G. Ruggie, Special Representative of the Secretary-General for Business and Human Rights', Geneva, 30 May 2011, www.ohchr.org/Documents/Issues/TransCorporations/HRC%202011_Remarks_Final_JR.pdf.
7   See, e.g. Global Policy Forum, *Corporate Influence on the Business and Human Rights Agenda of the United Nations* (June 2014), www.globalpolicy.org/home/221-transnational-corporations/52638-new-working-paper-corporate-influence-on-the-business-and-human-rights-agenda-of-the-un.html.
8   See J. Tasioulas, 'Human Rights, No Dogmas: The UN Guiding Principles on Business and Human Rights', http://jamesgstewart.com/human-rights-no-dogmas-the-un-guiding-principles-on-business-and-human-rights.
9   A. Sen, 'Elements of a Theory of Human Rights' (2004) 32 *Philosophy and Public Affairs* 319.
10 United Nations Sub-Commission on the Promotion and Protection of Human Rights, 'Norms on the Responsibilities of Transnational Corporations and Other Business Enterprises with Regard to Human Rights', UN Doc. E/CN.4/Sub.2/2003/12/Rev.2 (2003).
11 *International Covenant on Civil and Political Rights*, New York, 16 December 1966, in force 23 March 1976, 999 UNTS 171.
12 *International Covenant on Economic, Social and Cultural Rights*, New York, 16 December 1966, in force 3 January 1976, 999 UNTS 3.

13 International Law Commission, 'Fragmentation of International Law: Difficulties Arising from the Diversification and Expansion of International Law', UN Doc. A/CN.4/L.682 (13 April 2006).
14 Not everyone agrees. For an impassioned defence of deducing putative binding legal obligations from moral norms, see D. Bilchitz, 'A Chasm between "Is" and "Ought"? A Critique of the Normative Foundations of the SRSG's Framework and the Guiding Principles' in S. Deva and D. Bilchitz (eds), *Human Rights Obligations of Business: Beyond the Corporate Responsibility to Respect?* (Cambridge: Cambridge University Press, 2013) p. 107.
15 See United Nations Treaty Collection, Multilateral Treaties Deposited with the Secretary-General, https://treaties.un.org/Pages/DB.aspx?path=DB/MTDSG/page1_en.xml.
16 Kyoto Protocol to the United Nations Framework Convention on Climate Change, Kyoto, 11 December 1997, in force 16 February 2005, 2303 UNTS 162.
17 See, e.g. J. Pauwelyn, R. Wessel and J. Wouters (eds), *Informal International Lawmaking* (Oxford: Oxford University Press, 2012).
18 See J. Ruggie, 'Business and Human Rights: The Evolving International Agenda' (2007) 101(4) *American Journal of International Law* 819.
19 See Treaty Alliance, 'Enhance the International Legal Framework to Protect Human Rights from Corporate Abuse', www.treatymovement.com/statement.
20 M. Taylor, 'The Ruggie Framework: Polycentric Regulation and the Implications for Corporate Social Responsibility' (2011) 1 *Nordic Journal of Applied Ethics* 5.
21 EU Directive 2014/95/EU of the European Parliament and of the Council of 22 October 2014 amending Directive 2013/34/EU as regards disclosure of non-financial and diversity information by certain large undertakings and groups, OJ 2014 No. L 330, in force 6 December 2014.
22 See in this volume C. Rees and R. Davis, 'Salient human rights issues: when severe risks to people intersect with risks to business', p. 103; A. Mehra and S. Blackwell, 'The rise of non-financial disclosure: reporting on respect for human rights', p. 276.
23 See UN Guiding Principles Reporting Framework, www.ungpreporting.org.
24 See Institute for Human Rights and Business, 'Launch of the Corporate Human Rights Benchmark', 3 December 2014, www.ihrb.org/news/corporate-human-rights-benchmark-launch.html.
25 J. Ruggie and T. Nelson, 'Human Rights and the OECD Guidelines for Multinational Enterprises: Normative Innovations and Implementation Challenges' (CSRI Working Paper No. 66, 2015), www.hks.harvard.edu/content/download/76225/1711783/version/1/file/workingpaper.66.oecd.pdf.
26 See Foreign Affairs, Trade and Development Canada, 'Canada's Enhanced Corporate Social Responsibility Strategy to Strengthen Canada's Extractive Sector Abroad', www.international.gc.ca/trade-agreements-accords-commerciaux/topics-domaines/other-autre/csr-strat-rse.aspx?lang=eng.
27 J. Kurtz, 'The Use and Abuse of WTO Law in Investor-State Arbitration: Competition and Its Discontents' (2009) 20(3) *European Journal of International Law* 749.
28 P. Muchlinski, 'Implementing the New UN Corporate Human Rights Framework: Implications for Corporate Law, Governance and Regulation' (2012) 22(1) *Business Ethics Quarterly* 145.
29 Human Rights Council, 'Elaboration of an International Legally Binding Instrument on Transnational Corporations and Other Business Enterprises with Respect to Human Rights', UN Doc. A/HRC/26/L.22/Rev.1 (25 June 2014).
30 International Convention on the Protection of the Rights of All Migrant Workers and Members of Their Families, New York, 18 December 1990, in force 1 July 2003, 2220 UNTS 3.
31 See J.G. Ruggie, 'The Past as Prologue? A Moment of Truth for UN Business and Human Rights Treaty', Institute for Human Rights and Business, 8 July 2014, www.ihrb.org/commentary/past-as-prologue.html.
32 See W.S. Dodge in this volume, 'Business and human rights litigation in US courts before and after *Kiobel*', p. 244.
33 See J.S. Martinez, 'A First Step Is Better Than No Step at All', 3 February 2015, http://jamesgstewart.com/a--first-step-is-better-than-no-step-at-all.

Section 2.4

A business and human rights treaty

Justine Nolan

The push for a legally binding, comprehensive treaty on business and human rights began in the 1970s with an attempt at the United Nations (UN) to draft a code of conduct for transnational corporations. That push was revived in 2003 with the debate around the UN Norms on the Responsibilities of Transnational Corporations and Other Business Enterprises with Regard to Human Rights.[1] The private sector[2] has adamantly resisted the creation of a treaty, as have many governments.

The acceptance by the UN Human Rights Council in June 2014 of a resolution to pursue a business and human rights treaty revived this prickly debate. The 2014 resolution was sponsored by Ecuador and South Africa, among others. It called for the establishment of an open-ended intergovernmental working group on a legally binding instrument on transnational corporations and other business enterprises with respect to human rights. The mandate of this working group is to 'elaborate an internationally legally binding instrument to regulate, in international human rights law, the activities of transnational corporations and other business enterprises'.[3] This resolution was passed with what has been referred to as 'the thinnest of political mandates'.[4]

The adoption of the resolution immediately sparked strong and contrary views.[5] The International Organisation of Employers said in a statement that it

> deeply regrets that the adoption of the Ecuador initiative has broken the unanimous consensus on business and human rights achieved three years ago with the endorsement of the UN Guiding Principles on Business and Human Rights [and that it] is a genuine setback to the efforts underway to improve the human rights situation and access to remedy on the ground.[6]

A counter-movement was led by civil society organizations that favour such a treaty. A broad coalition of non-governmental organizations signed on to a joint statement supporting the development of a treaty because of 'the need to enhance the international legal framework to protect human rights in the context of business operations'.[7] The view presented by Arvind Ganesan,[8] below, is reflective of the general support among civil society advocates for a stronger legal framework; but he also expresses caution about the scope of the current resolution, which excludes national companies from scrutiny.[9]

Proponents of a treaty argue that the fundamental nature of human rights requires a binding instrument and that human rights need to be recognized on the same level as other obligations in the context of trade and investment.[10] As such, a treaty could recognize and clarify the legal obligations of business with respect to human rights. In addition, they argue that without legal compulsion corporate compliance with human rights is likely to be sporadic, inconsistent and largely dependent on the whims of business to ensure their operations are truly respectful of rights. The provision of a legal framework should not prevent the ongoing development of other national or soft-law mechanisms aimed at improving corporate respect for human rights.

Alternatively, critics point to the difficulty of drafting a treaty to cover the breadth of rights that apply in different industries. They also note that it is highly unlikely that a majority of governments will support such a treaty. Enforcement of a treaty (that aims to regulate the activities of tens of thousands of corporations) would also be a challenge because it would be predicated in part on the need to ensure that states exercise extraterritorial jurisdiction over their home country-based corporations that violate human rights. The current process for pursuing a business and human rights treaty is likely to take years to finish and it is unlikely that a majority of UN member states will endorse the final product. Some commentators note that the binding character of a treaty might be obtained only at the cost of diluted standards, as states awaken to some of the legal ramifications of a treaty entering into force; or a treaty might be 'strong' but fail to secure the participation of key states.[11]

But neither the length of the treaty drafting process nor the complexity of the process is a sufficient reason to derail the process at this stage. What is more important is to ensure that the process is carried out in collaboration with existing mechanisms such as the Guiding Principles, the OECD Guidelines, industry-focused standard-setting exercises and the development of multi-stakeholder initiatives, as well as other measures aimed at regulating the impact of corporate activities on human rights.[12]

A business and human rights treaty will never stand alone as a 'silver-bullet' solution to redressing corporate rights violations. In many ways, devotion to this mechanism harks back to an era before globalization gathered force and states were the pre-eminent enforcers of rights. The multi-stakeholder nature of the business and human rights landscape ensures that no single mechanism – whether an international or national legally binding instrument or voluntary initiatives – can act as a standalone device to hold corporations to account. However, the existence of an international legal framework could act in concert with and support the many other ongoing corporate responsibility initiatives that are currently in play around the world. The development of a business and human rights treaty should not be viewed as an either/or narrative[13] but rather as an additional mechanism that could help clarify the legal responsibilities of businesses, be used to encourage the development of consistent national laws and operate in conjunction with more practically focused industry-specific standards and metrics that are being developed from the ground up.

Notes

1 United Nations Sub-Commission on the Promotion and Protection of Human Rights, 'Norms on the Responsibilities of Transnational Corporations and Other Business Enterprises with Regard to Human Rights', UN Doc. E/CN.4/Sub.2/2003/12/Rev.2 (2003).

2 International Organisation of Employers and International Chamber of Commerce, 'Joint Views of the IOE and ICC on the Draft Norms on the Responsibilities of Transnational Corporations and Other Business Enterprises with Regard to Human Rights', UN Doc. E/CN.4/Sub.2/2003/NGO/44 (29 July 2003), www.unhchr.ch/Huridocda/Huridoca.nsf/0/918bbd410b5a8d2cc1256d78002a535a?Opendocument.

3 Human Rights Council, 'Elaboration of an Internationally Legally Binding Instrument on Transnational Corporations and Other Business Enterprises with Respect to Human Rights', UN Doc. A/HRC/26/L.22/Rev.1 (25 June 2014).

4 J. Ruggie, 'Quo Vadis? Unsolicited Advice to Business and Human Rights Treaty Sponsors', 9 September 2014, www.ihrb.org/commentary/quo-vadis-unsolicited-advice-business.html. The votes were: 20 in favour (Algeria, Benin, Burkina Faso, China, Congo, Côte d'Ivoire, Cuba, Ethiopia, India, Indonesia, Kazakhstan, Kenya, Morocco, Namibia, Pakistan, Philippines, Russia, South Africa, Venezuela, Vietnam); 14 against (Austria, Czech Republic, Estonia, France, Germany, Ireland, Italy, Japan, Macedonia, Montenegro, Romania, South Korea, UK, USA); and 13 abstentions (Argentina, Botswana, Brazil, Chile, Costa Rica, Gabon, Kuwait, Maldives, Mexico, Peru, Saudi Arabia, Sierra Leone, UAE). On 27 June 2014, the Council adopted by consensus a second resolution, sponsored by Norway, that requested a report considering, among other things, the benefits and limitations of legally binding instruments; see Human Rights Council, 'Human Rights and Transnational Corporations and Other Business Enterprises', GA Res. 26/3, UN Doc. A/HRC/26/L.1 (23 June 2014).

5 The Business & Human Rights Resource Centre's treaty page provides comprehensive coverage of statements and commentaries on the potential business and human rights treaty: http://business-humanrights.org/en/binding-treaty/statements-initiatives-commentaries.

6 International Organisation of Employers, 'Consensus on Business and Human Rights Is Broken with the Adoption of the Ecuador Initiative', 26 June 2014, www.ioe-emp.org/index.php?id=1238.

7 Treaty Alliance, 'Enhance the International Legal Framework to Protect Human Rights from Corporate Abuse', http://treatymovement.com/statement.

8   See A. Ganesan in this volume, 'Towards a business and human rights treaty?' p. 73.
9   A footnote to the Ecuador resolution defines 'other business enterprises' in a way that is intended to exclude
     national companies. It states: ' "Other business enterprises" denotes all business enterprises that have a
     transnational character in their operational activities, and does not apply to local businesses registered in terms
     of relevant domestic law.' Human Rights Council, 'Elaboration of an Internationally Legally Binding
     Instrument'.
10   D. Bilchitz, 'The Moral and Legal Necessity for a Business and Human Rights Treaty', Business & Human
     Rights Resource Centre, 10 February 2015, http://business-humanrights.org/en/treaty-on-business-human-
     rights-necessary-to-fill-gaps-in-intl-law-says-academic.
11   F. Megret, 'Would a Treaty Be All It Is Made up to Be?' 4 February 2015, http://jamesgstewart.com/would-a-
     treaty-be-all-it-is-made-up-to-be.
12   A. Mehra, 'The Caravan toward Business Respect for Human Rights', Institute for Business and Human
     Rights, 11 February 2015, www.ihrb.org/commentary/caravan-toward-business-respect-for-human-rights.
     html.
13   Ibid.

Section 2.5

Towards a business and human rights treaty?

Arvind Ganesan

In July 2014, the United Nations (UN) Human Rights Council stunned companies, some governments and many in civil society when they voted to start negotiations on a treaty to address corporate responsibility for human rights abuses. No one, including us at Human Rights Watch (HRW), thought that the Human Rights Council would authorize treaty negotiations concerning the liability of transnational corporations (TNCs). But, after a contentious and somewhat convoluted process, a resolution supporting the development of a treaty[1] emerged – as did a resolution to maintain the UN Working Group on Business and Human Rights.[2] In effect, the Human Rights Council chose to pursue two parallel paths towards corporate responsibility, or perhaps more accurately, two complementary paths.

Since the beginnings of the modern business and human rights movement in the 1990s, there has been a tension between voluntary initiatives that promote business adherence to human rights standards and expectations for mandatory rules requiring business compliance with human rights norms. Those tensions came to the forefront in 2003 when the now-defunct UN Sub-Commission on the Promotion and Protection of Human Rights released its Norms on the Responsibilities of Transnational Corporations and Other Business Enterprises with Regard to Human Rights, an expansive document that prescribed the human rights obligations of companies.[3] Civil society and others wanted strong standards while many business entities and governments objected to such rules. That disagreement led to a compromise arrangement: the creation of the mandate of the UN Special Representative on Business and Human Rights that would ultimately lead to the non-legally binding, but widely supported, UN Guiding Principles on Business and Human Rights[4] (Guiding Principles). While the Guiding Principles enshrined the idea that business has human rights responsibilities, they did not obviate the tension between voluntary and mandatory standards. In July 2014, that tension became apparent when the Human Rights Council established an intergovernmental working group to develop a legally binding instrument to regulate the activities of TNCs.

In reality, the two views are not in opposition, but reflect a steady evolution towards stronger standards. For example, HRW has long believed that legally binding norms are necessary to ensure that businesses respect human rights. For the last few years, voluntary and mandatory measures have been wrongly portrayed as mutually exclusive. In HRW's view, they are each evolutionary steps towards the same goal. Voluntary initiatives have often become the place where basic norms are developed and established. For example, the Voluntary Principles on Security and Human Rights[5] have established the basic norms on how human rights should be integrated into security arrangements; and the Global Network Initiative has provided the contours on how Internet and telecommunications companies should protect free expression and privacy. Such efforts also provide more detailed standards that specify how companies should comply with human rights norms and, in some cases, offer sophisticated monitoring mechanisms to help ensure compliance. The Guiding Principles provide broad guidance on the human rights responsibilities of business but do not provide detailed guidance for companies; nor do they attempt to monitor compliance. Rather, they set out the general roles and responsibilities of governments and business and provide guidance on how compliance can be achieved.

Both types of efforts are valuable, but fall short when it comes to enforcement or accountability when human rights problems occur. The Guiding Principles are not enforceable and, while multi-stakeholder initiatives offer some sanctions, the most serious often being expulsion from the initiative, such penalties may be inadequate in the face of serious human rights problems. Moreover, those rules only apply to the companies that are part of these efforts; for those that are not, there may be no accountability at all. Nonetheless, these efforts have been essential for establishing norms and creating new models of compliance. They are not, however, ideal for comprehensive enforcement of human rights standards.

For this reason, an evolution towards binding standards that involve laws and regulations requiring companies to respect human rights will be essential for meaningful accountability. But real regulation is far more polarizing and contentious than voluntary initiatives. This was evident at the Human Rights Council meeting concerning a treaty process, pitting many developing countries at the Council, led by Ecuador and South Africa, against the United States and the European Union. Critics warned that a treaty would face strong opposition from some of the world's largest companies and the governments where they are headquartered.[6] Western governments threatened to sit out the negotiations.

The Human Rights Council treaty meeting also exposed the problems caused by a narrow (and perhaps ideological) focus on TNCs, even though any company is capable of infringing human rights and most standards, including the Guiding Principles, do not draw this artificial distinction. The emphasis on TNCs occurred as a result of Ecuador's insistence, it being the lead sponsor of the treaty resolution. But this has created a situation where an international apparel company might be bound by human rights standards, while abusive local factories are not. A treaty with credibility must cover all businesses. This point does not excuse governments from enacting national laws to protect workers and others affected by miscreant business practices, or to allow victims to seek justice in national courts.

Despite the flaws in the Human Rights Council resolution, the reality is that a treaty negotiation process exists and now presents an opportunity to establish stronger human rights rules. Companies have been implicated in a litany of abuses around the world and rarely pay a price for them, because governments fail to impose even basic regulations, such as requiring businesses to review and monitor rights risks. The reality is that those rules may be fairly modest because of how contentious new international rules will be. The intergovernmental group met again in July 2015 to begin setting out the contours of the negotiations.

The momentum within civil society to push for a treaty may be traced in part to the Human Rights Council's 2011 approval of the Guiding Principles. The fact that the Guiding Principles include no firm requirements and no monitoring of progress may be seen as a sacrificing of compliance with standards in favour of recognition of standards. In light of this approach, it is no surprise that implementation of the Guiding Principles has been woefully inadequate. Nor is it a surprise that the Guiding Principles did not dissipate the pressure for a stronger instrument, especially in the face of continued business-related abuses.

The treaty resolution also reflects a parallel development at the national level: slowly but surely national laws and regulations are incorporating modest elements of the business and human rights agenda. In the United States, there are new human rights disclosure rules for conflict minerals and investments in Myanmar, as well as contentious rules on transparency in the extractive industries.[7] Similar rules have developed in the European Union. And other countries, such as India, are starting to require some reporting on socially responsible practices.[8] These developments suggest a slow evolution towards binding standards, at least for reporting. While reporting requirements are not a substitute for laws and regulations that require human rights compliance and create accountability for violations, the move towards mandatory reporting may be the first step in a new body of rules that ultimately amount to a comprehensive regime to ensure business adherence to human rights rules.

In this context, the treaty process represents an opportunity to more effectively safeguard communities and individuals around the globe from abuses involving companies. Perhaps the best outcome would involve governments negotiating transparently and consulting widely with all stakeholders to constructively identify areas that might be amenable to new rules. The worst case would be a highly politicized and contentious process that yields nothing and makes it even more difficult to develop new norms. In the short term, treaty negotiations could lead to standards that incorporate elements of the Guiding Principles and existing good practices that are increasingly recognized as essential for businesses to fulfil their obligations to respect human rights, such as mandatory human rights due diligence, public reporting on human rights compliance and accountability for non-compliance with those standards. Whatever the outcome, and no matter how necessary a binding instrument is, it is certain that treaty negotiations will be contentious and new norms may take years to emerge.

Notes

1   Human Rights Council, 'Elaboration of an Internationally Legally Binding Instrument on Transnational Corporations and Other Business Enterprises with Respect to Human Rights', UN Doc. A/HRC/26/L.22/Rev.1 (25 June 2014). The resolution, sponsored by Ecuador and South Africa, garnered 20 votes in favour, 13 abstentions and 14 votes against it.

2   Human Rights Council, 'Human Rights and Transnational Corporations and Other Business Enterprises', UN Doc. A/HRC/26/L.1/ (23 June 2014).

3   United Nations Sub-Commission on the Promotion and Protection of Human Rights, 'Norms on the Respons-
    ibilities of Transnational Corporations and Other Business Enterprises with Regard to Human Rights', U.N.
    Doc. E/CN.4/Sub.2/2003/12/Rev.2 (26 August 2003).
4   Human Rights Council, 'Guiding Principles on Business and Human Rights: Implementing the United Nations
    "Protect, Respect and Remedy" Framework', Report of the Special Representative of the Secretary-General on
    the Issue of Human Rights and Transnational Corporations and Other Business Enterprises, UN Doc. A/
    HRC/17/31 (21 March 2011).
5   Voluntary Principles on Security and Human Rights, www.voluntaryprinciples.org.
6   For further discussion on the development of a business and human treaty, see J. Ruggie, 'Quo Vadis? Unsolic-
    ited Advice to Business and Human Rights Treaty Sponsors', Institute for Human Rights and Business, 9 Sep-
    tember 2014, www.ihrb.org/commentary/quo-vadis-unsolicited-advice-business.html; D. Bilchitz 'The Moral
    and Legal Necessity for a Business and Human Rights Treaty', http://business-humanrights.org/sites/default/
    files/documents/The%20Moral%20and%20Legal%20Necessity%20for%20a%20Business%20and%20
    Human%20Rights%20Treaty%20February%202015%20FINAL%20FINAL.pdf; P.J. Selvanathan, 'Treaty Me
    Right', submission to 'The Business and Human Rights Treaty Debate: Is Now the Time?', Duke Human
    Rights Center, 2014, http://business-humanrights.org/sites/default/files/documents/IsNowtheTime_TreatyDe-
    bate.pdf. See generally the Business & Human Rights Resource Centre, 'Binding Treaty', http://business-
    humanrights.org/en/binding-treaty.
7   See A.P. Ewing in this volume, 'Mandatory human rights reporting', p. 284.
8   Ibid.

Chapter 3

Business and human rights

Implementation challenges

For most corporations, a systematic engagement with human rights is new territory. According to a report published by the Economist Intelligent Unit in 2015, the biggest current barrier in addressing human rights is the lack of understanding about what human rights responsibility entails for corporations. The report's survey of 853 senior corporate executives shows that despite a strong consensus on the relevance of human rights for business, the actual implementation presents a significant challenge.[1] This chapter focuses on these challenges from a conceptual and practical perspective.

In corporate practice, human rights are typically subsumed under what is termed 'Corporate Social Responsibility' (CSR) or 'Corporate Sustainability'. However, the academic debate on business and human rights (BHR) has developed largely independently from the more popular concept of CSR.[2] The CSR concept has evolved substantially over the past decades and has taken on different meanings in the United States (US) and Europe.[3] Particularly in the US, CSR has long emphasized philanthropic giving, community service and marketing.[4] BHR and some European concepts of CSR, in contrast, are more focused on where companies derive profits and how core operations affect human rights, particularly in places where states are not protecting the rights of their own people. The contribution of Florian Wettstein illustrates the more ambitious European perspective on CSR. He shows that the BHR concept, while distinct from CSR, could also profit from, for example, CSR's focus on company culture and values.

Some forward-looking companies are beginning to address human rights issues by aligning their organizational structures and procedures with their human rights commitment. Drawing on over 20 years of experience in the senior management team at General Electric, Ben W. Heineman Jr. outlines what it takes to create a culture of integrity that enables systematic respect for human rights. Christine Bader complements Heineman's institutional perspective by outlining typical challenges faced by individuals who are charged with the management of human rights in corporations.

To explain why addressing human rights makes good business sense for corporations, John Morrison outlines the concept of 'the social licence', while Rachel Davis and Caroline Rees outline the concept of 'saliency'. Both concepts show that ignoring human rights can be costly for corporations and 'salient' human rights risks are therefore also material business risks.

Notes

1   The Economist Intelligence Unit, 'The Road from Principles to Practices: Today's Challenges for Business in Respecting Human Rights', *The Economist*, 16 March 2015, www.economistinsights.com/business-strategy/analysis/road-principles-practice.
2   See F. Wettstein, 'CSR and the Debate on Business and Human Rights: Bridging the Great Divide' (2012) 22(4) *Business Ethics Quarterly* 739.
3   D. Matten and J. Moon, ' "Implicit" and "Explicit" CSR: A Conceptual Framework for Understanding Corporate Social Responsibility' (2008) 33(2) *Academy of Management Review* 404.
4   A.B. Carroll *et al.*, *Corporate Responsibility: The American Experience* (Cambridge: Cambridge University Press, 2012).

Section 3.1

From side show to main act: can business and human rights save corporate responsibility?

Florian Wettstein

1 Introduction

The idea of corporate social responsibility (CSR) has been around for some time. Howard Bowen's 1953 book *Social Responsibilities of the Businessman*[1] is generally seen as the first systematic engagement with the responsibilities of business to society.[2] However, despite the long history of CSR and the plethora of different interpretations and definitions that the discussion has produced over the years, the idea has proven surprisingly resistant towards human rights as a possible focus area.

The role of foreign multinationals in apartheid South Africa may have been the first major catalyst for questions about the human rights impact of business on a broader scale and inspired numerous works dealing with the subject.[3] However, while apartheid did eventually trigger a broad debate on divestment and the role of business in countries with authoritarian and oppressive governments, it did not spark a systematic debate concerning the relationship between business and human rights (BHR) in general because the doctrine of state-centricity in human rights matters was too rigid and too firmly established.[4] It took 20 more years for that doctrine to weaken and a systematic debate on the role of business in relation to human rights to emerge. The killing of Nigerian playwright and activist Ken Saro-Wiwa by the Abacha government, with alleged involvement and support of the oil giant Royal Dutch Shell, is commonly seen as the tipping point that triggered the debate.[5]

Interestingly, the debate on BHR that emerged during the 1990s evolved largely in parallel to the established debate on CSR.[6] Apart from some overlaps, for example in regard to sweatshop and child labour issues,[7] the debate was largely focused on legal arguments and driven by legal scholars, which may have moved the discussion outside the core competencies of CSR scholars. The debate started to become more diverse only recently with the inception of the mandate of the United Nations (UN)

Special Representative for Business and Human Rights (SRSG), John Ruggie, in 2005 and the subsequent publications of his two major reports: the UN 'Protect, Respect and Remedy' Framework for Business and Human Rights[8] and the UN Guiding Principles on Business and Human Rights[9] (Guiding Principles).

The aim of this chapter is to reflect on the rise of BHR against the background of existing conceptions of CSR, on their differences and commonalities and, most importantly, on the potential for a closer integration of the two. BHR is seen as an important step beyond CSR, but CSR also has lessons for BHR.

Snapshot

Shell in Nigeria[10]

On Tuesday, 31 October 1995, Nigerian playwright and minority-rights activist Ken Saro-Wiwa, along with eight of his followers, were sentenced to death by a specially convened tribunal of the Abacha regime in Nigeria. Saro-Wiwa was spearheading widespread protests against exploitation and environmental degradation by oil companies in the Ogoni land. Protests against the environmental destruction caused by oil companies had been growing throughout the Niger Delta since the 1970s. The most devastating of such protests occurred in January 1993. It was silenced violently by government forces, resulting in the destruction of countless villages, displacing tens of thousands of Ogoni villagers, and leaving some 2,000 people dead. The trial against Saro-Wiwa and his colleagues was widely condemned. Key witnesses had been bribed and the charges were perceived as fabricated. As a consequence, Shell also came under attack for its alleged complicity in the campaign against Saro-Wiwa. It was alleged that Shell had requested police interventions against protesters and many thought that the company, given its powerful position in the country, had a responsibility to denounce the arrest of Saro-Wiwa and to press for his release. However, Shell commented that it was not appropriate for a private company to become involved in Nigerian politics. In his closing statement to the tribunal, Ken Saro-Wiwa asserted that Shell's operations in the Delta would be called into question sooner or later and that the company's day in court would surely come. Saro-Wiwa's statement proved visionary. Not only was he correct about future litigation against Shell, but he also anticipated a future in which corporations in general would increasingly be held accountable for their involvement in human rights violations – a domain that, at the time, was widely thought to be relevant only for governments.

2 Differences at the normative level: the language of rights and its ethical implications

One may not readily see the difference between BHR and CSR; in fact, one may perceive them as addressing largely the same thing, just using different language. BHR, from that point of view, could be interpreted as a subset of CSR, specifically concerned with those social responsibilities that affect human rights. However, a closer look at the two concepts reveals that the differences cut deeper than mere semantics.

The semantic differences expressed through the language of rights point to more fundamental differences concerning the ethics underlying the two concepts.

One attribute that has characterized many interpretations of CSR to this day is the perceived voluntarism of such activity. In 2006, the European Commission denoted CSR as 'fundamentally voluntary business behavior'.[11] While this perceived voluntarism can be interpreted in a strictly legal sense – simply as those responsibilities that companies adopt on a voluntary basis beyond the law – it often is equated also with moral discretion. The legal interpretation would see as voluntary whatever is not legally required. A moral interpretation, however, would see it as optional also in a moral sense: the adoption of responsibility beyond the law may be desired and admirable, in some cases perhaps even expected, but hardly a 'must' for companies; that is, we cannot blame them for not taking action to ensure compliance with human rights standards. Early CSR approaches, which frequently equated the social responsibility of business with the charitable donation of some of a company's profits to social causes,[12] were prone to endorse such discretionary views of CSR. While this view has become less pervasive, it has not disappeared entirely.[13] 'Too much of the time when we think about ... corporate responsibility', as Sandra Waddock and Neil Smith suggest, 'we think about it as a discretionary responsibility.'[14]

Moral voluntarism of this sort does not sit well with a focus on human rights issues. The language of rights is also the language of obligation. Rights and obligations are two sides of the same coin, for otherwise the idea of a right as a particularly strong normative claim would be empty and meaningless. However, the very notion of an obligation conflicts with the perceived voluntarism of CSR, since it expresses 'something we conceive as *imposed* upon our inclinations, something we must do *whether we want to or not*'.[15] Thus, while CSR is often seen to deal with the supererogatory part of morality, that is, with those moral actions that lie beyond the call of duty, human rights responsibility deals with what we owe to each other in a morally obligatory sense.

Reducing BHR to a subset of CSR and thus applying this moral voluntarism to it may prove momentous from both a conceptual and a practical perspective. Conceptually, it will inevitably reduce human rights responsibility to mere acts of corporate goodwill. Shifting human rights from the domain of owed obligation into the domain of supererogatory moral discretion threatens to undermine the very core of what human rights aim to protect: the unconditional and equal dignity of all human beings. This is also of practical relevance: it results in public indifference towards corporate human rights conduct; it leads to corporations selectively meeting human rights standards based on economic incentives (the so-called 'business case for human rights responsibility'[16]); and it promotes hands-off public policy, which sees little need to hold companies accountable for their human rights impact.

3 Differences at the institutional level: bringing governments and the law back in

The difference between BHR and CSR at the normative level also translates into differences at the institutional level, particularly with respect to the role of government and the role of the law.

3.1 The role of government

There is a distinct difference in the ways that CSR and BHR respectively conceptualize the relationship between corporate and governmental responsibility. Conventional understandings of CSR commonly presuppose, at least implicitly, a functioning and well-ordered state as a background condition.[17] Because of this assumption, CSR commonly tends to adopt an isolated view of the corporation without having to engage extensively with the role of the state. That is, it defines corporate responsibilities largely without reference to the respective responsibilities of the state. Thus, conventional conceptions of CSR rely on a rather traditional separation of the public and private domains.[18] While the state organizes the public domain, companies and their respective social responsibilities are located squarely in the private realm.

BHR, on the other hand, does not take strong states for granted or separate the public and private domains. To the contrary, its very aim is to extend corporate responsibility into a domain that has long been viewed as the exclusive responsibility of the state and thus far into the public realm. From this perspective, it is perhaps unsurprising that CSR, with its clearly demarcated lines between private and public domains, has not intuitively embraced BHR until very recently.

The result of BHR's blurring of private and public is that it becomes necessary to consider corporate human rights responsibility in tandem with state obligations concerning human rights. We cannot extend corporate responsibility into the domain of human rights without addressing its relationship to the corresponding (pre-existing) responsibility of states. This is one of the quintessential insights of the Guiding Principles. While most CSR standards exclusively deal with business responsibilities, the Guiding Principles advance a framework to address both state and corporate responsibilities in an integrated way. This insight holds immediate practical implications: while governments have watched developments in the CSR field largely from the sidelines in the past, they are drawn squarely into the fold in BHR. Therefore, they face incentives and pressure to address the BHR issue head-on rather than being content with a role as mere observers. As a result, many (especially western European) governments have started to conduct gap and policy coherence analyses in regard to BHR; some have come out with – or are still developing – so-called National Action Plans, outlining their BHR roadmaps for the coming years.[19] This being said, the uptake and impact of such governmental activity is still small to date and it remains to be seen if the current momentum can be maintained.

3.2 The role of the law

CSR is often viewed as social responsibility that goes beyond the requirements of the law. Thus, the law is not a part of the CSR equation, but rather defines the boundaries or limits of CSR. Generally, (hard) law and CSR tend to be seen as two distinct and separate domains. At best, the law serves to facilitate and encourage CSR by creating favourable conditions, for example, by setting incentives for corporations to adopt responsible business practices. Therefore, the role of the law for CSR is seen as passive rather than active. The law does not actively intervene and enforce CSR, but rather provides a passive frame that shapes the context for the respective initiatives. Recent developments, especially in the realm of mandatory reporting or in regard to the enforcement of environmental responsibility, seem to indicate a move towards a more active role for the law in CSR. However, such tendencies may be rooted at least partly in the growing influence of the evolving BHR discussion.

The role of the law in BHR is more defining and fundamental. The very duty of governments to protect human rights requires them to assess the role of domestic and international legislation in order to determine whether to hold corporations accountable for their impact on human rights both within[20] and potentially beyond[21] their territory. The rise of human rights litigation against companies over the last two decades[22] illustrates a push for an increasingly active role for the law in regard to the direct enforcement of corporate human rights responsibilities.[23] The ongoing discussion at the UN about a legally binding international treaty on BHR bears witness to this more active and defining role, which does not merely shape the context or framework in which BHR takes place, but rather aims to directly establish and enforce human rights standards for business. Notwithstanding this trend, it is apparent that litigation has not thus far been an especially fruitful means of holding companies to account for human rights infringements. Similarly, it must be acknowledged that not all countries are actively improving this situation currently: while Europe seems to be pushing ahead, the United States is retreating.[24] However, despite such ups and downs in the short term, if we look at the rise of human rights litigation over the past 20 years, the long-term trajectory seems to point towards a steadily growing importance of litigation for BHR.

4 Differences at the operational level: implementing BHR and CSR

In addition to the normative and institutional differences between CSR and BHR, important differences are also apparent with respect to practical implementation. First and perhaps most important is the fact that human rights provide the kind of targeted reference point for practical tools and initiatives that has always been missing from CSR. In other words, the use of the language of rights matters not only at the normative level, but also at the operational one. For example, relying on the human rights stipulated in the International Bill of Human Rights,[25] the Guiding Principles provide a concrete and tangible reference point for practical initiatives for both governments and companies. The standards have the potential to spur the development of focused tools and instruments that, with some industry-specific adjustments, could cut across organizations and sectors. In contrast, CSR initiatives have always been scattered in terms of targets, instruments and audiences, reaching from the funding of cultural events and exhibitions to volunteering of employees to projects targeting water scarcity and waste reduction.

Second, BHR has succeeded in developing tools and instruments, such as human rights impact assessments or human rights due diligence, that have the potential to directly cut through to the core business processes of companies. Again, the uptake of such instruments by companies, while certainly increasing, seems to be small to date. However, the direct link between BHR and core business processes provides a significant advantage in terms of their promotion to companies over standard CSR 'tools'. Granted, CSR has never been shy about emphasizing its connection to companies' core business, but it has largely failed to come up with instruments that would implement that idea on a large scale. Organizational units, such as CSR departments, often fail to have a real and lasting impact on the organization as a whole; policies relating to CSR are often incoherent and conflict across departments and functions; and tools and instruments to tie CSR efforts closer to the core business are rare and seemingly unsystematic.[26]

5 What can we learn from CSR?

The previous sections outlined the shortcomings of CSR. However, BHR is by no means a perfect solution and may benefit from some of the lessons learned by CSR. Two aspects in particular stand out.

5.1 Responsibility beyond 'do no harm'

BHR has been preoccupied with negative responsibility, particularly since the beginning of the SRSG's mandate in 2005. A negative duty is a 'duty to ensure that others are not unduly harmed (or wronged) through one's own conduct'.[27] A positive duty, on the other hand, is a duty to 'benefit persons or to shield them from other harms'.[28] Thus, in the context of human rights, a negative responsibility is a responsibility not to violate human rights either directly or indirectly by being complicit in the abuse committed by another actor. It is a responsibility to respect human rights, which, symptomatically, the SRSG defined as a responsibility 'not to infringe on the rights of others – put simply, to do no harm'.[29]

This view of negative responsibility becomes increasingly problematic in today's context of globalization. The very nature of harm is changing in the process of a globalizing world. As Iris Marion Young[30] has argued, much of the suffering we observe in the world today is the result of the complex structural interplay of different actors rather than clearly identifiable acts by individual agents. Against this background, the normative potential of 'do no harm' provisions may be diminishing because they leave many of the more subtle structural effects of corporate activity unaddressed. Based on this, Young proposes to assign remedial responsibility based not on agents' direct causal contributions to the harms at stake, but based on their social connection to such harms through their position and participation in harmful structures. The more powerful an agent's position is within a respective structure, the greater its responsibility to bring about change. Thus, based on this model, corporations would have to shoulder their part of remedial responsibility irrespective of whether or not found legally complicit in causing harm in the first place.

5.2 From compliance checklists to cultures of integrity

A focus on liability and the active role of the law in enforcing human rights responsibilities brings with it the danger that businesses will perceive human rights as just another compliance issue. As a consequence, respect for human rights may turn into a checklist exercise handled by legal departments with little or no transformational impact on the organization itself. Paine has outlined the dangers of adopting too strict of a compliance focus at the expense of a deeper understanding of business integrity.[31] In her view, it is important to foster responsibility based not on compliance and control, but based instead on the cultivation of value-oriented corporate cultures, which permeate the identity of the organization in more profound ways. Such an approach may affect everything from the definition of business strategies through to the design of incentive systems and the recruitment and hiring of the 'right' people. It is safe to say that a lasting improvement of companies' human rights conduct hinges primarily on them being able to transform their culture rather than merely on the implementation of the right tools.[32]

In summary, CSR research has much to offer precisely in regard to proactive company engagement as well as to a focus on values and business culture. CSR has always put much weight on corporations' positive contributions to the improvement of society. While these contributions have often lacked coherence and stringency, they do express a basic belief and expectation that corporations ought to do more for society than merely not harming it. It is this aspirational spirit that has characterized CSR all along; it has extended its focus far beyond a narrow compliance orientation and always relied on a stronger role for values in shaping the respective CSR agendas. Frequent emphasis of business culture in CSR literature bears witness to this value perspective.[33]

6 Integrating BHR and CSR

Both BHR and CSR have their advantages and drawbacks. Thus, the 'solution' may be to take the best of the two approaches and to integrate them into a consistent philosophy of corporate responsibility for human rights.

An integrated approach would advance corporate responsibilities beyond 'mere' respect for human rights. Henry Shue convincingly argued that all human rights give rise to three categories of obligation: the negative obligation to respect, as well as the dual positive obligations to protect and realize human rights.[34] An integrated approach would support corporate responsibilities in all three categories.

6.1 Obligation to respect human rights

Corporations have a negative responsibility to respect human rights. This is the key insight advanced by the Guiding Principles. While the existence of a legally binding responsibility to respect human rights is still contested,[35] the moral case for corporate responsibility is, from a normative point of view, much stronger.[36] The duty to do no harm and thus to respect human rights is an agent-neutral responsibility. It does not matter whether we look at companies, governments or natural persons; it applies to every moral agent who, in principle, has the capacity to violate human rights through its actions (or lack thereof).[37]

6.2 Obligation to protect human rights

The Guiding Principles limit corporate human rights responsibilities to the negative responsibility to respect human rights. However, there is a growing consensus both in academia as well as in policy circles that corporations may also have responsibilities to protect human rights under certain circumstances. The International Council on Human Rights Policy,[38] for example, suggests that a company which 'is aware that human rights violations are occurring, but does not intervene with the authorities to try and prevent or stop the violations', risks becoming complicit in the abuse itself.[39] As this example suggests, the very line between respecting and protecting human rights is not clear-cut.[40] Thus, it may make little conceptual sense to limit corporate human rights responsibility to only one of the two categories at the outset, as the Guiding Principles do. A responsibility to protect does not apply to all moral agents equally, but depends on parameters such as proximity or connection of the agent to the abuse and its ability to mitigate or stop the violation.[41]

6.3 Obligation to realize human rights

Corporations have unique capacities and capabilities to address and contribute to the solutions for pressing human rights problems. These capabilities derive from their specific purpose and the productive nature of the corporation as a social institution. Thus, if we start our reflection on human rights responsibility with the purpose of the company, its potential to contribute to the realization of human rights turns into a central parameter of such responsibility. It is increasingly and sometimes painfully obvious that a growing number of global human rights problems, related to poverty or disease, for example, cannot be solved by governments alone; they crucially depend on the participation and contribution of a variety of institutions, among them companies.

7 Conclusion: towards shared responsibilities

I have argued that BHR has the potential to correct some of the main criticisms that are frequently voiced against CSR. On the other hand, CSR can enrich the BHR perspective, particularly in regard to its focus on values and culture and its stronger emphasis on positive responsibility. A closer integration of the two perspectives, as detailed in this chapter, will lead to a more expansive account of corporate human rights responsibility as it is advanced, for example, by the Guiding Principles. In addition to a responsibility to respect, companies may also have a responsibility to contribute to the protection and realization of human rights.

The point is not that all corporations necessarily have responsibilities in all three categories, but that it makes little sense to limit corporate human rights responsibility to any one of the three categories *at the outset*. The difficulty – and this is the real challenge in BHR – is to come up with models and concepts to hold corporations accountable for their (potential) responsibilities in all three categories without, however, confusing their role with that of governments along the way. Many pressing human rights problems can be solved only by collaborative efforts between institutions of all kinds and sectors. Initiating and participating in such collaborative efforts does not turn businesses into states, nor does it run against their purpose. Rather, a focus on the tripartite obligation to respect, protect and realize human rights represents an adequate expectation of these powerful institutions in the 21st century.

Notes

1   H.R. Bowen, *Social Responsibilities of the Businessman* (New York: Harper, 1953).
2   For a holistic overview of the history of CSR in the American context, see A.B. Carroll *et al.*, *Corporate Responsibility: The American Experience* (Cambridge: Cambridge University Press, 2012).
3   See, e.g. T. Donaldson, *The Ethics of International Business* (New York: Oxford University Press, 1989).
4   O. O'Neill, 'Agents of Justice' (2001) 32(1–2) *Metaphilosophy* 180.
5   See, e.g. G. Chandler, 'The Evolution of the Business and Human Rights Debate' in R. Sullivan (ed.), *Business and Human Rights: Dilemmas and Solutions* (Sheffield: Greenleaf Publishing, 2003) p. 22.
6   F. Wettstein, 'CSR and the Debate on Business and Human Rights: Bridging the Great Divide' (2012) 22(4) *Business Ethics Quarterly* 739.
7   See, e.g. D.G. Arnold, 'Moral Reasoning, Human Rights, and Global Labor Practices' in L.P. Hartman, D.G. Arnold and R.E. Wokutch (eds), *Rising above Sweatshops: Innovative Approaches to Global Labor Challenges* (Westport, CT: Praeger, 2003) p. 77; D.G. Arnold and L.P. Hartman, 'Worker Rights and Low Wage Industrialization: How to Avoid Sweatshops' (2006) 28(3) *Human Rights Quarterly* 676.
8   Human Rights Council, 'Protect, Respect and Remedy: A Framework for Business and Human Rights', Report of the Special Representative of the Secretary-General on the Issue of Human Rights and Transnational Corporations and Other Business Enterprises, John Ruggie, UN Doc. A/HRC/8/5 (7 April 2008).
9   Human Rights Council, 'Guiding Principles on Business and Human Rights: Implementing the United Nations "Protect, Respect, Remedy" Framework', Report of the Special Representative of the Secretary-General on the Issue of Human Rights and Transnational Corporations and Other Business Enterprises, UN Doc. A/HRC/17/31 (21 March 2011).
10 For a more extensive discussion of the case, see, e.g. Human Rights Watch, *The Price of Oil: Corporate Responsibility and Human Rights Violations in Nigeria's Oil Producing Communities* (New York: Human Rights Watch, 1999); F. Wettstein, 'Silence as Complicity: Elements of a Corporate Duty to Speak out against the Violation of Human Rights' (2012) 22(1) *Business Ethics Quarterly* 37, 49–52; E. Hennchen, 'Royal Dutch Shell in Nigeria: Where Do Responsibilities End?' *Journal of Business Ethics* (forthcoming, doi: 10.1007/s10551-014-2142-7); A. Rowell, *Green Backlash: Global Subversion of the Environmental Movement* (London: Routledge, 1996) p. 297; J. Sweeney and C. Duodu 'Nigeria? Business as Usual with the General, Chaps' (5 November 1995) *The Observer* 24; A. Rowell, 'Green Backlash', 308; E. Imomoh, General Manager, Eastern Division, Shell Petroleum. On Africa Express, Channel 4 TV, UK (18 April 1996). Quoted in C.L. Avery, *Business and Human Rights in a Time of Change* (London: Amnesty International UK, 2000), 22.
11 Commission of the European Communities, 'Implementing the Partnership for Growth and Jobs: Making Europe a Pole of Excellence on Corporate Social Responsibility', Brussels, 22 March 2006, p. 2.
12 A.B. Carroll, 'Corporate Social Responsibility: Evolution of a Definitional Construct' (1999) 38(3) *Business & Society* 268, 273.
13 See further A.P. Ewing in this volume, 'Mandatory human rights reporting', p. 284.
14 S. Waddock and N. Smith, 'Relationships: The Real Challenge of Corporate Global Citizenship' (2000) 105(1) *Business and Society Review* 47, 47.
15 J. Feinberg, *Rights, Justice, and the Bounds of Liberty: Essays in Social Philosophy* (Princeton, NJ: Princeton University Press, 1980) p. 136.
16 See D. Baumann-Pauly and M. Posner in this volume, 'Making the business case for human rights: an assessment', p. 11.
17 See A.G. Scherer and G. Palazzo, 'Toward a Political Conception of Corporate Responsibility: Business and Society Seen from a Habermasian Perspective' (2007) 32(4) *Academy of Management Review* 1096.
18 Ibid.
19 See C. Pitts in this volume, 'The United Nations "Protect, Respect, Remedy" Framework and Guiding Principles', p. 51.
20 See, e.g. International Council on Human Rights Policy, *Beyond Voluntarism: Human Rights and the Developing International Legal Obligations of Companies* (2002) p. 46; D.M. Chirwa, 'The Doctrine of State Responsibility as a Potential Means of Holding Private Actors Accountable for Human Rights' (2004) 5 *Melbourne Journal of International Law* 1; Human Rights Council, 'Business and Human Rights: Mapping International Standards of Responsibility and Accountability for Corporate Acts', Report of the Special Representative of the Secretary-General (SRSG) on the Issue of Human Rights and Transnational Corporations and Other Business Enterprises, UN Doc. A/HRC/4/35 (9 February 2007) p. 5; D. Augenstein and D. Kinley, 'When Human Rights "Responsibilities" Become "Duties": The Extra-Territorial Obligations of States That Bind Corporations' in

S. Deva and D. Bilchitz (eds), *Human Rights Obligations of Business: Beyond the Corporate Responsibility to Respect?* (Cambridge: Cambridge University Press, 2013) p. 271.

21 O. de Schutter, *Extraterritorial Jurisdiction as a Tool for Improving the Human Rights Accountability of Transnational Corporations* (2006); D. Augenstein and D. Kinley, 'When Human Rights "Responsibilities" Become "Duties"'.

22 J.C. Drimmer and S.R. Lamoree, 'Think Globally, Sue Locally: Trends and Out-of-Court Tactics in Transnational Tort Actions' (2011) 29(2) *Berkeley Journal of International Law* 456; A. De Jonge, *Transnational Corporations and International Law* (Cheltenham: Edward Elgar Publishing Limited, 2011).

23 See W.S. Dodge in this volume, 'Business and human rights litigation in US courts before and after *Kiobel*', p. 244.

24 See C. Kaufmann in this volume, 'Holding multinational corporations accountable for human rights violations: litigation outside the United States', p. 253.

25 The International Bill of Human Rights consists of: the *Universal Declaration of Human Rights*, Paris, 10 December 1948, GA Res. 217A(III); the *International Covenant on Economic, Social and Cultural Rights*, New York, 16 December 1966, in force 3 January 1976, 999 UNTS 3; and the *International Covenant on Civil and Political Rights*, New York, 16 December 1966, in force 23 March 1976, 999 UNTS 171, and its two Optional Protocols.

26 See, e.g. D. Baumann-Pauly, *Managing Corporate Legitimacy: A Toolkit* (Sheffield: Greenleaf Publishing, 2013).

27 T. Pogge, *World Poverty and Human Rights* (Cambridge: Polity Press, 2002) p. 130.

28 Ibid.

29 J.G. Ruggie, *Just Business: Multinational Corporations and Human Rights* (New York: W.W. Norton & Co., 2013) p. 100.

30 I.M. Young, 'Responsibility and Global Justice: A Social Connection Model' (2006) 23(1) *Social Philosophy and Policy* 102; I.M. Young, *Responsibility for Justice* (Oxford: Oxford University Press, 2011).

31 L.S. Paine, 'Managing for Organizational Integrity' (1994) 72(2) *Harvard Business Review* 106.

32 Ibid., 111. See further B.W. Heineman Jr in this volume, 'Implementing human rights in global business: high performance with high integrity', p. 88.

33 See, e.g. K.E. Goodpaster, *Conscience and Corporate Culture* (Oxford: Blackwell Publishing, 2007); D. Jondle, A. Ardichvili and J. Mitchell, 'Modeling Ethical Business Culture: Development of the Ethical Business Culture Survey and Its Use to Validate the CEBC Model of Ethical Business Culture' (2014) 119(1) *Journal of Business Ethics* 29; D.L. Swanson, *Embedding CSR into Corporate Culture: Challenging the Executive Mind* (New York: Palgrave Macmillan, 2014).

34 H. Shue, *Basic Rights: Subsistence, Affluence and US Foreign Policy* (Princeton, NJ: Princeton University Press, 1980).

35 For a sceptical view on this question, see Human Right Council, 'Business and Human Rights: Further Steps toward the Operationalization of the "Protect, Respect and Remedy" Framework', Report of the Special Representative of the Secretary-General on the Issue of Human Rights and Transnational Corporations and Other Business Enterprises, John Ruggie, UN Doc. A/HRC/14/27 (9 April 2010). For an affirmative view on this question, see D. Bilchitz, 'A Chasm between "Is" and "Ought"? A Critique of the Normative Foundations of the SRSG's Framework and the Guiding Principles' in Deva and Bilchitz (eds), *Human Rights Obligations of Business*, p. 106. For a comprehensive overview on this discussion, see, e.g. S. Joseph, *Corporations and Transnational Human Rights Litigation* (Portland, OR: Hart Publishing, 2004); J.A. Zerk, *Multinationals and Corporate Social Responsibility: Limitations and Opportunities in International Law* (Cambridge: Cambridge University Press, 2006).

36 See, e.g. D.G. Arnold, 'Transnational Corporations and the Duty to Respect Basic Human Rights' (2010) 20(3) *Business Ethics Quarterly* 371.

37 F. Wettstein, 'Normativity, Ethics and the UN Guiding Principles on Business and Human Rights: A Critical Assessment' *Journal of Human Rights* (forthcoming).

38 International Council on Human Rights Policy, *Beyond Voluntarism*, 133.

39 On silent complicity, see F. Wettstein, 'The Duty to Protect: Corporate Complicity, Political Responsibility, and Human Rights Advocacy' (2010) 96(1) *Journal of Business Ethics* 33; Wettstein, 'Silence as Complicity'.

40 See, e.g. J. Nolan and L. Taylor, 'Corporate Responsibility for Economic, Social and Cultural Rights: Rights in Search of a Remedy?' (2009) 87(2) *Journal of Business Ethics* 433.

41 See, e.g. Wettstein, 'The Duty to Protect'; Wettstein, 'Silence as Complicity'; S. Wood, 'The Case for Leverage-Based Corporate Human Rights Responsibility' (2012) 22(1) *Business Ethics Quarterly* 63; M.A. Santoro, *China 2020: How Western Business Can – and Should – Influence Social and Political Change in the Coming Decade* (Ithaca, NY: Cornell University Press, 2009).

Section 3.2

Implementing human rights in global
business: high performance with high
integrity

Ben W. Heineman Jr.

Introduction: high performance with high integrity

The foundational goals of the modern corporation should be the fusion of high performance with high integrity. High performance means strong sustained economic growth through provision of superior goods and services, which in turn provide durable benefits for shareholders and other stakeholders upon whom the company's health depends. Such performance entails an essential balance between risk-taking (the creativity and innovation so essential to economic growth) and economic risk-management (the financial, commercial and operational disciplines so essential to the soundness and durability of business institutions).

High integrity means robust adherence to the letter and spirit of formal rules, both legal and financial; voluntary adoption of global ethical standards that bind the company and its employees; and an employee commitment to core values of honesty, candour, fairness, trustworthiness and reliability. It involves understanding, and mitigating, other types of risk – beyond directly economic risk – that can cause a company catastrophic harm: legal, ethical, reputational, communications, public policy and country-geopolitical. Whether mandated by law or adopted voluntarily as global ethical standards, a corporation's protection of human rights is at the core of the fusion of high performance with high integrity.

The fusion of high performance with high integrity is not just about risk mitigation. It is about creating affirmative benefits in the company, in the marketplace and in the broader global society. Ultimately, high performance with high integrity creates the fundamental trust among shareholders, creditors, employees, recruits, customers, suppliers, regulators, communities, the media and the general public. This trust is essential to sustaining corporate power and freedom which drives the economy with widespread economic and social benefits – trust that in the past 10 years has dramatically eroded due to stark corporate scandals and unthinkable business failures. Nothing is more important in creating that trust than a corporation's commitment to human rights.

The core task of boards of directors, chief executive officers (CEOs) and top senior executives is to build a performance-with-integrity culture that permeates the corporation. Such a culture entails shared principles (values, policies and attitudes) and shared practices (norms, systems and processes). Although this culture must include elements of deterrence against legal, financial and ethical wrong-doing, it must, at the end of the day, be affirmative. An underlying tenet of this culture should be that people want to do the right thing – like protecting and advancing human rights – because leaders make it a company imperative and live it themselves. Clear expectations must be driven down into the company, and this must be a uniform global culture that applies in every nation and cannot be bent by corrupt local practices, regardless of short-term business costs. This culture is the foundation of a transnational corporation.

Based on my nearly 20 years as Senior Vice President – General Counsel at General Electric (GE), I believe that there are eight key principles which CEOs must implement to create this high-performance-with-high-integrity culture – and to assure corporate respect for, and commitment to, human rights.

Principle 1: Demonstrated commitment and consistent leadership

An unequivocal and unyielding leadership commitment is the beginning – and also the end – of creating a performance-with-integrity culture. This commitment is only understood and felt by the company when there is a seamless consistency between leaders' personal attributes, their public and private statements and their direct and indirect actions. High standards for employees demand high standards from senior leaders. Let me highlight six imperatives for corporate leaders.

A Leaders must lead

This sounds obvious, but it's not. GE often confronted a misperception that turns out to be endemic at many corporations: the notion that business leaders must focus on business – sales, marketing, new products, pricing, deals and the numbers – and that the staff (primarily finance, legal and human resources) owns the responsibility for integrity systems and processes. 'I just don't have the *time*' was the typical business leader's lament. The most important step a CEO can take is to reject that assertion – publicly and vehemently – and to make clear to the organization that the leaders at all levels of the corporation share the responsibility (along with the CEO) for communicating values and implementing related practices. There is no chance of fusing high performance with high integrity unless all executives understand that this is their most fundamental leadership task. It is the yardstick they must use as they hire people, build their organizations, set priorities and allocate resources – and by which they will be held accountable.

B Putting integrity first

Most companies have a short mission statement that commits the organization to broad goals like innovation, customer satisfaction, growth or specific personal traits (e.g. edge, energy, execution). One can debate whether these mission statements have any significant impact in and of themselves, but it is surely a glaring omission if the CEO does not make 'integrity' the foundational value upon which all others rest. CEOs must also make written corporate codes of conduct a core, personal message.

But the fundamental point is best delivered in person, in clear and unmistakable terms. At GE, the CEOs put special emphasis on two annual agenda-setting meetings of senior executives. They opened and closed each and every one of these meetings with strong statement about performance with integrity, centring on four main points:

- GE is built on our reputation as a world-class company. Our performance with integrity is the foundation of that reputation. That reputation is of tremendous benefit.
- Each senior leader in this room is personally accountable for the integrity of the company – it is the primary responsibility of GE business leaders. This means establishing the right systems and processes, and creating the right culture.
- No cutting of corners for commercial considerations will be tolerated. Integrity must never be compromised to make the numbers.
- For everyone in this room – those to whom the rest of the company looks for guidance – one strike and you're out. You can miss the numbers and survive; you cannot survive when you miss on integrity.

C Go beyond 'tone at the top'

The way that chief executives exercise moral judgement is much more important than company policy.[1] Specifically, the CEO must make clear that the top executives of the corporation will not be spared or favoured, but will be held every bit as accountable for lapses in integrity as they are for other performance failures. To cite a case in point, a seasoned GE business leader – operating in an emerging market under competitive pressures – wilfully sidestepped the company's due diligence procedures when shifting distribution from employees to a third party. An internal audit subsequently revealed serious misbehaviour by that third party. The upshot? The distribution arrangement was terminated, and the officer was compelled to resign, even though he was very 'successful' in a highly competitive market. There was no equivocation, or rationalization, or protracted weighing of the pros and cons. The executive had crossed a line that leaders should defend, not bend. The tough words delivered at senior leader meetings – competitive pressures never justify compromising integrity, and 'one strike and you're out' – were driven home by tough action.

D Communicate decisions candidly

The CEO gets the most impact out of disciplining senior executives when those actions are discussed candidly with top leadership. Delivering a positive message is equally effective. Shortly after becoming CEO in 2001, Jeff Immelt instituted Charmain's leadership awards that recognized top performers. Some awards go to the business unit with the best overall performance, others go the internal audit staff or to a successful environmental programme or to special actions protecting human rights – and this speaks volumes to company leaders about the core value of high performance with high integrity.

E Leaders must embody values

Companies are exquisitely attuned to hypocrisy on the part of their leaders. The CEO delivers a stirring call for 'performance with integrity!' at a large company meeting but then – at some smaller meeting – makes a cynical comment that points in the opposite direction. That second comment, too, flashes out across the organization, relayed, amplified, even distorted, by word of mouth. For employees who do not see the CEOs every day, loose language from the top is confusing (at best), and CEO cynicism or winks and nods are deadly. In other words, for CEOs, nearly every employee event is a 'public' meeting, demanding personal behaviour that is consistent with company values.

F Senior leaders must be both leaders and managers

Management is about coping with complexity in a large organization, through the disciplines of planning, goal setting, organizing, staffing, budgeting and auditing. Leadership is about coping with change, and expressing the powerful aspiration of fusing performance with integrity when markets, enforcement and public pressures are in constant motion. It is also about inspiring and energizing people – not just by pushing them in specific directions through controls, but by articulating a vision and satisfying the basic human need to belong in a strong culture that lets them live up to their ideals.

Principle 2: Manage performance with integrity as a business process

The hardest aspect of fusing high performance with high integrity is getting business leaders to invest the time and effort needed to embed key integrity principles and practices into business processes. The following six practices simplify this difficult process.

A Confront complexity

All companies struggle with the vast array of financial and legal rules that apply to their every activity. These rules are voluminous, multifaceted, ambiguous in interpretation and uncertain in application. For a transnational company like GE, which is subject not only to international law but also to the laws of more than 100 nations, rule complexity is immense. Many issues in practice are grey, rather than black and white, and require considerable judgement. Nevertheless, complexity must be confronted and overcome and existing rules need to be followed.

B Build the integrity infrastructure

The CEO's response to this complexity starts with building the integrity infrastructure: developing rigorous systems and processes to prevent, detect and respond. At GE, the shorthand for this task was to establish an integrity programme across each GE segment that

- Prevents ethics and compliance misses ... and when prevention fails...
- Detects misses as soon as possible ... and once they are detected...
- Responds quickly and effectively.

To prevent integrity lapses, risk assessments are the first critical step. This involves taking an inventory of the important financial and legal rules in all product lines and in all places where the corporation does business. The company must then review its different business processes and prioritize risks. The second critical prevention step is risk-abatement of mitigation. In general, this means building information tracking and control processes in all business functions (for example, sales, marketing, manufacturing, engineering, mergers and acquisitions (M&A), sourcing) for key risks. Company specialists need to develop customized tools so that employees in high-risk positions can handle complex general tasks and address sensitive issues. To detect potential issues as they emerge, robust internal systems need to be established. General management oversight and control processes help bring to the surface questions about integrity issues. But giving employees voice – through an ombuds system or other means – is also critical to detection.

Responding to concerns about possible improprieties has four basic dimensions: investigation, individual discipline, remediation within the business unit and remediation across the company when appropriate by identifying and addressing root causes.

C Merge business and integrity processes

It is the ultimate responsibility of the Profit and Loss (P&L) leadership team to embed the essential elements of the integrity infrastructure into all the business processes – from small units to larger divisions, from manufacturing and engineering to marketing and sales, from sourcing and information technology to M&A and research and development. This means integrating relevant abatement mechanisms into *each* basic operation.

As an example, GE sought to drive environmental health and safety issues deep into manufacturing, thereby making the plant managers and manufacturing leaders responsible for those issues, and the P&L leader ultimately accountable. Quarterly reports on each facility in each business on key parameters (spills, accident rates, notices of violations) were rolled up into a master matrix, and these cross-business comparisons were sent to the CEO. As one can imagine, landing in the bottom quartile provided the relevant business leaders with strong incentives for improvement!

D Deploy 'A' players – and adequate resources

Hiring 'A' experts on company-critical areas of financial and legal regulation inside the corporations is vital – and cost-effective – for risk assessment and abatement. The advantage of the inside experts is that they understand the company far better than any outsider, and they can act quickly, rather than calling outside for help. Bringing outside experts inside goes against the grain in many companies, but it often proves well worth the effort. There is also no way around paying for the infrastructure: funds must be found and spent to establish the fundamentals. Unless the CEO makes dedication of adequate resources a clear performance metric for business leaders, these costs inevitably get shoved to the bottom of the list.

E Make 'management integrity reviews' real events

Management integrity reviews are evaluations that business leaders use to drive accountability in their respective units, and that are subsequently used to drive accountability across the company. At GE, the business division leaders are responsible for separate, regular reviews of their adherence to controllership precepts, to legal and ethical rules and to environmental health and safety requirements. Each focuses on risks, abatement and results, as well as on controversies that raise systemic integrity issues. Each business reports integrity metrics, which are compared year over year. Some businesses have developed a best practice by merging integrity metrics with performance metrics and representing the results on the digital dashboards now used for continuous business assessments.

F Live by the vision of leadership and management

By embedding integrity processes inside business processes, the CEO and top business leaders show the company – in the most powerful, concrete terms – that 'high performance with high integrity' is not simply a slogan, but is in fact the company's foundation. Personal involvement of the CEO and the business leaders underscore the point: when they review risk-abatement plans for tough markets or new acquisitions, set integrity goals and objectives for key personnel, hold on-site integrity reviews and communicate personally about major misses, they send a basic message: It really matters.

Principle 3: Adopt global ethical standards

Adhering to legal standards is sometimes insufficient (for example, to ensure ethical sourcing policies, non-discrimination structures, the prohibition of bribes, a reduction of greenhouse gases). In these cases corporations need to go beyond the required duties and voluntarily impose a higher global ethical standard. An organized, systematic process is needed to decide whether to adopt such global standards. Once adopted, these standards have the same uniform application and implementation across business units, product markets and geographies as formal financial and legal rules.

To identify the issue areas that require the adoption of global standards, the corporation needs to understand the vital issues for key stakeholders and scan global ethics codes, guidelines and principles that have been promulgated by multinational organizations, non-governmental organizations (NGOs) or business groups. Among other virtues, this keeps the question of global standards grounded in company realities. At GE, the protection of human rights of employees and customers and suppliers was an area explicitly adopted as a core element of its ethical approach in global business.

Principle 4: Use early-warning systems to stay ahead of global trends and expectations

To avoid surprises, corporations need to gather information systematically on financial, legal and ethical trends and expectations. These 'early warning systems' can be put in place at all levels of the company. The signals they send can be invaluable. GE, for example, created systems for tracking fast-moving financial and legal rules. The system defined the kind of red flags to watch for and laid out ways for employees to stay well clear of ambiguous areas by generating proper documentation and by escalating troublesome issues to experts.

A similar early-warning process applies to demands that the corporation take 'ethical' actions extending beyond formal financial and legal requirements. These demands are emerging at an increasing rate from the stakeholder, NGO and academic communities. It is important to sort these emerging ethical issues according to the stakeholders affected, from employees to shareholders and from customers to suppliers. Increasingly, corporations have a vice president for corporate citizenship, who, in consultation with functional experts and affected business leaders, serves as the focal point for aggregating and ranking these issues. High-priority questions should be analysed thoroughly and then sent up to the CEO's corporate risk council for decisions about whether to accept voluntarily a new obligation not required by financial or legal rules. Scanning ethical risks is particularly relevant in nations with a weak rule of law and deciding whether or not to do business in a country with, for example, a weak human rights record needs to be carefully assessed.

Principle 5: Encourage the Chief Financial Officer and General Counsel to be both partner and guardian

The CEO can encourage the Chief Financial Officer (CFO) and the General Counsel (GC) to play a double role: as guardians of the corporation's integrity and reputation and as partners when difficult decisions are on the table. The fundamental job is to help the CEO decide by finding key facts and conducting potent analysis. Most business-integrity issues come cloaked in shades of grey. The task of the CFO and the GC in such cases is to give the CEO options that, while lawful and based on clearly articulated assumptions about the facts, entail varying degrees of legal, regulatory, ethical and reputational risk. The CEO must make clear to senior staff officers (GC, CFO, head of human resources) and senior business leaders that she expects them not only to advance business goals but to protect the company by taking strong, independent positions to preserve the company's integrity (adherence to formal rules, adoption of global ethical standards and promotion of core values).[2]

Principle 6: Foster employee awareness, knowledge and commitment

A high-performance-with-high-integrity culture rests on the commitments of all employees:

- to understand their formal and ethical obligations;
- to do things right by following those duties; and
- to do the right thing by living the values of candour, honesty, fairness, reliability and trustworthiness.

The most fundamental learning for employees comes from simply observing how their peers and leaders handle tough, stressful situations with integrity. But for many subjects, the company needs to help employees become aware of the risks, show them how to find the right answer and reinforce their commitment to do the right thing.

Educating employees about these issues is an extremely challenging proposition – one that is often paid lip service, but less often given creative thought. This is truly a lost opportunity. In a typical year, GE, for example, hires more than 20,000 professionals, takes on thousands more through acquisitions and promotes still others to new cross-border jobs. Many of these people joined the company to get education and training that could help advance their careers – for example, in engineering, finance, marketing, sales and technology development. CEOs proudly extol their company's 'learning culture'. But the typical 'integrity training' programme has less appeal. The CEO and the company's leaders must give equal pride of place to integrity skills and business skills; indeed, they must look for ways to teach these two kinds of skills together whenever possible. Such training must candidly confront the long-standing rationalizations that employees use for improper conduct, especially in emerging markets: it's the custom here; it's not really illegal; no one will know; the company condones it; there won't be consequences.[3]

To articulate *what people should do*, companies often adopt a code of conduct that lays out the basic aspirations of the company. A complementary policy guide sets forth basic integrity principles on specific themes. Such a guide should describe not only what to do, but what to watch out for (red flags). It should describe salient real-world problems and provide answers. At GE, we called our guide the *Spirit and Letter*, with the 'Spirit' setting out broad themes and core values like honesty, candour, fairness, reliability and trustworthiness, and the 'Letter' describing global integrity policies in detail on the Internet. The guide was translated into 31 languages. Additionally, more detailed implementation guidelines can be developed for thorny, recurring issues like improper payments, supplier relationships or fair competition. These guides need to explain not only what to do but also why it is important to the company. I believe that without these 'whys' the 'what' lacks punch. The reason? Because it fails to treat people with respect. People don't just want commands; they need explanations and understanding.

To effectively deliver the message, the essentials need to be built into orientation trainings of new hires and become part of the general training programme designed specifically for different functions that is tracked and tested. Case-based learning and learning from successes and failure have proven most effective at GE. Cultural differences need to be addressed head-on to underline the universal validity of rules. Leadership needs to be trained in separate and specifically tailored sessions that extend the specialist view of company leaders.

Principle 7: Give employees voice

One of the most powerful principles in creating a high-performance-with-high-integrity culture, and for ensuring accountability up and down the corporation, is to give every employee 'voice'. This means encouraging (and, indeed, requiring) the reporting of concerns about possible violations of financial, legal and ethical standards, and addressing those concerns promptly. The employee's voice can be expressed through at least five channels:

    i   The ombuds system based on a neutral intake person chosen on the basis of personal skills, rather than functional expertise, because trust is critical. The ombudsperson refers matters raising integrity concerns to financial, legal and human resources staff for investigation, tracks all such matters to ensure prompt close-out and keeps the employee up-to-date on the status of the concern. An effective ombudsperson system has the following elements:

        a   Employees should be strongly encouraged to report concerns immediately, through corporate or business ombudspersons or functional staff, using integrity helplines, letters, phone or email.

        b   Employees have a duty to report concerns – and not to retaliate.

        c   Finance and legal staff must fully, fairly and promptly investigate all concerns without fear or favour.

        d   The ombuds system's important cases and statistical summaries should be regularly reported to the CEO and the board.

   ii   Business bottom-up reviews in which any potential integrity issues are retrieved from employees and the risks are assessed regularly.

  iii   An elite corporate audit staff that spends its time auditing for adherence to global financial, legal and ethical standards. It reports regularly to the CFO, the company compliance review board and the audit committee both on systemic issues and on important questions raised by employees.

   iv   The strong dotted line in finance and legal departments to keep communication channels open for financial and legal staff to report up to top business leaders.

    v   By giving genuine voice to individuals throughout the company, and by treating their concerns with respect and professionalism, business leaders from the CEO down send a potent message about the importance of a self-cleaning culture: one that promptly surfaces what is wrong and candidly discusses what is right. At GE, reporting employees knew from long-standing company experience that their concerns would be handled independently, reviewed professionally and decided fairly on facts, not internal politics.

Principle 8: Pay for performance with integrity

The challenge for companies is not just to reward financial performance but to invent a compensation system that pays for performance with integrity. Of course, most companies *claim* that they build integrity issues into their compensation and promotion decisions. But how many companies use meaningful evaluation tools so that real accountability for integrity takes root? And how many companies extend the use of these beyond the corporate officers to the top echelon of P&L leaders or to key players on business teams? Four key practices can make this principle come alive:

i   *Use annual goals and objectives – and evaluations.* The place to start is building integrity issues into annual goals and objectives for senior leaders.

ii *Assess the leader's own programme.* Corporations need to evaluate business leaders on their efforts to create fundamental high-performance-with-high-integrity systems, processes and culture in the unit or division.

iii *Use comparative assessments.* A potent method of performance-with-integrity evaluation is to compare the leader's business with other businesses within the multi-business corporation or, where information is available, with peer companies. These comparisons can be based on the audit staff reviews of the whole company (e.g. which business has the most open audit issues), the overall number of relevant lawsuits filed or former regulators' assessment of a business against industry standards and best practices.

iv *Make it a clear factor in compensation and promotion.* Success in meeting annual goals, assessments of the overall programme both on its own terms and comparatively, qualitative evaluations of intensity and commitment: these measures can be used by the CEO and more to develop standards to pay for performance-with-integrity, working with the board's compensation committee. For example, expected performance in this area could constitute 20 to 30 per cent of both cash compensation (salary and bonus) and equity grants. Poor performance would diminish either the rate of increase or the absolute year-over-year amounts, or lead to a firing, if a senior leader violated integrity policies or failed to create an integrity culture. Conversely, superior performance – creating new systems and processes or working through a difficult problem that threatens the company's reputation – can be among the plus factors leading to positive annual increases and promotions. Of course, compensation and promotion decisions are always going to be matters of judgement. But personalized goals and objectives plus explicit integrity compensation guidelines – which affect a component of pay and are factors in promotions – provide the essential, real-world incentives that can have a significant role in creating the high performance-with-high-integrity culture. They can turn a corporate cliché – integrity is considered in compensation decisions – into a core corporate principle.

Conclusion

These eight principles provide guidance on how to address issues that are critical for the fusion of high performance with high integrity – the foundational goals, in my view, of global capitalism. Commitment to human rights is an essential dimension of corporate integrity standards. Since the UN Human Rights Council unanimously endorsed the Guiding Principles on Business and Human Rights[4] in 2011, the actual implementation of the 'corporate responsibility to respect human rights' is at the top of the agenda of many multinational companies. Indeed, GE has a special section of its *Citizenship Report* explicitly dedicated to human rights.[5] Recent business and human rights challenges like the collapse of Rana Plaza in Bangladesh or the discussion about the role of Internet service providers in autocratic regimes further emphasize the need for corporations to proactively address human rights and establish systems to manage their human rights impact through core business processes.

Notes

1   Enforcement elsewhere in the developed world is approaching levels in the United States, whether it involves privacy or cartel issues in the European Union or consumer protection in the United Kingdom or Japan. Government inquiries into integrity issues at Parmalat, Shell, Ahold, Volkswagen and Siemens illustrate the point. Indeed, investigations or controversies in one nation or jurisdiction are now often leveraged by regulators and enforcers in other jurisdictions or nations.
2   See, e.g. GE Sustainability, www.gesustainability.com/enabling-progress/human-rights.
3   These ageless rationalizations are discussed from a manager's perspective in S.W. Gellerman, 'Why "Good" Managers Make Bad Ethical Choices' (July 1986) *Harvard Business Review*.
4   Human Rights Council, 'Guiding Principles on Business and Human Rights: Implementing the United Nations "Protect, Respect, Remedy" Framework', Report of the Special Representative of the Secretary-General on the Issue of Human Rights and Transnational Corporations and Other Business Enterprises, UN Doc. A/HRC/17/31 (21 March 2011).
5   General Electric, 'Human Rights', www.gesustainability.com/enabling-progress/human-rights.

Section 3.3

Human rights 'intrapreneurs': challenges and keys to success

Christine Bader

1 Introduction

This scenario is based on the personal experience of the author driving change on human rights while working for BP, and of other 'intrapreneurs' similarly advocating for human rights in other companies. Some of the many issues faced include convincing colleagues of the universality of the imperative to respect human rights; the alignment of incentive structures; and ensuring that human rights are considered in key corporate processes.

2 The scenario

An up-and-coming executive in a large multinational corporation is charged with overseeing the company's initiatives to meet its responsibility to respect human rights. She has the support of her Chief Executive Officer, the catalyst of a recent human rights crisis at one of the company's sites (which led to her appointment), a solid track record in the company and an ample budget.

What could go wrong? And what should she do to manage the potential obstacles to success?

3 Challenges

3.1 The universality of the imperative is not clear

Problem: 'Sure, we had a crisis at one site', already overburdened managers might say. But they may just as quickly blame that crisis on the specifics of the location, or one rogue actor, or bad luck. Why should such an aberration necessitate yet another new policy or procedure?

Solution: Construct a compelling narrative of what has gone wrong elsewhere, emphasizing the commonality of factors from other locations.

Example: In 2000, as an executive working for BP in Indonesia, I was focused on the human rights challenges of the Tangguh liquefied natural gas (LNG) project: a resettlement of 127 households, a notoriously violent and corrupt military and weak state capacity. There were examples elsewhere in the country of how extractive projects go badly when human rights are not respected: Freeport-McMoRan's Grasberg copper and gold mine in Indonesia's Papua province has experienced decades of social strife and spends tens of millions of dollars annually on security; Exxon-Mobil's Arun LNG plant in Aceh had to halt production for four months in 2001 due to local conflict – which 11 Acehnese civilians accused the company of exacerbating in a lawsuit filed that year in US federal court.[1]

Both of those cases could have been attributed to the particular histories and contexts of those two projects. But discussing those cases in terms of broadly applicable factors, for example, the absence of clear terms of engagement with the military and a lack of proactive community engagement – led BP to address those issues at Tangguh early in the project's life cycle.[2]

3.2 Incentives are at cross-purposes with the responsibility to respect human rights

Challenge: An executive or team within a company can develop a human rights due diligence programme, but if managers are paid and promoted based on production or sales goals that undermine respect for human rights, even the best-written policies and tools will fail.

Solution: Examine performance contracts of groups and individuals relevant to the company's human rights impacts. Are there any targets that might undermine or preclude consideration of human rights? How can human rights be incentivized at the individual and team level?

Example: When GE Healthcare India discovered that its ultrasound machines were being used to detect the gender of foetuses that, if female, were then aborted, the company put in new requirements to certify that buyers would not use the machines for that purpose. The company also realized that it needed to emphasize to its sales force that they could not facilitate sales to suspect customers in order to meet sales targets.[3]

3.3 Human rights are considered after the fact, rather than before product launch or new market entry

Challenge: Once a project or product is launched, it can be difficult to retrofit existing operations to meet human rights requirements – and even harder to repair stakeholder relationships and remedy harms if problems have already ensued.

Solution: Examine the gateways for resource allocation and project approval and integrate requirements to assess how risks are being considered and mitigated before projects move forward.

Example: In 2010, Google shut down its Internet search engine in China after four tumultuous years dealing with government requirements to censor search results and hacker attacks.[4] In contrast, Yahoo! established a programme to conduct human rights impact assessments before launching new products or services in new markets; for example, it conducted one such assessment before expanding services in Vietnam, which led to the company deciding not to locate servers in that country for fear of threats to user free expression and privacy.[5]

4 Conclusion

Leading a company's efforts to respect human rights will be full of challenges – and should be, in any company with a diverse workforce and supply chain, and geographically dispersed operations and customer base. But it is possible to anticipate and prepare for those challenges, learning from good and bad examples from other companies and other industries. Understanding the various needs of internal constituencies, building networks both internally and externally and finding ways to embed human rights into existing policies and procedures can all support the intrapreneur charged with operationalizing respect for human rights inside her company.

Notes

1 On Freeport, see, e.g. S. Montlake, 'Cave in: Freeport-McMoran Digs a Heap of Trouble in Indonesia', *Forbes*, 13 February 2012. On ExxonMobil, see, e.g. Business & Human Rights Resource Centre, 'ExxonMobil Lawsuit (re Aceh)', http://business-humanrights.org/en/exxonmobil-lawsuit-re-aceh. As of December 2014, the case had yet to be settled or adjudicated.
2 For information about the Tangguh project, see BP Indonesia, 'Sustainability', www.bp.com/en_id/indonesia/sustainability/society.html.
3 General Electric Company and BSR, 'Promoting Ethical Ultrasound Use in India: A BLIHR Emerging Economy Case Study from GE', http://files.gecompany.com/gecom/citizenship/pdfs/ge_ethical_ultrasound_use_india_casestudy.pdf.

4 See, e.g. M. Helft and D. Barboza, 'Google Shuts China Site in Dispute over Censorship', *New York Times*, 22 March 2010.
5 C.M. Maclay, 'Protecting Privacy and Expression Online: Can the Global Network Initiative Embrace the Character of the Net?' in R. Deibert *et al.* (eds), *Access Controlled: The Shaping of Power, Rights, and Rule in Cyberspace* (Cambridge, MA: MIT Press, 2008).

Section 3.4

The social licence: one way of thinking about business and human rights

John Morrison

Mainstream approaches to corporate social responsibility (CSR) have come under increased criticism from both business and civil society over recent years, although for differing reasons. That is not to say that all CSR is bad. Rather, it is to say that CSR can, on the one hand, be ill-defined and poorly aligned with a company's business model; on the other hand, CSR may be criticized for being business-centric rather than society-centric. There has, therefore, been a tendency for many commentators to define business and human rights within its own terms rather than using the many and tattered coat-tails of CSR. But how then do we describe the societal and business benefits of the business and human rights agenda including, but not exclusively, in terms of the avoidance of harm?

The concept of 'social licence to operate' first arose in the 1990s in relation to the Australian and Canadian mining industries.[1] The concept can be traced back some 300 years to the social contract thinking of Thomas Hobbes, John Locke, Jean-Jacques Rousseau and Immanuel Kant (thinkers, among others, whose work forms the bedrock of modern human rights).[2] Today, the term 'social licence' is common in discussions in many parts of the world. The key elements of an approach based on social licence are:

*   The social licence cannot be self-awarded by any company in respect of its own activities; rather, the social licence describes an acceptance from society that must be freely given on an ongoing basis. The social licence is not written on a piece of paper, nor is it permanent. It is not an alternative to legal licence or political licence – both of which are also essential.
*   Any organization can best understand the circumstances required to maintain social licence for an activity by considering its relationship to the social contract that binds society and legitimizes the role of government itself. At a minimum, business must not undermine the social contract, and if the social contract is already weak or broken, a business must not seek to exploit such weaknesses.
*   A company cannot therefore manage its social licence directly but rather must consider key aspects such as trust, legitimacy and consent, as well as clarity about the social benefits of any activities, and how human rights risks will be avoided or mitigated, and how remedies for victims shall be ensured. Therefore, social licence is more than the legitimacy of an organization alone (although this is a key part of it) as it is activity-specific and depends much on how that

activity is undertaken. Accordingly, the best way of creating the conditions for a strong social licence is to engage fully in a business and human rights approach.[3]

• The social licence concept is relevant to any business sector and, in fact, relates to the activities of any organization. Governments also need social licence for key policy areas (winning an election is not always enough) and arguably non-governmental organizations (NGOs) need social licence the most (from where else do they draw their legitimacy?).

If this is an outline of a more credible definition that is aligned to core business impacts and is also society-centric, what does it mean in concrete terms for any given business? There are a number of well-known examples, including BP's mismanagement of the Deepwater Horizon disaster in the Gulf of Mexico,[4] and Shell's legacy in Nigeria,[5] that help illustrate the practical impact of a social licence. Below are two further examples from Myanmar:

1   The Institute for Human Rights and Business's work in Myanmar suggests that the social licence has concrete meaning in that state.[6] While it is possible to do business in Myanmar without trust, legitimacy or consent – in fact some companies continue to do so – such practices are typically unsuccessful. For example, soon after the commencement of work on the Myitsone Dam project, one of the world's largest hydroelectric schemes that involved Chinese investment for the purpose of generating power for Yunnan province in China, concerns were raised about the environmental and cultural impact of the project on the Irrawaddy Delta and its residents. Violent protests against the project took place in 2010. In 2011, the new president, Thein Sein, announced that the project would not continue during his term in office.[7] This decision on the part of the government of Myanmar may be seen as related to the absence of a social licence for the project to go ahead under present conditions.

2   Similarly, the violence that was meted out to protesters outside the Letpadaung copper mine in 2012 led to international condemnation and members of the local community withholding their consent to the project.[8] The planned expansion of the Heinda tin mines near Myanmar's border with Thailand has also resulted in protests by locals aggrieved at the environmental damage and consequent health issues said to result from the mines' operations. In 2014, protesters commenced legal proceedings in Dawei District Court seeking compensation for damage said to be the result of wastewater from the mines.[9]

These examples suggest that an important adjunct to foreign investment in Myanmar is acceptance of the presence and operations of foreign corporations by local populations – that is, companies require a social licence as well as formal governmental approval.

Social licence is not just important in fragile investment environments. In Western democracies, there are also controversial issues that call into question companies' social licences. For example, gas exploration and fracking in the United Kingdom (UK) has increasingly faced local opposition despite scientific evidence suggesting the risks remain comparably low.[10] Governments and business should learn from their experience across a number of multi-stakeholder approaches to proactively disclose risks and propose mitigating action before negative repercussions arise – to make such knowledge pre-competitive and available to all. We are likely to see more and more social licence discussions beyond the extractives sector, on issues such as food and nutrition (and the role of fast-food companies) or the big data and privacy implications of new household or automotive technologies.

Social licence is one door into substantive discussions about the human rights impacts of business activities. It offers more than mainstream CSR as it looks first to state duties in relation to society in general and analyses corporate impacts through this lens – at a minimum the business should not further weaken the pre-existing social contract or exploit such weakness for economic gain. Myanmar and the UK are examples of this, but there are many more. Essentially, social risk needs to be pre-competitive to be publicly available and such knowledge needs to be available to all relevant stakeholders, and most importantly rights-holders themselves. If a business enjoys social licence for any particular activity, it is because they have understood that legitimacy, trust and consent are built on real knowledge, real transparency and shared decision-making.

Notes

1   J. Morrison, *The Social License: How to Keep Your Organization Legitimate* (London: Palgrave Macmillan, 2014) pp. 14–28.
2   Ibid., pp. 23–6.
3   See, e.g. Institute for Human Rights and Business, www.ihrb.org.
4   Morrison, *The Social License*, pp. 5–11.
5   Ibid.
6   The Institute for Human Rights and Business works through the Myanmar Centre for Responsible Business based in Yangon, and was co-founded by the Danish Institute for Human Rights in 2013, www.myanmar-responsiblebusiness.org.
7   See, e.g. P. Hadfield, 'Burmese Villagers Exiled from Ancestral Home as Fate of Dam Remains Unclear', *Guardian*, 4 March 2014, www.theguardian.com/environment/2014/mar/04/burma-village-myitsone-dam-project-china.
8   See, e.g. Amnesty International, *Open for Business? Corporate Crime and Abuses at Myanmar Copper Mine* (2015).
9   See Business and Human Rights Resource Centre, 'Myanmar Pongpipat Lawsuit (re Environmental & Health Impact of Heinda Tin Mine)', http://business-humanrights.org/en/myanmar-pongpipat-lawsuit-re-environmental-health-impact-of-heinda-tin-mine-0.
10 See, e.g. British Geological Survey, 'Shale Gas', www.bgs.ac.uk/shalegas.

Section 3.5

Salient human rights issues: when severe risks to people intersect with risks to business

Caroline Rees and Rachel Davis

Any large company today is at risk of involvement with multiple human rights impacts across its operations and supply chain. Complex supply chains, weak laws or enforcement, local or regional conflicts, corruption and other factors make that a fact of doing business. So prioritization becomes essential. By prioritizing its 'salient human rights issues' a company identifies not only those human rights issues it needs to focus its resources on addressing first, but also those human rights issues that will represent greatest risk to the business and those that it will be most relevant for the company to address in its public disclosure.

This concept of salient human rights is central to putting the United Nations Guiding Principles on Business and Human Rights[1] (Guiding Principles) into practice. The Interpretive Guide on the corporate responsibility to respect human rights issued by the Office of the High Commissioner for Human Rights states: 'The most salient human rights for a business enterprise are those that stand out as being most at risk.'[2]

As the first step in due diligence, a company needs to identify the range of negative impacts on human rights with which it could be involved, whether through its own activities or its various business relationships. Some issues are evident based on a company's sector and are already the subject of voluntary standards, such as security and human rights for extractive companies; freedom of expression and privacy for information and communication technology (ICT) companies; labour rights for brand and retail companies, and so forth. Others will vary depending on the company's sourcing or operating countries, the type of business partners it has and the presence of certain vulnerable groups in different parts of its value chain.

The due diligence process is a way for each company to understand and internalize the full range of potential impacts and how they change over time. Yet in order not to become paralysed by the scale of the task, most (especially large and multinational) companies will have to prioritize which impacts they address first. Guiding Principle No. 24 states that where prioritization is necessary, 'business enterprises should first seek to prevent and mitigate those that are most severe or where delayed response would make them irremediable'. 'Severe' impacts are defined as those that are most grave, most widespread and/or most difficult to remedy. This means that companies should ensure that their efforts start with those impacts.

This focus is not to the exclusion of other issues – salience is not a cut-off line, but a principled basis for sequencing how resources get applied. It is not based on biggest spend, risk to business or what it is easiest to do (though easy issues need not be delayed). And it does not suggest one human right is more important than another; each company's salient human rights issues will be particular to them and will reflect their sector, operating context(s), an understanding of the perspective of potentially affected groups, inputs from internal and external experts and other relevant factors.

Once a company has identified its salient human rights issues this informs the rest of the due diligence process, from taking action to address these issues as a priority, to tracking and communicating about the effectiveness of those efforts.

Salient human rights issues, left unaddressed, translate into real costs. Both research and case-based evidence repeatedly show that where companies are involved with severe impacts on human rights they expose their own businesses to risk as well. One in-depth study, co-authored by Shift, shows that costs to extractive companies of conflict with communities over alleged impacts are substantial when aggregated from across the budget lines in which they typically occur. For example, for a world-class mining operation with capex of US$3–5 billion, temporary shutdowns or delays to operations can mean a loss of US$20 million per week in net present value terms.[3]

A 2012 study modelled the costs of conflict over land tenure between communities and companies in infrastructure, mining, agriculture and forestry. It suggested that 'the potential for bottom-line financial damage range[s] from massively increased operating costs – as much as 29 times over a normal baseline scenario ... – to outright abandonment of an up-and-running operation'.[4]

Reputational risk is another significant factor for many companies. A 2014 analysis found that across the FTSE350 an average of 38 per cent of a company's market capitalization was directly attributable to the confidence instilled by its reputation.[5] Company reputations have been substantially exposed where they have been involved with deaths in supplier factories in Bangladesh, China and Pakistan, or with forced labour in the Thai fishing industry, or construction in the Middle East.

These are just a few examples of the burgeoning evidence demonstrating that risk to people and risk to business are not parallel tracks, but converge strongly around salient human rights issues.

It is for all these reasons that the Guiding Principles Reporting Framework, which Shift developed jointly with Mazars through a two-year multi-stakeholder process, calls upon companies to focus their human rights reporting on their salient human rights issues.

Human rights reporting remains – with a few notable exceptions – the weakest area of non-financial disclosure. It often focuses on philanthropic projects or staff volunteering activities unrelated to core business. Where reporting does address human rights risks, it is typically patchy, centred, for example, around supply chain audit results or community engagement processes.[6] This makes it hard for investors and other stakeholders to understand how well companies are managing risks to human rights.

Traditional approaches to identifying relevant information for reporting have served companies and their shareholders poorly, let alone other stakeholders. Most materiality assessments discount human rights issues, sometimes due to flawed assumptions that there are no human rights risks associated with the business, that these are unrelated to risk to the business or that past impacts are sufficient to understand future risk. Those companies that grasp the greater complexity often still lack the internal processes to assess these risks effectively and lean heavily on inputs from select external stakeholders. Yet those stakeholders are often chosen based on their expertise in issues that are presumed to be relevant, thus reinforcing blind spots; and they are rarely given sufficient insight into the company to move beyond statements of the obvious or assertions of their own particular interest.

By contrast, the concept of salience offers far greater rigour and consistency for a company to identify which issues are most important for disclosure. It helps ensure principled prioritization and is informed at every stage by the perspectives of stakeholders, from those directly affected through to issue-specific experts. It focuses the company's efforts and attention on the most severe human rights issues, rather than the easiest or most popular topics. Therein lies the power of salience.

Notes

1   Human Rights Council, 'Guiding Principles on Business and Human Rights: Implementing the United Nations "Protect, Respect and Remedy" Framework', Report of the Special Representative of the Secretary-General on the Issue of Human Rights and Transnational Corporations and Other Business Enterprises, UN Doc. A/HRC/17/31 (21 March 2011).
2   Office of the High Commissioner for Human Rights, 'The Corporate Responsibility to Respect Human Rights: An Interpretive Guide', HR/Pub/12/02 (2012) p. 8.
3   R. Davis and D.M. Franks, *Costs of Company–Community Conflict in the Extractive Sector*, CSR Initiative Report No. 66 (Cambridge, MA: Harvard Kennedy School, 2014) p. 8.
4   The Munden Project, *The Financial Risks of Insecure Land Tenure: An Investment View* (December 2012) p. 2, www.rightsandresources.org/documents/files/doc_5715.pdf.
5   Reputation Dividend, *The 2013–2014 UK Reputation Dividend Study* (2014) p. 2, www.reputationdividend.com/files/2413/9029/4988/2013-14_UK_Reputation_Dividend_Report.pdf.
6   Shift, *Evidence of Corporate Disclosure Relevant to the UN Guiding Principles on Business and Human Rights* (New York, 2014).

Chapter 4

Defining and implementing human rights standards industry by industry

This chapter analyses multi-stakeholder initiatives (MSIs) as a new governance form for human rights. When states fail to provide basic rights, collaborations between private actors, and sometimes public and private actors, have in many key industries become the default response to regulating corporate human rights conduct.

Dorothée Baumann-Pauly, Justine Nolan, Sarah Labowitz and Auret van Heerden first explore the MSI model and its current status. This is followed by a series of case studies of MSIs in different industries by Auret van Heerden (manufacturing), Michael Samway (information and communication technology), Scott Jerbi (extractives) and Anne-Marie Buzatu (private security contractors). Each of these chapters points to the potential and the challenges of this new governance form.

Michael Posner then highlights the current developments in the agriculture sector, a key sector in which no overarching MSI has formed yet. To conclude the chapter, Joanne Bauer describes a more recent initiative in the agricultural sector developed by the Coalition of Immokalee Workers.

Section 4.1

Setting and enforcing industry-specific standards for human rights: the role of multi-stakeholder initiatives in regulating corporate conduct

Dorothée Baumann-Pauly, Justine Nolan, Sarah Labowitz and Auret van Heerden

1 Introduction

Globalization creates governance challenges that are testing the limits of state-based systems of global business regulation.[1] Voluntary, multi-stakeholder initiatives (MSIs) that include a mix of private (and sometimes public) actors have emerged to address the governance gaps that exist when transnational companies (TNCs) conduct operations in states that cannot or will not fulfil their obligations to protect the rights of their own people.

In the absence of other viable regulatory options, particularly in developing country markets that are increasingly important for global companies, MSIs have become a default response to business and human rights challenges. For example, after the tragic collapse of the Rana Plaza complex in Dhaka, Bangladesh, over 200 Western brands formed two collaborative initiatives to address the governance gap in the context of workplace safety.[2]

Over the last two decades, MSIs have formed across different business sectors – from telecommunications to apparel to private security contracting – and appear to be an enduring feature in regulating global corporate conduct on human rights. While MSIs are increasingly recognized as institutions that respond to and shape the global governance landscape,[3] there is still a lack of clarity about the factors that potentially make MSIs a legitimate governing force when it comes to business and human rights.[4]

MSIs typically form in moments of crisis affecting a particular industry – situations in which corporations are under pressure to respond to public human rights allegations that no actor alone can effectively address. Their origins in industry-specific crises often mean that the players in each emerging MSI may 'reinvent the wheel' when it comes to developing the parameters for the structure, governance, funding and activities of the new initiative. Subject-matter experts negotiating the formation of a new MSI do not usually possess expertise about MSIs broadly and their role in filling governance gaps. There is a lack of accessible research that examines MSIs as an emerging norm of global governance.

In this introductory chapter, we provide an overview of the typology and history of MSIs that have emerged over the past two decades. Within this typology, we focus our analysis on those MSIs that serve a governance function by setting and enforcing standards among competitors in a particular industry.

2 Typology of MSIs

2.1 Definition and typology

There is no single definition of what constitutes an MSI. The term 'multi-stakeholder initiative' is often used to refer to voluntary initiatives where two or more stakeholders cooperate to address some area of sustainability, corporate social responsibility (CSR), the environment and/or human rights. Such stakeholders include some combination of companies, industry associations, non-governmental organizations (NGOs), trade unions, government agencies, investors, academics and international organizations.

Despite the proliferation of initiatives that could be labelled MSIs, there is currently no widely acknowledged typology of MSIs. Introducing criteria by which MSIs can be distinguished is an important step in identifying and analysing those initiatives that have the potential to fill governance gaps. While there is a wide range of initiatives that fall under the broad heading of 'MSI', our analysis focuses on those that have the potential to effectively address governance gaps and regulate corporate conduct in markets where governments cannot or will not protect human rights.

By no means do all MSIs aim to achieve this objective. Some MSIs convene stakeholders across industry, civil society and government to broadly promote principles of sustainability, or to provide a forum for companies to share best practices and self-report on their sustainability activities. The United Nations Global Compact, for example, includes more than 8,000 corporations, in addition to governments and labour and civil society organizations.[5] While it includes multiple stakeholders and works to encourage business to adopt policies related to sustainability and social responsibility, it does not seek to regulate their conduct by setting standards, monitoring implementation of the standards, assessing overall company performance or issuing sanctions for non-compliance. We refer to this subset as 'best-practice sharing' MSIs.

There is another subset of MSIs devoted to certification. These initiatives, which we refer to as 'certification MSIs', do assess performance against standards, but the scope of their assessment is focused on individual suppliers in a TNC's supply chain rather than the multinational buyer company itself. For example, the Forest Stewardship Council's (FSC) forest certification programme assesses individual farms' compliance with the FSC forest management standard.[6] This can be aggregated to a chain-of-custody certification[7] for a global retailer or brand. Similarly, Social Accountability International (SAI) assesses and trains individual factories in the manufacturing supply chains of large multinational brands and retailers against its SA8000 standard for decent work.[8] Both of these initiatives are multi-stakeholder in nature and include representatives from industry, trade unions and civil society organizations. TNCs are involved in setting standards and promote their membership in these organizations, but the conduct of TNCs is not governed by the certification scheme; rather it is *suppliers'* conduct that is subject to certification.

Table 4.1.1 Types of MSIs

Best-practice sharing	Certification	Human rights governance
• UN Global Compact • Global Reporting Initiative	• Forest Stewardship Council • Social Accountability International • International Standards Organization • Roundtable on Sustainable Palm Oil • RugMark	• Fair Labor Association • FairWear Foundation • Global Network Initiative • International Code of Conduct for Private Security Providers[a] • Voluntary Principles on Security and Human Rights[b]

Notes

a As of July 2015, it is not yet clear whether the International Code of Conduct for Private Security Providers will evolve beyond a code of conduct to govern members' conduct.

b The Voluntary Principles were established to regulate corporate conduct in the energy and mining sectors, but have not fully evolved beyond the negotiation of a standard.

The subject of our analysis is a third category of MSIs: voluntary initiatives that seek to govern the human rights conduct of TNCs in their global operations by creating binding and enforceable rules[9] for groups of competitor companies in the same industry. Bernstein and Cashore define these initiatives as 'deliberative and adaptive governance institutions designed to embed social and environmental norms in the global marketplace, that derive authority directly from interested audiences, including those they seek to regulate, not from sovereign states'.[10] We refer to this type as 'human rights governance' MSIs.

2.2 Alternative regulatory approaches and the case for MSIs

Before moving to a discussion of industry-specific MSIs that seek to govern the human rights conduct of corporations, it is important to briefly consider the legislative or voluntary regulatory alternatives.

Legislation by home or host countries that aims to regulate the human rights impact of TNCs has many potential benefits including providing binding rules, government oversight of corporate conduct and the potential to 'level the playing field'.[11] Legislation, however, often also lacks the specificity that may be required to meaningfully constrain corporate behaviour. Most existing legislation in this area simply asks for disclosure of corporate practices, without setting a public reporting and evaluation standard that would enable consumers, regulators or investors to compare the performance of one company against another.

For example, in the United States (US), s. 1502 of the Dodd–Frank Wall Street Reform and Consumer Protection Act[12] imposes a new reporting requirement on publicly traded companies that manufacture products using certain conflict minerals. Under s. 1502, companies must report to the US Securities and Exchange Commission on whether the sourcing of the minerals originated in the Democratic Republic of Congo and bordering countries. This, in essence, requires TNCs to take on dual roles as both the 'regulatee' and 'regulator' of its supply chain and institute adequate 'due diligence processes' to ensure its reporting is accurate.

A recent study shows that such legislative reporting requirements have had limited impact and only '7% of companies [are] in strong compliance based on the level of due diligence measures that companies have reported in their 2014 Conflict Minerals Reports'.[13] Reporting and disclosure do not, by themselves, result in accountability. Such reporting requirements would benefit from clear industry-specific metrics and a framework that allows external stakeholders to evaluate corporate compliance with standards and creates a mechanism for sanctioning or correcting non-compliance.[14]

The timeframe for negotiating legislative text is also often an issue. It is not a process that can be established spontaneously, for example, to respond to a particular human rights crisis. Similarly, the process that has started around the concept of developing a treaty on business and human rights has no defined timeline and is likely to be lengthy. The time taken to develop legislative approaches – either domestically or internationally – is not a reason to discredit such processes, but it does highlight the need to ensure alternative mechanisms are in place in the interim. MSIs are one such alternative and are useful not only as a stop-gap measure but also as a regulatory mechanism that is likely to have greater industry-specific resonance even if such legislation is developed.[15]

In contrast to legally mandated human rights due diligence, voluntary CSR initiatives, like the United Nations (UN) Global Compact,[16] are particularly popular with companies. They give corporations visibility as being committed to human rights while providing ample flexibility in terms of the actual implementation process. Such initiatives are based on broad principles and while these may assist in raising awareness for specific issues (for example, human rights), they are generally insufficient for regulating corporate conduct.[17] Voluntary CSR initiatives are not set up to provide effective enforcement and oversight mechanisms.[18] For example, the principal accountability mechanism of the UN Global Compact to date is an annual mandatory reporting requirement. By participating, companies agree to incorporate the principles in their day-to-day operations and issue an annual public Communication on Progress, which reports on their progress in implementing the 10 principles. A failure to report could eventually lead to the expulsion of the company from the Global Compact.[19] Indeed, between 2008 and 2012, the Compact delisted over 3,000 companies due to corporate participants' failure to even meet this basic reporting requirement.[20] Delisting is a crude instrument and it does not help to assess the actual status of implementation of remaining participants.[21] The type of transparency that voluntary CSR initiatives such as the UN Global Compact provide does not significantly contribute to greater corporate human rights accountability.

Similarly, since the adoption of the UN Guiding Principles on Business and Human Rights[22] (Guiding Principles) in 2011, many companies have begun to assert their compliance with the principles through voluntary reporting, in their sustainability reports or other reports devoted specifically to the Guiding Principles.[23] In this context, companies often refer to themselves as being 'on a journey towards implementing human rights'.[24] While the implementation of human rights policies and procedures is an ongoing process, the notion of an individually defined 'journey' is a clear example of the limits of voluntarism. In this framework, companies are not required to provide a clear roadmap of the efforts that they are undertaking or to ensure that other companies in the same industry have a common understanding of the journey ahead and travel on the same path, according to the same rules. The human rights issues, the responses and the metrics or indicators of progress are left to individual companies to define and disclose. This produces a relativism that can lead to confusion and dilution of the notion of 'respect' for human rights.

Industry-specific MSIs that collaboratively design standards and monitoring mechanisms may compensate for some of the shortcomings posed by either by a purely legislative or voluntary approach:

- Industry-specific MSI processes integrate industry expertise to define concrete and industry-appropriate standards that create a level playing field for all companies in one industry context. Consensus building around a common code in the formative stage of an MSI is not easy. However, given the public pressure to which participating parties are generally exposed, agreement is still likely to be reached faster than legislation can be enacted.
- Industry-specific MSI processes can couple rigorous standards with monitoring mechanisms to which every member must commit. Membership thus hinges on agreement with accountability mechanisms and thus effectively rules out freeriding.

- Industry-specific MSIs that, based on common standards, define benchmarks against which the implementation status can be assessed ensure that progress can be tracked and company performance can be measured and compared with industry peers. Comprehensive reporting based on agreed indicators can enable public accountability of company performance.

3 Human rights governance MSIs: form and function

If MSIs are to fill human rights governance gaps, they must be able to govern or regulate corporate conduct in their form and function. Broadly speaking, governance includes three primary functions: legislative, executive and judicial.[25] When they work well, industry-specific, standards-based MSIs support these functions by concretely defining human rights standards in a specific industry context; operationalizing the standard into measurable benchmarks that allow for independent and public assessment of a member company's performance against the standard; and establishing processes for sanctioning non-compliance and providing access to remedy.

The MSIs that exist in different sectors perform these functions with varying degrees of rigour. Before turning to a discussion of how human rights governance MSIs organize themselves, the following presents a brief history of the evolution of MSIs over the last two decades. This history includes best-practice sharing and certification initiatives as well as the human rights governance MSIs that are the focus of this chapter:

- The Rainforest Alliance emerged in the late 1980s as a response to the impact of business on the environment and the perceived lack of regulatory response. It was followed by the Forest Stewardship Council in 1993, which originated in the United Kingdom when the World Wide Fund for Nature developed a code of conduct in partnership with timber traders, who agreed to purchase sustainably managed and certified forest products.
- Between 1993 and 1998 a number of diverse initiatives emerged, including the Marine Stewardship Council (1997), Social Accountability International (1997) and the Ethical Trading Initiative (1998).
- In 1996, in response to public concerns about sweatshop practices in the apparel industry's global supply chain, the US government served as a catalyst for the creation of a new MSI called the Fair Labor Association (FLA), which established a code of conduct for the apparel industry.[26]
- In a series of resolutions adopted from 1998 to 2005, the UN Security Council condemned the sale of conflict diamonds from Angola, Sierra Leone, Liberia and Côte d'Ivoire and called for the creation of a voluntary regulatory body for the diamond industry, which became the Kimberley Process.[27]
- In 2000, following a proposal from Secretary-General Kofi Annan to the World Economic Forum, the UN Global Compact was launched as a multi-sector voluntary corporate sustainability initiative intended to provide a 'leadership platform' for developing socially responsible corporate policies and practices.

- As it was leaving office at the end of 2000, the Clinton administration launched a set of Voluntary Principles on Security and Human Rights (Voluntary Principles) intended to set standards for security around extractive operations in the energy and mining sectors.[28] The Obama administration reinvigorated the initiative beginning in 2010, leading to its formal incorporation as a non-profit entity and a process to establish voluntary implementation and evaluation guidelines.
- Following media exposés of trafficked children forced to work in cocoa production in Côte d'Ivoire, US Congressional Representative Eliot Engel introduced an amendment to the 2002 Agricultural Appropriations Bill for funding to develop 'slave free' labelling requirements on cocoa products. Cocoa companies stopped passage of the bill by promising to adopt voluntary standards, which became the International Cocoa Initiative in 2002.
- Beginning in 2006, Yahoo!, Google and Microsoft joined with human rights groups, academics and social investors to form the Global Network Initiative (GNI), which was launched in 2008. The initiative aims to provide a set of global principles that address free expression and privacy issues on the Internet. The GNI completed its first assessments of the three founding companies in 2015.[29]
- The International Code of Conduct for Private Security Providers (ICoC) was launched in 2010. It arose in response to the perceived impunity of private security contractors operating in conflict zones, such as a 2007 incident in which Blackwater (a private security contractor contracted to guard a military convoy) opened fire in Nisour Square in Baghdad, killing 17 people and injuring 24 others.[30]

Subsequent chapters present in-depth analysis of several of these MSIs at different stages of development. Here, we present a three-part framework concerning the governance functions of MSIs that seek to regulate corporate conduct on human rights: (1) setting standards; (2) enforcement; and (3) sanctioning non-compliance and providing access to remedy. We also discuss operational challenges MSIs face in their efforts to fill the governance gap and regulate the human rights effects of TNCs.

3.1 Setting standards, making rules

The challenges that MSIs are established to address generally arise in an industry-specific business context. For example, in 2006, Google, Yahoo!, Cisco and Microsoft came under congressional scrutiny as a group for their activities in facilitating censorship and surveillance in China.[31] The GNI was born out of recognition that all companies in the information and communication technology (ICT) industry would face similar challenges when seeking to do business in countries where governments constrain the free expression and privacy rights of their own citizens. While the US Congress convened several hearings on the subject and drafted the Global Online Freedom Act of 2013, it was not able to enact legislation to govern corporate conduct in the sector.[32] One of the criticisms of the draft legislation was that it did not reflect the rapidly changing business realities of the companies it sought to regulate. The formation of the GNI was a way to develop industry-specific standards and implement guidelines that could adapt to a rapidly evolving sector.

The first task of the stakeholders that formed the GNI – and one that applies to any newly formed MSI – was to negotiate a standard that applies to all member companies and that reflects the specific challenges of their industry context. One of the advantages of MSIs is that they level the playing field by identifying common standards, rooted in existing international instruments and norms. For example:

- Fair Labor Association:

   > The FLA Workplace Code of Conduct defines labor standards that aim to achieve decent and humane working conditions. The Code's standards are based on International Labor Organization standards and internationally accepted good labor practices.[33]

- Global Network Initiative:

   > These Principles are based on internationally recognized laws and standards for human rights, including the Universal Declaration of Human Rights ('UDHR'), the International Covenant on Civil and Political Rights ('ICCPR') and the International Covenant on Economic, Social and Cultural Rights ('ICESCR').[34]

- Voluntary Principles on Security and Human Rights:

   > [T]he rights of individuals should not be violated while exercising the right to exercise freedom of association and peaceful assembly, the right to engage in collective bargaining, or other related rights of Company employees as recognized by the Universal Declaration of Human Rights and the ILO Declaration on Fundamental Principles and Rights at Work.[35]

However, the combination of utilizing these 'soft-law' standards and enforcement by private actors attracts reasonable criticism around the potentially selective nature of the standards monitored and the perennial problems of leaving the 'fox guarding the hen house'.[36] In some cases, the standards monitored by some MSIs set a lower bar than that required by local law[37] and some initiatives lack independent auditing and transparency.[38] Some of the codes that have multiplied in the last three to four decades exhibit these types of problems.

Negotiating the standard, or what might be called the 'constitutional' phase in the development of an MSI, often takes significant time. The origins of the FLA were in the Apparel Industry Partnership convened by the Clinton White House in 1996. The FLA Code was adopted three years later in 1999.[39] Similarly, negotiations around the GNI principles began in 2006 and were adopted in 2008. Over the course of 2014 and 2015, GNI participants have been renegotiating the standard with a group of telecommunications companies to apply the GNI principles to them.

As the subsequent chapters on the experience of individual MSIs illustrate, one of the key challenges during this stage is to build trust among competitor companies and other stakeholders. Many of the organizations that participate in MSIs are not accustomed to the kind of cooperation required to set rules for corporate conduct. In addition, the negotiation is conducted with stakeholders from civil society, academia and sometimes governments. These players do not necessarily have experience sitting at the table with companies in a cooperative, rule-setting context.

A healthy degree of tension among the different stakeholders can help maintain the rigour that makes MSIs appealing to the different stakeholders.[40] But arriving at that healthy tension – a point where companies and other stakeholders can cooperate while preserving their core interests – often takes place over a series of time-consuming and difficult negotiations during which time participants work towards an emerging shared vision for the organization.

For some advocacy organizations, this tension has been difficult, and sometimes impossible, to manage. During the development of the FLA, unions that had been part of the original group of stakeholders negotiating the code of conduct withdrew from the partnership before it launched the FLA. Likewise, Oxfam America, Amnesty International and Human Rights First have withdrawn from the Voluntary Principles in recent years.

Once the constitutional phase has been completed and the participants have launched or adopted a standard, participants in an MSI must then turn to implementing rules that operationalize that standard. The FLA maintains and regularly updates a set of 'Compliance Benchmarks' that provide guidance about how the standard applies in practice to member companies and their suppliers.[41] Similarly, the GNI maintains 'Implementation Guidelines' that 'provide further details on how participating companies will put the Principles into practice'. It describes the purpose of the Guidelines as being to:

- Describe a set of actions which constitute compliance with the Principles.
- Provide companies with guidance on how to implement the Principles.
- As described in the accompanying Governance, Accountability and Learning Framework, each participating company will be assessed on their progress implementing the Principles after two years and annually thereafter.[42]

While the Voluntary Principles were adopted in 2001, they were launched solely as a set of principles, without accompanying guidance for implementation. In 2011–12, the initiative undertook a joint project with the International Finance Corporation, the International Council on Mining and Metals, IPIECA (an industry association for the energy sector) and the International Red Cross to develop voluntary implementation guidelines.[43] While the development of these tools met a long-standing need for greater clarity about what it means for members to implement the Voluntary Principles, the guidance document makes it clear that the tools 'are non-prescriptive and provid[e] a range of different tools on which companies may draw, according to their individual needs and circumstances'.[44] The tools fall short of setting common operational protocols for addressing human rights issues in the energy and mining sectors.

Similarly, the participants in the more recently developed ICoC remain engaged in an as-yet unresolved debate about guidelines for implementation and how companies are accredited as participants in that MSI.

3.2 Enforcing the standard: independent monitoring and reporting

For voluntary regulation to be effective, compliance with the standard must be verified.[45] Absent verification, an initiative is simply a standard-setting body or a forum for shared learning about common challenges. These are useful activities, but they do not on their own regulate or constrain corporate behaviour with respect to human rights, nor do they allow companies to compare their performance on human rights to their competitors. A precondition for verification is increased transparency over corporate conduct. To verify compliance with the standard, the MSI needs insights into corporate operations (for example, participating companies need to share the locations of all supplier facilities with the MSI). When the MSI is allowed to report publicly about its findings, the compliance review also enables public accountability.

MSIs vary widely in their approach to verification and the degree of independence in their verification mechanisms. They also vary in how they publicly report on the findings of verification efforts. The FLA features one of the more advanced systems of independent verification: it conducts independent, unannounced assessments of a percentage of its member companies' supply chains, as well as an in-depth assessment of member companies themselves every three years. It posts audit reports on its website and includes longer reporting on individual company performance in its annual report.

The GNI also has a system of verification, though it is less developed than the FLA's. Companies directly engage independent monitoring organizations that have been accredited by the GNI Board to conduct an assessment of their internal processes for addressing free expression and privacy risks, as well as selected cases that illustrate the outcomes of these processes. The assessors' reports are shared with the company that is being assessed before a version that redacts commercially sensitive information is shared with the GNI Executive Director. An even more redacted version is shared with the GNI Board, which votes on the member company's compliance with the standard. The GNI completed its first full round of assessments in 2013 for the three founding companies, Microsoft, Google and Yahoo!. The GNI published a report on the assessment process in January 2014, but the report mostly comprised aggregated information and included barely two-and-a-half pages that discussed the specific performance of the three companies.[46]

The Voluntary Principles only began to develop a verification framework in 2011, more than a decade after the initiative launched.[47] In 2015, it released for the first time a 'Corporate Pillar Verification Framework' document.[48] The document was the result of an effort over several years by a majority of the corporate pillar participants to develop Key Performance Indicators (KPIs) 'to validate their commitments to the VPs'.[49] At the time the KPI project was launched, 14 of the then 20 corporate participants volunteered for the project.[50] The American oil companies (Chevron, ConocoPhillips, ExxonMobil, Hess Corporation, Marathon Oil and Occidental Petroleum Company) declined to participate. The framework that resulted from the pilot and which was published in 2015 is an important step forward in verifying corporate performance against the Voluntary Principles' standard, but it remains an 'opt-in' framework in which each company can choose its own indicators and which relies on self-reporting by companies, with no external verification of implementation of the KPIs. Today, many energy and mining companies that are not members of the initiative identify themselves as implementing the Voluntary Principles, despite the fact that they are not one of its 29 company members. For example, Kosmos Energy, which is not a participant, asserts that it 'will implement the Voluntary Principles on Security and Human Rights' as an element of its sustainability strategy.[51] In the absence of mandatory verification frameworks with some element of independence, the Voluntary Principles are merely a set of principles, which allows many companies to act as freeriders.

3.3 Sanctioning non-compliance and providing access to remedy

Sanctioning and correcting non-compliance with standards is the third leg of the governance stool, and MSIs must serve this function in order to fill the governance gap.[52] Sanctions give the other functions meaning, deter actions that would undermine human rights and discourage freeriding among competitors. In addition to the public reporting of corporate compliance levels, grievance mechanisms serve to increase the accountability of MSIs to those for whom they are established to benefit by providing an avenue for individuals, civil society and community groups to access remedies for violations of the standard.[53]

With the exception of the FLA and potentially the GNI, the MSIs surveyed in the subsequent chapters have yet to mature to the point where sanctions or correction of non-compliance are a serious prospect.

Determination of compliance with the standard is a necessary precursor to any sanction. The FLA assesses compliance on an ongoing basis through supply-chain monitoring and periodic assessments of performance at the headquarters level of its highest-level members. It also conducts special investigations into specific allegations of non-compliance.

Every three years, the FLA assesses and publicly reports on whether a member is in compliance with FLA standards based on the member's internal compliance programme and the findings of the FLA's supply-chain monitoring. Members found to be non-compliant are placed under a period of so-called 'Special Review'. If a member fails to effectively address the identified compliance issues during the Special Review period, the FLA Board may then vote to terminate its affiliation.[54] The FLA Board has voted to single out member companies on several occasions by placing the company on Special Review. In 2006, for example, Gildan was placed on special review as a result of violations of workers' rights at one of its Honduran factories.[55] In late 2012, the FLA terminated the affiliation of knitwear manufacturer Hey Tekstil due to persistent non-compliance with the FLA's Code of Conduct in relation to payment of wages and severance benefits to workers.[56]

The FLA also has a robust mechanism for third-party complaints that has been tested many times over the life of the organization.[57] Under its complaints procedure, 'any person, group or organization [can] report serious violations of workers' rights in facilities used by any company that has committed to FLA labor standards'.[58] The mechanism is not intended as a substitute for factory-, company- or national-level grievance processes but rather as an instance of last resort if those mechanisms are not effective or appropriate. If the complaint meets the FLA's criteria, the organization investigates, sometimes assigning an ombudsperson, and identifies and monitors a remediation plan.

The GNI is just beginning to test its assessment processes. Its first report on company compliance, *Public Report on the Independent Assessment Process for Google, Microsoft, and Yahoo*, was more a report on the *process* of assessment than on the companies being assessed. The report contains some information about the companies that could be useful to consumers, investors and other stakeholders, and is an early effort at testing the GNI's mechanisms for evaluating compliance. The GNI Board assessed compliance according to the following standard:

A finding of compliance indicates that the GNI Board believes the companies has committed to our Principles by adopting policies and procedures to implement them; and
based on the cases reviewed is making a good faith effort to implement and apply
them and improve over time.[59]

This language reflects the tensions many MSIs face between evaluating company
policy or procedure and evaluating the outcomes of those processes. In the negotiations that formed the GNI, NGOs fought for the assessment process to include
evaluation not only of process, but also outcomes. The extent to which the public
reports of the case reviews are redacted and aggregated limits transparency into the
outcomes of companies' policies and procedures to protect freedom of expression
and privacy. As the GNI assessment process matures, increasing transparency and
developing complementary procedures for correcting non-compliance will be
important milestones.

Given that the Voluntary Principles and the International Code of Conduct
Association (ICoCA) have yet to develop mechanisms for evaluating compliance,
there are neither examples nor the possibility of sanctioning or correcting non-
compliance in either initiative. The Voluntary Principles' reporting and auditing
framework, which was released in May 2015 and targets member companies, offers
the possibility of assessing compliance in the future, but it remains to be seen
whether and how the initiative will address findings of non-compliance, especially
because companies can opt out of the process.

3.4 Organizational challenges

As they have evolved, each of the MSIs discussed in the following chapters has
faced a common set of operational challenges that their members will have to overcome if these organizations are to reach their potential.

3.4.1 Resources and staffing

MSIs, like any organization, require resources and capacity to implement the agreements and procedures that its members negotiate. There is significant variation in the
funding and organizational models among the MSIs profiled in the subsequent chapters. Unsurprisingly, the FLA's large budget and staff undergird its ability to execute
consistent, in-depth processes that support its objectives of improving the lives of
workers in its members' supply chains. The GNI, in contrast, has survived for the
first five years of its existence on a shoestring budget, barely able to sustain three
full-time staff positions. The Voluntary Principles was only incorporated as a non-
profit organization in 2012.[60] Prior to that point, members funnelled contributions
through one member company, which supported the bare minimum consulting services required to convene meetings and conference calls. The ICoCA has started on
a much stronger financial footing and has a full-time staff in Geneva courtesy of
funding primarily from the Swiss government.

3.4.2 Sustaining a strong NGO voice

The multi-stakeholder nature of these initiatives is what gives them strength and
credibility, and ongoing NGO participation is an essential element of their success.
But many MSIs have struggled to establish and maintain a group of NGOs with the

knowledge, resources and capacity to sustain engagement around difficult issues over time.

NGOs consistently report that MSIs take significant staff time and that the foundations that support them do not reward work on MSIs.[61] One NGO participant in the Voluntary Principles recounted how her time spent on the Voluntary Principles was considered personal time, despite its relevance to her main job functions, because it did not fall within any funded programme.[62] The ICoCA and the FLA are the only MSIs that underwrite NGO participation in board meetings and other events. The absence of funding for NGO participation in MSIs taxes their organizations and reduces their effectiveness in advancing respect for human rights in difficult business environments.

In addition, not all NGOs view MSIs as valuable or legitimate in achieving their advocacy objectives. Amnesty International, Oxfam America and Human Rights First each left the Voluntary Principles between 2013 and 2015. In its statement announcing its withdrawal, Amnesty highlighted the failure of the MSI to establish accountability mechanisms for company performance, saying it believed 'extractive companies and security providers should be held to account for involvement in human rights abuses. We do not believe this objective can be realised through our ongoing membership of the VPs'.[63]

For the last decade, United Students Against Sweatshops has maintained a website entitled 'FLA Watch: Monitoring the "Fair" Labor Association'.[64] The objective of the site is to expose the FLA as a 'public relations mouthpiece of the apparel industry'.[65] In a lengthy 1999 article laying out the rationale for walking away from the negotiations that led to the formation of the FLA, Alan Howard of the United Needletrades, Industrial, and Textile Employees (UNITE) put it simply: 'The labor movement is not interested in top-down, paternalistic solutions to workers' problems.'[66]

These sentiments reflect the challenge facing NGOs that decide to stay at the table with companies to negotiate and enforce standards. Their role is important in a governance context to serve as a check on corporate power within the initiatives, yet they also face strong critiques from NGOs that have chosen to advance their missions from outside MSIs.

In the context of limited resources and contentious debates about whether they should participate at all, NGOs have struggled to maintain a strong voice in MSIs. The same representatives have filled the NGO pillar in the FLA for many years, and three of the six representatives are retired or are academics serving in a personal capacity. While other initiatives may have more NGO members, participants report that it often falls to one or two organizations to do the heavy lifting on particularly contentious or important debates. In addition, with the exception of Human Rights Watch (and previously Human Rights First), there are almost no NGOs[67] that participate in more than one MSI across industries.

Conflict of interest remains another contentious debate when it comes to NGO participation in MSIs. For example, with the departure of Amnesty, Oxfam and Human Rights First, the NGO pillar of the Voluntary Principles largely consists of NGOs that are funded by the same governments and/or companies that are members of the organization. Similar arguments about which organizations qualified for participation based on their funding models played out in the early negotiations of the ICoCA and the GNI.

Table 4.1.2 MSI resources and staffing (status at June 2015)[a]

MSI	Annual budget (approximate)	Staff	Funding sources	Annual member dues
Fair Labor Association	$6,600,000	55 staff, with an executive director	• Membership fees • Programme services, such as factory audits paid for by company members ($4,000–6,000 per audit) • Contributions, gifts and grants from governments and other organizations • Founded with significant funding from the Clinton Administration	*Suppliers* • 0.00184% per million of gross annual revenues. Minimum fee of $5,000 and a maximum of $250,000; plus at least one audit per year *Brands and retailers* • 0.18% of gross annual revenues. Minimum fee of $5,000 plus at least one audit per year; maximum fee of $250,000 *Licensees* • Minimum fees of $100, $500 and $5,000 based on annual revenue category; plus a percentage of annual revenue (0.0001 and 0.00001%) for larger licensees
Global Network Initiative	$733,295	3 full-time staff, with an executive director	• Membership fees • Contributions, gifts and grants from foundations; recently opened to government and private donors	*Companies* • Sliding scale according to revenue • Initial sponsor companies (Google, Yahoo!, Microsoft): $100,000 • New members: $35,000 • Companies engage and pay assessors bilaterally *Non-companies* • Nominal contribution of $100–$1,000

	Amount	Staff / structure	Funding sources	Fees
Voluntary Principles	$700,000	2.5-person part-time secretariat managed by DC-based law firm Foley Hoag	• Membership fees	• Companies: $18,000 • Governments: $18,000
International Code of Conduct for Private Security Service Providers	$1,166,000	3 full-time staff, with an executive director, plus 2.5 staff on detail from Geneva-based NGO Democratic Control of Armed Forces (DCAF)	• Membership fees • Government contributions • ICOCA is able to receive foundation funding, but has not to date • Founded with significant funding from the Swiss government	*Companies* • Company joining fee: $1,000 • Company fees: By year two, $3,000, $6,000 or $10,000 based on company size *Governments* • A voluntary basis, but with an expectation that governments will commit funds. ICOCA estimates an average of $750,000 from governments collectively per year *Civil society* • No fee; suggested $100 contribution

Note
a All amounts in US$.

Finally, none of these MSIs have yet effectively incorporated civil society voices from the communities most affected by TNCs in their governance structures. MSIs are established to address rights violations in difficult operating environments, so it follows that rights holders should have a voice in the operation of the initiatives. The absence of NGOs from Africa, Asia or Latin America has been a long-standing critique of many MSIs.[68]

3.4.3 Conveying meaningful information to the public

Another operational challenge facing all MSIs is how to convey information about their members in a way that is useful to consumers, investors, regulators and affected communities. At a basic level, the websites of some MSIs are often difficult to navigate and feature heavy text that is obscure to most non-experts seeking simple information about a member company.

Even an MSI like the FLA, which collects significant independent information about a wide array of companies and makes it available to the public, has struggled to distil this information into easily understood indicators that compare the performance of one of its member companies against another. While the FLA website contains large quantities of data about individual company performance – including factory audit reports, headquarter-level assessments, reports on complaints and special projects and assessments – it is difficult for even an expert to understand the meaning of all this information when it comes to making purchasing or investment decisions and comparing the performance of FLA member companies. Critically, this also limits the benefits to companies that are in compliance with the standards because it is difficult to distinguish them from those that do not comply.

MSIs are not well understood by funders and, as illustrated in Table 4.1.2, have struggled to attract support from foundations and other independent sources. More funding for communication, reporting and the development of meaningful indicators of their members' performance on human rights would make all MSIs stronger.

3.4.4 Best-practice sharing and 'shared learning'

Company members often seek to direct MSIs towards activities that focus on best-practice sharing and shared learning. Of course, one valuable purpose of MSIs is the opportunity for companies to collaborate with their competitors and other stakeholders on issues of human rights. In the FLA, for example, the Monitoring Committee convenes three times a year for a day-long meeting focused on the details of implementing programmes to advance labour rights in member supply chains. The FLA is well resourced to staff this kind of collaboration, which makes its members and the FLA better equipped to achieve its objectives. In the Voluntary Principles or the GNI, which operate on much smaller budgets, shared learning often comes at the expense of the initiatives' potential to fulfil regulatory functions.

4 Critiques of the MSI model

While MSIs have advantages as a practical mechanism to fill governance gaps, they are the subject of targeted critique from advocates and academics.[69] The three most common points raised against MSIs are the following.

Voluntary standards: Critics of MSIs argue that participation and compliance in MSIs is voluntary and therefore will not result in lasting change.[70] They often advocate for binding legislation or agreements between global unions and companies (which may or may not be incorporated as legally binding agreements) as viable alternatives.

Participation in an MSI, however, is quite different from a voluntary CSR commitment and the voluntarism critique does not account for the quasi-binding arrangements that some MSIs have developed.[71] For example, according to the Global Reporting Initiative, reporting has developed into an expected minimum 'requirement' for many TNCs.[72] For participants in MSIs, compliance with the standard is also not strictly voluntary. Peer control can, in this context, serve as a powerful means to hold corporations accountable.[73] However, both the standards and the rigour of monitoring mechanisms can vary considerably across MSIs. Given the large variety of MSIs, the dichotomy of voluntary vs mandatory standards seems overly simplistic as it does not capture the quasi-binding arrangements that some MSIs have developed.

Lack of representation from affected communities: In many MSIs, critical stakeholders are not represented in the governing body. Sometimes critical stakeholders are only represented in an advisory body; sometimes they are not represented at all. A report by MSI Integrity, for example, highlighted the lack of representation of affected communities in the Extractive Industries Transparency Initiative (EITI):

> The EITI Standard and related guidance material contain no indication that local actors, especially affected communities, are crucial stakeholders to the EITI process; indeed, the assumption throughout the EITI Standard that an MSG consists only of government, industry, and civil society may have an exclusionary effect on community-based organizations or community leaders seeking to participate.[74]

The lack of union involvement in some of the labour rights-focused MSIs has also been a particularly contentious issue. For example, organizations such as FLA Watch argue that the FLA is not representative of workers because unions are not participating in the initiative.[75] Unions are indeed critical stakeholders in the labour context, but unionization is not the only strategy to make progress towards an improvement of workers' rights and different approaches can complement each other in the workplace. The involvement of workers' representatives is a valuable strategy for ensuring that workers' voices are heard.

Co-option by corporations ('fox guarding the henhouse'): Some critics argue that the self-selective nature of the standards created by MSIs plays into the hands of corporations that seek to privatize and shape a government function.[76] In addition, NGOs may not often have the resources to fully participate in MSIs and hence corporations, who often provide large portions of the funding for the MSIs, have a greater say in how the standard and its monitoring mechanisms are designed. While ensuring a balance of power is critical, many MSIs have aligned their standards with international human rights and labour standards (for example, ILO fundamental conventions) and thus they do not require less from their members than governments. Several MSIs also ensure that all representatives of different stakeholder groups have equal voting rights in their governing body. Thus, while informal power imbalances cannot fully be excluded (and much is contingent on the strength of those individual members), there are at least formal mechanisms that ensure equal decision-making power.

The design of monitoring mechanisms, however, varies greatly. Whether the differences in approach are the result of corporate lobbying inside MSIs is a plausible yet unproven explanation.[77] MSIs that drive down standards by relying on softer monitoring mechanisms are a threat to the credibility of MSIs more generally because the small but critical differences are often invisible to consumers and investors.

These critical arguments show that MSIs have struggled to convey their value and point to several risk factors that may undermine the MSI model as a potential governance mechanism.[78] Most importantly, however, they further emphasize the need to differentiate among different types of MSIs. The arguments of MSI critics often refer to MSIs broadly and hence it is important to differentiate between types of MSIs. In our view, the greatest potential lies with industry-specific MSIs that aim to regulate corporate human rights conduct.

5 Conclusion

None of the MSIs discussed in subsequent chapters are a perfect governance solution to the human rights challenges that arise when TNCs operate in markets where governments cannot or will not protect the rights of their own people. In an ideal world, all governments would fulfil their responsibilities to protect rights – at work, at home, online and in local communities. That ideal is unlikely to be realized any time soon and, as such, MSIs hold promise as a collaborative governance model that can regulate global companies and their effects on human rights. If MSIs are able to achieve the governance functions described above – standard-setting, enforcement and sanctioning or correcting non-compliance – they hold the promise and possibility of filling governance gaps. MSIs can complement ongoing efforts to strengthen host- and home-country regulation, hold companies accountable for violations through judicial mechanisms and improve individual companies' programmes for strengthening rights protections.

The case studies in the following chapters explore MSIs in four different industries: manufacturing (FLA), ICT (GNI), extractives (Voluntary Principles, EITI) and private security (ICoC/ICoCA). We also discuss the lack of an overarching MSI in the agriculture sector but highlight the relatively recent establishment of the Campaign for Fair Food as an innovative strategy in one particular sector for protecting the rights of workers. The MSI case studies show that these organizations are all at different stages of their institutional development. Some are more mature than others and for all of them significant practical implementation challenges remain. The authors of these case studies have all been instrumental in establishing and/or managing these MSIs. Their insights into how these MSIs formed, how industry-specific human rights standards were developed and how these initiatives ensure accountability are unique and can inform the future development of MSIs.

Notes

1   J. Braithwaite and P. Drahos, *Global Business Regulation* (Cambridge: Cambridge University Press, 2000).
2   J. Reinecke and J. Donaghey, 'After Rana Plaza: Complementary Consumption and Production Based Mobilization for Global Labour Rights' (2015) *Organization* (forthcoming); D. Baumann-Pauly, S. Labowitz and N. Banerjee, 'Closing Governance Gaps in Bangladesh's Garment Industry: The Power and Limitations of Private Governance Schemes' (SSRN Working Paper, March 2015), http://papers.ssrn.com/sol3/papers.cfm?abstract_id=2577535.
3   Y. Papadopoulos, 'The Challenge of Transnational Private Governance: Evaluating Authorization, Representation, and Accountability' (LIEPP Working Paper, February 2013, No. 8), www.sciencespo.fr/liepp/sites/sciencespo.fr.liepp/files/WP8.pdf.
4   D. Baumann-Pauly *et al.*, 'Industry-Specific Multi-Stakeholder Initiatives That Govern Corporate Human Rights Standards: Legitimacy Assessment of the Fair Labor Association and the Global Network Initiative' (SSRN Working Paper, March 2015), http://papers.ssrn.com/sol3/papers.cfm?abstract_id=2576217.
5   As of May 2015, the United Nations Global Compact listed over 8,000 non-business participants on their Participants and Stakeholder site, www.unglobalcompact.org/ParticipantsAndStakeholders/index.html.
6   Forest Stewardship Council, 'Certification', https://us.fsc.org/certification.194.htm.
7   Forest Stewardship Council, 'Chain of Custody Certification', https://us.fsc.org/chain-of-custody-certification.201.htm.
8   Social Accountability International, 'About Us', www.sa-intl.org/index.cfm?fuseaction=Page.ViewPage&pageId=1365.
9   S. Bernstein and B. Cashore, 'Can Non-State Global Governance Be Legitimate? An Analytical Framework' (2007) 1 *Government and Regulation* 4, 347–71.
10 Ibid.
11 O. de Schutter *et al.*, *Human Rights Due Diligence: The Role of States* (ICAR, European Coalition for Corporate Justice, Canadian Network on Corporate Accountability, 2012) p. 44; E.R. George, 'Influencing the Impact of Business on Human Rights' in L. Blecher, N. Kaymar Stafford and G.C. Bellamy (eds), *Corporate Responsibility for Human Rights Impacts: New Expectations and Paradigms* (Chicago: American Bar Association, 2014) p. 271.
12 Pub. L. 111-203, 124 Stat. 1376 (2010). Section 1502 is codified at 15 USC §78m(p). See further A.P Ewing in this volume, 'Mandatory human rights reporting', p. 284.
13 G. Sarfaty, 'Shining Light on Global Supply Chains' (2015) *Harvard International Law Journal* (forthcoming).
14 See S. Zadek in this volume, 'The meaning of accountability', p. 284.
15 See in this volume A. Ganesan, 'Towards a business and human rights treaty?', p. 73; K. Genovese, 'Access to remedy: non-judicial grievance mechanisms', p. 266.
16 UN Global Compact, www.unglobalcompact.org.
17 D. Baumann-Pauly, *Managing Corporate Legitimacy* (Sheffield: Greenleaf Publishing, 2013) p. 71.
18 See B. Skorpen Claeson, 'Emerging from the Tragedies in Bangladesh: A Challenge to Voluntarism in the Global Economy' (2015) 24(4) *New Solutions*, 495, 201, for a summary of arguments against voluntary initiatives in the apparel sector, www.laborrights.org/sites/default/files/publications/New_Solutions_-_Claeson_-_Accord_-_2015.pdf.
19 J. Lee, 'UN Global Compact Expels Hundreds for Non-Compliance', Triple Pundit, 22 January 2015, www.triplepundit.com/2015/01/un-global-compact-expels-members-non-compliance (reporting that the UN Global Compact expelled 657 companies in 2014 for not submitting their Communication on Progress).
20 J. Confino, 'Cleaning up the Global Compact: Dealing with Corporate Free Riders', *Guardian*, 27 March 2012, www.theguardian.com/sustainable-business/cleaning-up-un-global-compact-green-wash.
21 Baumann-Pauly, *Managing Corporate Legitimacy*, p. 108.
22 Human Rights Council, 'Guiding Principles on Business and Human Rights: Implementing the United Nations "Protect, Respect and Remedy" Framework', Report of the Special Representative of the Secretary-General on the Issue of Human Rights and Transnational Corporations and Other Business Enterprises, UN Doc. A/HRC/17/31 (21 March 2011).
23 See, for example, Shift's 2013 assessment of Gap Inc.'s efforts under the Guiding Principles (http://business-humanrights.org/en/abn-amro-first-financial-institution-to-commit-to-using-un-guiding-principles-reporting-framework) and ABN AMRO's announcement that it will be the first financial institution to use the UN Guiding Principles Reporting Framework in its forthcoming 2015 sustainability report (www.abnamro.com/en/newsroom/newsarticles/abn-amro-first-financial-institution-to-report-on-human-rights-efforts.html).
24 See, for example, Coca-Cola's description of their human rights journey (http://assets.coca-colacompany.com/cd/7b/f4a72bc449619980f688c1394a3d/human-rights-journey-since-2005-updated-december-2014.PDF) or that of Nestlé (www.nestle.com/asset-library/documents/library/documents/corporate_social_responsibility/nestle-hria-white-paper.pdf, p. 6).
25 J. Braithwaite, *Responsive Regulation: Transcending the Deregulation Debate* (New York: Oxford University Press, 1992) p. 4.
26 See A. van Heerden in this volume, 'The Fair Labor Association: improving workers' rights in global supply chains', p. 128.
27 See S. Jerbi in this volume, 'Extractives and multi-stakeholder initiatives: the Voluntary Principles on Security and Human Rights; the Extractive Industries Transparency Initiative; the Kimberley Process Certification Scheme', p. 147.

28   See ibid.
29   See M. Samway in this volume, 'The Global Network Initiative: how can companies in the information and communications technology industry respect human rights?', p. [x].
30   See A.-M. Buzatu in this volume, 'The emergence of the International Code of Conduct for Private Security Service Providers', p. 160.
31   T. Zeller Jr., 'House Member Criticizes Internet Companies for Practices in China', *New York Times*, 15 February 2006, www.nytimes.com/2006/02/15/technology/15cnd-internet.html.
32   Global Online Freedom Act 2013, HR 491 (113th Congress, 2013–14).
33   FLA, 'Workplace Code of Conduct and Compliance Benchmarks', p. 1, www.fairlabor.org/sites/default/files/fla_complete_code_and_benchmarks.pdf.
34   Global Network Initiative, 'Principles on Freedom of Expression and Privacy', http://globalnetworkinitiative.org/sites/default/files/GNI_-_Principles_1_.pdf.
35   Voluntary Principles on Security and Human Rights, www.voluntaryprinciples.org/what-are-the-voluntary-principles.
36   Commission on Human Rights, 'Interim Report of the Special Representative of the Secretary General on the Issue of Human Rights and Transnational Corporations and Other Business Enterprises', UN Doc. E/CN.4/2006/97 (22 February 2006), para. 53.
37   For example, the FLA Workplace Code required a maximum of 60 hours worked per week (regular and overtime), while Chinese law limits work to 40 hours per week and a maximum of 36 hours overtime per month, potentially meaning a maximum of 49 hours per week. The reality is that the Chinese legal limits are not enforced and thus set a theoretical rather than practical limit: Fair Labor Association, *Independent Investigation of Apple Supplier, Foxconn* (March 2012), www. fairlabor.org/sites/default/files/documents/reports/foxconn_investigation_report.pdf, p. 8.
38   See, e.g. Worldwide Responsible Accredited Production (WRAP), www.wrapapparel.org.
39   See A. van Heerden in this volume, 'The Fair Labor Association: improving workers' rights in global supply chains', p. 128.
40   J. Nolan, 'The China Dilemma: Internet Censorship and Corporate Responsibility' (2009) 4(1) *Asian Journal of Comparative Law*, article 3.
41   Fair Labor Association, 'Principles of Fair Labor and Responsible Sourcing and Production', ww.fairlabor.org/our-work/principles.
42   Global Network Initiative, 'Implementation Guidelines', http://globalnetworkinitiative.org/implementation-guidelines/index.php.
43   Voluntary Principles on Security and Human Rights, 'Implementation Guidance Tools', www.voluntaryprinciples.org/wp-content/uploads/2013/03/VPs_IGT_Final_13-09-11.pdf.
44   Ibid., p. 3.
45   M.E. Conroy, *Branded! How the 'Certification Revolution' Is Transforming Global Corporations* (Gabriola Island, BC: New Society Publishers, 2007) p. 10; Bernstein and Cashore, 'Can Non-State Global Governance Be Legitimate?', p. 350; D. Kinley and J. Tadaki, 'From Talk to Walk: The Emergence of Human Rights Responsibilities for Corporations at International Law' (2004) 44(4) *Virginia Journal of International Law* 931, 956; L.W. Fransen and A. Kolk, 'Global Rule-Setting for Business: A Critical Analysis of MSI Standards' (2007) 14(5) *Organization* 667, 677.
46   Global Network Initiative, *Public Report on the Independent Assessment Process for Google, Microsoft, and Yahoo* (January 2014), http://globalnetworkinitiative.org/sites/default/files/GNI%20Assessments%20Public%20Report.pdf.
47   US Department of State, Bureau of Democracy, Human Rights, and Labor, '2012 Report of the US Government for Voluntary Principles on Security and Human Rights Initiative', 12 March 2013, www.state.gov/j/drl/rls/vprpt/2012/206029.htm.
48   Voluntary Principles on Security and Human Rights, 'Corporate Pillar Verification Framework', www.voluntaryprinciples.org/resources.
49   US Department of State, '2012 Report of the US Government for Voluntary Principles on Security and Human Rights Initiative'.
50   According to the US Government's 2012 annual report to the Voluntary Principles, the 14 companies included in the pilot were: Anglo American, AngloGold Ashanti, Barrick Gold Corporation, BG Group, BHP Billiton, BP, Freeport-McMoRan Copper & Gold, Inmet Mining Corporation, Newmont Mining Corporation, Rio Tinto, Shell, Statoil, Talisman Energy and Total. Ibid.
51   See, e.g. Kosmos Energy, 'Statement of Business Principles', Principle No. 5 – Kosmos in Society, www.kosmosenergy.com/business-principles/index.html.
52   Bernstein and Cashore, 'Can Non-State Global Governance Be Legitimate?', p. 349; Kinley and Tadaki, 'From Talk to Walk', p. 956.
53   J. Bendell, 'In Whose Name? The Accountability of Corporate Social Responsibility' (2007) 15(3) *Development in Practice* 372.
54   FLA, 'Charter Document' (as amended 12 February 2014), www.fairlabor.org/sites/default/files/fla_charter_2-12-14.pdf.
55   FLA, 'El Progreso Factory in Honduras', 14 December 2006, www.fairlabor.org/report/el-progreso-factory-honduras.
56   FLA, 'FLA Board Terminates Affiliation of Participating Supplier Hey Tekstil', 8 January 2013, www.fairlabor.org/press-release/hey-tekstil-affiliation-terminated.
57   The FLA website lists 27 third-party complaints in the period June 2012–June 2015: FLA, 'Third-Party Complaint Tracking Chart', www.fairlabor.org/third-party-complaint-tracking-chart.

58 FLA, 'Third Party Complaint Process', www.fairlabor.org/third-party-complaint-process.
59 Global Network Initiative, *Public Report on the Independent Assessment Process for Google, Microsoft, and Yahoo*, p. 3.
60 Voluntary Principles on Security and Human Rights, 'The Voluntary Principles Initiative Announces the Formation of the Voluntary Principles Association: New Organization Will Facilitate Efforts by Extractive Sector Companies to Protect Human Rights', press release, 21 November 2012, www.voluntaryprinciples.org/wp-content/uploads/2013/03/Voluntary_Principles_Association_Press_Release_-_November_21_2012.pdf.
61 Survey conducted by Sarah Labowitz in May 2015 with NGOs that participate in the Voluntary Principles.
62 Ibid.
63 Amnesty International, 'Amnesty International Withdrawal from the Voluntary Principles on Security and Human Rights', public statement, 3 June 2013, www.amnesty.org/en/library/asset/IOR40/003/2013/en/20db4 d7c-ee09-4a98-aab0-1016f2ebac42/ior400032013en.pdf.
64 FLA Watch, http://flawatch.usas.org.
65 FLA Watch, 'About FLA Watch', http://flawatch.usas.org/about.
66 A. Howard, 'Why Unions Can't Support the Apparel Industry Sweatshop Code' (1999) 3(2) *Working USA* 46.
67 The Center for Business and Human Rights at NYU Stern School of Business also participates in the FLA, ICoCA and GNI as an academic or civil society member.
68 N. Kearney, 'Codes and Partnerships: Experience of the Trade Union Movement' in 'Commerce with Conscience: Options for Business in the Global Economy', *Rights & Democracy*, 25 February 1999.
69 Fransen and Kolk, 'Global Rule-Setting for Business'. See also American Federation of Labor–Congress of Industrial Organizations (AFL-CIO), *Responsibility Outsourced: Social Audits, Workplace Certification and Twenty Years of Failure to Protect Worker Rights* (2013), www.aflcio.org/Learn-About-Unions/Global-Labor-Movement/Responsibility-Outsourced-Report.
70 C. Albin-Lackey, 'Without Rules: A Failed Approach to Corporate Accountability', in Human Rights Watch, *World Report 2013* (2013) p. 29.
71 P. Utting, *Rethinking Business Regulation: From Self-Regulation to Social Control*, United Nations Research Institute for Social Development, Technology, Business and Society Programme Paper No. 15, September 2005, www.unrisd.org/80256B3C005BCCF9/%28httpAuxPages%29/F02AC3DB0ED406E0C12570A10029 BEC8/$file/utting.pdf.
72 A 2013 KPMG survey showed that 93 per cent of the world's largest 250 companies issue a corporate responsibility report, of which 82 per cent refer to the GRI Guidelines. See KPMG, *The KPMG Survey of Corporate Social Responsibility Reporting 2013* (2013), www.kpmg.com/Global/en/IssuesAndInsights/ArticlesPublications/corporate-responsibility/Documents/kpmg-survey-of-corporate-responsibility-reporting-2013.pdf.
73 See A. van Heerden in this volume, 'The Fair Labor Association: improving workers' rights in global supply chains', p. 128.
74 MSI Integrity, *Protecting the Cornerstone: Assessing the Governance of EITI Multi-Stakeholder Groups* (February 2015), www.msi-integrity.org/wp-content/uploads/2015/02/MSI-Integrity-Summary-Protecting-the-Cornerstone-EN.pdf.
75 See FLA Watch, 'What's Wrong with the FLA?', http://flawatch.usas.org/about/events.
76 See AFL-CIO, *Responsibility Outsourced*.
77 See J. Merk and I. Zeldentrust, *The Business Social Compliance Initiative (CSI): A Critical Perspective* (June 2005), https://archive.cleanclothes.org/documents/05-050bsci_paper.pdf.
78 To address the question of MSI effectiveness, in 2013 a project entitled 'MSI-Integrity' was founded in conjunction with Harvard Law School's International Human Rights Clinic. The project is dedicated to 'understanding the human rights impact and value of voluntary initiatives that address business and human rights'. The initiative developed 400 indicators intended to evaluate the effect of MSIs and launched a series of pilot assessments against these indicators. The pilot reports, however, failed to distinguish the effectiveness of different MSIs, in part because the reports were mainly based on publicly available data and most MSIs do not do a good job in public reporting; in addition, the sheer volume of indicators obscures meaningful distinctions. See MSI Integrity, www.msi-integrity.org.

Section 4.2

The Fair Labor Association: improving workers' rights in global supply chains

Auret van Heerden

1 Introduction

The Fair Labor Association (FLA) was the outcome of a meeting convened by President Clinton at the White House in 1996 between industry, trade unions, non-governmental organizations (NGOs) and government representatives to discuss the disturbing persistence of human rights abuses in global supply chains making brand-name products. The meeting followed a series of exposés of human and labour rights abuses in the global supply chain that included instances in the United States (US).[1]

Robert Reich, the US Secretary of Labor at the time, had already launched a number of initiatives to try to eradicate sweatshop production, including a 'No Sweat' campaign that aimed to tackle the problem through a combination of enforcement, education and recognition of good practice.[2] Reich invited retailers to sign voluntary agreements with the US Department of Labor (DoL), under which retailers pledged to monitor their suppliers. Reich also publicly supported local monitoring initiatives such as the Los Angeles Compliance Alliance, but the limits of this strategy soon became apparent and the DoL began to 'name and shame' retailers who were sourcing from factories found to be violating labour standards. For example, the discovery of Thai workers in conditions of virtual slavery in El Monte, California in August 1995 prompted Reich to name the retailers involved and to propose a 'Retail Summit' in New York City in September 1995.[3] While the retailers were furious at the negative publicity, Reich argued that it was the only way to enforce a response.[4] The DoL also launched partnerships with the National Retail Federation, the American Apparel and Footwear Association and the National Consumers League to mobilize the private sector to combat labour abuses; it also began publishing a list of 'Trendsetters' – manufacturers and retailers who pledged to eradicate sweatshops in their supply chains.

However, it was the Kathie Lee Gifford case that arguably tipped the scales in favour of action. A television personality, Gifford had launched a clothing line that was sold at Walmart. In May 1996, the National Labor Committee (NLC) published evidence that the clothes were stitched by girls as young as 13 in Honduras.[5] Gifford's media profile turned the case into a national controversy and her defiant response enflamed it even more.[6] In addition, the label in her apparel line stated that a portion of the proceeds of each garment would be donated to various children's charities.[7] Furthermore, DoL inspectors raided a sweatshop in Manhattan producing for the Kathie Lee brand and found a practice of excessive working hours and low wages.[8]

Reich seized upon the issue. In July 1996, he testified before Congress[9] that he was convening a Fashion Industry Forum bringing together industry, labour, consumer and government representatives to explore ways of eliminating sweatshops and child labour. He posited the creation of a Rugmark-type[10] international label that would certify that a product was free of child, forced or exploited labour. President Clinton had already announced a set of Model Business Principles[11] to guide companies in developing codes of conduct for their global supply chains. However, the Principles had not gained traction and so, in August 1996, President Clinton convened industry, labour, trade union, consumer, NGO and government leaders and challenged them to come up with a system to prevent such abuses. This disparate group formed themselves into the Apparel Industry Partnership (AIP) and, over the next three years, it negotiated a workplace code of conduct. Signatory companies agreed to take steps to ensure that suppliers comply with the code, to check this through internal audits and to allow external audits of supplier facilities to verify the integrity of the system.[12] The FLA was set up to conduct those external audits. In 1999, it was incorporated as a non-profit company, making it tax-exempt under the Internal Revenue Code.[13] The FLA commenced its monitoring activities in 2001.[14]

Snapshot

FLA affiliates

The FLA has over 40 participating companies, some 200 colleges and universities and literally thousands of university licensees affiliated with it. The apparel industry is strongly represented, and the sporting goods and athletic footwear sector even more so, with companies including Adidas, Nike and Puma. Other major corporate affiliates include Apple and Nestlé.[15]

2 Developing standards

The AIP developed proposals for the code of conduct and monitoring system by studying United Nations (UN) and International Labour Organization (ILO) Conventions and Recommendations and company codes of conduct and monitoring programmes. A subcommittee on independent monitoring, led by the representative of the Interfaith Center on Corporate Responsibility (ICCR), conducted extensive stakeholder consultations before formulating its proposals. AIP members also conducted field tests on different monitoring methodologies and audit instruments in order to define the approach they wanted to take. Those Principles of Monitoring were then included in the FLA Charter.[16] Because the AIP made decisions by consensus, progress was often slow and agreement could not be reached on all issues. After six months of sometimes fierce debate, the AIP had missed its initial deadline and seemed to be in danger of collapsing. At that point, a new scandal broke concerning a Nike supplier in Vietnam.[17] The resulting public controversy, and a scathing letter to Nike from some of the NGO participants,[18] appeared to galvanize the company caucus and the AIP announced a month later that it had reached agreement on the terms of the AIP Workplace Code of Conduct and Principles of Monitoring (AIP Code).[19]

Snapshot

The evolution of the FLA Charter

Having reached agreement on the AIP Code, the negotiations turned to the question of implementation. Once again, disagreement on technical issues hampered progress. Some NGO and trade union participants felt that the companies were hesitating and accordingly increased public pressure in order to force them to act. Their campaign was spearheaded by the NLC and other NGOs that had not joined the AIP; it is likely, though, that they were in consultation with the labour groups in the AIP. This external pressure was not all positive for trust-building within the AIP. Many company participants reacted angrily to the continued NGO campaign focus on them. They also argued that by targeting companies that were already at the table, the NGOs were scaring off potential company recruits. The negotiations with AIP participants continued into 1998 but were clearly losing momentum. So, in the summer of 1998, an informal grouping of nine members convened to tackle the unresolved issues over which the AIP had deadlocked.

By October 1998, this leadership group of companies and civil society actors had agreed on the modalities for implementing and monitoring the code and the structure of the FLA to oversee the process. These nine actors then asked other companies to sign on; four did so. At this point, however, the unions and the ICCR decided to withdraw in protest at the failure to agree on living wages, how to address limitations on freedom of association in China and other places and disclosure of supplier factory locations. After the first year of monitoring, the FLA Board adopted a set of resolutions to strengthen many of the FLA Charter provisions that had been agreed by the AIP and a resolution to continue to explore means of defining and monitoring a living wage.

What is remarkable is that the AIP parties were able to continue negotiating, despite sometimes intense disagreements and decisions by some participants to leave the initiative. The AIP also managed to achieve sufficient momentum to set up the FLA to implement and monitor the AIP Code, a step that many other multi-stakeholder initiatives have found particularly challenging. Three factors appear to have been critical to this success:

- The role of government as convener, which laid a foundation of cooperation and trust on which the AIP was able to build and added a moral imperative to an agreement.
- The role of public opinion, which appears to have motivated the process in times of uncertainty.
- The informal network and collaboration that developed between companies and NGOs. These trusted relationships were crucial in getting the final agreement.

3 Enforcing compliance with the FLA Charter

The FLA Charter sets out the 'Obligations of Companies' that join the FLA, the requirements for accrediting independent external monitors and the 'Principles of Monitoring' that should guide the independent external monitoring events organized by FLA staff. The FLA Charter also provides for third-party complaints to be lodged directly with FLA staff.[20] At the beginning of every year, member companies are required to submit their factory lists to FLA staff who draw a random, risk-weighted sample of 5 per cent for independent external monitoring (IEM) conducted by accredited auditors selected and paid by the FLA.

In 2002, the initial FLA Charter provisions were strengthened to give FLA staff freedom to choose which sites to monitor on an unannounced basis, greater control over the selection of independent monitors and the ability to publish summaries of the results on the FLA website.[21] Once an IEM has been conducted, a member company is required to work with the supplier concerned to develop a remedial action plan that has to be approved by FLA staff. Companies have to update FLA staff on their progress in implementing the action plans and the FLA in turn updates the information published on the website. All of these steps have defined time periods to ensure that they occur in a reasonable time. The FLA also arranges verification audits of up to 1 per cent of companies in the original 5 per cent sample to ensure that the action plans were indeed implemented and to assess the degree to which the remedies were effective.

Snapshot

FLA monitoring

In the years following its creation, the FLA developed new monitoring tools and techniques to complement the IEM questionnaires administered by accredited monitors. These tools included management self-assessments, worker surveys and case studies. After a decade of monitoring, the FLA in 2008 moved beyond compliance audits to an assessment methodology that used a one- to five-point scale rather than pass–fail tests to assess the actual situation on a given FLA Charter benchmark. This Sustainable Compliance Initiative (SCI) is designed to score where the supplier facility lies along a continuum and to identify the capacity-building support they need in order to improve their performance.

All of these monitoring activities are backed by a complaint system whereby third parties who have reason to believe that egregious or persistent violations of the workplace code of conduct are occurring at a supplier facility may use the Third Party Complaint mechanism to complain. The FLA has tests that it applies in deciding whether to accept the complaint; if it does, the complaint is taken up with the member company that sources from that supplier.[22] If the member company fails to remedy the violation the FLA may commission an independent investigation into the case and publish a report. The member company concerned is required by the FLA Charter to remedy any FLA Charter violations confirmed by the report.

Snapshot

Third-party complaint: Honduras Russell

The Russell Athletic case was a peculiarly complex one. It actually involved two distinct but linked allegations and the FLA commissioned two independent investigators to determine whether: (a) the closure of Jerzees de Honduras (JdH) was a legitimate business decision (or designed to break the union that had formed there); and (b) the FLA Charter had been violated in other actions taken by the company prior to closure. This investigation was unique because the FLA Charter does not cover production decisions about which factory to use or close, except where it implies an alleged violation of workers' freedom of association. The investigations covered allegations of mandatory overtime, harassment by supervisors, discrimination against pregnant workers, unhygienic restrooms, dismissal of workers trying to form a union, late payment of wages and closure of the factory to avoid dealing with the trade union.

In early 2009, the FLA Board of Directors and Russell Athletic agreed on a remedial action plan; its implementation was tracked by the FLA and verified through announced and unannounced audits.[23] The FLA Board was concerned about the degree of implementation and, on 25 June 2009, decided to place Russell Athletic on a 90-day period of Special Review. This was extended for another 45 days on 28 October 2009. The Special Review procedure places a company on notice that if it does not implement specified remedial actions to the satisfaction of the Board within a defined period its participation in the FLA may be terminated.[24] The Board was particularly concerned that Russell Athletic should engage in good faith negotiations with the Central General De Trabajadores (CGT) union about issues of reinstatement and compensation of workers whose freedom of association had been violated, establishing an environment in which freedom of association could be enjoyed by disciplining certain managers, abolishing the system of collective pacts (*pactos colectivos*) and providing training to all workers and managers.

On 14 November 2009, Russell Corporation, SITRAJERZEES and the CGT concluded an agreement that met all of the FLA Board's requirements and the Board ended the Special Review. The FLA investigations and Special Review process lasted some 18 months, during which time NGOs, trade unions and student groups campaigned against Russell Athletic. Over 60 colleges and universities cut their contracts with Russell, placing the company's collegiate business in jeopardy. In the end, the JdH facility was reopened and a collective agreement was signed with the union. Russell Athletic and its parent company, Fruit of the Loom, agreed to work with unions at all their Honduran facilities.

4 Accountability through FLA mechanisms

There are four layers of accountability built into the FLA Charter that, taken together, arguably represent one of the most comprehensive and demanding set of requirements to be found in any multi-stakeholder monitoring initiative:

1　Oversight exercised by the FLA Board of Directors, which comprises representatives from six companies, six NGOs and six university representatives, as well as an independent Chair. The Board is a governing board, not simply an advisory one, and sets policy, decides the budget, votes on applications for membership, receives reports on monitoring activities and third-party complaints and decides whether to accredit companies that have completed their implementation periods.

2　Independent monitoring organized by FLA staff, which tests the degree to which companies have implemented the FLA Charter at the supplier level.

3　Public reporting on company performance, including the publication of company monitoring and assessment results, third-party complaint reports and the FLA's annual report. All reports including monitoring and assessment results are available on the FLA website.

4　The third-party complaint mechanism and the Special Review clause in the FLA Charter allows the Board to place a company on 90-day notice of expulsion if it fails to remedy violations identified in monitoring or third-party complaint reports. The Special Review clause has only been used twice in the history of the FLA, and in both cases (Gildan Activewear and Russell Athletic) it resulted in the companies making very significant changes in order to meet the remedial requirements set by the FLA Board and avoid expulsion for noncompliance. The resolution of certain third-party complaints has also led to the appointment by the FLA of ombudsmen to monitor implementation of agreements and to ensure timely responses to alleged breaches. Ombudsmen were also appointed in Guatemala and El Salvador due to the high number of complaints emanating from those jurisdictions.

This four-layered accountability system is clearly defined and programmed. Companies joining the FLA commit to implement the Obligations of Companies set out in the FLA Charter over the course of an 'implementation period' that is normally two or three years. This commitment is set down in a resolution adopted by the FLA Board of Directors and contained in a binding Monitoring Services Agreement signed by the company and the FLA Executive Director. The progress of the company is tracked by FLA staff who in turn report to the Monitoring Committee of the Board of Directors. At the end of the implementation period, a full review of the companies' performance is conducted by FLA staff who decide whether to recommend the company to the Board of Directors for accreditation. The Accreditation Reviews are now also published on the FLA website.[25]

5　Critical assessment of the FLA

The transparency of the FLA accountability mechanisms should prevent any significant departure from the FLA Charter requirements. In practice, though, there are some areas of weakness. While the system of tripartite Board representation depends on creative tension between company, civil society and university representatives, the NGO bench has often been weakened because of vacant seats or overstretched directors who cannot fulfil their Board obligations. This imbalance is even more noticeable at the committee level where specific technical knowledge and a substantial time commitment are required. The specific timeframes for submitting monitoring reports, corrective action plans and updates and publishing tracking charts have proven hard to maintain and all parties (independent auditors, supplier and brand representatives and FLA staff) often run well behind schedule. The result is that many issues are not remedied or reported in a timely fashion and this leaves the interested observer in some doubt as to the status of the remediation. Finally, reporting is a necessary but insufficient condition for accountability. The FLA reports extensively on company performance but if external stakeholders do not engage and use that information (or lack of it) to drive accountability, then transparency and accountability remain somewhat theoretical.

There are also limits to what the third-party complaints procedure can achieve. While the complaints process has proven to be very effective when the member company concerned cooperates fully and the complainants are well organized, there are a substantial number of cases where the system has not worked because one of those conditions was absent. Of the 23 cases that were lodged between February 2012 and February 2015, 16 were not accepted.[26] A particular feature worth noting about the operation of the third-party complaint system is that a number of complaints were lodged by member companies themselves in order to clear up allegations of FLA Charter non-compliance at supplier facilities. In this way, the buyer is able to commission an independent investigation to resolve controversies concerning a supplier.

6 Conclusion

There has been a wide range of initiatives in recent years, all designed to bring together different stakeholders to prevent violations of workers' rights in global supply chains, and it is clear that this is a work in progress. After 20 years of implementing codes of conduct, violations of human and labour rights continue to be found in every audit conducted by the FLA. This is not to say that such initiatives have failed, only that protecting rights in global supply chains is a process of progressive realization. The monitoring initiatives help to internalize human rights norms within corporations and confirm that corporations have duties with respect to shareholders *and* stakeholders, including workers in their supply chain. These processes help to shape the standards of care that are legally expected of business,[27] particularly with regard to workers. Unfortunately, not all initiatives have the same criteria for participation and certification or accreditation and there are significant differences that create code confusion and fatigue, as well as cynicism. Suppliers and consumers alike expect brands and retailers to handle human rights questions consistently and fairly but there is as yet no definitive model for doing so. The FLA is one example of how corporations can be both *principally* and '*principledly*' engaged in the business of human rights.

Notes

1   B. Wallace, '70 Immigrants Found in Raid on Sweatshop/Thai Workers Tell Horror Stories of Captivity', *San Francisco Gate*, 4 August 1995, www.sfgate.com/news/article/70-Immigrants-Found-In-Raid-on-Sweatshop-Thai-3026921.php; S. Strom, 'A Sweetheart Becomes Suspect: Looking behind Those Kathie Lee Labels', *New York Times*, 27 June 1996, www.nytimes.com/1996/06/27/business/a-sweetheart-becomes-suspect-looking-behind-those-kathie-lee-labels.html.
2   D.L. Spar, 'The Spotlight and the Bottom Line: How Multinationals Export Human Rights', *Foreign Affairs*, March–April 1998, www.foreignaffairs.com/articles/53800/debora-l-spar/the-spotlight-and-the-bottom-line-how-multinationals-export-huma.
3   R.M. DeWinter-Schmitt, 'Business as Usual? The Mobilization of the Anti-Sweatshop Movement and the Social Construction of Corporate Identity', PhD thesis, The American University (2007) p. 206.
4   P.J. McDonnell and P. Feldman, 'New Approaches to Sweatshop Problem Urged', *Los Angeles Times*, 16 August 1995, http://articles.latimes.com/1995-08-16/news/mn-35752_1_el-monte.
5   See, e.g. Strom, 'A Sweetheart Becomes Suspect'. In 2006, the National Labor Committee made fresh allegations concerning child labour against Walmart and other companies: National Labor Committee, *Child Labor Is Back: Children Are Again Sewing Clothes for Major US Companies* (2006).
6   US Department of Labor, Bureau of International Labor Affairs, *The Apparel Industry and Codes of Conduct: A Solution to the International Child Labor Problem?* (1995).
7   See, e.g. Institute for Global Labour and Human Rights, 'Behind the Labels: Made in China', 1 March 1998, www.globallabourrights.org/reports/behind-the-labels-made-in-china.
8   See R.A. Greenwald, 'Labor, Liberals, and Sweatshops', in D.E. Bender and R.A. Greenwald (eds), *Sweatshop USA: The American Sweatshop in Historical and Global Perspective* (New York: Routledge, 2003) pp. 77, 80–1.
9   US House of Representatives, Committee on International Relations, Subcommittee on International Operations and Human Rights, 'Child Labor Hearings', 104th Cong., 2nd sess., 11 and 15 June 1996, www.archive.org/stream/childlaborhearin00unit/childlaborhearin00unit_djvu.txt.
10 Rugmark (now known as GoodWeave) is a network of non-profit organizations working at ending illegal child labour in the rug-making industry. It provides a certification programme that allows companies that pass inspection to attach a logo certifying that their product is made without child labour. See GoodWeave, www.goodweave.org.
11 P. Lewis, 'US Provides First Details of Its Business Ethics Code', *New York Times*, 27 May 1996, www.nytimes.com/1995/05/27/business/us-provides-first-details-of-its-business-ethics-code.html.
12 Apparel Industry Partnership's Agreement, 'Workplace Code of Conduct', www.uiweb.uidaho.edu/fcs223/AIP%20Workplace%20Code%20of%20Conduct.htm.
13 See 26 USC §501(c)(3).
14 For a discussion of the build-up of the anti-sweatshop movement, see DeWinter-Schmitt, 'Business as Usual?'.
15 Fair Labor Association (FLA), 'Affiliates', www.fairlabor.org/affiliates?page=10.
16 FLA, 'Charter Document' (as amended 12 February 2014), www.fairlabor.org/sites/default/files/fla_charter_2-12-14.pdf.
17 S. Greenhouse, 'Nike Shoe Plant in Vietnam Is Called Unsafe for Workers', *New York Times*, 8 November 1997, www.nytimes.com/1997/11/08/business/nike-shoe-plant-in-vietnam-is-called-unsafe-for-workers.html.
18 Letter from L. Golodner *et al.* to P. Knight, 29 January 1999, www.saigon.com/nike/aipletter.html.
19 See US Department of Labor, 'Apparel Industry Partnership's Agreement', http://training.itcilo.it/actrav_cdrom1/english/global/guide/apparell.htm. See also FLA, 'Workplace Code of Conduct and Compliance Benchmarks', www.fairlabor.org/sites/default/files/fla_complete_code_and_benchmarks.pdf.
20 FLA, 'Charter Document'.
21 FLA, 'Tracking Charts', www.fairlabor.org/transparency/tracking-charts.
22 FLA, 'Third Party Complaint Process', www.fairlabor.org/third-party-complaint-process.
23 FLA, *FLA Report on the Closure of Jerzees de Honduras* (2009), www.fairlabor.org/sites/default/files/documents/reports/fla_report_jdh_01.28.09.pdf.
24 FLA, 'Frequently Asked Questions on Special Review', www.fairlabor.org/sites/default/files/documents/reports/special_review_faqs.pdf; Maquila Solidarity Network, *Fair Labor Association lifts Special Review for Russell Athletics Membership* (3 December 2009), http://en.maquilasolidarity.org/node/911; See, for example, the decision of Michigan University to end the licensing deal with Russell Athletic (Steve Greenhouse, *New York Times*, 23 February 2009), www.nytimes.com/2009/02/24/business/24sweat.html?_r=0; Russell Athletic and Union Announce Landmark Agreement (17 November 2009), http://en.maquilasolidarity.org/sites/maquilasolidarity.org/files/2009-11-17%20Jerzees%20Public%20Announcement.pdf.
25 FLA, 'Accreditation', www.fairlabor.org/accreditation.
26 FLA, 'Third Party Complaint Tracking Chart', www.fairlabor.org/third-party-complaint-tracking-chart.
27 H. Ward, *Legal Issues in Corporate Citizenship* (Swedish Partnership for Global Responsibility, 2003).

Section 4.3

The Global Network Initiative: how can companies in the information and communications technology industry respect human rights?

Michael Samway

1 Introduction

Over the past two decades, companies in the information and communications technology (ICT) sector have designed, developed and distributed online tools that have allowed citizens across the globe to share information and communicate in unprecedented and extraordinary ways. At the same time, governments around the world have developed increasingly effective methods for filtering information and monitoring users' online habits and communications. These sometimes competing and sometimes complementary forces often threaten the internationally recognized rights to free expression and privacy.

While the duty to protect these rights for citizens rests squarely on the shoulders of governments, ICT companies are increasingly at risk of becoming complicit in government efforts to censor information and disclose online user activity, in particular in places where the rule of law is weak. This chapter considers the emergence of the Global Network Initiative (GNI) as a multi-stakeholder response to evolving threats to freedom of expression and privacy in the ICT industry and as an initiative designed to encourage responsible company decision-making through developing standards, creating an evaluation and learning process and serving as a platform for collective advocacy.

2 Origins of the Global Network Initiative

Rapid global expansion by ICT companies headquartered in the United States (US) in the early 2000s led to conflicts between US law, other countries' domestic laws and practices, and international laws and norms. Though business and policy challenges from these conflicts arose across the world for the ICT industry – including in places like France,[1] Australia,[2] Turkey,[3] Argentina,[4] Russia[5] and Thailand[6] – the issues for this sector were most acute, and most heavily studied and reported, in China.[7]

China was undergoing significant economic transformation, integrating more deeply with the global system of trade and witnessing the rise of a large class of citizens with easy and inexpensive access to technology, the Internet and accompanying information and communications opportunities. During this period, the Chinese government developed a technologically sophisticated and multi-layered system known as the Golden Shield, which employed technology, manpower and political and legal pressure to censor online information.[8] Using traditional legal and regulatory systems of compelled information disclosure as well as an evermore sophisticated technical capacity for intercepting electronic information, the Chinese government, in similar ways to governments across the globe, grew increasingly capable of following its citizens' activities online. Although a number of Western technology companies had operated in China over the previous decade, the human and machine architecture in China built into and around the Internet created new intersection points between business and human rights – in particular around the rights to freedom of expression and privacy.

A number of incidents in China involving American corporations helped galvanize global public opinion on issues of online censorship and surveillance and possible corporate complicity in the actions of governments against their own citizens.[9] Microsoft's decision, at the behest of the Chinese government, to remove from its local service the blog of Chinese political journalist Michael Anti in late 2005 led to significant public criticism of Microsoft.[10] Google's decision to enter the Chinese market and offer its search services in early 2006, with its announcement that it would limit the display of certain search results based on Chinese censorship requirements, led to similar criticism from media, civil society and the US Congress, among others.[11] Human rights organizations and journalists also noted publicly that technology hardware manufacturer Cisco – notwithstanding its defence that it was providing an off-the-shelf product permissible under US export regulations – was supplying sophisticated network management equipment to the Chinese government, which in turn was using the technology as part of an elaborate programme of domestic censorship and surveillance inside China.[12]

The issue that might have been a tipping point for public concern over the Internet and risks of corporate complicity was the case of Chinese journalist Shi Tao.[13] In 2004, Yahoo!'s corporate subsidiary in Beijing complied with a valid Chinese law-enforcement demand for user account data, which ultimately led the Chinese police to Shi Tao, a journalist who was accused of disclosing state secrets by sending to a US-run website his notes regarding official Chinese press coverage rules distributed by the Chinese government on the 15th anniversary of the tragic events in Tiananmen Square. Mr Shi was arrested and sentenced to 10 years in prison. When his trial documents were discovered, translated and released in autumn 2005, Shi Tao's case gave a name, face and personal tragedy to the argument that US technology companies were complicit in certain governments' failure to protect the rights of their own citizens.

Each American high-tech company operating in China felt pressures from users, employees, the public, civil society and socially responsible investors, as well as from legislators in the US and Europe. The US House of Representatives held a hearing in February 2006 in which executives from Cisco, Google, Microsoft and Yahoo! were excoriated for being complicit in the Chinese government's unjust online censorship and surveillance.[14] Congressman Chris Smith (R-NJ) and others proposed draft legislation to regulate American companies doing business in so-called Internet-restricting countries.[15] The US Department of State, under then Secretary of State Condoleeza Rice, created the Global Internet Freedom Taskforce in the State Department's Bureau of Democracy, Human Rights and Labor to address challenges around the globe to freedom of expression and the free flow of information on the Internet.[16]

International stakeholders across civil society, investors, academics and some governments were increasingly convinced that there was a growing governance gap globally (not just in China) between corporate practices and international and national human rights laws and norms regarding freedom of expression and privacy in the ICT sector that certain governments were not upholding. These stakeholders believed that existing regulatory frameworks, at least as applied and enforced, were not holding companies accountable for their actions and that those companies could be considered complicit in various governments' restrictions of their own citizens' fundamental human rights.

By early 2006, three separate and loosely organized groups – one principally composed of ICT companies and two others comprising a mix of human rights groups, academics and investors – had formed to assess, and try to address, these issues. These groupings of stakeholders generally paralleled the participant groups found in multi-stakeholder initiatives (MSIs) addressing human rights issues in other industries. Although the participants were not in consensus on developing a code of conduct or MSI, each group understood that the meetings were intended to develop mechanisms – whether voluntary practices, industry standards or legislation – to address the issue of corporate complicity in violations of the rights to freedom of expression and privacy. By summer 2006, the three groups, in recognition of the common human rights concerns, growing public awareness of the issues and a belief in the strength of diversity and collective work, agreed to work together in a multi-stakeholder dialogue, with the various constituencies on equal footing. A number of the key participants in the new coalition brought extensive experience from involvement in other MSIs, including the Fair Labor Association, the Voluntary Principles on Security and Human Rights, and the Extractive Industries Transparency Initiative.

The parties agreed that the dialogue would be co-facilitated by the San Francisco-based consultancy Business for Social Responsibility and the Washington, DC-based civil liberties group Center for Democracy & Technology. The Berkman Center for Internet & Society at Harvard University, a co-founding participant in the dialogue as an academic stakeholder, also played a quasi-official and critical facilitating role throughout the new multi-stakeholder dialogue. Not only did the newly formed group have to overcome the traditional distrust between human rights groups and companies, it also had to contend with deep distrust between companies themselves in a fiercely competitive and often-secretive industry.

The new unified group faced difficult decisions around what specific sectors within the rapidly evolving technology industry to include as part of the scope of the discussions. The group generally agreed to consider three broadly defined sectors – Internet, telecommunications and hardware. In addition to the involvement of Google, Microsoft and Yahoo! from the beginning of the discussions, four European telecommunications companies joined the dialogue and remained involved for nearly two years before concluding that the multi-stakeholder dialogue was not in their companies' best interests, leading them to withdraw before the GNI's formal launch in autumn 2008. Despite requests to join the discussion and pressure from civil society and US lawmakers, hardware manufacturers like Cisco did not participate in the dialogue and did not join the GNI, noting the fundamental differences in their business models from the other participants as well as their existing internal and external commitments to human rights including free expression and privacy.[17]

Unlike in some other multi-stakeholder dialogues, all parties in the unified dialogue process agreed that governments should not be participants. This view was taken principally because the participants believed that governments, through weak rule of law in particular, created the environment that led to violations of rights to freedom of expression and privacy and put companies at risk of complicity in those human rights violations.

During the period between 2006 and 2008 – a period that included three US Congressional hearings on the subject of Internet freedom, threatened US Congressional legislation, European Union hearings, an unsolicited bid by one participant company (Microsoft) to take over another (Yahoo!) and deep scepticism among civil society and other stakeholders – the participants continued to negotiate intensively until they finally reached agreement in 2008 on a set of principles, implementation guidelines and a governance, accountability and shared learning framework. The Global Network Initiative launched publicly in October 2008.[18]

Snapshot

GNI membership

The GNI's membership is as follows:

- Companies: Facebook, Google, LinkedIn, Microsoft, Procera Networks and Yahoo!
- Civil society organizations: Bolo Bhi, Center for Democracy & Technology, Center for Internet & Society, Committee to Protect Journalists, Human Rights First, Human Rights in China, Human Rights Watch, Index on Censorship, Institute for Reporters' Freedom and Safety, International Media Support, Internews and PEN American Center.
- Socially responsible investors: Boston Common Asset Management, Calvert Group, Church of Sweden, Domini Social Investments, EIRIS Conflict Risk Network, F&C Asset Management, Folksam, Trillium Asset Management and Walden Asset Management.
- Academic institutions: Berkman Center for Internet & Society at Harvard University; Center for Business and Human Rights at New York University's Stern School of Business; Centro de Estudios en Libertad de Expresion, Universidad de Palermo; George Washington University Law School; Nexa Center for Internet & Society, Politecnico di Torino; Research Center for Information Law, University of St Gallen; and University of California, Berkeley School of Information.
- Individual experts: Christine Bader, Philip Howard, Rebecca MacKinnon and Ernest Wilson.

3 How the GNI developed industry standards

The GNI framework was developed through lengthy and good faith negotiations, which included the inevitable ebb and flow of tense and heated debate and near break-ups. Although all participants agreed to make it their common cause to protect user rights globally, each stakeholder constituency faced both internal and external pressures regarding the shape of the discussions and, in many cases, around continued involvement itself in the multi-stakeholder dialogue. This was the case inside both companies and civil society groups and is a tension that exists up to the present. Given the rapidly evolving nature of technology and online tools, growing threats to freedom of expression and privacy, diversity and difference of opinions of stakeholders, and the geographic reach of the companies' products and services, the GNI's 2008 launch was an important milestone in recognizing and collectively working to protect the rights of citizens around the world using the Internet.

The Preamble to the GNI Principles explains the initiative's foundation in international laws and norms including the Universal Declaration of Human Rights[19] and its two implementing treaties, the International Covenant on Civil and Political Rights[20] and the International Covenant on Economic, Social and Cultural Rights.[21] Though the United Nations Guiding Principles on Business and Human Rights[22] (Guiding Principles) were not released until 2011, the GNI framework was influenced by the work that served as the foundation for the Guiding Principles.[23] The Preamble to the GNI Principles states:

> The duty of governments to respect, protect, promise and fulfill human rights is the foundation of this human rights framework. That duty includes ensuring that national laws, regulations and policies are consistent with international human rights law and standards on freedom of expression and privacy.[24]

The GNI Principles further articulate that ICT 'companies have the responsibility to respect and protect the freedom of expression and privacy rights of their users'.[25] The GNI Principles and Implementation Guidelines take as their starting point international laws; however, they are specifically directed towards the ICT industry and have become standards referenced by international organizations[26] as well as by other initiatives regarding the protection of these particular rights.[27]

Snapshot

GNI Principles excerpts

Preamble

The duty of governments to respect, protect, promote and fulfill human rights is the foundation of this human rights framework. That duty includes ensuring that national laws, regulations and policies are consistent with international human rights laws and standards on freedom of expression and privacy.

Information and Communications Technology (ICT) companies have the responsibility to respect and protect the freedom of expression and privacy rights of their users. ICT has the potential to enable the exchange of ideas and access to information in a way that supports economic opportunity, advances knowledge and improves quality of life...

Freedom of Expression

Freedom of opinion and expression is a human right and guarantor of human dignity. The right to freedom of opinion and expression includes the freedom to hold opinions without interference and to seek, receive and impart information and ideas through any media and regardless of frontiers...

Participating companies will respect and protect the freedom of expression of their users by seeking to avoid or minimize the impact of government restrictions on freedom of expression, including restrictions on the information available to users and the opportunities for users to create and communicate ideas and information, regardless of frontiers or media of communication.

Participating companies will respect and protect the freedom of expression rights of their users when confronted with government demands, laws and regulations to suppress freedom of expression, remove content or otherwise limit access to information and ideas in a manner inconsistent with internationally recognized laws and standards.

Privacy

Privacy is a human right and guarantor of human dignity. Privacy is important to maintaining personal security, protecting identity and promoting freedom of expression in the digital age.

Everyone should be free from illegal or arbitrary interference with the right to privacy and should have the right to the protection of the law against such interference or attacks...

Participating companies will employ protections with respect to personal information in all countries where they operate in order to protect the privacy rights of users.

Participating companies will respect and protect the privacy rights of users when confronted with government demands, laws or regulations that compromise privacy in a manner inconsistent with internationally recognized laws and standards.

The GNI Principles work in tandem with the GNI Implementation Guidelines[28] and are divided into five broad sections, each with subcategories of obligations for companies to uphold. While the Principles cover general obligations and also comprise the standards by which companies are evaluated by GNI accredited and independent assessors, the Implementation Guidelines lay out clear steps that companies should take to fulfil their obligations under the Principles. Set out below are those broad categories, with a brief description of some of the areas covered by the Implementation Guidelines.

- The *Freedom of Expression* guidelines cover: (a) company obligations for careful scrutiny of, and a willingness to challenge, government demands to limit content; and (b) a commitment by companies to transparent communication with users on freedom of expression risks and company practices.
- The *Privacy* guidelines cover: (a) company obligations around the collection of user data; (b) company obligations for careful scrutiny of, and a willingness to challenge, certain governments' demands to disclose user data; and (c) a commitment by companies to transparent communication with users on privacy risks and company practices.
- The *Responsible Company Decision Making* guidelines cover: (a) requirements for board oversight and leadership; (b) obligations to conduct human rights impact assessments; (c) partner, supplier and distributor responsibilities; and (d) obligations to integrate human rights responsibilities into business operations.

- The *Multi-Stakeholder Collaboration* guidelines cover: (a) a commitment to engage in public policy work advocating for freedom of expression and privacy; (b) the requirements to engage with a multi-stakeholder advisory forum on global decisions around freedom of expression and privacy; and (c) a commitment to engage in external multi-stakeholder learning forums.
- *Governance, Accountability and Transparency* guidelines cover: (a) the commitment to further develop an effective system of governance for the initiative; (b) company and GNI transparency and reporting obligations on implementation of the Principles; and (c) the requirements and process for independent assessment and evaluation in order to hold companies accountable.

The GNI Principles and Implementation Guidelines were ultimately developed in a multi-stakeholder setting with a focus on the companies that remained at the table through the GNI's launch in 2008. Although the GNI Principles also apply generally to telecommunications companies and technology hardware manufacturers, the fact that those two sectors either did not participate at all or did not ultimately join the initiative meant that the participants understood that the GNI Implementation Guidelines might need to be supplemented for more specific application to these types of companies in the future. While each company that did not participate in meetings or join the GNI likely had its own reasons for doing so – ranging from confidence in their existing human rights policies to a desire to maintain a low-profile position outside of the public eye on human rights issues – the principal reason seemed to be rejection of the type of framework ultimately agreed across diverse stakeholders for independent and external assessment of the company's policies, practices and results.

Several telecommunications companies, including four European companies who were involved in the early stages of the multi-stakeholder dialogue that became the GNI, as well as four other telecommunications companies, are currently participating in a Telecommunications Industry Dialogue on Freedom of Expression and Privacy launched in March 2013 and is affiliated with the GNI.[29] In February 2016, seven of the eight members of this Industry Dialogue joined the GNI as official observers with the agreed aim that in March 2017 the seven companies would become full GNI members.

4 How the GNI ensures accountability

The most contentious aspect of the GNI negotiations – perhaps the case in most MSIs – involved agreeing and structuring periodic and independent evaluation of company processes and practices, including review of case outcomes, as measured against a set of ICT industry standards. The coalition of diverse stakeholders looked to the monitoring and auditing models employed in other MSIs, like the Fair Labor Association[30] and the Voluntary Principles on Security and Human Rights.[31] However, the independent review process that would form the core of the accountability process and be used to assess freedom of expression and privacy in the ICT industry was, in many ways, a distinct field given the novelty, complexity and global scale of the technology sector.

Issues in the negotiations ranged from who would select the assessors, to what company information the assessors would be permitted to review, to who would make the determination of company compliance or non-compliance and how accountability reports would be communicated publicly. Finding effective mechanisms to review a selection of specific cases, among a universe of hundreds of millions or even billions of users, also presented the group with unique challenges in the field of company assessment. While companies were concerned about the nature of any outside assessment, including of their free expression policies, practices and outcomes, the companies were most concerned about potentially intrusive assessment processes, particularly with respect to companies' privacy practices and outcomes, given the highly sensitive nature of government requests for individual user data from companies.

Ultimately, the participants agreed that an important goal of the accountability mechanism would be to provide practical feedback and guidance to the companies on the most effective practices employed to protect the free expression and privacy rights of the companies' users in the face of threats from governments – instead of serving as an investigative effort focused on exposing missteps by the companies. All stakeholders that remained participants through the GNI's launch in 2008 agreed the process would not be a so-called 'gotcha' or 'name and shame' exercise.

Civil society and investor groups in the dialogue emphasized that a credible accountability process required tangible consequences for companies that did not achieve compliance with the standards over time. A determination of non-compliance can eventually lead to a company's removal from GNI and criticism from internal and external stakeholders at the company's failure to satisfy its obligations to its users as set out in the GNI Principles. Conversely, a determination of compliance with the GNI Principles would provide to the public, and in particular to a company's users, a strong sense that a company is making substantial and effective efforts to protect the free expression and privacy rights of its users.

Transparency is a central feature of the GNI multi-stakeholder framework, including in the following ways, among others: (a) standards that require company transparency with users when content is restricted or data is disclosed; (b) company transparency to the public with respect to law-enforcement demands or content-removal requests; or (c) transparency around public disclosure by GNI of findings based on independent evaluations of the companies. All participants agreed on the importance of assuring the public that company assessments are independent, expert, credible and focused on a meaningful examination of company policy, practice and the outcomes of company decisions. Another area of tension between the companies and other participants was the level of detailed reporting that would be made available to the public regarding the assessment results.

The most sensitive area from the companies' perspective continued to be privacy and the practices and outcomes with respect to government demands for user data. In 2009, Google issued the ICT industry's first-ever transparency report, detailing information about the number of government demands for user data and demands to remove content. Each of the GNI companies now also issues transparency reports – as do dozens of other ICT companies. While a tension remains among GNI participants on how the GNI assessments themselves are reported to the public, the transparency-reporting process spear-headed by Google is now becoming the industry norm.

The assessment process, as set out when the GNI launched in 2008, was divided into three phases:

1   *Capacity building:* In this phase, each founding company put in place internal policies and procedures necessary to implement the GNI Principles over a two-year period, reporting annually to the GNI on its progress.
2   *Independent process review:* In this second phase, the independent assessors reviewed each company's policies and procedures for implementing the GNI Principles. The GNI executive director, with input from the GNI Board, then issued a report on the findings of the assessors. Learning from the first and second phases, the company participants incorporated lessons in order to develop clear, achievable guidelines for the third phase of the assessment process.
3   *Independent process and case review:* The third phase involved an evaluation of specific cases and government demands that implicate freedom of expression or privacy and the effectiveness of the company's response in relation to the GNI Principles. The assessors prepared detailed evaluation reports based on their independent review, and the GNI Board determined that each of the founding GNI companies – Google, Microsoft and Yahoo! – was in compliance with the GNI Principles. This determination and the details behind this first complete cycle of GNI independent assessments were made public in a January 2014 report issued by the GNI.[32]

5 The GNI's strategic review[33]

In 2014, the GNI Board[34] undertook a strategic review of the initiative to evaluate progress and explore ways to enhance the GNI's effectiveness. The review came on the completion of the first full cycle of assessments of the three founding companies (Google, Microsoft and Yahoo!), the addition of three new member companies (Facebook, LinkedIn and Procera Networks), the intense global focus on surveillance issues prompted principally by the Edward Snowden revelations, and the increasing global threats to freedom of expression and privacy.

The strategic review focused on four themes:

•   *Organizational capacity and fundraising:* The Board recognized, as a high priority, the need to grow the GNI's resources to give it more institutional capacity to pursue its many objectives, in particular in the policy, learning and communications areas. As one response, the Board developed a new policy[35] aimed at increasing and diversifying the GNI's funding sources, the vast majority of which comes from company contributions. Diversifying the funding base means soliciting private funding from individuals and foundations; there is also the possibility of receiving government funding under certain conditions.
•   *Learning and policy:* The Board agreed to redouble GNI efforts as an organization committed to learning and policy advocacy, building on its prior success and focusing on advancing concrete public policy approaches where the collective strength of the GNI will be most effective.

- *Communications:* The Board agreed to a strategic communications plan focused on advancing the global adoption of the GNI Principles and influencing government policy around the world to create an environment in which ICT companies are able to successfully implement the GNI Principles.
- *Accountability and assessment:* In reviewing the accountability process, the Board agreed that the assessment process should be more efficient, effective and transparent and should also be a process that feeds learning among the GNI's stakeholders. The revised assessment process now combines process and case review into a single assessment that occurs every other year. Companies will also report publicly on the assessment.

To concretely reflect the strategic review recommendations agreed in 2014, the Board approved revisions in early 2015 to the Governance Charter and Accountability, Learning and Policy Framework.

6 The GNI moving forward

As the GNI approaches the end of 2015 – a decade since many of the current participant organizations began meeting in small groups to find ways to collectively address the challenging global issues of censorship and surveillance – it faces internal and external challenges. At the same time, and often for the same reasons, the GNI is presented with promising opportunities to make a meaningful and sustainable impact on responsible ICT company decision-making on free expression and privacy issues around the globe.

While an ongoing and even healthy tension exists across and sometimes between stakeholder groups inside the GNI, the collective trust built over nearly a decade of engagement on difficult legal, policy and human rights issues has helped the GNI make meaningful progress on encouraging, shaping and assessing responsible company decision-making for the member companies. One of the GNI's principal challenges continues to be attracting additional companies as members. While only six companies have joined the GNI as full members as of January 2016, the collective user base of these six is in the billions and their coverage spans the globe. Although the GNI has many international participants, each current full-member company is a US-headquartered business. The GNI's efforts in bringing onboard – in each case as official observers for a one-year period – Change.org in September 2015 and seven Industry Dialogue companies from Europe in February 2016 has helped diversify the GNI's membership. Nevertheless, in order to make its message of responsible company decision-making more global, regional and local, the GNI still needs to bring on board more companies, more types of ICT companies, earlier stage companies and more companies from outside the US.

The GNI, like other MSIs, must also develop a more secure, sustainable, diverse and robust funding base. While the companies themselves are likely to remain the principal financial contributors to the organization for the foreseeable future, the GNI's ability to influence company and government decisions on free expression and privacy depends on it building and sustaining the human, capital and organizational resources to staff and finance its core functions. In short, the GNI needs additional resources. It needs a larger staff – currently there is an executive director, a policy and communications director and a graduate student intern – with more funds to attract and retain top talent in the field and to equip itself to shape company decision-making and government policy.

The GNI must also continue to explore ways to make independent evaluation of the companies both efficient and meaningful. The GNI must contain the costs associated with assessment and increase its value through a continued commitment to transparency and an emphasis on learning, teaching, sharing and advocating collectively on the issues that most deeply and directly impact the free expression and privacy rights of users online. The GNI must create a virtuous cycle where assessment feeds learning, innovation and problem-solving and provides a foundation for collective advocacy. Each of these areas must in turn inform the independent assessment process.

Notwithstanding the formidable global challenges to free expression and privacy, as well as the GNI's own current organizational constraints, the GNI has become a leading MSI by increasing awareness of the issues at stake and by promoting meaningful improvements to companies' practices on human rights issues globally. Companies in the ICT sector remain outside the GNI at their own, and their users', peril.

Notes

1   *Yahoo! Inc. v La Ligue Contre Le Racisme et L'antisemitisme; L'union des Etudiants Juifs de France*, 433 F.3d 1199 (9th Cir. 2006).
2   Inquisitr, 'The Economic Cost of Internet Censorship in Australia', 5 February 2009, www.inquisitr. com/17448/the-economic-cost-of-internet-censorship-in-australia.
3   J. Rosen, 'Google's Gatekeepers', *New York Times*, 28 November 2008, www.nytimes.com/2008/11/30/magazine/30google-t.html.
4   J. Katz, 'Google and Yahoo in Battle over Internet Search Freedom in Argentina', Finding Dulcinea, 17 November 2008, www.findingdulcinea.com/news/technology/2008/November/Google-and-Yahoo-in-Battle-over-Internet-Search-Freedom-in-Argentina.html.
5   BBC, 'Russia Internet Blacklist Law Takes Effect', 1 November 2012, www.bbc.com/news/technology-20096274.
6   O. Luft, 'Thai Government Tries to Shut down 400 Websites', *Guardian*, 3 September 2008, www.theguardian.com/media/2008/sep/03/digitalmedia.thailand.
7   OpenNet, *Internet Filtering in China in 2004–2005: A Country Study* (14 April 2005), https://opennet.net/studies/china.
8   X. Qiang, 'How China's Internet Police Control Speech on the Internet', Radio Free Asia, 24 November 2008, www.rfa.org/english/commentaries/china_internet-11242008134108.html.
9   Human Rights Watch, *'Race to the Bottom': Corporate Complicity in Chinese Internet Censorship* (Vol. 18, No. 8(C), August 2006), www.hrw.org/reports/2006/china0806/china0806web.pdf.
10 R. MacKinnon, 'Microsoft Takes down Chinese Blogger', RConversation, 2 January 2006, http://rconversation.blogs.com/rconversation/2006/01/microsoft_takes.html.
11 C. Thompson, 'Google's China Problem (and China's Google Problem)', *New York Times*, 23 April 2006, www.nytimes.com/2006/04/23/magazine/23google.html.
12 S.L. Stirland, 'Cisco Leak: Great Firewall of China Was a Chance to Sell More Routers', Wired, 20 May 2008, www.wired.com/2008/05/leaked-cisco-do.
13 R. MacKinnon, 'Shi Tao, Yahoo!, and the Lessons for Corporate Social Responsibility' (Working Paper, 30 December 2007), http://rconversation.blogs.com/YahooShiTaoLessons.pdf.
14 T. Zeller Jr., 'House Member Criticizes Internet Companies for Practices in China', *New York Times*, 15 February 2006, www.nytimes.com/2006/02/15/technology/15cnd-internet.html.
15 S. Stecklow, 'Bill Would Curb Exports of Spyware', *Wall Street Journal*, 1 December 2011, www.wsj.com/articles/SB10001424052970204012004577070280402066106.
16 US Department of State, Global Internet Freedom Task Force (Archive), http://2001-2009.state.gov/g/drl/lbr/c26696.htm.
17 J. Earnhardt, 'Cisco Q&A on China and Censorship', Cisco Blogs, 2 March 2006, http://blogs.cisco.com/gov/cisco_qa_on_china_and_censorship. See also S. Finkelstein, 'The Difference between Politics and Pornography Is a Social One', *Guardian*, 29 May 2008, www.theguardian.com/technology/2008/may/29/censorship.humanrights.
18 Global Network Initiative, 'Diverse Coalition Launches New Effort to Respond to Government Censorship and Threats to Privacy', press release, 26 October 2008, www.globalnetworkinitiative.org/newsandevents/Diverse_Coalition_Launches_New_Effort_To_Respond_to_Government_Censorship_and_Threats_to_Privacy.php.

19 Paris, 10 December 1948, GA Res. 217A (III).
20 New York, 16 December 1966, in force 23 March 1976, 999 UNTS 171.
21 New York, 16 December 1966, in force 3 January 1976, 999 UNTS 3.
22 Human Rights Council, 'Guiding Principles on Business and Human Rights: Implementing the United Nations "Protect, Respect, Remedy" Framework', Report of the Special Representative of the Secretary-General on the Issue of Human Rights and Transnational Corporations and Other Business Enterprises, UN Doc. A/HRC/17/31 (21 March 2011).
23 Some of the language in the GNI Principles is indicative of the 'Protect, Respect, Remedy' formula established in the Guiding Principles. See Special Representative of the Secretary-General on Human Rights and Transnational Corporations and Other Business Enterprises, *The UN 'Protect, Respect and Remedy' Framework for Business and Human Rights* (September 2010), http://198.170.85.29/Ruggie-protect-respect-remedy-framework.pdf.
24 GNI Principles, 'Preamble', https://globalnetworkinitiative.org/principles/index.php.
25 Ibid.
26 See Human Rights Council, 'The Right to Privacy in the Digital Age', UN Doc. A/HRC/27/37 (30 June 2014), www.ohchr.org/EN/HRBodies/HRC/RegularSessions/Session27/Documents/A.HRC.27.37_en.pdf.
27 See, e.g. Ranking Digital Rights, 'Our Mission', https://rankingdigitalrights.org.
28 GNI Implementation Guidelines, https://globalnetworkinitiative.org/implementationguidelines/index.php.
29 Telecommunications Industry Dialogue, http://telecomindustrydialogue.org.
30 Fair Labor Association, www.fairlabor.org.
31 Voluntary Principles on Security and Human Rights, www.voluntaryprinciples.org.
32 Global Network Initiative, *2013 Annual Report: Protecting and Advancing Freedom of Expression and Privacy in Information and Communication Technologies* (2013), http://globalnetworkinitiative.org/sites/default/files/2013%20Annual%20Report.pdf.
33 Global Network Initiative, 'GNI Strategic Review: Outcomes and Next Steps', 7 April 2015, http://globalnetworkinitiative.org/news/gni-strategic-review-outcomes-and-next-steps.
34 The author was engaged by the GNI Board to assist with the Strategic Review.
35 Global Network Initiative, 'GNI Fundraising Policy and Procedure', https://globalnetworkinitiative.org/sites/default/files/GNI%20Fundraising%20Policy%20and%20Procedure%20-%20Final.pdf.

Section 4.4

Extractives and multi-stakeholder initiatives: the Voluntary Principles on Security and Human Rights; the Extractive Industries Transparency Initiative; the Kimberley Process Certification Scheme

Scott Jerbi

1 Introduction

Leading companies from the extractives sector have been among the most actively involved in the development of multi-stakeholder initiatives (MSIs). These initiatives, which see governments, firms and civil society actors working collaboratively as co-participants, tend to focus on responding to dilemmas associated with extractive operations in areas experiencing conflict and in countries with weak governance systems. Companies from extractive industries have caused or contributed to tensions at local or national levels leading to conflict and human rights violations in a significant number of cases. A 2012 report sponsored by the United Nations (UN) and European Union (EU) identified a number of drivers of conflicts linked to the extractives sector including: poor engagement with communities and other stakeholders, inadequate benefit sharing, mismanagement of funds and weak institutional and legal frameworks.[1]

This chapter looks at three MSIs established to address such issues: the Voluntary Principles on Security and Human Rights (VPs); the Extractive Industries Transparency Initiative (EITI); and the Kimberley Process Certification Scheme (KPCS). The chapter briefly discusses the origins of these initiatives, all of which were created in the period 2000–03. Each section provides an overview of the approach the respective MSIs take to questions of standards and governance. Concluding reflections focus on commonly referenced criticisms facing these MSIs as well as future prospects. It should be noted that while each of the initiatives discussed is unique in its mandate and governance structure, all are of particular relevance in better understanding the appropriate human rights roles and responsibilities of the extractives sector.

2 The Voluntary Principles on Security and Human Rights

2.1 Origins

The VPs[2] were launched in 2000 by the governments of the United States (US) and United Kingdom (UK) with a small group of extractive industry leaders and nongovernmental organizations (NGOs). Companies such as BP, Chevron and Royal Dutch Shell were increasingly aware at the time of the legal and reputational risks associated with reliance on public and private security forces to protect operations in multiple operating environments, often in countries facing conflict or weak governance. This reality made the aim of shared industry standards on security matters a subject of growing urgency.

The US State Department and the UK Foreign Office convened and facilitated (often contentious) dialogue between the extractives sector companies and NGOs that originally agreed to develop the new initiative. These two governments had clear economic and political interests in encouraging extractive companies based within their countries to avoid involvement in human rights abuses when operating abroad. For their part, participating companies and NGOs saw benefits from the participation of governments in negotiating the VPs' standards. Official involvement provided additional legitimacy for the new initiative, as well as useful leverage for participating companies in their interactions with host country governments whose own human rights performance affected operational realities on the ground.

The genesis of the VPs initiative is linked directly to the adverse impacts of major oil and mining operations in conflict or weak governance zones. For example, UK-based company BP faced scrutiny in the late 1990s over the hiring of security forces in Colombia known to have been complicit in human rights abuses in communities where BP operated. In its 1999 *World Report*, Human Rights Watch noted 'reports of killings, beatings, and arrests committed by those forces responsible for protecting the companies' installations' and called on oil companies operating in Colombia to 'implement contractual and procedural structures to ensure respect for human rights as a result of their security arrangements'.[3] Similarly, Royal Dutch Shell faced public criticisms of its operations in the Niger Delta, including alleged involvement in the 1995 execution by a Nigerian military tribunal of activist Ken Saro-Wiwa, who had led a campaign demanding action in response to the negative environmental and social impacts of oil companies operating in the region. Lawsuits brought against Shell in US courts alleged that company officials provided Nigerian police with weapons, hired government forces to shoot at protesters around pipeline operations and were complicit in decisions concerning the execution of opponents of the industry.[4]

Snapshot

Participants in the VPs

At present, 28 companies participate in the VPs, including Anglo American, BHP Billiton, BP, Chevron, ExxonMobil, Rio Tinto, Shell, Statoil and Total.[5]

Government participants include Australia, Canada, Colombia, Ghana, the Netherlands, Norway, Switzerland, the UK and the US.

NGO participants include Fund for Peace, Human Rights Watch, International Alert, Pax and Search for Common Ground.

2.2 Standards and implementation

The VPs do not seek to address all issues relating to extractives sector companies and the local communities in which they operate. Instead, those involved in the initiative agreed to focus on creating guidance for companies on managing security arrangements in difficult environments. The VPs are therefore framed around three sets of issues. The first involves criteria that companies should consider when assessing their risk of complicity in human rights abuses in connection with security arrangements, including relationships with local communities and other diverse stakeholders. The second addresses relations between companies and state security forces, both military and police. The third area focuses on company relations with private security forces. The overall aim is to incorporate respect for international human rights standards into company policies and operational decision-making around the world.

In terms of governance, a tripartite steering committee made up of between two and four representatives of each stakeholder group – corporate, government and NGO – serves as the main executive body of the VPs initiative. Members of the steering committee are selected by their respective stakeholder groups that together make up the plenary, the initiative's main decision-making body which meets annually. A government representative is selected by participating governments to chair the plenary for a one-year period. The secretariat manages the day-to-day operational matters of the initiative. This role is currently outsourced to a Washington, DC-based law firm so the VPs themselves do not have any direct staff. Corporate and government participants pay annual contributions for secretariat services.

The question of how participants actually demonstrate that they are making good faith efforts to implement the VPs has been a subject of ongoing debate; the withdrawal of two key NGO participants in 2013 (Amnesty International and Oxfam) highlights the frustration of some of the VPs' participants with this process. In 2014, participants updated the initiative's governance rules and set out a number of expected actions for all actors, including to:

1   publicly promote the VPs and proactively implement or assist in their implementation;

2   attend the annual plenary meeting;

3   communicate publicly, at least annually, on efforts to implement or assist in the implementation of the VPs as well as prepare and submit to the VPs' Steering Committee an annual report on efforts to implement or assist in the implementation of the VPs;

4   participate in dialogue with other participants and provide timely responses to reasonable requests for information from other participants.[6]

In recent years, greater efforts have been made to assess company efforts to implement the VPs.[7] A subgroup of participating companies has been involved in developing key performance indicators with the aim of improving tracking and communication of implementation actions. Greater in-country action has also taken priority in recent years, given the extent to which companies face similar challenges within countries as well as limited engagement on security issues between home governments of extractive companies and governments of countries of operation.

Internal studies indicate that participating companies believe the VPs have provided critical guidance in their operations.[8] However, the initiative continues to be criticized for inadequate monitoring and reporting requirements as well as for a lack of effective accountability mechanisms. In 2013, one of the VPs' founding NGO participants, Amnesty International, announced that it was withdrawing from the initiative. While stressing that it remained committed to the value of the principles themselves, Amnesty explained that its decision to terminate its membership in the initiative was the result of lack of progress in developing 'robust accountability systems for member companies', which brought the credibility and effectiveness of the initiative into question.[9] Oxfam America also withdrew in 2013 citing

> frustration at the lack of meaningful progress in independent assurance, despite more than ten years of deliberation and discussion.... We believe that independent assurance – as a condition of membership – is essential to building and maintaining the credibility of the VPs and strongly encourage members to push for its adoption.[10]

Other civil society actors have pointed to related concerns, noting that participants' annual reports are not made publicly available and that reporting criteria remain vague. The absence of an external grievance mechanism is also seen as a major shortcoming in the eyes of civil society critics.[11] Despite such criticisms, it should be noted that the VPs initiative continues to expand its membership, with 28 companies currently participating as well as the addition of a number of governments including Canada, Colombia, the Netherlands, Norway, Switzerland and, most recently, Ghana, in addition to the UK and US. The initiative has stressed its renewed commitment to increasing the number of developing country government participants and to developing more effective community and civil society engagement around the world.

3 The Extractive Industries Transparency Initiative

3.1 Origins

The proposal for the EITI[12] was initially presented by then UK Prime Minister Tony Blair at the 2002 UN World Summit on Sustainable Development in Johannesburg. The EITI's founding principles were agreed in 2003 at a meeting between the original country, company and civil society participants hosted by the UK government.

The EITI is not based on a specific human rights-focused mandate, but instead aims to 'promote open and accountable management of natural resources'.[13] It came about in part as a response to calls by a civil society coalition known as the Publish What You Pay[14] campaign, which demanded greater transparency around the relationships between major extractive companies and governments in resource-rich countries. While the campaign pressured companies to disclose payments to governments, the EITI emerged as an MSI chiefly seeking to influence state performance and reporting as opposed to the largely company-oriented focus of the VPs.

The EITI was initially aimed at countries seen as facing the so-called 'Resource Curse', which links natural resource wealth in developing countries with political instability, corruption and conflict.[15] The underlying theory of the initiative suggests that widely available information on state revenues from business activities will improve public financial management, strengthen civil society oversight of those in positions of authority and help foster more equitable and sustainable long-term economic growth within countries. The EITI model sees each implementing country establish a national-level multi-stakeholder group of representatives from government, extractives industry companies and civil society and the publication of reports disclosing state revenues from natural resource extraction as well as company reports on payments to governments.

The different EITI stakeholders voluntarily agree to participate because developing country policy-makers generally see net positive links between EITI participation and greater foreign investment with limited costs of compliance. Industrialized country governments view the EITI as providing an additional tool to change social conditions in some developing countries without direct conditionality. Extractives industry executives acknowledge positive public relations benefits from involvement and believe the EITI does not impede their competitiveness as they seek new sourcing locations in countries around the world, many of which may have weak governance or oversight systems in place. Civil society and international donors welcome the EITI's role in increasing access to information, which supports democratic accountability and encourages governance learning.[16]

Snapshot

Participants in the EITI

Currently 32 countries are listed as being in compliance with EITI requirements, including Albania, Azerbaijan, Chad, Ghana, Iraq, Liberia, Mozambique, Mongolia, Nigeria, Norway and Peru. A country is designated as EITI compliant when the Board agrees that it has met all of the initiative's requirements.[17] The EITI stresses that compliance does not mean full transparency by a country but does indicate 'satisfactory levels of disclosure and openness in the management of the natural resources, as well as a functioning process to oversee and improve disclosure'.[18]

Currently 91 companies participate in EITI, including Anglo Gold Ashanti, AREVA, BG Group, DeBeers, Glencore, Kosmos Energy, Maersk Oil, Norsk Hydro, Petrobras, Tata Steel, Trafigura and Vale.

Current civil society EITI participants include CAFOD, Global Witness, Natural Resource Governance Institute, Open Society Institute, Oxfam, Publish What You Pay and Transparency International.[19]

Currently 94 institutional investors participate in the EITI, including Allianz Global Investors, Aviva, CalPERS, Calvert Group, Domini Social Investments, Fidelity Investments, HSBC, Standard Life Investments and Swiss Re Asset Management.

3.2 Standards and implementation

In contrast to the VPs, which focus specifically on standards that participating companies agree to implement in their own operations, the EITI only requires companies operating in EITI-implementing countries to disclose their payments to those governments participating in the initiative. In other words, the reporting requirement applies to all companies operating in EITI-implementing countries regardless of whether those companies have independently chosen to become 'supporting corporations' in the initiative. The EITI Standard[20] was most recently updated in July 2013, as part of the 10th anniversary of the initiative. Its core requirements for participating governments include: timely publication of accessible EITI reports that include full government disclosure of extractive industry revenues and disclosure of all material payments to government by oil, gas and mining companies; a credible assurance process overseen by an independent administrator (typically an auditing firm) appointed by the required in-country multi-stakeholder group and responsible for applying international standards; and follow-up steps at the national level to act on lessons learned and to review outcomes and the impact of EITI implementation.

Snapshot

EITI requirements[21]

The EITI requires:

1   effective oversight by the multi-stakeholder group;
2   timely publication of EITI Reports;
3   EITI Reports that include contextual information about the extractive industries;
4   the production of comprehensive EITI Reports that include full government disclosure of extractive industry revenues, and disclosure of all material payments to government by oil, gas and mining companies;
5   a credible assurance process applying international standards;
6   EITI Reports that are comprehensible, actively promoted, publicly accessible and contribute to public debate;
7   that the multi-stakeholder group takes steps to act on lessons learned and review the outcomes and impact of EITI implementation.

The current EITI system requires participating governments to complete an independent assessment every five years in order to move from 'candidate' to 'compliant' status within the initiative. This mechanism is not an audit but it does aim to evaluate implementation of the EITI Standard at the national level in consultation with relevant stakeholders. Accredited EITI validators[22] are selected to work with national-level multi-stakeholder groups to undertake this assessment. To date, 31 countries have achieved 'compliant' status and 17 countries are listed in the 'candidate' category, indicating involvement in the initiative without having yet met all requirements.[23]

Since 2006, the EITI has been overseen by a Board comprising an independent chair (currently Clare Short, former UK Secretary of State for International Development) and 20 individuals representing implementing countries, supporting countries, civil society organizations, industry and investment companies. An international secretariat made up of approximately 20 people based in Oslo, and hosted by the Norwegian government, is accountable to the Board. The overall budget of approximately US$3 million is funded by supporting governments and countries and covers core operating costs for the initiative. A World Bank-managed Multi-Donor Trust Fund provides technical assistance to countries in EITI implementation.[24]

An independent evaluation[25] in 2011 concluded that the EITI had established itself as an important international initiative, seen by many as a strategic entry point for strengthening global consensus around greater democratic control of resources. Its multi-stakeholder approach is credited with enhancing the voice and legitimacy of civil society in countries around the world. It is noteworthy that the EITI has been publicly supported by the G20 group of governments and that a growing number of Western nations, such as France, Italy, the UK and the US, have all committed in recent years to implementing the EITI Standard, with a number of others considering implementation.[26]

The EITI has also faced criticisms. For example, it has been suggested that it enables donors to link calls for democratization and 'good governance' with those for economic liberalization. Some argue this in part explains why countries such as Angola, Algeria, Iran and Saudi Arabia, which together represent an estimated 90 per cent of the global production of oil and gas, are not participating in the initiative. Similarly, only a small number of state-owned oil companies are participants in the EITI.[27]

Other critiques have focused on EITI national-level multi-stakeholder groups. A recent assessment of EITI implementation efforts concluded that significant governance challenges such as lack of transparency, inadequate independence and effectiveness of civil society participants and limited monitoring and incentives for robust governance at national level all required action.[28] It is noteworthy in this context that in April 2015 the EITI Board for the first time downgraded a country from 'compliant' to 'candidate' status. It did so in the case of Azerbaijan following 'deep concern' with respect to the ability of civil society groups to engage critically in the EITI process at country level.[29]

Although the EITI does not claim to be a human rights-focused initiative, rights issues have been very much a part of recent debates over its impact and future. In 2013, Human Rights Watch (HRW), which is not a civil society participant in the EITI, issued a report[30] that highlighted government constraints on civil society activities in some EITI participating countries, which are seen as putting at risk the legitimacy of its multi-stakeholder implementation processes at the national level. HRW argued that EITI should incorporate human rights in order to improve governance and that 'transparency alone does not improve governance'.[31] HRW recommended that the EITI expand its consideration of country contexts to include issues such as the environment for freedom of information, expression, association and assembly, in addition to assessing the degree to which civil society can operate freely within a given country. Other recent civil society reports have called on EITI participants to disclose all contracts governing extractives exploration and production and to disaggregate payment and receipt data by project.[32]

4 The Kimberley Process Certification Scheme

4.1 Origins

A third MSI addressing the impacts of a different part of the extractives industry is the KPCS to certify diamonds.[33] By the end of the 1990s, civil society[34] and subsequent UN expert reports[35] had brought to light widespread human rights abuses linked to the rough diamond trade and African conflicts. As Ian Smillie, a member of the UN expert panel that studied the issue and a key leader in the establishment of the KPCS framed the challenge:

> rebel armies in Angola, Sierra Leone, and the Democratic Republic of the Congo – bereft of Cold War financial support – turned to the exploitation of natural resources to finance their wars. Diamonds soon became the most expedient vehicle for purchasing illicit weapons in a post-Cold War world awash in cheap AK-47s.[36]

The KPCS initiative has its origins in UN Security Council resolutions calling for national certification schemes for the diamond trade in Angola, Sierra Leone and Liberia.[37] These resolutions proved ineffective in addressing the connection between rough diamonds sales and ongoing conflicts in these countries. Concerns within the diamond industry about a consumer backlash, as well as fears on the part of producing countries over the potential for significant loss of revenues, brought about a multi-stakeholder process to develop a global certification scheme aimed at eliminating so-called 'conflict diamonds'. The Kimberley Process takes its name from an initial meeting in South Africa in 2000 that launched a series of follow-up meetings to develop the initiative. UN backing for the KPCS and an exemption from the World Trade Organization were both seen as crucial steps in legitimizing the initiative, which, after three years of negotiations, officially launched in early 2003.

Snapshot

A rough trade

In 1998, the NGO Global Witness released a report entitled *A Rough Trade*, which exposed the role of the diamond trade in funding the civil war in Angola. The report was widely seen as shining a light for the first time on the practices of the diamond industry and the lack of effective international controls and oversight.

Along with the work of other civil society organizations and UN expert bodies, such reports brought the issue of 'conflict diamonds' to a global audience and resulted in public demands for action to address the problem, eventually leading to the development of the KPCS. According to the report:

> The importance of diamonds in funding UNITA'S [National Union for the Total Independence of Angola] war effort over the last decade is well known and fairly well understood. Diamond revenue became increasingly important for a number of reasons including the political changes in the post-Cold War era. Diamonds have provided the majority of UNITA's funding although gold, coffee and particularly in the late 1980's wildlife products and timber were all sources of funds. Between 1992 and 1998 UNITA obtained an estimated minimum revenue of US$3.72 billion from diamond sales...
>
> The international trade in diamonds has become a major obstacle to any possible progress towards peace; and has played the major role in enabling UNITA to restock its munitions and maintain a flow of supplies which in turn has enabled it to disregard the 1992 election results and to avoid meeting its obligations under the Lusaka Protocol.
>
> The workings of the international diamond trade are opaque and difficult to penetrate. However, it is clear that 80 per cent of the trade is controlled by De Beers through the CSO. It is also clear that the key role of the outside (unofficial) market in controlling the world price of diamonds needs to be re-examined.
>
> To the millions of Angolans who have survived the repeated years of conflict and the estimated 300,000 that died violently between late 1992 and 1995, the workings of the international diamond trade may seem an abstraction, but the revenue that UNITA has been able to generate from diamonds and the direct and indirect impacts of this revenue are real enough.[38]

Snapshot

Participants in the KPCS

Currently 54 governments participate, including Angola, Australia, Botswana, Brazil, Cambodia, Canada, China, Democratic Republic of Congo (DRC), the EU (counting as a single participant), India, Israel, Japan, Malaysia, the Russian Federation, South Africa, Switzerland, Turkey, the US and Zimbabwe.

Current observers include the African Diamonds Producers Association, the Diamond Development Initiative, the World Diamond Council and the Civil Society Coalition (comprising 10 NGOs including Partnership Africa Canada and nine African-based organizations). Global Witness, a key NGO in the development and early stages of the initiative, withdrew in 2011 over what it viewed as serious shortcomings of the KPCS in a number of countries, most notably Zimbabwe.

4.2 Standards and implementation

KPCS participants commit to ensuring that all rough diamond exports from their territory carry a certificate confirming the origins of those diamonds as 'conflict free'. The KPCS Core Document[39] sets out the initiative's minimum requirements for these certificates and includes a series of recommendations for participating governments on issues such as management of the certification scheme, controls on diamond mines and oversight of rough diamond buyers, sellers and exporters. In addition to imposing requirements on states, the KPCS includes provisions for industry self-regulation based on a system of warranties and verification by independent auditors of individual companies as well as internal penalties set by industry, all with the aim of helping to facilitate the full traceability of rough diamond transactions by government authorities.

The KPCS currently has 54 participants, representing 81 countries, with the EU and its Member States counting as a single participant. Instead of individual companies taking part as members, the World Diamond Council acts as representative of the international diamond industry along with the African Diamonds Producers Association, the Diamond Development Initiative and a number of civil society organizations, all of which participate in the initiative, but only in an observer capacity. The KPCS is chaired annually, on a rotating basis, by participating governments. States including Canada, China, the DRC, India, Israel, Russia, South Africa and the US have served as chairs. Angola chairs the initiative in 2015. Participating countries and industry and civil society observers meet twice per year and take part in a series of working groups and committees.

Requirements concerning legislative action at the national level are a distinguishing feature of the KPCS. In terms of monitoring state implementation, the founding agreement of the initiative refers only to 'review missions by other Participants or their representatives where there are credible indications of significant non-compliance'.[40] Such reviews are carried out by a peer-review mechanism overseen by a Working Group on Monitoring. This Working Group organizes review visits in participating countries and conducts assessments of participants' annual reports. Detailed information on such visits is not widely accessible, thus raising questions about the process and follow-up of recommendations. The process of involving other KPCS participants in the composition of monitoring groups has also raised concerns about the mechanism's impartiality.

The KPCS has been credited with helping reduce the market for illicit diamonds.[41] Yet despite these trends, the initiative has faced strong criticism in recent years, including from stakeholders who played key roles in its early stages of development. In 2011, Global Witness announced[42] that it was withdrawing from the KPCS over what it viewed as a series of initiative failures in specific country situations, most notably in Zimbabwe.

The withdrawal of Global Witness followed a decision by the KPCS to authorize exports from two companies operating in the Marange diamond fields in Zimbabwe,[43] despite widespread violence and repression of opponents of Zimbabwe's President Robert Mugabe. After extensive debate and strong support from African governments, KPCS participants decided that the Marange fields diamonds were not 'conflict diamonds' within the meaning of the KPCS because the term refers to 'rough diamonds used by rebel movements or their allies to finance conflict aimed at undermining legitimate governments'.[44]

In this context, it should also be noted that in 2012, the US government Chair of the KPCS proposed a more expansive definition for the term 'conflict diamond' under the initiative.[45] The proposed new definition would have included situations relating to violence affecting diamond mining areas. However, no consensus was reached on a revised definition at the 2012 plenary and the matter continues to be debated by KPCS participants.[46]

Critics have also raised strong concerns about the KPCS's functioning, for example, pointing to evidence of corrupt bureaucrats providing KPCS certificates without proper procedures[47] and urging more direct links between state human rights obligations and the implementation of commitments made under the KPCS.[48] There is, however, an understandable concern that excluding specific states from legitimate diamond trading due to rights violations may in some cases inadvertently aid those who benefit from illicit trade. This issue can be seen, for example, in the current debate within the KPCS over whether the ban imposed in 2013 on diamond exports from the Central African Republic (CAR) due to the conflict in the country should now be lifted. The CAR is the world's 10th largest diamond producer and experts estimate 30 per cent of these diamonds leave the country without any certification as to their origins. At the same time, the country's transitional government views renewed diamond exports as being of critical importance to restoring its economy and to rebuilding following the conflict.[49]

As one civil society report has summed up the challenges ahead for the initiative:

> On the one hand, the KPCS represents a significant focal point for efforts to stem the flow of blood diamonds.... On the other, it faces serious challenges. Its consensus decision making may render radical change in the KP[CS] impossible in the absence of external stimulus.[50]

5 Conclusions

This chapter has highlighted the efforts of three very different MSIs involved in addressing the adverse impacts of business operations linked to natural resources extraction. In different ways, each of these initiatives seeks to support companies to engage responsibly in difficult operating contexts; all look to establish legitimacy through the negotiation of mutually agreed principles and standards and the participation of civil society actors; and all face common governance challenges on issues such as ensuring active, diverse and independent stakeholder participation, providing robust reporting and monitoring as well as in developing empowered and adequately funded secretariats and appropriate accountability mechanisms for non-compliance. It is an open question as to what extent each MSI achieves these goals.

As a recent conference on increasing the effectiveness of MSIs noted, growing reliance on such initiatives does not mean they are necessarily better ways of addressing complex governance challenges.[51] Indeed, despite over a decade of experience in some cases, MSIs addressing human rights-relevant concerns remain experiments in governance requiring further analysis, greater capacity and sharing of lessons learned in order for policy-makers and other stakeholders to fully understand their place within broader governance frameworks nationally and at the global level.

For example, while the importance of transparency is a key theme and operational imperative for each of the initiatives discussed in this chapter, MSIs will increasingly need to develop effective implementation tools to ensure robust reporting, monitoring and assessment of member performance, which is so critical to bolstering perceived legitimacy and ensuring long-term impact. These initiatives will also need to give greater consideration to how they can play a more active role earlier in the investment cycle to prevent corporate involvement in human rights abuses. In the case of natural resources-related initiatives, this obligation would extend, for example, to the negotiation by countries and companies of contracts for the terms of specific extractive projects.

The role of civil society is another critical challenge for MSIs in this area, given the trend in a number of countries towards reducing the public space for civil society actors generally,[52] as well as reports of growing threats to human rights defenders engaging on issues relating to natural resources governance and corporate accountability.[53] This trend makes effective community engagement and dialogue, which MSIs can help to facilitate, all the more critical.[54] It also highlights the importance of effective judicial and non-judicial grievance mechanisms as set out in the UN Guiding Principles on Business and Human Rights.[55]

Addressing conflict and rights violations linked to natural resource extraction through multi-stakeholder action will undoubtedly continue to expand in the future. National legislation in a small but growing number of countries, regional developments through initiatives such as the OECD Due Diligence Guidance for Responsible Supply Chains of Minerals from Conflict-Affected and High-Risk Areas[56] and new industry efforts point to a future in which all extractive sector companies will be expected to conduct business responsibly and face real financial, legal and reputational consequences for failing to do so.[57]

Notes

1 UN Interagency Framework Team for Preventive Action, *Extractive Industries and Conflict: Toolkit and Guidance for Preventing and Managing Land and Natural Resources Conflict* (2012), http://commdev.org/userfiles/GN_Extractive_Consultation.pdf.
2 Voluntary Principles on Security and Human Rights, www.voluntaryprinciples.org.
3 Human Rights Watch, *World Report 1999* (1999), www.hrw.org/legacy/worldreport99/special/corporations.html.
4 C. Kaeb, 'Emerging Issues of Human Rights Responsibility in the Extractive and Manufacturing Industries: Patterns and Liability Risks' (2008) 6(2) *Northwestern Journal of International Human Rights* 327, 332.
5 A full list of corporate participants can be found at Voluntary Principles, 'For Companies', www.voluntaryprinciples.org/for-companies.
6 See VPs, 'Governance Rules', Appendix 2: Participation Criteria, www.voluntaryprinciples.org/wp-content/uploads/2014/06/VPs_Governance_Rules_-_as_posted_June_2014.pdf.
7 See, e.g. Voluntary Principles Information Working Group, 'Overview of Company Efforts to Implement the Voluntary Principles', http://voluntaryprinciples.org/files/vp_company_efforts.pdf.
8 Ibid.
9 Amnesty International, 'Amnesty International Withdrawal from the Voluntary Principles on Security and Human Rights', public statement, 3 June 2013, www.amnesty.org/en/library/asset/IOR40/003/2013/en/20db4d7c-ee09-4a98-aab0-1016f2ebac42/ior400032013en.pdf.
10 See Business & Human Rights Resource Centre, 'Oxfam Leaves Voluntary Principles for Security and Human Rights Multi-Stakeholder Initiative', 17 April 2013, http://business-humanrights.org/en/oxfam-leaves-voluntary-principles-for-security-and-human-rights-multi-stakeholder-initiative.
11 See, e.g. EarthRights International and the Centre for Environment, Human Rights and Development, *Assessing and Improving the Voluntary Principles on Security & Human Rights: Lessons from the Nigerian Experience* (2013), http://dg5vd3ocj3r4t.cloudfront.net/sites/default/files/documents/assessing-and-improving-voluntary-principles.pdf. See also S. Tripathi, 'Have the Voluntary Principles Realized Their Full Potential?' Institute for Human Rights and Business, 17 March 2010, www.ihrb.org/commentary/voluntary-principles-10th-anniversary.html.

12   Extractive Industries Transparency Initiative (EITI), www.eiti.org.

13   EITI, *The EITI, NOCs & The First Trade* (2015), https://eiti.org/files/EITI_Brief_NOC_FirstTrade_March 2015.pdf.

14   Publish What You Pay is a global coalition of civil society organizations (with more than 800 participants) that call for an open and accountable extractive sector, www.publishwhatyoupay.org.

15   See, e.g. Global Witness, *Building for the Long-Term: Avoiding the Resource Curse in Afghanistan* (2014), www.globalwitness.org/campaigns/afghanistan/building-long-term.

16   Adapted from S.A. Aaronson, 'Limited Partnership: Business, Government, Civil Society, and the Public in the Extractive Industries Transparency Initiative (EITI)' (2011) 31(1) *Public Administration and Development* 50, 57.

17   There are seven requirements for EITI compliance that are outlined in EITI, 'The EITI Standard' (2013), https://eiti.org/files/English_EITI%20STANDARD_11July_0.pdf.

18   EITI, 'Frequently Asked Questions', 'What does it mean to be EITI compliant?', https://eiti.org/faqs# EITICompliant.

19   Some of the major international human rights organizations are not participants in the EITI. In 2013 Human Rights Watch issued a report arguing for greater incorporation of human rights into the EITI Standards: Human Rights Watch, *A New Accountability Agenda: Human Rights and Extractive Industries Transparency Initiative* (2013), www.hrw.org/sites/default/files/related_material/A%20New%20Accountability%20Agenda %2C%20Human%20Rights%20and%20the%20EITI.pdf.

20   EITI, 'The EITI Standard'.

21   Ibid., p. 10.

22   See EITI, 'EITI Validators', https://eiti.org/validation/validators.

23   See EITI, 'EITI Countries', https://eiti.org/countries.

24   See EITI, 'How We Are Funded', https://eiti.org/about/funding.

25   Scanteam, *Achievements and Strategic Options: Evaluation of the Extractive Industries Transparency Initiative* (2011), http://eiti.org/files/2011-EITI-evaluation-report.pdf.

26   See, e.g. EITI, 'G20 Reaffirms Support for EITI', 9 September 2013, https://eiti.org/news/g20-reaffirms-support-eiti.

27   L.C. Mouan, 'Exploring the Potential Benefits of Asian Participation in the Extractive Industries Transparency Initiative: The Case of China' (2010) 19(6) *Business Strategy and the Environment* 367.

28   Institute for Multi-Stakeholder Integrity, *Protecting the Cornerstone: Assessing the Governance of the Extractive Industries Transparency Initiative Multi-Stakeholder Groups* (2015), www.msi-integrity.org/wp-content/uploads/2015/02/MSI-Integrity-Protecting-The-Cornerstone-Report.pdf.

29   EITI, 'Azerbaijan Downgraded to Candidate Country', 15 April 2015, https://eiti.org/news/azerbaijan-downgraded-candidate-country.

30   Human Rights Watch, *A New Accountability Agenda*.

31   Ibid., p. 1.

32   See, e.g. the 2013 position paper issued by the civil society members of EITI, 'Enhancing the Extractive Industries Transparency Initiative', 18 February 2013, www.lutahamutukinstitute.org/document/index/page/10.

33   The Kimberley Process, www.kimberleyprocess.com.

34   Global Witness, *A Rough Trade: The Role of Companies and Governments in the Angolan Conflict* (1998), www.globalwitness.org/library/rough-trade.

35   Letter dated 10 March 2000 from the Chairman of the Security Council Committee established pursuant to Resolution 864 (1993) concerning the situation in Angola addressed to the President of the Security Council, annexing Letter dated 28 February 2000 from the Chairman of the Panel of Experts established by the Security Council pursuant to Resolution 1237 (1999) addressed to the Chairman of the Security Council Committee established pursuant to Resolution 864 (1993) concerning the situation in Angola, UN Doc. S/2000/203; Letter dated 19 December 2000 from the Chairman of the Security Council Committee established pursuant to Resolution 1132 (1997) concerning Sierra Leone addressed to the President of the Security Council (in accordance with Resolution 1306 (2000)), UN Doc. S/2000/1195.

36   I. Smillie, *Diamonds* (Cambridge: Polity Press, 2014) p. 3.

37   Security Council Resolution 1173, UN Doc. S/Res/1173 (12 June 1998) (Angola); Security Council Resolution 1306, UN Doc. S/Res/1306 (5 July 2000) (Sierra Leone); Security Council Resolution 1343, UN Doc. S/Res/1343 (7 March 2001) (Liberia).

38   Global Witness, *A Rough Trade*, p. 4.

39   See KPCS, 'Core Document', www.kimberleyprocess.com/en/kpcs-core-document.

40   Ibid., s. VI, para. 13(b).

41   In 2006, Global Witness commissioned an independent three-year review evaluating the effectiveness of the KPCS. The report stated that conflict diamonds may have represented as much as 15 per cent of total global trade in the mid-1990s, declining to 4 per cent by the beginning of the new decade and declining further to under 1 per cent by 2006. While pointing out a range of shortcomings that needed to be addressed to ensure a robust initiative, and noting that quantifying the value of the KPCS is difficult, the report affirmed that, 'Quite simply, Kimberley is driving the illicit part of the diamond industry above ground.' Global Witness, *An Independent Commissioned Review Evaluating the Effectiveness of the Kimberley Process* (2006) p. 4, www.globalpolicy.org/images/pdfs/04globalwitness.pdf.

42   Global Witness, 'Why We Are Leaving the Kimberley Process: A Message from Global Witness Founding Director Charmian Gooch', 5 December 2011, www.globalwitness.org/library/why-we-are-leaving-kimberley-process-message-global-witness-founding-director-charmian-gooch.

43 KPCS, 'Administrative Decision on Marange' [Zimbabwe], 001_2011, www.kimberleyprocess.com/en/0012011-administrative-decision-marange-zimbabwecompendium.

44 KPCS, 'Core Document', s. 1 (definition of 'Conflict Diamonds').

45 See, e.g. A. Krawitz, 'Kimberley Process Chair Proposes New Conflict Diamond Definition', Diamonds.Net, 14 May 2012, www.diamonds.net/News/NewsItem.aspx?ArticleID=40092.

46 See Final Communiqué from Kimberley Process Plenary Meeting, Washington, DC, 30 November 2012, www.kimberleyprocess.com/en/2012-plenary-washington-plenary-communique, para. 31: 'discussions were guided by the proposals regarding a revised definition of "conflict diamond." After lengthy discussions, no consensus was reached on whether or not to change the definition.'

47 See, e.g. V. Haufler, 'Orchestrating Peace? Civil War, Conflict Minerals and the United Nations Security Council' in K. Abbott *et al.* (eds), *International Organizations as Orchestrators* (Cambridge: Cambridge University Press, 2015).

48 See, e.g. Partnership Africa Canada, *A Guide to the Kimberley Process* (2013) p. 27, www.pacweb.org/images/PUBLICATIONS/Conflict_Diamonds_and_KP/A_Guide_to_the_Kimberley_Process.pdf.

49 See E. Giokos, 'CAR Sees Diamond Export Ban Lift on Review', Mineweb, 24 April 2015, www.mineweb.com/news/diamonds-and-gems/car-sees-diamond-export-ban-lift-on-review.

50 F. Southward, *Kimberley Process: Observations from the Sidelines – Part I* (IPIS, 2013), http://ipisresearch.be/publication/ipis-insights-kimberley-process-observations-sidelines-part. IPIS is an independent research institute.

51 UK Foreign and Commonwealth Office & Wilton Park, *Increasing the Effectiveness of Multi-Stakeholder Initiatives through Active Collaboration* (Conference Report, WP1314, September 2014), www.wiltonpark.org.uk/wp-content/uploads/WP1314-Report1.pdf.

52 See, e.g. Freedom House, *Freedom in the World 2015: Discarding Democracy – Return to the Iron Fist* (2015), https://freedomhouse.org/sites/default/files/01152015_FIW_2015_final.pdf.

53 See, e.g. Summary of discussions of the Forum on Business and Human Rights, prepared by the Chair, Mo Ibrahim (advance edited version), UN Doc. A/HRC/FBHR/2014/3 (5 February 2015), paras 78–80, www.ohchr.org/Documents/Issues/Business/ForumSession3/A-HRC-FBHR-2014-3_en.pdf.

54 See, e.g. P. Stevens *et al.*, *Conflict and Coexistence in the Extractive Industries* (London: Chatham House, 2013), www.chathamhouse.org/sites/files/chathamhouse/public/Research/Energy%2C%20Environment%20and%20Development/chr_coc1113.pdf.

55 Human Rights Council, 'Guiding Principles on Business and Human Rights: Implementing the United Nations "Protect, Respect and Remedy" Framework', Report of the Special Representative of the Secretary-General on the issue of Human Rights and Transnational Corporations and Other Business Enterprises, UN Doc. A/HRC/17/31 (21 March 2011).

56 OECD Due Diligence Guidance for Responsible Supply Chains of Minerals from Conflict-Affected and High-Risk Areas, www.oecd.org/corporate/mne/mining.htm.

57 See further M. Wachenfeld, L.F. de Angulo and D. Kemp, *Promoting Human Rights, Ensuring Social Inclusion and Avoiding Conflict in the Extractive Sector* (paper presented to the United Nations Development Programme and Government of Brazil, Brasilia, 3–5 December 2014), www.extractivedialogue.com/wp-content/uploads/2014/12/PromotingHumanRights.pdf.

Section 4.5

The emergence of the International Code of Conduct for Private Security Service Providers

Anne-Marie Buzatu

1 Introduction

Since the end of the Cold War, private security companies (PSCs) have increasingly been involved in armed conflict and other complex environments.[1] This is largely due to two trends: (1) the shifting of functions traditionally carried out by the state to the private sector, with the United States (US) taking the lead in the 1980s; and (2) the downsizing of state armed forces after the end of the Cold War. Taken together, these two trends have put pressure on government authorities to make up for security sector shortfalls by contracting them out to the private sector.[2]

PSCs came to international notice in the early 1990s, particularly in the context of armed conflicts in the former Yugoslavia and Africa.[3] They subsequently gained further attention – and grew in numbers – during the Afghan and Iraqi wars of the 2000s. Due to their involvement in a number of high-profile incidents resulting in death and serious injury, notably the 2007 Nisour Square incident,[4] PSCs gained a reputation for providing security services with little respect for human rights.[5] The apparent failure of state mechanisms to effectively oversee and hold PSCs accountable for human rights abuses further fuelled public outrage, leading to claims that PSCs operated with impunity.[6] In response, the International Code of Conduct for Private Security Service Providers (ICoC)[7] and its oversight body, the International Code of Conduct Association (ICoCA),[8] were launched by the Swiss government with the aim of improving the protection of human rights by PSCs.

Snapshot

What's in a name? Mercenaries v PMCs v PMSCs v PSCs

Despite much discussion around the terms 'mercenaries', 'private military companies' (PMCs), 'private military security companies' (PMSCs) and PSCs, a common understanding is yet to emerge concerning what each of these terms mean. Instead, various laws and international instruments use different names to describe private actors offering security-related services on an international scale.[9] For example, the term 'mercenaries' has been defined in the United Nations (UN) International Convention against the Recruitment, Use, Financing and Training of Mercenaries,[10] in the Additional Protocol to the Geneva Conventions,[11] in the Organization of African Unity Convention for the Elimination of Mercenarism in Africa,[12] and in South African legislation.[13] The term PMSCs has been used in the Montreux Document[14] and in the UN Draft International Convention on the Regulation, Oversight and Monitoring of Private Military and Security Companies (Draft PMSC Convention).[15] The term PMCs has been primarily used in academic publications.[16] The term PSCs has been used in the Swiss federal law on private security services provided abroad (2013) and in the ICoC/ICoCA. The Voluntary Principles on Security and Human Rights[17] shortens it to just 'private security'.

2 How did the ICoC initiative develop?

The appearance of significant numbers of PSCs providing services in the context of armed conflict provoked a contentious debate on the risks and benefits of such actors, including discussion on how to effectively regulate PSCs.[18] Investigative reports citing a long string of violent incidents in which PSCs were not held accountable[19] led to public outcry against private security personnel who seemed to be willing and even predisposed[20] to violate the human rights of civilian populations.[21] The fact that many of these actors appeared to evade the usual oversight and accountability frameworks that apply to state security forces[22] further increased public outrage, with some organizations calling for PSCs to be banned entirely.[23] Some authors claimed that PSCs operate in a 'legal vacuum',[24] referring to the idea that, as non-state actors, PSCs are not typically the subjects of laws that regulate public security actors, including both national and international regulation. Furthermore, even in some areas where there is applicable regulation, transnational commercial actors providing security services often have not been held accountable, particularly where the rule of law is weakened.[25] These elements point to the existence of *governance gaps* in the effective regulation of the PSC sector.

At the same time, another, more pragmatic approach to PSCs emerged that viewed PSCs as fulfilling a legitimate role in an increasingly politically complex world. Following this line of thinking, PSCs are well-suited to performing the 'messy' humanitarian interventionist tasks that state military forces do not want to take on, so long as services are provided within an international system of regulation taking into account international norms and values including transparency and respect for human rights.[26] A number of scholars called for the development of additional regulatory frameworks using human rights-based standards with some kind of international oversight body for PSCs in which both state and non-state stakeholders would participate,[27] with suggestions that such a body could be housed under the institutional auspices of the UN,[28] or within unconventional multi-stakeholder frameworks inspired by the emerging area of business and human rights.[29] Furthermore, initiatives were launched by the Swiss government and the UN Working Group on the use of mercenaries as a means of violating human rights and impeding the exercise of the rights of peoples to self-determination (UN Working Group on the use of mercenaries) with a view to clarifying international legal obligations of states in regards to private security personnel.[30]

Snapshot

Nisour Square incident

On 17 September 2007, personnel from the PSC Blackwater, who were guarding a military convoy, opened fire in Nisour Square, Baghdad, killing 17 people and injuring 24 others.[31] Although accounts vary, an oncoming civilian car that did not move out of the way of the convoy apparently sparked the incident. Blackwater's response was considered by many to be disproportionate to the potential threat.[32] After an investigation, the US filed a criminal case against Blackwater personnel, which was subsequently dismissed in December 2009 by a US District Court on grounds that State Department investigators had offered the suspects immunity during their inquiry.[33] In 2011, the Court of Appeal for the Third Circuit reinstated the case.[34] A petition to the US Supreme Court to dismiss the reinstated case was rejected.[35] On 22 October 2014, more than seven years after the incident, one guard was convicted of first-degree murder with three others receiving convictions for manslaughter and for using a machine gun to commit a crime.[36] In April 2015, the guard convicted of murder was sentenced to life imprisonment, while the other guards received sentences of 30 years' imprisonment.[37] However, during the many years in which it was not clear whether the case would come to trial, the incident came to be emblematic of the difficulties in holding accountable private actors who conduct activities extraterritorially.

Against this backdrop, it became clear that a new regulatory approach was needed to establish standards and an accountability framework for PSCs. The emerging field of business and human rights was producing various multi-stakeholder initiatives (MSIs), such as the Fair Labor Association, which offered the promise that something similar and perhaps even more robust could be developed for the private security industry. Such an initiative would aim to overcome two principal challenges facing the PSC field:

- *The problem of perceived impunity:* This issue is epitomized by the Nisour Square incident, which gained further notoriety when it came to light that investigations of the incident had been compromised, casting doubt on whether the contractors would be held accountable in a court of law.
- *The failure of conventional international regulations:* The Draft PMSC Convention proposed by the UN Working Group on the use of mercenaries[38] had a divisive effect on the international community, as it was widely supported by the G77 group of states, but strongly opposed by developed countries, in particular the US and the United Kingdom (UK).

As guardians of the Geneva Conventions,[39] the Swiss government had already led and concluded the Montreux Document, which clarified governmental obligations vis-à-vis private military and security companies in times of armed conflict. In September 2008, at the adoption meeting of the Montreux Document, several large PSCs asked the Swiss government if it would lead an initiative to develop standards and more effective accountability for the private security industry. The Swiss government responded to this call by launching the ICoC Initiative in January 2009.

Snapshot

Challenges in enforcing national regulations extraterritorially: South Africa

Accountability of private military and security companies has been a priority of the South African government post-apartheid. This is largely due to the activities of South African companies such as Executive Outcomes that were founded by former members of apartheid-era South African Defence Forces (SADF), and which fought in conflicts on the African continent.[40] In response, South Africa has enacted stringent national legislation regulating 'mercenary' and private security and military activities beyond its borders,[41] but it has had little success in their enforcement. The laws aim to prohibit mercenary activities[42] and to regulate all forms of military assistance offered by persons[43] with ties to South Africa in countries experiencing armed conflict, including private security services. Taking an approach similar to arms export regimes, the Regulation of Foreign Military Assistance Act (No. 15 of 1998) requires that persons obtain authorization from the South African National Conventional Arms Control Committee (NCACC) before providing military and security services outside South Africa. While wide-reaching in scope and purpose, there has yet to be a conviction under this law resulting from a trial;[44] the few convictions under the Act have taken the form of plea-bargains where defendants paid fines and served no jail time.[45] Scholars speculate that the lack of convictions is due in part to the possibly unconstitutional nature of the legislation, as well as the practical difficulties of enforcing legislation extraterritorially.[46]

3 How did the ICoC Initiative develop standards?[47]

The development of the ICoC Initiative involved two distinct standard-setting phases:

1 Development of the ICoC, which articulates human rights-compliant principles and standards for the provision of private security services, as well as specific commitments by management to support implementation of the ICoC into a company's operations and policies.
2 Development of the ICoCA, or the framework for the multi-stakeholder governance and oversight body tasked with overseeing the ICoC.

3.1 ICoC: setting standards for PSC operations

3.1.1 Process

The development of the ICoC between January 2009 and November 2010 consisted of meetings and interviews with different relevant stakeholders that were organized by a neutral facilitator – in this case the Swiss government, supported by the Geneva Centre for the Democratic Control of Armed Forces (DCAF). This project can be divided into three phases:

1 *Exploratory phase* (January–May 2009). In this phase, different relevant stakeholders were identified and then invited to participate in meetings in which primarily one stakeholder took part, such as members of industry or members from civil society.[48]
2 *Consensus-building phase* (June–September 2009). This phase brought all stakeholders together to discuss and identify challenges posed by PSCs as well as possible ways to respond to them. Of note was a meeting organized by Wilton Park conference services which was held in Nyon, Switzerland. The three-day conference resulted in the Nyon Declaration in which industry participants stated their intention to pursue an international code of conduct compliant with human rights and international humanitarian law.[49]

Snapshot

Nyon Declaration industry statement

> Mindful of the Montreux Document which focused on the obligations of states and situations of armed conflict, and following discussions at the Nyon conference, the industry representatives now present at the conference consider it time to pursue and develop an international code of conduct for the companies themselves in all situations.
>
> Following a collective process involving pertinent stakeholders, we have achieved a broad consensus that an international code of conduct must be compliant with Human Rights and IHL. Further, there is a clear necessity for effective oversight, accountability and operational standards in such a code.

> Together with their involved partners, the Swiss government has played a crucial role in ensuring this process is inclusive, valid and dynamic.
>
> We see this process as an opportunity to enhance our ability to address broader stakeholder concerns and to serve all our clients, government and otherwise, in a transparent, professional and ethical manner.

The industry statement was issued in Nyon on 6 June 2009 by the International Peace Operations Association, the British Association of Private Security Companies and the Pan African Security Association, in the presence of participants of the Wilton Park Conference, 'PMSCs: Working Towards an International Code of Conduct'.

3   *Standard-developing phase* (June 2009–November 2010). During this phase of the ICoC Initiative, the text articulating human rights standards for PSCs was developed. Based on the consultations from the first two phases, the Swiss government and DCAF developed a draft text that was then shared with and further developed by multi-stakeholder participants in several workshops held during this time. These consultations resulted in two draft versions of the ICoC that were released for public comment in January 2010 and August 2010. The final draft was agreed at a September 2010 workshop and was subsequently formally adopted at a Signatory Conference held on 9 November 2010 in Geneva. At that conference, 58 PSCs signed the ICoC and publicly proclaimed that they would operate in compliance with it.

3.1.2 Standards

The standards contained in the ICoC can be divided into two categories:

1   *Specific principles regarding the conduct of personnel.* This category describes how services provided by PSCs should be carried out in accordance with international human rights standards, including the use of force and prohibitions on torture and human trafficking.
2   *Specific commitments regarding management and governance.* This category sets out practices and policies to be implemented by management that help to reduce the likelihood that personnel will violate human rights in the course of their duties, and to foster a human rights-respecting corporate culture. These policies include vetting and training of personnel and subcontractors, weapons management requirements, as well as incident reporting and grievance procedures.

Snapshot

Provisions of the ICoC

The ICoC takes a pragmatic approach to regulating PSC behaviour by both limiting the kinds of activities they can perform and closing some of the loopholes that private actors use to evade responsibility. This approach is illustrated by the following examples:

1   *Use of force by PSCs.*[50] The ICoC takes a very restrictive approach to the use of force by PSCs,[51] limiting it to circumstances of self-defence or defence of

others – a right to use force that all civilians possess. This approach reaffirms the civilian nature of PSCs, underlining that they do not have any additional privileges or rights to use coercive force, and distinguishing between PSCs and state police and military forces.

2 *Subcontractors.* The ICoC includes several provisions to help ensure that all subcontractors are accountable according to the same requirements and standards as the member PSC contractor. Paragraphs 16 and 18 of the ICoC state the general rule that Signatory Companies must require all subcontractors and other parties carrying out security services under their contracts to comply with the ICoC, and that this compliance must be an integral part of contractual agreements with subcontractors. Paragraphs 50 and 51 go into more detail regarding what is required of PSCs when selecting and vetting subcontractors. Paragraph 50 states that PSCs must 'exercise due diligence in the selection, vetting and ongoing performance review of all subcontractors performing Security Services'. Paragraph 51 specifies that if a PSC contracts with another company that is unable to fulfil the selection, vetting and training principles contained in the ICoC, the contracting company will 'take reasonable and appropriate steps to ensure that all selection, vetting and training of subcontractor's Personnel is conducted in accordance with the principle contained in this Code', thereby putting the responsibility on the contracting company to ensure the subcontractor's compliance with these elements of the Code.

3.2 Governance

Once the standards for PSCs had been adopted in the ICoC, attention turned to the development of the oversight mechanism. This task was entrusted to the multi-stakeholder Temporary Steering Committee (TSC), in which industry, government and civil society organization (CSO) representatives had equal representation, with three members from each stakeholder group participating. In order to ensure that each stakeholder group was represented in decision-making, the TSC adopted a weighted voting system that required a two-thirds majority of those members present with at least one member from each stakeholder group voting in favour. This system ensured that no decision could be taken without representation and some support from all three pillars. More practically, the stakeholder weighted voting approach *encouraged consensus-building*, as no decision by the TSC actually went to a vote. Instead, when there was disagreement within the TSC on an issue, the group worked together to find a solution with which all stakeholders felt reasonably comfortable.

While the representatives in the TSC each had a wealth of relevant experience within their stakeholder area of expertise, they also recognized the need for more expertise to develop a viable oversight mechanism. To that end, they reached out to the larger stakeholder communities to create three multi-stakeholder working groups composed of experts in specific subject matters to consider in more depth the following areas:

- Assessment, Reporting and Internal and External Oversight (Working Group 1).
- Resolution of Third-Party Grievances (Working Group 2).
- Independent Governance & Oversight Mechanism Structure, Governance and Funding (Working Group 3).

Drawing on a broader spectrum of expertise, the Working Group discussions helped to lay the foundations for the ICoCA oversight body.

The TSC produced two draft texts for public comment of the framework for the ICoCA, the entity that would oversee and administer the ICoC. The first draft text, which was released in January 2012, received more than 800 comments from more than 40 contributors including PSCs, governments, CSOs, academics, non-state clients and industry organizations. Taking these comments into account, the TSC then held several outreach meetings in May and June 2012 in order to discuss stakeholder concerns face-to-face. The TSC also created several three-person subgroups composed of one representative from each stakeholder group to work on specific sections of the draft text. The second draft of the oversight mechanism framework was released for public consideration in January 2013, serving as the basis for discussion at a multi-stakeholder drafting conference held in Montreux, Switzerland in February 2013. That conference resulted in the final version of the oversight mechanism which was formally adopted as the Articles of Association for the ICoCA, launched in September 2013.[52]

3.3 ICoC initiative: multi-stakeholder decision-making

One of the areas where the true multi-stakeholder nature of the ICoCA is apparent is in the area of decision-making and voting. Both the Board of Directors and the General Assembly have adopted a weighted stakeholder vote approach in order to ensure that all stakeholder groups are able to influence decisions.

For a motion to pass the Board of Directors, it must receive the support of eight out of 12 Directors, including a minimum of two out of four votes from each of the three stakeholder pillars. Since the Board is the 'executive decision-making body' of the ICoCA, with important powers related to operations including financial decisions, oversight functions, membership, suspension and termination, ensuring balanced stakeholder influence and participation is critical to the multi-stakeholder process.

In the General Assembly, industry members currently outnumber by several times the other CSO and government members.[53] If all members voted together equally in one body it is likely that industry interests would dominate and the other two stakeholder groups would not have much influence on decisions. The ICoCA tackled this problem by creating a three-pillar structure in the General Assembly, requiring a majority within each pillar for a vote to succeed. To give an example of how this would work in practice, in the case of an industry pillar containing 150 industry members, a CSO pillar of 13 organizations and a state pillar of six states, a decision to approve certification procedures would require at the most 76 companies, seven CSOs and four states voting in favour. Only in the case of votes to amend the ICoC or the ICoCA Articles of Association is there a higher threshold of two-thirds of members present and eligible to vote, requiring in this example a maximum of 100 companies, nine CSOs and four states voting for the amendments.[54]

4 Oversight and accountability in the ICoC Initiative

The ICoCA created three mechanisms to oversee and hold PSCs accountable:

1 *Certification* is a process where the ICoCA verifies that a member company's systems and policies meet ICoC requirements.[55]
2 *Reporting, Monitoring and Assessing Performance* describes the processes through which the ICoCA oversees the performance of member companies, including gathering data on their activities and conducting field visits, as well as receiving information from the companies themselves on their performance pursuant to a transparent set of criteria.[56] Importantly, under this article, the Board may suspend membership of companies for failure to act in good faith to remedy non-compliance.
3 *The Complaints Process* sets out a procedure where the member company's internal grievance mechanism is the normal forum of first instance to hear complaints.[57] However, in cases where the complainant alleges that the company's grievance mechanism does not offer an effective remedy, or is otherwise not compliant with the ICoC, the ICoCA Secretariat will perform a review of the internal grievance process which could have several follow-on effects, including recommending other fora such as mediation, or offering the 'good offices' of the ICoCA to help resolve complaints.

The Board of the ICoCA is empowered to suspend or terminate a company's membership if it fails to act in good faith to remedy non-compliance with the ICoC, including when it fails to offer an effective remedy. At the time of writing, the procedures for these functions are still under development, and there has yet to be field monitoring or use of the complaints process. These should gradually become available during 2016–17, at which point the ICoCA should be operational.

Snapshot

'Hardening' soft law and the power of the client

Since the finalization of the ICoC, a number of important, mostly government clients have strongly encouraged or required membership of the ICoCA as a condition for awarding contracts, as well as including compliance with the ICoC within contracts. These include the Swiss government, which has passed a law requiring membership of the ICoCA for Swiss-based PSCs operating in 'complex environments' as well as for those companies hired by Swiss entities located in 'complex environments',[58] the Australian government, the UK government, the US Department of State[59] and the UN.[60]

By incorporating ICoC incentives and requirements into procurement contracts, these clients are helping to further 'harden' the soft-law standards contained in the ICoC, providing consequential carrots and sticks that encourage companies to join the ICoCA and to operate in compliance with the ICoC.

5 ICoC Initiative: current challenges

The ICoC Initiative is still relatively new, with the procedures for its oversight functions still under development. However, in the course of its short lifespan, it has already encountered a number of challenges. One significant challenge is the lack of diversity of members, particularly in the government pillar, which, at the time of writing, has a membership of only European and North American governments. Both the industry and CSO pillars have a preponderance of members from developed nations, particularly the UK and the US, but they have been only moderately successful in attracting members from other regions, including Africa and Latin America. Having a more diverse pillar does bring its own challenges, such as fully integrating non-English speaking members in the discussions. The ICoCA has addressed this challenge by using simultaneous translation services at Board and General Assembly meetings – a very high expense in a fairly limited budget. Currently, the Swiss government is providing financial support for CSO participation including translation costs, but the high cost of diverse participation is only likely to grow in the years ahead.

On a related note, another area that is likely to be challenging for the ICoCA is that of funding. To date, the ICoCA has been fortunate to receive generous contributions from several governments in addition to the revenue generated from company joining fees and membership dues. However, in the years to come, when the operating costs of the ICoCA increase as its monitoring functions commence, the current level of funding is unlikely to cover those costs, which will require the ICoCA to find additional sources of income.

Another pressing challenge the initiative has faced in its nascent history is the turnover of Board members. After just a year of operations, two of the four industry members left their positions at participating security companies, which then required a special industry Board member election. Since the Board is very active, losing the experience and institutional memory acquired by a member can be a significant loss. In this particular instance, the Board lost a member who had more than five years' experience participating in the ICoC Initiative.

Another challenge, potentially common to many MSIs, is having strong and equal participation from each of its stakeholder groups. The number of civil society and government members is dwarfed by industry participation but the natural 'check and balance' to this situation is to try to ensure the inclusion and equal participation of a multiplicity of stakeholders in the design, implementation process and governance processes of the particular MSI. Equal participation of all stakeholders is not easily achieved and the power balance may at times veer towards powerful corporate and government participants who may assume principal responsibility for implementing the standards at ground level. The multi-stakeholder governance processes established by the ICoCA is attempting to ensure all voices are considered as equally powerful in the initiative.

6 Effectiveness: what has the ICoC Initiative achieved and what are its limitations?

As a young MSI, the ICoC Initiative has seen the most success in bringing together – and building consensus among – different stakeholders. As such, it presents a good model for how to build an MSI from the ground up. Through inclusive and transparent processes, the ICoC Initiative has developed human rights compliant principles and standards for the provision of private security services, and has developed a governance framework that embodies *true multi-stakeholderism*. Importantly, in carrying out these processes, the ICoC Initiative has built trust across different a number of stakeholder groups, including members of industry, civil society and governments. At the same time, the number of civil society and government participants is still quite small. As the initiative grows in scope and in impact, other relevant stakeholders including territorial states and non-state clients may be less favourably disposed towards the initiative, particularly once the ICoCA's monitoring functions commence.

Furthermore, the ICoC Initiative is not a state enforcement mechanism and therefore does not have powers of arrest or to conduct criminal investigations. As a soft-law mechanism, it largely relies on the willingness of PSCs to participate. However, this 'voluntariness' of participation is diminished as more states, international organizations and other clients favour or require membership of the ICoCA in their procurement practices and include them in their contracts. Importantly, contractual obligations are easier than national law to enforce across borders.

These efforts are emblematic of an emerging consensus that governance of transnational commercial actors, in particular efforts to prevent violations of human rights by private actors, can be more effective when regulatory efforts include relevant non-state actors. In this context, MSIs such as the ICoC Initiative can play an important role in filling some of the governance gaps arising out of activities of these actors, helping both to prevent human rights abuses and to improve accountability.

Notes

1 H. Born, M. Caparini and E. Cole, *Regulating Private Security Companies in Europe: Status and Prospects* (Geneva Centre for the Democratic Control of Armed Forces (DCAF), Policy Paper No. 20, 2007) p. 1. See also P.W. Singer, *Corporate Warriors: The Rise of the Privatized Military Industry* (Ithaca, NY: Cornell University Press, 2003) pp. 9–11.

2 H. Born and A.-M. Buzatu, 'New Dog, Old Trick: An Overview of the Contemporary Regulation of Private Security and Military Contractors' (2008) 28(4) *Security and Peace* 185, www.sicherheit-und-frieden.nomos.de/fileadmin/suf/doc/SuF_08_04.pdf.

3 See Singer, *Corporate Warriors*.

4 See Section 2, below.

5 See, further, Human Rights First, *Private Security Contractors at War: Ending the Culture of Impunity* (2008), www.humanrightsfirst.org/wp-content/uploads/pdf/08115-usls-psc-final.pdf.

6 See, e.g. P.W. Singer, 'War, Profits, and the Vacuum of Law: Privatized Military Firms and International Law' (2004) 42(2) *Columbia Journal of Transnational Law* 521; D. Isenberg, *Shadow Force: Private Security Contractors in Iraq* (Westport, CT: Greenwood Publishing, 2009).

7 International Code of Conduct for Private Security Service Providers, www.icoc-psp.org.

8 The term 'ICoC Initiative' will be used to refer jointly to the ICoC and the ICoCA.

9 The terms as used in these documents are distinguished from PSCs offering domestic security services in areas where security risks are low.

10 New York, 4 December 1989, in force 20 October 2001, 2163 UNTS 75.

11 Protocol Additional to the Geneva Conventions of 12 August 1949, and relating to the Protection of Victims of International Armed Conflicts (Protocol I), Geneva, 8 June 1977, in force 7 December 1978.

12 Libreville, 3 July 1977, in force 22 April 1985, CM/817 (XXIX) Annex II Rev 1.

13 Regulation of Foreign Military Assistance Act (No. 15 of 1998) (FMA Act); Prohibition of Mercenary Activities and Regulation of Certain Activities in Country of Armed Conflict Act (No. 27 of 2006) (Prohibition Act). At the time of writing, the Prohibition Act was not yet in force as it was still awaiting promulgation of regulations by the South African president.

14 Montreux Document on pertinent international legal obligations and good practices for States related to operations of private military and security companies during armed conflict, UN Doc. A/63/467-S/2008/636 (17 September 2008).

15 Human Rights Council, 'Report of the Working Group on the Use of Mercenaries as a Means of Violating Human Rights and Impeding the Exercise of the Right of Peoples to Self-Determination', UN Doc. A/HRC/15/25 (2 July 2010), Annex 1, Draft of a possible Convention on Private Military and Security Companies (PMSCs) for consideration and action by the Human Rights Council.

16 See, e.g. Raenette Taljaard, who uses the terms PMC and PSC, R. Taljaard, 'Private and Public Security in South Africa' in S. Gumezde (ed.), *The Private Security Sector in Africa* (ISS Monograph Series No. 146, July 2008). Other scholars, notably Peter Singer, use the term 'private military firm'. See P.W. Singer, 'War, Profits, and the Vacuum of Law'.

17 Voluntary Principles on Security and Human Rights, http://voluntaryprinciples.org.

18 See, e.g. J. Kelly, 'Safety at a Price: Security is a Booming, Sophisticated, Global Business', *Pittsburgh Post Gazette*, 13 February 2000; J. Kelly, 'Safety at a Price: Executive Protection a Fast Growing Sector in Security Boom', *Pittsburgh Post Gazette*, 14 February 2000; J. Kelly, 'Safety at a Price: Military Expertise for Sale or Rent', *Pittsburgh Post Gazette*, 15 February 2000.

19 See e.g. J. Scahill, *Blackwater: The Rise of the World's Most Powerful Mercenary Army* (London: Profile Books, 2008).

20 Given the large numbers of private security personnel present in the Iraq and Afghanistan wars, it is reasonable to say that the vast majority of these actors performed security services without incident. However, the apparent impunity for those actors who were involved in incidents made the lack of an effective oversight and governance regime particularly obvious.

21 See, e.g. Snapshot: Nisour Square incident, below.

22 See Human Rights First, *Private Security Contractors at War*.

23 War on Want, '"Ban UK Mercenaries" Call after New Shootings', www.waronwant.org/component/content/article/15036.

24 See, e.g. Singer, 'War, Profits, and the Vacuum of Law'.

25 See, further, Human Rights First, *Private Security Contractors at War*.

26 D.D. Avant, *The Market for Force* (Cambridge: Cambridge University Press, 2005) pp. 53–6, quoting D. Shearer, *Private Armies and Military Intervention*, Adelphi Paper 316 (Oxford: Oxford University Press, 1998) pp. 69–72. See also D. Brooks, 'Messiahs or Mercenaries: The Future of International Peacekeeping' (2000) 7(4) *International Peacekeeping* 129; N. Rosemann, *Code of Conduct: Tool for Self-Regulation for Private Military and Security Companies* (Geneva Centre for the Democratic Control of Armed Forces, Occasional Paper No. 15, 2008) pp. 6–7, 24–7.

27 See, e.g. Rosemann, *Code of Conduct*; J. Cockayne, *Beyond Market Forces* (New York: International Peace Institute, 2009).

28 Singer, 'War, Profits, and the Vacuum of Law', pp. 545–7; C. Holmqvist, *Private Security Companies: The Case for Regulation* (Stockholm International Peace Research Institute, Policy Paper No. 9, 2005) p. 46.

29 See, e.g. Cockayne, *Beyond Market Forces*.

30 In the period 2005–08, the Swiss government developed the Montreux Document, while in July 2010 the UN Working Group on the use of mercenaries released its recommendations to the Human Rights Council: Human Rights Council, 'Report of the Working Group on the Use of Mercenaries'.

31 CNN, 'Joint Iraqi–US Review Begins in Wake of Blackwater Firefight', 8 October 2007, http://edition.cnn.com/2007/WORLD/meast/10/07/iraq.main/?iref=mpstoryview.

32 An FBI investigation found that of the 17 killed, at least 14 were killed without cause. The Iraqi government claimed that the killings were unprovoked and three Blackwater guards who witnessed the event reportedly believed the shootings were unjustified: J. Risen, '3 Blackwater Guards Called Baghdad Shootings Unjustified', *New York Times*, 16 January 2010.

33 *United States v Slough*, 677 F. Supp. 2d 112, 116 (DDC 2009). See D. Johnston, 'Immunity Deals Offered to Blackwater Guards', *New York Times*, 30 October 2007.

34 *United States v Slough*, 641 F.3d 544 (DC Cir. 2011).

35 See, e.g. R. Devereaux, 'Blackwater Guards Lose Bid to Appeal Charges in Iraqi Civilian Shooting Case', *Guardian*, 5 June 2012.

36 M. Apuzzo, 'Blackwater Guards Found Guilty in 2007 Iraq Killings', *New York Times*, 22 October 2014.

37 M. Apuzzo, 'Ex-Blackwater Guards Given Long Terms for Killing Iraqis', *New York Times*, 13 April 2015.

38 Human Rights Council, 'Report of the Working Group on the Use of Mercenaries', Annex 1.

39 The four Geneva Conventions of 1949, along with Protocols I, II and III, and associated customary law, form what is known as international humanitarian law (IHL) or the law of armed conflict (LOAC).

40 Specifically in Angola and Sierra Leone. See further Singer, *Corporate Warriors*, pp. 101–18.

41 See FMA Act and Prohibition Act.

42 Defined in the FMA Act as 'direct participation as a combatant in armed conflict for private gain': s. 1(iv).

43 'Person' is defined in the FMA Act (s. 1(vi)) as

> a natural person who is a citizen of or is permanently resident in the Republic, a juristic person registered or incorporated in the Republic, and any foreign citizen who contravenes any provision of this Act within the borders of the Republic.

44 In fact, in the small number cases in which defendants were tried under the law on the merits, defendants were acquitted: S. Bosch and M. Maritz, 'South African Private Security Contractors Active in Armed Conflicts: Citizenship, Prosecution and the Right to Work' (2011) 14(7) *Potchefstroom Electronic Law Journal* 71, 100–1.

45 Ibid.

46 Ibid. See also D. Abrahams, 'Brief Legal Commentary on PMSCs in South Africa', http://psm.du.edu/media/documents/national_regulations/countries/africa/south_africa/south_africa_legal_commentary_by_david_abrhams_2008-english.pdf.

47 See generally A.-M. Buzatu, *Towards an International Code of Conduct for Private Security Providers: A View from inside a Multi-Stakeholder Process* (Geneva: DCAF, SSR Paper No. 11, 2015).

48 For example, the first stakeholder meeting was organized in March 2009 in London and brought together PSC stakeholders to discuss industry concerns and perspectives. A second meeting in April 2009 brought together academics and NGOs. A third meeting between states and representatives of international organizations occurred in May 2009.

49 Pan-African Security Association, Independent Policing Oversight Authority and British Association of Private Security Companies, 'Industry-Statement', June 2009 (Nyon Declaration), www.dcaf.ch/Event/Working-Towards-an-International-PMSC-Code-of-Conduct.

50 ICoC, paras 30–2.

51 Paragraphs 30–2 were based on the commonly accepted standards for the use of force in self-defence under criminal law, and the Basic Principles on the Use of Force and Firearms by Law Enforcement Officials, adopted by the Eighth United Nations Congress on the Prevention of Crime and the Treatment of Offenders, Havana, Cuba, 27 August to 7 September 1990.

52 ICoCA, 'Articles of Association', www.icoca.ch/en/articles_of_association.

53 The current list of ICoCA members is available at www.icoca.ch.

54 Article 6.8 of the ICoCA Articles of Association states that the 'quorum for proceedings of the General Assembly shall be established by the participation in the meeting of at least twenty-five percent of the Members in each of the three stakeholder pillars'.

55 ICoCA, 'Articles of Association', art. 11.

56 Ibid., art. 12.

57 Ibid., art. 13.

58 The Swiss law also forbids Swiss companies from directly participating in hostilities in an armed conflict, www.admin.ch/opc/fr/federal-gazette/2013/6577.pdf.

59 The bidding process for US Department of State's Worldwide Protective Services contracts requires private security companies to be a member in good standing with the ICoCA: US Department of State, Federal Business Opportunities, www.fbo.gov/index?s=opportunity&mode=form&id=6247a35a5d9816a4b5e4f067b8758ecc&tab=core&_cview=0.

60 See United Nations Department of Safety and Security, 'Guidelines on the Use of Armed Security Services from Private Security Companies', 8 November 2012, www.ohchr.org/Documents/Issues/Mercenaries/WG/StudyPMSC/GuidelinesOnUseOfArmedSecurityServices.pdf.

Section 4.6

Standard setting for agriculture

Michael Posner

An examination of business and human rights practices would not be complete without reflection on agriculture, which in many countries is the largest commercial sector. Despite massive migration from rural to urban areas over the last 30 years, in many less developed countries most people still work on farms. According to the Food and Agriculture Organization there are more than 570 million farms in the world, 90 per cent of which are run by individuals or families.[1] This sector is a significant driver of development, poverty reduction and food security for hundreds of millions of people, many of whom live in the most impoverished places on our planet.[2] More than one billion people, a third of the global workforce, earn their livelihood through agricultural employment opportunities, producing 80 per cent of the world's food.[3] In Sub-Saharan Africa, to cite one example, more than 60 per cent of the workforce is involved in agriculture.[4]

Yet for the majority of people working on these farms and/or in food production, wages are low and there is little job security. This is especially true for vulnerable populations such as migrant and child workers. Inhumane working conditions are also a widespread and chronic problem. According to the International Labour Organization, 60 per cent of all child labourers in the world work on farms – an estimated 98 million boys and girls.[5] Compounding these problems is the sheer volume of small and family farms, which makes efforts to establish industry standards and to provide any meaningful regulation or oversight of this industry challenging.

But increasingly, food production and agricultural supply chains are an important part of a globalized economy. Surpluses of cheap labour, easy access to land and climates conducive to food production and improved transportation capacity allow farm products to be shipped across the globe quickly and at low cost. These factors have led to the creation of massive global supply chains in recent decades. Now more than ever, multinational companies in the food and beverage sector routinely confront social, environmental and political risks that directly clash with their business models and pose complicated operational hurdles. Globally, food and beverage companies confront a range of vexing challenges including the widespread use of child labour on family farms, dismal wages, excessive work hours and unsafe working conditions. In many poor countries, people who depend on their land for their livelihood are being evicted by their own governments, which are seeking to accommodate multinational corporations that need land for export farming. Though women make up 43 per cent of the agriculture workforce, they are often powerless to control their own resources and discriminated against when they seek financing and opportunities to purchase land. Global food and beverage companies also use excessive amounts of water in regions, leaving little behind for the local population.[6] These and other challenges have been widely documented by a range of civil society organizations.[7]

To their credit, some of these companies, like Coca-Cola and Unilever, have taken early steps to seriously address these challenges. Two other global brands, Syngenta Seed and Nestlé, have joined the Fair Labor Association and are participating in its standards-based oversight programme.[8] However, unlike the manufacturing, energy or information and communication technology sectors, there is still no overarching multi-stakeholder organization, and no agreed industry standards, metrics or oversight of this vast and critically important sector. This is a gaping hole, and one that the food and beverage industry needs to address in the future.

In the absence of this type of initiative, several civil society organizations have independently developed initiatives to benchmark company conduct across the sector. An example of such an effort is Oxfam's 'Behind the Brands' campaign.[9] Launched in 2013, the online scorecard assesses the performance of 10 leading food and beverage companies across six major human rights and environmental categories. Companies receive a numerical score in each category, which contributes to the overall grade based on their composite performance. The 'Behind the Brands' initiative demonstrates Mehra and Blackwell's assertion that company reporting enables accountability and ultimately improvement on human rights issues.[10] Similarly, the Good Guide rates consumer products on a 1–10 scale based on health (ingredients, health impacts, certifications), environmental (resource use, environmental impact, transparency) and societal impact (worker safety, community) indicators.[11] Initiatives such as these, as well as bottom-up, grass-roots movements such as the Fair Food Program,[12] which seeks to educate fellow labourers on their rights and the resources to protect them, are important and are beginning to gain momentum. Joanne Bauer goes into further detail on the success of the Coalition of Immokalee Workers in Florida to negotiate with growers and retailers to raise wages and improve working conditions.[13]

Notes

1   Food and Agriculture Organization of the United Nations (FAO), *The State of Food and Agriculture* (2014) p. 9.
2   FAO, *FAO Statistical Yearbook 2013*, p. 18, http://issuu.com/faooftheun/docs/syb2013issuu.
3   Ibid.
4   Ibid.
5   International Labour Organization, 'Child Labour in Agriculture', www.ilo.org/ipec/areas/Agriculture/lang--en/index.htm.
6   See D. Hall and E. Lobina, *Conflicts, Companies, Human Rights and Water: A Critical Review of Local Corporate Practices and Global Corporate Initiatives* (Public Services International Research Unit, 2012) p. 9, www.world-psi.org/sites/default/files/documents/research/psiru_conflicts_human_rights_and_water.pdf. The largest corporate users of water are companies selling soft drinks or beer, including Coca-Cola, PepsiCo, Nestlé and Unilever. There have been a number of conflicts in India between local communities and drinks companies abstracting water. Three examples involve bottling plants of Coca-Cola, which led to deterioration in groundwater levels, so that local people, in particular farmers, were left with less water for their own needs.
7   See, e.g. Human Rights Watch, *Ripe with Abuse: Human Rights Conditions in South Africa's Fruit and Wine Industries* (2011), www.hrw.org/reports/2011/08/23/ripe-abuse; Ethical Trading Initiative, *Living Wages in Global Supply Chains: A New Agenda for Business* (2015), www.ethicaltrade.org/sites/default/files/resources/living_wages_in_global_supply_chains.pdf; MercyCorps, 'Agricultural Development', www.mercycorps.org/research-resources/agricultural-development; Grain and RIAO-RDC, *Agro-Colonialism in the Congo: European and US development Finance Is Bankrolling a New Round of Colonialism in the DRC* (June 2015), www.grain.org/article/entries/5220-agro-colonialism-in-the-congo-european-and-us-development-finance-bankrolls-a-new-round-of-agro-colonialism-in-the-drc; UNICEF, 'Factsheet: Child Labour', www.unicef.org/protection/files/child_labour.pdf; National Center for Farmworker Health, *A Profile of Migrant Health: An Analysis of the Uniform Data System, 2010* (2014), http://issuu.com/ncfh/docs/a_profile_of_migrant_health_4.1.
8   Fair Labor Association, 'Participating Companies', www.fairlabor.org/affiliates/participating-companies?page=2.
9   Oxfam, 'Behind the Brands', www.behindthebrands.org/en-us/about.
10 A. Mehra and S. Blackwell in this volume, 'The rise of non-financial disclosure: reporting on respect for human rights', p. 276.
11 Good Guide, www.goodguide.com.
12 Fair Food Program, www.fairfoodprogram.org. See, further, G. Asbed and S. Sellers, 'The Fair Food Program: Worker-Driven Social Responsibility for the 21st Century', Moyers & Company, 29 May 2014, http://billmoyers.com/2014/05/29/the-fair-food-program-worker-driven-social-responsibility-for-the-21st-century.
13 See J. Bauer in this volume, 'The Coalition of Immokalee Workers and the Campaign for Fair Food: the evolution of a business and human rights campaign', p. 175. See, further, Alliance for Fair Food, 'Who We Are', www.allianceforfairfood.org/who-we-are.

Section 4.7

The Coalition of Immokalee Workers and the Campaign for Fair Food: the evolution of a business and human rights campaign

Joanne Bauer

Some human rights advocates working side-by-side communities that have been harmed by business operations have successfully used the logic of the market to shift power imbalances and coax companies into upholding human rights standards. An example is the Campaign for Fair Food (Campaign) of the Coalition of Immokalee Workers (CIW) in the United States (US). The Campaign, driven by farmworkers themselves, has relied on strong alliance-building with consumer groups and human rights activists to persuade major brands to take steps to end farmworker exploitation. Having witnessed how weakly legislation is enforced even in the US, CIW focuses its campaign instead on using contract law to bind large food retailers to a set of rules and standards that determine the growers from which the companies source crops. The Campaign demonstrates tenacity – workers and their allies sticking with the Campaign until harmful corporate practices have ceased and adequate redress has been made. This is significant, since non-governmental organization (NGO) watchdogs, collectively tasked with monitoring millions of firms worldwide, are often under pressure to launch their reports documenting corporate abuses and then move on to the next bad actor.

Until the Campaign, working conditions for 80,000 tomato pickers in the state of Florida, where 90 per cent of American winter tomatoes are grown, were 'horrid'.[1] As the *New York Times* reported in a 2014 front-page story:

> ... crew leaders often hectored and screamed at the workers, pushing them to fill their 32-pound buckets ever faster ... migrant workers picked without rest breaks, even in 95-degree heat. Some women complained that crew leaders groped them or demanded sex in exchange for steady jobs.[2]

Most shockingly, the Florida tomato fields were also the sites of nine cases of human slavery involving over 1,200 workers, as documented by the US Department of Justice.[3]

The Campaign grew out of CIW, a workers' rights movement co-founded by Mexican immigrant Lucas Benitez and labour activist Greg Asbed in 1992 to end abusive working conditions in America's agricultural sector. After a period of organizing strikes, the workers began to set their sights on the market that created the conditions for their exploitation:

> After a decade of brilliant farmworker organizing and direct action targeting growers throughout the 90s – including 3,000 person general strikes, a 234-mile march and a 30 day hunger strike – the CIW identified that the root of their exploitation actually lay in the increasing degree of consolidation in the retail food industry and that systematic change in the agricultural industry would only be achievable through subverting the

mammoth corporate power at the top of the supply chain. In 2001, the CIW subsequently fixed a new gaze on food retail giants and launched the Campaign for Fair Food.[4]

The Campaign is an alliance CIW forged between farmworkers and consumers, including religious groups, student groups and environmental and labour activists. Throughout the Campaign, CIW leveraged the power of brands to change the conduct of the grower with an irresistibly simple idea: to ask fast food chains and supermarkets to pay merely a penny per pound more for their tomato purchases and improve working conditions. They created an arrangement whereby that penny paid by corporate buyers is passed on directly from growers to workers as a separate line item on their paychecks, nearly doubling the pay workers receive. Brands that joined the programme agreed to contract only with participating growers, thereby penalizing growers that did not comply.

It is noteworthy that the CIW consciously refers to its partners as 'allies' rather than 'advocates'. CIW views this terminology as essential to ensuring the relationship is built on a foundation of dignity and equality as opposed to advocating 'for' or supporting a campaign that is only about farmworkers. The term 'allies' recognizes that the Campaign is also about the partners as consumers, as both farmworkers and consumers are part of the larger market-driven food system.

The first target of the Campaign in 2001 was Taco Bell, part of Yum! Brands, the largest fast food conglomerate in the world. When the company refused to engage with workers and their allies, CIW launched a national boycott, which involved four major Taco Bell 'Truth Tours' that ended in protests outside Taco Bell's headquarters in Irvine, California, and at Yum!'s global headquarters in Louisville, Kentucky.[5] As part of the Campaign against Taco Bell, CIW staged a 10-day hunger strike in 2003 and a 44-mile protest march in 2004.

Through these Campaign activities the number of supporters grew; key among them were Interfaith Action, which worked with churches nationwide to pass resolutions supporting the Taco Bell boycott, and the Student/Farmworker Alliance (SFA), which formed in response to the movement. With a presence on 300 university campuses and at 50 high schools, the SFA launched their own 'Boot the Bell' campaign and managed to get 25 of those schools to sever their contracts with Taco Bell. Finally, in March 2005, the effort paid off when Taco Bell signed a landmark agreement to pay the additional penny-per-pound to workers and pledged to work with CIW to improve working conditions.[6] The agreement was celebrated in statements by former US President Jimmy Carter, as well as rock guitarist Tom Morello, one of a long line of celebrities who would come to be outspoken supporters of the Campaign.[7]

In the years that followed, three other fast food chains, McDonald's, Burger King and Subway, joined the Fair Food Program, while the SFA's 2009 'Dine with Dignity' campaign to bring on board campus food providers yielded its own wins: Bon Appetit Management Company, Aramark, Sodexo and Compass Group USA. As part of its agreement with CIW, McDonald's pledged to work with CIW to develop an independent third-party mechanism to monitor complaints. With these brands on board, in 2010 Pacific Tomato Growers became the first grower to sign an agreement with CIW. An even bigger breakthrough was soon to follow: the Florida Tomato Growers Exchange, representing 90 per cent of the Florida tomato industry, signed an agreement to establish a system of implementation for the programme.

The Florida Tomato Growers Exchange agreement institutionalized the Fair Food Program (Program), deepening and expanding the human rights standards of CIW's fair food agreements. A centrepiece of the Program is the Fair Food Code of Conduct,[8] to which all participating companies must submit, in addition to paying the Fair Food Premium, the additional penny per pound. The Code requires that growers observe all applicable local, state and federal laws regarding wages and benefits and equal opportunity and employee and product safety, and contains a zero tolerance policy for forced labour, systemic child labour, use or threat of violence, use or display of weapons for the purpose of intimidation, or sexual harassment. Negotiated among and supported by farmworkers, growers and buyers, the Code is considered a 'living document', shaped by ongoing dialogue and needs. In addition, the Program includes point-of-hire education and worker-to-worker education sessions, which are run by CIW, participatory health and safety committees and a complaints mechanism. It is overseen and monitored by a separate non-profit, the Fair Food Standards Council (FFSC), which also conducts comprehensive audits of the growers.

In this way, farmworkers participated in the design of their own human rights risk prevention and remedy system, and food companies were transformed from once corporate adversaries to corporate allies. As such, the Program is a model for two tools, considered critical in upholding corporate respect for human rights: multi-stakeholder initiatives (MSIs) and operational-level grievance mechanisms (OGMs). Both tools have been criticized as 'undemocratic' and 'replicating existing power structures';[9] OGMs, in particular, are widely regarded as a corporate human rights due diligence function.[10] The Fair Food model alters the power imbalance by empowering rights holders as full participants in MSI and OGM design. At the same time, the model provides incentives for powerful corporate buyers to become forces for raising standards for workers by knitting those standards to improved market performance.[11]

In the words of CIW's Greg Asbed, this is not corporate social responsibility (CSR) but 'worker driven social responsibility' (WSR):

> If a human rights program is to be effective, the humans whose rights are in question must be key players in – the architects, not the objects of – the design and implementation of the program ... The fundamental difference between ... CSR and ... WSR – the difference from which all other distinctions logically flow – lies in the question of who is at the helm.[12]

This WSR model appears to be effective. In its 2014 Annual Report, the FFSC proudly touted the following findings from their most recent audits: zero cases of forced labour or slavery; zero cases of sexual assault; zero cases of violence against workers; and US$15 million in Fair Food premiums that went into the workers' pay cheques.[13]

Despite the establishment of the Fair Food Program, the Campaign continues to pressure additional buyers. Corporate buyers themselves are beginning to understand the value of WSR. In January 2014, Walmart, the largest company in the world by revenue,[14] joined the Program 'without a single public protest'.[15] Walmart is now working with the CIW and the FFSC to expand the Program beyond Florida and to other crops so that other agricultural workers can enjoy the human rights now afforded to tomato pickers.

Notes

1   S. Greenhouse, 'In Florida Tomato Fields, a Penny Buys Progress', *New York Times*, 24 April 2014.
2   Ibid.
3   See CIW, 'Slavery in the Fields and the Food We Eat', www.ciw-online.org/Resources/tools/general/10Slavery%20in%20the%20Fields.pdf.
4   Alliance for Fair Food, 'Who We Are', www.allianceforfairfood.org/who-we-are/#.
5   Ibid.
6   In Spring 2007, Yum! Brands extended the agreement to all of its restaurants, which also includes KFC, A&W and Pizza Hut.
7   Alliance for Fair Food, 'Who We Are'.
8   Fair Food Standards Council, 'Fair Food Code of Conduct and Selected Guidance', www.fairfoodstandards.org/code.html.
9   J. Gordon and G. Asbed, 'The Problem with Multi-Stakeholder Initiatives', Addresses to the Open Society Institute, 11 June 2014, www.opensocietyfoundations.org/events/problem-multi-stakeholder-initiatives.
10 See Human Rights Council, 'Guiding Principles on Business and Human Rights: Implementing the United Nations "Protect, Respect, Remedy" Framework', Report of the Special Representative of the Secretary-General on the issue of Human Rights and Transnational Corporations and Other Business Enterprises, UN Doc. A/HRC/17/31 (21 March 2011). Guiding Principle No. 29 states that OGMs are a 'non-state based grievance mechanism' that is 'typically administered by enterprises'. Guiding Principle No. 20 considers OGMs as a means for corporations to track their impacts.
11 Jennifer Gordon and labour scholars refer to this method of improving labour standards as creating 'joint liability' of the buyers at the top of the supply chain so that they become forces for driving compliance by those directly employing the workers, in this case the tomato growers. See J. Gordon, 'Joint Liability Approaches for Regulating Recruitment' (Fordham Law Legal Studies Research Paper No. 2518519, 2014).
12 CIW, 'Worker-Driven Social Responsibility (WSR): A New Idea for a New Century', 16 June 2014, http://ciw-online.org/blog/2014/06/wsr.
13 Fair Food Standards Council, *Fair Food Program 2014 Annual Report*, http://fairfoodstandards.org/reports/14SOTP-Web.pdf.
14 *Fortune*, 'Global 500 2014', http://fortune.com/global500.
15 Alliance for Fair Food, 'Who We Are'.

Chapter 5

Key constituents that drive the implementation of business and human rights

Governments have the primary duty to protect the rights of their own people. The United Nations Guiding Principles on Business and Human Rights[1] starts from this premise but also recognizes that in today's globalized economy, many governments are unable or unwilling to fulfil this obligation. In a world where global companies wield increasing power and influence, the relationship between weak states and powerful companies is increasingly important. When serious human rights issues arise out of commercial activity, the question is: Who will address the governance gap and take responsibility for addressing these human rights challenges? A range of actors is helping to shape and influence this debate. This chapter examines the roles played by civil society organizations, trade unions, consumers and investors.

Chris Jochnick and Louis Bickford examine the role of civil society organizations that are strong advocates for a rights-based perspective. A rights-based approach is founded on the conviction that every person, by virtue of being human, is a holder of rights and that governments have an obligation to respect, promote, protect and fulfil these rights. If governments fail, civil society organizations can empower rights holders to claim their rights. By monitoring corporate operations through their global networks, civil society organizations have the ability to report on company actions, which is an important part of holding them accountable. By participating in multi-stakeholder initiatives, civil society organizations can also contribute to regulating human rights issues in specific industries. By engaging with companies, some civil society advocates also provide guidance and expertise to companies that are seeking to incorporate human rights standards into their business models.

Guido Palazzo, Felicitas Morhart and Judith Schrempf-Stirling explore how consumers are increasingly involved in factoring human rights considerations into their purchasing decisions. In today's increasingly connected world, dominated as it is by the Internet and social media, consumers, especially younger consumers, have become more sensitive to corporate human rights and environmental issues. Increasingly, they expect global brands to address these issues as a business priority. Palazzo *et al.*, however, highlight the gap between consumers' intention to purchase responsibly and their actual purchasing decisions. They suggest the need for consumers to focus on their own intrinsic values to break current consumption habits that negatively affect human rights.

The role of investors in advancing the implementation of human rights is a rapidly developing field. An increasing number of investors include ESG data – data that captures the environmental, social and governance aspects of corporations – in their decision-making. Currently, 59 per cent of European assets are in sustainable investments while in the United States (US), US$1 in every US$6 of assets in the US under professional management is invested in a responsible investment strategy.[2] Though much of this investor activity focuses on climate change and the environment, the connection between human rights and investments is also coming into sharper focus. Mary Dowell-Jones provides an overview of this developing trend and Mattie J. Bekink examines the need for investors to adopt longer-term investment horizons to allow human rights considerations to take hold.

The global labour movement also plays an essential role in giving workers a voice in the emerging global economy. Empowering workers to organize locally is often the most effective way to ensure that their core rights are protected. Barbara Shailor describes the current state of the international labour movement and considers its future role.

While each of these actors can potentially establish incentives for corporations to make progress on human rights, their success hinges upon the availability of human rights data. Consumers need accessible and comparable human rights data on companies in each industry to make informed purchasing decisions; investors also need to be able to assess the human rights performance of corporations to be able to factor human rights into their investment decision-making. Currently, however, the social dimension of ESG is weakly developed and consumers often have to rely on information from a company's own website. Civil society organizations and the media are assisting in increasing transparency through reports and projects, yet these efforts rarely enable consumers and investors to systematically compare the human rights performance of companies.[3] Developing industry standards and key performance indicators to measure the degree of compliance with particular standards would create comparable data to empower consumers, investors and civil society/labour organizations to differentiate their purchasing, investing and campaigning strategies. The development of such indices will be an important part of the future of business and human rights.

Notes

1   Human Rights Council, 'Guiding Principles on Business and Human Rights: Implementing the United Nations "Protect, Respect and Remedy" Framework', Report of the Special Representative of the Secretary-General on the issue of Human Rights and Transnational Corporations and Other Business Enterprises, UN Doc. A/HRC/17/31 (21 March 2011).
2   US SIF Foundation, *Report on US Sustainable, Responsible and Impact Investing Trends* (10th ed., 2014) pp. 12–13, www.ussif.org/Files/Publications/SIF_Trends_14.F.E.S.pdf.
3   A notable exception is Oxfam's 'Behind the Brands' project, which assesses the agricultural sourcing policies of the world's 10 largest food and beverage companies: www.behindthebrands.org.

Section 5.1

The role of civil society in business and human rights

Chris Jochnick and Louis Bickford

1 Introduction

Civil society organizations (CSOs) play a critical role in promoting and ensuring human rights with respect to companies. The work of CSOs in business and human rights (BHR) has become all the more important in light of the shrinking influence of governments and the growing power of multinational companies. CSOs have flourished in number and influence over the past three decades and are commonly viewed as a third pillar or 'third force' alongside the public and private sectors.[1] This chapter provides background on the ebb and flow of corporate–civil society engagement; a breakdown of civil society actors; common approaches to corporate advocacy and engagement; and future challenges and opportunities for corporate watchdogs.

2 History of civil society–corporate engagement

Alongside great wealth and progress, corporations have long brought violence, exploitation and protests. Modern civil society debates over BHR echo these original struggles. The abuses of the British and Dutch East India companies provoked church protests and consumer boycotts in 17th-century Britain and 18th-century Massachusetts, and gave rise to the Boston Tea Party. The rise of powerful independent corporations in the late 19th century provoked a wave of bloody worker–company confrontations and led to the modern-day labour movement.[2] In the 20th century, corporations were implicated in various anti-colonial struggles and coups in places like Cuba, Haiti, Zaire, Nicaragua, Guatemala and Chile.[3]

Today's corporate campaigns are fought over similar issues – exploitation of natural resources, land grabs, abuses of workers and communities and corruption. Organized campaigning by corporate watchdogs emerged in the late 1960s and 1970s. In the United States (US), Cesar Chavez led boycotts against the grape industry, Ralph Nader targeted General Motors and the auto industry and Saul Alinsky launched one of the first shareholder activist campaigns against Eastman Kodak.[4] As new technologies and liberalized trade spurred multinational corporate expansion, it also paved the way for North–South collaboration among civil society groups. Early global campaigns were fought over ITT Corporation's role in the Chilean coup, foreign investments in apartheid South Africa, the use of sweatshop labour by the likes of Nike and Gap, Dow's production of napalm for use in Vietnam and the horrific chemical explosion killing thousands in Bhopal, India. The apex of these campaigns was reached around the anti-globalization protests in Seattle in 1999, where the full range of activists and corporate targets were on display.[5]

Despite the evident connection to human rights, the mainstream human rights movement was largely absent from these early corporate campaigns. As a product of Cold War politics, Western funding and liberal ideologies, mainstream human rights groups adopted a narrow vision of human rights that was limited to state actors and largely excluded economic and social rights (the terrain of most corporate abuses).[6] It took the high-profile killing of Shell Oil campaigners Ken Saro-Wiwa and others in Nigeria in 1996 to spark significant interest among the likes of Amnesty International (Amnesty) and Human Rights Watch (HRW).[7] Early forays into the corporate sphere by these groups focused on the repression of individual activists, rather than the underlying corporate abuses, and BHR never became more than a marginal activity. More robust corporate advocacy instead came from a new wave of Southern-based human rights groups, with closer ties to local communities and social movements, and which were open to challenging the full range of corporate abuses as matters of human rights.

3 Composition of BHR-focused CSOs

The international human rights movement currently comprises hundreds if not thousands of organizations, from small grass-roots civil society groups to large international players.[8] These include a visible and influential set of formal and professionalized non-governmental organizations (NGOs) that self-identify as 'human rights organizations' and operate at various levels of engagement (international, regional, national) and have different theories of change and strategies.[9]

3.1 Non-governmental organizations

The story of human rights-based NGOs can be traced back to abolitionist groups acting throughout the world in the 19th century, as well as the international Anti-Slavery Society, founded in Britain in 1839.[10] In the 20th century, a global human rights system began to emerge that included national NGOs that worked to document human rights abuses in their home countries, and international NGOs (INGOs) that could operate from the relative safety and security of Northern headquarters, such as New York or London, while partnering with national and regional groups in the global South.[11]

National NGOs are widely diverse, from small grass-roots or highly localized groups and associations, to better-resourced, more internationally connected organizations that often serve as bridges or 'translators' between international institutions and national concerns.[12] Importantly, the flow of information, ideas and innovation in the human rights movement has often emerged from these bridge groups.[13] Many of these NGOs, including the Kenya Human Rights Commission, SERAC (Nigeria), CDES (Ecuador), Dejustica (Colombia), Aprodeh (Peru), CELS (Argentina), the Democracy Center (Bolivia), Conectas (Brazil) and PODER (Mexico), have developed programming in BHR.

In the early 1990s, following the Vienna Conference,[14] a set of human rights-focused INGOs were launched with missions going beyond traditional civil and political rights. These groups, including Global Witness, the Center for Economic and Social Rights and EarthRights International, opened up some of the earliest work on BHR. Companies in extractives industries such as Texaco (operating in the Amazon) and Unocal (operating in Burma) provided the most salient targets for this initial work. More recently, a cohort of INGOs has been established to focus on the information communication and technology (ICT) sector and human rights.[15]

Within the mainstream human rights movement, arguably the two most influential organizations, Amnesty and HRW, started taking corporations into account only towards the end of the 20th century.[16] Amnesty's early years were characterized by an emphasis on human rights violations committed by states against individuals, including campaigns around prisoners of conscience, stopping torture and ending the death penalty. The Bhopal disaster[17] and the killing of Ken Saro-Wiwa forced the organization to address company actors directly. Amnesty established a BHR advisory group in the late 1990s and started researching and campaigning around corporate accountability, including the small arms trade and the extractives industries. Today, Amnesty's work often targets corporations for human rights abuses.

Consistent with its mission to 'investigate abuses, expose the facts widely, and pressure those with power to respect rights and secure justice', HRW has occasionally touched on themes related to BHR, often through the lens of worker or children's rights. HRW established a BHR unit in the mid-1990s and has since expanded its work to include reports targeting extractive industries, tobacco companies, corruption, labour conditions in the garment sector and business practices in the US that impact the poor.[18]

For most NGOs at both the international and national levels the basic operating mode has been to publish hard-hitting investigative reports about the ways in which business practices have violated rights, and to push for more effective government oversight and changes in business behaviour. Other NGOs such as Interights, the Legal Resources Centre (South Africa), the Center for Constitutional Rights (CCR), the Center for Justice and International Law (CEJIL) and EarthRights International (ERI) have focused on strategic litigation and legal standard-setting to strengthen BHR jurisprudence.

3.2 International networks and movement builders

The International Federation of Human Rights (FIDH, by its French initials), with over 150 members in every world region, self-identifies as a movement builder, facilitating South–South exchange, cross-national strategy and solidarity. By 2009, the FIDH Secretariat in Paris noted that members were increasingly focused on the impacts of economic globalization and the responsibilities of business enterprises. FIDH's work on BHR has included promoting the recognition of extraterritorial obligations of states; greater corporate accountability; and the rights of victims to remedy and reparation. Other regional or global networks that have developed BHR programming include the International Commission of Jurists (ICJ), which convenes lawyers, judges and legal scholars from around the world; the International Network for Economic, Social and Cultural Rights (ESCR-Net), a membership association of over 200 organizations; and the Asian Forum for Human Rights and Development (FORUM-Asia), which has dozens of NGO members throughout Asia.

Movement builders play an important role in providing guidance and disseminating information. The Business & Human Rights Resource Centre (BHRRC),[19] established in 2002, has been at the forefront of those efforts, providing original research and analysis, a clearing house of BHR materials and a platform highlighting CSO allegations and responses from companies. Other important players in this respect include the International Corporate Accountability Roundtable (ICAR),[20] the Institute for Human Rights and Business (IHRB),[21] Shift[22] and the Centre for Research on Multinational Corporations (SOMO),[23] all providing important critical resources and guidance around BHR.[24]

3.3 NGOs outside the mainstream human rights movement

Advocacy around the human rights implications of corporate activity can also be traced to global NGOs not typically associated with the human rights movement. Campaigns by the likes of Greenpeace, Rainforest Action Network, ForestEthics, Friends of the Earth and AmazonWatch have long targeted corporations for both environmental and human rights impacts. These organizations can be credited with some of the most innovative and effective corporate campaigns to date.[25] Likewise, humanitarian and development groups like Oxfam, ActionAid and Christian Aid have successfully campaigned against pharmaceutical, mining, oil, agriculture and retail corporations, going back at least as far as the iconic campaign against Nestlé for marketing baby formula, launched in the mid-1970s.[26]

3.4 Social movements

Throughout history, social movements comprising community groups, indigenous organizations, student groups, workers and unions, the landless, women's organizations and others have targeted businesses, corporate power and corrupt relationships between businesses and governments. The country-specific acts of a single company like Union Carbide in India, Texaco in Ecuador, Nike in Indonesia, Bechtel in Bolivia, Coca-Cola in Colombia and Vedanta Mining in India, as well as the global operations of companies such as Dow in respect of Agent Orange, Nestlé in relation to infant formula and Monsanto in relation to its use of genetically modified organisms, have been enough to ignite social movement pressure. More often, movements have focused on the complicity of industry leaders with abusive governments (IBM in Nazi Germany, banks and others in apartheid South Africa, ICT companies in Libya and China) or in fomenting conflict (blood diamonds in Angola and conflict minerals in the Democratic Republic of Congo). Anti-globalization movements like the protests against the World Trade Organization in the late 1990s and the more recent Occupy Wall Street movement (and their INGO allies like Public Citizen, Corporate Accountability International and Rights and Accountability in International Development) have focused on trade regimes, the international banking system, multinational corporations (MNCs) and neoliberalism as drivers of injustice. These movements offer powerful opportunities to deploy BHR instruments, but are often weakly informed or sceptical about the United Nations or other multilateral regimes.

3.5 Labour movement

The international labour movement has been fighting BHR issues from its beginning, but almost completely outside the formal human rights realm.[27] Potential connections between the labour movement and the human rights movement – for example, around labour conditions, child labour, forced/slave labour, migrant labour, collective bargaining rights and freedom of expression and assembly – have rarely been realized. Until fairly recently, labour rights activists largely ignored international human rights instruments and bodies, and the human rights movement largely ignored worker rights.[28] That began to change in the 1990s with the iconic anti-sweatshop campaign against Nike and others.[29] Labour and human rights groups joined forces to push Western transnational corporations (TNCs) to account for rights abuses among workers in overseas factories.[30] The campaign against Coca-Cola for the killing of union leaders at a local bottling plant in Colombia in the early 2000s demonstrated a growing interest of mainstream human rights groups in threats to labour activists.[31] More recently, human rights groups and local labour advocates have brought global attention to worker rights following the Rana Plaza disaster in Bangladesh,[32] and have forced major (mostly European) TNCs to sign onto legally binding obligations covering abuses by independent suppliers.[33]

Spectrum of engagement

- Direct action to shut down a business or project.
- Litigation.
- Less formal grievance mechanisms.
- Calls for boycotts/divestments.
- Shareholder activism.
- 'Naming and shaming' via media.
- Supply chain or investor/bank pressure.
- Investigations and reports.
- Appeals to public bodies for greater oversight or enforcement.
- Participation in certification/auditing or ratings/indexing initiatives.
- Public events to raise awareness about BHR and corporate abuses.
- Supporting and strengthening civil society engagement.
- Strengthening BHR norms.
- Providing BHR resources, information and platforms for discussion.
- Dialogue/stakeholder engagement.
- Advisory services to companies and governments.
- Formal partnerships.
- Paid contracting.

4 Modes of engagement

Corporate human rights abuses have sparked all manner of engagement from civil society – from violent protests to collaborative partnering. Because human rights instruments were long construed to apply only to states, human rights groups traditionally focused on states' obligations to regulate companies. Early petitions to human rights bodies highlighted the neglect of or active participation of governments in abuses committed by companies. Approaches targeting companies directly have only come under the rubric of human rights in the last 15 years. Today's corporate campaigning and corporate social responsibility initiatives make ample use of human rights language, instruments and legal architecture, creating a broad range of BHR approaches that can be mapped on a spectrum running from adversarial to collaborative.[34] The approaches can be roughly grouped into 'corporate advocacy' – pressuring and influencing companies for reforms or rights vindication; 'collaboration' – working constructively with already agreeable companies; and 'building the field' – strengthening norms, advocates and platforms (see box above for full spectrum).

4.1 Corporate advocacy

Advocacy for responsible corporate activity has come of age over the last 40 years. Today's campaigners enjoy greater legitimacy, more space among business actors, new constituencies, new tools and new legal instruments to pursue their advocacy efforts. Human rights have lent support to these trends. Campaigners have turned to the language of human rights to help frame corporate abuses and campaign demands, providing critical legitimacy. Human rights norms and standards have penetrated laws and rules governing corporate practices, conditioning business expectations and offering new legal hooks.[35]

Corporate advocacy shares much in common with traditional human rights work, including fact-finding, reporting, mass communications, mobilizations, public events and legal petitions. At the same time, it confronts a wider range of targets and networks, governed by different legal regimes and social expectations. Campaigners will typically seek an actor or actors vulnerable to pressure and with influence over relevant business partners, industry or government – a calculus that will often lead to targeting high-profile Western brands that represent a particularly visible part of the problem, such as Nike, Apple or Shell.

Campaigners have a variety of means to influence their corporate targets, most of them relying on commercial or financial pressure (so-called 'market campaigns').[36]

4.1.1 Reputational risk

A company's reputation can be its single greatest asset and can be quickly undermined by public scandal. Activists will draw attention to corporate misdeeds through their research and reports, public events, direct action, grass-roots mobilizations and mainstream media. As Naomi Klein describes it in her path-breaking book *No Logo*, 'multinational brands, because of their high profile, can be far more galvanizing targets than the politicians whom they bankroll'.[37] The advent of social media and online activist platforms (for example, SumOfUs and Avaaz) has been a game-changer for these 'brand-based campaigns'. With far fewer resources, campaigners from any part of the world can quickly threaten corporate reputations. Social media has helped small NGOs compete against the public relations war chests of major corporations.

4.1.2 Access to finance

Campaigners will often engage investors, lenders and shareholders to influence corporate targets. Industry standards like the Equator Principles[38] and the UN Principles for Responsible Investment[39] require banks and investors to address environmental and social risks of clients. Multilateral investors like the International Finance Corporation offer additional 'hooks' for pressuring companies. Campaigners can rely on progressive shareholders among the socially responsible investor community to bring additional pressure.[40]

4.1.3 Supply chain pressure

Often the best way to pressure corporate abusers at a local level is via global supply chain partners. Worker rights groups, unions and sweatshop campaigners have long targeted global brands like Nike, the Gap and Walmart to address labour abuses in supply chains.[41] Major multinationals have adopted supply chain codes and auditing protocols as a matter of standard operating practices and increasingly frame these codes under a broader commitment to human rights.

4.1.4 Direct action

Unions have long relied on direct action in the form of strikes to pressure companies. Communities threatened by land grabs, environmental destruction and evictions have adopted similar tactics such as marches, protests and takeovers. This sort of direct action comes at great risk to local activists, but is often the only effective means to force corporate change. INGOs have supported these actions by bringing pressure on governments and company headquarters to ward off conflict and violence.

Snapshot

Points of leverage

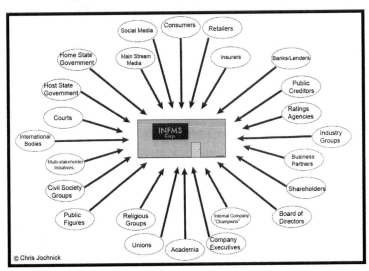

Figure 5.1.1 Points of leverage (source © Chris Jochnick)

Each corporate campaign offers additional avenues of influence. Formal remedies can be sought through courts in both home and host states[42] and through emerging grievance mechanisms at the global, industry and company levels.[43] It is becoming easier to harness consumer and public pressure through social media, new technologies and coalitions. Eager allies can be found among universities, civic groups, celebrities, progressive industry bodies and faith-based groups. Activists will seek internal corporate 'champions' for their issues and will address ethical appeals directly to employees, executives and board members. These various avenues of influence can be mapped on a chart like that above and are well represented in Oxfam's 'Behind the Brands' campaign targeting the largest food and beverage companies.[44]

Snapshot

'Behind the Brands'

In 2013, Oxfam launched a campaign targeting the 10 largest food and beverage companies for their treatment of workers, women and communities in their supply chains. The campaign demands were aligned with the UN Guiding Principles on Business and Human Rights (Guiding Principles),[45] and included a focus on due diligence and disclosure ('knowing and showing'), supply chain commitments and public support for human rights principles. The campaign brought public attention to, and pressure around, corporate failings and human rights abuses through investigations and reports, an interactive scorecard covering seven dimensions, public events, earned media, social media, shareholder resolutions, investor support, celebrity and NGO allies and consumer outreach. Oxfam campaigners spent over a year engaging each of the 10 companies and building ties with senior executives and CEOs.

After a year of campaigning, the campaign had generated over 700,000 online actions, gained the support of investors with US$1.4 trillion in assets under management and had been cited in hundreds of mainstream media stories across dozens of countries. Each of the targeted companies made significant commitments to abide by human rights principles, including gender rights, land rights, community rights and greater disclosure and public rights advocacy. While it continues to rank and pressure the companies, Oxfam is also following the various commitments, offering guidance and facilitating collaborations with other NGOs on implementation.

4.2 Collaboration

For many human rights activists, the idea of partnering with large corporations smacks of capitulation, and many CSOs will shun corporate partnerships or industry initiatives.[46] Nonetheless, NGO–corporate collaborations have become far more common in the last 20 years, even among advocacy-based NGOs.[47] This trend has been driven by recognition among some companies that they need NGO allies to solve critical challenges, and an appreciation among NGOs that some companies are willing to play a more constructive role in addressing human rights issues. Both sides have become more sophisticated about one another, with INGOs hiring from Wall Street and companies hiring NGO employees to join their growing sustainability units.

Advocacy-based NGOs will jealously guard their independence and will be attuned to potential greenwash risks in any collaboration. Because of those risks, some NGOs will avoid formal partnerships or initiatives like the UN Global Compact that offer brand enhancement for relatively light demands.[48] That still leaves much room for collaboration among the more risk-averse NGOs, through less formal or un-branded means of engagement, or through multi-stakeholder initiatives (MSIs).

Successful corporate advocacy campaigns have gone far towards incentivizing collaborations. Once a company meets the demands of advocates, it will inevitably seek NGO partners to implement any commitments. And those advocacy-based NGOs looking to turn successful individual victories into more systemic, industry-wide change will likewise seek to work with corporate leaders to move laggards, or companies and factories further down the supply chain. These sorts of collaborations have spurred a proliferation of MSIs, some with formal certification processes.[49]

As detailed in Chapter 4 of this volume, CSOs can play many roles in an MSI, from helping to establish it, to running the secretariat, to being an active or passive member. Advocacy-minded NGOs wary of partnering with particular MNCs may be willing to collaborate with them via MSIs given the multiplicity of participants, the mutually agreed upon set of principles or standards and the existence of account-ability mechanisms (in the form of reporting, certification requirements, independent assessments and/or grievance mechanisms). While Amnesty, HRW and Oxfam would be unlikely to collaborate formally with the likes of Chevron or Exxon, they worked alongside these and other oil and mining companies as active participants in the Voluntary Principles on Security and Human Rights.[50]

CSOs must weigh various factors in deciding whether to participate in MSIs. MSIs may offer a relatively safe and cost-effective way to engage, get familiar with and influence powerful MNCs. They may serve to develop and legitimize higher standards that can be incorporated into contracts, investment agreements, judicial decisions and even regulations and laws. But MSIs can also create a smokescreen or distraction, channelling civil society outrage away from legal reforms towards voluntary schemes. Advocacy-oriented CSOs in particular will be mindful of the risk that an MSI serves to protect corporate participants from greater scrutiny rather than truly catalysing or demanding higher standards of conduct.

Many companies are still at the front end of understanding and engaging with human rights; there is, accordingly, a high demand for guidance. Companies regularly consult with NGOs around human rights issues, from the development of human rights policies to more intensive guidance around how to manage conflicts or how to design grievance mechanisms. NGOs may offer this guidance in an ad hoc, unpaid, non-public manner, or may establish more formal partnerships with companies.[51] NGOs may also seek to leverage the influence of corporate 'champions' around human rights challenges. In campaigns directed at state actors, for example, to reform or implement laws relating to corporate governance, corporate allies and investors can play a critical role. One of the largest global mining companies, Newmont Mining, for example, broke from industry groups in supporting critical legislation to require revenue transparency for all publicly listed extractive industry companies under US legislation.[52] Alongside progressive investors and NGOs, Pepsi-Cola has been a public champion for the human right to water, and Coca-Cola for land rights.[53] Opportunities for these sorts of collaborations will grow as Western TNCs realize that institutionalizing best practices through regulations creates a more level playing field for them, and NGOs.[54]

4.3 Building the field

Civil society groups are engaged in a variety of efforts to build the field of BHR beyond advocacy and collaboration, targeting companies directly. For much of the last decade, these efforts were focused on normative development, in particular ensuring a robust and effective global framework for BHR via the six-year term of the UN Special Representative on Business and Human Rights, John Ruggie. National and international NGOs took part in consultations, offered guidance, advocated publicly and engaged government representatives to influence the final shape of the Guiding Principles and the mandate of the UN Working Group on the issue of human rights and transnational corporations and other business enterprises (Working Group).[55] Many of these groups continue to take part in public discussions around interpretations and implementation of BHR norms at the annual UN Forum on Business and Human Rights, in consultation with the Working Group and in numerous other fora.

Well-resourced NGOs and NGO networks,[56] academic centres[57] and foundations[58] have an interest in building a stronger civil society movement around BHR. To that end, they may undertake training, provide guidance documents and professional support and offer public platforms for amplifying reports/grievances and spurring discussions. The annual People's Forum on Human Rights & Business, arranged on a rotating basis in different regions of the global South, serves to strengthen collaboration and increase opportunities for CSOs. The BHRRC has been a leader in curating resources and promoting engagement between advocates and corporations. Shift and the IHRB were both established to provide expert guidance around BHR, aimed at governments, companies and civil society. ICAR and ICJ have also launched initiatives aimed at fleshing out critical gaps in the field, including remedies, National Action Plans and due diligence.

5 To campaign or collaborate?

CSOs that engage with companies must constantly choose between adversarial and collaborative tactics. Institutional factors such as funding sources, board composition and resource constraints, as well as political climate and ideology, will all play a role in these decisions. Mainstream NGOs will tend to be more dependent upon 'market-friendly' funders (large foundations, Western governments, high net-worth individuals), more comfortable with the language and culture of Wall Street and better resourced to engage in corporate collaborations. Smaller NGOs, and CSOs closer to the grass roots, will draw on more activist circles – staff, board, allies, networks and movements – with a sceptical view of the market and a greater focus on power imbalances.[59] Any close collaboration by these groups with or funding from large corporations can put the reputation, staff morale and key relationships at risk, making formal partnerships almost impossible, especially in conflictive environments, where these collaborations are often most needed.[60]

That being said, BHR-minded NGOs increasingly mix adversarial and collaborative approaches ('insider–outsider'). Activists rightly recognize that deep reforms in industry behaviour will not come about without aggressive pressure;[61] but converting that pressure into sustainable and systemic changes will often require negotiations and partnerships. As companies have become more sensitive and open to activist demands, space has opened for innovative, industry-wide collaborations and multi-stakeholder initiatives.[62]

6 Conclusion

The BHR field has grown enormously in recent years as organized actors from civil society have become more assertive, visible, effective and numerous.[63] CSO engagement has increased alongside an expanding body of international norms and laws, and new avenues for pursuing claims, largely outside the judicial sphere. Policymakers, progressive business leaders and an expanding range of allies have opened new opportunities for CSO influence. Private foundations, bilateral agencies and even corporations have opened new streams of funding, and academic centres promoting BHR are flourishing. While they still face enormous challenges, the moment is propitious for CSOs[64] and their involvement and influence in BHR will likely expand for years to come.

Notes

1 See, e.g. A.M. Florini, 'Lessons Learned' in A.M. Florini (ed.), *The Third Force: The Rise of Transnational Civil Society* (Tokyo and Washington, DC: Japan Center for International Exchange & Carnegie Endowment for International Peace, 2000) p. 211; M. Yaziji and J. Doh, *NGOs and Corporations: Conflict and Collaboration* (Cambridge: Cambridge University Press, 2009).

2 J. Micklethwait and A. Wooldridge, *The Company* (New York: Modern Library, 2003).

3 S. Kinzer, *Overthrow: America's Century of Regime Change from Hawaii to Iraq* (New York: Times Books, 2006).

4 C.A. Harwell Wells, 'The Cycles of Corporate Social Responsibility: An Historical Retrospective for the Twenty-First Century' (2002) 51 *Kansas Law Review* 77; D. Rothkopf, *Power, Inc.: The Epic Rivalry Between Big Business and Governments – and the Reckoning That Lies Ahead* (New York: Farrar, Straus and Giroux, 2012).

5 Naomi Klein, *No Logo* (Toronto: Knopf, 2000).

6 M. Mutua, *Human Rights: A Political and Cultural Critique* (Philadelphia: University of Pennsylvania Press, 2002); C. Jochnick, 'Confronting the Impunity of Non-State Actors: New Fields for the Promotion of Human Rights' (1999) 21(1) *Human Rights Quarterly* 56.

7 C. Avery, *Business and Human Rights in a Time of Change* (London: Amnesty International UK, 1999); Sir G. Chandler, 'The Evolution of the Business and Human Rights Debate' in R. Sullivan (ed.), *Business and Human Rights: Dilemmas and Solutions* (Sheffield: Greenleaf Publishing, 2003) ch. 3.

8 The human rights movement is part of a broadly defined 'civil society' as understood within social science literature. See, e.g. J. Hall (ed.), *Civil Society: Theory, History, Comparison* (Cambridge: Polity Press, 1995).

9 The number of organizations working in this field is too vast to cover in one chapter. A broader list of 'NGOs and organizations working in the field of human rights and the global economy' can be found in D. Caliguire, *Advancing Human Rights Accountability for Economic Actors: An Introductory Field Guide for Funders* (SAGE Fund, 2015) pp. 66–72.

10 The history of formal NGOs is nicely captured in W. Korey, *NGOs and the Universal Declaration of Human Rights: A Curious Grapevine* (New York: St Martin's Press, 1998). To get a sense of the multiplicity of strategies used by human rights organizations, see the New Tactics in Human Rights Project, *New Tactics in Human Rights: A Resource for Practitioners* (Minneapolis: The Center for Victims of Torture, 2004). See also A. Prakash and M.K. Gugerty (eds), *Advocacy Organizations and Collective Action* (Cambridge: Cambridge University Press, 2010).

11 See M.E. Keck and K. Sikkink, *Transnational Advocacy Networks in Regional and International Politics* (Paris: UNESCO Working Paper 155/1999). It should be noted that many observers have identified important shifts in these dynamics. See, e.g. C. Rodriguez-Garavito, 'The Future of Human Rights: From Gatekeeping to Symbiosis' (2014) 11(20) *SUR – International Journal on Human Rights* 499.

12 In Sally Engel Merry's words, these organizations 'refashion global rights agendas for local contexts and reframe local grievances in terms of global human rights principles and activities': S. Engel Merry,

'Transnational Human Rights and Local Activism: Mapping the Middle' (2006) 108(1) *American Anthropologist* 38.

13 These 'bridge' NGOs have been described as ' "solid organizations" in a "liquid world" of social movements, grassroots groups, and other more fluid and ephemeral organizational forms'; L. Nader, 'Solid Organisations in a Liquid World' (2014) 11(20) *SUR – International Journal On Human Rights* 483.

14 See Vienna Declaration and Programme of Action, adopted by the World Conference on Human Rights, Vienna, 25 June 1993. The Declaration called for the establishment of a High Commissioner for Human Rights by the General Assembly, which subsequently created the post on 20 December 1993; UN Doc. A/Res/48/141 (7 January 1994).

15 See, e.g. Business & Human Rights Resource Centre (BHRRC), *Information Technology: The Power and Responsibility of Business* (2014), http://business-humanrights.org/sites/default/files/media/documents/information-technology-briefing-feb-2014.pdf.

16 Amnesty International was founded in London in 1961. Human Rights Watch was preceded by Helsinki Watch (1978) and Americas Watch (1981). See A. Neier, *The International Human Rights Movement* (Cambridge: Cambridge University Press, 2012) chs 8, 9.

17 See S. Deva in this volume, 'Bhopal: the saga continues 31 years on', p. [x].

18 Human Rights Watch, Business and Human Rights, www.hrw.org/topic/business.

19 BHRRC, http://business-humanrights.org.

20 ICAR, http://accountabilityroundtable.org.

21 IHRB, www.ihrb.org.

22 SHIFT, www.shiftproject.org.

23 SOMO, http://somo.nl/themes-en/human-rights-grievance-mechanisms.

24 For a fuller listing of movement builders, see BHRRC, 'International Business and Human Rights Organizations', http://business-humanrights.org/en/international-business-and-human-rights-organizations.

25 Among them, campaigns against paper and pulp companies linked to deforestation by groups like Rainforest Action Network, Greenpeace and ForestEthics led to significant reforms. See generally M.E. Conroy, *Branded! How the 'Certification Revolution' Is Transforming Global Corporations* (Gabriola Island, BC: New Society Publishers, 2007).

26 See M. Muller, *The Baby Killer* (London: War on Want, 1974), http://archive.babymilkaction.org/pdfs/babykiller.pdf.

27 Given the vast history and diversity of the labour movement, any generalizations must be treated with caution. To the extent that labour advocates have referenced international instruments, they have focused on the International Labour Organization (where unions constitute one of three pillars) rather than United Nations or regional human rights bodies. Labour rights figured prominently in the 1977 Sullivan Principles for South Africa, which was the first corporate code of its kind. At the national level, many organizations such as CEDAL (Peru) and CIW (US) bridge human rights and labour rights.

28 J.A. Gross and L. Compa (eds), *Human Rights in Labor and Employment Relations: International and Domestic Perspectives* (Ithaca, NY: Cornell University Press, 2009) pp. 2–3; G.W. Seidman, *Beyond the Boycott: Labor Rights, Human Rights and Transnational Activism* (New York: Sage, 2007); A. Burkeen, 'Private Ordering and Institutional Choice: Defining the Role of Multinational Corporations in Promoting Global Labor Standards' (2007) 6(2) *Washington University Global Studies Law Review* 205.

29 See A.P. Ewing in this volume, 'Mandatory human rights reporting', p. 284.

30 Groups like the International Labor Rights Fund, the National Labor Committee and the Clean Clothes Campaign have worked with unions like the International Confederation of Free Trade Unions (ICFTU), the American Federation of Labor and Congress of Industrial Organizations (AFL-CIO), the International Trade Union Confederation (ITUC) and IndustriALL on various campaigns since the 1990s under a labour and human rights rubric. See generally D. Eade and A. Leather (eds), *Development NGOs and Labor Unions: Terms of Engagement* (Hartford, CT: Kumarian Press, 2005). Portals like Labour Start (www.labourstart.org/news) serve this movement.

31 The Colombia campaign was pre-dated by similar campaigning by Amnesty International and unions in Guatemala in the 1980s. See H. Veltmeyer, 'Civil Society and Social Movements: The Dynamics of Intersectoral Alliances and Urban–Rural Linkages in Latin America' (Programme Paper No. 10, October 2004), United Nations Research Institute for Social Development.

32 See J. Nolan in this volume, 'Rana Plaza: the collapse of a factory in Bangladesh and its ramifications for the global garment industry', p. 27.

33 See Accord on Fire and Building Safety in Bangladesh, http://bangladeshaccord.org.

34 See Yaziji and Doh, *NGOs and Corporations*, pp. 123–44.

35 The BHRRC maintains a comprehensive listing of global efforts to hold companies legally accountable for human rights violations; see BHRRC, http://business-humanrights.org.

36 A variety of references exist for corporate campaigners, including: Rainforest Action Network, 'Corporate Campaigning Activist Manual'; and the Democracy Center, *Beating Goliath: A Resource for Corporate Campaigners* (2011), http://democracyctr.org/wp/wp-content/uploads/2011/11/Beating-Goliath-resource-for-corporate-campaigners-fixed-2.pdf. See further M. Winston, 'NGO Strategies for Promoting Corporate Social Responsibility' (2002) 16(1) *Ethics & International Affairs* 71; D.L. Spar and L.T. La Mure, 'The Power of Activism: Assessing the Impact of NGOs on Global Business' (2003) 45(3) *California Management Review* 78.

37 Klein, *No Logo*, p. 342.

38 Equator Principles, www.equator-principles.com.

39 UN Principles for Responsible Investment, www.unpri.org.
40 See M. Dowell-Jones in this volume, 'Investors: models and strategies for engaging with human rights', p. 209.
41 See J. Nolan in this volume, 'Rana Plaza: the collapse of a factory in Bangladesh and its ramifications for the global garment industry', p. 27.
42 See in this volume C. Kaufmann, 'Holding multinational corporations accountable for human rights violations: litigation outside the United States', p. 253; W.S. Dodge, 'Business and human rights litigation in US courts before and after *Kiobel*', p. 244.
43 See K. Genovese in this volume, 'Access to remedy: non-judicial grievance mechanisms', p. 266.
44 Similar notable efforts to rank corporate actors include: Access to Medicines Index, www.accesstomedicine index.org; Ranking Digital Rights, https://rankingdigitalrights.org; and the Corporate Human Rights Benchmark, http://business-humanrights.org/en/corporate-human-rights-benchmark.
45 Human Rights Council, 'Guiding Principles on Business and Human Rights: Implementing the United Nations "Protect, Respect and Remedy" Framework', Report of the Special Representative of the Secretary-General on the issue of Human Rights and Transnational Corporations and Other Business Enterprises UN Doc. A/HRC/17/31 (21 March 2011).
46 Corporate–NGO collaborations have spurred a rich literature. See, e.g. Yaziji and Doh, *NGOs and Corporations*; L. Zandvliet and M.B. Anderson, *Getting It Right: Making Corporate–Community Relations Work* (Sheffield: Greenleaf Publishing, 2009).
47 For a good overview of recent corporate–NGO collaborations around BHR, see BHRRC and Global Business Initiative on Human Rights, *Respect in Practice* (Report on UN Annual Forum on Business and Human Rights, 2015), www.global-business-initiative.org/wp-content/uploads/2015/03/Respect-in-Practice-Report. pdf. Additional longer-term collaborations are described in Conroy, *Branded!*
48 Many NGOs protested the launch of the UN Global Compact as mere 'blue washing'. See, e.g. K. Bruno and J. Karliner, *earthsummit.biz: The Corporate Takeover of Sustainable Development* (Oakland, CA: Food First Books, 2002). Similarly, many NGOs stayed on the sidelines or pushed back against the UN Special Representative on Business and Human Rights' consultations and the Guiding Principles.
49 See S. Jerbi in this volume, 'Extractives and multi-stakeholder initiatives: the Voluntary Principles on Security and Human Rights; the Extractive Industries Transparency Initiative; the Kimberley Process Certification Scheme', p. 147. This process of campaigns leading to collaboration on MSIs is well documented in Conroy, *Branded!*
50 As discussed by Jerbi in this volume, 'Extractives and multi-stakeholder initiatives', there are times when NGOs will also prefer an 'external role' if they are unsatisfied with the progress of the MSI. For example, Amnesty and Oxfam have now both left the Voluntary Principles.
51 Organizations such as Business for Social Responsibility, the Danish Institute for Human Rights, Business in the Community (BitC), Ethical Corporation, Good Corporation and 20/50 all offer BHR guidance for companies.
52 Dodd–Frank Wall Street Reform and Consumer Protection Act, Pub. L. No. 111-203, 124 Stat. 1376 (2010), s.1504.
53 C. Jochnick, 'Why Is Coca Cola Championing Land Rights at the UN?', Oxfam, 16 May 2014, http://oxfam-blogs.org/fp2p/why-is-coca-cola-championing-land-rights-at-the-un.
54 Yaziji and Doh, *NGOs and Corporations*, pp. 175–82.
55 Human Rights Council, 'Human Rights and Transnational Corporations and Other Business Enterprises', UN Doc. A/HRC/Res/17/4 (6 July 2011).
56 For example, the International Corporate Accountability Roundtable (ICAR); the International Commission of Jurists (ICJ); the International Network for Economic, Social, and Cultural Rights (ESCR-Net); and the International Federation of Human Rights (FIDH).
57 BHR-minded academic human rights centres and clinics have proliferated in the last two decades, including, among others, the Centre for Applied Legal Studies (CALS) at the University of the Witswatersrand in South Africa, and the Law School of the Federal University of Juiz de Fora in Brazil. Although these centres are usually at law schools, a new Business and Human Rights Center has also been established at Stern School of Business at New York University. A network of BHR professors/lecturers maintained through Columbia University has grown from fewer than a dozen five years ago to well over 100 today.
58 According to a recent report by the International Human Rights Funders Group (IHRFG), in 2011, private foundations alone (i.e. not including bilateral funders or individuals) allocated more than US$1.7 billion in support of human rights. See IHRFG, 'Advancing Human Rights: Update on Global Foundation Grantmaking', http://humanrights.foundationcenter.org. Although it is difficult to estimate the percentage of funding that goes into BHR, major funders, including the Ford Foundation and the Open Society Foundations, have supported many of the NGOs discussed in this chapter.
59 The ideological schism between NGOs is echoed in debates around globalization, trade, corporate social responsibility and corporate voluntary initiatives, as well as in the recent discussions over the UN Norms on the Responsibilities of Transnational Corporations and Other Business Enterprises with Regard to Human Rights, U.N. Doc. E/CN.4/Sub.2/2003/12/Rev.2 (2003), the UN Global Compact and the push for a BHR treaty. See C. Jochnick, 'Challenging Corporate Power through Human Rights' in C. Rodriguez-Garavito (ed.), *Business and Human Rights: Beyond the End of the Beginning* (forthcoming 2015).
60 C. Jochnick, 'How Can Campaigners Tap Corporate Largesse without Undermining Their Credibility? Unlocking Millions for Advocacy', Oxfam, 12 December 2013, http://oxfamblogs.org/fp2p/can-corporate-campaigners-tap-corporate-largesse-unlocking-millions-for-advocates.

61 As Martin Luther King Jr stated in his Birmingham Letter, 'History is the long and tragic story of the fact that privileged groups seldom give up their privileges voluntarily.' Letter from Martin Luther King Jr to Bishop C.C.J. Carpenter *et al.*, 16 April 1963, p. 5, http://mlk-kpp. 01.stanford.edu:5801/transcription/document_images/undecided/630416-019.pdf.
62 See, e.g. Conroy, *Branded!*
63 See L. Bickford, 'Reflections on "Business and Human Rights: Beyond the End of the Beginning"' in Rodriguez-Garavito (ed.), *Business and Human Rights.*
64 See Caliguire, *Advancing Human Rights Accountability for Economic Actors*, p. 5.

Section 5.2

Workers' rights in the business and human rights movement

Barbara Shailor

1 The establishment of workers' rights

Worker organizations – unions and new forms of worker mobilization – are central forces in developing human rights and corporate accountability. Untrammelled competition among businesses can lead to a race to the bottom; accordingly, markets are always bounded by laws to protect competition (anti-trust law), to enforce agreements (contract law) and to protect other social values (environmental, consumer and worker protection laws). The struggle to define those legal boundaries is often contested; and workers and their organizations and allies are the driving force in much of that effort.

Trade unions have their 'foundation ... firmly planted within the grass roots of society (for, after all, the overwhelming majority of citizens in any country are workers)'.[1] Worker organization grew with the advent of the industrial era. Early efforts took many forms and were often met with fierce resistance. In the United States (US), early unions were treated as a violation of anti-trust law.[2] But, eventually, in the US as in other advanced industrial nations, unions grew, becoming in most nations one of the largest independent membership organizations. And, as such, they came to, and continue to, serve as a continuing and powerful force for human rights, particularly basic economic rights.

Out of worker struggles came the basic concepts of economic rights – decent hours and wages, prohibitions against child labour, protections against discrimination, workplace safety and eventually health care and retirement security; central to advancing all of these rights is the right of workers to organize and bargain collectively.[3] Often progress came from an outraged response to tragedy. The horror of the Triangle Shirtwaist fire – when a group of workers comprising primarily female immigrants faced a raging fire with the doors of their factory locked and had little choice but to jump to their deaths – triggered massive demonstrations that transformed labour laws in New York and the US.[4]

Worker rights were increasingly seen as central to deepening democracy. Workers organized at the workplace – often across lines of national origin, race, religion and gender – and learned democracy in practice, even while joining together to gain greater voice outside the workplace in the political debate.

This understanding was increasingly incorporated into international and national laws. Haunted by the horrors of the First World War, world leaders understood that 'universal and lasting peace can be established only if it is based on social justice',[5] and that social justice depended upon a strong voice for workers. That belief was incorporated into the Treaty of Versailles, formally ending the war, and the founding of the International Labour Organization (ILO) in 1919, which provided workers with an equal seat at the table with governments and employers.

After the Great Depression and the Second World War, the United Nations (UN), guided by Eleanor Roosevelt, adopted the Universal Declaration of Human Rights, promising respect for political, civil and economic rights, including 'the right to form and to join trade unions'.[6] This right became an essential element in the reconstruction of Europe and the economy of Germany through the Marshall Plan.

> Trade unionists sat as representatives of the United States on the Economic Cooperation Administration (ECA) ... in 1948 the AFL founded the European Recovery Program Trade Union Advisory Committee (ERPTUAC), a transnational trade union organization dealing with matters of the Marshall Plan.... Trade union officials took part in the occupation of Germany, in the Office of Military Government (OMGUS) and the US High Commission for Germany (HICOG), where it was their task to supervise and promote the reconstruction of the German labour movement.[7]

Franklin Roosevelt famously declared, 'If I went to work in a factory the first thing I'd do is join a union.' In the US during the postwar period, workers did just that – with unions organizing 35 per cent of the workforce, contributing to the longest period of sustained growth and rising productivity in US history.[8] During this period of strong growth and near full employment, union contracts set standards that even non-union employers had to respect. Unions were central to efforts to lift the minimum wage, enforce hours and overtime and curb workplace hazards. Unions provided resources and allies for the civil rights movement that ended segregation and reaffirmed equal protection under the law.[9]

2 The impact of globalization

As globalization accelerated in the 1980s, companies found that they could escape regulation and counter worker pressure by outsourcing work abroad. Stable regimes with disciplined workforces and few regulations attracted investments. Once more, democratic movements, mirroring the earlier campaigns of workers and progressives at the turn of the century, were needed to extend the guarantee of basic human rights. Again, worker movements were central to those struggles. Again, workplace tragedies and abuses stoked the outrage that drove the debate for labour and human rights for workers around the world.[10]

These movements of labour, human right activists and students launched campaigns to 'name and shame' companies and industries that did not recognize basic human rights. Activists began to expose extreme labour abuses in factories producing for well-known global brands, holding corporations responsible for their suppliers, demanding changes in the way companies do business around the world.[11]

As the movement grew, some corporate leaders understood the need to respond to the pressure. New initiatives were launched to address business practices and new commitments were made to monitor employment practices. Many of these initial responses were public relations gestures, but over time more lasting and successful programmes have begun to develop through multi-stakeholder processes. The more successful of these have been tripartite initiatives where business and labour are equal partners. The OECD Guidelines on Multinational Enterprises have evolved over many years and were updated in 2011 for the fifth time since they were first adopted in 1976.[12] Multi-stakeholder processes have been less successful when the influence and resources of business dominated the decision-making process.

> This fact is a clear example of a fundamental problem in the assessment of multi-stakeholder partnerships. The quality and extent of the assessment depends hugely on the terms of reference of whoever commissioned the study, which is inherently guided by the interest of the commissioning party.[13]

Often international institutions reflect the evolving consensus on workers' rights. Through tripartite negotiations over several years, the ILO developed, and in 1998 adopted, a landmark Declaration on Fundamental Principles and Rights at Work, which identifies four universally accepted workplace human rights as core labour rights:

- Freedom of association and the effective recognition of the right to collective bargaining.
- The elimination of all forms of forced or compulsory labour.
- The effective abolition of child labour.
- The elimination of discrimination in respect of employment and occupation.[14]

In 2000, the UN launched the Global Compact with 10 principles including basic labour rights.[15] The UN Guiding Principles on Business and Human Rights further defined the responsibility of business enterprises to respect human rights, incorporating those rights detailed in the ILO.[16] Each of these initiatives establishes broad frameworks that clearly reaffirm the right of workers to organize and bargain collectively as a central human right. But neither the Global Compact nor the Guiding Principles go far enough in prescribing what companies must do in practice to uphold these rights. Thus, while a growing number of companies pay lip service to these aspirational documents, they continue to adhere to business models that contest the applicability of core labour rights in their daily operations and those of their business partners.

Without this formal enabling right of workers to organize and act collectively, the drive for all other basic workers' rights – against forced labour, child labour, discrimination, decent hours and wages and more – is weakened. And not surprisingly, in a global economy of mass unemployment and widespread poverty, with worker organizations under severe pressure, we have witnessed the repeat of human tragedy and the spread of abuse – migrant labour, sex trafficking, forced labour, harsh discrimination and more.[17]

3 Workers' rights under pressure

Driven by increased investigative journalism into corporate practices, expanded campaigning by non-governmental organizations (NGOs), and labour and student movements from across the world, new initiatives for broader civil society participation have urged governments, trade unions and businesses to come together to improve conditions for workers. These efforts take form in countries across the globe, particularly those that are most vulnerable to corporate pressures to adopt 'low road' economic policies.

Myanmar is a test case for internationally respected worker rights. After many years of trade unions, businesses and governments working to address forced labour in Myanmar through the ILO, in 2003 the ILO Governing Body invoked art. 33 of its constitution, for the first time in its history. That article reads:

> In the event of any Member failing to carry out within the time specified the recommendations, if any, contained in the report of the Commission of Inquiry, or in the decision of the International Court of Justice, as the case may be, the Governing Body may recommend to the Conference such action as it may deem wise and expedient to secure compliance therewith.[18]

In 2012, the government of Myanmar, anxious to comply with ILO conventions on forced labour, revised parts of its labour laws and the first steps were taken to lift sanctions imposed by the US and the European Union (EU).[19] These steps accelerated a political and economic reform process, which is continuing today and includes drafting new labour law legislation.[20] The rights contained in these new laws will be essential to development of a sustainable and equitable economy. With the lowest wages in the region and a large unemployed workforce, international companies could easily take the low road and profit from an undeveloped labour relations and regulatory system. The ILO continues to provide a platform that will address labour reform by bringing together stakeholders to draft labour law reforms and oversee their implementation. Worker and human rights organizations will have an important role to play in monitoring and exposing violations.[21]

Bangladesh has also been a focus of worker and human rights activity.[22] After the horrific building collapse at Rana Plaza in Bangladesh (killing 1,134 people), several trade union, NGO and business initiatives were launched. The Accord on Fire and Building Safety in Bangladesh was signed and brought together over 200 companies with the trade unions and NGOs representing garment workers.[23] The Alliance for Bangladesh Worker Safety, a business coalition, brought together 26 companies with global sourcing. The Bangladesh Sustainability Compact was also launched in 2013.[24] It was negotiated between the government of Bangladesh, the EU, the US and the ILO with input from the private sector, civil society, human rights groups and labour (International Trade Union Confederation). The Compact's goal is to improve working conditions and respect for labour rights in Bangladesh's ready-made garment industry. To do this, the Compact is built on short- and long-term commitments related to three interlinked pillars: (1) respect for labour rights; (2) structural integrity of buildings and occupational safety and health; and (3) responsible business conduct.[25] However, a measure of uncertainty attends the ongoing existence of the Compact because funding is heavily dependent on external financial support. This is also true for the Accord and the Alliance.

In Brazil, the Partido dos Trabalhadores (Workers' Party), led by Luiz Inácio Lula da Silva, consolidated political power throughout the 1990s and Lula was eventually elected president in 2003. One result has been an acceleration of efforts to crack down on slave labour. The Brazilian National Pact for the Eradication of Slave Labour[26] began as a multi-stakeholder effort involving the ILO and over 240 organizations including unions, civil society organizations and business. Since 2005, the National Pact has rescued 40,000 workers from slavery.[27] It has been promoting responsible labour practices throughout global supply chains by working with signatories that have agreed not to purchase from suppliers on the government 'dirty list', and to allow independent monitoring of that commitment.

In 2000, the media began reporting that children were being trafficked and employed in large numbers in hazardous work and in slave-like conditions in West Africa.[28] Faced with the risk of boycotts and/or sanctions in the US and the United Kingdom, representatives of the cocoa industry met with a number of trade union and consumer organizations and NGOs and codified a protocol to eliminate the worst forms of child labour from the cocoa and chocolate sector. In 2002, the International Cocoa Initiative was launched with the cocoa industry, civil society and national governments (the ILO partnership formula) to work on the elimination of child labour.[29] This tripartite ILO partnership model is significant in addressing child labour, trafficking and many of the abuses in the informal sector around the world, where worker organizations are weak or nonexistent.[30]

4 Emerging initiatives

Today, ongoing efforts to influence business practices concerning labour are continuing through many of the established tripartite multilateral organizations, including the ILO, the UN Global Compact, the UN Working Group on Business and Human Rights, the OECD and its Guidelines on Multinational Enterprises and annual meetings, and working groups at the World Bank, the International Monetary Fund and the G20.

New labour initiatives have also developed to address specific industry practices, including several originated by industry specific unions. International framework agreements (IFAs) are a comparatively recent instrument in setting standards for labour policies. These agreements are an approach developed by global union federations operating in specific sectors to negotiate agreements with multinationals to implement cross-border components of labour relations. They include the internationally codified social human rights, in particular, the core labour standards defined by the ILO.[31]

New coalitions of activists are also emerging to campaign for the protection of migrants that now fuel much of the global economy. There were an estimated 232 million migrants in 2013, with a large proportion moving for work-related reasons.[32] They are domestic workers, construction and agricultural workers, factory and service workers, teachers and professionals, many of whom encounter harsh working conditions.[33]

Worker protest will continue to drive business responses, as the recent campaigns around raising the minimum wage in cities and states across the US have shown. A year ago no one would have thought that the largest Big Box retailer in the world, whose very business model has been based on driving down costs and wages, is now touting the benefits of raising wages for their workers.[34]

Human rights will always be contested. This is particularly true of basic economic rights – and most particularly of the internationally recognized right of workers to organize and bargain collectively. To protect and expand those rights will require the enforcement by governments of national laws and regulations, new corporate responsibility and business and human rights practices, and most of all a vigilant civil society comprising worker organizations, acting as watchdogs, whistleblowers, negotiators, organizers and citizens.

Notes

1 B.J. Fick, 'Not Just Collective Bargaining: The Role of Trade Unions in Creating and Maintaining a Democratic Society' (2009) 12(2) *WorkingUSA: The Journal of Labor and Society* 249, 250.
2 J.L. Greenslade, 'Labor Unions and the Sherman Act: Rethinking Labor's Nonstatutory Exemption' (1988) 22 *Loyola of Los Angeles Law Review* 151.
3 See J. Nolan in this volume, 'Mapping the movement: the business and human rights regulatory framework', p. [x].
4 Remembering the 1911 Triangle Factory Fire, http://trianglefire.ilr.cornell.edu/story/introduction.html.
5 ILO Constitution (1919), Preamble.
6 Universal Declaration of Human Rights, Paris, 10 December 1948, GA Res. 217A (III), art. 23(4).
7 J. Angster, '"The Finest Labour Network in Europe": American Labour and the Cold War' in H. Laville and H. Wilford (eds), *The US Government, Citizen Groups and the Cold War: The State–Private Network* (Abingdon: Routledge, 2006) pp. 102–3.
8 S. Greenhouse, 'Union Membership in U.S. Fell to a 70-Year Low Last Year', *New York Times*, 21 January 2011.
9 R. Siegal, 'Labor Movement Was Critical Ally to Civil Rights Movement', NPR, 27 August 2013, www.npr.org/templates/story/story.php?storyId=216191855.
10 For example, the Bhopal disaster in India in 1984 generated protests against miscreant corporate practices. See S. Deva in this volume, 'Bhopal: the saga continues 31 years on', p. 22.
11 See, e.g. Naomi Klein, *No Logo* (Toronto: Knopf, 2000).
12 OECD Guidelines on Multinational Enterprises, www.oecd.org/corporate/mne.
13 J. Martens, *Multistakeholder Partnerships: Future Models of Multilateralism?* (Dialogue on Globalization, Occasional Papers No. 29, 2007).
14 ILO Declaration of Fundamental Principles and Rights at Work (1998), www.ilo.org/declaration/lang--en.
15 UN Global Compact, www.unglobalcompact.org.
16 Human Rights Council, 'Guiding Principles on Business and Human Rights: Implementing the United Nations "Protect, Respect and Remedy" Framework', Report of the Special Representative of the Secretary-General on the issue of Human Rights and Transnational Corporations and Other Business Enterprises, UN Doc. A/HRC/17/31 (21 March 2011).
17 US Department of State, Bureau of Democracy, Human Rights and Labor, 'Country Reports on Human Rights Practices for 2014', Introduction, www.state.gov/j/drl/rls/hrrpt/humanrightsreport/index.htm#wrapper.
18 ILO Constitution, art. 33.
19 S. Mahtani, 'Sanctions Lifted against Myanmar', *Wall Street Journal*, 22 April 2013.
20 See the Settlement of Labour Dispute Law, Law No. 5/2012, www.altsean.org/Docs/Laws/Labor%20Dispute%20Settlement%20Law.pdf.
21 Office of the United States Trade Representative, 'Fact Sheet: New Initiative to Improve Labor Rights in Burma', https://ustr.gov/about-us/policy-offices/press-office/fact-sheets/2014/November/New-Initiative-to-Improve-Labor-Rights-in-Burma.
22 See J. Nolan in this volume, 'Rana Plaza: the collapse of a factory in Bangladesh and its ramifications for the global garment industry', p. 27.
23 Accord on Fire and Building Safety in Bangladesh, http://bangladeshaccord.org.
24 Alliance for Bangladesh Worker Safety, www.bangladeshworkersafety.org/about/about-the-alliance.
25 European Commission, *Bangladesh Sustainability Compact: Technical Status Report* (24 April 2015) p. 1.
26 National Pact for the Eradication of Slave Labor, www.ilo.org/wcmsp5/groups/public/---dgreports/---ilo-washington/documents/genericdocument/wcms_189835.pdf.

27 Ibid.
28 For an overview, see Anti-Slavery International, *The Cocoa Industry in West Africa: A History of Exploitation* (2004).
29 International Cocoa Initiative, www.cocoainitiative.org/en.
30 ILO, International Programme on the Elimination of Child Labor (IPEC), www.ilo.org/ipec/lang--en/index.htm.
31 H.W. Platzer and S. Rüb, 'International Framework Agreements: An Instrument for Enforcing Social Human Rights?' (January 2014), http://library.fes.de/pdf-files/iez/10474.pdf.
32 See United Nations General Assembly, 'International Migration and Development', Report of the Secretary-General, UN Doc. A/69/207 (30 July 2014).
33 D. Batty, 'Call for UN to Investigate Plight of Migrant Workers in the UAE', *Guardian* (14 September 2014), www.theguardian.com/global-development/2014/sep/13/migrant-workers-uae-gulf-states-un-ituc.
34 See S. Ramakrishnan, 'Wal-Mart to Raise Wages for 100,000 U.S. Workers in Some Departments', Reuters, 2 June 2015.

Section 5.3

Shopping for a better world: how consumer decisions can help to promote sustainability and human rights

Guido Palazzo, Felicitas Morhart and Judith Schrempf-Stirling

1 Introduction

Recent decades have seen a greater acceptance of the notion that multinational corporations are morally responsible for the harm that occurs along their supply chains even if the harm is attributable to one of their suppliers or the supplier of a supplier.[1] In the early 1990s, the first companies that were attacked for human rights violations, such as Nike, defended themselves by arguing that it was not their responsibility to provide decent working conditions, but that of their independent contractors. In contrast, many multinational corporations have now accepted that they are co-responsible for the whole value chain – from resource extraction to recycling.[2] Today, across diverse industries, corporate social responsibility (CSR) is considered relevant to the decisions made by multinational corporations along the scale of their *production* activities.

Despite this supply-side development, the *consumption* side of the problem has been largely neglected in this debate.[3] The argument put forth in this chapter is that consumers are also responsible for human rights violations because consumption habits have a considerable bearing on social problems. Human rights violations in global production networks (so-called sweatshops) can be partly attributed to the overall tendency of consumers in Western capitalist societies to buy more products at lower prices and at an increasing speed. Put differently: consumers want more stuff, cheap stuff and new stuff. This pressure on costs and delivery time translates into pressure on suppliers of global brands to produce goods more quickly and cheaply. It puts pressure on factory owners to outsource production to smaller producers, which, in some countries like Bangladesh, has led to the development of a large illegal network of shadow factories with substandard working conditions.[4]

Consumer decisions are thus strongly connected to problems in factories, on fields and in mines. As a consequence, a *'responsibilization'* of consumer habits could be an important factor in the overarching debate on business and human rights.

One of our key consumption decisions – buying clothes – makes this connection evident. Many consumers ardently make use of 'fast fashion' – the ability to buy the latest fashion trends every two to three weeks for little money. This philosophy is at the core of mass retailers such as Zara, Forever 21 and H&M, which are especially popular among young and income-scarce consumers.[5] The strategy of these companies centres on fast production in low-cost sites (for example, Bangladesh) and keeping inventory to a minimum to increase turnaround. By demanding instant gratification in the form of the latest fashion here and now and for the lowest price, consumers themselves turn fashion into a disposable good and buy into an environmentally harmful throw-away mindset. For example, Zara estimates that its clothes are not worn more than seven times.[6] At the same time, consumers condone potentially bad labour conditions and depressed wages in the low-cost countries as long as they refuse to acknowledge the impact of their decisions on these conditions.

Surprisingly, the discussion on CSR in general and on human rights in particular has been quiet about the power of the consumer. By and large, the consumer has been portrayed as someone who only *reacts* to CSR activities of corporations according to a simple stimulus–response model.[7] The assumption is that an inherently responsible consumer exists: consumers make rational decisions based on available information, and metes out punishment or reward based on corporate performance. In reality, however, very few consumers make decisions based on ethical considerations.[8] After more than two decades responsible consumption still seems to be a niche phenomenon despite debates and campaigns for more decent global production; as such, corporations have generally failed to translate their CSR engagement into customer loyalty.[9] The growing awareness of sustainability concerns has not yet triggered changes in behaviour. In the United Kingdom, for instance, the world's largest fair trade market, only 4 per cent of consumers engage in responsible consumption on a regular basis.[10] However, if consumption is a key driver of human rights violations, it is important not only to change production conditions, but also to transform consumer habits and mindsets. In this chapter, we propose a three-step process to promote human rights and sustainable purchasing by consumers based on intrinsic values and the creation of new consumption habits.

2 Sustainable consumption: the big misunderstanding

Current approaches to changing consumption behaviour are quite naive. They are mostly based on the idea that providing information on a firm's CSR performance and the 'responsible' attributes of a product (brand or corporation) will motivate consumers to reward the company with loyalty and brand preference. It seems that for many years, non-governmental organizations (NGOs) have assumed that their pressure on corporations to change production conditions will automatically lead to a transformation of consumer habits as well. Their campaigns rarely challenge the habits of the consumers and rather invite them to punish companies, mainly focusing on the leading brands in the targeted industries.[11] Similarly, corporations seriously engaged in protecting human rights throughout their global operations provide information to their customers and assume that those customers will reward them for their effort. The assumption therein is that consumers are in principle willing to consider responsibility criteria. In this thinking, consumers are simply *consumers of CSR*. Consequently, consumers are not actively engaged in the practice of CSR in a strict sense. Instead, consumers are assigned a reactive role.

The problem with an information-based approach, though, is that in actual decision-making situations, most consumers might lack the ability, time and willingness to process the information necessary to consider human rights in their decision-making. Given that consumers make thousands of decisions on products with myriad social and environmental problems, it is obvious that the impact of information on forced labour, unfair wages or slavery in remote countries on the decisions of Western mainstream consumers will be limited. Apart from the fact that information on the human rights conditions in global production is often absent, incomplete or distorted, even perfect information would not automatically change behaviour. It is apparent that the attempt to use information to break deep consumption habits, which have been promoted by marketing efforts and routinized often over decades, has failed. Several recent studies on responsible consumption demonstrate this failure.[12]

3 Consumers in power

Consumers are no longer passive receivers of corporate information. The Internet has led not only to an increase in power for corporations who act on a global level but also to a countervailing increase in power for consumers who have also become globally networked. This newly gained power manifests in at least four ways: decision; investigation; communication; and networking power.

3.1 Decision power

The Internet has exponentially increased the consumption choices available to consumers. While in the pre-Internet era consumers were mainly dependent upon physical stores, e-stores and e-commerce now enable consumers to choose and buy from a vast array of providers and products from around the world. This marks an important shift from a seller's market to a buyer's market, in which companies have to compete for consumers' favour. Today, consumers have significant purchasing freedom and they are in a strong position to determine what and how goods and services should be offered in the marketplace. In the end, it is demand that decides shelf and retail space. Consumer power is exercised through choice, for example, when a consumer decides to purchase fair trade coffee or sustainably sourced clothing over fast fashion.

3.2 Investigation power

The Internet provides unprecedented transparency regarding company behaviour. Beyond companies' polished websites, consumers can inform themselves about a company's value for money compared to its competition, first-hand customer experiences with products and company staff, internal company issues through discussion forums and blogs by previous and current employees, and responsibility ratings by independent consumer associations.[13] Initiatives such as Codecheck[14] and Oxfam's 'Behind the Brands'[15] make it easier to compare the responsibility performance of corporations. 'Behind the Brands' enables users to check the agricultural procurement practices of food and beverage companies operating in developing countries, while Codecheck uses the barcode of products to track the social and environmental performance of their producers. As a consequence, companies have lost control over what is being said about them (and their brands) to consumers and their associations.

3.3 Communication power

The Internet has not only made it more difficult for companies to tell blatant lies or hide serious shortcomings from the public; it has also made such practices more risky. Through Web 2.0 and the development of user-friendly interfaces to produce and manage their own communication content, consumers have stepped out of their former role as mere audience or users of prefabricated messages and have instead become creators of their own content. In addition, social media platforms such as Facebook and YouTube put consumer content providers (so called 'prosumers') in direct contact with a theoretically global audience. Such potential media exposure is a strong motivation for consumers to share their content. The combined power of investigation and communication enable consumer activism. By controlling their own content and media, consumers have a powerful weapon with which to hold companies accountable for misbehaviour.

Recent viral campaigns against Amazon for worker exploitation and Abercrombie & Fitch for discriminative practices are examples of how consumers have used their communication power to put pressure on companies.[16] Activist consumers can also exert power through reward campaigns by actively promoting companies that demonstrate good practice, and by stimulating demand for their products. The slow fashion movement, for instance, supports consumer habits that reduce the pressure on factories to manufacture goods in a rapid-response framework, and promotes brands with responsible production practices.

3.4 Networking power

Another manifestation of consumers' increased power is their potential to convoke and organize large groups of peers. Through social media platforms, individuals or small groups can mobilize and coordinate like-minded individuals across borders and time zones. A paradigm example is the Occupy Wall Street (OWS) movement, which is inspired 'by popular uprisings in Egypt and Tunisia, and aims to fight back against the richest 1% of people that are writing the rules of an unfair global economy'.[17] The movement began in autumn 2011 in Liberty Square in Manhattan's Financial District after an online call for action by the anti-consumerist magazine *Adbusters* in summer 2011 (see the original call: www.adbusters.org/blogs/adbusters-blog/occupywallstreet.html). Organized around its central website, occupywallst.org, the campaign has spread to more than 100 cities in the US and mobilized actions in over 1,500 cities worldwide, ranging from mere protests to concrete 'move your money' actions where OWS supporters withdrew their money from commercial banks to cooperative banks or even helped private debtors through peer-to-peer financial support. On a local scale, consumers may also reward companies for their human rights engagement. The development of 'Carrotmob' (see Snapshot below) is an example of a consumer-driven reward scheme. Networking power can also be used to withdraw from traditional consumer markets altogether and develop alternative forms of consumption.[18] Take, for instance, the recent popularity of clothing swaps and circles in which participants can either meet in person or online to exchange clothes, try new styles and literally change their closet every month without the harmful consequences of commercial fast-fashion business.[19]

Snapshot

Carrotmob

Brent Schulkin believes in the power of carrots rather than sticks. In 2008, he founded Carrotmob Inc (www.carrotmob.org) under the motto 'Let's use the power of our money to change business for the better'. Carrotmob allows individuals and organizations to organize 'buycott' campaigns (in contrast to boycott campaigns) to reward businesses' commitments to socially responsible change. Supported issues include civil liberties, climate change, environment, fair trade, food, health and safety, human rights, job and workplace security, local economy and social justice.

In a Carrotmob buycott, businesses compete to be the most responsible business with regards to a particular issue. A network of consumers ('the mob'), mostly convened through social media, then spends money to support the winner. As of today, more than US$1 million has been spent through more than 250 campaigns in more than 20 countries around the world.

Carrotmob rewards not just responsible for-profit businesses, but any venture that promotes responsible change. For example, Carrotmob recently teamed up with 18 Reasons, a non-profit culinary school, to fight childhood obesity. During the Carrotmob campaign, 18 Reasons committed to devoting 100 per cent of the proceeds of its US$50 memberships to creating and developing a scholarship programme to enable at-risk and low-income children to attend a healthy-eating summer camp in partnership with Slow Food San Francisco.

4 Transforming consumer behaviour: key actors

It is our contention that consumers share responsibility for human right violations. Accordingly, responsible consumption practices are a crucial aspect of ensuring corporate respect for human rights. Thus far, responsible consumption has failed to affect mainstream consumption practices. However, in principle, consumers are able to use their increasing market power in favour of responsible business practices or against irresponsible practices. Accordingly, it is important to understand how consumers can be motivated to use this power. Put differently: How can consumer behaviour be transformed in a way that aligns responsible production and responsible consumption? In our view, the process needs to be driven by three key actors.

4.1 Civil society

Civil society has proved on various occasions that it is able to develop campaigns to which consumers react. This ability could be used not only to pressure corporations into more responsible forms of production, but also to trigger self-reflection on the part of consumers about their own contribution to the harms they perceive as being the result of poor corporate behaviour. Consumer decisions have always been powerful elements in processes of political resistance against repressive systems – from the boycotts of the American colonies to Gandhi's boycott of English goods.[20] Consumers can shop for a better world, as shown by a recent anti-Mafia campaign in Sicily. Campaigns can either promote the boycott of companies for their irresponsible business practices or the buycott of companies. In the latter case, consumers reward responsible companies.

Snapshot

Addiopizzo

One of the key driving forces of human rights violations is the private use of violence in contexts where governments are either unwilling or unable to protect citizens. While situations of this sort arise more commonly in developing countries, the developed world also encounters these situations. For instance, in countries with a strong organized crime presence, governments often struggle to defend citizens against violence. A recent anti-Mafia campaign in Sicily suggests that consumer campaigns can be a powerful tool. For more than 150 years, shop-owners in Sicily have paid protection money to the Mafia. Attempts to break this illegal practice normally ended with the death of those who challenged it. A few years ago, however, a group of young students created an organization called Addiopizzo (meaning farewell protection money) and convinced numerous shop-owners to stop the payments. This was only possible because they first convinced consumers to exercise their power to purchase goods at stores with an anti-Mafia label in the window. Thousands of Sicilian consumers turned into anti-Mafia activists; their consumption decisions became a political vote against organized crime.[21]

4.2 Governments

Governments can establish incentives for consumers to engage in more sustainable consumption habits. The fight against the tobacco industry is an example of how governments can influence consumer habits. The effective combination of anti-tobacco communications and limiting the public spaces where smoking is still possible has reduced smoking (in particular among younger people) in Europe and the US to a considerable degree.[22]

4.3 Corporations

Corporations should aim to transform consumer habits as part of their own CSR strategy. With their powerful marketing machinery, corporations can influence their clients' mindsets and transform their behaviour. While this would considerably enlarge the scope of corporate responsibility by shifting attention and resources from production to consumption, it would be in the interests of the corporations themselves because such practices may increase brand loyalty. Some companies such as Barilla, Puma and Patagonia have indeed started to see the education of their customers towards more sustainable consumption habits as a key element of their CSR strategy. Such ambitious initiatives, however, require the cooperation of companies, civil society, governments and international organizations.

Snapshot

Educating customers

As the World Health Organization argues, 'the enjoyment of the highest attainable standard of health is one of the fundamental rights of every human being'.[23] A company that has taken this route is the Italian food company Barilla with their credo 'We help people live better by bringing well-being and the joy of eating into their everyday lives.' Although Italian food is probably the epitome of indulgence and pleasure in many people's eyes, Barilla augments the otherwise mundane claim of joy with a more holistic interpretation of well-being. Barilla has an institute for conducting research on healthy food and healthy lifestyles; it collaborates with universities and uses the results of its research to improve its own products. By first framing their communication around healthy nutrition and then connecting this value to consumers' well-being, Barilla makes this value relevant for consumers and at the same time opens their eyes to a broader form of well-being beyond mere joy. In fact, what Barilla powerfully showcases to consumers is that pursuing an intrinsic value like health does not mean a sacrifice for them. Health and the pleasure of eating can be combined.

5 Transforming consumer behaviour: key strategies for corporations

How can consumer habits be transformed? In order to answer that question, we first have to understand what drives those habits in the first place. Behind routinized practices, there are the values and beliefs that create those practices and drive them. As soon as the practices transform into a habit, the underlying values and beliefs might be removed from the consciousness of the consumer.[24] There are two principal ways habits might be transformed. First, one can try to directly manipulate the practices themselves. For example, one might simply forbid certain practices (e.g. smoking in restaurants). The second way in which habits might be altered is through a focus on values. It is these values-based concerns with which we are concerned.

Values may be understood as 'desirable, trans-situational goals, varying in importance, that serve as guiding principles in people's lives'.[25] Values are at the core of a person's identity; they can be activated; and their salience can be manipulated, since the different values human beings hold can collide.[26] Changes based on values are likely to be more enduring than external prohibitions[27] (for example, presenting smoking as 'uncool' will probably be more effective with teenagers than simply banning it). The relevance of these points in the context of responsible consumption is that products and brands are laden with cultural meaning and values and provide a source for self-definition.[28] Since consumers – when it comes to brand preferences – are most likely to buy products from those corporations whose values match their own,[29] a focus on consumer values is an important element in shifting consumer behaviour towards those companies that are behaving in a sustainable and rights-respecting manner.

5.1 A three-step model to activate consumers' human rights consciousness

We propose a three-step process to promote and protect human rights by focusing on consumers' values. First, corporations activate intrinsic values. Second, corporations provide consumers with the opportunity to apply those activated values to their purchasing decisions. Third, corporations embed their efforts within a larger sustainability narrative to strengthen new sustainable consumption routines beyond their own brands and products. Ideally, as we have argued, corporations launch such initiatives in close cooperation with other companies and/or actors such as civil society, governments and international institutions.

Step 1: Activate intrinsic values

The starting point is the activation of the kinds of values that have been shown to precede responsible consumption, including a concern for human rights. The key is that consumers grasp the importance and meaning of intrinsic values to accept them as their own and make them part of their identity. Intrinsic values include self-acceptance, affiliation, community feeling, justice and physical health.[30] They are congruent with many core human rights issues. People with strong intrinsic values consume less, have more prosocial concerns and are more ecologically responsible.[31] Accordingly, activating intrinsic values in consumers is likely to engender more responsible consumption and concern for human rights.

Step 2: Provide opportunities for new practices

Many consumers make decisions based on habit. To the extent that habits are preventing consumers from making more sustainable choices, it is important to disrupt consumption habits and inculcate a concern for more sustainable consumption. Corporations that intend to promote more sustainable practices have to provide enabling environments for alternative behaviours (which then eventually become new habits). For instance, the convenient but unsustainable use of plastic bags might be disrupted by no longer offering such bags. Consumers might accept, for instance, alternative options for carrying their purchases home if an alternative is provided that does not disturb shopping convenience. New habits will develop if the repetition of a new behaviour in stable circumstances anchors new associations in the memory of consumers.[32]

Step 3: Contribute to a larger human rights movement

The final step deals with the challenge of anchoring human rights considerations in consumer habits beyond the efforts of individual corporations. It is necessary to create a broader vision and narration of a society with decent production conditions and to embed corporate efforts within a larger movement. Valuable lessons can be learnt from large-scale initiatives such as the slow food movement, which was founded in 1989 in response to the social and environmental problems of industrial-ized food production.[33] Targeting a set of self-transcending values such as respect and solidarity, this movement aims to re-educate consumers with regard to food con-sumption, trying to break the habit of prioritizing price over sustainability. The movement offers a strong narrative that relates production conditions to consump-tion, aims at the promotion of local communities, local cultural heritage and biodi-versity, and also highlights the pleasure of eating. Many different actors from different industries (from restaurants to hotels) can connect to this narrative, thus strengthening the movement and promoting their own particular business at the same time.

6 Conclusion

As consumers, we are part of a globalized production system that is out of (political) control and increasingly results in severe human rights violations. Thus far, consum-ers have not reacted by changing their habits towards more mindful consumption decisions. However, in order to make the economy more sustainable it is insufficient to just focus on the conditions of production. A parallel transformation of consump-tion habits is necessary as well. Our chapter makes a proposition on how such a transformation might be promoted.

Notes

1 J. Schrempf-Stirling and G. Palazzo, 'Upstream Corporate Social Responsibility: From Contract Responsib-ility to Full Producer Responsibility', *Business and Society* (forthcoming, doi: 10.1177/0007650313500233).
2 S. Zadek, 'The Path to Corporate Responsibility' (2004) 82(12) *Harvard Business Review* 125.
3 R. Caruana and A. Crane, 'Constructing Consumer Responsibility: Exploring the Role of Corporate Commu-nications' (2008) 29 *Organization Studies* 1495.
4 S. Labowitz and D. Baumann-Pauly, *Business as Usual* Is *Not an Option* (New York: New York University, Stern Center for Business and Human Rights, 2014).
5 I.M. Taplin, 'Who Is to Blame? A Re-examination of Fast Fashion after the 2013 Factory Disaster in Bangla-desh' (2014) 10 *Critical Perspectives on International Business* 72.
6 P. Ghemawat and J.L. Nueno, 'Zara: Fast Fashion', Harvard Business School Case 9-703-497 (Cambridge, MA: Harvard Business School Publishing, 2006).
7 T.M. Devinney, P. Auger and G.M. Eckhardt, *The Myth of the Ethical Consumer* (Cambridge: Cambridge University Press, 2010).
8 M.J. Carrington, B.A. Neville and G.J. Whitwell, 'Why Ethical Consumers Don't Walk Their Talk: Towards a Framework for Understanding the Gap between the Ethical Purchase Intentions and Actual Buying Behaviour of Ethically Minded Consumers' (2010) 97 *Journal of Business Ethics* 139.
9 J. Bray, N. Johns and D. Kilburn, 'An Exploratory Study into the Factors Impeding Ethical Consumption' (2011) 98 *Journal of Business Ethics* 597.
10 D. Blackmore, *Consumer Trends: Quarter 4* (London: Office of National Statistics, 2009).
11 See Schrempf-Stirling and Palazzo, 'Upstream Corporate Social Responsibility'.
12 Ibid. See also the *McKinsey Quarterly*, 'Addressing Consumer Concerns about Climate Change' (2008).
13 See, e.g. Green America, 'Responsible Shopper', www.responsibleshopper.com; The Good Shopping Guide, www.thegoodshoppingguide.com; Ethical Consumer, www.ethicalconsumer.org.
14 See Codecheck, www.codecheck.org.
15 Oxfam, 'Behind the Brands', www.oxfam.org/en/campaigns/behind-brands.
16 J. Conroy, 'Would You Boycott Amazon This Christmas?', Newstalk, 2 December 2014, www.newstalk.com/POLL:-Will-you-be-boycotting-Amazon-this-Christmas.
17 Occupy Wall Street, http://occupywallst.org.
18 P.A. Albinsson and Y. Perera, 'Alternative Marketplaces in the 21st Century: Building Community through Sharing Events' (2012) 11 *Journal of Consumer Behaviour* 303.

19   Ibid., p. 340.

20   See, for instance, the role of consumer boycott in the revolution of the American colonies against Great Britain. The boycott of British goods (in particular tea) in Boston in 1774 united thousands of Americans from all social classes and promoted the formation of an American identity. T.H. Breen, ' "Baubles of Britain": The American and Consumer Revolutions of the Eighteenth Century' (1988) 119 *Past & Present* 73.

21   N. Vaccaro and G. Palazzo, 'Violence against Values: Institutional Change in Societies Dominated by Organized Crime' (2015) 58 *Academy of Management Journal* 1075–1101

22   J.P. Pierce, V.M. White and S.L. Emery, 'What Public Health Strategies Are Needed to Reduce Smoking Initiation?' (2012) 21 *Tobacco Control* 258.

23   Constitution of the World Health Organization, New York, 22 July 1946, in force 7 April 1948, Off. Rec. Wld Hlth Org., 2, 100 (*Basic Documents*, 45th ed., Supplement, October 2006).

24   R. Greenwood, R. Suddaby and C.R. Hinings, 'Theorizing Change: The Role of Professional Associations in the Transformation of Institutionalized Fields' (2002) 45(1) *Academy of Management Journal* 58; S. Hitlin and J.A. Piliavin, 'Values: Reviving a Dormant Concept' (2004) 30 *Annual Review of Sociology* 359.

25   S.H. Schwartz, 'Value Priorities and Behavior: Applying a Theory of Integrated Value Systems' in J.O.C. Selilgman and M. Zanna (eds), *The Psychology of Values: The Ontario Symposium, Vol. 8.* (Mawhah, NJ: Lawrence Erlbaum, 1996) pp. 1–24.

26   B. Verplanken and R.W. Holland, 'Motivated Decision-Making: Effects of Activation and Self-Centrality of Values on Choices and Behavior' (2002) 82(3) *Journal of Personality and Social Psychology* 434.

27   S. Hitlin and J.A. Piliavin, 'Values: Reviving a Dormant Concept' (2004) 30 *Annual Review of Sociology* 359.

28   C.B. Bhattacharya, 'Introduction to the Special Section on Stakeholder Marketing' (2010) 29(1) *Journal of Public Policy and Marketing* 1.

29   C.B. Bhattacharya and S. Sen, 'Consumer–Company Identification: A Framework for Understanding Consumers' Relationships with Companies' (2003) 67 *Journal of Marketing* 76.

30   In contrast, extrinsic values appeal to hedonistic pleasure, power or individual achievements. Extrinsic values manifest, for example, in the bonus systems of corporations or the hedonistic promises of happiness brands make to consumers.

31   M. Vansteenkiste, B. Soenens and B. Duriez, 'Presenting a Positive Alternative to Strivings for Material Success and the Thin Ideal: Understanding the Effects of Extrinsic Relative to Intrinsic Goal Pursuits' in S.J. Lopez (ed.), *Positive Psychology: Vol. 4 – Exploring the Best in People* (Westport, CT: Greenwood Publishing Company, 2008) p. 57.

32   C. Duhigg, *The Power of Habit: Why We Do What We Do in Life and Business* (New York: Random House, 2014).

33   B. Pietrykowski, 'You Are What You Eat: The Social Economy of the Slow Food Movement' (2004) 62(3) *Review of Social Economy* 307.

Section 5.4

Investors: models and strategies for engaging with human rights

Mary Dowell-Jones

1 Introduction

Investors play a fundamental role in funding economic activity through channelling capital into corporations, and they have been a target of campaigns by social activists and others as a tool to uphold human rights and ethical business practices for several decades.[1] This chapter provides an overview of efforts to embed human rights into investment processes. In particular, it focuses on two areas where human rights engagement between investors and companies has been especially robust: project finance and ethical investing. Even in these areas, though, the debate about the most appropriate and effective role of investors in addressing human rights and other concerns related to sustainability is still evolving. There remain many outstanding issues, such as how human rights risks can be measured and captured by investors; what human rights risks are relevant to investment mandates; and what processes should be used to best manage them. The chapter also looks beyond project finance and ethical investing to the large swathes of the financial markets that are still largely untouched by human rights analysis, and the scope for significant negative impacts by investment activities on human rights in a globalized economy created by this lacuna.

2 The investment and human rights debate: some background

Investors deploy capital across the world's markets using different investment strategies and objectives, but with the general aim of earning returns for themselves or their clients. For example, pension funds that need to generate stable returns over the long run may be engaged in straightforward buy-and-hold investments in the equity and bonds of corporations listed on stock exchanges. In contrast, hedge funds and traders acting on their own account often rely on complex strategies involving computer trading software, algorithms, derivatives and a rapid turnover of positions to generate the highest returns on capital.

In economic theory, the activities of investors in pursuit of their own individual strategies and objectives will promote a general increase in global welfare by putting the world's pool of capital to its most productive use through the millions of investment decisions made each day across the world's financial markets. In practice, investors are faced with a global economy that is characterized by widespread denial of basic economic and social rights despite the existence of a larger pool of investment capital than ever before – one that appears to be generating growing levels of inequality and entrenched poverty rather than inclusive, sustainable economic growth.[2] Investors also focus largely on financial returns, which can obscure the social impacts of their investments in their analysis.

In this context, embedding human rights standards into investment processes is essential to building a sustainable global economy for two reasons: it helps to protect and promote human rights in the global economy by ensuring that investors pay attention to the non-financial, social costs of their activities and that companies respect human rights; in addition, where companies have a negative human rights impact, the existence of human rights standards in investment processes may help to protect investors from risks arising from rights infringements.[3] In the aftermath of the 2007–09 Global Financial Crisis (GFC), leading financial regulators have recognized that liberal financial markets depend upon a foundation of ethics to maintain trust and build cohesive, socially inclusive capitalism.[4] The United Nations (UN) Guiding Principles on Business and Human Rights (Guiding Principles) also recognize that corporate respect for human rights is essential to building 'socially sustainable globalization'.[5] However, the diversity and complexity of investment products and strategies mean that human rights processes need to be tailored to particular investors' requirements and we are still a long way from fully embedding human rights standards across the investment universe.[6]

The starting point for linking investors and human rights was the recognition that because investors control a huge pool of global funds, their influence over corporations could be an important avenue in defending human rights from harmful business conduct and an important source of leverage in fostering respect for human rights. Investors were seen as providing 'the means for front-line industries to operate',[7] and, as such, could be seen as vicariously responsible for the human rights impacts of the companies in which they invested. Efforts were then directed at understanding what role they could play in supporting human rights in the conduct of businesses in other sectors (for example, mining, pharmaceutical, manufacturing) in which they had invested or to which they had made loans.[8] This process in itself raised many challenges, in particular defining standards and metrics for capturing human rights risks in corporate conduct and knowing how investors could manage those risks when they did arise.

Over the last decade, interest in investors' responsibilities for respecting human rights has grown substantially within the human rights community, as well as among investment managers and customers seeking investment funds that have ethical or human rights standards as part of their investment strategy. There has also been an expansion in the issues that are now included within the ambit of responsible investment, from a narrow focus on excluding arms and tobacco companies, to a much broader range of issues including a focus on improving corporate governance and funding renewable energy.

However, there is a lack of consensus on key definitions and it is particularly difficult to quantify and measure human rights risks in a robust manner. A key challenge in this area has been defining a common framework of standards and developing a reliable, credible corporate reporting framework for human rights risks that investors can use to assess investments. Beyond egregious violations such as forced labour, there is scope for broad ethical judgement in the application of human rights assessments to corporate operations, and investors have struggled with understanding how exactly to apply human rights to their investment decisions.[9] There are currently human rights benchmarking initiatives in development that aim to help investors by producing a transparent measurement system for companies' human rights records, but these are still at early stages.[10] The EIRIS Global Platform, for example, offers investors a platform with dashboards of indicators on various environmental, social and governance (ESG) issues and over 3,000 companies, which can be tailored to investors' particular interests.[11] The Global Reporting Initiative has developed a human rights reporting guide and an analysis of human rights reporting trends.[12] Similarly, the United Nations Environment Programme (UNEP) Finance Initiative has developed a 'Human Rights Guidance Tool for the Financial Sector'.[13] However, a former head of responsible investment at an institutional investor has argued that a central obstacle to the full engagement of investors with human rights continues to be 'the lack of consensus and clarity around the human rights expectations of companies and specifically, the absence of an agreed normative framework against which corporate human rights performance can be assessed'.[14] As a result of this lack of clarity, investor engagement with human rights can span a spectrum of engagement. On the one hand, funds can limit their ethical policy to exclusion of certain industries such as armaments.[15] On the other hand, investors can pursue a much broader remit. For example, the Church of England pension fund's 'Statement of Ethical Investment Policy' is supported by 16 subpolicies relating to areas of concern, from weapons to supply chain issues to property and high interest rate lending.[16]

Snapshot

Responsible investment: defining terms, capturing risks

The responsible investing universe is heterogeneous. The various terms used in this space – 'responsible investment', 'socially responsible investment', 'sustainable and responsible investment', 'environmental, social and governance investment', 'sustainable investing' and 'ethical and socially responsible investment' – hint at the inherent diversity of this field and the lack of concrete, harmonized approaches. Eurosif, for instance, has argued that 'no consensus on a unified definition of SRI [sustainable and responsible investment] exists within Europe, regardless of whether that definition focuses on the processes used, societal outcomes sought or the depth and quality of ESG analysis applied'.[17]

Arguably, one reason for the rapid growth in responsible investing over recent years is the breadth of the definition of what counts as 'responsible investment' – including a focus on enhanced corporate governance – that allows more funds to fall under this umbrella.[18]

Human rights can be particularly problematic because there is a wide range of interpretations of what falls within their scope, and what should be excluded on human rights grounds. While a survey of fund managers by BNY Mellon found that human rights were the single most important issue that clients were focused on in the ESG space, this related mostly to excluding companies implicated in human rights violations, supporting certain regimes or having a detrimental impact on local communities. The main countries excluded were Sudan and Iran; China, however, was not on the list despite its record of serious human rights violations.[19]

Assets under management (AUM) in the responsible investment space, which broadly covers ESG factors including human rights, have grown substantially over the last decade. Responsible investment funds are now estimated to hold approximately US$45 trillion in AUM,[20] and there has been widespread commitment by mainstream asset managers, pension funds and major banks with asset management arms to include human rights as part of their responsible investment processes and policies. Although there is wide diversity in what is included in a 'responsible investment' strategy and the integration of human rights, AUM in the responsible investment space have grown approximately tenfold since 1995.[21]

However, total global financial assets are estimated at approximately US$242 trillion. Global derivatives exposures are hundreds of trillions of dollars more again (in excess of US$700 trillion). So, while AUM of US$45 trillion in the responsible investing space seems large, it is apparent that huge swathes of the financial markets remain untouched.[22] The GFC, for example, revealed a large gap between actual financial engagement with human rights and the vast range of potential negative impacts that can flow from financial markets. In particular, abuses of individual rights through systematic mis-selling of subprime mortgage products in the United States, the global impact on living standards of the systemic mismanagement of risk at major financial institutions, and the global recession that this triggered, highlight the need for targeted analysis of the far-reaching and subtle linkages between human rights enjoyment and financial markets in a globalized economy.[23]

The scale and depth of modern financial markets, and the complexity and intractability of the global human rights situation, creates complicated layers of interaction between human rights impacts and investment activity. Accordingly, investors can be exposed in multiple ways to human rights risks, and building robust, effective processes across all layers of interaction between investors and rights will be a multi-year task.

3 Engagement strategies in project finance and ethical investing

Over the last 15 years, as investment activity has become more global in scope, civil society groups and conscientious investment funds seeking to use investment as a lever to improve human rights in business practices coalesced around an approach to investor engagement that prioritized soft-law, stakeholder-led initiatives. These initiatives aimed to develop voluntary sets of principles with benchmarks for ethical conduct in different areas of investment practice. Leading stakeholder initiatives include:

- the Equator Principles,[24] founded in 2002 by four banks (ABN AMRO, Barclays, Citi and West LB) to develop a credit risk management framework, including human rights standards, for major project loans;
- the UN Principles for Responsible Investment (UNPRI),[25] developed in 2005 by institutional investors as a means to embed ESG and human rights principles in the asset management business;
- the UNEP Finance Initiative,[26] founded in 1992 as a collaboration between the UN and the financial sector to address climate change, but which also has a human rights work-stream that looks at how human rights can be embedded within the banking sector;
- the Sustainable Stock Exchanges Initiative (SSE),[27] founded in 2009 as a collaboration between stock exchanges, regulators and investors to investigate how listed companies could enhance corporate governance and ESG performance;
- the Global Compact,[28] launched in 2000 as a collaboration between the UN and global businesses to explore practices to uphold human rights and sustainability in business conduct;
- the Global Reporting Initiative,[29] founded in 1997 by two American non-governmental organizations to champion sustainability reporting in corporate conduct.

These initiatives bring together stakeholders to draw up targeted standards and processes and to develop accountability mechanisms; they have engaged mainly with banks, asset managers, pension funds and sovereign wealth funds, particularly in the areas of project finance and ethical investing.

At the outset, when human rights defenders began to examine the impact of investors on human rights, investors posed a challenge because they generally did not engage directly with communities and were not assumed to cause direct human rights harm (the role of asset managers and other financial institutions in generating financial crises and their consequent human rights impacts were not immediately included in the analysis). Investors were viewed as simply the providers of the investment funds that companies needed to operate their businesses, although the actions of companies could generate risks for investors via the negative human rights impacts of corporate operations. This approach to engagement with investors over human rights reflected a concern with the direct human rights impacts of front-line companies in other sectors, such as the extractives industry, garment manufacturing or pharmaceuticals.

Subsequently, the focus shifted towards encouraging investors to incorporate an assessment of human rights issues into their investment/funding decisions, to monitor on an ongoing basis a company's human rights performance and to encourage management to address any issues that may arise. The ethos behind this approach was that investors should not benefit financially from a company that was perpetrating human rights violations, and that as owners of the company by virtue of their investments, investors were uniquely placed to foster respect for human rights among companies through engagement with company management and shareholder activism. For example, in 2015, the German Association of Ethical Shareholders filed a shareholders' resolution at the Annual General Meeting of the German company BASF urging it to engage with the miner Lonmin, from which it bought substantial amounts of metals, over the 2012 massacre of striking miners at its platinum mine in South Africa. Shareholders were quoted as saying: 'It is a disgrace that BASF, which bought for €450 million platinum group metals from Lonmin in 2014, did nothing to share responsibility up to date.'[30] The Chief Executive Officer of BASF stated that the company was unable to act until the release of the report of the Marikana Commission of Inquiry, but shareholders stressed that they would be closely watching the response of the company to the report.

From this perspective, investors are, in effect, a means for ensuring that front-line companies in other sectors responsibly manage their human rights impacts. The impacts of investors' activities on human rights through other means were not immediately in the picture. However, there is a growing interest in other areas in which investors can impact human rights.

Snapshot

Layers of investor–human rights interaction

The impact of human rights-focused investment activities can be immediate, such as a loan to or investment in the equity of a mining company that is polluting a village's water source and using security forces to quell any protests from the villagers. This is one of the most widely studied areas of investor–human rights interaction and it is the most easily managed through human rights due diligence or screening processes.[31]

Alternatively, investment can be remote from immediate harm but nevertheless part of the collective action of markets in undermining human rights. For example, a trader's bet on a complicated financial instrument such as a commodity derivative may have negative impacts if the instrument is linked to food. There is debate over the role of these products and investors in rising food prices and the right to food, but the link between an individual investor's activity and its impact on an individual's right to food is difficult to prove.[32] It is likely that action is required at the level of market structure, such as position limits on commodity derivatives, alongside building tailored human rights processes for funds that invest in commodities.[33] The former UN Special Rapporteur on the Right to Food, Olivier de Schutter, campaigned to link investors' activities in the commodity derivatives markets with the human right to food.[34]

An investor's role in negative human rights outcomes can also be product-specific, but intermediated through connected market-wide failings. For instance, structured mortgage-related products triggered the GFC, which in turn had various human rights impacts that were tied to issues of financial market structure and functioning that are complex and difficult to untangle.[35] Where financial crises result from layers of interacting dynamics and products across the world's financial markets, it is clear that simply overlaying a human rights due diligence process is an insufficient tool of risk mitigation. An overhaul of the architecture of financial regulation and market rules, which builds in an understanding of the possible human rights impacts of financial market failures, is also essential. The work of the Financial Stability Board on misconduct risk, though not framed directly in human rights terms, is a step towards this.[36]

The remainder of this section examines steps taken to embed human rights into project finance and ethical investing, and issues that are emerging from this process.

3.1 Project finance

The Equator Principles is one of the earliest stakeholder-led initiatives in this area, having been founded in 2002 under the auspices of the International Finance Corporation (IFC) with four major banks.[37] At the time, rights activists were focusing heavily on the negative human rights impacts of the structural adjustment programmes promoted by the World Bank and International Monetary Fund (IMF). This focus led to a concern with the impacts of large mining and infrastructure projects that were promoted as part of these policies on the environment and communities in which the projects were undertaken, and the banks that were funding them.

The Equator Principles were designed as a credit risk management framework for major project loans (such as mining or infrastructure projects) and to encourage banks lending to such projects to ensure the proper management of social and environmental risks. Signatory banks commit to ensuring that the company operating the project will perform an environmental and social impact assessment of the project, which includes human rights risks; that affected communities will be consulted in 'a structured and culturally appropriate manner' to allow them to freely raise concerns, and that risks identified will be appropriately addressed; that the project company will establish a grievance mechanism for affected stakeholders to raise issues during the operation of the project; and that an independent environmental and social expert will be retained for the life of the project to monitor its impacts.[38] Compliance with these principles can be made part of the bank's requirements on the borrower, which embeds protections for human rights in the framework of the loan agreement. Disbursements of tranches of funding can then be made conditional on effective management of human rights issues.

The Equator Principles have a high industry profile, and have helped to establish social and environmental issues, including human rights, as a legitimate aspect of project risk management for banks, although their success in reducing human rights impacts of major projects is a matter of debate.[39] There are currently 80 member banks from around the world[40] and the Principles were updated in 2006 and in 2013. However, a key limitation is that the Principles only cover specific types of activities:

- project finance and project finance advisory services with project capital costs in excess of US$10 million; and
- project-related corporate loans where the majority of the loan relates to a single project and the total aggregate loan amount is in excess of US$100 million.[41]

These limitations exclude many smaller projects with lower costs, and projects that are funded in different ways – for example, through the issuing of corporate bonds or syndicated loans to the company. As a consequence, there are major global banks that are not members of the Principles, such as the Swiss banking giant UBS. Although banks such as UBS have their own corporate human rights policies, they are not yet fully embedded across all of their business activities and funding to projects with human rights risks can slip through their due diligence processes. That is, certain financial products are understood as more closely associated with potential human rights risks, and so will be subject to a human rights risk assessment prior to a deal or investment being undertaken. Other, more technical areas of finance such as syndicated loans may not be understood as directly relevant to a bank's human rights policies and so may not be subject to the same level of scrutiny.[42]

Given the scale and complexity of today's financial markets, there are many different ways in which investors can fund projects. The human rights protections set out in the Equator Principles framework can easily be circumvented either by investors who have not committed to supporting human rights or through the use of products or funding strategies that so far have not been brought within the ambit of human rights due diligence. Banks funding such projects have also complained that it is sometimes difficult to find human rights specialists who can undertake the stakeholder consultation process effectively.[43]

3.2 Ethical investing

Engagement with investment intermediaries such as asset managers, pension funds and institutional investors has been another core focus of efforts to embed human rights into financial processes. According to the Institute for Human Rights and Business:

> Investors can play a major role in drawing attention to human rights issues, using their influence as shareholders. As owners of capital, they can encourage companies to prevent, mitigate and address the negative human rights impacts of their activities, and take advantage of opportunities to create positive impacts. They have the power to influence the way investment managers address human rights and other environmental, social and governance (ESG) issues with investee companies through their mandate, contractual arrangements and oversight. Equally important, investors themselves have a responsibility under the UN Guiding Principles to respect human rights in their operations and their business relationships with the companies in which they invest.[44]

'Ethical investing' has its origins in the Sullivan Principles and campaigns for divestment from apartheid-era South Africa in the 1990s.[45] Similarly, the MacBride Principles on fair employment became a widely accepted code of conduct for American companies doing business in Northern Ireland following a campaign that targeted investors. In the last decade, the drive to embed human rights in investment processes gained momentum in the face of a growing concern over responsible business practices.

An ongoing debate on the question of a fund manager's fiduciary duty to his or her clients has shaped the field of ethical investing since the beginning. Under their fiduciary duty, fund managers are legally required to maximize returns on funds under management and are not at liberty to take ancillary, ethical considerations into account unless their mandate specifically requires them to do so. Human rights issues cannot be taken into consideration in the investment process simply because the manager considers it desirable to do so.

In 2005 and 2009, the UNEP Finance Initiative responded to this characterization of fiduciary duty by issuing two reports that asserted the principle of materiality of ESG considerations, including human rights, to investment mandates, and their place within an investor's fiduciary duty. The basis for this claim was that human rights play a role 'in the proper analysis of investment *value*'.[46] That is, human rights are material to a company's share price and therefore its potential to generate future returns can be affected by human rights impacts and other ESG criteria. Accordingly, these criteria should be included as part of the assessment of an investment's future potential and, on this basis, proper attention to ESG risks is part of an institutional investor's obligation to properly discharge his or her fiduciary duty.

For example, a company that is embroiled in disputes with a local community over a mining project, that has allowed contaminated water to leak from reservoirs and that shows little regard for stakeholders can be subject to protests by the local community which disrupt production at the mine. The company may also be subject to regulatory action by government agencies, to complaints to courts or alternative dispute resolution mechanisms and to awards of damages for affected communities, and even the revocation of the licence for the project. Each of these potential outcomes will affect the financial performance of the company, the company's share price and returns to investors.

Today, the question of whether a fund manager's fiduciary duty encompasses ESG considerations remains unsettled. The United Kingdom's (UK) Local Government Pension Scheme (LGPS) Advisory Board, which represents approximately £180 billion in local government pension funds in the UK, recently sought legal advice on the nature of its fiduciary duty and 'what considerations may legitimately influence the exercise of investment decisions'.[47] Given that breach of a fiduciary duty can give rise to a claim for compensation or disgorgement of profits, and most LGPS funds are in significant deficit, it was important to clarify the scope of the funds' duties to minimize risks to the scheme. Members of the scheme are all government bodies, and therefore are bound under s. 6 of the Human Rights Act 1998 (UK) to act in accordance with the rights guaranteed by the European Convention on Human Rights.[48] The legal advice given was that 'the administering authority is ... under no legal *obligation* to consider investment decisions from a perspective other than the maximisation of returns',[49] but that ESG criteria could be taken into account at the margins when there was little difference between investment choices and it would result in no material financial detriment to the fund: '[I]f tobacco investments were seen as deleterious to the health of the population, they could be avoided if but only if that did not endanger the diversity of investments or the returns likely to be achieved.'[50]

The UNEP Finance Initiative has conducted a follow-up inquiry into ESG and fiduciary duties in 2015, as it acknowledges that it remains a key issue for investors in considering whether to commit to including ESG criteria in their investment decision-making.[51]

The UNPRI, established in 2006, is another initiative designed to explore how investors can take ESG considerations into account. The Principles set out a series of expectations that investors will: incorporate ESG criteria in their investment analysis and decision-making; incorporate ESG issues into their stock-ownership practices and policies; seek appropriate disclosure on ESG issues from the companies they invest in; promote and support the Principles in the investment industry; and report on their activities under the Principles.[52] Human rights are included in the social part of 'ESG'. Although the UNPRI themselves are very brief, the initiative has engaged with the investment community and other stakeholders to develop tools and practical understanding of how ESG criteria can be applied in investment methodology.[53] For example, since 2011, a UNPRI working group has been looking at how asset managers can integrate ESG criteria into their investments in hedge funds.[54]

While the UNPRI have been widely adopted, with 1,369 signatories, there are significant obstacles to them becoming a driving force for change in corporate practice to encourage greater respect for human rights. In particular, the UNPRI has not defined how human rights should be measured and applied in investment processes, and there is little consensus among signatories in their approaches on human rights, either in terms of the range of human rights issues that they consider or the methodology they use to address human rights risks.[55] Moreover, signatories commit to publicly reporting on their activities relative to the Principles every year, and the reports are published on the UNPRI website. However, while external stakeholders can scrutinize public reports, there is no audit or assurance framework for the reports. That is, there is no formalized verification procedure to ensure the reporting companies are upholding the Principles. Therefore, while there is broad commitment among institutional investors to applying human rights principles in their investment processes, there is no agreed framework by which they are expected to do this and it is largely left up to individual investors' discretion.

In practice, human rights risks in an investment process can be managed through various approaches:

- *passive screening*: where a fund will track an ethical index that includes human rights, such as FTSE4Good or the Dow Jones Sustainability Index;
- *positive screening*: where a fund manager will positively identify companies to invest in that have a list of specified criteria, for example, a company human rights policy, a stakeholder engagement system, protection of labour rights for workers and a good human rights record;
- *negative screening*: where companies are excluded from the portfolio on the basis of identified human rights concerns, such as poor labour rights practices, links to the manufacture of cluster munitions or other weapons, involvement in industries or countries with known human rights concerns;

- *shareholder engagement*: where human rights issues arise in a company in which the investor has already invested, they can use their influence as shareholders/bondholders to raise the matter with senior management and press for change; institutional investors can also engage in public policy debates on ESG issues;
- *thematic funds*: where funds are tailored to a particular ESG focus, such as investment in renewable technology or social impact investing, where funds look to support positive social outcomes such as investments in social infrastructure.

Snapshot

Norway's Government Pension Fund

Norway has set up a government pension fund using the revenue from its oil reserves. Norges Bank Investment Management (NBIM) was established in 1998 and has generated an annual return of 5.8 per cent from its establishment to the end of 2014.[56] Overall responsibility for managing the Government Pension Fund Global (Fund) falls to the Ministry of Finance, which created a Council on Ethics in 2004 to advise on and oversee the Fund's Ethical Guidelines, which include human rights. The overall mandate of the Fund is that positive financial returns are 'deemed to be contingent on a sustainable development in economic, environmental and social terms, and on well-functioning, efficient and legitimate financial markets'.[57] Ethics is therefore at the heart of the Fund's vision.[58]

The Fund's Ethical Guidelines provide that companies can be put under observation or excluded from the Fund if there is an unacceptable risk that they contribute to or are responsible for serious or systematic human rights violations; serious violations of the rights of individuals in situations of war or conflict; severe environmental damage; gross corruption; or other particularly serious violations of fundamental ethical norms.[59] The Council on Ethics makes recommendations to the Ministry of Finance concerning companies that fall within these provisions, and a publicly available list of excluded companies is maintained.[60]

For example, in June 2011, the UK mining company Randgold Resources Ltd was put under observation due to concerns that its establishment of a gold mine in the Democratic Republic of the Congo could involve serious violations of the rights of individuals in situations of war or conflict. In January 2014, the period of observation ended as it was determined that there was no longer a risk that the company could be involved in such violations.[61]

In January 2014, Sesa Sterlite was excluded from the Fund. Sesa Sterlite is a subsidiary of the Indian mining conglomerate Vedanta Resources plc, which has been involved in a long-running controversy over the environmental and human rights impacts of some of its Indian projects. Vedanta had already been excluded from the Fund, and Sesa Sterlite was a newly established subsidiary that would be operating some of the Indian mines. The Ethics Council's assessment was that these operations 'present[ed] an unacceptable risk of environmental damage and serious violations of human rights'.[62]

4 The value argument and long-term vs short-term investing

Although moves to date to incorporate an assessment of human rights in investment processes are a major step towards embedding human rights standards into corporate conduct and financial market activity, there remain many challenges. Critically, the value argument for including a human rights assessment in investment processes hinges upon the argument that human rights risks affect a company's operations and profits, and therefore its share price and returns to investors. Investing for sustainable long-term returns requires the selection of companies that take a proactive approach to managing these risks, or avoiding those that commit human rights violations. On this basis, human rights considerations are part of the evaluation of a company's potential investment value rather than simply a desirable ethical overlay. While this approach can overcome narrow constructions of fiduciary duties, and the more general 'why?' of mainstream fund managers, there are two basic problems with this type of analysis: (1) it depends upon an investor taking a long-term approach to investing; and (2) it automatically excludes large swathes of investment activity that do not take a long-term approach. As noted by the Danish Institute for Human Rights:

> Actors and assets such as *hedge funds, brokerage houses, insurance, derivatives, private equity and variable income investments* have proved difficult to include in the present [report]. Hedge funds involve a great deal of short-term products, and the actors and the assets are not compatible with long-term only thinking. Structured finance, built on a series of complex intermediate operations linking one asset to multiple others, to future dividends, or to funds of funds, makes it difficult to create a feasible methodology that includes social concerns, considered not to be significant to valuation. The high frequency of transactions and the volatility of these assets also make long-term thinking irrelevant. Moreover, it is a considerable challenge to track financial operations and movements of capital which may span several territorial sites and pass through various financial entities, especially considering operations with private equity. For these reasons, this survey focuses on long-term-only actors and assets.[63]

While the value approach has built a basis of acceptance of human rights as a material issue among investors, it is a methodology that has clear limits. In particular, it limits the range of financial products that can be included in the methodology. It effectively looks at points in the financial system where human rights due diligence can be tailored to fit, rather than working from the top down to capture and address the range of human rights risks raised across the financial markets.

While long-term investment approaches clearly strengthen the possibility of respect for human rights in business operations, and have certainly increased the visibility of human rights as a material issue for corporations and investors, the broader trend over the last decade is towards short-term investments, either through the buying and selling of positions held by a fund or by computer-based trading (or high-frequency trading). This type of trading is thought to account for approximately 70 per cent of equity trading in the US, 30–40 per cent in Europe and 10 per cent in Asia, where it is still in its infancy.[64] Asset managers routinely turn over their portfolios (or buy and sell the stocks in their portfolio) rather than simply holding individual stocks for long periods. This generates extra fees for the funds and helps them track benchmarks against which their performance is assessed on a quarterly basis, and it can also dilute the incentive for them to meaningfully engage with companies in their portfolio over their human rights impacts. As a result, their holding periods for stocks can be quite short. The Kay Review into UK equity market structure, which was commissioned by the UK government after the GFC, highlighted the problem of short-term behaviour by asset managers and investors and the impact it had on market performance and incentives.[65]

Similarly, as people have grown disillusioned with the high fees and disappointing performance offered by active asset managers, there has been a move to cheaper alternatives such as Exchange Traded Funds (ETFs), which offer an electronically managed basket of stocks. Many ETFs simply track a benchmark such as the FTSE 100 Index, and although they are standard equity products, it is more difficult to include human rights criteria in their activity than it is in the area of active fund management. Trading in equity derivatives also has an impact on the materiality of human rights to an equity's value: investors and traders will buy stocks of companies to offset some of the risks of their derivatives exposures, based purely on quantitative assessments of how much risk they need to offset. As demand in the market is a key determinant of an equity's price, this activity can generate substantial price movements without any reference to the underlying company's human rights policies. Thus, the size of this trading can itself influence the price of stock, and it takes no account of ethical, human rights or ESG criteria.

Arguably, in practice, financial markets are pulling in two different directions. On the one hand, there is a lot of attention being paid to responsible and sustainable finance and the need for a long-term investing focus that includes the social and human rights risks within an assessment of long-term value. On the other hand, a huge amount of investment activity remains either indifferent to human rights concerns, or is based on products and processes that are difficult to marry with human rights. This results in a classic conundrum – ultimately the best sanction an investor has is divestment, but the huge volume of short-term and human rights-agnostic finance can easily overwhelm investors with good intentions. If investors with human rights concerns sell a stock and the price falls relative to corporate valuation metrics, other investors will simply buy the stock hoping to make a return. The power of responsible investing to improve corporate human rights performance lies in the power of collective action by fund managers who share the same ethical concerns. However, with responsible investors controlling only US$45 trillion of global markets that are worth upwards of US$700 trillion,[66] their current scope to produce better human rights outcomes is necessarily limited.

Snapshot

Vedanta Resources plc

Vedanta Resources is an Indian mining conglomerate listed on the London Stock Exchange with operations in various countries. A proposed bauxite-mining project in the Niyamgiri Hills in Odisha, India, caused significant human rights and environmental controversy due to its location in an important environmental corridor that is home to the Dongria Kondh tribe, who are subject to special protection under Schedule 5 to the Indian Constitution. Other mining operations run by the company nearby had caused serious pollution and human rights violations. A complaint against Vedanta was upheld by the UK's OECD National Contact Point for the OECD Guidelines on Multinational Enterprises, with which the company failed to comply. The Indian government eventually cancelled the licence for the mine over concerns of 'utter contempt' for the law shown by the company.

Due to the global commodities boom, the company was earning annual revenues in excess of US$10 billion, and had a high share price. Although a handful of principled investors including the NBIM Fund divested from the stock – after corporate management simply refused to engage with them to discuss human rights concerns – the stock price was not badly affected due to investor demand for profitable global mining stocks. Leading global banks also organized huge loans and bond issues for the company (US$12.3 billion of financing over four years) and won industry awards for doing so, despite their own commitments to upholding universal human rights.[67] Investor activity around the company did not seem to make much difference to its human rights performance.

5 Conclusion

Over the last decade, there has been significant progress in raising awareness of human rights issues among investors, as part of a growing focus on ESG issues. Whereas 10 years ago, very few investors would have had a statement on ESG and/or human rights, such statements are now commonplace and the UNPRI has attracted many signatories among asset managers. However, critical issues and challenges remain. While initiatives such as the Equator Principles have begun to impose human rights requirements on some investments, these remain a relatively small part of the investment landscape, especially with such a wide array of sources of finance available in an increasingly diversified financial marketplace. Efforts to infuse investment with an ethical lens have largely focused on broad statements of principle and general awareness-raising about the importance of human rights in ESG. There is no clear framework on how human rights apply to corporate operations that can be used by investment managers, nor any agreed set of metrics to capture human rights risks that can be applied in investment decision-making. As a result, there is a large degree of discretion involved in how human rights are integrated into investment analysis, and a lack of coherence in what counts as a commitment to human rights by investors.

Looking forward, there is a need to develop clear, industry-specific standards and metrics that can be applied in the investment process to measure corporate performance on human rights. There is also a need for broader engagement by investors with human rights, and investigation of how human rights can be applied effectively to different types of investment products and activities.

Notes

1   R. Sparkes, *Socially Responsible Investment: A Global Revolution* (Chichester: John Wiley & Sons, 2003).
2   T. Piketty, *Capital in the Twenty-First Century* (Cambridge, MA: Harvard University Press, 2014); R. Fuentes-Nieva and N. Galasso, *Working for the Few: Political Capture and Economic Inequality* (Oxford: Oxfam International, 2014).
3   The financial cost of social risks is an issue that has now been recognized by some banking regulators as material to financial risk. The Peruvian and Brazilian central banks, for example, require banks to manage 'socioeconomic credit risk', that is, to make sure that projects they lend to are engaging properly with communities affected by their projects and taking steps to address any social/human rights risks. They recognize that if such risks are ignored, any resulting social conflict can delay or derail projects, affecting a company's financial situation and thereby its ability to finance its loans. See D.M. Schydlowsky and R.C. Thompson, 'Reducing the Financial Risk of Social Conflict' (Spring 2014) *Americas Quarterly* 82.
4   M. Carney, 'Inclusive Capitalism: Creating a Sense of the Systemic', speech delivered by Mark Carney, Governor of the Bank of England, at the Conference on Inclusive Capitalism, London, 27 May 2014.
5   Human Rights Council, 'Guiding Principles on Business and Human Rights: Implementing the United Nations "Protect, Respect, Remedy" Framework', Report of the Special Representative of the Secretary-General on the issue of Human Rights and Transnational Corporations and Other Business Enterprises, UN Doc. A/HRC/17/31 (21 March 2011).
6   R. Sullivan and N. Hachez, 'Human Rights Norms for Business: The Missing Piece of the Ruggie Jigsaw – The Case of Institutional Investors' in R. Mares (ed.), *The UN Guiding Principles on Business and Human Rights: Foundations and Implementation* (Leiden: Brill, 2012) p. 217.
7   Human Rights Council, 'Report of the United Nations High Commissioner on Human Rights on the Sectoral Consultation Entitled "Human Rights and the Financial Sector" 16 February 2007', UN Doc. A/HRC/4/99 (6 March 2007), para. 6.
8   Global Compact, *Who Cares Wins: Connecting Financial Markets to a Changing World* (New York: United Nations, 2004).
9   F. Haines, K. Macdonald and S. Balaton-Chrimes, 'Contextualising the Business Responsibility to Respect: How Much Is Lost in Translation?' in Mares, *The UN Guiding Principles on Business and Human Rights*, p. 107 (examining reasons for the diversity in interpretations of the business responsibility to respect).
10 For example, the Corporate Human Rights Benchmark was launched in December 2014. See Business & Human Rights Resource Centre, http://business-humanrights.org/en/corporate-human-rights-benchmark.
11 www.eiris.org/asset-managers/products-services/eiris-global-platform.
12 Global Reporting Initiative, *Indicator Protocol Set: Human Rights* (Amsterdam: Global Reporting Initiative, 2010–11), www.globalreporting.org/resourcelibrary/G3.1-Human-Rights-Indicator-Protocol.pdf.
13 UNEP Finance Initiative, 'Human Rights Guidance Tool for the Financial Sector', www.unepfi.org/humanrightstoolkit.
14 Sullivan and Hachez, 'Human Rights Norms for Business', pp. 217–18.
15 See, e.g. LYXOR Asset Management, 'Socially Responsible Investments: LYXOR SRI Principles in Brief', www.lyxor.com/about-us/sri.
16 See Church of England, 'Ethical Investment Policies', www.churchofengland.org/about-us/structure/eiag/ethical-investment-policies.aspx.
17 Eurosif, *European SRI Study 2012* (Brussels: Eurosif, 2012) p. 7.
18 R. Watson, 'Ethical and Socially Responsible Investment Funds: Are They Ethically and Responsibly Marketed?' (2011) 19(2) *Journal of Financial Regulation and Compliance* 100.
19 G. Stewart, S. Berard and E. Fruscella, *Trends in Environmental, Social and Governance Investing* (New York: BNY Mellon, 2012) pp. 12, 14, www.bnymellon.com/_global-assets/pdf/foresight/trends-in-environmental-social-and-governance-investing.pdf.
20 AUM held by signatories of the United Nations Principles on Responsible Investment. See UNPRI, 'PRI Fact Sheet', www.unpri.org/news/pri-fact-sheet.
21 US SIF Foundation, *Report on US Sustainable, Responsible and Impact Investing Trends, 2014* (Washington, DC: US SIF Foundation, 2014) pp. 12–13, www.ussif.org/Files/Publications/SIF_Trends_14.F.ES.pdf.
22 Deutsche Bank Research, *The Random Walk: Mapping the World's Financial Markets 2014* (London: Deutsche Bank, 1 April 2014) figures 1, 13, http://etf.deutscheawm.com/DEU/DEU/Download/Research-Global/47e36b78-d254-4b16-a82f-d5c5f1b1e09a/Mapping-the-World-s-Financial-Markets.pdf.
23 M. Dowell-Jones and D. Kinley, 'The Monster under the Bed: Financial Services and the Ruggie Framework' in Mares, *The UN Guiding Principles on Business and Human Rights*, p. 193; M. Dowell-Jones, 'International Finance and Human Rights: Scope for a Mutually Beneficial Relationship' (2012) 3(4) *Global Policy* 467.
24 Equator Principles, www.equator-principles.com.
25 UN Principles for Responsible Investment, www.unpri.org.
26 UNEP Finance Initiative, www.unepfi.org.
27 Sustainable Stock Exchanges Initiative, www.sseinitiative.org.
28 UN Global Compact, www.unglobalcompact.org.
29 Global Reporting Initiative, www.globalreporting.org.

30   Dachverband Kritische Aktionäre, 'BASF Challenged to Share Responsibility for Marikana Massacre', Press Release No. 10, 1 May 2015, https://basflonmin.files.wordpress.com/2015/04/pr_english_picture_basf_30042015.pdf.

31   See, e.g. K. Verhoef and J. de Wilde, *Case Study: Extractives and Human Rights – A Case Study for the Dutch Fair Bank Guide and the Dutch Fair Insurance Guide* (Amsterdam: Profundo, December 2013). See also Banktrack, www.banktrack.org.

32   A. Horwood, 'Food, Markets and Human Rights: The Role of Speculation in Food Crises' (2014) 6(4) *Quarterly Access* 12; International Swaps and Derivatives Association, *Regulation of Commodity Derivatives Markets within MiFID: Price Formation Drivers* (New York: ISDA Position Paper, November 2011).

33   Letter from Righting Finance to C. Kirkpatrick, 'Re: Comment on the Position Limits Proposal: RIN 3038', www.rightingfinance.org/wp-content/uploads/2015/03/Read-full-submission.pdf.

34   O. de Schutter, *Food Commodities Speculation and Food Price Crises: Regulation to Reduce the Risks of Price Volatility* (UN Special Rapporteur on the Right to Food, Briefing Note 02, September 2010), www2.ohchr.org/english/issues/food/docs/Briefing_Note_02_September_2010_EN.pdf. See also N. Mahajan and K. Singh, *A Beginner's Guide to Indian Commodity Futures Markets* (New Delhi: Madhyam, April 2015), www.madhyam.org.in/wp-content/uploads/2015/04/Commodity-Guide.pdf.

35   Dowell-Jones and Kinley, 'The Monster under the Bed'.

36   Letter from M. Carney to G20 Finance Ministers and Central Bank Governors, 'Re: Financial Reforms – Progress on the Work Plan for the Antalya Summit', 9 April 2015, www.financialstabilityboard.org/wp-content/uploads/FSB-Chairs-letter-to-G20-April-2015.pdf.

37   See S. Leader and D. Ong (eds), *Global Project Finance, Human Rights and Sustainable Development* (Cambridge: Cambridge University Press, 2011), for an analysis of the Equator Principles' development and ongoing challenges.

38   The June 2013 Equator Principles are available at www.equator-principles.com/resources/equator_principles_III.pdf.

39   Leader and Ong, *Global Project Finance*.

40   For a list of member banks see Equator Principles, 'Members & Reporting', www.equator-principles.com/index.php/members-reporting.

41   For the scope of the Equator Principles see Equator Principles (2013 ed.), p. 3.

42   M. Dowell-Jones, 'Financial Institutions and Human Rights' (2013) 13(3) *Human Rights Law Review* 423.

43   D. Kinley and B. Meyersfeld, 'Financial Institutions and Human Rights: A South African Experiment' (2015) *SUR – International Journal on Human Rights* (forthcoming).

44   Institute for Human Rights and Business, *Investing the Rights Way: A Guide for Investors on Business and Human Rights* (2013) p. 3.

45   M.P. Mangaliso, 'South Africa: Corporate Social Responsibility and the Sullivan Principles' (1997) 28(2) *Journal of Black Studies* 219.

46   Freshfields Bruckhaus Deringer and UNEP Finance Initiative, *A Legal Framework for the Integration of Environmental, Social and Governance Issues into Institutional Investment* (2005) p. 11 (emphasis in original); see also UNEP Finance Initiative, *Fiduciary Responsibility: Legal and Practical Aspects of Integrating Environmental, Social and Governance Issues into Institutional Investment* (2009).

47   Nigel Giffen QC, *Duties of Administering Authorities under the Local Government Pension Scheme* (London: LGPS Board, 25 March 2014) p. 5, www.lgpsboard.org/images/PDF/Publications/QCOpinionApril2014. See also D. Clarke, 'Legal Opinion on Ethical Investing Is Welcome but Confusion Remains', *Pension Insight*, 16 April 2014, www.pensions-insight.co.uk/legal-opinion-on-ethical-investing-is-welcome-but-confusion-remains/1474024.article.

48   Convention for the Protection of Human Rights and Fundamental Freedoms, Rome, 4 November 1950, in force 2 June 1952, 213 UNTS 221.

49   Giffen, *Duties of Administering Authorities under the Local Government Pension Scheme*, p. 10 (emphasis in original).

50   Ibid., p. 8.

51   UNEP Finance Initiative, *Complying with Your Fiduciary Duty: A Global Roadmap for ESG Integration – Freshfields: 10 Years On* (2015), www.unepfi.org/fileadmin/documents/complying_with_fiduciary_duty.pdf.

52   UNPRI, 'The Six Principles', www.unpri.org/about-pri/the-six-principles.

53   UNPRI, 'Publications', www.unpri.org/publications.

54   UNPRI, 'Hedge Funds', www.unpri.org/areas-of-work/implementation-support/hedge-funds.

55   There is very little material available on the UNPRI website that is focused specifically on human rights, apart from the Institute for Human Rights and Business, *Investing the Rights Way*.

56   NBIM, 'Government Pension Fund Global', www.nbim.no/en/the-fund.

57   Government of Norway, 'The Government Pension Fund', www.regjeringen.no/en/topics/the-economy/the-government-pension-fund/id1441.

58   L. Backer, 'Sovereign Investing and Markets-Based Transnational Rule of Law Building: The Norwegian Sovereign Wealth Fund in Global Markets' (2013) 29(1) *American University International Law Review* 1; G. Vasudeva, 'Weaving Together the Normative and Regulative Roles of Government: How the Norwegian Sovereign Wealth Fund's Responsible Conduct Is Shaping Firms' Cross-Border Investment' (2013) 24(6) *Organization Science* 1662.

59   Government of Norway, 'Guidelines for Observation and Exclusion from the Government Pension Fund Global', s. 3, www.regjeringen.no/en/topics/the-economy/the-government-pension-fund/responsible-investments/guidelines-for-observation-and-exclusion/id594254.

60   See NBIM, 'Exclusion of Companies', www.nbim.no/en/responsibility/exclusion-of-companies.

61 Government of Norway, 'Decisions about Completed Observation and Reinclusion of Companies in Government Pension Fund Global (GPFG)', 10 December 2014, www.regjeringen.no/en/aktuelt/Decisions-about-completed-observation-and-reinclusion-of-companies-in-Government-Pension-Fund-Global-GPFG-/id2344678.

62 Government of Norway, 'New Decisions about the Government Pension Fund Global', 30 January 2014, www.regjeringen.no/en/aktuelt/new-decisions-about-the-government-pensi/id750091.

63 R. Roca and F. Manta, *Values Added: The Challenge of Integrating Human Rights into the Financial Sector* (Copenhagen: Danish Institute for Human Rights, 2010) p. 19 (emphasis in original).

64 A.G. Haldane, 'Patience and Finance', speech delivered to the Oxford China Business Forum, Beijing, 2 September 2010, www.bankofengland.co.uk/archive/Documents/historicpubs/speeches/2010/speech445.pdf.

65 J. Kay, *The Kay Review of UK Equity Markets and Long-Term Decision Making: Final Report* (London: Department for Business, Innovation and Skills, July 2012), www.gov.uk/government/uploads/system/uploads/attachment_data/file/253454/bis-12-917-kay-review-of-equity-markets-final-report.pdf.

66 Deutsche Bank Research, *The Random Walk*.

67 See Dowell-Jones, 'Financial Institutions and Human Rights', pp. 457–64 for an analysis of the Vedanta controversy; Amnesty International, *Don't Mine Us Out of Existence: Bauxite Mine and Refinery Devastate Lives in India* (London: Amnesty International, 2010); *Final Statement by the UK National Contact Point for the OECD Guidelines for Multinational Enterprises: Complaint from Survival International Against Vedanta Resources plc* (London: Department for Business, Innovation and Skills, 25 September 2009); *Follow Up to the Final Statement by the UK National Contact Point for the OECD Guidelines for Multinational Enterprises* (London: Department for Business, Innovation and Skills, 12 March 2010); *Report of the Four Member Committee for Investigation into the Proposal Submitted by the Orissa Mining Company for Bauxite Mining in Niyamgiri Submitted to the Ministry of Environment & Forests, Government of India* (New Delhi: Ministry of Environment and Forests, 16 August 2010).

Section 5.5

Thinking long-term: investment strategies and responsibility

Mattie J. Bekink

1 Introduction

In recent years, two seemingly contradictory trends have emerged in the investment world. The first is the increased focus by investors and corporate executives on short-term financial returns.[1] The second is the movement to include considerations of environmental, social and governance (ESG) performance in investment decision-making.[2] Ethical or socially responsible investors are making the case that over the long term companies that pay greater attention to environmental and social issues will develop sustainable business models that are both financially strong and good for society.[3] The portion of funds devoted to this longer-term, sustainable-investing model is still very small in terms of the overall global investment universe; nevertheless, it is growing.

Driven in large measure by the growing global concerns about climate change and the environment, the amount of funds invested 'responsibly' – in some manner considering or incorporating ESG issues – has grown approximately tenfold in the United States (US) alone since 1995.[4] In the past two years, US-domiciled sustainable, responsible and impact investing has grown substantially, with total assets under management incorporating responsible investment strategies growing from US$3.73 trillion at the start of 2012 to US$6.57 trillion at the start of 2014, a total gain of 76 per cent.[5] This asset class represents 18 per cent of the US$36.8 trillion in assets under management in America. By the end of 2013, US$1 in every US$6 of assets under professional management in the US was being invested using some kind of sustainable investing strategy.[6] And the US is not the country most active in this space. Investors in European nations are leading the way, accounting for roughly 65 per cent of the known global sustainable investing assets under management.[7]

Despite this impressive growth, responsible or ethical investing is still confined to a narrow slice of the investment world. Globally, there is approximately US$45 trillion in assets under management held by signatories to the United Nations Principles on Responsible Investment,[8] who presumably employ some sort of responsible investment strategy. This is nonetheless a small fraction of the approximately US$242 trillion in total global financial assets.[9] There is also a lack of clarity around definitions, approaches and metrics in responsible investment. As Michael Schröder, head of the finance department at the Centre for European Economic Research (ZEW), explained to the *Financial Times*: 'There is no common definition. It's easy to get agreement that it's about social, ethical, environmental and long-term economic issues, but what lies behind those terms is very subjective.'[10] And yet this field is growing[11] and is the subject of increasing interest.[12]

Mainstream investors are also beginning to show interest in sustainability issues.[13] This presents an opportunity to explore whether and how long-term investing in sustainable business models that embrace commitments to the environment and human rights can become a more significant component of the investment universe. Accordingly, this chapter considers increasing investor interest in long-term strategies; the institutional investors who already adopt a long-term approach that includes a focus on responsible investing; whether responsible investment is profitable in the long term; and the implications of long-term responsible investment.

2 Short-termism in investment

Traditionally, those engaged in responsible or ethical investing have focused on social as well as financial returns,[14] which allows for more patient capital.[15] When investment decisions are made not solely in terms of financial risk and return but also with attention to 'some combination of ethical, religious, social, and environmental concerns',[16] the focus on financial results can be softened. For many mainstream investors, however, a myopic focus on short-term results and immediate returns, encouraged by regulatory reporting requirements for companies and corporate incentive structures for asset managers, is an obstacle to taking a long-term view and promotes short-termism.[17] Causes of short-termism include the pressures imposed on corporations by the excessive expectations of capital markets, the narrow financial focus of performance indicators, the short-term incentive structures applied to fund managers and corporate executives and the resulting individual orientations and organizational cultures that develop in this context.[18]

The wisdom of short-termism is, however, being challenged, even by leaders in the commercial investment community. In April 2015, Larry Fink, the Chief Executive Officer (CEO) of the world's largest asset manager, BlackRock,[19] took aim at short-termism in the investment world. Fink issued a public letter to S&P 500 CEOs in the US, urging business leaders to move away from a preoccupation with short-term results.[20] Fink explained that for several years BlackRock has 'engaged extensively with companies, clients, regulators and others on the importance of taking a long-term approach to creating value' and did so 'in response to the acute pressure, growing with every quarter, for companies to meet short-term financial goals at the expense of building long-term value'.[21]

In the last few years, other analysts, executives and investors have similarly found fault with a focus on short-termism, emphasizing that it inhibits corporate development, innovation and long-term growth.[22] Nevertheless, a focus on short-term results persists. In 2013, McKinsey and the Canada Pension Plan Investment Board (CPPIB) conducted a *McKinsey Quarterly* survey of more than 1,000 global board members and senior executives on issues related to the time horizon in their management decision-making.[23] The survey found that the majority of respondents felt the pressure to generate short-term results but felt that 'using a longer time horizon to make business decisions would positively affect corporate performance in a number of ways, including strengthening financial returns and increasing innovation'.[24] The results of this survey led McKinsey and CPPIB to establish a joint initiative, Focusing Capital on the Long Term,[25] which focuses on advancing practical actions to focus business and markets on the long term.[26]

2.1 A shift towards long-term investment strategies

Mainstream investors and analysts are not criticizing short-termism because they are concerned about corporate human rights performance. They are more concerned about the long-term health of financial markets and corporations, and creating opportunities for increasing wealth and innovation. An investment strategy that focuses on the long term may allow for consideration of non-financial data that has implications for financial returns. For example, a February 2015 study by the Coller Institute of Private Equity at London Business School suggests that institutional investors are increasingly taking this long-term view and demanding that private equity firms adopt ESG policies in their investment processes.[27] The study reveals that, due to pressure from institutional investors, ESG is increasingly a core value-creation strategy at private equity firms. Ioannis Ioannou, Assistant Professor of Strategy and Entrepreneurship at London Business School and one of the study's authors, noted that ESG is moving 'from a purely compliance and risk mitigating strategy to a key long-term strategy [for] ... value creation'.[28]

The world's largest asset owners – pension funds, sovereign wealth funds, mutual funds, family offices, university and philanthropic endowments – are perhaps best positioned to think in the long term because of their scale and time horizons, given that their fiduciary responsibilities may stretch over generations. Indeed, it is among these asset owners and institutional investors where we see the most long-term thinking and thus an emerging focus on sustainability, including human rights.

3 Examining the long-term approach: public pension funds and university endowments

Strong and consistent financial returns are fundamental to the investment industry. However, certain investors, including some public pension funds, are leading the move towards more long-term, sustainable approaches. According to Mirjam Staub-Bisang, CEO of Independent Capital Group and an expert on sustainable investing, many of the world's leading public funds are 'focusing on the long term rather than the short term' and thus 'integrating sustainability criteria into their investment decisions, benefiting beneficiaries, society and the environment'.[29]

3.1 Pension funds

One especially noteworthy example is Norway's Government Pension Fund. With assets of approximately US$890 billion, it is one of the largest pension funds in the world. It is guided by an entity that explicitly screens for human rights issues and has generated an annual return of 5.8 per cent from its establishment in 1998 to the end of 2014.[30] In June 2015, the fund announced that it would sell off many of its investments related to coal.[31] Marthe Skaar, a spokeswoman for Norges Bank Investment Management, which manages the fund, described the decision as 'safeguarding and building financial wealth for future generations in Norway', adding that the reasons for divesting include 'long-established climate-change risk-management expectations'.[32]

The Norwegian fund is not the only public pension fund to consider human rights, focus on ESG integration and adopt a long-term approach. PGGM, the leading Dutch multi-employer pension plan, with assets of over €130 billion, applies exclusion criteria focused on human rights and considers sustainability issues in its investment activities.[33] The fund makes thematic investments in sustainable forestry, climate projects, renewable energy infrastructure, clean technology and microfinance. As an active shareholder PGGM engages with companies on ESG issues. For example, when oil company PetroChina was operating in Sudan, a country with 'a government responsible for large-scale human rights abuses', and PGGM felt that there were 'insufficient indications that the company has taken adequate measures to prevent involvement in this abuse or to contribute constructively to the peace process in Sudan',[34] it 'sought to enter into dialogue with PetroChina'.[35] When the firm did not sufficiently engage with PGGM and address its human rights concerns, PGGM decided to add the company to its list of excluded companies and withdraw its €37 million investment in PetroChina.[36]

California Public Employees Retirement Scheme (CalPERS), the largest US pension fund, has a long history of using its shareholding in companies in an activist manner, asserting its demands as to how it believes those companies should be governed and engaging with companies over issues of concern.[37] CalPERS adopts a long-term approach to investment and embraces a concept of 'sustainability' that is focused on 'long term value creation' or the maintenance of profitability over a long period by companies.[38] In September 2013, CalPERS adopted a statement on 'Investment Beliefs' that referenced 'human capital' and 'fair labor' practices as relevant to long-term value creation by companies, though it does not define those terms.[39] The statement suggests that CalPERS is concerned with situations where human rights could affect financial returns due to effects on supplier productivity or corporate reputation as well as working conditions in supply chains.[40] CalPERS CEO Anne Stausboll recently emphasized the fund's long-term approach as she publicly defended its decision not to divest from fossil fuels by emphasizing its commitment to engagement, saying, '[a]s a long-term investor, a seat at the table is the most effective way to shape how our investment capital gets put to use in a sustainable manner'.[41]

3.2 University endowments

University endowments, especially in the US,[42] represent another class of large investors who are active in the conversation about responsible investment and long-term thinking. Proponents of using investments to influence social change, including human rights issues, have long targeted American university endowments, which control US$516 billion in assets.[43] In addition to representing a large quantity of capital, university endowments are uniquely situated given that they have stakeholders who are sensitive to the social and political implications of their investments and who may be poised for long-term thinking. An increasing number of US universities have established advisory committees to examine the impact of their portfolios on social and environmental issues and have adopted statements on responsible investment policies.[44] Advocates have urged universities to do more and 'move from the defensive, fending off divestment campaigns, to a more affirmative approach, examining how they can maximize their investments in companies that adopt longer-term business models that embrace sustainable environmental and human rights business practices'.[45]

Engaging US universities on human rights or ESG issues through their endowments has seen varying degrees of success. In 1987, the American Medical Association campaigned for American medical schools and their parent universities to divest from tobacco stocks. In 1989, environmentalists called on universities to divest from oil stocks following Exxon's handling of the Valdez oil spill. Entertainment companies have been targeted in response to the release of violent songs and movies; debt and liquor companies, computerized trading platforms and companies that engage in trade with China, Israel, Sudan and Nigeria have also been the focus of divestment campaigns.[46] Perhaps the best-known effort of social activists to engage universities regarding their investment practices was the anti-apartheid divestment movement focused on South Africa. A total of 155 institutions undertook either full or partial divestment of South African assets by 1988.[47] Currently, there is a divestment movement targeting universities in both the US and the United Kingdom (UK),[48] calling for divestment from fossil fuels. With few notable exceptions,[49] most universities are not currently divesting from fossil fuels even if they have some policy on responsible investing.

Stanford University, with an endowment of US$21.4 billon, announced in May 2014 that it would not make direct investments in coal mining companies.[50] Stanford is the only university with an endowment in the top 150 to make a commitment related to fossil fuels.[51] This decision was made based on a recommendation from Stanford's Advisory Panel on Investment Responsibility and Licensing (APIRL). APIRL includes representatives of students, faculty, staff and alumni. The panel conducted an extensive review over several months of the social and environmental implications of investment in fossil fuel companies before making its recommendation. APIRL acts in accordance with Stanford's 'Statement on Investment Responsibility',[52] which it originally adopted in 1971 and subsequently amended, most recently in June 2015.

Even if it is the only university with a very substantial endowment to take a position on fossil fuel divestment, Stanford's approach to responsible investing is consistent with that at other universities with policies on responsible investing for their endowments. The Harvard Management Company (HMC), which manages

Harvard's endowment, is committed to 'investing for the long term' and 'integrating ESG factors' into its investment choices.[53] HMC uses ESG metrics, along with financial and operating business factors, to weigh the risks of potential investments. It also has a policy for 'active ownership' focused on how to exercise Harvard's shareholder voting rights and engage in private dialogue with select portfolio companies on ESG risks.[54] In 2005, Harvard announced its decision to divest its PetroChina stock because of the human rights crisis in the Darfur region of Sudan and the extensive role played by PetroChina's closely affiliated parent company, China National Petroleum Corporation, as a leading partner of the Sudanese government in the production of oil in Sudan.[55] This was an instance where 'the extraordinary combination of circumstances presented in the case of PetroChina warrant[ed] the rare step of divestment' despite the university's 'strong institutional presumption against divesting stock for reasons unrelated to investment purposes'.[56]

4 Long-term, responsible investment strategies and returns

Though some advocates have argued that sustainable investments outperform the markets, data on the performance of responsible investments is inconclusive.[57] What does seem true is that sustainable investment strategies can show at least comparable return potential over the long-term.[58] This is not surprising given that studies show that passively managed index funds tend to perform as well as actively managed funds (or better, especially when management fees are counted against returns).[59] Responsible investment strategies are simply another form of actively managing funds, making predictive choices based on data, whether financial or non-financial.

There is no clear data conclusively establishing that responsibly invested funds perform well.[60] There is nonetheless 'significant and growing evidence from a large number of research studies that companies that are more socially responsible, or more responsible in general to all their stakeholders, perform at the same level or somewhat better than less responsible companies'.[61] For example, a 2015 report by Morgan Stanley analysed the performance of more than 10,000 mutual funds and found that sustainable equity funds met or exceeded median returns of traditional equity funds during 64 per cent of the time periods examined.[62]

Studies examining data over a long time horizon demonstrate the most positive results for sustainable investment. The success of these strategies was perhaps most conclusively shown by a recent Harvard Business School study where the share price performance of 180 companies was analysed over 18 years.[63] Between 1993 and 2011, the portfolio of 90 companies that were at the forefront of implementing sustainability programmes achieved nearly 50 per cent higher performance than the comparison group.[64] The study divided the 180 companies into two groups: those that were labelled 'high sustainability' had voluntarily adopted sustainability policies by 1993; a matched sample of companies that adopted almost no sustainability policies were labelled 'low sustainability'. In addition to significant discrepancies in terms of institutional structure, the study provides evidence that sustainability pays. The 'high sustainability' companies significantly outperformed their counterparts over the long term, both in terms of stock market and accounting performance.[65]

Moreover, responsibly invested funds may perform better in times of crisis by anticipating risk. Considering ESG factors may allow investors to outperform the market by identifying risk characteristics that others overlook. Studies have shown that responsibly invested funds have lower risk, and as a result perform better during periods of market crisis.[66] In practical terms, the case for taking non-financial factors, such as risk, into account becomes obvious when looking at examples.

The case of BP's 2010 oil spill in the Gulf of Mexico is illustrative. The spill was the worst in US history, and BP has set aside US$43 billion to cover fines, legal settlements and clean-up costs.[67] However, it would not have come as a surprise to anyone monitoring BP's ESG performance. As described in an analysis of the matter by the *Financial Times*:

> The explosion there was not an isolated incident. It was preceded by a series of environmental and safety issues, including breaches of safety laws at Grangemouth in 2000, the 2005 Texas City refinery explosion, the subsequent Alaska oil spill and Azerbaijan gas leak, along with several violations of the US Clean Water Act and penalties from the Occupational Safety and Health Administration. These were risks that clearly affected value at BP (shame the analysts did not notice). It would clearly have made sense for trustees to weigh them when considering an investment in the company.[68]

There were serious consequences for investors as a result of the oil spill. BP's stock fell by 52 per cent in 50 days on the New York Stock Exchange, going from US$60.57 on 20 April 2010, to US$29.20 on 9 June, its lowest level since August 1996. By June 2010, investors saw their holdings in BP shrink to US$27.02, a nearly 54 per cent loss of value in 2010.[69] By July 2010, the company's loss in market value totalled US$60 billion, a 35 per cent decline since the explosion. At that time, BP reported a second-quarter loss of US$17 billion, its first loss in 18 years.[70] By 2013, BP had dropped from the second to the fourth largest of the four major oil companies.[71] In September 2014, when BP was found guilty of gross negligence and wilful misconduct under the Clean Water Act, the company's shares lost 6 per cent of their value.[72] As of 15 June 2015, BP's stock price was US$40.80, still well below the US$60.57 pre-spill price.[73]

It is not possible to know whether investors could have avoided losses sustained as a result of the Gulf of Mexico oil spill by screening based on environmental and safety practices in place at BP, or by requiring more from the company in this regard. It is nonetheless clear that investors sustained losses due to BP's insufficient oversight of environmental and safety issues in its operations.

5 Conclusion: looking ahead

Investing responsibly and maximizing profits may not be mutually exclusive. Active, long-term efforts by universities and pension funds indicate a move towards responsibility in the interest of profits. While responsible investing still represents a small portion of the financial world, 'sustainability' and 'ESG' are increasingly commonplace terms. And an increasing number of mainstream commercial investors are now focusing on ESG in a more integrated manner. By thinking long term, investors motivated primarily by returns attempt to incorporate as much data as they can into their decision-making. As such, both financial and non-financial data can prove material to predictability, anticipating change and smart investing. This can include corporate human rights performance.

The efforts by large institutional investors and others to take a long-term perspective indicate that these responsible investing practices will continue to develop. The next challenge to mainstreaming long-term, responsible investing that considers human rights is the development of comprehensive, credible metrics for evaluating corporate behaviour in order to guide investment decision-making. Currently, environmental metrics measuring the 'E' and standards for the governance 'G' of ESG are more developed than those measuring human rights, a component of 'S'. This may be because governance structures are more easily discernible and regulations more clearly identify the consequences and costs of environmental negligence. The social aspect of ESG may be more difficult to quantify. The 'S' metrics are still emerging and going forward there need to be more clear, industry-specific standards on human rights performance as well as credible assessment processes for these issues to be practically embraced by mainstream investors.

Notes

1 See A. Rappaport, *Saving Capitalism from Short-Termism: How to Build Long-Term Value and Save Our Financial Future* (New York: McGraw Hill, 2011); D. Barton and M. Wiseman, 'Focusing Capital on the Long Term' (January–February 2014) *Harvard Business Review.*
2 Global Sustainable Investment Alliance, *Global Sustainable Investment Review 2014*, www.gsi-alliance.org/wp-content/uploads/2015/02/GSIA_Review_download.pdf.
3 See, e.g. Morgan Stanley Institute for Sustainable Investing, 'The Business Case for Sustainable Investing', 28 April 2015, www.morganstanley.com/ideas/business-case-for-sustainable-investing; S. Waddock and N. Smith, 'Corporate Responsibility Audits: Doing Well by Doing Good' (Winter 2000) *Sloan Management Review.*
4 US SIF Foundation, *Report on US Sustainable, Responsible and Impact Investing Trends* (10th ed., 2014) pp. 12–13, www.ussif.org/Files/Publications/SIF_Trends_14.F.E.S.pdf.
5 Ibid.
6 Ibid. See also H. Boerner, 'Sustainable & Responsible Investing: It's Now $1-in-$6 in the US Capital Market', CSRwire, 8 December 2014, www.csrwire.com/blog/posts/1478-sustainable-responsible-investing-it-s-now-1-in-6-in-the-us-capital-markets.
7 W. Vissar, I. Magureanu and K. Yadav, *The CSR International Research Compendium: Vol. 1 – Governance* (London: Kaleidoscope Futures, 2015) p. 364.
8 UNPRI, 'PRI Fact Sheet', www.unpri.org/news/pri-fact-sheet.
9 Total global financial assets are estimated at approximately US$242 trillion and global derivatives exposures are hundreds of trillions of dollars more again (approximately US$700+ trillion). Deutsche Bank Research, *The Random Walk: Mapping the World's Financial Markets 2014* (London: Deutsche Bank, 1 April 2014) figures 1, 13.
10 S. Grene, 'A Socially Responsible Mission Impossible', *Financial Times*, 13 July 2008, www.ft.com/intl/cms/s/0/7b142854-4f70-11dd-b050-000077b07658.html#axzz3d8tKM59q.
11 See US SIF Foundation, *Report on US Sustainable, Responsible and Impact Investing Trends.*
12 In addition to the growth statistics noted herein, a 2014 survey of TIAA-CREF (Teachers Insurance and Annuity Association – College Retirement Equities Fund) retirement plan participants found that 60 per cent of participants who had not already invested in responsible investing funds were 'very interested' in such opportunities, indicating a strong potential for continued growth in the sector. TIAA-CREF Asset Management, *Socially Responsible Investing: Strong Interest, Low Awareness of Investment Options* (2014), www.tiaa-cref.org/public/pdf/survey-of-TIAA-CREF-retirement-plan-participants.pdf.
13 See, e.g. F. Cornelli, I. Ioannou and T. Zhang, *ESG Moving out of the Compliance Room and into the Heart of the Investment Process* (London Business School, Coller Institute of Private Equity, February 2015), www.collerinstitute.com/content/userdocuments/newsdocuments/25.pdf (noting an increased focus on ESG integration in private equity).

14 S.J. Schuer, 'Socially Responsible Investing in the United States' in P. Camejo (ed.), *The SRI Advantage* (Gabriola Island, BC: New Society Publishers, 2002) pp. 115–22; K.K. White (ed.) and L.A. Duram (contributing ed.), *America Goes Green: An Encyclopedia of Eco-Friendly Culture in the United States* (Santa Barbara, CA: ABC-CLIO, 2013) p. 215.

15 White and Duram, *America Goes Green*, p. 215. Patient capital is sometimes used as another word for long-term capital, whereby an investor makes an investment focusing not on a quick profit, but on more substantial returns in the long run. In the world of sustainable or ethical investing the term also refers to a willingness to forgo financial returns in the name of social impact and longer time horizons for a return on investment.

16 L. Kurtz, 'Socially Responsible Investment and Shareholder Activism' in A. Crane *et al.* (eds), *The Oxford Handbook of Corporate Social Responsibility* (New York: Oxford University Press, 2008) pp. 249, 250.

17 See, e.g. Investment Leaders Group, *The Value of Responsible Investment: The Moral, Financial and Economic Case for Action* (University of Cambridge Institute for Sustainability Leadership, 2014), www.cisl.cam. ac.uk/publications/publication-pdfs/ilg-the-value-of-responsible-investment.pdf.

18 D. Marginson and L. McAulay, 'Exploring the Debate on Short-Termism: A Theoretical and Empirical Analysis' (2008) 29(3) *Strategic Management Journal* 273. See also J. Aspara *et al.*, 'Explaining Corporate Short-Termism: Self-Reinforcing Processes and Biases among Investors, the Media and Corporate Managers' (2014) 12(4) *Socio-Economic Review* 667.

19 BlackRock 'is trusted to manage more money than any other investment firm' (based on US$4.65 trillion assets under management as of 31 December 2014); BlackRock, 'Who We Are', www.blackrock.com/corporate/en-gb/about-us.

20 ValueWalk, 'BlackRock CEO Larry Fink: The Effects of the Short-Termism', 15 April 2015, www.value walk.com/2015/04/blackrock-larry-fink-on-activism.

21 Ibid.

22 See, e.g. D. Barton, 'Capitalism for the Long Term' (March 2011) *Harvard Business Review*; S. Denning, 'Why Can't We End Short-Termism?' *Forbes*, 22 July 2014; Rappaport, *Saving Capitalism from Short-Termism*; R. Della Croce, F. Stewart and J. Yermo, 'Promoting Longer-Term Investment by Institutional Investors: Selected Issues and Policies' (2011) 1 *OECD Journal: Financial Market Trends* 1.

23 Barton and Wiseman, 'Focusing Capital on the Long Term'. The survey results indicated that: (1) 63 per cent of respondents said the pressure to generate strong short-term results had increased over the previous five years; (2) 79 per cent felt especially pressured to demonstrate strong financial performance over a period of just two years or less; (3) 44 per cent said they use a time horizon of less than three years in setting strategy; (4) 44 per cent said they use a time horizon of less than three years in setting strategy; (5) 73 per cent said they should use a time horizon of more than three years; (6) 86 per cent declared that using a longer time horizon to make business decisions would positively affect corporate performance in a number of ways, including strengthening financial returns and increasing innovation.

24 Ibid.

25 Focusing Capital on the Long Term, www.fclt.org/en/theinitiative.html.

26 Ibid.

27 Cornelli *et al.*, *ESG Moving out of the Compliance Room*.

28 London Business School, 'Investors Are Driving Increased Adoption of ESG Policies', 23 February 2015, www.london.edu/news-and-events/news/investors-are-driving-increased-adoption-of-esg-policies#. VYPjxl7oCbB.

29 M. Staub-Bisang, 'Public Pension Funds: Sustainable Investment Pioneers', *Guardian*, 8 August 2013, http://theguardian.com/sustainable-business/public-pension-funds-sustainable-investment-pioneers.

30 Norges Bank Investment Management, 'The Fund', www.nbim.no/en/the-fund.

31 J. Schwartz, 'Norway Will Divest from Coal in Push against Climate Change', *New York Times*, 5 June 2015, www.nytimes.com/2015/06/06/science/norway-in-push-against-climate-change-will-divest-from-coal.html?hp&action=click&pgtype=Homepage&module=first-column-region&region=top-news&WT.nav=top-news&_r=0.

32 Ibid.

33 PGGM, *PGGM Beliefs and Foundations for Responsible Investment* (May 2014), www.pggm.nl/english/what-we-do/Documents/PGGM-Beliefs-and-Foundations-for-Responsible-Investment_May-2014.pdf.

34 PGGM, 'Statement PetroChina', www.pggm.nl/english/what-we-do/exclusions/Pages/statement-PetroChina. aspx.

35 Ibid.

36 See also L. Preesman, 'PGGM Divests on PetroChina Because of human Rights', Investments & Pensions Europe, 18 January 2008, www.ipe.com/pggm-disinvests-on-petrochina-because-of-human-rights/26791. fullarticle.

37 G. Huppé and T. Hebb, 'The Virtue of CalPERS' Emerging Equity Markets Principles' (2011) 1(1) *Journal of Sustainable Finance and Investment* 62, 62.

38 Ibid.

39 CalPERS, *CalPERS Beliefs*, 'Investment Belief 4', p. 6, www.calpers.ca.gov/eip-docs/about/pubs/calpers-beliefs.pdf.

40 See ibid., 'Investment Belief 3', p. 5, which provides that investment decisions may reflect wider stakeholder views provided they are consistent with its fiduciary duty to members and beneficiaries; 'materiality' is a factor to be considered, specifically, whether the issue has the potential for an impact on portfolio risk or return.

41 A. Stausboll, 'Selling out of Fossil Fuels No Solution for Climate Change', *Financial Times*, 22 March 2015, www.ft.com/intl/cms/s/0/def47f8c-bb8d-11e4-b95c-00144feab7de.html?siteedition=intl#axzz3VP6jgxaP.

42   US universities are not the only institutions to divest from fossil fuels. In October 2014, the University of Glasgow became the first university in the UK to divest from fossil fuels: University of Glasgow, 'Glasgow Becomes First UK University to Divest from Fossil Fuel Industry', www.gla.ac.uk/news/headline_364008_en. html.

43   National Association of College and University Business Officers, 'Building on 11.7% Gain in FY2013, Educational Endowments' Investment Returns Averaged 15.5% in FY2014', 29 January 2015, www.nacubo. org/About_NACUBO/Press_Room/2014_NACUBO-Commonfund_Study_of_Endowments_(Final_Data). html.

44   M. Posner, 'Universities Can Put Their Economic Clout to Good Use', *Chronicle of Higher Education*, 17 November 2014, http://chronicle.com/article/Universities-Can-Put-Their/150071.

45   Ibid.

46   S.H. Teoh, I. Welch and C.P. Wazzan, 'The Effect of Socially Activist Investment Policies on the Financial Markets: Evidence from the South African Boycott' (1999) 72(1) *Journal of Business* 35.

47   R. Knight, 'Sanctions, Disinvestment, and US Corporations in South Africa' in R.E. Edgar (ed.), *Sanctioning Apartheid* (Trenton, NJ: Africa World Press, 1990) pp. 67, 69.

48   Fossil Free UK, http://gofossilfree.org/uk.

49   See generally E.J. Mandrey, 'The Missing Campus Climate Debate', *New York Times*, 1 November 2014, www.nytimes.com/2014/11/02/opinion/sunday/the-missing-campus-climate-debate.html?smprod=nytcore-ipad&smid=nytcore-ipad-share.

50   Stanford Report, 'Stanford to Divest from Coal Companies', 6 May 2014, www.news.stanford.edu/news/2014/may/divest-coal-trustees-050714.html.

51   Mandrey, 'The Missing Campus Climate Debate'.

52   Stanford, 'Statement on Investment Responsibility', https://web.stanford.edu/group/apir-l/docs/public/Stanford%20University%20Statement%20on%20Investment%20Responsibility.pdf.

53   Harvard Management Company, 'Investing for the Long-Term: Integrating ESG Factors', www.hmc.harvard.edu/investment-management/sustainable_investment.html.

54   Ibid.

55   *Harvard Gazette*, 'Harvard Announces Decision to Divest from PetroChina Stock', 4 April 2005, http://news.harvard.edu/gazette/story/2005/04/harvard-announces-decision-to-divest-petrochina-stock.

56   Ibid.

57   A 2009 Mercer report consolidated 16 academic studies going as far back as 2001 and covering data collected as far back as 1989. Of the 16 reports selected for the study, 10 found evidence of a positive relationship between some type of ESG screening and financial performance. Two studies found 'negative-neutral' relationships, and four found a neutral relationship. Mercer, *Shedding Light on Responsible Investment: Approaches, Returns and Impacts* (2009), www.law.harvard.edu/programs/lwp/pensions/conferences/cm_europe12_09/Shedding_light_on_responsible_investment_free_version.pdf. A 2011 academic study of French socially responsible investment (SRI) funds found the differences in performance between SRI funds and matched samples to be statistically insignificant. P. Leite and M.C. Cortez, *Performance and Performance Persistence of European Socially Responsible Funds: French Evidence* (2011), www.efmaefm.org/0EFMAMEETINGS/EFMA%20ANNUAL%20MEETINGS/2012-Barcelona/papers/EFMA2012_0131_full-paper.pdf. That work was expanded upon in 2013 and the authors reached a similar conclusion when they included a more geographically diverse set of data covering all of Europe. P. Leite and M.C. Cortez, 'Style and Performance of Internationally Socially Responsible Funds in Europe' (2014) 30(C) *Research in International Business and Finance* 248.

58   Mercer, *Shedding Light on Responsible Investment*; Leite and Cortez, 'Style and Performance of Internationally Socially Responsible Funds in Europe'.

59   For example, a 2014 report entitled *The Case for Index-Fund Investing* by Vanguard concluded that

>   (1) the average actively managed fund has underperformed various benchmarks, (2) reported performance statistics [of actively managed funds] can deteriorate markedly once 'survivorship bias' is accounted for … and (3) persistence of performance among past winners is no more predictable than a flip of a coin.
>
>   (C.B. Philips *et al.*, *The Case for Index-Fund Investing* (Vanguard Research, 2014).

>   Additional support for the thesis that active investment management is no better than passive investing comes from B.G. Malkiel, *A Random Walk down Wall Street: The Time-Tested Strategy for Successful Investing – Completely Revised and Updated Edition* (New York: W.W. Norton & Co., 1973, 2003). Malkiel, a Professor of Economics at Princeton University, outlines the 'random walk' market theory: that sophisticated stock pickers perform no better and no worse than a randomly selected, diversified set of stocks. In Malkiel's words:

>   The evidence from several studies is remarkably uniform. Investors have done no better with the average mutual fund than they could have done by purchasing and holding an unmanaged broad stock index. In other words, over long periods of time mutual-fund portfolios have not outperformed randomly selected groups of stocks. Although funds may have very good records for certain short time periods, there is generally no consistency to superior performance.
>
>   (Ibid., p. 187)

60   Mercer, Shedding Light on Responsible Investment.

61   S. Waddock, 'Strategic Corporate Social Responsibility' in R. Kolb (ed.), *Encyclopedia of Business Ethics and Society* (Thousand Oaks, CA: Sage, 2007) p. 2008.

62   Morgan Stanley Institute for Sustainable Investment, 'Sustainable Investing's Performance Potential', 2 April 2015, www.morganstanley.com/ideas/sustainable-investing-performance-potential.

63 R.G. Eccles, I. Ioannou and G. Serafeim, 'The Impact of Corporate Sustainability on Organizational Processes and Performance' (2014) 60(11) *Management Science* 2835.
64 Ibid.
65 Ibid.
66 See, e.g. J. Nofsinger and A. Varma, 'Socially Responsible Funds and Market Crises', paper presented at Geneva Summit on Sustainable Finance, 24 December 2012, www.geneva-summit-on-sustainable-finance.ch/wp-content/uploads/2013/03/nofsinger.pdf; R. Briand, R. Urwin and P.C. Chin, MSCI, 'Integrating ESG into the Investment Process: From Aspiration to Effective Implementation', August 2011, www.msci.com/www/research-paper/integrating-esg-into-the/014288982.
67 BBC News, 'BP Found "Grossly Negligent" in 2010 Gulf Oil Spill', 4 September 2014, www.bbc.co.uk/news/business-29069184.
68 J. Plender, 'Trustees of the Non-Financial Revolution', *Financial Times*, 26 October 2014, www.ft.com/intl/cms/s/0/37d8339c-5936-11e4-a33c-00144feab7de.html?siteedition=intl#axzz3HGLVMTEE.
69 P. Tharp, 'Stormy Weather: BP's Stock Hits New Low', *New York Post*, 25 June 2010, http://nypost.com/2010/06/26/stormy-weather-bps-stock-hits-new-low.
70 Associated Press, 'BP Replaces CEO Tony Hayward, Reports $17 Billion Loss', *Times-Picayune*, 27 July 2010, www.nola.com/news/gulf-oil-spill/index.ssf/2010/07/bp_replaces_ceo_tony_hayward_r.html.
71 A. Callus, 'Smaller BP's Profits down as Oil Spill Trial Looms', Reuters, 5 February 2013, www.reuters.com/article/2013/02/05/us-bp-results-urgent-idUSBRE91409C20130205?irpc=932.
72 *New Orleans Sun*, 'BP Found "Grossly Negligent" in Gulf of Mexico Oil Spill', 4 September 2014, www.neworleanssun.com/index.php/sid/225407625.
73 Google Finance, 'BP plc', www.google.com/finance?q=NYSE:BP.

Section 5.6

Investors and human rights: values, risk and materiality[1]

Bennett Freeman

1 Introduction

Human rights have been a concern to certain investors, especially those motivated by socially responsible and faith-based values, for over three decades. Ending apartheid in South Africa was the cause that crystallized and galvanized the power that divestment could make to the liberation of a people. A generation later that movement had its echo in the face of another morally compelling human rights challenge on the same continent, when the genocide in Darfur spurred divestment from companies contributing significant revenues or other capabilities to the government of Sudan.[2] Both issues compelled action on the part of individual and institutional investors, especially public pension funds as well as college and university endowments, which felt a moral imperative or political impetus to act.[3]

A wide range of human rights issues also began to emerge over the last two decades that not only challenged corporate responsibility but also presented investors with an opportunity to address human rights. Some investors have responded creatively and constructively, from adding human rights to investment selection criteria and shareholder-advocacy agendas to raising standards through multi-stakeholder and public policy initiatives.

Four sectors – extractives, footwear and apparel, information and communication technology (ICT) and food, beverages and agriculture – have been the focus of particular attention from investors, as well as non-governmental organizations whose reports and campaigns have played an instrumental role in highlighting human rights issues. Two of those sectors were on the front lines of scrutiny by human rights activists beginning in the mid-1990s. Extractives (oil, gas and mining) companies operating in conflict zones, in countries with repressive governments and unaccountable security forces, or in proximity to Indigenous communities, came under heavy criticism in Nigeria, Indonesia and Colombia, among other countries.[4] Around the same time, footwear and apparel companies such as Nike[5] and retailers such as Walmart[6] were the subjects of allegations of labour rights and workplace safety violations throughout their global supply chains.[7] More recently, the ICT sector has come under scrutiny, with human rights issues ranging from labour rights and workplace safety to surveillance and censorship threats.[8] The food, beverage and agriculture sector also faces human rights issues related to supply chain labour rights, conflict zones and security forces, Indigenous communities and land rights.[9]

2 Materiality

The circle of responsible investors is no longer confined to those whose moral or political perspective compels them to embrace human rights, whether in the context of apartheid South Africa, Sudanese divestment movements, or in connection with issues that are prevalent in the sectors mentioned above. Some individuals and institutions continue to invest in accordance with their values in order to acknowledge and further improve the social performance of individual companies and even entire industries. But a growing number of investors[10] view non-financial environmental, social and governance (ESG) factors, including human rights, as prisms through which they can see around corners and over horizons, to focus on risks and opportunities that may affect company valuations and investment performance. This convergence of values and valuations, whereby human rights considerations may be conjoined with financial fundamentals, is sharpening the focus on human rights as an investment factor across asset classes and among asset owners and managers alike.

Human rights-related investment risk is gaining recognition among analysts and portfolio managers.[11] But its materiality (strictly defined as the potential of a particular factor to affect valuations of companies and overall performance of portfolios) has yet to be fully accepted, at least quantitatively. Intangible reputational risk is easier to identify, while financial or operational impact is harder to demonstrate.

The extractives sector is the most prone to material human rights issues with financial and operational dimensions. One major oil company saw its share price sag in part due to severe criticism of its operations in Sudan.[12] Disruption of oil production in the Niger Delta due to poor governance, community unrest and violent incidents should be seen as a material risk to oil companies operating there.[13] Similarly, the 2011 suspension of a US$4.8 billion mining project in the Andean highlands of Peru due to conflicts over land with local Indigenous communities and clashes with security forces indicates the materiality of human rights concerns for mining companies in that region.[14] A recent study has illuminated the risks posed to several hundred extractive projects around the world from Indigenous community opposition and potential violation of Indigenous peoples' rights.[15]

Material risk is becoming increasingly apparent beyond the extractives sector. Disruption of complex, highly time-sensitive supply chains due to labour and safety issues in Chinese consumer electronics factories may be material not only when valuable global brands can be tarnished with some consumers, but when product delivery is affected at times of peak market demand.[16] The revelation that surveillance by the United States (US) National Security Agency extends throughout US ICT networks not only diminished user trust in the companies operating those networks but also had the more tangible result of a loss of customers and overseas contracts.[17] These very different issues in the ICT sector reflect the growing human rights-related risks that may be material for some investors to the extent that they focus on the standards and deploy the tools now at their disposal.

A growing range of international normative standards and operational tools is evolving to help companies and industries address their human rights-related issues and responsibilities, and these standards are increasingly well known by investors and used as baselines from which to assess material risk across their portfolios. In particular, the United Nations Guiding Principles on Business and Human Rights[18] contain a due diligence framework to address human rights risks and responsibilities, which also provides investors with the basis to conduct initial due diligence on companies they may own or be interested in owning.[19] In addition, investors can take advantage of new reporting and benchmarking frameworks,[20] as well as sector-specific human rights indicators such as those developed by the Global Reporting Initiative (GRI),[21] as well as the more recent, investor-led International Integrated Reporting Council (IIRC)[22] and Sustainability Accounting Standards Board (SASB)[23] initiatives. Despite this progress, investor awareness and acceptance of these standards and tools remains uneven, even among 'responsible' investors whose focus on human rights varies among asset owners and managers in different markets.

Responsible investors should care about both values and valuations, about both the moral and material dimensions of human rights; yet too few understand and embrace the importance of non-monetary incentives. While there should be no need for anything but a moral case for human rights, as the late Sir Geoffrey Chandler insisted, most investors have distance to travel.[24] Attention to human rights-related risk on the part of investors will be most persuasive when the materiality of those risks can be not only explained but also demonstrated.[25] Yet even as progress is being made on the part of business in respecting human rights, investors will have the opportunity – and the responsibility – to take human rights into account for the foreseeable future.

Notes

1   This chapter was adapted from the author's 'Investors and Human Rights' blog contributed to the LSE Measuring Business and Human Rights Project, February 2014.
2   The United States passed the Sudan Accountability and Divestment Act 2007, which permitted state and local governments to divest assets in companies operating in Sudan, and made it easier for funds to sell investments in Sudan or in companies with ties to Sudan. See S.G. Stolberg, 'Bush Signs Bill Allowing Sudan Divestment', New York Times, 1 January 2008, www.nytimes.com/2008/01/01/world/africa/01sudan.html?_r=0.
3   See M.J. Bekink in this volume, 'Thinking long term: investment strategies and responsibility', p. 225.
4   See S. Jerbi in this volume, 'Extractives and multi-stakeholder initiatives: the Voluntary Principles on Security and Human Rights; the Extractive Industries Transparency Initiative; the Kimberley Process Certification Scheme', p. 147.

5   See A.P. Ewing in this volume, 'Mandatory human rights reporting', p. 284.
6   See A. van Heerden in this volume, 'The Fair Labor Association: improving workers' rights in global supply chains', p. 128.
7   See generally N. Klein, *No Logo* (Toronto: Knopf, 1999).
8   See in this volume J. Nolan, 'Business and human rights in context', p. 2; S. Samway, 'The Global Network Initiative: how can companies in the information and communications technology industry respect human rights?', p. 136.
9   See J. Bauer in this volume, 'The Coalition of Immokalee Workers and the Campaign for Fair Food: the evolution of a business and human rights campaign', p. 175; D. Hall and E. Lobina, *Conflicts, Companies, Human Rights and Water: A Critical Review of Local Corporate Practices and Global Corporate Initiatives* (Public Services International, 2012), www.world-psi.org/sites/default/files/documents/research/psiru_conflicts_human_rights_and_water.pdf.
10 The United Nations Principles for Responsible Investment (UNPRI) have attracted signatories among asset owners and managers collectively representing US$59 trillion in assets: UNPRI, 'PRI Fact Sheet', www.unpri.org/news/pri-fact-sheet. Similarly, US SIF – The Forum for Sustainable and Responsible Investment estimates that nearly US$5 trillion in assets are subject to at least some form of ESG criteria: US SIF Foundation, *Report on US Sustainable, Responsible and Impact Investing Trends* (10th ed., 2014), www.ussif.org/files/publications/sif_trends_14.f.es.pdf.
11 See, e.g. LYXOR Asset Management, 'Socially Responsible Investments: LYXOR SRI Principles in Brief', www.lyxor.com/about-us/sri. See also EIRIS, www.eiris.org. See generally M. Dowell-Jones in this volume, 'Investors: models and strategies for engaging with human rights', p. 209.
12 Canadian oil company Talisman sustained a prolonged drop in its share price in 2000–01 partly due to divestment campaigns spurred by its operations in Sudan, which it terminated in 2002. See J.T. Lawrence and P.W. Beamish, *Globally Responsible Leadership: Managing According to the UN Global Compact* (Thousand Oaks, CA: Sage, 2013) p. 201. See further Human Rights Watch, *Sudan, Oil, and Human Rights* (2003) pp. 416–36, www.hrw.org/reports/2003/sudan1103/sudanprint.pdf; E. Rocha and S. Haggett, 'Talisman Shares Drop as Investors Question Icahn Effect', Reuters, 8 October 2013, www.reuters.com/article/2013/10/08/us-talisman-icahn-idUSBRE9960VR20131008.
13 Between 2005 and 2010 unrest caused Nigerian production to be diminished by as much as 25 per cent. See M. Farivar, 'Nigeria Unrest Dims Outlook on Oil Prices', *Wall Street Journal*, 25 June 2007, www.wsj.com/articles/SB118272703249446497.
14 Newmont Mining's Conga mine, valued at US$4.8 billion, has been suspended since November 2011. See *Forbes*, 'Newmont's Conga Project in Peru Faces Uncertain Fate', 12 April 2013, www.forbes.com/sites/greatspeculations/2013/04/12/newmonts-conga-project-in-peru-fates-uncertain-fate.
15 First Peoples Worldwide, *Indigenous Rights Risk Report* (2014), www.firstpeoples.org/images/uploads/Indigenous%20Rights%20Risk%20Report%281%29.pdf.
16 Foxconn, the largest manufacturer of consumer electronics products in China, was reported to have faced production interruptions in 2012. See *New York Times*, 'Foxconn Denies Report of Unrest at iPhone Factory', 6 October 2012, www.nytimes.com/2012/10/07/business/foxconn-denies-report-of-unrest-at-iphone-factory.html.
17 Verizon, for example, was reported to have lost a public procurement contract with the German government in mid-2014. See *New York Times*, 'Sen. Wyden: NSA Tech Spying Hurts Economy', 8 October 2014, www.nytimes.com/aponline/2014/10/08/technology/ap-us-tec-wyden-surveillance-hurts-economy.html. In 2013, Microsoft General Counsel Brad Smith called governmental interception and collection of private data an 'advanced persistent threat' to the security and privacy of online communications: B. Smith, 'Protecting Customer Data from Government Snooping', Official Microsoft Blog, 4 December 2013, http://blogs.microsoft.com/blog/2013/12/04/protecting-customer-data-from-government-snooping.
18 Human Rights Council, 'Guiding Principles on Business and Human Rights: Implementing the United Nations "Protect, Respect and Remedy" Framework', Report of the Special Representative of the Secretary-General on the issue of Human Rights and Transnational Corporations and Other Business Enterprises, UN Doc. A/HRC/17/31 (21 March 2011).
19 Institute for Human Rights and Business, *Investing the Rights Way: A Guide for Investors on Business and Human Rights* (2013). The report was published by the IHRB in cooperation with the Interfaith Center on Corporate Responsibility and Calvert Investments to focus investors on the accessibility and utility of the Guiding Principles due diligence framework as well as other recent standards and initiatives that can help investors to identify and diminish risk.
20 See UN Guiding Principles on Business and Human Rights Reporting Framework, www.ungpreporting.org; Business & Human Rights Resource Centre, Corporate Human Rights Benchmark Initiative, http://business-humanrights.org/en/corporate-human-rights-benchmark.
21 Global Reporting Initiative, www.globalreporting.org/Pages/default.aspx.
22 International Integrated Reporting Council, http://integratedreporting.org.
23 Sustainability Accounting Standards Board, www.sasb.org.
24 Sir Geoffrey Chandler, 'Challenges of Globalisation: The Flaw of the "Business Case"', speech delivered to the Environment Foundation's Windsor Consultation, Windsor, UK, 12 December 2001, www.environment-foundation.net/reports/2001-geoffrey-chandler.htm ('unless principle precedes profit – in other words you don't accidentally kill or poison people in your employment because it's bad for business, but because it's wrong – public suspicion of business is understandably reinforced').
25 See D. Baumann-Pauly and M. Posner in this volume, 'Making the business case for human rights: an assessment', p. 11.

Chapter 6

Accountability and remedy

This chapter examines how corporations can be held accountable for their human rights conduct and how effective remedies should be available when companies violate human rights. These concerns are central to the business and human rights debate. Enhancing corporate accountability, and with it corporate human rights practice, is the ultimate objective of human rights advocates. Despite a range of early efforts, corporate human rights accountability to date rests upon an incomplete patchwork of legal and non-legal requirements.

The term 'accountability' means dramatically different things to different people. The definitional challenges are compounded in practice by individually defined reporting and due diligence processes. If each company has the latitude to define its own human rights programme without reference to an agreed-upon industry standard, corporate human rights performance does not have a reference point, nor can consumers or investors compare companies in the same industry. At this point, existing measures or structures do not provide the kind of transparency that is likely to lead to enhanced corporate accountability.

Simon Zadek's contribution outlines the foundations of the accountability concept. He observes that 'continuous improvement in accountability is not to be assumed'.[1] He argues that new and more effective accountability mechanisms need to be invented or perfected. These accountability measures need to fit into today's globalized economy, and they must recognize that private actors are assuming what we think of as public functions. Mindful of these changes, we need to develop accountability measures that respond to this evolving reality. The chapters on legal and non-legal remedial mechanisms, as well as on human rights reporting, echo Zadek's conclusion by illustrating the imperfect designs of current accountability mechanisms.

Note

1   S. Zadek in this volume, 'The meaning of accountability', p. 240.

Section 6.1

The meaning of accountability

Simon Zadek

1 Essentials of accountability

Accountability, quite literally, describes a relationship between those who have power to act and influence others, and those who are affected by their actions. Usually, it is considered to consist of one or both of two elements: 'answerability' (making power-holders explain their actions) and 'enforceability' (punishing poor or criminal performance), often described in shorthand as 'soft' and 'hard' account-ability, respectively. Accountability can usefully be thought of as the temporary accommodation between the needs of power and the claims of justice. Society or groups of stakeholders cede authority, willingly or otherwise, to those with power. In return, conditions are imposed on those with power – the priest, the general, the poli-tician and a company's board of directors – who seek to ensure that defined interests of those impacted by their actions are adequately served and protected. Such accom-modations, or deals, are temporary because accountability mechanisms often degrade over time and need renewing, sometimes peaceably but at times requiring violence.

Accountability in public debate is often framed as concerning its absence or inadequacy – that the company, or government official, or sometimes civil society organization, are not being held effectively to account. But more often than not, the problem is not that the person or organizations are unaccountable – it is that their accountability is not aligned with some stakeholders' interests. Human rights failures by business can of course happen by mistake, but more often they happen because the business is responding to demands from those to whom it is accountable, such as investors. Business is certainly accountable, but legally and otherwise, in ways that more often privilege their shareholders over their customers, employees or wider society, and privilege financial returns over human rights that carry no legal or penal-izing obligation. So when we say that a business is unaccountable, we generally mean that they are exercising their authority, and fulfilling their accountability, in ways that result in unjust and so illegitimate outcomes.

Accountability is universal in that every society has embedded accountability practices that set out the consequences of transgressing defined norms of behaviour and so establish what is considered 'just' or at least acceptable. Such norms and the basis and effectiveness of accountability evolve over time. Limited liability is perhaps the most significant accountability innovation underpinning the modern cor-poration, incorporated into law for the first time in England as the Limited Liability Act 1855 (18 & 19 Vict c. 133). The United Nations Guiding Principles on Business and Human Rights[1] are a marked development in the application of international human rights norms, with a varied and still-evolving basis of accountability, from self-regulated principles to 'civil regulation' (broadly the responses of wider society to perceived transgression of acceptable norms) and the legislated rule of law.

2 A short history of accountability

Societies' histories are marked by the history of accountability, and broader historical trends are equally underpinned by accountability innovations. A short history of accountability must begin with the family. Families are our most basic organizational unit, and continue to be a hotbed of experimentation. Experiments like polygamy, primogeniture and the allocation of domestic labour are all means of establishing legitimate authority, and so accountability, between the sexes, within and between communities and over generations. Promises too are one of the most basic of innovations in accountability, providing us with our oldest historical records of accountability. They start from the most basic level at which accountability can exist: between two people. They emphasize the interpersonal nature of the fundamentals of accountability. And yet contracts often involve witnesses to stabilize the promise in an inalienable public space, rendering accountability a communal affair. Money is one of society's most important mutual accountability innovations, enabling people who do not know each other to exchange goods and services with an intrinsically worthless promise by society at large that the equivalent value can be called upon from another, equally anonymous producer or trader. Religious institutions have provided some of the most successful and widespread means of establishing accountability because of the effectiveness of this feeling of accountability to a god or gods. Accountability in its most modern forms appears in diverse ways, from the limited liability company to democracy and the norms and at times legal accountabilities established by and as a result of United Nations declarations and agreements.

3 Making accountability work

Accountability requires that we can know and decide on certain things, and act accordingly. First, calls for accountability assume someone can be held accountable for a given action, which in turn requires that we can know *who* is accountable. Accountability requires, second, that we have the capability to do something about it, that there is some level of consensus about the action that needs to be accounted for and the penalties for failure. Accountability requires, third, a reasonably well-defined 'community' that can reach such decisions. Someone can only be unaccountable if they are part of that community where the rules have been generally accepted, adopted and can be enforced.

What is challenging is how we negotiate accountability with and between groups with whom we share only slim common interests and identity. More formally, we can understand this problem as concerning the need to balance the dynamic of *intensive* (homogeneous accountability holders) and *extensive* (heterogeneous accountability holders) accountability. Company boards, conventionally, are responsible for the business's financial success, a mandate often embodied in law. Broader stakeholder interests, such as the rights of consumers and workers, are in that context instrumentally relevant to the board fulfilling its duties and basis of accountability. Impacted stakeholders, whose well-being contributes nothing to or even costs the company, are hard to accommodate, unless the scope of either soft or hard account-ability is broadened, or else the company's underlying ethos or values dictate actions beyond the satisfaction of external accountability holders.

Globalization and scaled effects require us to resolve the fact that distant, *extensive* relationships often produce effects normally reserved for more proximate, *intensive* relationships. Climate change caused by carbon emissions from one community impacts distant, otherwise unrelated communities, creating huge challenges in forging workable accountabilities – from the attribution of cause and effect to the valuation of impact to the means by which one will be held accountable for impacts elsewhere. Just as global supply chains required and drove the cutting edge of accountability innovations from the early 1990s onwards, and new technologies are already raising a multitude of challenges in determining rights and accountabilities, so climate change and other 'public goods' (outcomes that cannot be exclusively privately or often through choice consumed) are generating the new envelope of innovation for the determination of rights and accountabilities.

4 Business, human rights and accountability

Continuous improvement in accountability is not to be assumed. This is true whether its application is to business and human rights, to the matter of citizens' choice over their governments, or the ability of citizens as consumers to hold businesses to account. Increasing pressure on campaigning organizations in some countries demon-strates that the spheres of application and effectiveness of accountability are in con-tinual contestation, from constraining legislation and judicial action driven by governments and businesses, to illegal harassment, imprisonment and worse. Several decades of concerted focus on using transparency as a core accountability mech-anism has in many respects been disappointing, despite many business- and situation-specific successes in exposure leading to improved practices. Corruption, an invidious source of human rights abuse, has by all accounts increased over the period, just as most indexes of freedoms and rights have levelled off or declined after decades of uninterrupted improvements.

On the other hand, accountability innovations are a continuous feature of vibrant societies, as new norms, political and broader institutional forms, and technologies interact in the context of evolving economic and ecological conditions. Electronic communications such as social media provide inspiration and platforms for new accountability mechanisms, engaging hitherto excluded or apathetic citizens in actions intended to hold those with power to account. Increased transparency of busi-nesses, and proactive actors who want to make use of such information, from inves-tors to regulators, consumers and voters, can make a difference. Corporate governance models that drive extended interests can make a major difference, from B corporations (with multi-purpose or 'beneficial' mandates) to the growth of state-directed enterprises and sovereign wealth funds. Countries that have lagged behind in advancing rights in modern times are struggling with the political risks of system-atically weak legal systems, and are often focusing improvements particularly on corporate accountability.

Note

1   Human Rights Council, 'Guiding Principles on Business and Human Rights: Implementing the United Nations "Protect, Respect and Remedy" Framework', Report of the Special Representative of the Secretary-General on the issue of Human Rights and Transnational Corporations and Other Business Enterprises, UN Doc. A/HRC/17/31 (21 March 2011).

Introduction to Sections 6.2–6.4

Litigation and access to non-judicial remedy

While guidelines and principles espousing corporate responsibilities for human rights have proliferated in recent years, mechanisms for providing victims with remedies when such norms are violated are less commonplace. The right to an effective remedy is an essential component of human rights. The third pillar of the United Nations Guiding Principles on Business and Human Rights[1] demands access to judicial or non-judicial remedies. However, to date the mechanisms employed to provide effective remedies vary greatly in both their scope and effectiveness. It is clear that more work needs to be done to transform 'access to remedy' from mere principles to practice.

One remedial tool is litigation. Lawsuits have been used as a potential 'stick' to compel corporations to uphold human rights standards or face damages claims if they fail to do so. In particular, litigation brought under the Alien Tort Statute (ATS)[2] in the United States (US) (or perhaps more accurately the threat of such litigation) has been one of the principal tools for advocates who seek compensation from businesses for their actions that violate human rights standards. ATS litigation has attracted inordinate attention in the business and human rights field. While these lawsuits often garner significant corporate attention, very few cases have brought relief to the plaintiffs. According to Harold Koh, the ATS is 'an extremely limited, highly conditional, litigable instrument of last resort'.[3] As detailed in the chapter by William Dodge, a series of decisions by the US Supreme Court – including its 2013 ruling in *Kiobel v Royal Dutch Petroleum Co*[4] – has placed substantial limits on such litigation and may well mean that business and human rights litigation in US courts will need to identify and rely on different legal approaches.

Recent developments outside the US, particularly in Europe and Canada, seem to offer somewhat better prospects for using national courts as a means to hold corporations legally accountable for actions in their global operations. But such cases are far from being straightforward. Christine Kaufmann discusses some of the principal challenges to establishing legal accountability, especially in European courts. Among these challenges are problems in establishing the jurisdiction of national courts to hear claims based on harms that have occurred elsewhere, and the difficulty in attributing legal liability to parent companies based on the actions of their subsidiaries or subcontractors.

In Europe and the US, litigation is a long and arduous process with multiple challenges. Too often those who have been harmed by corporate activity have very limited capacity to file lawsuits or to pursue other avenues of redress. Recognizing this gap, a number of people have begun to develop non-judicial grievance mechanisms (NJGMs) for victims seeking redress. As discussed by Kristen Genovese, 'in an ideal world, NJGMs would supplement judicial mechanisms, but the reality is that in many jurisdictions judicial remedies are ineffective or non-existent,[5] and NJGMs are, in practice, the only option for those affected by business-related human rights abuse'.[6] NJGMs vary widely in terms of their scope, process and outcomes. The very characteristic that might attract victims to attempt litigation – the legally binding nature of a judgment – is absent in the case of many NJGMs. However, some NJGMs, particularly those set up within established multistakeholder initiatives, have proven to be effective and 'socially binding'.

As with litigation, these non-judicial remedies also have a history of inconsistent 'success'. In sum, none of the current avenues that are available to victims seeking to right corporate wrongs provide consistent, reliable or effective remedies.

Notes

1   Human Rights Council, 'Guiding Principles on Business and Human Rights: Implementing the United Nations "Protect, Respect and Remedy" Framework', Report of the Special Representative of the Secretary-General on the issue of Human Rights and Transnational Corporations and Other Business Enterprises, UN Doc. A/HRC/17/31 (21 March 2011).
2   28 USC §1350.
3   H. Koh, 'Separating Myth from Reality about Corporate Responsibility Litigation' (2004) 7(2) *Journal of International Economic Law* 263, 269, referred to in D. Kinley, *Civilising Globalisation* (Cambridge: Cambridge University Press, 2009) p. 193.
4   133 S. Ct. 1659 (2013).
5   G. Skinner, R. McCorquodale and O. de Schutter, *The Third Pillar: Access to Judicial Remedies for Human Rights Violations by Transnational Business* (International Corporate Accountability Roundtable, CORE and European Coalition for Corporate Justice, 2013) p. 66.
6   K. Genovese in this volume, 'Access to remedy: non-judicial grievance mechanisms', p. 266.

Section 6.2

Business and human rights litigation in US courts before and after *Kiobel*

William S. Dodge

1 Introduction

In the United States (US), litigation brought by private parties under the Alien Tort Statute (ATS)[1] has been one of the principal tools for business and human rights accountability. But a series of decisions by the US Supreme Court – including its 2013 ruling in *Kiobel v Royal Dutch Petroleum Co*[2] – has placed substantial limits on such litigation and may well bring the era of business and human rights litigation in US courts to an end. This chapter describes the emergence of ATS litigation against corporations in the US before *Kiobel*, as well as developments in US courts after that case.

2 Emergence of the ATS as a tool of accountability

The ATS was part of the Judiciary Act of 1789 that first established the federal courts in the United States.[3] As codified today, the provision reads: 'The district courts shall have original jurisdiction of any civil action by an alien for a tort only, committed in violation of the law of nations or a treaty of the United States.'[4] The ATS lay dormant in American law until 1980, when the Court of Appeals for the Second Circuit held in *Filartiga v Pena-Irala*[5] that the statute provided a federal forum for human rights claims.

Joel and Dolly Filartiga were the father and sister of Joelito Filartiga. They alleged that Americo Pena-Irala, a police inspector in Paraguay, had tortured Joelito to death in retaliation for his father's political activities.[6] Pena later came to the US, where he overstayed his visa and was sued by the Filartigas before being deported to Paraguay. Backed by a memorandum filed by the US government, the Second Circuit held that the ATS gave the District Court jurisdiction over the case because the Filartigas were aliens, the claim was in tort and official torture violated customary international law, the modern equivalent of the 'law of nations' to which the ATS refers.[7] *Filartiga* thus began the era of human rights litigation in US courts.

That era nearly ended prematurely in 1984 with *Tel-Oren v Libyan Arab Republic*.[8] In that case, plaintiffs sued the Palestine Liberation Organization (PLO) for a terrorist attack in Israel.[9] The three-judge panel agreed that the case should be dismissed, but could not agree on the reason for dismissal. Judge Edwards agreed with *Filartiga* that *official* torture violated customary international law but he did not think that *unofficial* acts by the PLO implicated the law of nations.[10] Judge Bork, on the other hand, argued that plaintiffs lacked a 'cause of action' – or right to sue – because neither international law nor federal common law created one.[11] Congress responded to Judge Bork's opinion in 1992 by passing the Torture Victim Protection Act (TVPA),[12] which grants an express cause of action for torture and extrajudicial killing under colour of foreign law and extends that cause of action not just to aliens but also to US citizens.

3 Suits against corporations and *Sosa*

The first suits against corporations under the ATS were filed in 1996.[13] The most famous is *Doe v Unocal*, in which villagers from Myanmar alleged that an American oil company had aided and abetted the Myanmar military in subjecting them to forced labour, murder, rape and torture while Unocal built a pipeline. These corporate cases raised new issues, in particular whether a corporation could be held liable not for committing human rights violations directly but for aiding and abetting government actors in doing so. In *Unocal*, the Ninth Circuit held that aiding and abetting human rights violations was itself a violation of customary international law and therefore actionable under the ATS.[14]

In the meantime, the ATS reached the US Supreme Court for the first time in *Sosa v Alvarez-Machain*.[15] *Sosa* was not a corporate case. It was brought by a

Mexican doctor abducted at the behest of the US Drug Enforcement Agency (DEA) to stand trial for involvement in the murder of a DEA agent. But Sosa's counsel was also counsel to Unocal and advanced an argument that would not only have won the case for Sosa but would also have put an end to the corporate cases. Echoing Judge Bork's opinion in *Tel-Oren*, Sosa argued that the ATS was strictly jurisdictional and did not create a cause of action.[16] The Bush administration supported this argument and added that inferring a cause of action would violate the so-called 'presumption against extraterritoriality' – the presumption that US law applies only within the territory of the US.[17]

The Supreme Court rejected Sosa's 'cause of action' argument and did not address the United States' extraterritoriality argument. The court held that federal courts could recognize a cause of action under federal common law for violations of international law, but only if the international law norm was as generally accepted and specifically defined as the norms against piracy and violations of the rights of ambassadors that Congress had in mind when it passed the ATS in 1789.[18] The claim in *Sosa* – arbitrary detention – did not meet this standard, so the defendant Sosa won his case.[19] But the court seemed to endorse the *Filartiga* line of cases, and suits against corporations continued.

After *Sosa*, both plaintiffs and defendants viewed the question of aiding and abetting liability through *Sosa*'s lens. Plaintiffs argued that aiding and abetting should be governed by federal common law – like the ATS cause of action – while defendants argued that aiding and abetting should be governed by international law and was not well enough established to meet the *Sosa* standard.[20] Courts generally concluded that aiding and abetting was actionable but divided on the standard for liability: the Second and Fourth Circuits held that corporations would be liable only if they acted with the 'purpose' of providing substantial assistance to the human rights violation;[21] the DC and Eleventh Circuits held that 'knowledge' of the substantial assistance was sufficient for liability.[22]

By 2012, approximately 60 cases alleging violations of international law had been filed against corporations under the ATS.[23] Many were dismissed for lack of jurisdiction or on other threshold grounds, but about 20 led to extended litigation.[24] A few settled, including *Doe v Unocal*[25] and *Wiwa v Royal Dutch Petroleum Co*,[26] a case alleging involvement in the Nigerian military's attacks on civilians protesting the company's oil operations.

4 *Kiobel v Royal Dutch Petroleum Co*

In 2014 it was another case against Royal Dutch Petroleum Co that brought the ATS back to the US Supreme Court. Nigerian nationals brought a class action[27] alleging that the defendant had aided and abetted the government's human rights violations in the Ogoni region of Nigeria. On appeal, the Second Circuit surprisingly held that corporations could not be sued at all under the ATS because 'customary international law has steadfastly rejected the notion of corporate liability for international crimes'.[28] Other circuits disagreed.[29] They recognized that the correct approach was not to consider corporate liability or non-liability in the abstract – divorced from the particular norms alleged to be violated – but rather, as the Ninth Circuit put it, to 'consider separately each violation of international law alleged and which actors may violate it'.[30]

Snapshot

Kiobel v Royal Dutch Petroleum Co

Nigerian nationals brought suit under the ATS against Royal Dutch Petroleum Company (a Dutch company), Shell Transport and Trading Company (a British company) and their subsidiary Shell Petroleum Development Company of Nigeria (a Nigerian company). The plaintiffs alleged that the defendants had enlisted the Nigerian government to suppress demonstrations against its oil operations in the Niger Delta. The Nigerian military and police allegedly attacked Ogoni villages, beating, raping and killing their residents, while the defendant companies allegedly allowed their property to be used as staging areas for attacks and provided food, transportation and payment.

The District Court for the Southern District of New York dismissed the Nigerian subsidiary for lack of personal jurisdiction, but held that aiding and abetting claims could be brought against its parent companies.[31] On appeal the Second Circuit held that corporations could not be sued under the ATS because international law does not recognize corporate liability.[32] Ultimately, the US Supreme Court dismissed the case on a different ground – that the claims did not touch and concern the territory of the US with sufficient force to displace the presumption against extraterritoriality.

The Supreme Court took the case to decide whether corporations could be sued under the ATS. But after oral argument, the court directed the parties to brief the additional question whether courts may recognize causes of action for violations of international law within the territory of a country other than the US. Writing for the majority, Chief Justice Roberts answered with a qualified 'no'.[33] Under the so-called 'presumption against extraterritoriality', US statutes are presumed to apply only within the territory of the US unless there is a clear indication to the contrary.[34] Roberts CJ acknowledged that the presumption does not typically apply to jurisdictional statutes like the ATS, but he reasoned that 'the principles underlying the canon of interpretation similarly constrain courts considering causes of action that may be brought under the ATS'.[35] He found nothing in the text, history or purposes of the ATS to rebut the presumption.[36] But the majority opinion did not close the door to all cases against corporations or to all cases involving violations of human rights outside the US. In the final paragraph of his opinion, the Chief Justice said:

> On these facts, all the relevant conduct took place outside the United States. And even where the claims touch and concern the territory of the United States, they must do so with sufficient force to displace the presumption against extraterritorial application. Corporations are often present in many countries, and it would reach too far to say that mere corporate presence suffices. If Congress were to determine otherwise, a statute more specific than the ATS would be required.[37]

Kiobel's final paragraph, which was likely added to secure Justice Kennedy's crucial fifth vote, appears to leave open a number of possibilities. First, in some cases – even in some cases against foreign corporations – some 'relevant conduct' might occur in the US although the human rights violation itself did not. Second, in some cases the defendant might be a US corporation rather than a foreign corporation. If 'mere corporate presence' does not suffice, perhaps corporate domicile does. Third, in some cases the defendant might be an individual rather than a corporation. Corporations 'are often present in many countries', but individuals are not, and *Kiobel* reserves the possibility that *Filartiga*-type suits against individuals might proceed. Whether any of these possibilities – alone or in combination – might make a claim 'touch and concern the territory of the United States' with enough force to displace the presumption against extraterritoriality has been the principal question in ATS litigation since *Kiobel*.

Justice Kennedy's one-paragraph concurring opinion confirms that *Kiobel* 'leave[s] open a number of significant questions regarding the reach and interpretation of the Alien Tort Statute'.[38] Ironically, so does Justice Alito's concurrence. Justice Alito would have held that the presumption against extraterritoriality bars an ATS cause of action 'unless the domestic conduct is sufficient to violate an international law norm that satisfies *Sosa*'s requirements of definiteness and acceptance among civilized nations'.[39] The fact that only Justice Thomas joined Justice Alito highlights that the majority did not hold that the conduct violating international law had to occur in the US, as Justice Alito would have held. On the other side of the court, Justice Breyer and the three justices who joined him (Ginsburg, Sotomayor and Kagan JJ) would have recognized a cause of action if the tort occurred in the US, if the defendant were a US national or if recognizing a cause of action were necessary to prevent the US from becoming a safe harbour for human rights violators.[40] Thus, if Justice Kennedy decides that a cause of action should exist in any of the circumstances left open by *Kiobel*, there appear to be four justices ready to join him.

Before turning to the post-*Kiobel* cases, it is necessary to mention two other Supreme Court decisions that have shaped the landscape. First, the year before *Kiobel*, in *Mohamad v Palestinian Authority*,[41] the court unanimously held that the TVPA – the statute Congress passed in 1992 to create express causes of action for torture and extrajudicial killing under colour of foreign law – was limited to suits against natural persons. Therefore, although the TVPA plainly applies extraterritorially, it cannot be used to sue corporations. Second, the year after *Kiobel*, in *Daimler AG v Bauman*,[42] the court held by a vote of 8–1 that courts in the US may not exercise personal jurisdiction over claims unrelated to the forum unless the defendant has enough contacts with the forum state to render it 'at home' there.[43] The court suggested that only corporations that are incorporated in or have their principal place of business in the US would be subject to general jurisdiction of this sort,[44] placing a further limit on plaintiffs' ability to sue foreign corporations on claims that arise abroad, including human rights claims.[45]

5 The landscape after *Kiobel*

Four questions dominate the legal landscape for business and human rights cases in US courts after *Kiobel*: (1) personal jurisdiction; (2) corporate liability; (3) the standard for aiding and abetting liability; and (4) what will satisfy *Kiobel*'s 'touch and concern' test.[46]

5.1 Personal jurisdiction

The fact that transnational corporations often operate through locally incorporated subsidiaries can make them hard to sue in the US. In *Kiobel*, for example, the parent companies ran their oil operations in Nigeria through a Nigerian subsidiary, which was removed as a defendant at an early stage in the litigation because it did not have sufficient contacts with the US to subject it to personal jurisdiction. The British and Dutch parent companies did not challenge personal jurisdiction in *Kiobel*, but they certainly would today because under *Daimler* there is no chance they would be considered 'at home' in the US. An American parent company would, of course, be subject to general jurisdiction by US courts. But even in that case, a court would have to find either that the parent company itself engaged in conduct giving rise to liability or that the subsidiary's conduct was attributable to the parent. Thus, rules of personal jurisdiction pose a substantial barrier to business and human rights litigation in US courts. Moreover, these rules apply not just to suits in federal courts under the ATS but also to any suits that might be brought in US state courts.

5.2 Corporate liability

As noted above, the Second Circuit held in *Kiobel* that corporations could not be sued at all under the ATS, while other circuits held that corporations are liable to suit.[47] Chief Justice Roberts' discussion of corporations in the last paragraph of his *Kiobel* opinion – and particularly his statement that 'it would reach too far to say that mere corporate presence suffices'[48] – suggests that corporations may be sued. But the Second Circuit has adhered to its position 'that corporate liability is not presently recognized under customary international law and thus is not currently actionable under the ATS'.[49] The Ninth Circuit has similarly reaffirmed its holding that a corporation can be sued if it violates an international law norm that applies to all actors, and has held that the prohibition against slavery is such a norm.[50] Thus, the circuits continue to be divided on the question of corporate liability.

5.3 Aiding and abetting

Before *Kiobel*, the Courts of Appeals had held that claims for aiding and abetting human rights violations could be brought under the ATS, but had divided on whether liability required a showing of knowledge or purpose.[51] This split has also persisted after *Kiobel*, with the Second Circuit adhering to its purpose standard,[52] the Eleventh Circuit adhering to its knowledge standard[53] and the Ninth Circuit continuing to reserve the question.[54]

5.4 'Touch and concern'

Four circuits have had occasion to apply the 'touch and concern' test to corporations since *Kiobel*.[55] The Second Circuit has held that 'neither the US citizenship of defendants, nor their presence in the United States, is of relevance for jurisdictional purposes'.[56] Therefore, 'if all the relevant conduct occurred abroad, that is simply the end of the matter under *Kiobel*'.[57] The Fourth, Ninth and Eleventh Circuits, on the other hand, have held that the US nationality of the defendants is *relevant* to the 'touch and concern' analysis but not sufficient by itself.[58]

The principal question in the cases decided so far has been how much US conduct is required, and of what character. Many of the cases allege conduct in the US that aids and abets human rights violations abroad. As the Fourth Circuit has noted, 'it is not sufficient merely to say that because the actual injuries were inflicted abroad, the *claims* do not touch and concern United States territory'.[59] Each of the circuits to have considered the question has indicated that decision-making in the US *may* be sufficient to satisfy the 'touch and concern' test.[60] But most have found such claims lacking in some respect. In *Mujica v AirScan, Inc*, the Ninth Circuit found claims of planning from the US to be 'speculation'.[61] In *Doe v Drummond*, the Eleventh Circuit weighed the alleged planning in the US against the execution of those plans in Colombia and concluded that 'the domestic location of the decision-making alleged in general terms here does not outweigh the extraterritorial location of the rest of Plaintiffs' claims'.[62] And in *Mastafa v Chevron Corp*, the Second Circuit required that the alleged conduct in the US itself constitutes a violation of international law,[63] a position that comes quite close to Justice Alito's concurring opinion in *Kiobel*.[64]

Snapshot

Cardona v Chiquita Brands International, Inc

Colombian nationals brought suit under the ATS and TVPA against Chiquita Brands International, Inc and Chiquita Fresh North LLC, both companies incorporated in the US. Plaintiffs alleged that defendants from their offices in the US approved payments to the terrorist organization Autodefensas Unidas de Colombia (AUC) and facilitated shipments of weapons and ammunition with the purpose of aiding and abetting extrajudicial killings to suppress labour activism and local competition. In a separate criminal prosecution brought by the US, Chiquita pleaded guilty to making illegal payments to the terrorist organization but argued that it did so because of threats to its employees and property.

On appeal, the Eleventh Circuit concluded without explanation that, as in *Kiobel*, all the relevant conduct took place outside the US.[65] The court further concluded that the US nationality of the defendants was not sufficient by itself to displace the presumption against extraterritoriality and that the case should therefore be dismissed. The US Supreme Court denied review.

In only one post-*Kiobel* case has a Court of Appeals found that the claims involving human rights violations abroad 'touch and concern' the US with sufficient force to displace the presumption against extraterritoriality. In *Al-Shimari v CACI Premier Technology, Inc*, the Fourth Circuit allowed an ATS suit to proceed against a US military contractor for torture at Abu Ghraib prison in Iraq.[66] The court cited, among other things, the US nationality of both the corporation and its employees, its contract for interrogation services with the US government and the allegations that managers in the US gave tacit approval to the torture.[67] But these facts are not typical of the business and human rights cases brought under the ATS.

6 Conclusion

The number of business and human rights cases that survived a motion to dismiss or resulted in a settlement before *Kiobel* was small, and the number seems bound to shrink in the wake of that decision. Plaintiffs must squeeze through a number of doors – establishing personal jurisdiction, convincing the court that corporations are liable to suit under the ATS, proving the facts necessary to meet the applicable standard for aiding and abetting liability and showing that conduct in the US is sufficient to displace the presumption against extraterritoriality. Unless and until the Supreme Court takes another corporate ATS case and opens some of these doors a little wider, the number of cases likely to succeed seems small indeed.

Notes

1   28 USC §1350.
2   133 S. Ct. 1659 (2013).
3   For discussion of the history leading to the ATS, see W.R. Casto, 'The Federal Courts' Protective Jurisdiction over Torts Committed in Violation of the Law of Nations' (1996) 18 *Connecticut Law Review* 467.
4   28 USC §1350. There are 94 federal judicial districts in the United States, which are organized into 12 regional circuits. Each regional circuit has a court of appeals designated by a number (e.g. the Court of Appeals for the Second Circuit) or in one case by a geographic location (the Court of Appeals for the District of Columbia Circuit). The US Supreme Court hears appeals from the courts of appeals but has discretion whether to accept a case for review.
5   630 F.2d 876 (2d Cir. 1980). For a comprehensive account of the *Filartiga* case, see W.J. Aceves, *The Anatomy of Torture: A Documentary History of Filartiga v Pena-Irala* (Leiden: Brill, 2007).
6   *Filartiga*, 630 F.2d 876, 878–9.
7   Ibid., 880–5.
8   726 F.2d 774 (DC Cir. 1984).
9   The plaintiffs also sued Libya, but that claim was dismissed under the US Foreign Sovereign Immunities Act of 1976, 28 USC §§1330, 1332, 1391(f), 1441(d), 1602–11.
10   *Tel-Oren*, 726 F.2d 774, 788 (Edwards J concurring).
11   Ibid., 798–823 (Bork J concurring). Judge Robb thought the case should be dismissed as a political question: at 823–7.
12   28 USC §1350 note.
13   See *Beanal v Freeport-McMoRan, Inc*, 969 F. Supp. 362 (ED La. 1997); *Doe v Unocal Corp*, 963 F. Supp. 880 (CD Cal. 1997).
14   *Doe v Unocal Corp*, 395 F.3d 932, 947–9 (9th Cir. 2002). Judge Reinhardt concurred but thought the question of complicity should be governed by federal common law not international law: at 963. The Ninth Circuit vacated the panel opinion when it granted rehearing en banc: see *Doe v Unocal Corp*, 395 F.3d 978 (9th Cir. 2003). Ultimately, the parties settled the case, and the en banc court dismissed the appeal: see *Doe v Unocal Corp*, 403 F.3d 708 (9th Cir. 2005).
15   542 US 692 (2004).
16   Brief of Petitioner at 9–45, *Sosa*, 542 US 692.
17   Brief for the United States as Respondent Supporting Petitioner at 47–8, *Sosa*, 542 US 692.
18   *Sosa*, 542 US 692, 732.
19   Ibid., 738.
20   See W.S. Dodge, 'Alien Tort Litigation: The Road Not Taken' (2014) 89 *Notre Dame Law Review* 1577, 1599–602.
21   See *Presbyterian Church of Sudan v Talisman Energy, Inc*, 582 F.3d 244, 257–9 (2d Cir. 2009) (purpose standard under international law); *Aziz v Alcolac, Inc*, 658 F.3d 388, 401 (4th Cir. 2011) (same).
22   See *Doe v Exxon Mobil Corp*, 654 F.3d 11, 39 (DC Cir. 2011) (knowledge standard under international law); *Cabello v Fernandez-Larios*, 402 F.3d 1148, 1158–9 (11th Cir. 2005) (knowledge standard under federal common law); see also *Sarei v Rio Tinto, plc*, 671 F.3d 736, 765 (9th Cir. 2011) (en banc) (noting the question without resolving it). Professor Chimène Keitner has argued convincingly that aiding and abetting liability under international law requires only a showing of knowledge not purpose: C.I. Keitner, 'Conceptualizing Complicity in Alien Tort Cases' (2008) 60 *Hastings Law Journal* 61, 83–96; see also Dodge, 'Alien Tort Litigation', p. 1601, n.211 (collecting authorities).
23   See B. Stephens, 'The Curious History of the Alien Tort Statute' (2014) 89 *Notre Dame Law Review* 1467, 1518.
24   Ibid., pp. 1518–19.

25 See EarthRights International, 'Final Settlement Reached in Doe v Unocal', 21 March 2005, www.earthrights. org/legal/final-settlement-reached-doe-v-unocal. For further details, see also http://ccrjustice.org/newsroom/ press-releases/settlement-reached-human-rights-cases-against-royal-dutch/shell.

26 226 F.3d 88 (2d Cir. 2000). See Stephens, 'The Curious History of the Alien Tort Statute', p. 1519, n.283.

27 Class actions are representative proceedings brought by one or more persons on behalf of a group of people.

28 *Kiobel v Royal Dutch Petroleum Co*, 621 F.3d 111, 120 (2d Cir. 2010).

29 See, e.g. *Sarei*, 671 F.3d 736, 747–8; *Exxon Mobil*, 654 F.3d 11, 40–57; *Flomo v Firestone Natural Rubber Co*, 643 F.3d 1013, 1017–21 (7th Cir. 2011).

30 *Sarei*, 671 F.3d 736, 748. See also W.S. Dodge, 'Corporate Liability under Customary International Law' (2012) 43 *Georgetown Journal of International Law* 1045.

31 *Kiobel v Royal Dutch Petroleum Co*, 456 F. Supp. 2d 457 (SDNY, 2006).

32 *Kiobel*, 621 F.3d 111.

33 *Kiobel v Royal Dutch Petroleum Co*, 133 S. Ct. 1659, 1669 (2013).

34 See, e.g. *Morrison v National Australia Bank Ltd*, 561 US 247 (2010) (holding that anti-fraud provisions of the Securities Exchange Act of 1934 apply only to transactions in the US).

35 *Kiobel*, 133 S. Ct. 1659, 1664.

36 Ibid., 1665–9.

37 Ibid., 1669.

38 Ibid., 1669 (Kennedy J concurring).

39 Ibid., 1670 (Alito J concurring).

40 Ibid., 1674 (Breyer J concurring).

41 132 S. Ct. 1702 (2012).

42 134 S. Ct. 746 (2014).

43 Ibid., 760.

44 Ibid.

45 *Daimler* was a human rights suit under the ATS and TVPA: ibid., 751. But the court's holding did not depend on that fact.

46 Courts still sometimes dismiss ATS cases on other grounds. See, e.g. *Fischer v Magyar Allamvasutak Zrt*, 777 F.3d 847 (7th Cir. 2015) (affirming dismissal on *forum non conveniens* grounds); *Saldana v Occidental Petroleum*, 774 F.3d 544 (9th Cir. 2014) (affirming dismissal on political question grounds).

47 See notes 28–9 above and accompanying text.

48 *Kiobel*, 133 S. Ct. 1659, 1669.

49 *Chowdury v World Bangladesh Holding Ltd*, 746 F.3d 42, 49 n 6 (2d Cir. 2013); see also *Mastafa v Chevron Corp*, 770 F.3d 170, 179 n 5 (2d Cir. 2014); *Balintulo v Daimler AG*, 727 F.3d 174, 191 n 26 (2d Cir. 2013).

50 See *Doe v Nestle USA, Inc*, 766 F.3d 1013, 1022 (9th Cir. 2014).

51 See notes 21–2 above and accompanying text.

52 See *Mastafa*, 770 F.3d 170, 192–3.

53 See *Doe v Drummond Co*, 782 F.3d 576, 609 (11th Cir. 2015) (applying knowledge standard to TVPA claim).

54 See *Nestle*, 766 F.3d 1013, 1024. Contra at 1029 (Rawlinson J concurring in part and dissenting in part): 'Unlike the majority, I would definitely and unequivocally decide that the purpose standard applies to the pleading of aiding and abetting liability under the ATS.'

55 Although application of the 'touch and concern' test to individual defendants is beyond the scope of this chapter, courts appear to have applied it in the same way as to corporations. See, e.g. *Sikhs for Justice, Inc v Nath*, 596 Fed. Appx. 7, 10 (2d Cir. 2014): '[B]ecause all of the conduct relevant to the alleged ATS violations occurred abroad, defendants' alleged presence in the United States is insufficient to displace the presumption against extraterritoriality and to establish jurisdiction under the ATS.'

56 *Mastafa*, 770 F.3d 170, 188.

57 *Balintulo*, 727 F.3d 174, 190.

58 See *Drummond*, 782 F.3d 576, 596: 'Although the US citizenship of Defendants is relevant to our inquiry, this factor is insufficient to permit jurisdiction on its own'; *Mujica v Airscan Inc*, 771 F.3d 580, 594 (9th Cir. 2014): 'the fact that Defendants are both US corporations ... without more, is not enough to establish that the ATS claims here "touch and concern" the United States with sufficient force'; *Al-Shimari v CACI Premier Technology, Inc*, 758 F.3d 516, 527 (4th Cir. 2014): 'courts must consider all the facts that give rise to ATS claims, including the parties' identities and their relationship to the causes of action.'

59 *Al-Shimari*, 758 F.3d 516, 528; see also *Drummond*, 782 F.3d 576, 593 n 24: 'it would reach too far to find that the only *relevant* factor is where the conduct occurred, particularly the underlying conduct'; *Mastafa*, 770 F.3d 170, 185: 'the "relevant conduct" in a complaint' may be 'either a direct violation of the law of nations or ... conduct that constitutes aiding and abetting another's violation of the law of nations'.

60 *Drummond*, 782 F.3d 576, 597; *Mujica*, 771 F.3d 580, 591; *Mastafa*, 770 F.3d 170, 182–3, 185, 195; *Al-Shimari*, 758 F.3d 516, 530–1.

61 771 F.3d 580, 592.

62 782 F.3d 576, 598.

63 See 770 F.3d 70, 187.

64 See *Kiobel*, 133 S. Ct. 1659, 1670 (Alito J concurring) (presumption against extraterritoriality bars claim 'unless the domestic conduct is sufficient to violate an international law norm that satisfies *Sosa*'s requirements'); see also *Mastafa*, 770 F.3d 170, 184 n 11 (agreeing with Justice Alito).

65 *Cardona v Chiquita Brands International, Inc*, 760 F.3d 1185 (11th Cir. 2014).

66 *Al-Shimari*, 758 F.3d 516.

67 Ibid., 530–1.

Section 6.3

Holding multinational corporations
accountable for human rights violations:
litigation outside the United States

Christine Kaufmann

1 Introduction

This chapter provides an overview on the use of tort and civil action-based litigation outside the United States (US). It highlights some developments in Europe, Canada and Australia as typical home countries of multinational corporations (MNCs);[1] it also discusses selected cases from India, Peru and South Africa to illustrate challenges for access to remedy in host countries.[2]

Remedies for people who are affected by human rights infringements have only recently become a topic in the discussion on human rights and business. In line with the traditional notion of sovereignty and the related principle of territoriality, providing judicial mechanisms for reconciliation and compensation, as well as the prosecution of perpetrators, has been seen as a mainly domestic affair. States are responsible for implementing their international human rights obligations, including their duty to protect people against human rights violations by corporate actors, within their own territory. However, in many countries, particularly those with weak governments, in conflict-affected regions, or in a post-conflict context, local legal remedies are often absent or not efficient. For this reason, the third pillar of the United Nations (UN) Guiding Principles on Business and Human Rights[3] (Guiding Principles) upholds a joint responsibility for states and corporations to provide access to remedy for people affected by human rights infringements. This responsibility includes a state obligation to establish mechanisms for holding MNCs judicially liable for human rights violations. States should remove legal, practical and other barriers for actions against MNCs as part of their duty to protect as well as provide access to remedy according to the Guiding Principles. The obstacles for filing a complaint against an MNC locally (in the host country) are manifold and may include insufficient legal remedies, lack of resources and widespread corruption. One option to remedy this situation is to revise existing procedural rules at the local level in the host country. Some countries have considered including such a revision in their National Action Plan for implementing the Guiding Principles. In this regard, the example of South Africa is worth mentioning with its High Court recently being more open to accepting so-called class actions which allow victims to join forces to bring a lawsuit against a corporation.[4]

As a result, alternatives for holding MNCs accountable in their home countries, where the legal system may be more elaborate, are currently being discussed. However, the approaches taken by countries to hold corporations legally accountable vary greatly, as the following cases will illustrate. The cases demonstrate that it is essential to establish jurisdiction so that a court will look into the substance of a case. Related to the issue of jurisdiction is the question of whether parent companies can be held accountable for their foreign subsidiaries' actions. Given that alleged human rights violations by MNCs will regularly be of a transnational nature, involving not only different procedures but also different legal systems, it will not always be obvious what the applicable law is. This may be particularly relevant when the level of human rights protection or the extent of a corporate duty of care to prevent human rights infringements vary greatly between the host and the home country.

The following analysis focuses on three topics that are increasingly shaping the discussion around domestic civil liability for MNCs: the jurisdiction of national courts to hear claims based on harms that have occurred elsewhere; the liability of parent companies in respect of their own actions or omissions, or those of their subsidiaries; and the applicable law in domestic claims.

2 Jurisdiction

To be able to hear and decide a case, a court must have jurisdiction over it. It is generally accepted that courts in countries where human rights abuse, injury or damage has occurred (*host* countries) have jurisdiction to hear claims related to the harm based on the so-called principle of territoriality. This principle is one of the key elements of the traditional concept of a state under international law. It means that a state has jurisdiction over all persons, property and activities in its territory. For several reasons, including potentially more favourable applicable laws (for example, concerning parent company liability and the quantum of damages), victims might, however, want to bring cases in the state where the corporation is incorporated or domiciled. Under international law this would imply having to refer to another element for a state's jurisdiction (apart from territoriality): nationality. Since corporations do not have a passport, their home country is the country where they have been registered or have their headquarters. However, due to complex procedural requirements, the establishment of a forum in the *home* states of MNCs may be challenging and require a thorough analysis and argument as to why proceedings in the host country would not be more suitable. The necessity to decide between different available courts is inherent to any legal system and courts have been faced with it for centuries in different contexts. In order to resolve situations where different courts may be seized with a case, different approaches have been developed for determining the most appropriate venue, among them the *forum non conveniens* and *forum necessitatis* doctrines.

According to the *forum non conveniens* doctrine, courts have the discretion to grant a stay on proceedings despite a real and substantial connection between the forum and the subject matter of the claim, in favour of a forum in which the case may be 'tried more suitably for the interests of all the parties and the ends of justice'.[5] The doctrine is mostly applied by countries following a common law tradition.[6] Both plaintiffs and defendants regularly invoke the doctrine given the inherent tension between, on the one hand, providing plaintiffs with a choice of venue for claims where there may be more than one appropriate jurisdiction and, on the other hand, preventing so-called forum shopping, i.e. picking a court merely to gain an advantage in the proceedings.

Another important principle with regard to courts' discretion in adopting a case is the *forum necessitatis* doctrine, which is widely known in civil law jurisdictions.[7]

It allows a court to assert jurisdiction over a case even if the standard conditions for jurisdiction are not fully met as long as no other forum that is capable of providing a fair trial is reasonably available to the victim, there is some connection with the forum and it seems reasonable for the court to decide the case.[8]

While the principle of fairness serves as the legal backbone for both the *forum non conveniens* and the *forum necessitatis* doctrines, interpretations of the former vary among courts while the latter seems to be applied in a rather uniform way.[9] Given the relatively broad discretion for courts to adopt a case under common law rules, the jurisprudence may indicate some early trends for the role of the Guiding Principles' third pillar in establishing jurisdiction. While the decisions discussed below are of course only binding within their respective jurisdictions, they nevertheless tend to influence other courts in deciding on similar issues.[10]

Snapshot

Club Resorts Ltd v Van Breda

In its 2012 landmark decision, *Club Resorts Ltd v Van Breda*,[11] the Supreme Court of Canada provided clarification concerning the application of the *forum non conveniens* doctrine by Canadian courts. In particular, the court identified several presumptive factors that establish a real and substantial connection between the forum (in this case the corporation's home state) and the subject matter of the litigation, and which entitle a court to assume jurisdiction: the defendant is domiciled or resident or carrying on business in the Canadian province where jurisdiction is said to exist; the tort was committed in the province; or a contract connected with the dispute was concluded in the province.[12] Once such a connection is established a court may apply the *forum non conveniens* doctrine provided that it takes into consideration the impact of a transfer on the conduct of the litigation, the possibility of conflicting judgments and the principle of 'comity and an attitude of respect for the courts and legal systems of other countries'.[13] Although the case does not seem to refer to a typical business and human rights context at first glance, the joint intervention submitted by the Canadian Centre for International Justice, the Canadian Lawyers for International Human Rights and Amnesty International illustrates its potential relevance in ensuring access to justice for victims of corporate human rights abuses who may otherwise not have access to a court.[14] While the Supreme Court in its decision did not engage in a discussion on the interveners' detailed argument on the legal foundations of the *forum necessitatis* doctrine, it nevertheless confirmed that in the absence of a real and substantial connection to the home country, a court may still assert jurisdiction based on the doctrine.[15] In addition, by not addressing the Ontario Court of Appeals' reasoning that *forum necessitatis* is recognized by Canadian common law,[16] the Supreme Court let this precedent stand.[17]

This case arose out of injuries sustained by two Canadians in separate incidents while they were each on vacation in Cuba. Ms Van Breda suffered catastrophic injuries when a metal exercise structure that she was using on a private beach managed by Club Resorts Ltd collapsed on her. Mr Charron died while he was on a scuba diving trip organized by a resort managed by Club Resorts. Actions were brought in Ontario against a number of parties, including Club Resorts, which was incorporated in the Cayman Islands. Club Resorts sought to block those proceedings, arguing that the Ontario courts lacked jurisdiction and, in the alternative, that a Cuban court would be a more appropriate forum on the basis of the *forum non conveniens* principle.

On appeal by Club Resorts, the Supreme Court of Canada held that because each contract relied upon by the plaintiffs was entered into in Ontario, and since Club Resorts' commercial activities were also in Ontario, a presumption in favour of Ontario's courts having jurisdiction had been established. The Supreme Court then moved on to examine Club Resorts' claim for applying the *forum non conveniens* doctrine. It concluded that while a sufficient connection existed between Cuba and the subject matter of the litigation to support an action there, there were sufficient concerns regarding fairness to the parties and the efficient disposition of the claim to reject Club Resorts' claims in each case. In particular, the court emphasized that a trial held in Cuba would impose an unduly heavy burden on the plaintiffs.

In *Association Canadienne contre l'impunité (ACCI) v Anvil Mining Ltd*,[18] ACCI brought an action before the Superior Court of Québec on behalf of civilian victims of a military conflict in the Democratic Republic of Congo (DRC). They argued that the defendant, a corporation registered in Canada's Northwest Territories and listed in Ontario but with its head office in Australia (and also listed on the Australian Stock Exchange), had provided assistance to a military attack against a group of rebels resulting in 70 people being killed in a Congolese town. Québec's jurisdiction was said to arise because Anvil had established an office in Montreal. Thus, pursuant to art. 3148(2) of the Civil Code (which confers jurisdiction over legal persons with 'an establishment in Québec' and where 'the dispute relates to its activities in Québec'), it was argued that Anvil was established in Québec and the dispute related to its activities in Québec. This argument was accepted by the Superior Court, which held that Anvil's operations in Québec were 'necessarily linked' to the events in issue in the DRC, since mining was Anvil's primary activity. The Superior Court also rejected Anvil's *forum non conveniens* claim, which was based on art. 3135 of the Civil Code, finding that Australian and Congolese courts would not be in a position to secure victims' access to justice.[19] On appeal,[20] Anvil asserted the need for a nexus between the dispute and the jurisdiction in which a case is heard. It also revived its *forum non conveniens* claim. The Québec Court of Appeal found for Anvil on the basis that the case did not have a sufficient connection with Québec (in particular, Anvil's office in Montreal was established after the alleged conduct forming the basis of the claim) with the result that neither the *forum non conveniens* doctrine nor the *forum necessitatis* doctrine[21] applied.

In contrast, the Australian threshold for a stay on the grounds of *forum non conveniens* is stricter than in Canada because an action can only be dismissed on this basis if an Australian forum is 'clearly inappropriate'.[22] In *Dagi v Broken Hill Proprietary Co*, plaintiffs from Papua New Guinea (PNG) sued the Australian mining company BHP in the Supreme Court of Victoria because the defendant was incorporated in Victoria and had allegedly polluted a river in PNG by dumping waste and thereby compromised the livelihood of people living nearby.[23] Given its limited chance for success, BHP did not try to obtain a dismissal on the grounds of *forum non conveniens* even though the plaintiffs lived in PNG, the damage had mostly occurred there and most of the evidence was also there.[24] The case was eventually settled, an outcome that some observers interpreted as a result of Australia's restrictive approach to *forum non conveniens*.[25]

In the United Kingdom (UK), the discussion of *forum non conveniens* has taken a different route, not least in the light of recent European Union (EU) legislation. The classic interpretation was outlined in the leading case of *Lubbe v Cape plc*.[26]

Snapshot

Lubbe v Cape plc

Three workers from a South African mine operated by Cape plc's South African subsidiaries, and two villagers living near the mine, claimed damages in the English High Court from Cape plc, an MNC incorporated in the UK, for personal injuries said to be the result of exposure to asbestos. Subsequently, more than 3,000 additional plaintiffs joined the action. In light of the number of South African plaintiffs, the Court of Appeal[27] reconsidered an earlier decision[28] and stayed the proceedings on grounds of *forum non conveniens*. However, the House of Lords overruled this finding. In affirming its jurisdiction, the court reasoned that a case of such magnitude required effective legal representation as well as experts on technical and medical issues. Since South Africa, as the country where the injuries had taken place, was not in a position to fulfil these requirements, the application of the *forum non conveniens* doctrine would result in a denial of justice for the plaintiffs. Therefore, the case was to be heard by English courts.

The House of Lords in *Lubbe* did not deem it necessary to address the plaintiffs' motion that art. 2 of the Brussels Convention[29] would preclude the application of the *forum non conveniens* doctrine, or the defendant's argument that the court's discretion to grant a stay in favour of a forum in a non-contracting state was not affected by the Convention. Instead, the court held that it would defer the question to the European Court of Justice if it were relevant in the case at hand. The question was decided in 2005, when the European Court of Justice clarified in *Owusu v Jackson*[30] that the Brussels I Regulation provided that national courts within the EU had jurisdiction over *all persons* who are domiciled in their jurisdiction. With this decision, the doctrine of *forum non conveniens* lost its relevance in EU member states. However, the latest revision of the Brussels I Regulation provides member state courts with some discretion to stay proceedings in favour of a court in a third state provided that a stay is necessary for the 'proper administration of justice'.[31] It remains to be seen how these new provisions will be applied by courts in practice. In addition, the question of whether courts in a parent company's home state have jurisdiction over its foreign subsidiaries requires further clarification.

In sum, establishing jurisdiction is as challenging as it is essential in providing victims of corporate human rights abuses with access to remedy. While defendants' pleas for removal of cases on grounds of *forum non conveniens* are a legitimate instrument to prevent forum shopping by plaintiffs, such claims may not only limit plaintiffs' choice of venue but also – and more importantly – result in a denial of access to remedy for victims. This is particularly relevant in situations where legal redress is not available locally, i.e. in the host country where the human rights violation took place. Therefore, expanding the doctrine of *forum of necessity*, as it is already known in many civil law countries and arguably anchored in art. 6 of the

European Convention on Human Rights,[32] is an important instrument for fostering victims' access to legal remedies according to the Guiding Principles. The *forum necessitatis* doctrine allows courts to accept a complaint for corporate human rights abuses even if the standard conditions for jurisdiction are not fully met provided that no other forum is available. By providing a minimum standard for victims who would otherwise not have access to a court, the doctrine seems to follow a similar logic to the well-established concept of *ordre public* (public order), which provides that measures which may be formally legal must not be taken if they do not meet fundamental standards of the forum state. In cases of serious corporate human rights violations without adequate access to remedy for the victims, public order could be used as an additional argument for establishing a *forum necessitatis*.

3 Parent company liability

Holding a parent company accountable for human rights abuses can take two different forms: it can refer to either the company's *direct involvement* in the abuses or its responsibility for actions of its *subsidiaries*. Direct liability of the parent company may entail its actions as well as its omissions.

In general, subsidiaries are separate legal entities and therefore by definition legally distinct from their parent. Holding the parent company liable for actions of a subsidiary therefore requires reaching through the corporate legal structure, a so-called '*piercing of the corporate veil*'. This process is subject to strict conditions and mainly applies where the separate legal entity is established for the purpose of avoiding legal liability or a related abuse of legal rights. The specific requirements are defined by, and vary according to, domestic law.

Snapshot

Akpan v Royal Dutch Shell plc[33]

In 2008 five court procedures were initiated before a Dutch District Court in The Hague by four Nigerian villagers and Milieudefensie, a non-governmental organization, against Royal Dutch Shell plc (RDS), a company incorporated in the UK and headquartered in The Hague, and its Nigerian subsidiary, Shell Petroleum Development Company of Nigeria Ltd (SPDC).

According to the plaintiffs, oil had spilled from pipelines operated by SPDC in the Niger Delta and polluted farmlands and fish ponds, contaminated drinking water sources and, as a result, compromised their livelihoods. The plaintiffs argued that SPDC had neglected its duty of care by neither taking preventive measures nor undertaking to mitigate the effects of the oil spills and adequately clean up the contaminated sites. The plaintiffs also alleged that RDS had violated its duty of care since it did not exercise its control over SPDC to ensure the safety of the oil production.

In an interlocutory ruling in 2009, the court first confirmed that it had jurisdiction to hear the case not only against the Dutch-based RDS but also against its Nigerian subsidiary SPDC because the two companies were co-defendants and the claims against them were connected. In another interlocutory ruling in 2011, the court declared that Nigerian tort law, which follows English tort law, was the applicable law for the claims.

In 2013, the court eventually issued its decision on the merits. It concluded that the oil spills were the result of sabotage and vandalism and not of SPDC's actions. Since Nigerian law did not provide a general legal obligation for pipeline operators to prevent sabotage, the court dismissed all claims that were based on negligent maintenance except for one instance involving SPDC. Under that claim, SPDC was held accountable despite the oil spill being the result of sabotage because it had not taken adequate measures to secure an oil well after it was no longer used by SPDC. As for the claims against RDS, the court found that there was no legal obligation in Nigerian law for the parent company to prevent its subsidiaries from doing harm to third parties except in very special circumstances that were not at issue in this case. As a result, all claims against RDS were dismissed.

On appeal the Hague Court of Appeals recognized its jurisdiction for claims against RDS and ordered RDS to provide the court with documents to clarify its involvement in the oil spills.

The decision by the Dutch Court of Appeals in *Akpan* marks an important step in the quest to establish adequate mechanisms to hold business accountable for harm caused abroad. While the US Supreme Court in *Kiobel v Royal Dutch Shell Petroleum Co*[34] made it clear that it would not hear such a case due to the lack of a sufficient nexus with the US, the Dutch Court of Appeals held that the relationship between RDS and its Nigerian subsidiary was sufficiently close to establish the jurisdiction of Dutch courts. The court's approach takes into account the fact that people affected by human rights abuses in the context of corporate activities will often face difficulties in bringing a complaint in the country where the abuse occurred, not least because of ill-equipped judicial systems, widespread corruption or lack of funding.

Snapshot

Choc v Hudbay Minerals, Inc

Members of an indigenous group in Guatemala brought three related actions against the Canadian mining company Hudbay Minerals, Inc and its subsidiaries HMI Nickel, Inc and Compañía Guatemalteca de Níquel SA (CGN) in the Ontario Superior Court.[35] The plaintiffs alleged that human rights abuses had occurred in Guatemala during a forced removal from an area which local indigenous populations claimed were ancestral homelands but that was needed to facilitate the development of a mining project. The alleged abuses included shootings, killings and gang rapes by security personnel hired by the defendant and its subsidiaries. In addition, the plaintiffs submitted that the local community had not been consulted when the mining concession on their ancestral land was granted.

The defendants sought to have the case struck out on a number of grounds, most relevantly that the plaintiffs had failed to establish the conditions to pierce the corporate veil or the constituent elements for a claim of direct negligence by Hudbay.

In 2013, the court held that the plaintiffs' argument that CGN was an *agent* of Hudbay Minerals corresponded to one of the three exceptions for piercing the corporate veil. In the case at hand, this allegation was 'not patently ridiculous or incapable of proof'.[36] The court concluded that a duty of care on the part of Hudbay was not obviously absent, and the facts presented by the plaintiffs – if proven at trial – could establish that the harm complained of was the reasonably foreseeable consequence of the defendants' conduct. Finally, the court saw no obvious policy consideration to prevent the case from moving to trial.

The other claimed bases for dismissal were rejected.[37] As a result, the actions will move to trial.

In Canadian and English law, findings of negligence require that the damage suffered by the victim was 'reasonably foreseeable' to the defendant, that there is a relationship of proximity between the parties and that it is fair, just and reasonable to impose liability. To hold a parent company liable for actions of its subsidiaries on the basis of negligence, a duty of care must be proven. Furthermore, it must be shown that this duty was breached and that the breach resulted in damage or loss to the claimant. Finally, the claimant has to establish that the damage suffered was close enough to justify compensation in the circumstances.[38]

Snapshot

Bodo Community v Shell Petroleum Development Company (Nigeria) Ltd

In 2012, over 15,000 plaintiffs of the Bodo community in Nigeria sued Shell Petroleum Development Company (Nigeria) Ltd (SPDC) in the London High Court.[39] In return for SPDC submitting to the High Court's jurisdiction, the plaintiffs agreed not to pursue their claims against Royal Dutch Shell (RDS), SPDC's UK-based parent company. The plaintiffs sought compensation for the damage resulting from two oil spills in the Niger Delta in 2008 and 2009. In addition, they asked for a clean-up of the area. The oil spills caused damage to their health, livelihoods and land and had allegedly occurred due to the poor maintenance of out-of-date pipelines.

In a preliminary ruling in June 2014,[40] Justice Akenhead referred to s. 11(5)(b) of the applicable Nigerian Oil Pipelines Act 1956, which provides for compensation

> to any person suffering damage by reason of any neglect on the part of the holder or his agents ... to protect, maintain or repair any work, structure or thing executed under the licence, for any such damage not otherwise made good.

Justice Akenhead held that this provision involved a 'general shielding and caring obligation' for an oil company that could inter alia entail informing the police about known acts of sabotage or taking appropriate protective measures to prevent pipelines from leaking.[41] As a result, he found that SPDC could be held responsible for the oil spills if it did not undertake reasonable measures to protect them from malfunction or oil theft. Documents produced in November 2014 showed that SPDC had been warned about the risks of the pipeline prior to the oil spills. With regard to the acts of sabotage and oil thefts themselves, Justice Akenhead concluded that under the Oil Pipelines Act, the defendants could not be held responsible.

In January 2015, SPDC agreed to a substantial out-of-court settlement and pledged to clean up the Bodo Creek.[42]

Although the *Bodo* case was settled, it sparked a series of other lawsuits in the UK related to oil spills in the Niger Delta. It remains to be seen how courts will react to this new development and decide on their jurisdiction, which, owing to SPDC's acceptance of the High Court's jurisdiction, was not an issue in the *Bodo* case.

Another English case, *Chandler v Cape plc*,[43] provides guidance concerning the responsibility of a parent company for its subsidiary.

Snapshot

Chandler v Cape plc

Mr Chandler worked in a factory owned by Cape Building Products Ltd (Cape Products), a subsidiary of Cape plc (Cape) for several months in 1959 and 1961. During this time Mr Chandler was exposed to asbestos fibres. In 2007 he was diagnosed with asbestosis, a chronic lung condition caused by prolonged exposure to asbestos. Due to an exclusion clause for asbestosis in Cape Products' insurance policy, Mr Chandler brought a claim against his employer's parent company Cape plc in the Manchester County Court. He argued that Cape owed a direct duty of care to the employees of its subsidiary. In 2011, the Court of Appeals upheld the High Court's decision and confirmed Cape's liability.[44] The court developed a four-prong test to establish a parent company's responsibility for the health and safety of its subsidiary's employees:

> (1) the businesses of the parent and subsidiary are in a relevant respect the same; (2) the parent has, or ought to have, superior knowledge on some relevant aspect of health and safety in the particular industry; (3) the subsidiary's system of work is unsafe as the parent company knew, or ought to have known; and (4) the parent knew or ought to have foreseen that the subsidiary or its employees would rely on its using that superior knowledge for the employees' protection.[45]

Based on this test, the court concluded that Cape owed a *direct duty of care* to the employees of Cape Products.

It is important to note that *Chandler* was framed as an issue of direct liability and not of piercing the corporate veil. The Court of Appeal's approach was confirmed in a similar asbestos-related case, *Thompson v The Renwick Group plc*.[46] Again, the court made it clear that there was no general duty of care owed by the parent company to its subsidiary's employees but stated the inquiry in these terms:

> [W]hat one is looking for here is a situation in which the parent company is better placed, because of its superior knowledge or expertise, to protect the employees of subsidiary companies against the risk of injury and moreover where, because of that feature, it is fair to infer that the subsidiary will rely upon the parent deploying its superior knowledge in order to protect its employees from risk of injury.[47]

While Cape plc and the Renwick Group were both accused of being responsible for asbestos-related human rights infringements, the Renwick Group had not been involved in business operations but only held shares in its subsidiary. Therefore, the court decided that it did not owe a duty of care towards its subsidiary's employees.

The legal relationship between a parent company and its subsidiaries is relevant in a business and human rights context because it determines the attribution of responsibility. Since subsidiaries are formally independent legal persons, a parent company's responsibility for its subsidiary's actions requires a specific legal basis. Such a basis may be found in the parent company's negligence to oversee its subsidiaries or to intervene in cases of known negative human rights impacts such as safety and health issues in the production process. Another option is to argue for piercing the corporate veil and thereby considering the parent company and its subsidiaries as a (business) unit rather than as two separate legal entities. Both avenues require extensive knowledge of the parent company and its proximity to the subsidiaries, which may be difficult to obtain for the plaintiffs.

4 Applicable law

Once a court has asserted its jurisdiction it will have to identify the criteria for parent company liability. In the absence of an internationally agreed standard the specifics of a corporate duty of care or the conditions for piercing the corporate veil will therefore depend on the standards of the applicable national law.[48] Given the transnational context in which such situations occur, there are often several national laws involved in establishing different standards with regard to a parent company's duty of care or the conditions for piercing the corporate veil. Defining the applicable law can therefore be decisive for the merits of a case. Most courts will determine liabilities according to the law of the place where the injuries or damages were sustained (*lex loci delicti*). Accordingly, the Rome II Regulation obliges courts in the EU to apply the 'law of the country in which the damage occurs' unless the tort is manifestly more closely connected with another country, in which case the law of that other country is applicable.[49] In the context of international business activities this principle will often result in the law of the host country being applicable, as illustrated in some of the cases discussed above. From the Guiding Principles' perspective, applying the host country's law may hinder victims' access to remedy if the local standards are low. In addition, applying different legal standards to a parent company depending on the location of where the injury or the damage takes place is increasingly questioned as being in line with the spirit of the Guiding Principles' concept of a corporate responsibility to respect. This has sparked discussions on whether home countries of MNCs should establish duties of care for business activities conducted at home *and* abroad.[50] In several countries this discussion takes place in the context of developing a National Action Plan for implementing the UN Guiding Principles.

5 Conclusion

While the work on implementing the Guiding Principles has gained momentum with regard to their pillars one (state duty to protect) and two (corporate responsibility to respect), substantial progress in providing victims with efficient access to remedies has not yet been achieved. In many countries, particularly those that are rich in resources, affected by conflicts or with weak governments and widespread corruption, the local court system is not working efficiently, remedies may be lacking or not be accessible for victims of human rights abuses. Examples to illustrate these findings include cases regarding mining activities in Peru, where the government is not enforcing a law that imposes an obligation on mining companies to consult with indigenous communities prior to commencing operations.[51] A case involving a Korean company in a mining project in India reveals the complexity that complaints against corporate human rights abuses may involve: only rising public pressure together with statements by UN experts,[52] as well as discussions in several OECD National Contact Points, seem to have brought about a change of view in the Indian Supreme Court and the Indian government.[53] Yet, the affected local tribe had to fight over a period of more than 10 years and largely depended on external support.

A variety of reasons accounts for the inadequacies of local courts and remedies. Countries that are rich in resources are often affected by conflicts and weak governmental structures, which pave the way for corruption and may result in unequal access to court proceedings and the lack of an independent judiciary. In addition, inadequate protection of minorities and indigenous populations often goes hand in hand with the lack of opportunities to seek legal relief in cases of human rights violations, for example, in the context of large investment projects. Given the complexity of business-related human rights cases with different jurisdictions and different legal standards, legal knowledge may not always be sufficiently available for local communities and local judges.

In order to overcome these deficiencies and the resulting limited nature of access to remedies in countries where corporate human rights abuses take place, lawsuits are increasingly filed against parent companies in their home countries, sometimes including their subsidiaries as co-defendants. The cases discussed above point towards an emerging foreign direct liability for corporations, at least within Europe and Canada.

First, the doctrine of *forum non conveniens* is increasingly seen in combination with the need to establish a *forum necessitatis* to overcome some legal obstacles that prevent victims litigating in courts in a corporation's home country.

Second, complaints tend to focus on direct liability more often, particularly based on negligence, rather than aiming to pierce the corporate veil of a parent company. While the UK and Canada require a measure of proximity between a parent company and its subsidiaries, as well as the possibility of the parent company exerting influence over a subsidiary, establishing a breach of duty remains challenging for plaintiffs given that the relevant documentation is often not publicly available or may be difficult to obtain in discovery.

A third observation relates to applicable national law. Due to the widespread acceptance of the *lex loci delicti* principle, the applicable law for complaints filed against parent companies in their home country will often be the law of the country where the abuse took place, i.e. the law of the host country. However, applying different standards to a parent company depending on the geographical scope of its business activities raises concerns with regard to the feasibility and legitimacy of such an approach. Apart from applying a purpose-oriented perspective, which would treat the parent company and its subsidiaries as a business unit despite their formal legal independence and thus pierce the corporate veil, the so-called *ordre public* (public order) exception could be applied. The *ordre public* exception provides that laws which do not meet fundamental standards of the forum state must not be applied. The idea behind this concept is also reflected in Guiding Principle No. 12, which sets minimum human rights standards to be respected by corporations. While there is ample jurisdiction with regard to applying the *ordre public* exception in cases of inadequate fundamental human rights standards, for example, in extradition cases, its role with regard to access to remedy requires further exploration. One avenue to pursue could be to link the logic of the *ordre public* exception with the discussion on establishing a forum of necessity and argue that not accepting a complaint for serious corporate human rights abuses would result in depriving victims of their right to access to remedy. The ongoing discussions on how to include access to remedy measures in National Action Plans may provide a forum for such a discussion.[54]

Notes

1   MNCs and TNCs (transnational companies) are terms used interchangeably throughout this volume.
2   Criminal complaints, administrative law actions and claims based on false advertising are outside the scope of this chapter.
3   Human Rights Council, 'Guiding Principles on Business and Human Rights: Implementing the United Nations "Protect, Respect and Remedy" Framework', Report of the Special Representative of the Secretary-General on the issue of Human Rights and Transnational Corporations and Other Business Enterprises, UN Doc. A/HRC/17/31/Annex (21 March 2011).
4   *Gold Fields Limited & Ors v Motley Rice LLC* [2015] ZAGPJHC 62 (19 March 2015). The particular issue in this case is whether a specific litigation funder ought to be joined as a party (thereby enabling costs orders).
5   *Spiliada Maritime Corporation v Cansulex* [1987] AC 460, 476.
6   G.A. Bermann, 'Parallel Litigation: Is Convergence Possible?' (2011) 13 *Yearbook of Private International Law* 21, 23–6.
7   For example, in France, Germany, Netherlands, Ireland, Portugal, Switzerland and Canada (Quebec): C. Nwapi, 'Jurisdiction by Necessity and the Regulation of the Transnational Corporate Actor' (2014) 30 *Utrecht Journal of International and European Law* 24.
8   Ibid., p. 24.
9   A. Nuyts, *Study of Residual Jurisdiction: Review of the Member States' Rules concerning the 'Residual Jurisdiction' of Their Courts in Civil and Commercial Matters Pursuant to the Brussels I and II Regulations* (Final Report for the European Commission, 3 September 2007), http://ec.europa.eu/civiljustice/news/docs/study_residual_jurisdiction_en.pdf.
10 Studies show that in many countries domestic courts will increasingly consider decisions by foreign courts. For commentary on Europe, see M. Bobek, *Comparative Reasoning in European Supreme Courts* (Oxford: Oxford University Press, 2013). For commentary on the US, see E. Volokh, 'Foreign Law in American Courts' (2014) 66(2) *Oklahoma Law Review* 219.
11 *Club Resorts Ltd v Van Breda*, 2012 SCC 17.
12 Ibid., para. 90.
13 Ibid., paras 110, 112. This decision seems to depart from *Recherches International du Québec v Cambior, Inc* [1998] QJ No 2554, in which the Superior Court of Québec held that Guyana was the more appropriate forum for a class action against a Canadian mining company on behalf of Guyanese victims of a spill of toxic fluids that resulted in polluted water.
14 Factum of the Interveners, Canadian Centre for International Justice, Canadian Lawyers for International Human Rights and Amnesty International, SCC File No. 33692/33606 (7 March 2011), www.ccij.ca/programs/cases/index.php?DOC_INST=15.
15 *Club Resorts Ltd v Van Breda*, 2012 SCC 17, para. 100.
16 *Van Breda v Village Resorts Limited*, 2010 ONCA 84, paras 100, 109.
17 Ibid., paras 59, 82, 86, 100.

18 2011 QCCS 1966.
19 An attempt to bring a class action claim in Australia had earlier foundered following alleged interference by the DRC in the process of locating witnesses, and the ensuing withdrawal of the Australian law firm seeking to bring the case.
20 *Association Canadienne contre l'impunité (ACCI) v Anvil Mining Ltd*, 2012 QCCA 117.
21 Code civil du Québec, art. 3136.
22 *Voth v Manildra Flour Mills* (1990) 171 CLR 538.
23 *Dagi v Broken Hill Proprietary Co* (1997) 1 VR 428.
24 P. Prince, 'Bhopal, Bougainville and Ok Tedi: Why Australia's *Forum non Conveniens* Approach Is Better' (1998) 47(3) *International and Comparative Law Quarterly* 573, 594–5.
25 Ibid., 594.
26 [2000] 1 WLR 1545.
27 [2000] 1 Lloyd's Rep. 139, 155.
28 [1998] CLC 1559.
29 Brussels Convention on Jurisdiction and the Recognition and Enforcement of Judgments in Civil and Commercial Matters 1968, now replaced by Regulation (EU) No. 1215/2012 of the European Parliament and of the Council of 12 December 2012 on jurisdiction and the recognition and enforcement of judgment in civil and commercial matters, OJ L351, 20 December 2012, in force 10 January 2015.
30 *Owusu v Jackson* [2005] ECR 1383. The decision referred to the 2001 version of the Regulation: Council Regulation (EC) No. 44/2001 of 22 December 2000 on jurisdiction and the recognition and enforcement of judgments in civil and commercial matters, OJ L12, 16 January 2001.
31 Regulation (EU) No. 1215/2012 of the European Parliament, arts 33, 34.
32 Convention for the Protection of Human Rights and Fundamental Freedoms, Rome, 4 November 1950, in force 2 June 1952, 213 UNTS 221.
33 *Friday Alfred Akpan and Vereniging Milieudefensie v Royal Dutch Shell plc and Shell Petroleum Development Company of Nigeria Ltd*, C/09/337050/HA ZA 09-1580 (District Court of The Hague, 30 January 2013).
34 133 S. Ct. 1659 (2013). See further W.S. Dodge in this volume, 'Business and human rights litigation in US courts before and after *Kiobel*', p. 244.
35 *Choc v Hudbay Minerals Inc* [2013] ONSC 1414.
36 Ibid., para. 49.
37 The defendant argued that the limitation period for a claim based in negligence had expired. This was rejected on the basis that the claim dealt with sexual assault rather than negligent supervision and, accordingly, limitation periods did not apply: ibid., paras 82–4.
38 J. Zerk, *Corporate Liability for Gross Human Rights Abuses: Towards a Fairer and More Effective System of Domestic Law Remedies*, report prepared for the Office of the UN High Commissioner for Human Rights (2013) 44, 46, www.ohchr.org/Documents/Issues/Business/DomesticLawRemedies/StudyDomesticeLawRemedies.pdf.
39 *Bodo Community v Shell Petroleum Development Company of Nigeria Ltd* [2014] EWHC 1973.
40 Ibid.
41 Ibid., para. 92(g).
42 Leigh Day, 'Shell Agrees £55m Compensation Deal for Niger Delta Community', 7 January 2015, www.leighday.co.uk/News/2015/January-2015/Shell-agrees-55m-compensation-deal-for-Nigeria-Del.
43 [2012] EWCA Civ 525.
44 Ibid.
45 Ibid., para. 80.
46 [2014] EWCA Civ 635.
47 Ibid., para. 37.
48 Nigerian law was applied by a British court in *Bodo* [2014] EWHC 1973, and a Dutch court in *Akpan* C/09/337050/HA ZA 09-1580 (District Court of The Hague, 30 January 2013). In other cases, English law was applicable: see, e.g. *Connelly v RZT Corporation plc* [1997] 3 WLR 373; *Sithole & Ors v Thor Chemicals Holdings Ltd and Desmond Cowley* [2000] WL 1421183; *Guerrero v Monterrico Metals plc* [2009] EWHC 2475 (QB); [2010] EWHC 3228 (QB); *Vava v Anglo American South Africa Ltd* [2013] EWHC 2326 (WB).
49 Regulation (EC) 864/2007 of the European Parliament and of the Council of 11 July 2007 on the law applicable to non-contractual obligations (Rome II), OJ L199/40 (31 July 2007), art. 4.
50 An example is the proposed legislation for expanding large corporations' due diligence to their activities abroad. The proposal has been accepted by the French National Assembly in its first reading but rejected by the Senate. It is now pending with the National Assembly again: see *Proposition De Loi relative au devoir de vigilance des sociétés mères et des entreprises donneuses d'ordre*, 19 November 2015, www.assemblee-nationale.fr/14/propositions/pion3239.asp.
51 Republic of Peru, Defensoría del Pueblo, Oficio No. 629-2015, 26 May 2015, www.defensoria.gob.pe/modules/Downloads/documentos/Oficio-629-2015-DP-OD-LAMB.pdf.
52 Office of the High Commissioner for Human Rights, 'India: Urgent Call to Halt Odisha Mega-Steel Project amid Serious Human Rights Concerns', 1 October 2013, www.ohchr.org/en/NewsEvents/Pages/DisplayNews.aspx?NewsID=13805&LangID=E.
53 *Geomin Minerals & Marketing (P) Ltd v State of Orissa & Ors* [2013] INSC 553 (10 May 2013).
54 See C. Pitts in this volume, 'The United Nations "Protect, Respect, Remedy" Framework and Guiding Principles', p. 51.

Section 6.4

Access to remedy: non-judicial grievance mechanisms

Kristen Genovese

1 Introduction

There is no shortage of standards for corporate conduct. States have obligations under international human rights treaties to protect against human rights violations by corporations. Soft law and voluntary standards – on everything from the handling of toxic chemicals[1] to the conduct of private security firms[2] – have proliferated in the last few decades. However, too often these standards go unenforced at the national and international level. Those who have been harmed by corporate activity have nowhere to turn for redress.

The need for better access to remedy is reflected in the United Nations (UN) Guiding Principles on Business and Human Rights[3] (Guiding Principles), which provide that states and corporations must offer access to judicial and non-judicial grievance mechanisms (NJGMs) for those harmed by corporate conduct. In an ideal world, NJGMs would supplement judicial mechanisms, but the reality is that in many jurisdictions judicial remedies are ineffective or non-existent,[4] and NJGMs are, in practice, the only option for those affected by business-related human rights abuse. Although a few NJGMs are beginning to show potential in providing remedies, without significant reform to the system, they are not yet up to the task of providing victims with remedy.

2 Overview of non-judicial grievance mechanisms

The Guiding Principles offer the following definition for a NJGM: any routinized, state-based or non-state-based process through which grievances concerning business-related human rights abuse can be raised and a remedy can be sought.[5] Although it is sometimes assumed that NJGMs produce non-binding outcomes, there is nothing inherent in NJGMs that would prevent a binding outcome. For example, arbitration is a non-judicial process in which the parties have agreed to participate and be bound by the decision of a neutral third party. Even when the result is non-binding, NJGM processes can create incentives or consequences for the parties involved.

A wide array of NJGMs now exist that differ with regard to scope, procedures and outcome.[6] NJGMs can be categorized according to the actor that established and administers them. There are state-based NJGMs at the national, regional and international levels. Similarly, there are NJGMs established by non-state actors at all levels, from operational-level grievance mechanisms to those established at the sector level.

NJGMs handle complaints using either dialogue-based or adjudicatory processes.[7] Dialogue-based processes rely on methods that require the agreement and participation of both parties, such as mediation. Adjudicatory or compliance processes result in an investigation to determine if the corporation in question has breached applicable standards. Some NJGMs combine both functions.

According to the Guiding Principles, an effective NJGM is one that is: legitimate, accessible, predictable, equitable, transparent, rights-compatible, a source of continuous learning and – for operational-level mechanisms – based on engagement and dialogue.[8] Often, NJGMs cannot fulfil these criteria alone. Rather, the administering institution should share in the responsibility to fulfil these criteria.

3 Types of NJGMs

The range of NJGMs is evolving as new and different mechanisms are established. What follows is an overview of the NJGM landscape, describing their scope and relevance for the field of business and human rights. They range from international human rights bodies that can address recommendations only to states regarding their duty to protect against human rights abuses, to domestic state-based and non-state-based NJGMs that have jurisdiction over the business that is alleged to have caused the harm and are often narrower and more specific in their scope. The results of each mechanism depend heavily on its mandate and functions.

3.1 Human rights bodies

Within the UN system, there are treaty-based bodies[9] and charter-based bodies[10] that can receive complaints or communications from those harmed by business-related human rights abuses. At the regional level, NJGMs can be found within African and Inter-American systems of human rights.[11] The International Labour Organization's Committee on Freedom of Association accepts complaints from governments, trade unions or employers' organizations concerning violations of trade union rights by states.[12]

The scope of these mechanisms is limited to the actions or omissions of states. They can indirectly address cases involving human rights abuses committed by corporations by recommending that states regulate corporations within their jurisdictions. They cannot address recommendations directly to corporations. For example, in response to detailed information submitted by Austrian civil society organizations (CSOs) regarding the involvement of Austrian corporations in human rights abuses,[13] the Committee on Economic, Social and Cultural Rights made the general recommendation that Austria establish 'appropriate laws and regulations, together with monitoring, investigation and accountability procedures to set and enforce standards for the performance of corporations'.[14] Whether and how states implement those recommendations leaves much uncertainty for those seeking remedy. According to the same CSOs, Austria still lacks adequate legislation to regulate corporations and provide access to remedy.[15]

3.2 Development finance institutions

The private sector receives financing from development finance institutions (DFIs), which are funded in whole or in part by their member states. In response to pressure from CSOs,[16] the World Bank established the Inspection Panel in 1993 to receive complaints from individuals, communities and workers adversely affected by activities it finances. Since then, most multilateral development banks and a few national DFIs have followed suit. In 2004, these mechanisms created their own network, the Independent Accountability Mechanisms (IAMs) network, which meets annually to share experiences.[17] Almost every IAM offers both mediation and compliance functions.

IAMs can only hear complaints regarding harm that is caused by activities funded by their respective DFIs. Increasingly, though, private banks and other economic actors are financing development projects, but they have yet to establish similar mechanisms.[18] IAMs also face several challenges to their effectiveness. DFI clients are not required to inform affected communities about the availability of the mechanism, thus limiting its accessibility. More fundamentally, IAMs do not have the authority to suspend or terminate a project. They can make findings about whether the DFI complied with its environmental and social policies in the design, implementation and supervision of the project. However, the response to those findings is left to the board or senior management of the DFI, which is often the same body that approved the project.

Snapshot

International Finance Corporation's Compliance Advisor Ombudsman: Wilmar Group

In 2007 and 2008, community members in Indonesia filed complaints to the Compliance Advisor Ombudsman (CAO) regarding International Finance Corporation (IFC) investments in the Wilmar Group, a large agribusiness conglomerate specializing in palm oil. The complaints described the environmental and social impacts of the Wilmar Group's operations, including loss of community land. The CAO convened dialogue processes between the parties, resulting in agreements that partially restored the community land that was taken and provided compensation for appropriated land, among other benefits. A subsequent complaint filed in 2011 from some of the same communities[19] alleged that Wilmar's subsidiary had failed to honour Wilmar's earlier commitments, demonstrating the difficulties in ensuring adequate implementation of CAO agreements. In addition to facilitating mediation between the parties, the CAO also undertook an investigation and found that IFC had not adhered to its environmental and social policies.[20] In response to pressure from CSOs following the CAO's investigation report,[21] then president of the World Bank, Robert Zoellick, suspended all investments in palm oil worldwide by the entire World Bank Group until it had developed a strategy for investment in that sector.[22] However, the resulting palm oil strategy,[23] adopted in 2011, received a lukewarm response from civil society for its failure to ensure respect for indigenous rights and adequately address impacts along the entire supply chain.[24]

3.3 National Contact Points

The Organisation for Economic Co-operation and Development (OECD) Guidelines for Multinational Enterprises (OECD Guidelines) set forth state expectations for responsible business conduct on a variety of issues. The human rights chapter of the OECD Guidelines incorporates the Guiding Principles. OECD member and adhering states are obliged to set up a National Contact Point (NCP) to promote the OECD Guidelines.[25] States have flexibility in determining the structure and make-up of their NCPs. However, they should satisfy four functional equivalency criteria: visibility, accessibility, transparency and accountability.[26] Individuals, workers and communities can file a complaint or a 'specific instance', as they are referred to in the OECD Guidelines, at an NCP regarding the actions of a corporation operating in or from that country. Because the OECD Guidelines and the Guiding Principles require corporations to conduct human rights due diligence throughout their supply chains, complaints can be filed against a corporation regarding the human rights impacts of its subsidiary or supplier operating abroad. In response to a complaint, NCPs should use their 'good offices' to help the parties resolve the conflict and issue a final statement at the conclusion of the process. If the parties are unsuccessful in resolving the issue, the final statement should include recommendations, as appropriate, on the implementation of the OECD Guidelines.[27]

The NCPs are the international NJGM with the most comprehensive scope. The 46 NCPs, covering many of the jurisdictions where the most powerful corporations are headquartered, have received, to date, over 300 complaints from labour unions, civil society organizations, communities and individuals.[28] But only a fraction of the final statements in those cases include a rigorous analysis of the implementation of the Guidelines. Most NCPs do not make findings regarding compliance with the Guidelines, and a few do not publish final statements at all.[29] NCPs have also been criticized by CSOs for their lack of independence because they are often housed in government ministries such as finance or trade, whose mission is to support and encourage – not regulate – corporate investment abroad.[30]

3.4 National grievance mechanisms

National Human Rights Institutions (NHRIs) are bodies established by, but intended to be independent from, states, with a mandate to protect and promote human rights. Their core functions are complaint handling, human rights education and making recommendations on legal reform.[31]

As the most prominent state-based NJGM with a human rights mandate, NHRIs are increasingly seen as playing an important role within the area of business and human rights.[32] In 2010, NHRIs adopted the Edinburgh Declaration, welcoming the UN Framework on Business and Human Rights and committing to use their mandates to promote and protect human rights in the context of business-related human rights abuses.[33] The UN Working Group on Business and Human rights recommends that states collaborate closely with their NHRIs in elaborating their National Action Plans to implement the Guiding Principles and makes several suggestions for strengthening the mandate of NHRIs to receive complaints regarding business-related human rights abuses.[34] Currently, few NHRIs have an unlimited mandate to handle complaints against companies for human rights abuses.[35] A complaint handled by the National Human Rights Commission of India provides a positive example.

The complaint, filed by the Mine Labour Protection Campaign regarding the deaths of several mine workers from silicosis in private and state-owned sandstone quarries in Rajasthan, resulted in compensation being paid to the workers' families.[36]

3.5 Sector and multi-stakeholder grievance mechanisms

In response to the need for improved corporate conduct, sector and multi-stakeholder initiatives have been established to develop standards that member companies voluntarily commit to respect. Some of these initiatives have their own grievance mechanism to receive complaints from affected stakeholders when those standards are violated. For example, the Roundtable on Sustainable Palm Oil (RSPO), created in 2004 to establish sustainability principles and criteria for the production of palm oil, has established a system to handle complaints from communities alleging non-compliance with those standards.[37] It has handled 51 complaints,[38] with mixed results.[39]

These mechanisms can only address complaints that relate to the actions of its members. In the case of the RSPO, member companies are largely from Europe, the United States and Asia. However, palm oil production is expanding through Africa and Latin America, where there are fewer RSPO members. The mechanisms generally do not have the mandate to de-certify those who are found to be in breach of the standards. That decision is usually left to the governing body of the initiative, thus diminishing the effectiveness of the mechanism.[40]

3.6 Operational-level grievance mechanisms

Finally, many business enterprises have established their own operational-level grievance mechanisms that are available at the local level to those who might be adversely affected by their activities. Despite the Guiding Principles' effectiveness criteria and available guidance on best practice,[41] these mechanisms vary widely from well-established mechanisms to hotlines. In addition, because they are owned and operated by the same actors who have allegedly committed abuses, these mechanisms often lack the confidence of stakeholders.[42] They have also been criticized for being an inappropriate forum for addressing human rights abuses and for requiring complainants to waive their right to pursue future legal action against the company.

Snapshot

Barrick Gold Corporation: conditional remedy for victims at the Porgera mine

One controversial operational-level grievance mechanism is that established by mining company, Barrick Gold Corporation, after it was documented that its security personnel were involved in widespread sexual violence at its Porgera mine in Papua New Guinea. According to EarthRights International, which represents some of the victims, '[a]pproximately 200 women who survived brutal rapes by Barrick Gold's security guards in Papua New Guinea were asked to waive their legal rights in exchange for small "business grants" and "business training"'.[43] Documents obtained by EarthRights International show that in exchange for these benefits, the women had to promise not to sue Barrick. In response to requests from CSOs, the Office of the High Commissioner for Human Rights issued an opinion regarding the consistency of Barrick's remedial framework with international human rights standards, which states that:

> the presumption should be that as far as possible, no waiver should be imposed on any claims settled through a non-judicial grievance mechanism. Nonetheless, and as there is no prohibition per se on legal waivers in current international standards and practice, situations may arise where business enterprises wish to ensure that, for reasons of predictability and finality, a legal waiver be required from claimants at the end of a remediation process. In such instances, the legal waiver should be as narrowly construed as possible, and preserve the right of claimants to seek judicial recourse for any criminal claims.[44]

4 Outcomes

Although many of the NJGMs were created 10 to 20 years ago, it has only been in the last few years that a more consistent practice among NJGMs and a critical mass of cases have emerged.[45] The outcomes of NJGM processes can be categorized as follows: provision of benefits to the complainants; policy change at the company or institution in question; both; or no action.

Recent experience has shown that concrete benefits for complainants are more likely to result from mediation processes. The Office of the CAO of IFC has been a leader in this field, facilitating mediations that have resulted in economic compensation, land, improved health care and economic development projects, among others.[46] However, NJGMs that offer mediation, especially the NCPs, are still plagued by parties who are unwilling to engage because there is no incentive to do so.

In addition to providing benefits to complainants, NJGM processes can result in commitments to adopt new or modified policies or practices to prevent future harm from occurring. Here, NCPs have a better record than IAMs. However, as the example below demonstrates, those policy changes can come in the absence of any remedy for those harmed.

Snapshot

POSCO: precedent for financial institutions, but no remedy for communities

In October 2012, Lok Shakti Abhiyan (National Alliance of People's Movements in India) filed a complaint to the Korean, Norwegian and Dutch NCPs, with the support of NGOs in those countries, regarding the failure by POSCO – a large South Korean steel company – to conduct human rights due diligence on its proposed iron ore mine, steel plant and associated infrastructure in Odisha, India.[47] The complainants alleged that POSCO's plans would lead to, among other impacts, the physical and economic displacement of more than 20,000 people. Furthermore, the complaint argued that the Dutch pension fund, ABP, and the Norges Bank Investment Management (NBIM), which manages the Norwegian

Government Pension Fund Global, failed to undertake their own human rights due diligence before investing in POSCO.

The Korean NCP rejected the complaint against POSCO. The Dutch NCP, handling the case against ABP, successfully facilitated several meetings between the parties, resulting in a joint statement in which ABP committed to exercise its leverage to influence POSCO's business practices. NBIM refused to engage with the Norwegian NCP. The final statements of the Dutch and Norwegian NCPs affirmed that the OECD Guidelines apply to financial institutions, including minority shareholders. Because the OECD Guidelines incorporate the Guiding Principles, their finding meant that the human rights responsibility of financial institutions extends to the conduct of their clients. After that conclusion was challenged by different actors, OECD Watch – a civil society coalition – and then the OECD itself sought clarification from the UN High Commissioner for Human Rights, who confirmed that financial institutions, including minority shareholders, can contribute or be linked to human rights abuses through their investments and, thus, they should undertake human rights due diligence on their portfolios.[48] NBIM eventually divested from POSCO, but as a result of its investments in the palm oil sector not because of its operations in India.

Even though the case set an important precedent for financial institutions, the communities affected by POSCO's activities are no better off now than they were before they submitted the complaint. The case thus exemplifies the weakness of the NCP system's capacity to provide remedies to those harmed by corporate misconduct.

The most likely outcome for a complaint filed at an NCP by an NGO is that it will be rejected.[49] Similarly, IAMs reject a large proportion of the complaints that they receive.[50] Even when complaints are accepted, the process may not produce a result because the NJGM does not have the mandate or capacity to address the issues raised in the complaint. For NCPs that refuse to undertake investigations, they have little to offer if the conflict or the parties are not amendable to mediation. For IAMs, there appears to be a worrying trend that instead of addressing the findings of an investigation report, bank management ignores, refutes or denies them.[51] The result, in those cases, is that there is no change in the project design or implementation, no measures to address the concerns of the complainants and no change to policy or practice. Not only are the complainants left without a response to their concerns, this result also makes it less likely that they or other communities will use the mechanism in the future.[52]

5 Conclusion

The CAO's Wilmar case, described above, is one of the very few examples where there has been both concrete redress for complainants and changes in policy or practice as a direct result of an NJGM process. However, those few cases that do deliver show the promise and potential of NJGMs. More research is needed to understand under what conditions NJGMs can produce outcomes that result in both concrete benefits to complainants and policy changes that prevent future human rights abuses, but it appears that it is necessary for a complaint to go through both mediation and compliance processes. Ultimately, it may be necessary to strengthen the mandates of existing NJGMs and create new ones in order to ensure that complainants consistently receive remedies for corporate-related human rights abuses. The current process to negotiate a legally binding instrument on transnational corporations and other business enterprises with respect to human rights provides an opportunity to create a new grievance mechanism at the international level with a broader mandate and powers than the current NJGMs.

Notes

1   International Cyanide Management Code for the Manufacture, Transport, and Use of Cyanide in the Production of Gold, www.cyanidecode.org.
2   International Code of Conduct for Private Security Service Providers (2010), www.icoca.ch/en/the_icoc.
3   Human Rights Council, 'United Nations Guiding Principles on Business and Human Rights: Implementing the United Nations "Protect, Respect and Remedy" Framework', Report of the Special Representative of the Secretary-General on the issue of Human Rights and Transnational Corporations and Other Business Enterprises, UN Doc. A/HRC/17/31 (21 March 2011).
4   G. Skinner, R. McCorquodale and O. de Schutter, *The Third Pillar: Access to Judicial Remedies for Human Rights Violations by Transnational Business* (International Corporate Accountability Roundtable, CORE and European Coalition for Corporate Justice, 2013) p. 66.
5   Guiding Principle No. 25.
6   For more detailed information on the NJGMs mentioned here and others, see SOMO, 'Human Rights and Grievance Mechanisms', www.grievancemechanisms.org; Accountability Counsel, www.accountability counsel.org.
7   Guiding Principle No. 27, Commentary.
8   Guiding Principle No. 31.
9   There are 10 human rights treaty bodies that monitor the implementation of the treaty that established them. These include, among others: the Human Rights Committee, established by the International Covenant on Civil and Political Rights, New York, 16 December 1966, in force 23 March 1976, 999 UNTS 171; and the Committee on Economic, Social and Cultural Rights, established by the International Covenant on Economic, Social and Cultural Rights, New York, 16 December 1966, in force 3 January 1976, 999 UNTS 3.
10 These include the Special Procedures and the Complaint Procedure of the UN Human Rights Council.
11 These are the African Commission on Human and Peoples' Rights and the Inter-American Commission on Human Rights.
12 International Labour Office, *Freedom of Association: Digest of Decisions and Principles of the Freedom of Association Committee of the Governing Body of the ILO* (5th ed., rev.) (Geneva: International Labour Office, 2006) pp. 231–43.
13 FIAN Austria, *Parallel Report: Austria's Extraterritorial State Obligations on ESCR* (2013), www.fian.at/assets/PR-ESCR-ETOs-DRUCK-Nov13.pdf.
14 Committee on Economic, Social and Cultural Rights, 'Concluding Observations on the Fourth Periodic Report of Austria', UN Doc. E/C.12/AUT/CO/4 (13 December 2013).
15 Netzwerk Soziale Verantwortung, *Menschen. Rechte. Wirtschaft: Rechtsgutachten zum Menschenrechtsschutz bei Auslandsaktivitäten österreichischer Unternehmen* (2014), www.netzwerksozialeverantwortung.at/media/Studie_Menschen_Rechte_Wirtschaft_Web.pdf.
16 D. Clark, J. Fox and K. Treakle (eds), *Demanding Accountability: Civil Society Claims and the World Bank Inspection Panel* (Lanham, MD: Rowman & Littlefield, 2003).
17 K. Lewis, *Citizen-driven Accountability for Sustainable Development: Giving Affected People a Greater Voice – 20 Years On* (Independent Accountability Mechanisms Network, 2012) p. 2.
18 BankTrack, *Going around in Circles: An overview of BankTrack–EPFI Engagement on the Equator Principles 2003–2010* (2010) p. 4.
19 Compliance Advisor Ombudsman (CAO), *Assessment Report: Regarding Community and Civil Society Concerns of 3rd Complaint in Relation to Activities of the Wilmar Group of Companies in Indonesia* (2012).
20 CAO, *CAO Audit of IFC's Investments in: Wilmar Trading (IFC No. 20348); Delta–Wilmar CIS (IFC No. 24644); Wilmar WCap (IFC No. 25532); Delta–Wilmar CIS Expansion (IFC No. 26271)* (2009), www.cao-ombudsman.org/cases/document-links/documents/CAO_Audit_Report_C_I_R6_Y08_F096_ENG.pdf.
21 Letter from M. Colchester *et al.* to R. Zoellick, 14 August 2009, www.cao-ombudsman.org/cases/document-links/documents/ifc_ngo_let_cao_wilmar_14aug09_eng.pdf.
22 Letter from R. Zoellick to J. Kalafat, 25 November 2009, www.cao-ombudsman.org/cases/document-links/documents/ZoellickletterrewholeWBGfreezenov2009.pdf.

23 World Bank Group, *The World Bank Group Framework and IFC Strategy for Engagement in the Palm Oil Sector* (2011).

24 Bretton Woods Project, 'Open for Business: World Bank to Reinvest in Palm Oil amid Criticism', 14 April 2011, www.brettonwoodsproject.org/2011/04/art-568287.

25 OECD, *Guidelines for Multinational Enterprises* (2011 ed.).

26 Ibid., Commentary on Implementation Procedures, para. 9.

27 Ibid., Procedural Guidance, para.I(C)(3).

28 OECD, 'Database of Specific Instances', http://mneguidelines.oecd.org/database.

29 OECD Watch, *Assessment of NCP Performance in the 2013–2014 Implementation Cycle* (OECD Watch submission to the 2014 Annual Meeting of the National Contact Points, June 2014) pp. 23–4, http://oecdwatch.org/publications-en/Publication_4090.

30 Ibid., pp. 12, 34. A recent report published by OECD Watch found that of the 250 cases filed by communities, individuals and NGOs, only 35 have had some beneficial results for complainants. See, OECD Watch, 'Remedy Remains Rare' 19 (2015), available at http://oecdwatch.org/publications-en/Pub.

31 International Coordinating Committee of National Human Rights Institutions for the Promotion and Protection of Human Rights (ICCNHRI), 'Roles and Types of NHRIs', http://nhri.ohchr.org/EN/AboutUs/Pages/RolesTypesNHRIs.aspx.

32 German Institute for Human Rights, *Business and Human Rights: The Role of National Human Rights Institutions* (2014).

33 ICCNHRI, 'Edinburgh Declaration' (2010), http://scottishhumanrights.com/application/resources/documents/ENG_Sep_2010_Edinburgh_Declaration_FINAL_101010_1417h.doc.

34 UN Working Group on Business and Human Rights, *Guidance on National Action Plans on Business and Human Rights* (2014).

35 Office of the High Commissioner for Human Rights, 'Business and Human Rights: A Survey of NHRI Practices', 2008, www.reports-and-materials.org/OHCHR-National-Human-Rights-Institutions-practices-Apr-2008.doc.

36 Mine Labour Protection Campaign (MLPC), *Marble Quarry Workers of Makrana* (2014), www.mlpc.in/doc/MLPC%20Report%20on%20the%20Marble%20Mines%20of%20Makrana.pdf.

37 Roundtable on Sustainable Palm Oil, 'Complaints', www.rspo.org/members/complaints.

38 Ibid.

39 See M. Colchester, S. Chao and N. Jiwan, 'Conclusions and Recommendations' in M. Colchester and S. Chao (eds), *Conflict or Consent? The Oil Palm Sector at a Crossroads* (2013) p. 383, 390, www.forestpeoples.org/sites/fpp/files/publication/2013/11/conflict-or-consentenglishlowres.pdf.

40 For a discussion of a MSI grievance mechanism, see A. van Heerden in this volume, 'The Fair Labor Association: improving workers' rights in global supply chains', p. 128.

41 CAO, *A Guide to Designing and Implementing Grievance Mechanisms for Development Projects* (2008).

42 C. Freeman and E. de Haan, *Using Grievance Mechanisms: Accessibility, Predictability, Legitimacy and Workers' Complaint Experiences in the Electronics Sector* (Amsterdam: Centre for Research on Multinational Corporations (SOMO), 2014).

43 EarthRights International, 'Survivors of Rape by Barrick Gold Security Guards Offered "Business Grants" and "Training" in Exchange for Waiving Legal Rights', 21 November 2014, www.earthrights.org/media/survivors-rape-barrick-gold-security-guards-offered-business-grants-and-training-exchange.

44 See, e.g. Office of the High Commissioner for Human Rights, 'Allegations Regarding the Porgera Joint Venture Remedy Framework', July 2013, www.ohchr.org/Documents/Issues/Business/LetterPorgera.pdf.

45 The two largest categories of NJGMs, the IAMs and the NCPs, have received a combined total of over 600 complaints since their creation.

46 CAO, *2014 Annual Report* (2014), www.cao-ombudsman.org/documents/CAOANNUALREPORT2014_000.pdf.

47 *Lok Shakti Abhiyan et al. v POSCO*, www.oecdwatch.org/cases/Case_260/1046/at_download/file.

48 OECD, Global Forum on Responsible Business Conduct, *Expert Letters and Statements on the Application of the OECD Guidelines for Multinational Enterprises and UN Guiding Principles on Business and Human Rights in the Context of the Financial Sector* (2014), www.mneguidelines.oecd.org/globalforumonresponsiblebusinessconduct/GFRBC-2014-financial-sector-document-3.pdf.

49 OECD Watch, *Assessment of NCP Performance in the 2013–2014 Implementation Cycle*.

50 Accountability Counsel, *Recent Trends in Accountability: Charting the Course of Complaint Offices* (2014).

51 Letter from CSOs to President Kim, 'Re: Learning from Failure: Management Action Plans Needed in Response to Inspection Panel and CAO Investigations', 12 November 2013, www.ciel.org/Publications/CAO_WB_12Nov2013.pdf.

52 The two largest categories of NJGMs to date are the IAMs and NCPs and this section addresses their outcomes. In comparison, there have been far fewer complaints made to MSIs and there is currently insufficient data to more generally assess their effectiveness.

Introduction to Sections 6.5–6.6
Reporting

Reporting on the human rights performance of companies can take different forms, including voluntary self-evaluations by companies, reporting by companies and those monitoring them as a requirement of participation in multi-stakeholder initiatives, external evaluative reporting by civil society organizations, and reporting that is required by national governments through official reporting requirements that are mandated by law. Each of these reporting systems has a different purpose and the reports are directed at different audiences. Reporting by itself does not guarantee accountability. Rather, reporting is a tool that has the power to advance accountability by increasing transparency around corporate operations, which may then trigger pressure to improve corporate human rights performance.

The following two chapters examine some current aspects of reporting on business and human rights. They each provide an overview of the current state of play for both voluntary and mandated reporting of corporate human rights issues. Amol Mehra and Sara Blackwell examine the rise in voluntary (internal and external) reporting on human rights issues, and raise critical concerns about its utility in improving the human rights performance of individual companies. Anthony P. Ewing describes recent reporting requirements schemes that are required by national laws, such as the United States' disclosure requirement concerning the use of conflict diamonds in the Democratic Republic of Congo, found in the Dodd–Frank Act. Ewing concludes that 'legally mandated reporting to date is not yet aimed squarely at preventing the adverse human rights impacts of corporate activities'.[1]

It is not yet clear if these or other reporting systems and the greater transparency they promote have improved the protection of human rights on the ground. What is clear is that, at a minimum, increased transparency is a precondition for accountability. The examination of various reporting models in the following chapters also makes it clear that there is a need to develop clearer parameters for more meaningful reporting, both for companies and for others who use these reports, including both internal and external stakeholders. Further clarification is needed, including through the development of industry standards and metrics. There is also a need to move beyond self-selection by companies of the issues on which they are willing to report. Future reporting may need to be more narrowly tailored to a smaller but common set of issues on which industry competitors can be evaluated. Reports also need to focus not only on company processes and policies, but also the actual outcome of corporate actions, which is key to improving corporate human rights performance.

Note

1   A.P. Ewing in this volume, 'Mandatory human rights reporting', p. 285.

Section 6.5

The rise of non-financial disclosure:
reporting on respect for human rights

Amol Mehra and Sara Blackwell

1 Introduction

From the moment a corporation is registered, its directors and officers are required to report to regulators. These requirements are compounded if the corporation is publicly traded.[1] Outside of reporting to regulators, corporate reporting includes both internal and external reports that communicate how a company is addressing a particular challenge. Such reporting is often only thought of in terms of financial aspects, including company reporting in relation to annual fiscal performance. However, recent years have demonstrated a deepening practice among companies to also report on non-financial issues, including social disclosures, such as the human rights harms that a corporation is at risk of causing or contributing to. This is due at least in part to the increasing level of attention afforded to these issues by both internal and external stakeholders, including consumers, employees, investors and the media, all of whom may seek information concerning a company's human rights risks and impacts before making decisions to purchase, invest or support.[2]

With the rise in corporate reporting on human rights issues, however, comes critical concern over its utility in improving a company's human rights performance on the ground. The sheer number of reports being produced and the diverse topics that such reports aim to cover have created cottage industries for corporate social responsibility (CSR) consultancies while, at times, burdening in-house practitioners and overloading the consuming public. With all of this activity, a key question arises: does reporting lead to the establishment of strong systems and policies within companies that detect and mitigate actual or potential human rights impacts? If not, how can reporting be appropriately structured to deliver on these results? Do current reporting frameworks enable public accountability of corporate human rights conduct? If not, what needs to be done to enable accountability?

Ultimately, if reporting is refocused to address a number of key criteria, it can lead to improved human rights performance, thereby creating both internal systems and the accountability mechanisms needed to anticipate and address human rights harms and to communicate these efforts effectively.

2 The backstory: frameworks for reporting on corporate respect for human rights

A key part of the momentum of corporate reporting on human rights was the development of the United Nations (UN) Guiding Principles on Business and Human Rights[3] (Guiding Principles), which were unanimously endorsed by the UN Human

Rights Council in 2011 and which provide a widely agreed-upon set of principles for both governments and companies in ensuring that human rights are protected and respected in the context of business activity.

Snapshot

The Guiding Principles and Reporting on Human Rights

The Guiding Principles explicitly elaborate on the obligations of States and the responsibility of companies in terms of human rights reporting.

For example, within Pillar 1 of the Guiding Principles, which relates to the State duty to protect human rights, Guiding Principle 3 states that, '[i]n meeting their duty to protect, States should ... encourage, and where appropriate require, business enterprises to communicate how they address their human rights impacts'. Notably, the Commentary to Guiding Principle 3 articulates that '[f]inancial reporting requirements should clarify that human rights impacts in some instances may be "material" or "significant" to the economic performance of the business enterprise', demonstrating a key link between financial and non-financial information within the reporting realm.

Moreover, within Pillar 2, which relates to the corporate responsibility to respect human rights, Guiding Principle 21 states: '[i]n order to account for how they address their human rights impacts, business enterprises should be pre-pared to communicate this externally.' The Commentary to Guiding Principle 21 then explains that '[t]he responsibility to respect human rights requires that business enterprises have in place policies and processes through which they can both know and show that they respect human rights in practice'. The Com-mentary goes on to state that '[s]howing involves communication, providing a measure of transparency and accountability to individuals or groups who may be impacted and to other relevant stakeholders, including investors'.

However, the Guiding Principles are a general framework that offers a broad set of principles, leaving much to the discretion of companies in terms of their practical application, including the scope and scale of the reporting and the process for gathering and disclosing such information. As such, further specificity is needed to turn the Guiding Principles into a framework for reporting.

Snapshot

Reporting and Assurance Frameworks Initiative (RAFI)

Based on the Guiding Principles, the RAFI[4] attempts to elaborate further on what the responsibility to respect entails and asks companies to consider and report on key questions.

Launched in February 2015, the Reporting Framework (the first part of the two-part RAFI) aims to provide guidance to companies on how to disclose informa-tion concerning their human rights performance.[5] The Reporting Framework con-sists of 31 questions that are structured under three main parts: (A) governance of respect for human rights; (B) defining the focus of reporting; and (C) management of salient human rights issues.[6] Such reports are intended to define a minimum level of information and will be publicly available as they are developed.[7]

The Reporting Framework provided by RAFI has already been taken up by five companies in five industry sectors: Unilever (consumer goods); Ericsson (communications technology and services); H&M (retail clothing); Nestlé (food and beverage); and Newmont Mining Corporation (gold mining).[8] A lengthy list of investors – with US$3.91 trillion assets under management – have also formally expressed their support for the Reporting Framework.[9]

The RAFI provides a strong framework for reporting on human rights and could increasingly be used to track company performance on these issues. Critical to this is that under the Reporting Framework reporting must go beyond process and also include the risks and impacts that the company has in relation to human rights and how the company mitigates and addresses them.

Outside of the Guiding Principles, a number of initiatives have developed in the past several years, with varying ranges of specificity, in order to structure, and in some cases require, companies to report on human rights issues. Civil society groups, investors and even some companies and governments are engaged in emerging efforts to motivate greater transparency and accountability around business interaction with human rights.

2.1 Voluntary initiatives

Voluntary reporting initiatives take many forms and may be facilitated by either governmental or non-governmental entities and can focus on the national, regional or international levels. The voluntary nature of such reporting, however, often results in variances that make it a challenge for external stakeholders to compare and contrast as well as hold companies to account when they fail to report. Still, where voluntary initiatives are specific, clear and permit comparison between companies, they can be quite useful in driving at accountability.

Snapshot

Sustainability Accounting Standards Board (SASB)

The SASB was founded in 2011 with the aim of developing and disseminating standards for 'sustainability accounting' in a way that works within the current system of financial regulation.[10] A strength of this voluntary initiative is that SASB's standards are integrated into existing accounting standards currently used in public companies' mandatory financial reporting to the US Securities and Exchange Commission (SEC).[11] Moreover, SASB takes an industry-specific approach to reporting in order to enhance the usefulness of benchmarking against key performance indicators.[12] Through 2016, SASB will be developing sustainability accounting standards for approximately 80 industries in 10 sectors.[13]

2.2 Multi-stakeholder initiatives

Multi-stakeholder initiatives (MSIs) are efforts to bring diverse stakeholder groups together to develop a shared framework to improve company performance on human rights through, for example, joint standard-setting, certification and monitoring or oversight functions. Company reporting to an MSI along agreed-upon criteria is often a condition of membership, and the MSI itself can also issue public reports based on its own assessments of company performance.

Snapshot

International Code of Conduct for Private Security Service Providers Association (ICoCA) and the Fair Labor Association (FLA)

ICoCA and the FLA are two major MSIs where reporting enables mechanisms of accountability. These initiatives rely on two forms of reporting. First, an internal report from member companies is filed with each association with respect to the company's fulfilment of association standards. Second, each association itself then reports out to the public on member companies' performance. The mechanism of accountability is derived from the internal structure of each association, composed of multi-stakeholder representation with the ability to ensure compliance with human rights criteria.

Established in 2010, the ICoCA is an MSI that aims to set principles and standards, based on international human rights and humanitarian law, for the private security industry operating in complex environments.[14] ICoCA also aims to improve oversight over and accountability of these companies.[15] By signing the International Code of Conduct for Private Security Service Providers (ICoC) and becoming members of ICoCA, private security companies submit to an ongoing process of independent monitoring, auditing and verification. Companies are also required to report regularly on their performance.[16]

The FLA is a group of civil society groups, universities and companies that agree to uphold the Association's Workplace Code of Conduct and commit to its Principles of Fair Labor and Responsible Sourcing.[17] Member companies also agree to subject their supply chains to independent assessments and investigations, which are then publicly disseminated by the FLA to facilitate transparency and inform consumers.[18] The FLA also hosts a complaint mechanism, whereby any individual or organization can report serious worker rights violations associated with member companies.[19]

2.3 Mandated reporting[20]

Mandatory non-financial reporting requirements are appearing in several countries' laws. Some regulators have used securities laws to compel reporting. In the United States (US), for instance, s. 1502 of the Dodd–Frank Wall Street Reform and Consumer Protection Act[21] requires the SEC to promulgate regulations requiring listed companies that offer products containing conflict minerals to disclose on an annual basis whether any of those minerals originated in the Democratic Republic of the Congo (DRC) or an adjoining country.[22] Companies are already reporting, and advocacy groups and investors are tracking these responses.[23]

Outside of securities laws, there are other tools that regulators use to compel reporting. For example, the US Department of State issued the Burma Responsible Investment Requirements in May 2013.[24] These reporting requirements mandate that any US person (individual or entity) who invests US$500,000 or more in Myanmar (Burma), or who invests in Myanmar's oil and gas sector, is required to complete reporting requirements related to human rights, workers' rights, anti-corruption, the environment, property acquisition, arrangements with security providers and financial transparency.[25]

Mandatory non-financial reporting has also gained momentum outside the US. In December 2014, the European Commission's directive to its Member States on non-financial reporting took effect, requiring certain companies to disclose 'policies, risks, and outcomes as regards environmental matters, social and employee aspects, respect for human rights, anticorruption and bribery issues, and diversity in their board of directors'.[26] Although the directive will only cover certain large companies and leaves the specific reporting requirements to the discretion of individual Member States of the European Union (EU), this mandatory reporting initiative covers approximately 6,000 large companies across the EU region.[27]

3 The evaluators: assessing reporting of respect for human rights

Beyond voluntary, multi-stakeholder and regulatory requirements around human rights reporting, outside evaluators can play an important role in shaping the process and content of reporting and, more importantly, how a company should deliver in terms of respecting human rights in practice.

A number of civil society groups and other stakeholders have spearheaded recent initiatives to externally evaluate company reports and responses along human rights measures.[28] These initiatives seek to shift company practice by using performance data to drive a 'race to the top' that generates competition among companies for the most positive human rights records.

Snapshot

Oxfam's 'Behind the Brands'

Oxfam has developed a website and scorecard that ranks the world's 10 largest food and beverage companies based on specific indicators covering these companies' sourcing of agricultural commodities from developing countries.[29] Using only publicly available information, Oxfam's 'Behind the Brands' ranking criteria takes into account a number of issues, including transparency, women's rights, workers' rights, farmers' rights, land, water and climate.[30] Under each of these themes, the scorecard measures company performance using the indicator categories of awareness, knowledge, commitments and supply chain management.[31] Recent increases in companies' scores reflect that success is achievable when individuals leverage informational tools to pressure companies to improve their policies.[32]

4 Reporting as a benefit, not a burden

The examples detailed above represent a small selection of the various initiatives calling for reports by companies on human rights issues. It is important to consider that many companies will indeed be reporting along a number of such standardized reporting requirements, depending on their size, sector and areas of operation. Add to this various voluntary reporting and MSIs, and the complexity only increases. Clearly, there is the potential for reporting to become a burden, both for the company and for the potential stakeholders interested in ascertaining how a company engages with human rights issues internally and through its operations.

There is, therefore, a need to drive at more meaningful reporting both for the companies and for the users of the reports, be they internal or external stakeholders. Further clarification, including through the development of industry standards and metrics, are a critical way to go about addressing these challenges. Still, while these processes develop, three criteria must be considered to ensure more meaningful reporting. They are the 'Three Cs' of reporting: (1) the *content* of the report; (2) the *capacity* for human rights within the company; and (3) the *consideration* of the intended audience.

4.1 Content

The content of human rights reports varies greatly, particularly when there is no clear set of criteria to follow. More specifically, if there are no industry standards or benchmarks against which the quality of companies' reports can be measured, transparency initiatives run the risk of becoming overly general and disconnected from actual impacts on the ground. Some companies have voluntarily disclosed human rights-related information through external reporting. For example, in 2011, McDonald's began producing 'human rights due diligence' reports, which clarified the company's policies on human rights and disclosed steps taken by the company to minimize human rights impacts in its supply chain and through its franchises.[33] Other companies have adopted a more piecemeal approach to voluntary reporting on respect for human rights, focusing on specific social issue areas and how the company responds to them. For example, PepsiCo has been producing a 'Water Report' detailing the company's efforts to address the right to water in its operations and operating environments.[34]

Generally, and across all typologies of reporting, there are critical elements in terms of a report's content that need to be included to evidence how a company engages in respect for human rights. First, the content must show how human rights are embedded within a company's operations, detailing who has responsibility, oversight and accountability for human rights issues within the company. Next, the content must describe both the policies and processes that a company has with respect to human rights, including the steps they take to conduct human rights due diligence. Third, the company must report outcomes and impacts that they may be causing, and detail clearly how they will prevent, mitigate and address them. Finally, content must reveal how companies engage with remedial measures when violations do occur.[35]

4.2 Capacity

Critical to good reporting on human rights is clear internal capacity within the company. This not only includes capacity in terms of the preparation of reports, but also in terms of how the process of developing the reports and communicating about findings is centralized. Some companies use CSR divisions to detail their human rights reports. Other companies embed the human rights domain in their legal departments or use a cross-functional approach to managing human rights. Regardless of the structure, without such dedicated capacity, human rights issues risk being minimized or ignored, with the resulting potential downside being of significant cost to those affected and to the company itself.[36]

4.3 Consideration

Good reporting must show consideration by the company of the intended audience of the report and their expectations. Key questions to consider include: (1) Is the intended audience shareholders of a company who want to understand how to value a company based on considerations of human rights risks? (2) Is the audience a regulator or regulatory agency seeking information from a company to condition a benefit? (3) Is the audience or its representatives seeking to understand how a company addresses human rights in its specific environment? (4) Is the audience some combination of these, or another audience altogether? The intended audience will shape how the report should be presented in order to enable assessments of a company's respect for human rights.

5 Conclusion: reporting as accountability

A critical lesson is, no matter what the form, reporting is not accountability. Rather, reporting empowers stakeholders, both internal and external to the company, with a valuable process and information about how the company addresses human rights. Reporting therefore has the power to enable accountability. But it can only improve human rights outcomes for businesses and for affected individuals and communities through careful and thoughtful procedures whereby companies seek to 'know' the human rights impacts of their operations and then 'show' what these impacts are in ways that inform the company's own policies, processes and thinking, and empower stakeholders to use that information to assess the company's respect for human rights. With this in mind, and by carefully considering the three criteria above, the benefits of reporting can be unlocked for internal and external stakeholders alike.

Notes

1   For example, in the context of securities reporting in the United States (US), which aims both to ensure accurate marketplace pricing of securities and to improve business behaviours by exposing corporate conduct to public scrutiny, companies must file periodic reports with the US Securities and Exchange Commission (SEC) on a host of matters that are material to investors, including management's views in relation to the financial condition of the company, future prospects and a range of risks. See International Corporate

Accountability Roundtable (ICAR), *'Knowing and Showing': Using US Securities Laws to Compel Human Rights Disclosure* (2013) pp. 8, 10, http://accountabilityroundtable.org/wp-content/uploads/2013/10/ICAR-Knowing-and-Showing-Report5.pdf.

2   For instance, the garment industry has received widespread and largely negative attention after multiple deadly factory disasters in Bangladesh, including the Tazreen Fashions fire that killed 114 workers in Dhaka on November 24, 2012 and the Rana Plaza factory collapse on April 24, 2013 that left more than 1100 workers dead.... The extractives industry has similarly faced scrutiny for adverse working conditions, human rights abuses by security personnel at mines, forced labor and other modern forms of slavery, and the contamination of ground water supplies.

(Ibid., p. 5)

Moreover, investors have also demonstrated strong support for increased access to non-financial information, such as whether certain companies are sourcing from conflict-affected areas, following exposure of human rights violations associated with particular industries and regions. Such information has been claimed by leading socially responsible investor groups to be 'material information that is critical to their decision-making including brand valuation and risk assessment'. See, e.g. Responsible Sourcing Network, *Federal Court's Decision Allows SEC Conflict Minerals Disclosure Rule to Move Forward: But Investors Voice Concern over Invalidation of Key Requirement*, 15 April 2014, www.sourcingnetwork.org/storage/minerals-press-releases/federal_courts_decision_allows_sec_conflict_minerals_disclosure_rule_to_move_forward.pdf. See also A. Mehra and S. Winstanley, 'Respecting Human Rights: Shareholders Shift from Policy to Action', CSRwire, 22 April 2013, www.csrwire.com/blog/posts/812-taking-action-to-respect-human-rights-shareholders-shift-from-policy-to-action.

3   Human Rights Council, 'Guiding Principles on Business and Human Rights: Implementing the United Nations "Protect, Respect and Remedy" Framework', Report of the Special Representative of the Secretary-General on the issue of Human Rights and Transnational Corporations and Other Business Enterprises, UN Doc. A/HRC/17/31 (21 March 2011).

4   Shift, 'Human Rights Reporting and Assurance Frameworks – RAFI', www.shiftproject.org/project/human-rights-reporting-and-assurance-frameworks-initiative-rafi.

5   Shift and Mazars, *UN Guiding Principles Reporting Framework* (2015), www.ungpreporting.org/wp-content/uploads/2015/03/UNGPReportingFramework_Feb2015.pdf.

6   Ibid.

7   Shift, 'Human Rights Reporting and Assurance Frameworks'.

8   Ibid.

9   Ibid.

10   Sustainability Accounting Standards Board (SASB), 'Vision and Mission', www.sasb.org/sasb/vision-mission.

11   Ibid. See also SASB, 'Standards Download', www.sasb.org/standards/download.

12   SASB, 'Vision and Mission'. See also SASB, 'Using SASB Standards', www.sasb.org/standards/using-sasb-standards.

13   SASB, 'Vision and Mission'.

14   International Code of Conduct for Private Security Service Providers Association (ICoCA), 'International Code of Conduct Association (ICoCA): Core Documents, Frequently Asked Questions, Membership Requirements', 2010, p. 21, www.icoca.ch/sites/default/files/resources/ICoCA%20Brochure-OnlineDesigned.pdf.

15   Ibid.

16   Ibid., pp. 21–5. For example, art. 12.2.2 of the International Code of Conduct for Private Security Service Providers Articles of Association clarifies that 'Member companies shall provide to the Association a written assessment of their performance pursuant to a transparent set of criteria covered by necessary confidentiality and nondisclosure arrangements'. In addition, art. 12.3 notes that the Association will also 'report publicly, no less than annually, on its activities under this article'.

17   Fair Labor Association (FLA), 'Protecting Workers' Rights Worldwide', www.fairlabor.org/our-work.

18   FLA, 'Transparency', www.fairlabor.org/transparency.

19   FLA, 'Third Party Complaint Process', www.fairlabor.org/third-party-complaint-process.

20   See further A.P. Ewing in this volume, 'Mandatory human rights reporting', p. 284.

21   Pub. L. 111-203, 124 Stat. 1376 (2010). Section 1502 is codified at 15 USC §78m(p).

22   The term 'adjoining country' is defined in s. 1502(e)(1) of the Dodd–Frank Act as a country that shares an internationally recognized border with the DRC, which presently includes Angola, Burundi, Central African Republic, the Republic of the Congo, Rwanda, South Sudan, Tanzania, Uganda and Zambia.

23   See, e.g. Global Witness and Amnesty International, *Digging for Transparency* (2015), www.globalwitness.org/campaigns/democratic-republic-congo/digging-transparency; Responsible Sourcing Network and the Enough Project, *Expectations for Companies' Conflict Mineral Reporting* (2013), www.sourcingnetwork.org/1502-expectations-download-for.

24   US Department of State, Bureau of Democracy, Human Rights and Labor, 'Responsible Investment Reporting Requirements', OMB No. 1405-0209, www.humanrights.gov/wp-content/uploads/2013/05/responsible-investment-reporting-requirements-final.pdf.

25   Ibid., Reporting Questions 5–8. For a critical analysis of the quality of reports submitted by companies thus far, see US Campaign for Burma, *Report Card: US Companies Investing in Burma* (2014), www.uscampaignforburma.org/images/USCB_Report_Card_US_Companies_Investing_In_Burma.pdf.

26   European Commission, 'Banking and Finance: Non-Financial Reporting', http://ec.europa.eu/finance/accounting/non-financial_reporting/index_en.htm.

27 Ibid.
28 For example, the Business & Human Rights Resource Centre (BHRRC) launched an initiative in February 2015 that maps government and company actions with respect to business and human rights. It reflects the responses – and non-responses – of 101 governments and 180 companies to questionnaires targeting these stakeholders' efforts relating to the human rights impacts on business. The government and company 'action platforms' feature the ability to build comparisons of responses or to search responses by government, company, issue or type of action. See BHRRC, 'Government Action Platform', http://business-humanrights.org/en/government-action-platform; BHRRC, 'Company Action Platform', http://business-humanrights.org/en/company-action-platform. See further A. Mehra and E. Embree, 'Rankings, Benchmarks, Reporting, and More: Motivating Action on Business and Human Rights', *Huffington Post*, 26 February 2015, www.huffingtonpost.com/amol-mehra/rankings-benchmarks-repor_b_6761934.html.
29 Oxfam, 'Behind the Brands', www.oxfam.org/en/campaigns/behind-brands; Oxfam, 'Behind the Brands: About', www.behindthebrands.org/en-us/about.
30 Ibid.
31 Ibid.
32 Ibid.
33 See A. Mehra and N. Santiago, 'You Want Human Rights With That? McDonald's Serves up Due Diligence on Human Rights', *Huffington Post*, 25 March 2014, www.huffingtonpost.com/amol-mehra/you-want-human-rights-wit_b_5020908.html.
34 PepsiCo, *Delivering Access to Safe Water through Partnerships* (2014), www.pepsico.com/Assets/Download/PEP_WP14_Safe_Water_2014.pdf.
35 See K. Genovese in this volume, 'Access to remedy: non-judicial grievance mechanisms', p. 266.
36 See, e.g. R. Davis and D. Franks, *Costs of Company–Community Conflict in the Extractive Sector*, Corporate Social Responsibility Initiative Report No. 66 (Cambridge, MA: Harvard Kennedy School, 2014), www.hks.harvard.edu/m-rcbg/CSRI/research/Costs%20of%20Conflict_Davis%20%20Franks.pdf.

Section 6.6

Mandatory human rights reporting

Anthony P. Ewing

1 Introduction

More companies are communicating how they address their human rights impacts to meet escalating stakeholder expectations of corporate transparency. As voluntary reports proliferate,[1] states have begun to mandate corporate reporting on non-financial issues. In a growing number of jurisdictions where transnational corporations reside, including the United States (US), Europe and China, companies must disclose information relating to their human rights policies, due diligence and impacts.

Legally mandated reporting schemes vary in their objectives, scope, requirements and enforcement. Key variables are whether reporting requires disclosure on human rights issues specifically, or on 'corporate social responsibility' (CSR) more broadly; and to what degree reporting promotes human rights due diligence consistent with the United Nations (UN) Guiding Principles on Business and Human Rights (Guiding Principles).[2]

Mandatory reporting is relevant for both states and businesses under the Guiding Principles. To meet their duty to protect human rights, states should 'encourage, and where appropriate require, business enterprises to communicate how they address their human rights impacts', especially when operations pose a significant risk to human rights.[3] To meet their responsibility to respect human rights, business enterprises should 'account for how they address their human rights impacts'[4] – formal corporate reporting is expected where risks of severe human rights impacts exist.[5] Furthermore, '[p]olicies or laws … can usefully clarify what and how businesses should communicate, helping to ensure both the accessibility and accuracy of communications'.[6]

The number of companies worldwide subject to some form of mandatory human rights reporting is increasing with the introduction of new disclosure requirements by policy-makers seeking greater corporate transparency. Predominant forms of mandatory reporting are financial and non-financial reporting that may require corporate human rights disclosures. More recent regulations require companies to disclose information on their human rights policies, risks and due diligence.

As reporting is employed more widely as a policy tool, questions remain as to whether greater transparency leads to improved protection and provision of human rights. The principal objective of most mandatory reporting is information disclosure; regulations address whether companies should report on their human rights policies, not necessarily how, often adopting a 'comply or explain' model.[7] Current reporting requirements do not prescribe or evaluate what companies are doing about human rights impacts connected to their operations.[8] New requirements address how and what companies report about their human rights impacts, with disclosure intended to trigger public pressure for improved corporate human rights performance. Future disclosure may be more narrowly tailored to prescribe human rights due diligence as well as what companies must do to act on what they learn.

This chapter surveys current forms of mandatory reporting – financial, non-financial and human rights – that may require companies to address their human rights policies, due diligence and impacts. While mandatory human rights reporting has the potential to shape corporate behaviour, is raising expectations of greater corporate transparency and is beginning to produce information about corporate human rights policies and due diligence, the chapter concludes that legally mandated reporting to date is not yet aimed squarely at preventing the adverse human rights impacts of corporate activities.

2 Financial reporting

Under corporate and securities law in numerous jurisdictions, companies must report on issues considered to be material or significant for investors.[9] For example, when a human rights issue results in a major operations disruption or litigation exposure that meets financial materiality thresholds, it must be reported under US securities law.[10] There is limited regulatory guidance for companies, however, on when human rights impacts without a clear connection to the company's operations or financial performance become material, a gap noted in the Guiding Principles.[11] While there is a strong argument that human rights are increasingly materially relevant to investors,[12] securities regulators like the US Securities and Exchange Commission (SEC) have yet to adopt that view. The actual and potential human rights impacts connected to corporate operations generally do not trigger mandatory financial reporting requirements.

3 Non-financial reporting

The most common form of mandatory reporting relating to corporate human rights impacts requires companies to supplement financial reporting with non-financial information on 'social' or CSR issues. As early as 1977, France required companies with more than 300 employees to report on labour and employment-related indicators.[13] Today, certain French companies must disclose non-financial performance measures and comment on the 'social and environmental consequences of [their] activity and [their] social commitments in sustainable development', including human rights.[14] Canada's federal securities laws require disclosure of a company's CSR policies, which may include human rights policies.[15] Australian issuers of financial products must, if the product has an investment component, disclose the extent to which 'labour standards or environmental, social or ethical considerations' are taken into account in investments.[16] Pension funds in Belgium, Germany and the United Kingdom (UK) must reveal how social, environmental and ethical issues inform investment decisions.[17] A number of stock exchanges, in some instances implementing governmental policy,[18] require listed companies to report on social issues, which may include human rights impacts.[19] China has issued guidelines for state-owned enterprises that include reference to CSR information disclosure.[20] India encourages companies to report on human rights policies.[21] Other countries with some form of mandatory CSR reporting include Norway,[22] the Netherlands,[23] Spain[24] and Sweden for state-owned enterprises.[25] Even municipal jurisdictions may mandate non-financial corporate reporting. The City of Buenos Aires, for example, requires companies that employ over 300 people to prepare an annual report of their social, environmental and economic impact.[26]

Snapshot

Mandatory corporate responsibility in India

In 2013, India became the first country to mandate corporate philanthropy, adopting a provision that requires companies registered in India earning more than certain amounts to spend annually at least 2 per cent of the average net profits of the company over three years 'in pursuance of' CSR initiatives undertaken within India.[27] Activities that qualify as CSR are broadly defined, including corporate spending that relates to 'eradicating extreme hunger and poverty; promotion of education; [and] promoting gender equality and empowering women', as well as 'such other matters as may be prescribed'.[28] The Companies Act 2013, which took effect in April 2014, requires covered companies to form a 'CSR' committee of the board to 'formulate and monitor the company's CSR Policy'. An estimated 8,000 Indian companies qualify, representing some US$2 billion of potential charitable spending.[29]

Companies must disclose their CSR policy in the board's annual financial report and on the company's website. If a company fails to spend the required amount, it must provide the reasons in its report.[30] The first mandatory reports were due in April 2015.

The Indian legislation is noteworthy for mandating specific CSR performance, as opposed to solely requiring information disclosure. Even if the law works as intended,[31] however, the corporate philanthropy mandate is unlikely to have a meaningful impact on corporate human rights performance.[32]

Non-financial or CSR reporting mechanisms may or may not result in disclosure of human rights impacts related to a company's operations. Social issues or CSR, a voluntary concept, are often broadly defined. Companies may have wide discretion to choose which issues to address in their reporting. Under the Companies Act 2006 (UK), for example, companies listed on the London Stock Exchange must disclose in their annual strategic report information on environmental, workplace and social, community and human rights matters 'to the extent necessary for an understanding of the development, performance or position of the company's business'.[33] Unless human rights are specified as a required topic for disclosure, human rights reporting is effectively voluntary under most mandatory non-financial reporting mechanisms.

Snapshot

Human rights policy disclosure in Denmark

Since 2009, Danish companies above a certain size and certain financial enterprises must publish an annual CSR report summarizing their CSR policy or stating that they do not engage in CSR.[34] Under Danish securities laws, CSR includes the voluntary consideration of human rights conditions, among other topics. Companies that engage in CSR must report on how the business translates its CSR policies into action and evaluate what has been achieved through its CSR initiatives. Companies are free to choose how they publish their CSR report, and may meet the requirement by issuing a report under international guidelines.[35] The requirement covers approximately 1,100 large companies.[36] Non-compliance is subject to punishment by fine. Reports are subject to auditing for consistency, but not for performance.

The Danish Financial Statements Act was amended in 2013 to require companies to explicitly account for their policies on both human rights and climate change. In a subsequent implementation survey, two-thirds (66 per cent) of reporting companies surveyed disclosed a human rights policy (versus 77 per cent disclosing a CSR policy).[37] Of these, half (49 per cent) addressed how their human rights policies translate into action and evaluated progress.

While the amended Danish law requires companies to disclose whether a human rights policy exists, and evaluate the policy's impact, companies are not required to adopt a human rights policy in the first place. The content, scope, standards and integration of any corporate human rights efforts are left to the company.

A human rights policy is just one element of meeting the corporate responsibility to respect human rights.[38] More detailed human rights reporting promotes human rights due diligence by requiring companies to disclose information on how they identify, prevent and mitigate adverse human rights impacts connected to a company's operations.

4 Human rights reporting

A recently adopted European Directive (EU Directive 2014/95/EU),[39] which seeks to achieve consistent transparency of social and environmental reporting, goes further than non-financial reporting by mandating corporate disclosure of human rights due diligence and consideration of human rights risks, consistent with the Guiding Principles.

Snapshot

EU Directive on Non-Financial Reporting

Beginning in 2017, large publicly listed European companies must report annually 'on environmental, social and employee matters, respect for human rights, anti-corruption and bribery matters'.[40] These non-financial reports must include a 'description of the policies pursued' relating to respect for human rights, includ-ing 'due diligence processes implemented'; 'the outcome of those policies'; prin-cipal human rights risks linked to the company's operations, including its 'business relationships, products or services' likely to cause adverse impacts; and relevant non-financial performance indicators.[41] The Directive will cover approxi-mately 6,000 companies incorporated within the European Union.[42] While com-panies may choose how they report, the Directive references international frameworks such as the UN Global Compact,[43] the Guiding Principles and the Organisation for Economic Co-operation and Development (OECD) Guidelines for Multinational Enterprises.[44] Member states must implement the Directive through national legislation and are free to set more stringent disclosure requirements.[45] The European Commission is expected to issue non-binding guidelines for report-ing non-financial information. Member states must ensure that non-financial statements are provided; they may also require that the information be independ-ently verified.[46] There is no sanction at the European level for non-compliance.

EU Directive 2014/95/EU cites corporate actions taken to ensure gender equality, implementation of fundamental International Labour Organization Con-ventions and the prevention of human rights abuses as examples of information to be disclosed in non-financial reporting,[47] and emphasizes that companies should report risks of severe adverse impacts.[48]

The Directive gives companies reporting flexibility, following the 'comply or explain' model without sanction for non-compliance, and allows states to provide a non-disclosure safe harbour.[49]

The broad applicability of EU Directive 2014/95/EU will force many companies to address human rights impacts for the first time. By referencing business relation-ships, the Directive may also prompt European companies to address human rights risks linked to their global supply chains.[50]

Mandatory reporting mechanisms focused on specific sectors, issues and geog-raphies in which there are risks of severe human rights impacts require more detailed human rights due diligence disclosure.

Snapshot

Conflict minerals disclosure

As part of the 2010 Dodd–Frank Act,[51] the US SEC has promulgated rules that require all companies publicly listed in the US to examine their supply chains to determine whether they use certain 'conflict minerals',[52] such as coltan and gold, that originate in the Democratic Republic of the Congo (DRC) or adjoining countries.[53] The object of the rules is to encourage companies using minerals linked to funding for groups perpetuating conflict and human rights violations in the DRC to source them responsibly.[54] All issuers that manufacture, or contract to manufacture, products for which conflict minerals are necessary to functionality or production (like cellphones, computers and automobiles) must make disclosures.

Companies using these minerals must submit an annual report to the SEC detailing measures taken to exercise due diligence with respect to determining the source and chain of custody of its minerals, including whether products manufactured by the company are 'DRC conflict free'.[55] The three-stage disclosure process includes: (1) determining whether the company is subject to the provision; (2) if so, conducting a 'reasonable country of origin inquiry'; and (3) preparing a Conflict Minerals Report (CMR), if necessary.[56] Mandatory reporting is triggered in the second and third stages. The CMR must describe steps taken by the company to exercise due diligence in relation to the conflict minerals' source and chain of custody using a recognized due diligence framework, such as the OECD Due Diligence Guidance.[57] Reports must be independently audited and made public on the company's website. Issuers are subject to liability under US securities laws for fraudulent or false reporting.

The conflict minerals disclosure provisions have faced legal challenges and criticism from the business sector over the potential cost of corporate compliance.[58] In April 2014, a federal Circuit Court struck down the requirement that companies state whether their supply chains are 'DRC conflict-free' on grounds that it compelled speech contrary to the First Amendment to the US Constitution.[59] The SEC allowed Conflict Mineral Reporting to commence, waiving, for the time being, statements that products are 'DRC conflict undeterminable' or 'not found to be DRC conflict-free'.[60] The case will be reheard in light of a subsequent decision. The Conflict Minerals Disclosure Rules (Conflict Minerals Rules) took effect in 2013 and some 1,300 companies have submitted CMRs to date.

The Conflict Minerals Rules promote supply chain due diligence in one area where mining operations pose a significant risk to human rights.[61] Mandatory disclosure applies to a clearly defined set of corporate actors. The Conflict Minerals Rules limit disclosure to due diligence steps taken, without requiring companies to report any corporate actions flowing from that due diligence, such as concrete efforts to prevent or mitigate adverse human rights impacts once they are identified.

Because the Conflict Minerals Rules are narrowly tailored, and carry the prospect of enforcement under US securities laws, they have the potential to shape corporate behaviour.[62] The rules directly affect an estimated 6,000 companies, plus thousands of suppliers to these companies.[63] While advocates have criticized as inadequate some of the first CMRs submitted by companies,[64] the disclosure provisions may already be changing purchasing behaviour, such as by prompting Chinese buyers to ask African mineral exporters to provide information on mineral sourcing.[65]

The Conflict Minerals Rules have influenced similar requirements in other jurisdictions, including African states where mining companies operate. The DRC, for example, requires companies operating in its domestic mining sector to undertake and report on supply chain human rights due diligence, consistent with OECD standards.[66] In October 2014, the government-affiliated Chinese Chamber of Commerce of Metals, Minerals and Chemicals Importers and Exporters (CCCMC) issued Guidelines for Social Responsibility in Outbound Mining Investments (CCCMC Guidelines) that call on companies in that sector to 'conduct risk-based supply chain due diligence in order to prevent engagement with materials that may have funded or fuelled conflict'.[67] A footnote in the CCCMC Guidelines cites the OECD Due Diligence Guidance as good practice.[68] While voluntary for CCCMC members, the CCCMC Guidelines are likely to influence the business practices of Chinese companies.

Snapshot

California Transparency in Supply Chains Act

Since 2012, large retailers and manufacturers doing business in California have been required to disclose on their websites the extent to which the company engages in verification of product supply chains to address risks of slavery, forced labour and human trafficking.[69] Disclosures must describe steps taken, such as verifying product supply chains, auditing suppliers and requiring direct suppliers to certify that materials comply with local laws regarding slavery and human trafficking. There is no penalty for failing to take steps, only for failing to disclose whether a company engages in supply chain due diligence or not. The Act does not address what constitutes appropriate due diligence. The sanction for non-compliance is potential injunctive relief by the California State Attorney General.

Similar federal proposals that would require disclosures by companies relating to slavery conditions within product supply chains have been introduced, but have consistently failed to reach a vote, in the US House of Representatives.[70]

The UK's Modern Slavery Act mandates transparency in supply chains.[71] The Act requires companies to prepare an annual statement describing steps that the company has taken to ensure that slavery and human trafficking is not present in the company's operations or in any of its supply chains, and to publish it on the company's website.[72] The statement may include information about the company's policies, due diligence processes, risks, performance indicators and training relating to slavery and human trafficking.[73] If the company has not taken any such steps, it must issue a statement to that effect.[74]

Under US procurement regulations, federal contractors who supply products on a list published by the Department of Labor must certify that they have made a good faith effort to determine whether forced or indentured child labour was used to produce the items listed.[75] Federal contractors providing supplies acquired or services to be performed outside the US, with a value greater than US$500,000, must provide a compliance plan and certification, after completing due diligence, that no contractor or subcontractor is engaged in human trafficking.[76]

Like the Conflict Minerals Rules, the California Supply Chains Act, the corporate transparency element of the UK's Modern Slavery Act and similar provisions are designed principally to produce information about steps taken by companies to conduct supply chain due diligence on specific human rights issues, and to force companies that have not engaged in due diligence to say so publicly.[77] These mechanisms do not set mandatory standards for what due diligence must look like or for corporate conduct based on what companies learn about the risks in their supply chains; nor do they hold companies accountable for actual adverse human rights impacts connected to their operations.[78]

A reporting requirement that seeks to mandate corporate due diligence consistent with the Guiding Principles applies to US investors in Myanmar.

Snapshot

Responsible investment in Myanmar

Following signs of political reform in Myanmar, the US in 2012 modified sanctions prohibiting investment in that country.[79] Pursuant to a Presidential Executive Order, the Office of Foreign Asset Control adopted a reporting requirement for US individuals or entities making aggregate new investment in Myanmar of over US\$500,000, or investing in Myanmar's oil and gas sector.[80] Investors must report annually to the US Department of State on policies and procedures relating to their operations and supply chain in Myanmar, including policies on due diligence,[81] anti-corruption, community and stakeholder engagement, grievance mechanisms and 'global corporate social responsibility'.[82] If an investor has conducted human rights due diligence, they must summarize 'any risks and/or impacts identified and any steps taken to mitigate them'.[83] Investors must also report on any arrangement with security service providers,[84] on government payments[85] and, for certain land acquisitions, on efforts to 'ascertain land or other property ownership, use rights, dislocation, resettlement, or other claims'.[86]

Investors must submit two reports annually, one version for use by the US Government, and a second, shorter version that will be made public by the US Department of State.[87] Civil monetary penalties may be imposed for violating the requirements. Some 19 reports have been submitted to date.[88]

While the Myanmar investment requirements address due diligence and specific corporate human rights risks in one location where there are risks of severe human rights impacts, they are by definition a temporary measure, remaining in effect only as long as Myanmar is considered by the US government to be subject to 'national emergency' sanctions.

5 The impact of mandatory human rights reporting

Reporting has the potential to shape corporate behaviour. Disclosure requirements may lead companies to adopt human rights policies and conduct human rights due diligence consistent with the Guiding Principles.[89] Mandates with broad application like EU Directive 2014/95/EU will force many companies to consider their human rights impacts for the first time. Mandatory reporting has the power to 'cast a broader net to include companies that have resisted private regulation and also include sanctions for non-compliance that go beyond the reputational sanctions most commonly associated with private regulation'.[90] Similarly, the Conflict Minerals Rules have brought new companies into the conversation about supply chain monitoring. Measures that focus on human rights due diligence in global supply chains can have an impact beyond the covered company by triggering third-party suppliers to address human rights impacts.[91] Mandatory human rights disclosure may become a principal trigger for companies to address human rights impacts as perceived litigation exposure declines.[92]

Despite the wide-ranging quality of corporate reports,[93] mandatory reporting is producing more public information on corporate human rights policies, due diligence and impacts, especially in specific geographies (Central Africa, Myanmar[94]) and sectors (extractives, state-owned enterprises), and on specific issues (conflict minerals, human trafficking and labour standards in supply chains) with significant risks of human rights impacts. Reporting is reinforcing international standards for human rights due diligence by referencing frameworks like the Guiding Principles and OECD Due Diligence Guidance. Mandatory reporting also raises stakeholder expectations for corporate transparency on human rights issues, which may lead to broader acceptance of human rights practices as a material factor for investors.

However, a number of challenges may limit the impact of mandatory reporting. Disclosure requirements are shaped to a large extent by the body of law to which they are attached. Measures under securities or corporate law, like the US Conflict Minerals Rules or EU Directive 2014/95/EU on non-financial reporting, are aimed at providing information to investors, not ensuring that human rights are respected and fulfilled in practice.[95] Geographically specific regulations like the Myanmar investment requirements may not have a sustained impact unless they are made permanent.

Mandatory human rights reporting to date is focused on the process of disclosure, not the substance of improving corporate human rights performance. Enforcement is limited to penalties for companies that fail to report. Reporting relies on disclosure to trigger public pressure for better corporate human rights performance and accountability.[96] Civil society bears the burden of advocacy to highlight corporate disclosures and to use the information produced through mandatory reporting to push for corporate accountability.[97] One avenue for corporate accountability linked to corporate reporting is liability based on consumer protection provisions, such as the case brought against Nike under California law for false or misleading statements in its public disclosures.[98]

Snapshot

Kasky v Nike

In 1998, Nike was sued for unfair business practices under California state consumer protection law. The plaintiff, Marc Kasky, argued that Nike's advertising and public statements about working conditions in its supply chain had presented a deceptive image of the company, and that Nike had falsely claimed to protect workers through its code of conduct.[99] The legal question at the heart of the case was whether Nike's public statements about its labour practices should be considered commercial speech, like advertising, which the government can regulate for false or misleading statements, or free speech, which enjoys a higher level of protection under the US Constitution.[100] The California Supreme Court held that

Nike's statements were commercial in nature, intended to induce consumers to buy its products, and therefore the suit against the company could proceed.[101] Nike ultimately settled the case before it reached a jury.[102]

Mandatory reporting is not yet aimed squarely at preventing or mitigating the adverse human rights impacts of corporate activities. For transparency to lead to meaningful improvements in corporate human rights performance, reporting must prescribe human rights due diligence and be enforced consistently. By regulating the 'means and methods' of human rights disclosure, states can bolster the effectiveness and legitimacy of human rights due diligence.[103] States can strengthen human rights reporting by setting and enforcing minimum standards for reporting quality and content. A comprehensive policy approach would make human rights impacts material in financial reporting;[104] require disclosure in non-financial reporting of human rights policies, due diligence and actions taken to prevent or mitigate human rights impacts; and include narrowly tailored reporting requirements for specific geographies, sectors or issues where there is a high risk of severe human rights impacts.[105]

6 Conclusion

Mandatory human rights disclosure is no longer 'sporadic and anecdotal'.[106] Companies will face more requirements to disclose whether and how they address their human rights impacts. Mandatory human rights reporting is beginning to produce information about corporate human rights policies and due diligence, and is raising expectations of greater corporate transparency from companies on how they are managing the human rights impacts of their operations. Legally mandated reporting is one way states can prod companies to identify, prevent and mitigate adverse human rights impacts, helping them to meet their responsibility to respect human rights. If applied comprehensively, mandatory human rights reporting has the potential to improve corporate human rights performance and accountability.

Notes

1   I. Ioannou and G. Serafeim, 'The Consequences of Mandatory Corporate Sustainability Reporting: Evidence from Four Countries' (Harvard Business School Research Working Paper No. 11-100, 20 August 2014), p. 2, http://ssrn.com/abstract=1799589: 'While fewer than 100 firms globally reported such information twenty years ago, by 2013 more than 6,000 companies were issuing sustainability reports.'

2   Human Rights Council, 'Guiding Principles on Business and Human Rights: Implementing the United Nations "Protect, Respect and Remedy" Framework', Report of the Special Representative of the Secretary-General on the issue of Human Rights and Transnational Corporations and Other Business Enterprises, UN Doc. A/HRC/17/31 (21 March 2011). See especially Guiding Principle No. 17: 'In order to identify, prevent, mitigate and account for how they address their adverse human rights impacts, business enterprises should carry out human rights due diligence.'

3   Guiding Principle No. 3(d). See also A. Mehra and S. Blackwell in this volume, 'The rise of non-financial disclosure: reporting on respect for human rights', p. 276.

4   Guiding Principle No. 21 provides that external communication should 'be of a form and frequency that reflects the organization's human rights impacts and is accessible to its intended audiences'. Information provided should be 'sufficient to evaluate the adequacy of an enterprise's response to the particular human rights impact involved', and should 'not pose risks to affected stakeholders, personnel, or to legitimate

requirements of commercial confidentiality'. The Commentary to Principle 21 states: '[f]ormal reporting is itself evolving, from traditional annual reports and corporate responsibility/sustainability reports, to include online updates and integrated financial and non-financial reports'. See generally Office of the High Commissioner for Human Rights, *The Corporate Responsibility to Respect Human Rights: An Interpretative Guide* (2012) pp. 57–62.

5 Guiding Principle No. 21, Commentary.

6 UN Guiding Principle No. 3, Commentary. Communication features prominently in all three pillars of the Guiding Principles. Transparency is an effectiveness criterion for non-judicial grievance mechanisms, both state-based and non-state-based under the 'Access to Remedy' pillar, with respect to regular communication with parties to individual grievances, but also 'about the mechanism's performance to wider stakeholders … to demonstrate its legitimacy and retain broad trust'. See Guiding Principle No. 31(e) and Commentary.

7 Human Rights Council, 'Report of the Special Representative of the Secretary-General on the issue of human rights and transnational corporations and other business enterprises, John Ruggie, Addendum: Human rights and corporate law: trends and observations from a cross-national study conducted by the Special Representative', UN Doc A/HRC/17/31/Add.2 (23 May 2011), para. 129: 'This ["comply or explain" model] allows companies to decide whether or not to comply with specific social or environmental requirements, and if it has chosen not to comply, the company must explain the reasons why in its report.'

8 Under Guiding Principle No. 13, to meet their 'responsibility to respect human rights', companies must address adverse human rights impacts that they cause or contribute to 'through their own activities' and that are 'directly linked to their operations, products or services by their business relationships'.

9 Human Rights Council, 'Report of the Special Representative of the Secretary-General', p. 2. See also International Corporate Accountability Roundtable (ICAR), *Knowing and Showing: Using US Securities Laws to Compel Human Rights Disclosure* (2013) pp. 8–15.

10 Regulation S-K, 17 CFR §229 (2012). One mining company, for example, described as a risk factor in its financial reporting potential operational delays caused by community opposition or by imposition of 'additional requirements to protect human rights in the community' where it operates, having a potentially material adverse effect on the company's 'reputation, operations or profitability'. Goldcorp, *Annual Information Form for the Financial Year Ended December 31, 2011* (28 March 2012), pp. 95–6, www.goldcorp. com/files/FINAL%20_%20Goldcorp%20AIF%20SEDAR_v001_m4a6xy.PDF.

11 'Financial reporting requirements should clarify that human rights impacts in some instances may be "material" or "significant" to the economic performance of the business enterprise': Guiding Principle No. 3(d), Commentary. See also Human Rights Council, 'Report of the Special Representative of the Secretary-General', para. 208.

12 See, e.g. ICAR, *Knowing and Showing*; O. de Schutter *et al.*, *Human Rights Due Diligence: The Role of States* (ICAR, European Coalition for Corporate Justice, Canadian Network on Corporate Accountability, 2012) p. 44; E.R. George, 'Influencing the Impact of Business on Human Rights' in L. Blecher, N. Kaymar Stafford and G.C. Bellamy (eds), *Corporate Responsibility for Human Rights Impacts: New Expectations and Paradigms* (Chicago: American Bar Association, 2014) p. 271.

13 *Décret d'application de la loi sur le bilan social de 12 Juillet 1977.*

14 French Commercial Code, art. L225-102-1; Code de commerce, art. L225-102-1. The disclosure requirements apply to publicly trade limited liability companies and private companies with revenues exceeding €100 million and more than 500 employees.

15 Canada Business Corporations Act, RSC 1985, c. C-44, s.155(1). De Schutter *et al.*, *Human Rights Due Diligence*, p. 46.

16 Corporations Act 2001 (Cth), s 1013D(1)(l).

17 George, 'Influencing the Impact of Business', p. 285.

18 De Schutter *et al.*, *Human Rights Due Diligence*, p. 46. All companies listed on Bursa Malaysia must disclose CSR activities in their annual financial reports: ibid., pp. 45–6.

19 These include exchanges in Brazil, Indonesia, Malaysia, Singapore, South Africa, Thailand and Taiwan. See Shift, 'Update to John Ruggie's Corporate Law Project: Human Rights Reporting Initiatives' (New York, 2013) pp. 6–7.

20 Government of China, State-owned Assets Supervision and Administration Commission of the State Council, 'Guidelines to the State-owned Enterprises Directly under the Central Government on Fulfilling Corporate Social Responsibilities' (6 December 2011), para. 18:

> Enterprises having experienced [*sic*] in CSR work, should establish an information releasing mechanism, providing update and regular information about CSR performance and sustainable development, plans and measures in carrying out CSR. Meanwhile, a regular communication and dialogue mechanism concerning CSR should be established, so that the enterprise can have feedback from its stakeholders and give its response quickly. All the information and feedback should be publicized to receive supervision from stakeholders and society.

Furthermore, state-owned enterprises must 'disclose their decision-making process to make prudent decisions that comply with international treaties that China has ratified before investing overseas'. See ICAR, 'Overseas Investments by Chinese SOEs', http://hrdd.accountabilityroundtable.org/content/overseas-investments-chinese-soes#_msocom_1. Failure to report, or inaccurate or misleading statements, can result in revocation of the company's ability to make foreign investments for three years.

21 Government of India, Ministry of Corporate Affairs, *Corporate Social Responsibility Voluntary Guidelines* (2009), www.mca.gov.in/Ministry/latestnews/CSR_Voluntary_Guidelines_24dec2009.pdf. Article 4 of the

Implementation Guidance within the Guidelines states: 'The companies should disseminate information on CSR policy, activities and progress in a structured manner to all their stakeholders and the public at large through their website, annual reports, and other communication media.'

22 United Nations Environment Programme, Global Reporting Initiative, KPMG and the Centre for Corporate Governance in Africa, *Carrots and Sticks: Sustainability Reporting Policies Worldwide – Today's Best Practice, Tomorrow's Trends* (2013 ed.) p. 70.

23 Human Rights Council, 'Report of the Special Representative of the Secretary-General', p. 27.

24 De Schutter *et al.*, *Human Rights Due Diligence*, p. 46.

25 Government of Sweden, Ministry of Enterprise and Innovation, *Guidelines for External Reporting by State-Owned Companies* (11 December 2007), www.government.se/contentassets/b7ba2a84d9a1419caf2bb-605cf90488e/guidelines-for-external-reporting-by-state-owned-companies (requires annual sustainability report using GRI G3 Guidelines).

26 Failure to comply may result in criminal liability: De Schutter *et al.*, *Human Rights Due Diligence*, p. 43.

27 The Companies Act 2013, s.135.

28 Ibid., Schedule VII, cll. (i), (ii), (iii), (x). Human rights are not explicitly mentioned.

29 Esha Chhabra, 'Corporate Social Responsibility: Should It Be a Law?', *Forbes*, 8 April 2014.

30 Companies (Corporate Social Responsibility Policy) Rules, 2014. To qualify, public and private companies, including foreign companies conducting business in India, must meet or exceed certain thresholds of either net worth (Rs.5 billion), turnover (Rs.10 billion) or net profit (Rs.50 million) within any of the previous three financial years.

31 The purpose of the Companies Act 2013 is to encourage firms to undertake social welfare voluntarily and to attract investment. See A. Karnani, 'Mandatory CSR in India: A Bad Proposal', blog post, *Stanford Social Innovation Review*, 20 May 2013, www.ssireview.org/blog/entry/mandatory_csr_in_india_a_bad_proposal (quoting Sachin Pilot, India's Minister of State for Corporate Affairs).

32 Critics contend that without clear definitions or enforcement, the mandatory spending provision is unlikely to improve general welfare, constitutes a tax on large businesses and effectively privatizes the state responsibility to determine governmental spending priorities. See, e.g. ibid.

33 Companies Act 2006 (Strategic Report and Directors' Report) Regulations 2013, r.414C(7).

34 The Danish Financial Statements Act, Act No. 448 of 7 June 2001. See also de Schutter *et al.*, *Human Rights Due Diligence*, p. 45.

35 These include the UN Global Compact, the Principles for Responsible Investment or the Global Reporting Initiative: K. Buhmann, 'The Danish CSR Reporting Requirement as Reflexive Law: Employing CSR as a Modality to Promote Public Policy' (2013) 24(2) *European Business Law Review* 187.

36 B. Cooper, 'Non-financial Reporting: Learning from Denmark', Ethical Corporation, 10 March 2009.

37 Danish Business Authority, *CSR-Reporting: Impact Study of the Financial Year 2013* (2013), 'Executive Summary', http://csrgov.dk/documents/856499.

38 Guiding Principle No. 16.

39 EU Directive 2014/95/EU of the European Parliament and of the Council of 22 October 2014 amending Directive 2013/34/EU as regards disclosure of non-financial and diversity information by certain large undertakings and groups, OJ 2014 No. L 330, in force 6 December 2014. The EU Directive 2014/95/EU applies to 'public interest entities', EU companies with listed securities and all banks and insurers, whether listed or not, with more than 500 employees: Preamble, cl. 14. According to de Schutter *et al.*, *Human Rights Due Diligence*, p. 57, '[t]here is at present significant variation in the rules concerning reporting, the mechanisms through which companies are required to report and the criteria as to what constitutes effective disclosure for the purposes of human rights due diligence'.

40 EU Directive 2014/95/EU, art. 1.

41 Ibid.

42 European Coalition for Corporate Justice (ECCJ), 'EU Directive on the Disclosure of Non-Financial Information by Certain Large Companies: An Analysis', press release, 15 April 2014, www.corporatejustice.org/Press-release-European-parliament.

43 See, e.g. UN Global Compact, 'UN Global Compact Policy on Communicating Progress', updated 1 March 2013, www.unglobalcompact.org/docs/communication_on_progress/COP_Policy.pdf.

44 EU Directive 2014/95/EU, Preamble, cl. 9.

45 ECCJ, 'Corporate Transparency: Transposition of the New European Reporting Requirements into National Legislation', blog post, 10 December 2014, www.corporatejustice.org/Corporate-transparency.html.

46 EU Directive 2014/95/EU, art. 1.

47 Ibid., Preamble, cl. 7.

48 Ibid., Preamble, cl. 8.

49 If the disclosure would be 'seriously prejudicial' to the company's commercial interest: ibid., art. 1.

50 See, e.g. ECCJ, 'EU Directive on the Disclosure of Non-financial Information'. On May 20, 2015 the EU Parliament voted to require mandatory due diligence requirements similar to those contained in the Dodd–Frank Act. The European Parliament's vote legally requires that all EU companies processing, importing and using tin, tantalum, tungsten and gold (3TG) act responsibly and undertake due diligence to provide information on the steps they take to identify and address risks in their supply chains for the minerals and metals concerned. At the time of writing, the content of the law including the parameters of what constitutes due diligence was still being drafted. See European Parliament News, 'Conflict Minerals: MEPs Ask for Mandatory Certification of EU Importers', 20 May 2015, www.europarl.europa.eu/news/en/newsroom/content/20150513IPR55318/html/Conflict-minerals-MEPs-ask-for-mandatory-certification-of-EU-importers.

51   The Dodd–Frank Wall Street Reform and Consumer Protection Act, Pub. L. No. 111-203, 124 Stat. 1376 (2010) amends federal securities laws. See generally George, 'Influencing the Impact of Business', pp. 257–67.

52   Conflict minerals include: columbite-tantalite (coltan – the metal ore from which tantalum is extracted), cassiterite (the metal ore from which tin is extracted), gold, wolframite (the metal ore from which tungsten is extracted) or their derivatives, or any other mineral or its derivatives determined by the Secretary of State to be financing conflict in the DRC or an adjoining country: Dodd–Frank Act, s. 1502(e)(4).

53   Adjoining countries are those countries that share an internationally recognized border with the DRC: Angola, Burundi, Central African Republic, the Republic of the Congo, Rwanda, South Sudan, Tanzania, Uganda and Zambia: Dodd–Frank Act, s. 1502(e)(1).

54   Section 1502 of the Dodd–Frank Act is 'intended to curtail commercial complicity in international human rights violations': George, 'Influencing the Impact of Business', p. 260. A related provision, s. 1504, which is intended to decrease corruption by increasing transparency, requires resource-extraction issuers to disclose any payments made to a foreign government or the federal government: ibid., p. 268.

55   Products are conflict-free when they 'do not contain minerals that directly or indirectly finance or benefit armed groups in the DRC or an adjoining country': Dodd–Frank Act, s. 1502(b).

56   United States Federal Register, 'Conflict Minerals; Disclosure of Payments by Resource Extraction Issuers; Final Rules', 77 Fed. Reg. 56274 (12 September 2012) (to be codified at 17 CFR pts. 240, 249 and 249b). See generally George, 'Influencing the Impact of Business', pp. 253–64.

57   OECD, 'OECD Due Diligence Guidance for Responsible Supply Chains from Conflict-Affected and High Risk Areas' (2011).

58   *Nat'l Ass'n of Mfrs. v SEC*, No. 13-cv-635 (DDC, 23 July 2013) (dismissed); George, 'Influencing the Impact of Business', p. 270. See further S.M. Davidoff, 'Humanitarian Effort in Congo Puts Wall St. Regulator in Unintended Role', *New York Times*, 29 August 2012, p. B7.

59   J. Greene, 'DC Circuit to Give Second Look at SEC's Conflict-Minerals Rule', *National Law Journal*, 24 November 2014.

60   At the time of writing, an appeal by the SEC is possible, but unlikely.

61   'Section 1502 is the first regulation to create binding rules on due diligence with regard to a company's supply chain': G. Sarfaty, 'Human Rights Meets Securities Regulation' (2013) 54 *Virginia Journal of International Law* 97, 100.

62   According to the UN Group of Experts on the DRC, the US Conflict Minerals Rules generated a 'massive and welcome impact' requiring 'the world to take due diligence and conflict financing seriously': George, 'Influencing the Impact of Business', p. 266, citing Letter from Fred Robarts, Group of Experts on the DRC Coordinator, to Mary Schapiro, SEC Chairman (21 October 2011).

63   G. Sarfaty, 'Shining Light on Global Supply Chains' (2015) *Harvard International Law Journal* (forthcoming), 20, citing US Government Accountability Office, 'Report to Congressional Committees, SEC Conflict Minerals Rule: Information on Responsible Sourcing and Companies Affected' (2013), 21.

64   Amnesty International and Global Witness, *Digging for Transparency: How US Companies Are Only Scratching the Surface of Conflict Minerals Reporting* (April 2015).

65   See, e.g. Global Witness, *Tackling Conflict Minerals: How a New Chinese Initiative Can Address Chinese Companies' Risks* (October 2014) p. 18.

66   Ibid., p. 12. Rwanda has adopted a similar requirement: see Ministerial Regulations No. 002/2012/ MINIRENA of 28 March 2012 on the Regional Certification Mechanism for Minerals, Official Gazette No. 17 of 23 April 2012.

67   CCCMC Guidelines, cl. 2.4.6.

68   Ibid., p. 36, n 9. The OECD standard includes annual public reporting on supply chain due diligence as part of its framework.

69   California Transparency in Supply Chains Act, Ca. Civ. Code §1714.43. See George, 'Influencing the Impact of Business', pp. 276–9. See also Wilson Sonsini Goodrich & Rosati, 'New California Disclosure Requirements Regarding Slavery and Human Trafficking in Supply Chains to Take Effect on January 1, 2012' (October 2011). The Act applies to every retail seller or manufacturer operating in California with more than US$100 million in gross receipts.

70   Business Supply Chain Transparency on Trafficking and Slavery Act of 2014, House Bill 4842, HR 4842, (113th Cong., 2013–14) (applying to companies with receipts in excess of US$100 million). See also George, 'Influencing the Impact of Business', pp. 270–6.

71   Modern Slavery Act 2015 (c. 30) (UK), s. 54.

72   Ibid., s. 54(4), s. 54(7). The Act applies to companies with total turnover above an amount to be determined by the Secretary of State. Ibid., s. 54(2)(b).

73   Ibid., s. 54(5).

74   Ibid., cl. 54(4)(b). The Act provides for enforcement through injunction or specific performance. Ibid., s. 54(11).

75   US Department of State, Bureau of Democracy, Human Rights and Labor, *US Government Approach on Business and Human Rights* (2013).

76   United States Federal Register, 'Federal Acquisition Regulation; Ending Trafficking in Persons; Final Rule', 80 Fed. Reg. 4967 (2 March 2015).

77   De Schutter *et al.*, *Human Rights Due Diligence*, p. 46: '[I]t is a disclosure statute that simply asks companies to tell the public what they do, and to publish this on their website with a conspicuous link to the pertinent information.'

78   The US procurement regulation addressing human trafficking, however, contains the most detailed 'compliance plan' requirements and violations can result in termination of a federal contract.

79   US Department of the Treasury, Office of Foreign Asset Control (OFAC), Burma General License No. 17 (11 July 2012). See also OFAC, 'Burma Sanctions Program', 29 January 2014, www.treasury.gov/resource-center/sanctions/Documents/burma.pdf.

80   US Department of State, Bureau of Democracy, Human Rights and Labor, 'Responsible Investment Reporting Requirements', OMB No. 1405-0209, www.humanrights.gov/wp-content/uploads/2013/05/responsible-investment-reporting-requirements-final.pdf.

81   'Due diligence policies and procedures (including those related to risk and impact assessment) that address operational impacts on human rights, worker rights, and/or the environment in Burma.' Ibid., Reporting Question 5(a).

82   Ibid., para. II. Global CSR policies include 'those related to human rights, sustainability, worker rights, anti-corruption, and/or the environment': Ibid., Reporting Question 5(3).

83   Ibid., Reporting Question 11.

84   Ibid., Reporting Question 6.

85   Ibid., Reporting Question 8.

86   Ibid., Reporting Question 7(a).

87   Information omitted from the public report may include any military communications and any risks and/or impacts identified through human rights due diligence, and any steps to mitigate them: Ibid., Reporting Questions 10 and 11. The US Department of State will use the information 'to conduct informed consultations with US businesses to encourage and assist them to develop robust policies and procedures to address … impacts resulting from their operations and investments in Burma': US Department of State, Office of the Spokesperson, 'Burma Responsible Investment Reporting Requirements', press release, 23 May 2013, www.state.gov/r/pa/prs/ps/2013/05/209869.htm.

88   The first reports were submitted in 2013. Companies submitting reports to date include Gap Inc, Western Union Company and the Coca-Cola Company. For a current list, see Embassy of the United States, Rangoon, Burma, 'Reporting Requirements', http://burma.usembassy.gov/reporting-requirements.html.

89   Sarfaty, 'Human Rights Meets Securities Regulation', p. 101: 'Mandatory disclosure rules can provide teeth to international human rights norms and operationalize them into the day-to-day decision-making of companies.' See also J. Nolan, 'Refining the Rules of the Game: The Corporate Responsibility to Respect Human Rights' (2014) 30(78) *Utrecht Journal of International and European Law* 7, 15–16. Reporting need not be mandatory to prompt greater human rights transparency. See Ioannou and Serafeim, 'The Consequences of Mandatory Corporate Sustainability Reporting'.

90   Nolan, 'Refining the Rules of the Game', p. 19.

91   See, e.g. Sarfaty, 'Shining Light on Global Supply Chains'.

92   For instance, as the likelihood of litigation under the Alien Tort Statute, 28 USC §1350, decreases.

93   See, e.g. Global Witness, *Tackling Conflict Minerals*, p. 18 (noting that the quality and detail of company reporting under s. 1502 varies widely).

94   See, e.g. EIRIS, 'US Companies Report on Burma Investments', 1 July 2014, www.eiris.org/media/press-release/u-s-companies-report-burma-investments.

95   See, e.g. Sarfaty, 'Human Rights Meets Securities Regulation', p. 115:

> Carefully crafted securities regulation can bridge the translation gaps between the business and human rights communities, who hold divergent goals, are made up of distinct constituencies, and speak different languages. It can operationalize emerging international human rights norms through a domestic mechanism with real teeth. Moreover, given the materiality of human rights risks, securities regulation is an appropriate mechanism for conveying information about these risks to investors.

See also George, 'Influencing the Impact of Business', p. 255.

96   De Schutter *et al.*, *Human Rights Due Diligence*, p. 60: '[S]ecurities laws, consumer protection laws and reporting requirements for corporate social responsibility operate on the logic that information serves the interests and will prompt action by investors, regulators, and people who might be adversely affected by a business activity.' The US government's objective in its Myanmar investment requirements, for example, is 'to empower civil society to take an active role in monitoring investment in Burma': US Department of State, Office of the Spokesperson, 'Burma Responsible Investment Reporting Requirements', 23 May 2013.

97   See, e.g. Nolan, 'Refining the Rules of the Game', p. 18:

> [R]eporting requirements … indelibly link transparency with accountability, and in a field where accountability is arguably pursued by civil society with often greater vigor than states, the more information that is made available on global business operations, the more doable the work of these non-state actors becomes to privately regulate corporate activities.

98   See, e.g. S. Saadoun, 'Private and Voluntary: Are Social Certification Standards a Form of Backdoor Self-Regulation?' (2013) 45 *Columbia Human Rights Law Review* 281, 318–21. Similar claims could be brought against European companies under Directive 2005/29/EC of the European Parliament and of the Council of 11 May 2005 concerning unfair business-to-consumer commercial practices: Buhmann, 'The Danish CSR Reporting Requirement', p. 187.

99   *Kasky v Nike, Inc*, Cal. S087859, 119 Cal. Rptr. 2d 296 (2002).

100 US Constitution, Amend. I.

101 *Kasky v Nike, Inc.*

102 The US Supreme Court declined to review the decision of the California Supreme Court: *Nike, Inc v Kasky*, 539 US 654 (2003) (dismissing writ of certiorari). As part of the settlement, Nike agreed to pay US$1.5 million

to the Fair Labor Association: see L. Girion, 'Nike Settles Lawsuit over Labor Claims', *Los Angeles Times*, 13 September 2003.

103 De Schutter *et al.*, *Human Rights Due Diligence*, p. 63: 'Without regulation of the means and methods of disclosure, the effectiveness, and therefore legitimacy, of a company's human rights due diligence will remain in doubt.'

104 Cf. George, 'Influencing the Impact of Business', p. 257: 'The new disclosure regime contained in Dodd–Frank, in effect, makes matters that pertain to human rights material.'

105 One opportunity to strengthen national policy is by integrating mandatory reporting as part of state National Action Plans. See C. Pitts in this volume, 'The United Nations "Protect, Respect, Remedy" Framework and Guiding Principles', p. 51.

106 See, e.g. S. Lydenberg and K. Grace, *Innovations in Social and Environmental Disclosure outside the United States* (New York: Domini Social Investments, 2008).

Chapter 7

Global rules, private actors

Future challenges for business and human rights

Section 7.1

We live in a world of global supply chains

Richard M. Locke

1 Introduction

Globalization,[1] with its volatile mix of economic opportunity and social disruption, is redefining the boundaries of the firm, changing the dynamics among consumers, global corporations and their suppliers, and shaping the working conditions of the millions of individuals employed in today's global supply chains. The world of global supply chains links thousands of firms, large and small, across multiple cultural and political boundaries. The diffusion of global supply chains in an array of different industries – apparel, electronics, footwear, food, toys and so on – has provided developing countries with much-needed investment, employment, technology and access to international markets. As such, the integration of producers located in developing countries into global supply chains is having a catalytic and transformative effect on local economies, allowing poor countries to finally achieve their long-sought-after goal of development.[2] At the same time, however, the social and environmental consequences of this particular pattern of economic development have provoked significant controversies over the role of global brands and their local suppliers, often seen as exploiting developing countries' low wages and weak social and environmental regulation to produce low-cost goods at the expense of local workers' welfare. In fact, child labour, hazardous working conditions, excessive working hours and poor wages plague many workplaces in the developing world, creating scandal and embarrassment for the global companies that source from these factories and farms.[3]

2 The supply chain of everyday products

To get a better sense of this phenomenon, this section examines how two everyday products are manufactured in today's global supply chains. In her 2005 book, *The Travels of a T-Shirt in the Global Economy*,[4] Pietra Rivoli traces a t-shirt's supply chain journey from the cotton fields of Texas to the spinning, weaving and garment factories of China, back to consumer markets in the United States (US) and finally to the used clothing and rag markets in Africa. Each of these stages involves multiple firms and complex transactions. In many stages of this supply chain, workers toiled under difficult and precarious conditions. Borrowing from Rivoli's approach, this section examines the supply chain dynamics of two common products, athletic running shoes and mobile electronic devices, and their consequences for workers.

2.1 Athletic footwear

Early athletic footwear was manufactured in vertically integrated facilities located primarily in Europe and North America. Some of the first athletic shoes to be marketed in the US (in the early 1900s) were manufactured in the US. For example, the US Rubber Company introduced 'Keds' in 1916, using rubber originally produced for bicycle tyres for the soles of what became a classic athletic shoe.[5]

The production of athletic footwear today, in contrast, requires a much longer supply chain, involving dozens of component parts and materials from around the world, which are manufactured, assembled, transported and distributed by companies and workers across many national borders. While many brands maintain their national identity, more and more production is taking place in developing countries with lower production costs. These trends show no signs of slowing down and China and Indonesia continue to export a significant portion of footwear to the global market. In fact, an astonishing 86 per cent of all footwear sold in the US in 2009 was made in southern China.[6]

In their book *Stuff: The Secret Lives of Everyday Things*,[7] John Ryan and Alan Durning document the many components from which a typical pair of Nike 'cross-trainers' are made, and the many locations from which these components and their raw materials are sourced. In tracking the journey of a particular shoe, they found that it was 'manufactured' by a Korean-owned factory located in Tangerang, Indonesia – an industrial district outside of Jakarta. The shoe was made up of dozens of component parts, almost all of which were manufactured elsewhere and then shipped to Indonesia for final assembly. First, designers based at Nike's headquarters in Oregon sent product specifications for the shoe to a design firm located in Taiwan. The design company in Taiwan, in turn, sent the more developed plans on to engineers in South Korea. The Korean company then outsourced the actual production of the shoe to Indonesia.[8]

The cross-trainer in question had three main sections: the upper, the midsole and the outsole. The upper for this particular shoe was made primarily from leather, which came from cows slaughtered and skinned in Texas and then shipped to South Korea for tanning. Tanning itself is a 30-stage process. The tanned leather was then shipped to the factory in Indonesia. The midsection of the shoe was made from synthetic parts, including ethylene vinyl acetate (EVA) foam made from Saudi Arabian petroleum, refined and transformed into EVA foam in Korea, and subsequently shipped to the factory in Indonesia. Another component that provides cushioning under the heel was manufactured in the US. The outer soles of the shoes were made of rubber, again a by-product of petroleum, refined in Korea, processed into large sheets of rubber by another company in Taiwan and eventually shipped to the assembly plant in Indonesia to be cut, shaped and finally attached to the shoes.

All of these many parts were assembled in the Tangerang factory. Journalist Elizabeth Grossman recently picked up the shoe's story, visiting a similar Korean-owned factory in Tangerang that employs 18,000 people and produces about 300,000 shoes per week. Each shoe is assembled in pieces. First, workers (over 80 per cent are female) assemble the uppers of the shoe, made from fabric, synthetics and leather. Pieces are stitched together using specialized machines. Other, smaller pieces, including Nike's trademark 'swoosh', are sewn either by machine or by hand. The upper sections of the shoes are then placed on a conveyer belt, from which other workers apply glue and then attach the uppers to the soles of the shoe. Next, workers trim excess material from the shoe; this work is done by hand, using small electric tools. Finally, the shoes are polished and fitted with laces and insoles. All in all, factory management estimates that approximately 200 people are involved in making just one pair of shoes.[9] The shoes are then stuffed with tissue paper (made from Indonesian trees) and packed into boxes that were originally manufactured by a paper mill in New Mexico.[10] From there, the shoe begins its journey back to markets in the US, Europe and elsewhere.

2.2 Mobile electronic devices

Mobile electronic devices are today ubiquitous. These products, however, come with substantial costs to producers, workers and the environment, involving a complex flow of materials and products around the world. Raw materials for electronic components are extracted, often under harsh working conditions, from mines in Asia and Africa. These materials are refined and processed in Asia, and then sold to companies (Asian and Western) that manufacture component parts such as chips and circuit boards. These parts are then assembled, primarily in China, in large factories that employ hundreds of thousands of workers. The final products are then shipped back to consumer markets located for the most part in already developed economies. The shelf life of these mobile devices is relatively short, and the e-waste generated by consumers who dispose of their phones and other portable devices in exchange for newer models is, in turn, shipped back to Asia and Africa.

To better understand this complex supply chain and its consequences for workers, let's examine one of the industry's most high-profile producers: Apple.[11] Some of the most value-added parts of an Apple product, for example, its innovative software, are still produced in the US. Almost everything else, however, comes from overseas. A recent *New York Times* study of Apple's supply chain estimated that over 90 per cent of an iPhone's components are produced outside the US, in places ranging from Germany and Taiwan (where semiconductors are produced), Korea and Japan (for memory boards, display panels and circuits), Europe (data chips) and elsewhere in Asia and Africa (where rare metals are extracted and refined).[12] The hundreds of components that go into an iPhone or iPad are assembled in China. A huge industry has sprung up around the production of these electronic devices, providing Apple's suppliers with the parts they need. A former Apple executive explained:

The entire [assembly] supply chain is now in China. You need a thousand rubber gaskets? That's the factory next door. You need a million screws? That factory is a block away. You need that screw made a little differently? It will take three hours.[13]

The working conditions at Apple's suppliers have come under intense scrutiny, following a wave of suicides by factory workers at Foxconn – one of the largest manufacturers of iPhones and iPads. The *New York Times* published a series of articles on the working conditions at these factories, citing sources as varied as labour advocacy groups, anonymous workers and Apple's own, internal assessments of working conditions. In order to meet the high consumer demand for these Apple products, employees in these factories had to work long days with mandatory overtime and forgo their rest days. Conditions in these factories are harsh; workers are not rotated, but rather specialize in narrow tasks and therefore suffer from repetitive stress injuries.[14] Workers are also exposed to hazardous chemicals and unsafe conditions in the workplace. For example, in 2010, 137 workers were injured after using a toxic chemical to clean iPhone screens. More recently, there were several explosions at iPad factories in Chengdu, southwestern China in which four people were killed and 77 injured.[15]

In response to these scandals, Apple carried out its own internal audits of its suppliers and also engaged with the Fair Labor Association (FLA) to further investigate the working conditions among its lead suppliers in southern China. Together they have inspected hundreds of facilities including both first- and second-tier suppliers. Apple's internal audits found evidence of excessive work hours, failure to pay overtime, inadequate safety precautions and instances of child labour among some of its suppliers.[16] Even after several years of intense auditing of their suppliers, Apple's 2012 *Supplier Responsibility Report* found that although most of its suppliers were improving their compliance on key issues like underage labour, involuntary labour and anti-discrimination, many of these same suppliers continued to struggle with excessive working hours and low wages.[17] The FLA Report concerning three of Foxconn's factories in China, all major producers of Apple products, found that 'all three factories exceeded the FLA Code Standard and the requirements of Chinese law' relating to working hours, especially during peak production periods. Although 48 per cent of the workers employed in these factories reported in the FLA survey that they felt the working hours at Foxconn were 'reasonable', 64.3 per cent of these same workers also claimed that their salary was 'not sufficient to cover their basic needs'.[18]

Nor is this situation unique to Foxconn or other Apple suppliers. Over the last few years, the FLA conducted surveys among workers employed in Chinese factories supplying various global brands and found that an estimated 50 per cent of workers employed in the garment industry and 80 per cent of workers employed in the electronics industry work more than the legal limits of 60 hours per week. Of the 1,766 surveyed workers, 45 per cent claim that they need to work above 60 hours per week since their regular salaries are insufficient to cover their basic needs.[19]

The anecdotes presented above illustrate some of the salient features of most global supply chains – fragmented and globally dispersed production, multiple tiers and actors within each supply chain, suppliers producing for multiple brands, short lead times and tight margins, and the key role lead buyers play in orchestrating this entire process and even investing in their suppliers. As the above anecdotes also revealed, these underlying features create very real challenges for the millions of workers employed in supply chain factories, who every day struggle with poor working conditions, long working hours, low pay and a variety of other (minor and not so minor) injustices. According to the International Labour Organization (ILO), the rapid growth of cross-border trade and capital flows since 1990 has not led to improved employment conditions in developing countries. On the contrary, the ILO *Global Employment Report* found that over 486 million workers throughout the world do not earn enough to raise themselves or their families above the US$1 per day poverty rate and that another 1.3 billion people do not earn above US$2 per day.[20] More than half of all workers in most developing countries and over 70 per cent in some parts of South Asia and Sub-Saharan Africa find themselves in 'vulnerable employment', which is roughly defined as informal employment; employment that is poorly paid and that does not provide workers with fundamental labour rights, a 'voice' at work and job security.[21]

Of course, not all workers in developing countries are employed in factories or farms linked to global supply chains.[22] Because data on employment and labour conditions are collected either by country or by sector, we do not know precisely how many of these workers are actually employed at firms supplying global buyers. However, through various reports, published by the ILO, individual non-governmental organizations (NGOs) and even by global corporations, we are able to piece together an image of what working conditions and standards are like for the millions of workers employed in global supply chains. According to the ILO, throughout the world, 168 million children work. Of these, 85 million are engaged in 'hazardous work' in sectors such as agriculture, manufacturing and mining, which are deeply integrated into global supply chains.[23] Around 21 million people worldwide are victims of forced labour. Although most companies operating in global supply chains do not themselves employ forced labour, many have become implicated in such practices through their second- or third-tier suppliers and contractors.[24] These findings are echoed in the internal assessments of several global brands working in a variety of different industries. Female workers are especially hard hit since they occupy 60–90 per cent of the jobs in manufacturing and agricultural supply chains.[25] What, if anything, can be done to improve working conditions and promote worker rights in these global supply chains?

3 Private voluntary regulation as a 'second-best' solution

Throughout most of the 20th century, labour standards were regulated largely on a national basis, through a mixture of laws, union–management negotiations and company policies. Internationally, the conventions and technical services of the ILO provided an additional source of moral authority and advice but lacked significant enforcement power. The emergence of global supply chains, however, has rendered these national and international strategies inadequate since authority is dispersed not only across national regimes but also among global buyers and their myriad suppliers. It is in this context that private initiatives have emerged to fill this regulatory void.

A number of scholars have already documented the rise of private voluntary initiatives aimed at regulating global labour standards and thus the details of this process need not be repeated here.[26] Essentially, a series of separate but interrelated (and self-reinforcing) developments unfolded over the final decades of the 20th century that led to the increasing inability of both nation states and international organizations to regulate labour standards in the global economy. These developments include the shift of a substantial fraction of global manufacturing from the advanced industrial states (for example, the US, Europe and Japan) to several large developing countries (for example, China, India and Mexico). According to Meyer and Gereffi, by 2000, 50 per cent of the world's manufacturing production was located in developing countries.[27] This trend only increased over the last decade. Linked to this shift in the *locus* of global manufacturing were dramatic changes in the *organization* of production. In the past, most manufacturing was carried out by domestic companies and their suppliers located within the same country or by vertically integrated transnational corporations (TNCs) headquartered in the advanced industrial economies (and thus subject to their regulations) that owned (fully or partially) their subsidiaries located in foreign markets. Today, global production is organized primarily around global supply chains in which lead firms (brands, global buyers, large retail chains), while still based in the developed economies, are working with and coordinating the production of thousands of independent suppliers located for the most part in developing countries.

As described by Meyer and Gereffi, these changes in the locus and organization of global production had profound implications for labour regulation.[28] In a world where manufacturing occurred primarily within domestic firms and/or vertically integrated TNCs headquartered in the advanced industrial states, national governments could still regulate labour conditions in most factories. However, with the rise of global supply chains and the dispersion of production across multiple developing countries, these new sites of production escaped the regulatory reach of developed country governments. Moreover, in many cases, the national governments of the developing countries hosting these new factories either lacked the institutional capacities to fully regulate labour, health and safety, and environmental standards within these supply chain worksites or they intentionally chose not to enforce their own domestic laws and regulations for fear of driving up costs and thus driving away these sources of economic development, employment and taxation. As a result, the factories producing for global supply chains fell into a regulatory void in which labour laws and workplace standards were not being enforced by either host (developing) country governments or by the national authorities governing the large consumer markets absorbing much of this global production.

In an effort to remedy this situation and promote global labour standards among the thousands of geographically dispersed factories supplying global brands, various efforts were launched to include 'social' clauses within global trade agreements as well as to use access to the large consumer markets of the developed countries as leverage to compel developing country governments to enforce their own labour laws and thus drive improvements in working conditions within the supply chain factories located within their national boundaries.[29] Yet these efforts largely failed, primarily because they were blocked by developing country governments that argued that linking social and environmental standards to trade (or market access) was nothing short of protectionism. Several developing countries threatened to fight these efforts at the World Trade Organization, which had already signalled its unwilling-ness to support the inclusion of social clauses in global trade agreements. As a result of both this resistance by the developing countries and the growing popularity of neoliberal ideas among several influential developed country governments (espe-cially the US), the appetite for this alternative strategy waned.[30] Although 'social clauses' were included in a few bilateral trade agreements,[31] efforts to create an effective and truly global system of labour regulation through trade arrangements for the most part failed.

An alternative path involved efforts by the ILO and the United Nations to promote core labour standards through the establishment of 'decent work' conven-tions and the Global Compact. But these initiatives also lacked enforcement powers and thus offered little more than moral guidance for already committed governments and corporations.

In the absence of a strong system of global justice,[32] and given the limited ability (perhaps willingness) of many national governments to enforce their own labour laws, an array of different actors – both private and public – including transnational NGOs,[33] global corporations and industry associations,[34] multi-stakeholder initiatives (MSIs) and even a few developed country governments,[35] began to promote (some-times by themselves, other times in collaboration with other actors) a variety of private initiatives aimed at establishing and enforcing labour standards in global supply chains. Private voluntary regulation has many different forms. At times, it revolves around corporate codes of conduct in which lead buyers and brands articu-late their own internal standards governing, for instance, working conditions, wages, working hours and health and safety conditions, and require their suppliers to sign on to these standards. Other times, it entails monitoring programmes in which private auditors periodically inspect and assess factories in order to ensure that suppliers are in compliance with the corporate codes of conduct. And on still other occasions, private regulation involves certification mechanisms that label products 'sweat-free' and/or 'fair trade', thus signalling to consumers that certain products are allegedly made under fair and/or sustainable conditions. Notwithstanding, and perhaps because of this variation, private voluntary regulation has emerged as the dominant approach global corporations and labour rights NGOs alike embrace to promote labour stand-ards in global supply chains.

Given the diversity and often competing goals of these various initiatives,[36] this model of private voluntary regulation has provoked heated debates over the particu-larities of the actual programmes: how compliance programmes and certification schemes are designed and implemented; how factory auditors are trained and selected; how information generated from factory audits is shared – or their relation to other forms of regulation, especially state regulation; does private regulation crowd out or complement government regulation?[37] Because the debates are highly polarized, however, the basic question about the effectiveness of private regulation in improving labour standards has not been adequately evaluated.

I argue that regardless of the particular mission or leadership or organizational design or even resources underlying any of these private initiatives, they all inevit-ably produced limited or mixed results because they all confront a fundamental chal-lenge of reconciling diverse and conflicting interests among the key actors engaged in global supply chains. While most (although not all) of these actors may be genuinely interested in improving labour standards across the thousands of factories supplying global brands, conflicts of interest typically drive them in different directions about how best to achieve these goals. This is not to say that diverse interests can never be reconciled or that genuine progress towards promoting better working conditions within global supply chains is impossible. As some of my previous research[38] has shown, under certain conditions, these conflicting interests can be mediated and novel institutional arrangements and programmes that promote labour standards have, in fact, emerged. But these conditions are quite rare and the new institutional arrangements (and constellation of interests underlying them) rarely include only private actors.

4 Conflicting interests and collective action problems inherent in private voluntary initiatives

A quick and overly simplified description of the diverse and competing interests expressed by different actors engaged in global supply chains highlights the fundamental challenges faced by all private voluntary initiatives. Consider first the global brands and buyers sourcing their products through these global supply chains. On the one hand, these companies have an interest in obtaining high-quality products as quickly and cheaply as possible. At the same time, most reputation-conscious brands also have a genuine interest in ensuring decent labour practices among their suppliers for fear that harsh working conditions could (if discovered) create scandal and hence risk to their reputation and brand image. As such, they actively engage their suppliers in various private initiatives, be they monitoring efforts or certification schemes.[39] Yet because these brands and buyers are competing fiercely with one another, they are unwilling to pay extra for improved working conditions since this could erode their margins or lead to price increases that most consumers these days are unwilling to accept.[40] As a result, most companies are unwilling to fully redress workplace problems endemic in supply chain factories on their own, especially since most of these suppliers are also producing for their competitors.[41] Moreover, even when individual buyers or brands do invest in 'supplier responsibility' programmes – and many of them do – some of their 'downstream' business practices (i.e. product development, commercialization, purchasing) drive their suppliers to implement production and work systems that ultimately undermine these very same corporate responsibility efforts. In highly competitive markets, global brands and lead buyers face tremendous pressure to sell an increasing variety of products at ever-lower prices. In order to do this, they pressure their suppliers to reduce costs, shorten lead times and produce a variety of products in smaller batches. Suppliers, in turn, respond to these increased demands by paying their workers low base wages, limiting employee benefits and demanding excessive work hours simply to meet the shorter lead times their buyers require. Thus, even when global buyers do invest in programmes aimed at improving labour standards among their suppliers, their own 'downstream' business practices inadvertently undermine these efforts.

Suppliers, too, possess diverse and conflicting interests. Like the global buyers they work for, these independent contract manufacturers are also competing fiercely with one another for purchase orders from the large global brands. They have an interest in receiving orders that will utilize as much of their productive capacity as possible, for as much of the year as possible (in order to amortize their fixed costs) and that generate the highest margins. As such, they seek to win large orders with good mark-ups from high-end brands and/or large retailers. In an effort to reduce transaction costs and risk, they also attempt to develop long-term, stable relationships with these global buyers. To do this, they need to deliver (quickly and reliably) high-quality products at acceptable prices. They also need to make sure that their production and work practices do not create any reputation risks for their global customers. Yet, given that their margins result from the difference between the unit prices buyers are willing to pay for the products they order (less every year) and the total costs entailed in producing these goods (i.e. material costs, labour, overheads, transportation – all of which have risen in recent years), suppliers have a strong interest to contain or even reduce their production costs. As a result, they seek to restrain wage increases, limit overtime pay and benefits and under-invest in various services (canteens, dormitories, health clinics, recreation halls) for their workers. Moreover, in order to respond to the growing demands by buyers (both existing and potential new customers) for lower prices, smaller batches and shorter lead times, suppliers structure their production processes in ways that permit them to ramp up production quickly but without incurring additional fixed costs. This means imposing excessive overtime hours on their workers and relying on migrant and/or contract workers that they can quickly hire and fire, depending upon their production schedules. Thus, even when these suppliers embrace corporate responsibility programmes and engage in various private initiatives aimed at improving working conditions within their factories, the pressures they face often drive them to engage in various production and work practices that undermine these efforts.

Both workers and developing country governments also express complex and often contradictory interests. Developing country governments both have an interest in asserting their sovereignty and protecting the rights and welfare of their citizens by enforcing domestic laws that regulate workplace conditions, and, at the same time, because of the various economic and employment benefits generated by these new sites of global production, these same governments fear that by enforcing their own domestic laws, they could drive up costs and thus drive away these factories. As a result, even those governments with the institutional capacities to enforce their own laws often refuse to do so, or they do so in a non-systematic way by granting contract manufacturers exemptions (sometime full, other times partial) from various wage, work-hour and social insurance regulations in an effort to provide them with a more hospitable 'business environment'. Workers employed at these supply chain factories often come to these workplaces from rural villages (or in some cases, other less developed countries) in search of decent jobs with good wages. These workers often want to work overtime since overtime compensation permits them to supplement their base salaries. Given that these factory jobs are often preferable to whatever work opportunities were available in their home villages, many of these workers are willing to work long hours under stressful conditions.[42] Yet, at the same time, these workers want to be treated fairly. They want to be paid for the overtime work they do at the agreed-upon rates (not be cheated), they want to work in environments that do not jeopardize their personal safety and health, and they want to be treated with respect – to live in clean, not overly crowded dorms, eat nutritious and well-cooked food and have their personal dignity respected. Thus, while most supply chain factory workers are willing to repeat the same task for many hours, day in day out, under stressful working conditions and for low wages, they expect to be treated fairly and with respect. If not, they will either leave their employer as soon as they can and/ or engage in individual or even collective resistance.[43]

In sum, even a cursory examination of only a few of the actors involved in global supply chains reveals their divergent and often conflicting interests. How can any private voluntary initiative aimed at promoting improved working conditions and labour standards reconcile these interests and resolve the coordination/collective action problems this mix of actors and interests creates?

The problem of reconciling diverse and conflicting interests and overcoming obstacles to collective action is not new.[44] In the context of promoting standards through private voluntary initiatives, a number of mechanisms have been proposed to overcome these collective action problems. Some of these entail tapping into the enlightened self-interest of individual corporations by showing that investments in particular voluntary programmes will not only improve standards but also signal to potential buyers, rivals and even regulatory authorities certain distinctive attributes that will enhance the competitiveness of firms that choose to participate in these initiatives. For example, in a series of studies focused primarily on voluntary environmental initiatives, Aseem Prakash and Matthew Potoski have shown that under certain conditions – the home country of foreign investors or trading partners – increased foreign direct investment (FDI) and trade can lead to the diffusion of process standards like ISO 14001, a private, voluntary standard aimed at promoting improved environmental practices within individual firms. In their book *The Voluntary Environmentalists*,[45] they argue that voluntary regulatory programmes such as ISO 14001 can mitigate collective action problems by providing participating firms with shared, group benefits (what they refer to as 'club goods') like enhanced standing with stakeholders and improved brand image that are not available to firms that refuse to participate in these voluntary programmes.

Can similar mechanisms work in the case of labour, or is labour somewhat different? Unfortunately, the particular circumstances underlying the successful diffusion of voluntary environmental standards do not carry over to the field of labour. Unlike ISO 14001, which has established itself as the world's most successful private initiative for environmental standards, no such dominant initiative exists for labour standards. In fact, there exist multiple, competing voluntary programmes, each claiming to be more effective and/or rigorous than the other.[46] As a result, individual firms cannot signal anything distinctive about themselves simply by participating in any one (or the other) of these initiatives and, as a result, these voluntary labour initiatives are unable to provide exclusive 'club goods' for participating companies in their programmes. Moreover, whereas ISO 14001 signals that firms are making significant investments aimed at achieving specific process improvements, over and beyond what is expected of them by national legislation, most voluntary labour initiatives simply require participating firms to respect the local 'law of the land', which entails very different levels of commitment to labour rights and working conditions across the same supply chain. Finally, as we saw above, the collective action problems facing firms seeking to promote improved labour standards in global supply chains are more complex than those facing 'voluntary environmentalists' since they entail not simply collective action among rival firms but also coordination and collaboration challenges between global brands/buyers and their multiple suppliers dispersed across the world. As a result of these supply chain dynamics, promoting global standards through 'club goods' has not been as successful in the arena of working conditions and labour rights.[47]

If market signalling and segmentation appear unable to overcome the collective action problems plaguing private initiatives seeking to promote global labour standards, perhaps embedding these private initiatives within particular institutional arrangements capable of shaping firm behaviour in more constructive ways might help. A number of scholars[48] have described various institutional arrangements that in different ways promote 'credible commitments', 'trust', 'redundant capabilities' and particular 'equilibria' that promote collective action among private firms by modifying or suspending their individual short-term interests. Wolfgang Streeck,[49] for example, has written extensively on the institutional conditions required to support what he calls 'diversified quality production', a production system that for many years appeared to respond successfully to changing consumer tastes, price pressures, variable batch sizes and growing international competition while still delivering high-quality goods and empowering (rather than immiserating) the workers employed in these factories. Henry Farrell[50] has described a somewhat different set of institutions that exist in northern Italy and southern Germany that provide local firms with information about one another so that they can engage in inter-firm collaborations that would not be possible given their divergent interests and ambiguous circumstances.

Once again, the lessons for labour standards in global supply chains are not so clear, given the variation in political, economic and cultural circumstances covered by supply chains. The number of actors – both private and public – and the diversity of interests may simply be too complex (and evolving) to construct institutions that can provide either sufficient and accurate information about and/or redundant resources to the thousands of private firms involved in global supply chains so that they modify their self-interested, market-oriented behaviours in more labour-friendly ways. In fact, there appears to be some evidence that the original national/subnational institutional arrangements that have inspired these models are themselves facing difficulties in the face of globalization.[51]

Although it is usually the case that current institutional arrangements and/or market-based voluntary initiatives have not sufficed to reconcile the diverse interests and overcome the collective action problems inherent in global supply chains, I argue that under certain circumstances, and when combined with novel forms of public regulation, private voluntary programmes aimed at promoting labour standards can work.

5 The argument in brief

Private initiatives aimed at improving labour standards in global supply chains can succeed when global buyers and their suppliers establish long-term, mutually beneficial relations and when various public (authoritative rule-making) institutions help to both support these mutually beneficial buyer–supplier relations and resolve a set of collective action problems that private actors cannot overcome on their own.

As such, private voluntary regulation can best succeed when 'layered' on and interacting with public (state) regulation.[52]

If properly designed, private efforts aimed at promoting global labour standards can succeed by tapping into and shaping the self-interest of global buyers and their suppliers.[53] However, the benefits generated by these private initiatives do not merely revolve around brand image and/or positive stakeholder relations. Instead, I argue that under certain conditions (long-term relations, frequent interactions and mutually beneficial economic arrangements between buyers and suppliers) private voluntary initiatives can work in ways that both tap into and align the interests and incentives of private firms (by reducing information and transaction costs, developing new capabilities, promoting process and product innovations that enhance the competitiveness of both buyers and suppliers) while also generating positive results for workers through new work and production processes that improve wages, reduce excessive work hours and empower operators on the shop floor.[54]

In his study of buyer–supplier relations in the US, Germany and Japan, Gary Herrigel[55] describes a system in which buyers and suppliers learn from one another, experiment together and distribute the risks and rewards of doing business together. He shows how these patterns of buyer–supplier relations were not culturally or even institutionally determined but rather politically constructed over many years of struggle and compromise among these supply chain actors. In some of my previous research,[56] I have documented how several global buyers were able to establish similar collaborative and labour standards-enhancing relations with some (but by no means all) of their suppliers when these relations were based upon mutual gains, joint learning and long-term commitments. Like most global buyers, these companies engaged their suppliers in various compliance and capability-building programmes. But these more collaborative relations were based not solely on policing/deterrence or even capability building/technical assistance – although both of these elements existed in these particular buyer–supplier relationships – but rather on the mutual recognition that each party had to gain from the collaboration. These more collaborative buyer–supplier relations were based upon a fundamental understanding that both the risks and the rewards of doing business together would be distributed more or less fairly between the parties; the gains would not be captured nor the losses borne by one or the other party alone. It was this recognition and the positive spillovers it generated that created the real incentives for private firms to engage in the most effective private voluntary initiatives analysed in my previous work.

Although clearly beneficial to both global buyers and their suppliers, these more collaborative arrangements are rare within most supply chains. Moreover, because of the conflicting pressures facing both buyers and suppliers, where these mutually beneficial arrangements do exist, they remain unstable in the sense that each actor has a strong incentive to cheat or renege upon whatever commitments underlie these collaborations. Even in the most successful of these collaborations, moreover, some labour standards (for example, the right to associate freely into unions and bargain collectively) are not part of the understanding, but remain beyond the pale. In other words, these 'enabling rights' do not arise naturally from even these enlightened buyer–supplier relations. The only way these rights can be brought to life is when the law requires them. For this, the state needs to be brought into the realm of private governance negotiations. As a result, we need to bring in the state and embed these private initiatives within a system of authoritative rule-making and new forms of regulation that can enable them to consistently and sustainably promote labour standards within global supply chains.

Earlier I described the decline in the capacity of national governments, especially in the developing economies, to regulate labour standards as a consequence of competition for FDI. Recent research shows, however, that national governments – even in poor countries with few natural resources – have far more ability to impose their will on foreign investors than previously believed.[57] As a number of recent studies have shown, even when eager to attract foreign investment and constrained by global competition, national governments have underutilized capacity to protect worker rights and resolve some collective action problems among firms.[58] Since most private voluntary initiatives promoting labour standards in global supply chains simply require participating firms to adhere to local laws, having strong national labour, environmental and health and safety laws is crucial to the success of these programmes. And since monitoring for compliance with these laws is costly, with suppliers having limited incentives to fully enforce them and NGOs having limited capacity to do so, only national governments have sufficient power and legitimacy to enforce their own laws. Moreover, in most global supply chains, in which different buyers and suppliers have real incentives to circumvent any regulations that increase their costs, national governments are best positioned to prevent defections by individual firms and ensure that all producers within the same national or regional economy adhere to common standards. Yet how does one promote this type of government intervention/public regulation in a world of global supply chains?

Building on recent research on 'experimentalist governance'[59] and 'responsive regulation',[60] I argue that government, even in most developing countries, can play a positive role in promoting collaborative buyer–supplier relations and resolving collective action problems among different global buyers as well as between these buyers and their multiple suppliers. In explaining the features of experimentalist governance, Sabel and Zeitlin[61] describe a multi-level process in which government agencies, in collaboration with the private actors they regulate, engage in a process in which broad goals and metrics are developed and implemented in ways that promotes responsiveness to variation in local circumstances, learning and the diffusion of best practices across different private and public actors, and ever-increasing compliance with government regulations. As a result of this framework, European governments have been able to promote enhanced environmental standards both within the EU and among developing countries supplying forestry products to Europe. Potoski and Prakash[62] describe a similar process within the US, in which innovative state-level policies (i.e. lenient penalties in exchange for transparency and self-disclosure of problems) have encouraged private firms to enhance their compliance with environmental regulations. These innovations are not limited to the US and Europe but have also emerged in several developing countries, including Argentina,[63] Brazil,[64] Cambodia[65] and India.[66] In each of these cases, using different mechanisms and targeting different actors, national governments were able to promote labour and environmental standards by reconciling the competing interests of, and resolving collective action problems among, private firms that were violating these standards. In all cases this process involved not traditional command and control (deterrence) government regulation but rather a mix of carrots (in the form of capability-building/technical assistance programmes) and sticks (in the form of threatening sanctions and closing off 'low-road' options for domestic firms).

6 Conclusion

In *The Promise and Limits of Private* Power,[67] I analyse various compliance and 'beyond compliance' initiatives promoted by several global brands alone or in collaboration with other firms, NGOs and even international organizations like the ILO. The book makes three substantive points:

1   Traditional private compliance programmes are limited in their ability to promote labour justice in global supply chains. Notwithstanding years of efforts by various global companies to develop evermore comprehensive monitoring tools, hire growing numbers of internal compliance specialists, conduct hundreds (if not thousands) of factory audits and engage external consultants and even NGOs, working conditions and labour rights have improved somewhat among some of their suppliers but have stagnated or even deteriorated in many other supplier factories. After more than a decade of concerted efforts by global brands and labour rights NGOs alike, private compliance programmes appear largely unable to deliver on their promise of sustained improvements in labour standards in the new centres of global production. Compliance efforts have delivered some improvements in working conditions but these improvements seem to have hit a ceiling: basic improvements have been achieved in some areas (for example, health and safety) but not in others (for example, freedom of association, excessive working hours). Moreover, these improvements appear to be unstable in the sense that many factories cycle in and out of compliance over time.

2   'Beyond compliance' and capability-building programmes are also limited in their impact. Notwithstanding significant improvements over traditional compliance programmes, my research shows how many (but not all) capability-building initiatives suffer from their own shortcomings, especially their inability to address certain distributive issues and overcome various political hurdles necessary to achieve labour rights enforcement. Although capability-building programmes generated marked improvements for participating factories in terms of increased productivity and quality, and improvements for most workers in terms of health and safety conditions and, in some cases, greater autonomy and empowerment on the shop floor, these same initiatives – precisely because of their technocratic approach – eschewed more difficult, distributive issues (for example, living wages) and the enforcement of 'enabling rights' so that workers could organize to demand higher wages and better working conditions.

3   In response to both the limitations of these private voluntary programmes, and growing demands for more effective state enforcement of already existing labour and employment laws designed to protect workers employed in the factories and farms supplying global buyers, a number of new and/or reformed public regulatory initiatives aimed at promoting greater compliance with labour laws, health and safety standards and the ability of workers to freely organize themselves into independent unions have been launched in recent years. My research suggests that although the revival of labour inspection and the promotion of innovative regulatory initiatives in an array of different countries have certainly helped improve working conditions and labour rights in these

countries, these efforts also suffer various limitations in their organizational capacities and ability to adequately inspect, let alone redress, violations in all workplaces under their jurisdiction.

These organizational limitations could be overcome through complementary interactions with private voluntary initiatives. It is precisely these complementary private/public regulatory approaches that have the greatest potential to promote labour justice in a world of global supply chains. Even in today's world of global supply chains, a new form of labour regulation is possible and can be constructed through a sequential process that blends private interests and public intervention. Precisely how this takes place across different national, cultural, and economic contexts should be the focus of future research.

Notes

1   This chapter focuses on global supply chains and various outsourcing practices by global brands and large retail chains. Another important dimension of globalization, the rise of foreign direct investment by developed-country-based transnational corporations in developing countries (either through opening up their own subsidiaries or investing in joint ventures with local firms) is not covered in this chapter. For more on the labour implications for these alternative globalization strategies, see L. Mosley and S. Uno, 'Racing to the Bottom or Climbing to the Top?: Economic Globalization and Collective Labor Rights' (2007) 40(8) *Comparative Political Studies* 923; L. Mosley, *Labor Rights and Multinational Production* (New York: Cambridge University Press, 2011).

2   P. Collier and D. Dollar, *Globalization, Growth, and Poverty: Building an Inclusive World Economy* (World Bank Policy Research Report) (Washington, DC and New York: Oxford University Press and World Bank, 2002); T.H. Moran, *Beyond Sweatshops: Foreign Direct Investment and Globalization in Developing Countries* (Washington, DC: Brookings Institution Press, 2002).

3   Verité, *Excessive Overtime in Chinese Supplier Factories: Causes, Impacts, and Recommendations for Action* (2004), http://verite.org/sites/default/files/images/Excessive_Overtime_in_Chinese_Factories.pdf; D. Pruett, *Looking for a Quick Fix: How Weak Social Auditing Is Keeping Workers in Sweatshops* (Clean Clothes Campaign, 2005), www.evb.ch/fileadmin/files/documents/Konsum/Quickfix05.pdf; T. Connor and K. Dent, *Offside! Labor Rights and Sportswear Production in Asia* (Oxfam International, 2006); C. Kernaghan, *US–Jordan Free Trade Agreement Descends into Human Trafficking and Involuntary Servitude* (New York: National Labor Committee, 2006).

4   P. Rivoli, *The Travels of a T-Shirt in the Global Economy: An Economist Examines the Markets, Power, and Politics of World Trade* (Hoboken, NJ: John Wiley & Sons, 2005).

5   BBC, 'The History of Running Shoes', http://news.bbc.co.uk/sportacademy/hi/sa/athletics/features/newsid_3935000/3935703.stm.

6   C. Dubin, 'Snapshot: Footware', Inbound Logistics, December 2009, www.inboundlogistics.com/cms/article/snapshot-footwear.

7   J.C. Ryan and A.T. Durning, *Stuff: The Secret Lives of Everyday Things* (Seattle: Northwest Environment Watch, 1998).

8   Ryan and Durning describe how South Korea used to be a leading exporter of athletic shoes in the 1980s. But, by the 1990s, rising wages and labour unrest propelled many companies to shift their manufacturing base elsewhere, primarily to China and Southeast Asia. An estimated 400,000 Koreans employed in the shoe industry lost their jobs between 1990 and 1993. Ibid.

9   E. Grossman, '200 People per Shoe: Making Footwear in Tangerang, Indonesia', ScienceBlogs, http://scienceblogs.com/thepumphandle/2010/11/16/200-people-per-shoe-making-n.

10 Ryan and Durning, *Stuff*.

11 Apple, of course, is not the only company engaged in this kind of production. Dell, Hewlett-Packard, IBM, Lenovo, Motorola, Nokia, Sony, Toshiba and many others are engaged in very similar practices. Apple, however, is an industry leader in both design and profits. Since 2005, its share prices have risen from about US$45 to more than US$427.

12 C. Duhigg and K. Bradsher, 'How the US Lost out on iPhone Work', *New York Times*, 21 January 2012, www.nytimes.com/2012/01/22/business/apple-america-and-a-squeezed-middle-class.html?_r=3&hp=&pagewanted=all.

13 Ibid.

14 For a detailed description of working conditions in Foxconn factories in southern China, see P. Ngai and J. Chan, 'Global Capital, the State, and Chinese Workers: The Foxconn Experience' (2012) 38(4) *Modern China* 383. For a more nuanced view that illustrates both the difficult working conditions young migrant workers employed at these factories experience, as well as the freedoms they also enjoy living among thousands of

other young workers and away from their rural villages, see L.T. Chang, *Factory Girls* (New York: Spiegel and Grau, 2008).

15   C. Duhigg and D. Barboza, 'In China, Human Costs Are Built into an iPad', *New York Times*, 25 January 2012, www.nytimes.com/2012/01/26/business/ieconomy-apples-ipad-and-the-human-costs-for-workers-in-china.html.

16   Apple, *Supplier Responsibility: 2009 Progress Report* (2009), www.apple.com/supplier-responsibility/pdf/Apple_SR_2009_Progress_Report.pdf.

17   Apple, *Apple Supplier Responsibility: 2012 Progress Report* (2012), www.apple.com/supplier-responsibility/pdf/Apple_SR_2012_Progress_Report.pdf.

18   Fair Labor Association (FLA), *Independent Investigation of Apple Supplier, Foxconn* (2012), www.fairlabor.org/sites/default/files/documents/reports/foxconn_investigation_report.pdf.

19   FLA, *Wages along the Supply Chain: Trends, Progress and Looking Ahead* (2011), www.fairlabor.org/sites/default/files/wageforumreport_final.pdf.

20   International Labour Organization (ILO), *Global Employment Trends* (2008) p. 10.

21   Ibid., pp. 11, 46.

22   In fact, Mosley shows how the collective rights of workers employed in the subsidiaries of multinational corporations are significantly better than those of workers employed by local, independent suppliers or subcontractors. Mosley, *Labor Rights and Multinational Production*.

23   ILO, 'Child Labour', www.ilo.org/global/topics/child-labour/lang--en/index.htm.

24   ILO, 'Forced Labour, Human Trafficking and Slavery', www.ilo.org/global/topics/forced-labour/lang--en.

25   Oxfam International, *Trading away Our Rights: Women Working in Global Supply Chains* (2004), www.oxfam.org/sites/www.oxfam.org/files/rights.pdf.

26   V. Haufler, *A Public Role for the Private Sector: Industry Self-regulation in a Global Economy* (Washington, DC: Carnegie Endowment for International Peace, 2001); K.A. Elliott and R.B. Freeman, *Can Standards Improve under Globalization?* (Washington, DC: Institute for International Economics, 2003); D. O'Rourke, 'Outsourcing Regulation: Analyzing Nongovernmental Systems of Labor Standards and Monitoring' (2003) 31(1) *Policy Studies Journal* 1; T. Bartley, 'Institutional Emergence in an Era of Globalization: The Rise of Transnational Private Regulation of Labor and Environmental Conditions' (2007) 113 *The American Journal of Sociology*; R.B. Reich, *Supercapitalism: The Transformation of Business, Democracy and Everyday Life* (New York: Knopf, 2007); D. Vogel, 'Private Global Business Regulation' (2008) 11 *Annual Review of Political Science* 261; M. Mayer and G. Gereffi, 'Regulation and Economic Globalization: Prospects and Limits of Private Governance' (2010) 12(3) *Business and Politics*.

27   Mayer and Gereffi, 'Regulation and Economic Globalization'.

28   Ibid.

29   Bartley, 'Institutional Emergence in an Era of Globalization'; S. Charnovitz, 'Rethinking WTO Trade Sanctions' (2001) 94(4) *American Journal of International Law* 792; L. Compa and J.S. Vogt, 'Labor Rights in the Generalized System of Preferences: A 20-Year Review' (2001) 22(2–3) *Comparative Labor Law and Policy Journal* 199; Elliott and Freeman, *Can Standards Improve under Globalization?*; S. Polaski, 'Protecting Labor Rights through Trade Agreements: An Analytical Guide' (2004) 13 *UC Davis Journal of International Law & Policy* 13; Reich, *Supercapitalism*.

30   Bartley, 'Institutional Emergence in an Era of Globalization'; Vogel, 'Private Global Business Regulation'.

31   Polaski, 'Protecting Labor Rights through Trade Agreements'; S. Polaski, 'Combining Global and Local Forces: The Case of Labor Rights in Cambodia' (2006) 34(5) *World Development* 919; C. Doumbia-Henry and E. Gravel, 'Free Trade Agreements and Labour Rights: Recent Developments' (2006) 145(3) *International Labour Review* 185.

32   J. Cohen and C. Sabel, 'Extra Republicam Nulla Justita?' (2006) 34(2) *Philosophy & Public Affairs* 147.

33   M.E. Keck and K. Sikkink, *Activists beyond Borders: Advocacy Networks in International Politics* (Ithaca, NY: Cornell University Press, 1998); G.W. Seidman, *Beyond the Boycott: Labor Rights, Human Rights, and Transnational Activism* (New York: Russell Sage Foundation, 2007).

34   Haufler, *A Public Role for the Private Sector*; Bartley, 'Institutional Emergence in an Era of Globalization'; O'Rourke, 'Outsourcing Regulation'; Reich, *Supercapitalism*; Vogel, 'Private Global Business Regulation'.

35   Bartley, 'Institutional Emergence in an Era of Globalization'.

36   O'Rourke, 'Outsourcing Regulation'; K. Nadvi and F. Wältring, 'Making Sense of Global Standards' in H. Schmitz (ed.), *Local Enterprises in the Global Economy: Issues of Governance and Upgrading* (Northampton: Edward Elgar, 2004) p. 53; Bartley, 'Institutional Emergence in an Era of Globalization'.

37   J. Esbenshade, *Monitoring Sweatshops: Workers, Consumers, and the Global Apparel Industry* (Philadelphia: Temple University Press, 2004); Seidman, *Beyond the Boycott*; Reich, *Supercapitalism*.

38   R.M. Locke, *The Promise and Limits of Private Power: Promoting Labor Standards in a Global Economy* (New York: Cambridge University Press, 2013).

39   Haufler, *A Public Role for the Private Sector*; A. Heritier, A.K. Mueller-Debus and C.R. Thauer, 'The Firm as an Inspector: Private Ordering and Political Rules', (2009) 11(4) *Business and Politics*, art. 2; Mayer and Gereffi, 'Regulation and Economic Globalization'.

40   The research on consumer's willingness to pay more for products made under just working conditions presents a mixed picture, in which some consumers at higher income levels are willing to pay somewhat more for these 'ethically sourced' products whereas other consumers with less purchasing power are not willing to pay more for goods made under 'sweat-free' conditions. See J. Hainmueller and M.J. Hiscox, 'The Socially Conscious Consumer? Field Experimental Tests of Consumer Support for Labor Standards', MIT Political Science Department Working Paper Series, No. 2012-15 (3 June 2012).

41   For an interesting argument for why firms might take these actions, even if other competing firms do not, see F. Reinhardt, 'Market Failure and the Environmental Policies of Firms: Economic Rationales for "Beyond Compliance" Behavior' (1999) 3(1) *Journal of Industrial Ecology* 9. Reinhardt focuses on environmental standards but the parallels with labour standards are strong.

42   Rivoli, *The Travels of a T-Shirt in the Global Economy*; Chang, *Factory Girls*.

43   For interesting descriptions of this growing worker resistance, especially in China, see M. Gallagher, 'Changes in the World's Workshop: The Demographic, Social and Political Factors behind China's Labor Movement' in W. Huang and H. Zhou (eds), *Dragon versus Eagle: The Chinese Economy and US–China Relations* (Kalamazoo, MI: Upjohn Press, 2012) ch. 5; E. Friedman, 'Getting through the Hard Times Together'?: Chinese Workers and Unions Respond to the Economic Crisis' (2012) 54(4) *Journal of Industrial Relations* 1. In many ways, these worker protests resemble the social conflicts that emerged among migrant factory workers in Europe in the late 1960s–early 1970s. See C.F. Sabel, *Work and Politics* (New York: Cambridge University Press, 1982).

44   See, e.g. R. Axelrod, *The Evolution of Cooperation* (New York: Basic Books, 1984); J.R. Bowman, 'The Politics of the Market: Economic Competition and the Organization of Capitalists' (1985) 5 *Political Power and Social Theory* 35; E. Ostrom, *Governing the Commons: The Evolution of Institutions for Active Action* (Cambridge: Cambridge University Press, 1990); P. Swenson, 'Bringing Capital Back in, or Social Democracy Reconsidered: Employer Power, Cross-Class Alliances, and Centralization of Industrial Relations in Denmark and Sweden' (1991) 43(4) *World Politics* 513; R. Putnam, *Making Democracy Work: Civic Traditions in Modern Italy* (Princeton, NJ: Princeton University Press, 1994); F. Fukuyama, *Trust: The Social Virtues and the Creation of Prosperity* (New York: Free Press, 1995).

45   A. Prakash and M. Potoski, *The Voluntary Environmentalists: Green Clubs, ISO 14001, and Voluntary Environmental Regulations* (Cambridge: Cambridge University Press, 2006).

46   O'Rourke, 'Outsourcing Regulation'; Nadvi and Wältring, 'Making Sense of Global Standards'; T. Bartley, 'Transnational Private Regulation in Practice: The Limits of Forest and Labor Standards Certification in Indonesia' (2010) 12(3) *Business and Politics*.

47   Bartley, 'Transnational Private Regulation in Practice'.

48   D. North, *Institutions, Institutional Change and Economic Performance* (Cambridge: Cambridge University Press, 1990); J. Knight, *Institutions and Social Conflict* (Cambridge: Cambridge University Press, 1992); W. Streeck, 'The Uncertainties of Management in the Management of Uncertainty: Employers, Labor Relations and Industrial Adjustment in the 1980s' (1987) 1(3) *Work, Employment & Society* 281; W. Streeck, 'On the Institutional Conditions of Diversified Quality Production' in E. Matzner and W. Streeck (eds), *Beyond Keynesianism: The Socio-Economics of Production and Employment* (London: Edward Elgar, 1991) p. 21; P. Hall and D. Soskice, *Varieties of Capitalism: The Institutional Foundations of Comparative Advantage* (Oxford: Oxford University Press, 2001); K. Thelen, *How Institutions Evolve: The Political Economy of Skills in Germany, Britain, the United States and Japan* (New York: Cambridge University, 2004); H. Farrell, *The Political Economy of Trust: Institutions, Interests, and Inter-Firm Cooperation in Italy and Germany* (New York: Cambridge University Press, 2009).

49   Streeck, 'The Uncertainties of Management in the Management of Uncertainty'; Streeck, 'On the Institutional Conditions of Diversified Quality Production'.

50   Farrell, *The Political Economy of Trust*.

51   W. Streeck, *Re-forming Capitalism: Institutional Change in the German Political Economy* (Oxford: Oxford University Press, 2009).

52   For more on the 'layering' of private and public regulation, see D.M. Trubek L.G. Trubek, 'New Governance & Legal Regulation: Complementarity, Rivalry, and Transformation' (2007) University of Wisconsin Law School, Legal Studies Research Paper Series 1047; T. Bartley, 'Transnational Governance as the Layering of Rules: Intersections of Public and Private Standards' (2011) 12(2) *Theoretical Inquiries in Law* 6.

53   For various illustrations of how private initiatives can be designed in ways that align the self-interest of private forms with the broader goal of enhancing labour standards, see A. Fung, D. O'Rourke and C.F. Sabel, *Can We Put an End to Sweatshops? A New Democracy Forum on Raising Global Labor Standards* (Boston: Beacon Press, 2001); Elliott and Freeman, *Can Standards Improve under Globalization?*

54   This argument builds upon research on both collaborative manufacturing (see G. Herrigel, *Manufacturing Possibilities* (New York: Oxford University Press, 2010); G. Herrigel and V. Wittke, 'Mutually Beneficial Upgrading? China's Changing Relationship with Developed Country Manufacturing Multinationals', paper presented at the Beijing Forum, Beijing, China, 5–7 November 2010; C.F. Sabel and J. Zeitlin, 'Neither Modularity nor Relational Contracting: Inter-Firm Collaboration in the New Economy' (2004) 5(3) *Enterprise & Society*; I. Ivarsson and C.G. Alvstam, 'Local Technology Linkages and Supplier Upgrading in Global Value Chains: The Case of Swedish Engineering TNCs in Emerging Markets' (2009) 13(4) *Competition & Change* 368; I. Ivarsson and C.G. Alvstam, 'Supplier Upgrading in the Home-furnishing Value Chain: An Empirical Study of IKEA's Sourcing in China and South East Asia' (2010) 38(11) *World Development* 1575; I. Ivarsson and C.G. Alvstam, 'Upgrading in Global Value-Chains: A Case Study of Technology-Learning among IKEA-Suppliers in China and Southeast Asia' (2010) 10(2) *Journal of Economic Geography* 731) and relational contracts (G. Baker, R. Gibbons and K.J. Murphy, 'Relational Contracts and the Theory of the Firm' (2002) 117(1) *The Quarterly Journal of Economics* 39).

55   Herrigel, *Manufacturing Possibilities*.

56   Locke, *The Promise and Limits of Private Power*.

57   See, e.g. R.L. Wellhausen, *The Shield of Nationality: When Governments Break Contracts with Foreign Firms* (New York: Cambridge University Press, 2014).

58 M. Amengual, 'Complementary Labor Regulation: The Uncoordinated Combination of State and Private Regulators in the Dominican Republic' (2010) 38(3) *World Development* 405; S. Coslovsky, 'Relational Regulation in the Brazilian Ministério Publico: The Organizational Basis of Regulatory Responsiveness' (2011) 5(1) *Regulation & Governance* 70; R. Pires, 'Beyond the Fear of Discretion: Flexibility, Performance, and Accountability in the Management of Regulatory Bureaucracies' (2011) 5(1) *Regulation & Governance* 43.
59 C.F. Sabel and J. Zeitlin, 'Experimental Governance' in D. Levi-Faur (ed.), *The Oxford Handbook of Governance* (Oxford: Oxford University Press, 2012) ch. 12.
60 J. Braithwaite, 'Responsive Regulation and Developing Economies' (2006) 34(5) *World Development* 884; D. Graham and N. Woods, 'Making Corporate Self-Regulation Effective in Developing Countries' (2006) 34(5) *World Development* 868.
61 Sabel and Zeitlin, 'Experimental Governance'.
62 M. Potoski and A. Prakash, 'The Regulation Dilemma: Cooperation and Conflict in Environmental Governance' (2004) 64(2) *Public Administration Review* 152.
63 Amengual, 'Complementary Labor Regulation'.
64 Coslovsky, 'Relational Regulation in the Brazilian Ministério Publico'; Pires, 'Beyond the Fear of Discretion'.
65 Polaski, 'Combining Global and Local Forces'.
66 M. Tewari and P. Pillai, 'Global Standards and Environmental Compliance in India's Leather Industry' (2005) 33(2) *Oxford Development Studies*.
67 Locke, *The Promise and Limits of Private Power*.

Section 7.2

The future of business and human rights: challenges and opportunities

Dorothée Baumann-Pauly, Justine Nolan and Michael Posner

The various contributions to this volume are an accurate reflection of the contemporary discourse on business and human rights. In one sense, this debate has evolved substantially in the last decade, fuelled in part by today's rapidly expanding global economy, the exponential growth of the Internet and social media, and by a generational shift in our culture, with millions of young consumers, investors, bloggers and thought leaders eager to bring issues of business sustainability to the fore. The United Nations Guiding Principles on Business and Human Rights[1] (Guiding Principles) have also helped to lay the foundation for future action, based on a formula which holds that governments have the primary duty to protect human rights, and companies also have a corollary responsibility to address these issues in their core business operations. The adoption of the Guiding Principles in 2011 created the space for more open conversations about these complex and often sensitive issues among companies, governments and non-governmental organizations.

On the other hand, while states have the primary duty to protect human rights, a look around the world today makes clear that too often governments lack the will or capacity to do so. In the long term, efforts to strengthen state capacity and resolve may eventually provide the types of laws, regulations and judicial and administrative oversight that are needed to protect the rights of vulnerable populations everywhere. But given profound weaknesses in the state-based system, other actors, including businesses, will need to help fill governance gaps.

Corporations today are expected to proactively address and manage business-related human rights risks. Preparing the next generation of business leaders for this task will be of increasing relevance. A rapidly globalizing economy has offered breathtaking new opportunities to companies with global sourcing models, natural resource needs and the desire to expand their markets. On the positive side, these multinational companies have fuelled economic growth and helped create new jobs that have moved hundreds of millions of people out of extreme poverty. But all too often these same companies have built business models that benefit from weak local governance in the places they manufacture, farm, fish, extract minerals or otherwise do business. Globalization has resulted in an economy where companies and countries no longer trade simply in raw materials and final products; 'rather different firms and countries specialize not just in producing different products, but in different *parts* of different products, each focusing variously on design, assembly, marketing and so on'.[2] Global supply chains are characterized by relentless pressures on prices and lead times and the corresponding effect is the deterioration of working conditions at the bottom of the supply chain. In many industries these business models are the roots of the challenge; based on very tight margins, they result too often in exploitative practices, unsafe working conditions, risks to security or infringements on privacy. It is a significant challenge to alter these practices, and for companies to adopt new business models that correct the current imbalance between people and profits.

A number of leading global companies have begun to recognize their important role in the realization of human rights. But we are still in the early days of this emerging field, with a much longer road ahead than the distance already travelled. The challenges are immense. To begin with, many human rights problems are daunting for companies because they touch on subjects laden with risks to their brand reputations and which hold the prospect of adding costs to their operating budgets. While some companies are starting to make a strategic long-term business case for developing sustainable human rights and environmental practices, too few companies overall have as yet made this calculation or committed to this model.

Business models today are largely fuelled by an investment climate that typically rewards short-term financial earnings at the expense of long-term planning and decision-making. This investment culture, especially prevalent in the United States, is generating unrelenting financial pressure on corporate CEOs and boards that can undermine their prospects for building sustainable businesses. These pressures have been exacerbated in recent years by the rise in power and influence of investors that focus on short-term earnings. While the investment climate in Western Europe appears more amenable to incorporating environmental and social considerations into investment decisions, even there mainstream investors lack accessible human rights data to create the affirmative incentives that are needed to bring real change.[3]

To make further progress on human rights issues the current business paradigm needs to shift to a more inclusive model that integrates human rights. Against the background of the ideas espoused in this book, we envision a future business and human rights agenda that strategically focuses on three key aspects:

- development of measurable industry-specific standards;
- adoption of credible metrics that make transparent the extent of corporate compliance with human rights; and
- greater integration between public and private 'regulators' to improve collaboration and alignment between state and non-state governance mechanisms.

1 Industry specific standards

Companies need to move beyond broad generalized assertions of their commitment to human rights in which each individual company self-defines and self-assesses its own progress. Instead, companies should be called on to participate in the development of industry standards and metrics that will help define and measure their human rights performance. Companies generally rely heavily on metrics to design and chart their progress in a range of areas that are business priorities, such as efficiency, productivity, worker retention, workplace safety and quality control. Charting human rights progress needs to be assessed in the same rigorous way. This needs to happen on an industry-by-industry basis, as the human rights challenges facing each industry are often distinct. Leading companies in each industry need to be centrally involved in defining these standards, but companies cannot do this credibly and efficiently without the active participation of other key stakeholders. Some industries have begun to develop standards and metrics collaboratively in multi-stakeholder settings. The Fair Labor Association, created in 2000, and discussed by Auret van Heerden,[4] is perhaps the most advanced effort in this context to date and it may serve as a model for other industries. Multi-stakeholder initiatives to date struggle with a range of operational challenges, but this relatively new governance model has the potential to legitimately regulate corporate human rights conduct.

2 Credible and transparent metrics

Once industry-specific standards are developed, independent bodies need to assess company performance according to agreed-upon metrics. These evaluations of individual companies must capture companies' internal business structures and procedures as well as the outcomes of their efforts. Monitoring, evaluating and reporting on actual company practices and outcomes are essential for tracking both current compliance with human rights and designing improvements. Industry competitors need to be judged by the same standards, through assessment processes that are practical and fair, as well as credible and transparent to consumers, investors and other external stakeholders. If done well, these comparative evaluations of companies can potentially promote a race to the top, rewarding the best companies with greater consumer support in the marketplace and eventually leading investors to factor this data into their investment decision-making.

These evaluations of company human rights performance need to be distilled into ratings that are accessible, user-friendly and deemed credible by consumers, investors and other public actors. In today's business world rating agencies are increasingly important in evaluating a range of aspects of corporate performance. In an era of big data, economic analysts use increasingly sophisticated financial tools and models to rate and evaluate companies. An increasingly significant group of social investors are keen to obtain data on so-called ESG issues – environment and social governance. While a number of public and private groups are now busy measuring environmental standards and others have long studied and evaluated corporate governance, the 'S' in ESG is still ill-defined.[5] The development of human rights standards and metrics, and the rating of companies on those standards, will help fill the void and give meaning to the 'S' in ESG assessments.

On a parallel track, consumers also are increasingly interested in guidance on these issues. Efforts like Oxfam's 'Behind the Brands' and the Good Guide[6] provide early models of consumer-facing company ratings. In the years ahead, as these and other company ratings systems emerge and evolve and gain greater prominence and depth, the future of human rights will change, as global companies come to realize that good performance on these and environmental issues is imperative to maintaining their brand reputation and consumer trust.

3 Aligning public and private regulatory models

Finally, as Richard Locke notes in his thoughtful essay,[7] private efforts to shape and regulate corporate conduct need to be layered onto and interact with public engagement and regulation. What is becoming increasingly apparent is that for sustained improvements to occur in the protection of human rights, a multiplicity of stakeholders must be involved. As Locke rightly observes, adopting complementary private and public approaches provides the greatest potential to address the seemingly intractable challenges that dot our global landscape. All too often global businesses are operating in complex and very challenging places where they can and should play a constructive remedial role, but they cannot do so alone. Whether addressing recruiting practices in the construction industry in the Gulf, security risks in the energy sector in Africa or labour rights problems in manufacturing in Bangladesh, global companies confront systemic challenges that beg for innovative solutions based on a notion of shared responsibility among key actors in the industry.

The regulatory challenges in monitoring this vast network of specialized supply chains extend beyond the control of any one nation state and increasingly need to involve a variety of non-state actors. This book provides in-depth case studies of some multi-stakeholder initiatives at play in the manufacturing, Internet and communications technology, extractive and private security sectors that utilize a mix of private and public–private regulatory techniques. None of these initiatives is perfect and not everyone agrees that non-state governance is always either appropriate or effective for protecting human rights. Too often, though, criticisms are based on generalities and further study is warranted to develop a greater understanding of how improved collaboration and alignment between state and non-state governance mechanisms can be realized to better protect rights in the workplace.

A key example in this context are the efforts to establish labour rights in global supply chains. As argued by Leary, 'the status of workers' rights in a country is a bellwether for the status of human rights generally'.[8] The long-standing collaborations of public and private actors on this issue show that improving work conditions often is a process of progressive realization. While a diverse range of initiatives (some initiated by states and others by non-state actors) aimed at curbing violations of workers' rights have proliferated in recent decades, it is also clear that such initiatives have been unable to stem the flow of human rights violations. This should not be taken as an indication that such measures are altogether devoid of merit. Initiatives, including those highlighted in this book, that have relied on the development of soft law via such tools as codes of conduct can play a vital role in internalizing human rights norms within corporations and solidifying the notion that corporations have duties with respect to shareholders *and* stakeholders (including workers in their supply chain) alike – a process that, in time, can shape the standards of care that are legally expected of business. Laws, both at national and international levels, are also an important tool for shaping corporate behaviour. The best results are most likely when a multiplicity of tactics and actors are employed in the protection of human rights.

The business and human rights field presents an opportunity to create innovative global governance models of shared responsibility.[9] It offers the potential for the governments of leading economic powers to share the economic burdens of fixing broken systems in partnership with global companies, international financial institutions and local governments and companies in a fair and equitable way that distributes the burden and offers a practical pathway forward. Whether such models successfully catalyse practical progress on the implementation of human rights requires careful tracking as well as access to remedies. The enjoyment of rights depends on the existence of effective remedies[10] and progress is only measurable if corporations can be held to account. Companies committed to human rights need to support both the creation of channels for remedies as well as systems that enable greater accountability. Human rights advocates are just beginning to develop models of such shared responsibility, but we think these models offer real promise for the future. It is to that future and the business leaders who will help shape it that we dedicate this volume.

Notes

1   Human Rights Council, 'Guiding Principles on Business and Human Rights: Implementing the United Nations "Protect, Respect and Remedy" Framework', Report of the Special Representative of the Secretary-General on the issue of Human Rights and Transnational Corporations and Other Business Enterprises, UN Doc. A/HRC/17/31 (21 March 2011).
2   K. Macdonald, *The Politics of Global Supply Chains* (Cambridge: Polity Press, 2014) p. 2.
3   See M.J. Bekink in this volume, 'Thinking long term: investment strategies and responsibility', p. 225.
4   See A. van Heerden in this volume, 'The Fair Labor Association: improving workers' rights in global supply chains', p. 128.
5   D. Cassel and A. Ramasastry, *White Paper: Options for a Treaty on Business and Human Rights* (2015), http://business-humanrights.org/sites/default/files/documents/whitepaperfinal%20ABA%20LS%206%20 22%2015.pdf.
6   See M. Posner in this volume, 'Standard setting for agriculture', p. 172.
7   R.M. Locke in this volume, 'We live in a world of global supply chains', p. 299.
8   V. Leary 'The Paradox of Workers' Rights as Human Rights' in L. Compa and S. Diamond (eds), *Human Rights, Labour Rights and International Trade* (Philadelphia: University of Pennsylvania Press, 1996) p. 22.
9   The German government's 2015 G7 initiative to address global supply chain challenges as a collective problem may be an early example of the way forward. See G7 Germany 2015, 'The G7 Are Committed to Fair Trade and Sustainable Supply Chains', www.bmz.de/g7/en/Entwicklungspolitische_Schwerpunkte/ Menschenwuerdige_Arbeit/index.html; see also *WEF Shared Responsibility – A New Paradigm for Global Supply Chains* (2015) www3.weforum.org/docs/WEF_GAC_Supply_Chains_%20A_New_Paradigm_2015.pdf.
10 See L. Henkin, *The Age of Rights* (New York: Columbia University Press, 1990) p. 37.

Questions for discussion

Chapter 1: The relationship of human rights to business

1   Over the last 35 years there has been a dramatic expansion of the market-based global economy. In terms of human rights, what are the key positive and negative consequences of this globalized economy?
2   What will the global landscape for business look like in 2025? Are human rights considerations likely to be more prominent than they are today? If so, why? If not, why not?
3   As a future CEO or senior legal adviser to a large global business, how would you make the business case for investing in actions that are aimed at addressing human rights challenges faced by your company?

Chapter 2: Regulatory framework and Guiding Principles

1   The UN Guiding Principles on Business and Human Rights call on companies to 'respect human rights'. What does this mean for multinational companies? As the CEO, or senior adviser to the CEO, what actions are you compelled to take to respect human rights? What are the factors influencing your decision?
2   The Guiding Principles emphasize the importance of each company undertaking a 'due diligence' review of its operations. From within a company, how do you decide what constitutes 'due diligence'? What role should external stakeholders play in shaping this standard?
3   A number of NGOs and some governments have requested the UN to adopt a legally binding treaty on business and human rights. What are the advantages and disadvantages of this approach?

Chapter 3: Business and human rights: implementation challenges

1   Many companies now have corporate social responsibility (CSR) offices and experts. How does the notion of CSR overlap with business and human rights? How are they different?

2 For a company to address human rights issues most effectively, where should responsibility for these issues reside within the company?

3 What is a corporation's 'social licence'? What operational consequences can corporations derive from this concept? How would you rely on this concept in making the case for strong human rights standards within a company? How effective is this concept for those outside a company who are seeking to change corporate behaviour?

Chapter 4: Defining and implementing human rights standards industry by industry

1 How have industry-specific human rights standards been developed to date? How does this process compare with the development of human rights standards for governments? What is similar? What is different? How should these differences shape future advocacy?

2 What types of multi-stakeholder initiatives (MSIs) exist? What are the key attributes of human rights governance MSIs?

3 What are the key similarities of the MSIs described in this chapter? What are the key differences? What are the most important functions of these initiatives? In what respect are MSIs successful and what are their limitations?

4 How do/should MSIs relate to regulatory efforts by home and host governments?

Chapter 5: Key constituents that drive the implementation of business and human rights

1 How can civil society organizations (CSOs) advance the business and human rights agenda? Different CSOs play different roles, as watchdogs and reporters, public campaigners, advocates within MSIs, and as technical advisers and trainers to companies. How do these different organizations complement each other? What are the gaps? How well is the current system of different types of CSOs working to support the implementation of human rights and to hold corporations accountable?

2 What is the role of the global trade union movement? How has it evolved? How are local unions progressing in less developed states? What can be done to strengthen the voice of workers?

3 What types of information do consumers want and need to make informed purchasing decisions with respect to human rights? What will it take to develop such information? If such information does become available, do you think consumers will care? What factors will motivate them to consider human rights in their purchasing decisions?

4 Some company leaders say that many investors pay overwhelming attention to short-term profits, making it more difficult to develop strong environmental and

human rights policies. Despite the short-term investing model, a growing number of investors also are focusing on environmental and social governance (ESG) criteria. How is the 'S' currently being defined? How should it be defined? What will it take to encourage key actors in the investment community to adopt a longer-term investment horizon?

Chapter 6: Accountability and remedy

1 What is the responsibility of companies to provide effective remedies where rights violations are tied directly to their core business operations? How do you determine if violations are directly related to a particular company?

2 Over the last 20 years litigants have brought cases against corporations in US courts using the Alien Tort Statute as a basis for asserting extraterritorial jurisdiction. How effective has US litigation been in providing effective remedies? How has the US Supreme Court decision in the *Kiobel* case changed the US legal landscape?

3 How have courts outside the US addressed corporate violations of human rights? What trends are emerging in these places? Should US, European or other courts adjudicate corporate human rights cases by applying extra-territorial jurisdiction? What are the pros and cons of this approach?

4 What non-litigation remedy mechanisms set up by companies, NGOs and MSIs are available in the business and human rights sphere? How effective are these alternative remedies and what are their limitations? What can be done to strengthen them?

Chapter 7: Global rules, private actors: future challenges for business and human rights

1 Richard M. Locke describes the intersection between public and private efforts to advance the rights of workers. How can public and private efforts be integrated to better protect human rights?

2 What are the greatest opportunities for advancing the business and human rights agenda in the coming years? What are the most important factors in making these changes possible?

3 What are the most significant obstacles to progress on business and human rights issues? What needs to be done to overcome these obstacles?

Index

PROPERTY OF
SENECA COLLEGE
LIBRARIES
NEWNHAM CAMPUS